SAGE
Premium
Video

BOOST COMPREHENSION. BOLSTER ANALYSIS.

- SAGE Premium Video **EXCLUSIVELY CURATED FOR THIS TEXT**
- **BRIDGES BOOK CONTENT** with application & critical thinking
- Includes short, auto-graded quizzes that **DIRECTLY FEED TO YOUR LMS GRADEBOOK**
- Premium content is **ADA COMPLIANT WITH TRANSCRIPTS**
- Comprehensive media guide to help you **QUICKLY SELECT MEANINGFUL VIDEO** tied to your course objectives

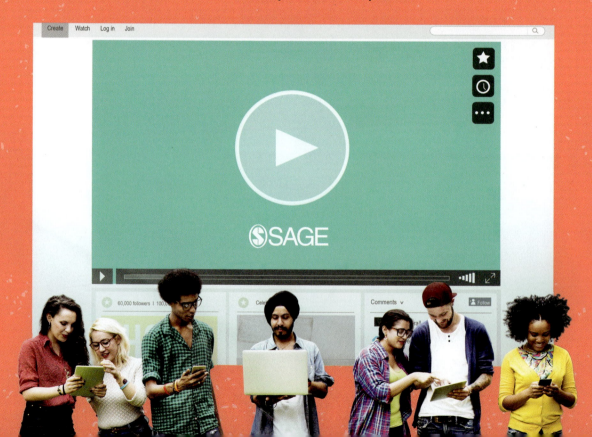

The
Hallmark
Features

A COMPLETE LEARNING PACKAGE

Fundamentals of Human Resource Management: People, Data, and Analytics provides a brief, cutting-edge introduction to the world of HRM with a special emphasis on how understanding data can help managers make better decisions about the people in their organizations.

- **HR IN ACTION** features at the beginning of each chapter help set the stage for students about why the topic matters to HRM.

- A chapter on **DATA MANAGEMENT AND HUMAN RESOURCE INFORMATION SYSTEMS** unpacks the increasingly important role of data in today's workplace.

- End-of-chapter **DECISION-MAKING AND ETHICAL MATTERS EXERCISES** help students grapple with HR in action.

- **REAL-WORLD CASES** spotlight organizations like Google, Igloo, Pinterest, and Chobani.

SAGE Publishing:
Our Story

At SAGE, we mean business. We believe in creating evidence-based, cutting-edge content that helps you prepare your students to succeed in today's ever-changing business world. We strive to provide you with the tools you need to develop the next generation of leaders, managers, and entrepreneurs.

- We invest in the right **AUTHORS** who distill research findings and industry ideas into practical applications.

- We keep our prices **AFFORDABLE** and provide multiple **FORMAT OPTIONS** for students.

- We remain permanently independent and fiercely committed to **QUALITY CONTENT** and **INNOVATIVE RESOURCES** .

Fundamentals of
Human Resource
Management

Fundamentals of
Human Resource Management
People, Data, and Analytics

Talya Bauer - Portland State University

Berrin Erdogan - Portland State University

David Caughlin - Portland State University

Donald Truxillo - University of Limerick

Los Angeles | London | New Delhi
Singapore | Washington DC | Melbourne

FOR INFORMATION:

SAGE Publications, Inc.
2455 Teller Road
Thousand Oaks, California 91320
E-mail: order@sagepub.com

SAGE Publications Ltd.
1 Oliver's Yard
55 City Road
London, EC1Y 1SP
United Kingdom

SAGE Publications India Pvt. Ltd.
B 1/I 1 Mohan Cooperative Industrial Area
Mathura Road, New Delhi 110 044
India

SAGE Publications Asia-Pacific Pte. Ltd.
18 Cross Street #10-10/11/12
China Square Central
Singapore 048423

Acquisitions Editor: Maggie Stanley
Content Development Editor: Lauren Gobell
Editorial Assistant: Janeane Calderon
Production Editor: Tracy Buyan
Copy Editor: Gillian Dickens
Typesetter: Hurix Digital
Proofreader: Alison Syring
Indexer: Will Ragsdale
Cover Designer: Scott Van Atta
Marketing Manager: Sarah Panella

Printed in Canada

Library of Congress Cataloging-in-Publication Data

Names: Bauer, Talya, author. | Erdogan, Berrin, author. | Caughlin, David Ellis, author. | Truxillo, Donald M., author.

Title: Fundamentals of human resource management : people, data, and analytics / Talya Bauer, Portland State University, Berrin Erdogan, Portland State University, David Caughlin, Portland State University, Donald Truxillo, University of Limerick.

Description: Thousand Oaks, California : SAGE Publishing, [2021] | Includes bibliographical references and index.

Identifiers: LCCN 2019031761| ISBN 9781544377728 (paperback) | ISBN 9781544397269 (epub) | ISBN 9781544397276 (epub) | ISBN 9781544397252 (ebook)

Subjects: LCSH: Personnel management.

Classification: LCC HF5549 .B3148 2021 | DDC 658.3—dc23
LC record available at https://lccn.loc.gov/2019031761

This book is printed on acid-free paper.

20 21 22 23 24 10 9 8 7 6 5 4 3 2 1

Brief Contents

Detailed Contents

Chapter 4 • Diversity, Inclusion, and Equal Employment Laws   73

Part II: Managing Across the Talent Life Cycle

Chapter 6 • Workforce Planning and Recruitment 121

Chapter 9 • Performance Management   201

Chapter 10 • Managing Employee Separations and Retention   227

Chapter 12 • Managing Benefits — 279

Chapter 15 • Opportunities and Challenges in International HRM 355

Preface

We are excited to introduce you to *Fundamentals of Human Resource Management: People, Data, and Analytics.* We wrote this book because human resource management (HRM) is important and has the potential to be an essential business partner in making data-informed decisions within organizations. In fact, the potential for HRM has never been greater than it is today. However, that potential will only be realized if business students are well versed in how people, data, and analytics work together. As you will read throughout this book, fluency with people, data, and analytics involves asking the right questions, gathering the right data to address questions, choosing appropriate analyses, and interpreting and communicating findings in a meaningful way. Recognizing and addressing ethical and legal challenges are critical for success. Today, organizations able to manage people, data, and analytics effectively are positioned to leverage HRM to inform and support organizational strategy.

A unique feature of this book is a focus on how HRM is rapidly evolving into a vibrant and data-rich field while also making sure that students are well versed in the basics of HRM. While the demand for data and analytic skills is growing (as evidenced by the 2019 glassdoor.com *50 Best Jobs in America* list with data scientist as #1 for the fourth year in a row, HR manager as #9, recruiter as #28, and data analyst as #31), business students will be well served if they understand HRM regardless of their intended major or work setting. As a result, this book is designed to help students utilize the principles of *people, data,* and *analytics* to focus on *leveraging data to inform decisions in business in general and HRM specifically.* At the same time, all the time-honored HRM concepts are covered for students studying all business functions, including HRM.

Concise, Modern, and Relevant

When it came to developing a textbook with a people, data, and analytics focus geared toward exposing students to the fundamentals of HRM in terms of core concepts and skills, we knew that designing experiences such as exercises that would support faculty and engage students in applying HRM concepts, regardless of their major, was essential. Our goal was to write about critical concepts in an accessible, compelling, and informative manner. We did this through three key approaches to the content of this book.

1. **An approachable writing style.** We carefully consider student perspectives and believe it is important that we make material accessible and engaging. We understand that some students have little or no work experience, others have work experience not related to HR, and others do have HR-related experience. Our goal is to appeal to all of these perspectives. We also recognize that some of those reading this book are doing so

as part of their coursework for a career in HR, while others are not. What matters to us is that we communicate the importance of HR-related decisions for everyone within organizations by equipping students with the tools to make high-quality decisions.

2. **Modern examples of HRM in practice.** Throughout the book, you will find concise examples of different types of organizations, individuals in different positions and levels within organizations, and examples of effective and ineffective HR decisions. All of these examples help attune readers to considerations, approaches to decision making, and best practices and help them avoid the mistakes made by some organizations. The examples bring material to life, make the material relevant, and help students learn from the experiences of other organizations.

3. **Evidence-based practices.** Like many areas of business, people who work in HR have traditionally made decisions based on a "gut feeling." While intuition can be an effective and efficient way to make low-stakes, moment-to-moment decisions, critical, high-stakes decisions informed by evidence and systematic problem solving help avoid failure. Evidence comes in different forms and from different sources, and our book reflects this. First and foremost, we review scholarly research to inform recommended practices and to understand and explain human behavior at work. Second, we showcase ways in which organizations have systematically analyzed and evaluated their own data to inform high-stakes HR decision making. Third, we provide opportunities for students to practice applying different approaches to collect, analyze, and interpret data.

What Makes Our Book Unique

We wanted to write a book that is modern, approachable, and effective at communicating the importance of HRM. In doing so, we believed it should describe the effective and evidence-based approaches to HRM. At the same time, we wanted to create a textbook that helps students understand the importance of people, data, and analytics for supporting the HRM functions within organizations. We are proud of the result. For example, this textbook is the first to include an entire chapter on data management and HR information systems (Chapter 3). This is an important feature given the pivotal space that data occupy in today's business landscape. We believe that upon reading this textbook, you will appreciate the importance of this innovation. We also highlight key trends in the people, data, and analytics space, such as the importance of online privacy for individuals and organizations. We feel that it is imperative for students to understand that just because something is possible using the most sophisticated analytic techniques does not mean it is ethical or even legal. One of our major goals is to highlight areas where the promise and the reality of people, data, and analytics have also produced challenges and ethical dilemmas for individuals and organizations alike.

We take a contemporary approach to HRM and its role in business regardless of one's formal position, title, or functional area. As HRM evolves, we are observing emerging pathways that are moving HRM beyond being simply transactional toward becoming more transformational and strategic in nature. People are the life force of organizations, and attracting, motivating, and retaining the best people is crucial for organizational success. HRM is uniquely positioned to inform the systems, policies, and practices organizations use to manage their people.

As we lay out in the next section, we accomplish this throughout the book via several approaches, including hands-on data and analytics exercises, spotlight features on data and analytics, and content, exercises, case studies, and spotlight features on legal and ethical issues throughout the book.

Textbook Features

In-Chapter Features

Each chapter includes features that stand alone and that also align with the Society for Human Resource Management's (SHRM's) nine competencies:

Source: Reprinted from *SHRM Competency Model* with permission of the Society for Human Resource Management (SHRM). © SHRM. All rights reserved.

- A short **opening case** focusing on key business and HR practices as well as the implications of data-informed decisions appears in every chapter to help students engage in *critical evaluation* and *business acumen* within a variety of organizations, including Costco, Procter & Gamble, ADP, Salesforce.com, L'Oréal, Gravity Payments, and much more. Our goal was to highlight small, medium, and large organizations; *Fortune* 500 organizations; family-owned businesses; not-for-profit organizations; and non-governmental organizations (NGOs) in a variety of industries and settings. Longer supplemental chapter cases appear in Appendix A at the end of the book.

- The **Manager's Toolbox** helps students gather tools and knowledge that will help readers become more effective now and in the future. Examples include tools to help individuals develop skills for making more effective decisions, developing effective organizational strategy, engaging in strong cybersecurity, avoiding illegal questions, choosing key performance indicators, structuring interviews, delivering feedback effectively, and retaining top talent.

- The **Spotlight on Data and Analytics** is a major feature of our book. HRM has become more focused on data. These features offer real-world examples of how companies have collected and analyzed HR data to inform decision making, as well as explanations of key data and analytics terms, concepts, and tools. Example topics include distinguishing between descriptive, predictive, and prescriptive analytics; aligning analytics with strategy; using analytics to improve retention; using performance metrics in screening job applicants; using sentiment analysis to assess engagement; using data and analytics to evaluate pay-for-performance programs; and measuring the antecedents of workplace accidents.

- The **Spotlight on Legal Issues** recognizes that HRM is influenced and shaped by laws. Specifically, legal issues around civil rights legislation have shaped today's approach to diversity management and elevated job analysis from a "nice to have" activity to a foundational legal underpinning of HRM, recruitment, and selection. These legal issues will continue to shape the HRM landscape. Such legislation also has implications for how individuals are trained, developed, managed, and rewarded; the benefits they receive; how their labor rights are managed and protected; and their occupational safety and health. And it is impossible to do work globally without understanding the laws of the countries within which one does business, an issue that is addressed in our chapter on global HRM. Examples of topics covered in these spotlight features include the legal issues associated with obtaining and maintaining data in organizations, the use of "data scraping" by organizations, and pay discrimination. In each chapter, we highlight important legal issues such as these.

- **HR Reasoning and Decision-Making Exercises** for each chapter put the student in the role of a decision maker. Each exercise describes a scenario and asks the student to make a decision that is fair and ethical, fosters healthy employer–employee relationships, and is evidence based. These exercises require students to read and understand the material discussed in each chapter but then also weigh the pros and cons of different alternatives to arrive at a decision that meets the needs of all stakeholders. We find this approach useful in our own teaching, so we included both a mini case study and a decision-making exercise at the end of each chapter.

- **Ethical Matters Exercises** for each chapter expose student to various ethical dilemmas. This exposure leads to a greater ethical understanding of HR concepts. Each exercise presents students with an ethical dilemma and accompanying questions that ask students what they would do when facing ethical issues.

- **Summaries** and **Key Terms** serve to help students master the critical terminology with ease. Learning the vocabulary of HR is important to be able to communicate with other HR professionals more efficiently and to access most up-to-date materials on a particular topic more easily.

Optional Data Exercises

- **Data and Analytics Exercises** for each chapter are also included for instructors to assign as they choose. These end-of-chapter activities provide illustrations and applications of how data can be used to answer a question relevant to the chapter content. The feature in the textbook can also be paired with lifelike data available to instructors in the Excel Extensions should they be interested in having students analyze the data to answer the question. Done individually or in teams, this allows students to engage in actual HRM decisions. Example exercises cover techniques like describing data using descriptive statistics and data visualizations, using regression to understand performance, determining the amount of turnover using metrics, and evaluating a merit pay program using data visualizations.

- **Excel Extensions** for each chapter are included for instructors to assign as they choose. They offer hands-on opportunities for students to practice using data analytics in Microsoft Excel to inform decision making. These activities extend the Data and Analytics Exercises.

Online Resources

SAGE edge™

SAGE edge for Instructors

A password-protected instructor resource site at **edge.sagepub.com/bauerbrief** supports teaching with high-quality content to help in creating a rich learning environment for students. The SAGE edge site for this book includes the following instructor resources:

- **Test banks** built on AACSB and SHRM standards, the book's learning objectives, and Bloom's Taxonomy provide a diverse range of test items. Each chapter includes 100 test questions to give instructors options for assessing students.

- Editable, chapter-specific **PowerPoint® slides** offer complete flexibility for creating a multimedia presentation for the course.

- **Lecture notes** for each chapter align with PowerPoint slides to serve as an essential reference, summarizing key concepts to ease preparation for lectures and class discussion.

- **Discussion questions** are used to further explore topics covered in the chapter.

- Carefully selected **video and multimedia content** aligned with the book's learning objectives enhances exploration of key topics to reinforce concepts and provide further insights.

- Author-created **supplemental exercises and activities** help students apply the concepts they learn to see how they work in various contexts, providing new perspectives.

- **Spotlight on HR Research, Small and Medium Businesses, and Global Issues** boxes highlight articles and research on new and exciting concepts in the field of HR such as the influence of technology on HRM and how data combination methods affect hiring decisions.

- **Tables and figures** from the book are available for download.

- **SAGE coursepacks** provide easy learning management system (LMS) integration.

SAGE edge for Students

The open-access companion website helps students accomplish their coursework goals in an easy-to-use learning environment with the following features:

- **Learning objectives** with summaries reinforce the most important material.
- Mobile-friendly practice **quizzes** encourage self-guided assessment and practice.
- Mobile-friendly **flashcards** strengthen understanding of key concepts.
- Carefully selected **video and multimedia content** enhances exploration of key topics to reinforce concepts and provide further insights.

SAGE coursepacks

SAGE coursepacks makes it easy to import our quality instructor and student resource content into your school's LMS with minimal effort. Intuitive and simple to use, **SAGE coursepacks** gives you the control to focus on what really matters: customizing course content to meet your students' needs. The coursepacks, created specifically for this book, are customized and curated for use in Blackboard, Canvas, Desire2Learn (D2L), and Moodle.

In addition to the content available on the SAGE edge site, the coursepacks include:

- **Pedagogically robust assessment tools** that foster review, practice, and critical thinking and offer a better, more complete way to measure student engagement, including:

  - **Diagnostic chapter tests** that identify opportunities for student improvement, track student progress, and ensure mastery of key learning objectives.

  - **Instructions** on how to use and integrate the comprehensive assessments and resources provided.

  - **Assignable video tied to learning objectives, with corresponding multimedia assessment tools**, that bring concepts to life that increase student engagement and appeal to different learning styles. The **video assessment questions** feed to your gradebook.

  - **Integrated links to the eBook version** that make it easy to access the mobile-friendly version of the text, which can be read anywhere, anytime.

Interactive eBook

Human Resource Management is also available as an **Interactive eBook** that can be packaged with the text or purchased separately. The Interactive eBook offers hyperlinks to original videos, including **Inside HR** video interviews of HR professionals and general managers at Blount International and Procore Technologies, Inc., explaining how concepts in the text are applied in a real-world organization. The Interactive eBook also includes additional case studies from the SAGE Business Case Collection, TED Talks, and carefully chosen articles from the web. Users will also have immediate access to study tools such as highlighting, bookmarking, note-taking/sharing, and more!

Acknowledgments

The authors thank the following people who supported this book both personally and professionally. We offer our heartfelt thanks to Maggie Stanley, our acquisitions editor at SAGE, who supported our vision along the way. It has been a great working relationship. Thanks are also due to Lauren Holmes, our development editor. It was a pleasure to work with you. We also thank our editorial assistant, Janeane Calderon, who kept us on track; our copy editor, Gillian Dickens; and our cover designer, Scott Van Atta. Tracy Buyan, our production editor, did a fantastic job keeping us on schedule throughout the process. We also send sincere thanks to Sarah Panella, our marketing manager, and marketing communications manager Andrew Lee. They helped champion this textbook and communicate our people, data, and analytics HRM approach. This talented SAGE team worked with us to develop compelling content and experiential exercises to help faculty teach the material and, more important, to help students learn to engage in HRM from a strategic and analytic perspective regardless of their position within the organization.

We give special thanks to Alex Alonso and Nancy Woolever at SHRM for the invaluable resources they provide to individuals and organizations to engage in effective HR practices. As the world's largest and leading organization for human resources, SHRM provides thought leadership, certification, community, and advocacy for the effectiveness and practice of organizations and HR individuals and functions. Throughout this book, we drew upon SHRM's guidance and competencies to outline the key HR practices and approaches to cover across the 15 chapters of this book.

No textbook acknowledgment is complete without recognizing the significant role that instructor feedback and reviews play in developing a vibrant, responsive, and useful book that helps faculty teach and students learn key concepts and to develop their skills in applying what they learn. With this in mind, we offer special thanks to the following reviewers for their expertise, insights, questions, and suggestions throughout the development of each chapter of this book as well as the themes.

The authors and SAGE thank the following instructors who participated in reviews and market development for this book:

Susan Flannery Adams, Sonoma State University

Joann Adeogun, Point University

Devi Akella, Albany State University

Ron Alexandrowich, York University

Lisa M. Amoroso, Dominican University

Stephanie Bae, East Carolina University

Stacy Ball, Southwest Minnesota State University

Rimjhim Banerjee, Santa Fe College

Linda Barrenchea, University of Nevada, Reno

Shari Benson, University of La Verne

Michael Bento, Owens Community College

Robyn Berkley, Southern Illinois University, Edwardsville

Mike Bojanski, Methodist College

Angela D. Boston, The University of North Texas–Dallas

Emmanuele Bowles, Florida International University

Yvonne Brinson, Union University

Ronald Brownie, Northern State University

Nina Burokas, Mendocino College

Antonio Cardona, Rutgers, Rider and Keen Universities

Otha Carlton Hawkins, Alamance Community College

Brian Cawley, Calvin College

Hyeran Choi, Columbus State University

Wendell Coleman Jr., University of La Verne

Gwendolyn M. Combs, University of Nebraska Lincoln

Joseph Cooper, University of Toledo

Cody Cox, St. Mary's University

Stan Dale, University of LaVerne

Diana L. Deadrick, Old Dominion University

Caitlin A. Demsky, Oakland University

Charlene Dybas, Fulton Montgomery Community College

Loren R. Dyck, University of La Verne

Karen Ehrhart, San Diego State University

Allison Ellis, California Polytechnic University, San Luis Obispo

Vicki Fairbanks Taylor, Shippensburg University

John Fazio, Marieta College

Matt Fuss, Geneva College

Diane D. Galbraith, Slippery Rock University

Bruce Gillies, California Lutheran University

Deborah Good, University of Pittsburgh

Patricia Greer, University of Denver

Sheri Grotrian, Peru State College

Bruce L. Haller, Molloy College

Robert W. Halliman, Austin Peay State University

Robert Hanks, Portland State University

Michael B. Harari, Florida Atlantic University

Kelli Hatin, SUNY Adirondack

Jeffrey Hefel, Saint Mary's University of Minnesota

Heidi Helgren, Delta College

Terrill C. Herring, Lindenwood University

Michael W. Hill, University of Georgia

Kevin J. Hurt, Columbus State University

Patricia A. Ippoliti, Rutgers University

Sayeedul Islam, Farmingdale State College

Robin James, William Rainey Harper College

Kathleen Jones, University of North Dakota

Jie Ke, Jackson State University

Kevin Knotts, Marshall University

Chris Krull, Indiana University–Purdue University Indianapolis

Jeffrey D. Kudisch, University of Maryland College Park

Ann Langlois, Palm Beach Atlantic University

Julia Levashina, Kent State University

Waheeda Lillevik, The College of New Jersey

Stefan Litz, St. Francis Xavier University

Kurt Loess, East Tennessee State University

Jeanne MacDonald, Minot State University

Erin E. Makarius, University of Akron

Elizabeth Malatestinic, Indiana University

Gery Markova, Wichita State University

Lowell Matthews, Southern New Hampshire University

Randy McCamey, Tarleton State University

Ralph E. McKinney Jr., Brad D. Smith Schools of Business at Marshall University

Jalane Meloun, Barry University

Ian Mercer, Auburn University

Mark S. Miller, Carthage College

Edwin Mourino, Rollins College

Steven Nichols, Metropolitan Community College

Lisa Nieman, Indiana Wesleyan University

Victor Oladapo, Webster University

Candice A. Osterfeld Ottobre, University of Akron

Deborah Powell, University of Guelph

Norma Raiff, Chatham University

Anushri Rawat, Eastern Michigan University

Kendra Reed, Loyola University of New Orleans

Julie Rothbardt, Monmouth College

Kate Rowbotham, Queen's University

Lou L. Sabina, Stetson University

Terry J. Schindler, University of Indianapolis

Lewis Schlossinger, Fordham University

Tom See, California State University, Bakersfield

Tushar R. Shah, University of Texas at Arlington

Denise Simion, Fitchburg State University

Joseph Simon, Casper College

Lauren Simon, University of Arkansas

Shamira Soren Malekar, City University of New York–Borough of Manhattan Community College

Alicia Stachowski, University of Wisconsin, Stout

Lisa Stamatelos, Pace University

Heather Staples, Texas A&M University

Steven Stovall, Southeast Missouri State University

Gary Stroud, Franklin University

Kyra Leigh Sutton, Rutgers University

Charmaine Tener, Thompson Rivers University

Neal F. Thomason, Columbus State University

Justice Tillman, Baruch College

Lee J. Tyner, University of Central Oklahoma

Stephen H. Wagner, Governor's State University

Carlotta S. Walker, Lansing Community College

Stacy Wassell, Frostburg State University

Brian D. Webster, Ball State University

Joseph R. Weintraub, Babson College

Don Wlodarski, Roosevelt University

Feirong Yuan, University of Texas at Arlington

Benjamin B. Yumol, Claflin University

We also thank Susan Schanne of Eastern Michigan University, Bruce Gillies of California Lutheran University, and Jessica McCulley at Graphic World, Inc. for contributing to the digital resources for this book.

Finally, we offer special thanks to the thousands of students we have taught over the years. Each one of you has made us better teachers and scholars.

Thank you!

About the Authors

Talya Bauer, PhD

Gerry & Marilyn Cameron Professor of Management

Talya Bauer earned her PhD in business with an emphasis in organizational behavior and human resources from Purdue University. She is an award-winning teacher who has received the Innovation in Teaching Award from the HR Division of the Academy of Management. She teaches HR analytics, introduction to HRM, training and development, organizational behavior, and negotiations courses and has also been recognized by the Society for Industrial and Organizational Psychology (SIOP) with the Distinguished Teaching Award. She conducts research about HR and relationships at work. More specifically, she works in research areas across the employee life cycle, including recruitment and selection, new employee onboarding, and coworker and leader relationships. This work has resulted in dozens of journal publications, book chapters, and research grants, including from the National Science Foundation and National Institutes of Health. She has acted as a consultant for government, *Fortune* 1,000, and start-up organizations. She has been quoted and her work covered in the *New York Times, Harvard Business Review, Wall Street Journal, Fortune,* the *Washington Post, Business Week, Talent Management, USA Today,* as well as appearing on NPR's *All Things Considered.* Previously, she worked as a computer consultant and as a trainer in California, Idaho, Oregon, and Hong Kong. She has been a visiting professor in France, Italy, Spain, and at Google, Inc. Talya is involved in professional organizations and conferences at the national level such as serving on the Human Resource Management Executive Committee of the Academy of Management and as SIOP president. She has received several Society for Human Resource Management (SHRM) research grants and authored SHRM's "Onboarding New Employees: Maximizing Success" and coauthored SHRM's "Applicant Reactions to Selection: HR's Best Practices" white papers. She is an associate editor for the *Journal of Applied Psychology,* the former editor of *Journal of Management,* and on the editorial boards for *Personnel Psychology, Journal of Management,* and *Industrial and Organizational Psychology: Perspectives on Science and Practices.* She has coauthored multiple textbooks, including *Organizational Behavior, Principles of Management,* and *Psychology and Work: Introduction to Industrial and Organizational Psychology.* She is a fellow of SIOP, APA, APS, and IAAP.

Berrin Erdogan, PhD

*Express Employment Professionals Professor
of Management*

Berrin Erdogan completed her PhD in human resource management at the University of Illinois, Chicago. She is Professor of Management at Portland State University, Distinguished Research Professor at the University of Exeter Business School (UK), and visiting scholar at Koç University (Turkey). Prior to her graduate studies, she worked as a corporate trainer at a private bank. She teaches human resource management, performance management and compensation, and global human resource management at the undergraduate and graduate levels, and is the recipient of Innovation in Teaching Excellence Award at Portland State University. Her research focuses on the flow of people into and out of organizations, with a focus on applicant reactions to employee selection systems, newcomer onboarding, manager–employee relationships and skill utilization, and employee retention. Her studies have been conducted in a variety of industries, including manufacturing, clothing and food retail, banking, health care, education, and information technology in the United States, the United Kingdom, Turkey, Spain, India, China, France, Germany, and Vietnam. She has authored more than 60 articles and book chapters that appeared in journals, including *Academy of Management Journal, Journal of Applied Psychology, Journal of Management, Personnel Psychology,* and *Human Resource Management,* and have been discussed in media outlets, including the *New York Times, Harvard Business Review, Wall Street Journal, BBC Capital,* and *The Oregonian.* In addition, she coauthored several textbooks including *Organizational Behavior, Psychology and Work: Introduction to Industrial and Organizational Psychology,* and *Principles of Management.* She is the current editor of *Personal Psychology,* served as an associate editor for *Personnel Psychology* and *European Journal of Work and Organizational Psychology,* and has served on numerous editorial boards. She is a fellow of APS and SIOP. She was a visiting scholar and gave invited talks at universities in Australia, Canada, Greece, Singapore, Spain, Turkey, the United Kingdom, and the United States.

David Caughlin, PhD

*Daimler Trucks Professor of Analytics, Instructor
of Management*

David Caughlin earned his master's degree in industrial and organizational psychology from Indiana University Purdue University–Indianapolis and his PhD in industrial and organizational psychology with concentrations in quantitative methodology and occupational health psychology from Portland State University. He has taught a number of courses related to human resource management (HRM) and data analytics, such as introduction to HRM, reward systems and performance management, HR information systems, HR analytics, organizational behavior, organizational psychology, practical statistical skills in psychology, and research methods in psychology. In his HR analytics courses, David teaches students how to use the statistical programming language R to manage, analyze, and visualize HR data to improve high-stakes decision making; in the process, students build their data literacy and develop valuable critical thinking and reasoning skills. He has been recognized by the School of Business at Portland State University with the Teaching Innovation Award and the Extra Mile in Teaching Excellence Award. David conducts research on topics related to supervisor support, employee motivation, and occupational safety and health. As a faculty member, he is affiliated with Portland State University's Advancement of Interdisciplinary Methodology for Social Science. He has worked with a variety of organizations on projects related to employee selection, performance management, compensation, organizational culture, mistreatment prevention, and employee survey development. His work has been published in academic journals such as the *Journal of Applied Psychology, Journal of Occupational Health Psychology*, and *Stress & Health*.

Donald Truxillo, PhD

Professor of Work and Employment Studies

Donald Truxillo earned his PhD from Louisiana State University. He is a professor at the Kemmy Business School, University of Limerick, Ireland. Previously, he worked in the areas of selection, employee development, and promotions in the public sector as an industrial psychologist and as a professor in the industrial/organizational psychology program at Portland State University. He studies the methods employers use to hire workers and the experiences of job applicants during recruitment and hiring. In addition, Donald examines issues related to workplace safety and health as well as age differences at work. He served as associate editor for the *Journal of Management* and is currently an associate editor at *Work, Aging and Retirement*. He is a member of nine editorial boards, including *Journal of Applied Psychology, Personnel Psychology,* and *Human Resource Management Review*. He is the author of more than 100 peer-reviewed journal articles and book chapters. Donald is the recipient of SIOP's 2017 Distinguished Teaching Contributions Award and a coauthor of the textbook *Psychology and Work: Introduction to Industrial and Organizational Psychology*. His research has been supported by the SHRM Foundation, the National Institute of Occupational Safety and Health (NIOSH), and the National Science Foundation (NSF), most recently to study privacy and security issues associated with online hiring. He has taught courses in human resource management, training and development, research methods, and industrial psychology. He has received three Fulbright grants to study abroad and has visited at universities in Germany, Ireland, Italy, Portugal, Spain, and Switzerland. Since 2010, he has been a member of the Doctoral Training Committee, Department of Psychological Science and Education, University of Trento, Italy. He is a fellow of SIOP, APA, APS, and IAAP.

Sara Miller McCune founded SAGE Publishing in 1965 to support the dissemination of usable knowledge and educate a global community. SAGE publishes more than 1000 journals and over 800 new books each year, spanning a wide range of subject areas. Our growing selection of library products includes archives, data, case studies and video. SAGE remains majority owned by our founder and after her lifetime will become owned by a charitable trust that secures the company's continued independence.

Los Angeles | London | New Delhi | Singapore | Washington DC | Melbourne

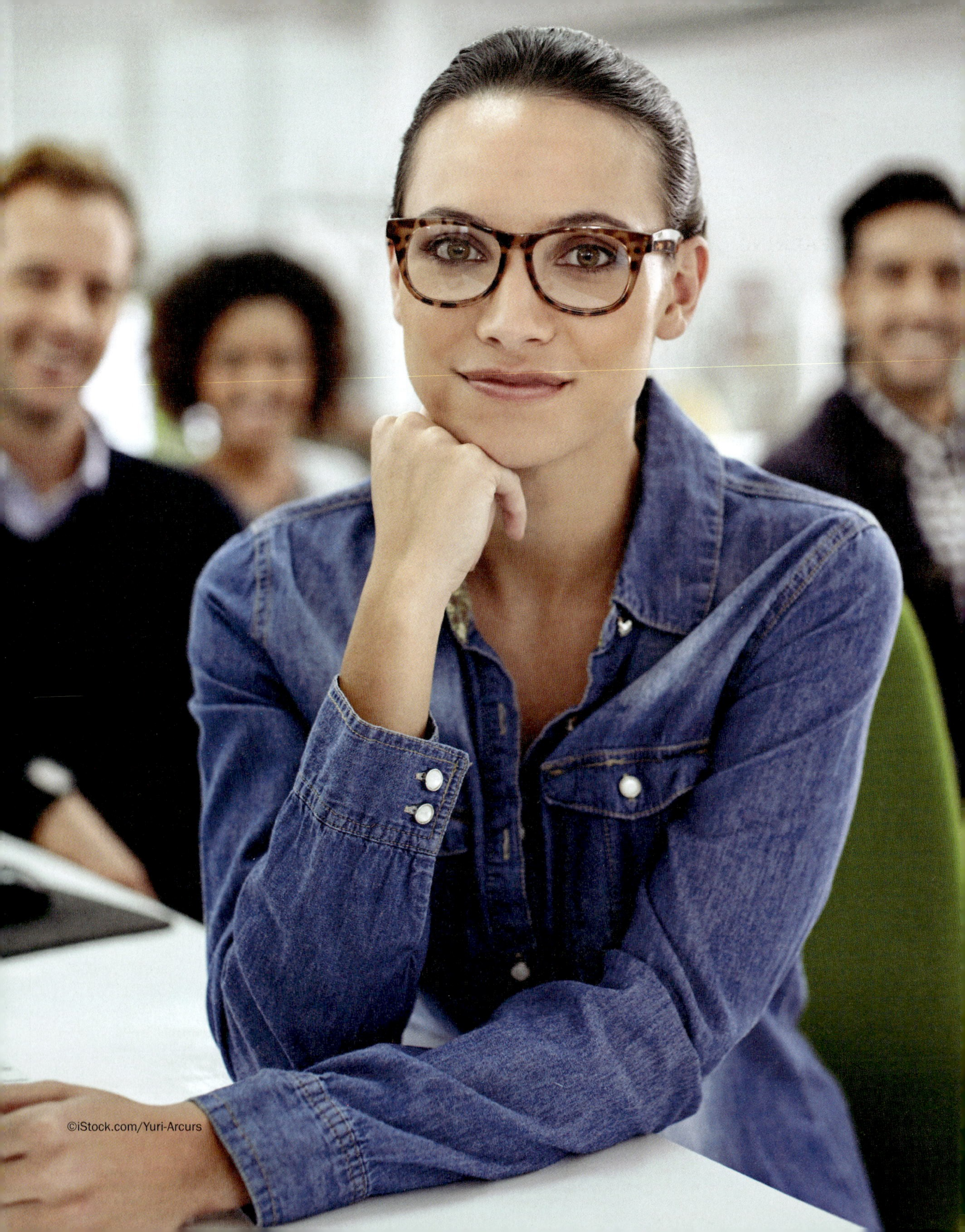

1 Human Resource Management

LEARNING OBJECTIVES

After reading and studying this chapter, you should be able to do the following:

1.1 Understand the definition of human resource management (HRM).

1.2 Articulate why HRM matters.

1.3 Explain the changing context of HRM.

1.4 Summarize the HRM profession.

HR in Action: The Case of Costco

Costco is known as a desirable employer. This is partly because it pays an average of $21 per hour to employees in retail environments where $10.50 is the average hourly pay. Costco also covers 90% of health insurance expenses for both full-time and part-time employees, which is rare. James Sinegal, former CEO of Costco, is quoted as saying, "When employees are happy, they are your very best ambassadors." Although HR at Costco is not directly run by its CEO, you can imagine how such a strong set of values at the executive level influences all human resource (HR) practices at Costco. These values, together with the facts that Costco promotes from within, encourages and listens to employee suggestions, and gives managers autonomy to experiment with their departments and stores with an eye toward increasing sales and/or reducing costs (as long as products are never marked up more than 15%), and the fact that he made a modest salary as CEO, are among the reasons why Sinegal was named one of the 100 Most Influential People in Business Ethics in 2008. As a founder and CEO, he made a big profit for the company while putting people first, so it is hard to argue with his success. Although Costco pays considerably more than the industry average, including bonuses and other incentives, its revenues and stock price continue to grow. In fact, the value of Costco stock from 1985 until Sinegal's retirement in 2012 increased by 5,000%. The next

Barry Sweet/Bloomberg via Getty Images

Former Costco president and CEO James Sinegal pictured in one of the company's stores near its headquarters in Issaquah, Washington.

CEO, Craig Jelinek, continued this trend. In 2015, Costco's stock rose more than 15% under his leadership, and he was named CEO of the Year by CNN. Costco's stock price has continued to be strong in subsequent years.[1]

Case Discussion Questions

1. Why do you think Costco is able to make a profit while paying their employees more than the average wages and benefits?

2. Do you think that Costco's approach could work in other industries?

3. What do you think would happen to Costco's sales and profits if they were to change their HR policies and not offer such attractive benefits to employees?

HRM relates to all aspects of organizational life and is everyone's responsibility. The first chapter of this book gives you an overview of what HRM is and why it is important regardless of what area of business you are pursuing.

Defining Human Resource Management

LO 1.1   Understand the definition of human resource management (HRM).

This textbook provides an introduction to the field of human resource management (HRM). This includes what HRM is, the evolving context and landscape of HRM, best practices, and some of the issues and controversies associated with HRM today. We suspect that, unlike some other areas of study in business, HRM is a subject you already know a great deal about even before reading this book or taking this class. For example, if you have ever filled out a job application or been interviewed for a job, you have been exposed to a major function within HRM called *selection*. Even if you have never applied for a job, you have still interacted with thousands of people who have. Every teacher you have had in the classroom and every customer service interaction you have encountered were the result of HRM in some way or another: Teachers and customer service specialists are hired, trained, paid, and managed via their organization's HRM system. Interactions such as these may have given you some preconceived notions of what HRM is all about. This is a great thing because it means you can jump right in and start participating and discussing the material. But we suspect, as you progress through this book, you will also find yourself seeing the strategic value of HRM practices and why HRM is a key factor in organizational success regardless of the area of business that you intend to focus on in your own career. That is why we set out to write this book.

The world of HRM is changing in new and innovative ways. Much like the *Industrial Revolution* of the mid-1800s, when machines changed the way that manufacturing work was done, we are currently in the midst of a *knowledge revolution*. Never before in history has it been easier to access information, connect globally, and manage employees remotely. We discuss the implications of this recent shift in this chapter, and it is integrated throughout the book. Chapter 2 specifically addresses how this knowledge revolution has created exciting opportunities for HRM to become invaluable within organizations in a variety of ways, including informing managers with best practices and data to aid decision making throughout the organization. As valued business partners, HRM specialists and generalists can span the range of activities from following procedures to creating and testing hypotheses regarding the most effective ways to manage employees. It is clear that there is a lot to learn, so let us get started with addressing the basic question of what HRM is, who is involved, and where HR is located within organizations.

Human resource management (HRM) refers to the constellation of decisions and actions associated with managing individuals throughout the employee life cycle to maximize employee and organizational effectiveness in attaining goals. This includes functions that range from analyzing and designing jobs; managing diversity and complying with local, national, and global employee laws; recruiting individuals to apply for jobs; selecting individuals to join organizations; training and developing people while they are employed; helping to manage their performance; rewarding and compensating employee performance while maintaining healthy labor relations and helping keep them safe; and managing their exit, or departure, from the organization.

Ultimately, HRM is about making decisions about people. This decision-making process involves many questions that those within an organization must ask and answer. Over time, the answers may change as the firm experiences growth or decline, external factors change, or the organizational culture evolves. For example, those involved in HRM need to address questions such as these:

- Where will we find the best employees?
- How can we help them be safe at work?
- How should we motivate and reward employees to be effective, innovative, and loyal?
- What training do our employees need, and how can we further develop them?
- How can we help ensure that employment relations between employees and managers remain healthy?
- What can we do to ensure that employees engage in ethical decision making and behaviors?
- What do we need to do to remain competitive locally and globally?
- Why are employees leaving, and what can we learn from their exits?

All of these questions and more are part of managing the HRM system of decisions and actions associated with managing individuals throughout the employee life cycle (see Figure 1.1), from the hiring stage through the exit of an employee through voluntary or involuntary turnover.

Viewing HRM from a decision-making perspective has important implications for the success of employees and organizations. HRM systems can help overcome **biases**—types of favoritism or prejudice—that can be inherent in organizational decisions. Evidence indicates that individuals have biases, often unconscious, when engaging in decision

Human resource management (HRM) The decisions and actions associated with managing individuals throughout the employee life cycle to maximize employee and organization effectiveness

Biases A tendency, feeling, or opinion, especially one that is preconceived, unreasoned, and unsupported by evidence

Availability bias The tendency to rely more on information that is more readily available than alternative information

■ **FIGURE 1.1**   Key Aspects to Manage During the Employee Life Cycle

A critical aspect of HRM is managing key aspects of work throughout the entire employee life cycle.

making. Each of these biases represents a shortcut to making decisions. Based on years of experience, each of us has developed the ability to sort through huge amounts of information to arrive at decisions. Some are small, and we hardly ever give them a thought, but those can be dangerous decisions because biases such as availability, anchoring, or confirmation can influence the outcome unconsciously. Other choices, such as whether to hire one of three candidates, also have consequences.

For example, consider the **availability bias**, which is the tendency to rely more on information that is readily available to us, and we discount alternative information. To the degree that the information relating to the job candidates is subjective, such as when interviews are used, our past experiences will influence us to a greater degree, and bias can creep into the process. The bias might be subtle, such as your recollection that the last employee you hired from State University has done a great job. This might lead you to lean toward the one candidate on your short list from this same school. But is this a reasonable thing, given that State University graduates 8,000 students per year and the other two candidates graduated from schools from which your company has employed dozens of successful candidates? It probably is not. To avoid this as well as the other types of biases, take concrete steps, including recognizing that such biases exist; taking the other side of your argument, including others in the decision making; assigning a devil's advocate; and considering the consequences of a suboptimal hire. In other words, one of the functions of HRM is to be aware of and design systems that prevent systemic biases from exerting undue influence over decision making, resulting in better decisions. **Anchoring bias**, the tendency to rely too much on the first piece of information given, can be just as dangerous, as your decision can be influenced simply by the way others present information. Finally, **overconfidence bias**, the tendency to seek confirmation of one's own beliefs or expectations, can shortcut the exploration of a full range of options. All of these biases can hurt the quality of decisions made.

Manager's Toolbox
AM I MAKING A GOOD DECISION?

Making decisions is not easy. Research shows that only about 50% of all decisions made within organizations are successful.[2] To help you understand whether a particular decision has the hallmarks of success, it makes sense to consider the following key characteristics. Doing so won't guarantee success, but it can help you develop more robust decision-making criteria that help to meet the needs of the entire organization rather than just solving a problem today that may create a larger problem tomorrow.

Ask yourself these questions:

- *Is this course of action legal? Is it ethical? Is it fair?* Just being legal is a good first step, but it is not enough. How would you feel if your course of action were shared on the Internet or on the front page of your local newspaper? If the answer is "not so great," that's an indication that the course of action you are considering may be legal but may not be ethical or fair.

- *Is this decision based on evidence and data?* While decisions should not be made solely based on prior evidence and relevant data, they should consider both and try to leverage what is possible to know to rule out alternative courses of action.

- *Will pursuing this course of action help to make the organization healthier?* It is easy to make decisions and pursue courses of action in isolation from the larger organization. Doing so can create problems. Stopping to consider whether you are doing something that is likely to help or hinder positive employee–employer relations is helpful in avoiding problems down the line.

- *Is this course of action time and resource efficient?* If the course of action you are considering is not time or resource efficient, it is not likely to be sustainable over time. This can lead to resource

(Continued)

(Continued)

constraints, including employee energy and burnout as well as financial constraints.

- *Does this course of action take a systematic perspective and consider various stakeholders?* You might have all the information necessary to make a good

decision. But you might not. And even if you do have the relevant information, including stakeholders in the decision-making process is a helpful way of securing acceptance of a decision. Skipping this step will most likely lead to less effective decisions in the long run.

HRM Matters

LO 1.2   Articulate why HRM matters.

You might be taking this class because it is required at your school even if you are not an HRM major. Regardless of your major, HR is valuable for you and your career. For example, knowing about HR policies and practices is important because as a manager or future manager, you will be required to make employee-related decisions. You might be involved in recruiting and hiring employees, and in fact, you will be on the front line of the hiring process. You may play an important role in managing the performance of employees and allocating rewards. You may need to discipline employees or manage their exit. Your decisions, actions, and inactions will be used to assess compliance with the law. Much of the information included in this book is relevant as you build your managerial skills. For any HR practice to be implemented effectively, HR and line managers will need to be partners. This involves each party understanding the rationale behind each practice, line managers remaining true to the spirit of the system in place and giving feedback to HR, and HR departments designing systems that meet the needs of line managers. If you end up working in an area outside of HR, such as accounting or marketing, you will still be a consumer of the HR systems and services available at your organization. For example, your department may require a new training program, and it will be essential to partner with the HR department to design and implement the new training program. It is important to understand how HR systems and services work. In short, even if you have no interest in working in HR, learning about HRM will be a good investment of your time.

People Matter

A-S-A framework The process of attraction, selection, and attrition that defines an organization's culture

It is well documented that the individuals who work within an organization matter when it comes to what an organization is like as a place to work and what it is able to do. Individuals influence its culture, informal rules, how hard individuals work, how they should treat one another, how much risk employees should take, and what is considered acceptable in terms of performance and ethics. Influence happens through who is attracted to join the organization, who is selected to join the organization, and who decides to remain or leave the organization. Benjamin Schneider called this the **A-S-A framework**, standing for attraction-selection-attrition in organizations. In other words, organizations vary in terms of the human capital they have access to based on whom they attract, hire, and retain. Human capital refers to the knowledge, skills, and abilities, as well as other characterristics (KSAOs), embodied in people.[3] As you might imagine, human capital might refer to the KSAOs of a handful of people when a company is starting out to thousands of employees if and when the organization grows. It is clear that human capital needs of organizations change over time.

Richard Branson, founder of the Virgin Group, famously said, "Take care of your employees, and they'll take care of your business."[4] He argues that creating a great place to work involves a work climate where people are appreciated, engaged in their work, productive, and thriving rather than simply surviving. Research supports this idea, showing that large percentages of disengaged employees (68% to 70% of survey respondents) cost U.S. businesses up to $550 billion per year in lost productivity. Disengaged employees also have 49% more accidents on the job and 60% more errors in their work, and their companies have a 65% lower share price over time than those with more engaged employees. Organizations increasingly understand that treating individuals isn't just about "being nice" to them; it is a win-win, as those employees who feel valued also tend to be more engaged and productive. And we know that organizations that value their employees are more profitable than those that do not.[5]

If employing people who are valued, highly supported, and engaged at work promotes company success, why don't all organizations create such cultures? That is a great question. The answer is complex, but reasons include not understanding or believing the connection between organizational culture and success and not knowing how to create this connection.

Organizational Culture Matters

Organizational culture refers to shared, "taken-for-granted" assumptions that members of an organization have that affect the way they act, think, and perceive their environment.[6] Because of this, organizational culture influences how decisions are made within organizations, and it is also influenced by those decisions. For example, if being polite is highly valued within an organization, the approach taken when giving performance feedback would be much different than in an organization that values directness. During the initial pilot of a managerial training program, which involved a simulation and role-play conducted with employees at Hewlett Packard in the 1990s, the entire role-play had to be rewritten when the participants insisted that the role of an employee who argues with their manager vigorously just would never happen. As participants explained, they didn't know how to react to this because it was so far out of the norm of their business. Since that time, HP's culture has evolved to be more in line with other cultures, which are more direct and aggressive. This is a useful reminder of how powerful cultures can be. It makes sense to take some time to understand the different types of organizational cultures that exist within organizations.

Organizational culture
Assumptions shared by organization members, which affect their actions, thoughts, and perceptions

Types of Organizational Culture

One popular typology of organizational cultures, called the Competing Values Framework, characterizes organizations by their emphasis on collaboration, creating, controlling, or competing.[7] The Competing Values Framework identifies four different types of organizational cultures:

- **Clan cultures** are collaboration oriented and characterized by valuing being cohesive, people oriented, team players, and empowering employees. Examples of organizations that can be seen as having clan cultures are Costco, Southwest Airlines, and SAS Institute.
- **Adhocracy cultures** focus on creating and emphasize being entrepreneurial, being flexible, taking risks, and being creative. Examples of adhocracy cultures are 3M, Google, and Facebook.
- **Market cultures** are characterized by competition and value being aggressive, competitive, and customer oriented. Examples of companies showing signs of a market culture are Amazon, Intel, and Netflix.
- **Hierarchy cultures** focus on controlling and value being efficient, timely, and consistent. Organizations such as Walmart and Boeing are examples of this type of culture.

HRM and Organizational Culture

No one type of culture leads to success and happy employees. The examples given for different cultures are all successful businesses in their industries. It is important to remember that there is a close connection between company culture and HR practices adopted, and in turn, the HR practices adopted will influence and shape the culture into the future. Company HR practices are often a reflection of company culture. For example, Marriott developed an online recruiting platform called "My Marriott Hotel": Candidates manage different areas of the hotel's operations, where they lose or gain points for customer satisfaction and profitability. Such a recruitment tool reflects the company's values, such as being results and customer oriented.[8] You would not expect to see such a system in place in a company that emphasizes efficient and cost-effective hiring to fill specific positions.

Similarly, the HR practices in use will shape a company's culture. For example, imagine a company that adopts a performance review system that involves ranking employees on a bell curve and distributing rewards accordingly, such as Yahoo's adoption of such a system in 2013. Requiring managers to compare employees with each other will shape the culture of the company toward a market culture, as survival in such a system will require competition among employees. Effective HR decisions will need to consider the implications of every decision for the culture the company has and the culture the company would like to have.

Macro Changes and HRM

LO 1.3   Explain the changing context of HRM.

Human resource management does not exist in a vacuum. Companies have gone from personnel departments exclusively using paper forms and tracking benefits to HR becoming a strategic partner in organizational decisions. Because of this, as the world and the fundamental characteristics of work continue to evolve, so must human resource

---

Clan culture
Organizations with clan cultures are collaboration and people oriented and value cohesion, employee empowerment, and team players

Adhocracy culture
Organizations with adhocracy cultures are creation focused and emphasize entrepreneurship, flexibility, risk taking, and creativity

Market culture
Organizations with market cultures are characterized by competition and are characterized as aggressive, competitive, and customer oriented

Hierarchy culture
Organizations with hierarchy cultures focus on control and value being efficient, timely, and consistent

■ **FIGURE 1.2**   Macro Changes Affect HRM

Forces shaping human resource management continue to evolve.

Changing Demographics	Emerging Gig Economy	Increasing Globalization
© /Shutterstock	© Prostock-studio/Shutterstock	© Lightspring/Shutterstock

Technology	Availability of Data	Ethical and CSR Challenges
© Scorpp/Shutterstock	© wk1003mike/Shutterstock	© arfa adam/Shutterstock

management. This section outlines a number of these important changes in the contextual landscape that have major implications for HRM. These include changing demographics, the emerging gig economy, increased globalization, technology, the availability of data, and the ongoing and rising importance of ethics and corporate social responsibility (see Figure 1.2).

Demographics Are Changing

One of the largest impacts on HRM is that of the increasingly changing demographics of individuals in the United States and around the world (see Figure 1.3). Changes include the aging population and increasing demographic diversity. Given how prevalent this topic is, you are probably aware that the American workforce is aging. By 2030, 20% or more of those in the United States are projected to be aged 65 or older, which is more than double the percentage in 1970.[9] This represents a major shift in the working population, as nearly 75 million baby boomers (those born between 1946 and 1964) are expected to retire in the next 25 years, with only 46 million new workers from later generations joining the organizational ranks.

■ FIGURE 1.3 Percent Age 65 and Older by Race and Hispanic Origin for the United States: 2012 and 2050 (percent of each group's total population)

The distribution of U.S. population is projected to change, which has implications for HR.

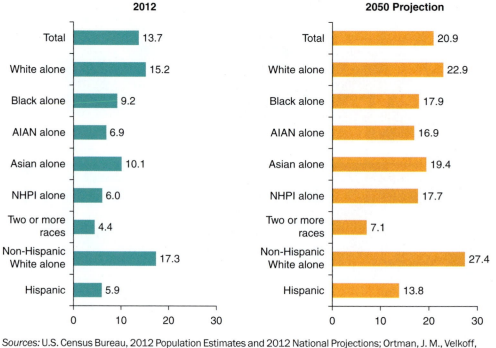

Sources: U.S. Census Bureau, 2012 Population Estimates and 2012 National Projections; Ortman, J. M., Velkoff, V. A., & Hogan, H. (2014). An aging nation: The older population in the United States. U.S. Department of Commerce. Retrieved August 2, 2019, from https://www.census.gov/prod/2014pubs/p25-1140.pdf

Note: AIAN = American Indian and Alaska Native; NHPI = Native Hawaiian and Other Pacific Islander.

Increasing diversity in the workplace is also an aspect of the changing demographic landscape, which has implications for HRM. For example, race is an area where we still see challenges with equal pay for equal work. Research finds that ethnic subgroups experience both an earnings gap and a glass ceiling. In 2015, for every dollar a Caucasian male employee made, Asian males made $1.20, whereas African American males made around 76 cents, and Hispanic employees made 69 cents.[10] In 2019, only three *Fortune* 500 companies (Merck & Co, Inc., JCPenney's, and TIAA) were run by African American chairpersons and CEOs. It is interesting that although, as a group, ethnic subgroups face challenges in terms of pay and promotion, the demographic trends are such that by 2055, Caucasians are estimated to constitute less than one half of the population in the United States.[11] This demographic shift has already taken place in some parts of the United States, such as the Los Angeles area, where only 29% of the population is Caucasian, non-Hispanic.[12]

Such core changes in who is available to work have major implications for how to recruit, select, train, reward, and manage the workforce. Given that HRM is responsible for these functions, being aware of the changes as well as their associated challenges and opportunities is essential for organizations to remain competitive.

The Gig Economy Is Growing

A **gig economy** is characterized by the prevalence of temporary employment positions, and individuals are employed as independent workers rather than actual employees of an organization. And a gig is defined as a single project or task that a worker is hired to do on demand. Think of Uber drivers or substitute teachers. In 2018, of the 161 million employed in the United States, nearly 21 million (or 13%) reported working part-time jobs for noneconomic reasons.[13] A survey found that 75% of full-time and 68% of part-time freelance employees noted scheduling flexibility as a key reason for their attraction to freelance work.[14] Other positives reported are variety and the ability to pursue one's interests. Reported downsides include inconsistency in pay and scheduling and the lack of benefits associated with this type of employment contract. As the U.S. Department of Labor noted about the gig economy, "These workers often get individual gigs using a website or mobile app that helps to match them with customers. Some gigs may be brief. . . . Others are much longer but still of limited duration, such as an 18-month database management project. When one gig is over, workers who earn a steady income this way must find another. And sometimes, that means juggling multiple jobs at once."[15] Some occupations are more likely than others to employ contract workers. Arts and design, computer and information technology, construction and extraction, media and communications, and transportation and material moving are industry sectors at the top of the list for contract work. The implications of the emerging gig economy are vast. Because this class of employment is so relatively new, the legal environment has not yet kept up, and it remains an area that is unclear.

Globalization Is Increasing

U.S.-based businesses recognize the importance of international business and international presence. India and China are the fastest growing economies, each of them being home to around 18% of the world's population. Major U.S. businesses are realizing that a big portion of their revenues comes from overseas. For example, Intel receives 82% of its revenue from overseas. For Qualcomm, this ratio is over 98%. Half the revenue of Dow Chemical, Exxon Mobil, Apple, and Johnson & Johnson comes from overseas.[16] If you are not convinced that international business is here to stay, consider these iconic, everyday brands normally associated with the United States: Budweiser, 7-Eleven, Holiday Inn, Shell, and T-Mobile. All of these are foreign owned. Globalization of business introduces a number of HRM challenges. Businesses recruit and hire employees from a more diverse pool of applicants given the realities of global mobility of potential employees. Businesses will need to consider the local laws and regulations in the different operations they run. It is also important to consider the role of cultural differences in the use of different HRM practices around the world. It is tempting to transport best practices developed in corporate headquarters, but

Gig economy
The prevalence of temporary employment positions, where individuals are employed as independent workers instead of actual employees of an organization

such efforts, without sensitivity to the local culture, are often doomed to fail. As a result, in companies operating worldwide, effective HRM takes into account local differences in local laws and norms to create an effective global organization.

Technology Is Rapidly Evolving

Technology has been evolving at a rapid pace. A key reason behind this can be explained via Moore's Law, put forth in 1965, which states the capacity of computer chips would double roughly every 2 years at around the same cost. George E. Moore was the cofounder of Intel Corporation. As part of its 50-year celebration of Moore's Law, Intel calculated that if fuel efficiency were to improve at the same rate as the law over 50 years, a person could drive their car for a lifetime on a single tank of gas.[17] Moore's Law is important to HRM because it illustrates how rapidly technology will continue to evolve as the cost and availability of processing power become increasingly accessible. This aligns with the increasing rate of technology's impact on HRM processes and procedures. As you will see throughout this book—and especially in Chapter 3—technology matters a great deal when it comes to HRM.

Availability of Data Is Increasing

It may seem like everyone is talking about big data. We discuss this in greater detail in the next two chapters, but for now, it is helpful to know that *big data* refers to data that are large in volume, variety, and velocity. Technology has allowed for greater and greater computing power, and the Internet has generated so much data that recent estimates are that Amazon, Facebook, Google, and Microsoft stored at least 1,200 petabytes among them in 2013 alone. A petabyte is 1 million gigabytes. Every second, there are over 8,000 tweets, nearly 1,000 Instagram photos uploaded, over 1,500 Tumblr posts, 3,600 Skype calls, over 72,000 Google search queries, and 2.8 million e-mails sent. These numbers continue to grow over time.[18] That's a lot of data. In addition, companies often gather annual opinion surveys, as well as other employment data from millions of workers each year. As more and more transactions, communications, and shopping move online, more information is available each day. Over 70% of business executives are investing, or plan to invest, in analytics related to big data, but only 2% say they have yet achieved what they called "broad, positive impact."[19]

Ethical Challenges and Corporate Social Responsibility

Business ethics is a system of principles that govern how businesses operate, how decisions are made, and how people are treated. It includes the conduct of individual employees as well as the entire organization. These concepts should look familiar from our earlier discussion of the characteristics of effective HRM decision making. The concept of business ethics arose in the 1960s and 1970s in the United States as values shifted from strict loyalty to the organization to a stronger loyalty toward one's own guiding principles and ideals.[20] This manifested itself through environmental issues, increasing employee-versus-employer tension, human rights issues surrounding unfair and unsafe labor practices, and civil rights issues. Over time, additional issues surfaced, such as bribes and illegal contracting practices, deception in advertising, and lack of transparency in business transactions.

Business ethics A system of principles that govern how business operates, how decisions are made, and how people are treated

By the early 2000s, concerns regarding business scandals such as financial mismanagement, increased corporate liability for personal damage, and fraud had come to the forefront. Such scandals led to several changes on the global stage, such as the UN Convention Against Corruption and the 2004 Global Compact adopting the 10th principle against corruption, and the Association of Advanced Collegiate Schools of Business (AACSB) included ethics as part of an accredited business education, including a key provision on the importance of ethical decision making.[21] Given that HRM is defined as the constellation of decisions and actions associated with managing individuals throughout the employee life cycle, addressing ethical challenges and corporate social responsibility are key aspects of HRM. You will find an exercise called *Ethical Matters* in each chapter of this book. We encourage you to take the time to consider the ethical challenges you have and may encounter at work.

This book explicitly focuses on the importance of data in making effective HRM decisions. We offer examples and insights throughout the book as well as special features to help bring data analytics to help you become more familiar and more effective at thinking about and leveraging the availability of data. Knowing that technology and big data are major trends that affect HRM throughout the world are the key points we want you to take way from this section.

Spotlight on Data and Analytics

DESCRIPTIVE, PREDICTIVE, AND PRESCRIPTIVE ANALYTICS

A survey of business leaders conducted by Deloitte found that concerns exist regarding the gap between the perceived need for data-driven approaches to HR and the existing skill base. Of the companies surveyed, 75% reported a belief that HR analytics is important, but just 8% reported a belief that their own organization is strong in this area.[22] A Society for Human Resource Management (SHRM) Foundation report on analytics found that two key skills are lacking: analytics skills and the ability to present findings in a convincing way to senior executives.[23] As more organizations such as Pfizer, AOL, and Facebook continue to focus on analytics, we suspect that other organizations will continue to follow suit.

As you consider how analytics in general and HR analytics in particular may play a role in your future, keep in mind these different levels of

analytics: *descriptive, predictive,* and *prescriptive. Descriptive analytics* is focused on understanding what has happened. By definition, it is focused on understanding the past. Descriptive analytics might include understanding what percentage of an employee sample has a college education versus a high school education. *Predictive analytics* focuses on what is likely to happen given what is known. By definition, it is forward looking. For example, predictive analytics might focus on understanding how going to high school versus continuing to college relates to job performance based on probabilities. *Prescriptive analytics* focuses on what should be done in the future based on what is known. By definition, it is also forward looking. Prescriptive analytics might focus on what the best mix of high school– versus college-educated employees the firm *should* have for optimal firm performance.

(Continued)

(Continued)

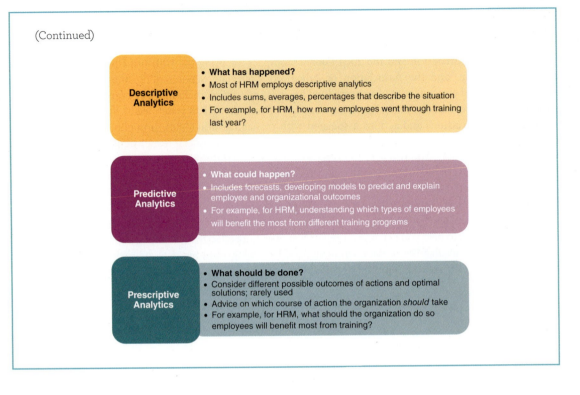

The Profession of HRM

LO 1.4   Summarize the HRM profession.

We realize that not every person reading this book plans to go into HRM as a profession. Nevertheless, understanding who is involved in HRM, the types of HR careers available, and what the core HRM competencies are should be helpful to all interested in business. We start with an overview of who is involved in HRM.

Who Is Involved in HRM?

The short answer to this question is everyone within an organization. This is because everyone is responsible for helping the organization be successful. Some individuals, groups, and departments are more involved in HRM decision making and actions on a day-to-day basis than others. These include CEOs and the associated leadership team, HR managers, line managers, and HR specialists and generalists. In addition, other areas of the organization, such as information systems technology, play an important role in making sure the right people have the right information in place to make the most effective decisions possible. The marketing of products influences whether potential applicants know about and are attracted to the organization. The accounting and finance functions are critical to the fiscal health of an organization and also play an important role in keeping the organization's finances supporting human capital. They may be involved in compensation and benefits-related decisions as well. And every one of these departments also has managers who oversee them. It would be a missed opportunity to *only* focus on what happens within the Department of Human Resource Management within an organization.

Because this book is written with a special focus on best practices and functions of HRM, we focus primarily on the ways in which four important groups affect the culture and functioning of HRM within an organization. These include the top management leadership team, line managers, HRM practitioners, and, finally, HR departments.

Enrique Washington is an executive talent acquisition leader. In the past, he has recruited executives at sports organizations such as the Trail Blazers, video game maker Electronic Arts, and Nike. A key part of his job is advising hiring leaders on establishing role requirements to identify, assess, select, and integrate new executive leaders in alignment with their business goals.

Top Management Teams

The top members of the organizational team, such as the CEO, top management team, and/or owner of the organization, set the tone for HR and how much or how little human capital is valued. They also set the tone for how much HRM is valued as a strategic function to enhance the organization's effectiveness. The organization's chief human resource officer (CHRO) is also critical in this regard. Organizations often use executive recruiting functions within their organizations or hire external search firms to help them find the right talent at this level.

HR Managers

An HR manager is someone who oversees the personnel department or HR functions within a group. The degree to which they are passive versus proactive in terms of asking questions, gathering data, and helping to address the major challenges and opportunities of the organization can influence how effective HRM and, relatedly, the organization ultimately becomes. One of the other major functions of these individuals is to partner with other managers across the organization. This is a critical coordination function. These individuals might hold a variety of job titles such as HR manager/director, which is the most frequently advertised job position in HR.

Line Managers

Managers also play a critical role in making people decisions. For example, a hiring manager's opinion can be the difference between a person being hired, promoted, or fired. Managers also play a critical day-to-day role in managing workflows, helping support new employee development, and developing talent for greater responsibilities over time. Managers help to set the tone of a work group or department. Research shows that the climate managers set can influence the level of innovation, safe behaviors, and ethical behaviors within the group.[24] Most position announcements for HR manager require 3 to 5 years of HR-related experience to be considered for the job.

HR Careers

HR practitioners work on HR-related activities and regularly engage in HR-related strategic and process-related people or personnel decisions within the organization. They might be called HR manager, HR partner, or HR specialist. Each of these titles connotes different aspects of the HR practitioner's core job functions. And each might perform an **HR specialist** function where they attend to all aspects of one specific HRM function, such as recruitment, compensation, or training. Or they might be an **HR generalist** function where they span the multiple HR functions. As you might imagine, the needs for specialists versus generalists are related to the size and scope of the HR function, as well as the industry the organization is in. The larger the organization is, the more likely it is to employ specialists. You might see job titles such as recruiter, compensation analyst, or HR analyst.

HR Business Partners

HR business partner (HRBP) is the second most frequently advertised job position in HR. An **HR business partner** is a more recent term and refers to someone who serves as a consultant to management on HR-related issues. As the Society for Human Resource Management notes, the "HRBP is responsible for aligning business objectives with employees and management in designated business units. . . . The successful HRBP will act as an employee champion and agent of change." The key aspect of HRBPs is that their role is to anticipate HR-related needs, as well as being available to share advice and proactively address small problems before they become big ones.

What Employers Look for in HR Applicants

The answer to this question depends on the level of the HR position in the organization, as well as the degree to which HR plays a strategic role within the organization. For example, an HR assistant position typically only requires a high school diploma. To move up in the organization, a college degree can make a big difference. An analysis of HR position announcements for jobs found that the top requested areas of college study included human resource management, business administration, psychology, and organizational development. Getting the first job and some HRM experience is only the first step. Those in HR need to stay up to date on the latest developments—especially as they relate to the ever-shifting legal environment.

Organizations can help HR practitioners stay informed of best practices and up to date on the latest trends that might affect HR. One such organization is the Society for Human Resource Management (SHRM). SHRM is the world's largest HR professional society, representing 285,000 members in more than 165 countries. Its headquarters are located in Alexandria, Virginia, and it has 575 affiliated local chapters throughout the United States, China, India, and the United Arab Emirates.[25] One of the key benefits of such professional organizations is that they have a wide view of what it takes to be effective in HRM. In fact, SHRM has spent a great deal of time and energy studying just that, as seen in the section on competencies.

Salary and Job Outlook

The Bureau of Labor Statistics reports that the median pay for an HR manager in 2017 was $110,120 per year, which equals $52.94 per hour. Moving up to become an HR manager happens, on average, about 5 years after starting out. In addition, job growth is projected to be 9% in the next 10 years, which is above the average for all jobs that year.[26] Overall, HRM is considered to have solid career prospects and to be an attractive job. For example, a 2018 survey by Glassdoor.com found that human resource manager was the fifth-best job based on job projections, median base salary, and career opportunity ratings.[27]

HRM certifications. The two major certifications in HRM are administered by SHRM (SHRM-CP and SHRM-SCP) and the HR Certification Institute (SPHR and PHR). One

HR specialist
A person who fulfills an HR specialist function attends to all aspects of one specific HRM function

HR generalist
A person who fulfills an HR generalist function attends to multiple HR functions

HR business partner Someone who serves as a consultant to management on HR-related issues

question that those interested in business and HRM practitioners alike ask is the value of HRM certifications. In an analysis of job postings for HRM, 42% noted a preference or requirement for certification. Further, some positions, such as HR business partner, were more likely than not to require certification, which indicates that certification may be beneficial in securing a job.[28] In addition, having a deeper knowledge of HRM should help the individual to master the HRM knowledge domain more fully and signals a deeper interest in HRM than noncertified individuals.[29]

HR Competencies

You probably know what it means to be competent. A person who is competent is perceived to be able to perform specific functions reasonably well. A **competency** is a cluster of knowledge, skills, abilities, and other characteristics (KSAOs) necessary to be effective at one's job. Competencies are much like this but at a broader level, as they refer to a set of technical or behavioral KSAOs that, together, help to define what it takes to be successful within a specific job, organization, or profession.[30]

SHRM developed its competency model to create a model that is applicable to all HR professionals regardless of characteristics such as job function or career level, organization size, industry, or location. What emerged was a set of core technical competencies called *HR expertise/knowledge.* In addition, it identified eight behavioral competencies that form three additional clusters of competencies with *interpersonal competencies,* including relationship management, communication, and global and cultural effectiveness; *business competencies,* including business acumen, critical evaluation, and consultation; and *leadership competencies,* including leadership and navigation and ethical practice (see Figure 1.4).

Staying Up to Date: Evidence-Based Management

We have seen how important learning the functions of HRM is. It is also important to stay abreast of changes in

Competency
A cluster of knowledge, skills, abilities, and other characteristics (KSAOs) necessary to be effective at one's job

■ **FIGURE 1.4**   SHRM Competency Model

SHRM developed the SHRM Competency Model. Technical competencies are encompassed within HR expertise/knowledge. Interpersonal competencies include relationship management, communication, and global and cultural effectiveness. Business competencies include business acumen, critical evaluation, and consultation. Leadership competencies include leadership and navigation and ethical practice.

Source: Reprinted from *SHRM Competency Model* with permission of the Society for Human Resource Management (SHRM). © SHRM. All rights reserved.

the field as they evolve by taking workshops and education courses (and continuing education) separately or as part of being certified. Another important way that managers, HRM practitioners, consultants, and researchers stay up to date on the latest findings and changes in the field is by learning about research findings conducted by others. In this way, practitioners can learn best practices to give their organization a competitive advantage by saving time by learning from others' mistakes and considering their successes.

Information regarding HRM comes from three main places. First, organizations often engage in benchmarking. **Benchmarking** refers to a measurement of the quality of an organization's practices in comparison with peer organizations using similar metrics. The best benchmarking follows the standards of good decision making and includes identifying the goal and parameters of the benchmarking, gathering data, analyzing data, and communicating the results. Benchmarking might occur within a specific industry sector or across functions such as HRM benchmarking. Benchmarking is often done at different levels as well, with *Fortune* 500 organizations often benchmarking against one another. For example, asking what the top 10 best companies in your industry do in terms of surveys with departing employees could be useful information if you are planning to make changes to your own exit process. One thing to keep in mind is that simply meeting benchmarks is not an advantage, but understanding them and moving beyond them can be.

Second, reports are written based on surveys and trends by HR organizations, such as SHRM, The Conference Board, or the Association for Talent Development, and HR consulting firms, such as PwC, SAP/SuccessFactors, and Aberdeen Group. These findings might be shared at industry conferences or in practitioner outlets such as *HR Focus, HR Magazine, Harvard Business Review, People Management, Workforce*, and *T+D*, as well as via blogs or newsletters. These outlets may be reviewed but do not go under the same scrutiny as peer-reviewed research articles.

Third, researchers within universities and in industry in the fields of HRM and industrial-organizational (I-O) psychology[31] generate new knowledge about best practices through their research streams. The findings are published in academic journals, which are peer reviewed by experts in that research area who evaluate the rigor of the studies and their contribution to the research and practice of HRM. Research findings are also presented at annual conferences such as the Academy of Management and Society for Industrial and Organizational Psychology.[32] Papers presented at these particular conferences are also peer reviewed but with less detailed peer review than for a journal, and attending sessions at conferences allows HRM practitioners and researchers to learn what some of the most current research is on a given topic. And of course, books on HRM topics are also important ways to stay up to date.

Given how important we feel evidence-based practice is, we include research findings throughout the book. When we can, we focus on key findings from meta-analyses in each chapter. Although we base much of this textbook on findings across many individual studies, a meta-analysis is unique in that it summarizes and synthesizes everything that researchers have found on a given topic up to that point using a statistical process. Another way to think about staying up to date is to follow the scientific process in gathering information within your own organization.

Benchmarking
The measurement of the quality of an organization's practices in comparison with those of a peer organization

Spotlight on Legal Issues
U.S. EQUAL EMPLOYMENT OPPORTUNITY COMMISSION

The U.S. Equal Employment Opportunity Commission (EEOC) is the primary federal agency responsible for handling workplace discrimination claims. In 2017, the agency received over 84,000 individual filings. In the United States, federal law prohibits discrimination in employment decisions based on protected characteristics. These laws are referred to as equal employment opportunity (EEO) laws. Most EEO laws pertaining to private, government, and state institutions are monitored and enforced by the EEOC, which is an independent federal agency. The EEOC ensures compliance with the law, in addition to providing outreach activities and preventing discrimination from occurring in the first place. EEO laws typically apply to organizations with 15 or more employees and cover businesses, private employers, government agencies, employment agencies, and labor unions and aim to prevent discrimination against employees, job applicants, and participants in training and apprenticeship programs. You will learn more about the laws that the EEOC covers in Chapter 4, but for now, the key point is to understand that this agency exists.[33]

CHAPTER SUMMARY

HRM influences a company's success from start-up through years of expansion, including successes and setbacks. At this point, you know a great deal about what HRM is, why it matters, and different types of organizational cultures. We also covered an overview of six key aspects of the changing context of HRM, including changing demographics, the emergence of a gig economy, globalization, technology, availability of data, and ethical challenges and corporate social responsibility. The overview of HRM as a profession included understanding who is involved in HRM, different aspects of HRM careers, and HRM competencies. Finally, Spotlights on the manager's tool box, data and analytics, and legal issues, as well as HR in Action, highlighted key points and examples.

KEY TERMS

human resource
   management (HRM)   5
biases   5
availability bias   6
anchoring bias   6
overconfidence bias   6
A-S-A framework   8

organizational
   culture   9
clan culture   10
adhocracy culture   10
market culture   10
hierarchy culture   10
gig economy   13

business ethics   14
HR specialist   18
HR generalist   18
HR business
   partner   18
competency   19
benchmarking   20

$SAGE edge™

Get the tools you need to sharpen your study skills. SAGE edge offers a robust online environment featuring an impressive array of free tools and resources.

Access practice quizzes, eFlashcards, video, and multimedia at **edge.sagepub.com/bauerbrief**

HR REASONING AND DECISION-MAKING EXERCISES

EXERCISE 1.1: SEEKING INFORMATION AS A NEW EMPLOYEE

You have started work at a small company, Johnson Natural Shoes, which designs and produces children's shoes. The company has an innovative approach and uses all-natural materials. Its product has been increasing in demand in the few short years since it began. The company was founded by Shannon McKenzie. You found out about the position because you are friends with Shannon's daughter, who is an old friend of yours from high school. You were hired after you met with the founder, who remembered you from soccer games and birthday parties.

You do not have a job description or formal job title. But you are the only person in the organization with a degree in business, and Shannon mentioned to you that you were hired in the hopes you could help the company manage its rapid growth. At this point, the company is on track to double in size this year compared with last year, when it had only 28 employees.

You notice from the first days on the job that employees enjoy collaborating and making decisions together, and you feel welcomed right away. You see great things in the company's future and want to help make Johnson Natural Shoes an international brand. You can't wait to start making a contribution.

Now it is your turn to decide how to help.

Questions

1. Given that you are still new to the company, how would you approach learning more about the company and its employees?
2. What are specific key questions you might want to ask employees about the company?
3. Based on your knowledge of business, what would you advise Shannon to consider as HR priorities as the organization experiences high growth?

EXERCISE 1.2: THE CHANGING CONTEXT OF HRM

Making HRM decisions is often a group activity, as seldom does one person have all the required information, context, and expertise to tackle every HR issue. Working in a group, review the six trends we identified as affecting HRM today and into the future (changing demographics, the emerging gig economy, increasing globalization, technology, availability of data, and ethical and corporate social responsibility challenges).

Questions

1. Form your group.
2. Decide if there are additional trends your group believes might be as important or more important than these six.
3. As a group, decide which trend your group collectively feels is the *most* important factor that will influence HRM. It is as important to justify your answer in terms of your selection of the most important factor as it is to defend why the others are not seen as equally important.

ETHICAL MATTERS EXERCISE: SHRM CODE OF ETHICS

Ethics is critically important to the effective practice of HRM. Ethical decisions and actions lead to greater trust and engagement within organizations and allow for all types of information to emerge, which is important for effective decision making. Given the importance of ethics to HRM, the Society for Human Resource Management (SHRM), which is the world's largest professional society for human resource management, developed a code of ethics. We encourage you to read this code of ethics whether you are an aspiring manager or HRM professional or one who is seasoned. The core principles noted are easily transferable to different organizational roles, and following them can help you avoid serious problems as you are faced with ethical dilemmas and decisions throughout your career. The six core principles described in the code provisions include the idea that professionals should engage in their work with a focus on professional responsibility, professional development, ethical leadership, fairness and justice, conflicts of interest, and use of information.

Questions

1. Describe a hypothetical scenario in which you would benefit from applying certain principles from the SHRM Code of Ethics.

2. Choose a business situation from the news or the HR literature where principles from the SHRM Code of Ethics could have made a difference. Specifically, what did the decision makers do right, or what could they have done better?

Professional Responsibility
As HR professionals, we are responsible for adding value to the organizations we serve and contributing to the ethical success of those organizations. We accept professional responsibility for our individual decisions and actions. We are also advocates for the profession by engaging in activities that enhance its credibility and value.

Professional Development
As professionals, we must strive to meet the highest standards of competence and commit to strengthen our competencies on a continuous basis.

Ethical Leadership
HR professionals are expected to exhibit individual leadership as role models for maintaining the highest standards of ethical conduct.

Fairness and Justice
As human resource professionals, we are ethically responsible for promoting and fostering fairness and justice for all employees and their organizations.

Conflicts of Interest
As HR professionals, we must maintain a high level of trust with our stakeholders. We must protect the interests of our stakeholders as well as our professional integrity and should not engage in activities that create actual, apparent, or potential conflicts of interest.

Use of Information
HR professionals consider and protect the rights of individuals, especially in the acquisition and dissemination of information while ensuring truthful communications and facilitating informed decision making.

2

Strategic HRM, Data-Driven Decision Making, and HR Analytics

LEARNING OBJECTIVES

After reading and studying this chapter, you should be able to do the following:

2.1 Identify the steps for formulating and implementing a strategy.

2.2 Explain the importance of strategic HRM for realizing employee, operational, stakeholder, and financial outcomes and for sustaining a competitive advantage.

2.3 Demonstrate the use of data-driven decisions in realizing organizational strategy and contrasting different HR analytics competencies and levels of HR analytics.

2.4 Summarize the arguments for a scientific, ethical, and legally compliant approach to HR decision making.

2.5 Manage the components of a successful HR analytics function.

HR in Action: The Case of Procter & Gamble

Many human resource departments use strategy when implementing initiatives or plans to achieve organizational objectives. As a major strategic initiative, in 2005, Procter & Gamble (P&G) reached a deal to purchase the Gillette Company for approximately $57 billion in stock, thereby strengthening P&G's reputation as a consumer products giant and surpassing Unilever as the world's biggest consumer products conglomerate. The

merger brought together household brands like P&G's Crest and Tide and Gillette's Right Guard and Duracell under the umbrella of a single company. The move provided P&G with more pricing leverage for its products with large retailers like Walmart and with a stronger negotiating position when buying advertising from media companies.

Even though mergers and acquisitions present opportunities for achieving a competitive advantage,

©iStock.com/jetcityimage

they can also be quite disruptive for the people who work for the companies involved. Careful attention must be paid to integrating distinct companies with sometimes different values, norms, policies, and systems. To ensure success, P&G took several steps to calm employee fears and to integrate Gillette employees into the P&G workforce and culture. For instance, P&G gradually introduced Gillette employees to the P&G performance management and reward systems so that they had time to learn P&G's business strategy and objectives. In addition, although P&G had a reputation for promoting from within, management decided to replace many lower-performing P&G employees with higher-performing Gillette employees. This, in turn, signaled to employees that P&G valued the quality of the people who came from Gillette. Finally, as evidence of P&G's merger success, P&G met financial targets in the year following the merger.[1]

Case Discussion Questions

1. What might have been some arguments for and against changing P&G's usual promotion pattern to give Gillette employees an advantage?

2. If you were an HR manager in a large company that was acquiring a smaller one, how might you apply lessons from the P&G case?

3. How should a company go about communicating its strategy to new employees?

Simply put, people matter. Jim Goodnight, CEO of SAS Institute, Inc., is quoted as saying, "Ninety-five percent of my assets drive out the gate every evening. It's my job to maintain a work environment that keeps those people coming back every morning."[2] This chapter focuses on the role HR plays in managing people to achieve organizational success. **Strategic human resource management** is the process of aligning HR policies and practices with the objectives of the organization, including employee, operational, stakeholder, and financial outcomes. This chapter explains how strategy is combined with HRM to achieve organizational success and how organizations can make data-driven decisions that are accurate, fair, ethical, and legal—considerations that are becoming increasingly important as our society pushes forward into an era of big data.

Strategic human resource management
The process of aligning HR policies and practices with the objectives of the organization, including employee, operational, stakeholder, and financial outcomes

Defining Strategy

LO 2.1   Identify the steps for formulating and implementing a strategy.

Central to strategic human resource management—and to strategic management in general—is the concept of a strategy. What is a strategy? Think of a **strategy** as a well-devised and thoughtful plan for achieving an objective.[3] A strategy is inherently future oriented and is intended to provide a road map toward completion of an

Strategy
A well-devised and thoughtful plan for achieving an objective

objective. Strategy reflects the manner in which a unit, department, or organization coordinates activities to achieve planned objectives in both the short and long term.[4] Strategy can be paired with data analytics and scientific process to make data-informed decisions, which improve the likelihood of achieving strategic objectives and sustaining a competitive advantage.

Some firms keep their strategies relatively private, but others, like Tesla Motors, Inc., announce their strategy to the world. With a mission to "accelerate the world's transition to sustainable energy," Tesla's strategy is multiphased and is referred to as the *Tesla Motors Master Plan* by provocative and often controversial company cofounder and CEO Elon Musk, who settled Securities and Exchange Commission fraud charges in 2018.[5] Musk unveiled Tesla's strategy in 2006, describing the overall purpose of the company as expediting a shift from a hydrocarbon (fossil fuel) economy to a solar-electric (clean energy) economy. For the first phase, Musk outlined the company's plan of initially producing a high-end electric car called the Tesla Roadster, which reached the market in 2006 and was rated the second-best invention by *Time* magazine in 2008. (The retail DNA test developed by 23andMe took top honors that year.)[6]

Using revenue and interest generated from the Tesla Roadster, the original plan was to develop increasingly more affordable cars and, ultimately, affordable family cars. So far, Tesla has followed through on the first-phase strategy. In 2012, a higher-end, yet more accessible, model called the Model S rolled out of production plants, and in 2017, the even more affordable Model 3 went into production, albeit with some initial newsworthy delays.[7] Based on these achievements, Tesla not only formulated a viable strategy but, to date, has largely followed through on the implementation of most aspects of its strategic plan. In 2016, Musk set the second phase of Tesla's strategy into motion by announcing plans for Tesla to acquire SolarCity, a company that produces solar panels.[8] By combining Tesla and SolarCity, Musk intends to stay true to the overall purpose of his company: shifting the world to clean energy. That is, when Tesla electric cars are charged with solar electric energy, they become truly clean-energy vehicles, and in the process, Tesla follows through on its strategy and leaves its mark as an industry disrupter with its innovative approaches to car design and energy.[9]

Developing and Refining a Strategy: Strategy Formulation

The Tesla example illustrates two important aspects of strategy: formulation and implementation. Strategy formulation involves planning what to do to achieve organizational objectives—or in other words, the development and/or refinement of a strategy. To achieve its overarching goal of shifting consumers toward clean-energy transportation and living solutions, Tesla formulated a rational and methodical strategy with multiple preplanned phases. Strategy formulation often follows the steps depicted in Figure 2.1, which ultimately set the stage for strategy implementation.

Create a Mission, Vision, and Set of Values

A **mission** describes a core need that an organization strives to fulfill and represents the organization's overarching purpose. Recall that Tesla's espoused mission is to "accelerate the

Mission
A core need that an organization strives to fulfill and represents the organization's overarching purpose

■ **FIGURE 2.1**   Steps for Strategy Formulation

Formulating an organization strategy requires decision making regarding the mission, vision, values, and strategy type; analyzing the internal and external environments; and defining objectives designed to satisfy stakeholders.

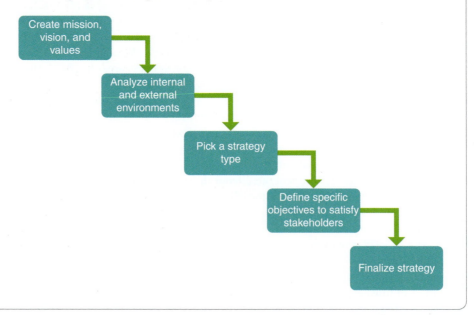

world's transition to sustainable energy," and as you have probably observed, many organizations feature their mission statements prominently on their websites. Tesla is no exception. In addition to having a mission, strategy formulation also involves stating a vision and values. An organization's **vision** is an extension of the mission and describes what the organization will look like or be at some point in the future. Creating a set of core **values** provides the organization with parameters and guidelines for decision making and bringing its vision to life.

Analyze Internal and External Environments

As the next step in strategy formulation, an organization must look both internally and externally to understand how to bring its mission, vision, and values to life. That is, an organization must analyze the internal *strengths* and *weaknesses* that are under its control and the external *threats* and *opportunities* that are beyond its direct control—a process commonly referred to as a SWOT analysis.[10] By analyzing the internal environment, an organization comes up with a plan for how to leverage its strengths and improve on its weaknesses. By analyzing the external environment, an organization identifies opportunities and threats with respect to the state of its industry and competitors, as well as other external factors like the labor market, unemployment rate, and the general state of the local, national, and/or global economies.

Vision An extension of an organization's mission that describes what the organization will look like or be at some point in the future

Values Parameters and guidelines for decision making that help an organization realize its vision

Pick a Strategy Type

After analyzing internal and external environments, an organization is ready to select a strategy type. A strategy type provides a general approach for how an organization will bring its mission, vision, and values to life while at the same time leveraging its strengths and improving its weaknesses. Examples include the following:[11]

- **Differentiation:** The organization creates a product or service that is different from competitors' products or services and warrants a higher price or more attention from consumers.

- **Cost leadership:** The organization identifies ways to produce a product or provide a service at a lower cost compared with competitors. This can help the organization increase its margin or sell the product or service at a cheaper price than competitors.

- **Focus:** The organization uses differentiation or cost leadership but identifies a narrow consumer base to appeal to a specific product or service type that might not be produced or sold by competitors.

Define Specific Objectives to Satisfy Stakeholders

Ultimately, an organization formulates a strategy to meet the needs of key stakeholders and—above all—to be competitive. That is, strategic objectives should be designed to satisfy different stakeholders. **Stakeholders** include a number of different groups that an organization must appeal to, such as

- customers,
- investors and shareholders,
- employees, and
- communities.

Finalize Strategy

Once an organization defines its mission, vision, and values; analyzes the internal and external environments; chooses a general strategy type; and defines its strategic objectives, it is ready to finalize the strategy. That is, the organization must create a clear plan for the future before progressing to strategy implementation.

Bringing a Strategy to Life: Strategy Implementation

During **strategy implementation,** an organization follows through on its plan. It is during this stage that an organization builds and leverages the capabilities of its human resources (which collectively are called **human capital**) to enact its strategy. The following section discusses how to align an organization's HR policies and practices with its strategy and how a well-designed system of HR policies and practices can improve human capital capabilities within an organization and, ultimately, performance.

Stakeholders
A number of different groups that an organization must appeal to, including customers and investors

Strategy implementation
The enactment of a strategic plan

Human capital
The knowledge, skills, and abilities that people embody across an organization

Manager's Toolbox
CONTRIBUTING TO YOUR ORGANIZATION'S STRATEGY

After the formulation stage, the strategy must be implemented, which requires the coordination and cooperation of employees and managers at all levels of the organization. As you might imagine, sometimes there are disconnects between an organization's official strategy and how managers interpret and implement that strategy. Here are some actions you can take as a manager to effectively bring your organization's strategy to life.[12]

1. *Know what your organization's strategy is.* In a survey of employees from 20 major Australian corporations, only 29% of respondents were able to identify their company's strategy from a list of six choices. Take the following steps to understand your organization's strategy:

   - Review your organization's mission statement, vision, and values.
   - Ask your manager to explain how you can contribute to strategic objectives.

- Pay attention to formal communications from executives and upper management.
- Stay on top of changes to your firm's strategy.

2. *Align your own goals with your organization's strategic objectives.* As a manager, it is important to align your self-interests with the interests of the organization. Specifically, set goals that describe how you and your team can contribute to organizational objectives, such as decreasing turnover or increasing productivity.

3. *Communicate the strategy to your employees.* Explain the strategy to your employees, and engage them in activities that help them understand how they can contribute to the organization's strategic objectives. Remember, as a manager, you play an essential role in communicating company strategy to employees.

Linking Strategy With HRM: Strategic HRM

LO 2.2 Explain the importance of strategic HRM for realizing employee, operational, stakeholder, and financial outcomes and for sustaining a competitive advantage.

The beginning of this chapter defines *strategic HRM* as the process of aligning HR policies and practices with the strategic objectives of the organization, including achieving employee, operational, stakeholder, and financial outcomes to achieve and sustain a competitive advantage. An important implication of strategic HRM is that HR practices and employees are company assets that add value and not merely costs.[13]

The Origins of Strategic HRM

HRM activities have changed over the years. A growing number of organizations now focus on *strategic* HRM and using HR data to make better organizational decisions. Traditionally, HRM focused mostly on transactional and administrative activities (e.g., recordkeeping)

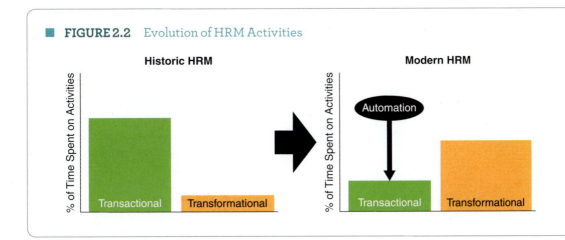

■ **FIGURE 2.2** Evolution of HRM Activities

and employee relations activities. However, the amount of time spent on transactional activities has decreased over the past century as more HR functions become automated, freeing up more time for transformational activities that help the organization leverage its human resources to achieve strategic objectives (see Figure 2.2). This change has expanded our view of managing people from that of a cost to that of an asset and corresponds with advances in information systems.[14]

The focus on strategic HRM has also expanded the responsibilities of the HR function. According to Ulrich's model of strategic HRM, the HR function should play the roles of administrative expert, employee advocate, change agent, and business partner (see Figure 2.3). This approach to HRM has expanded the influence of the HR function, such that the deployment of HR practices and human resource capabilities can be used to realize strategic change initiatives, such as mergers, acquisitions, reorganizations, and restructurings, as well as gain a "seat at the table" during key business decisions. With greater influence comes greater responsibility, which means that the modern HR function now faces greater pressure to link HR activities and responsibilities to organizational performance.

Organizational Performance and the Balanced Scorecard

Historically, organizational performance was defined in terms of financial indicators, such as return on assets, return on equity, and market return. While achieving financial outcomes is indeed a worthwhile and necessary objective, other indicators of firm performance must also be considered. The introduction of the balanced scorecard was a game-changer because it made the case for considering nonfinancial indicators when defining organizational success.[15] The balanced scorecard is used to evaluate organizational performance based on the extent to which the organization satisfies different stakeholder needs, such as the needs of customers, investors and shareholders, employees, and the broader community. For example, an employee survey can be administered to understand how well the organization is meeting the learning and development needs of its employee stakeholders.

■ **FIGURE 2.3**   Ulrich's Model of Strategic HRM

Ulrich's model indicates that HRM should provide administrative expertise, serve as an employee advocate, be an agent of change, and serve as a strategic business partner.

Source: Adapted from Ulrich, D. *Human resource champions: The next agenda for adding value and delivering results.* Cambridge, MA: Harvard Business School Press.

Identifying Best Practices

Some HR practices can be thought of as *universal best practices* because implementing them often leads to improved organizational performance, regardless of the organization. In HRM, evidence-based universal best practices include enhancing perceptions of job security among employees, promoting from within the organization, providing financial incentives linked to performance, offering training, and providing flexible work arrangements.[16] And such practices are often referred to as **high-performance work practices**.[17] Recent meta-analytic evidence indicates that certain well-designed individual HR practices generally have positive effects on organizational outcomes.[18] For examples of evidence-based high-performance work practices, refer to Figure 2.4.

Systems Thinking: Considering the System and Context

In addition to identifying universal best practices, such as high-performance work practices, it is important to consider how these practices and others fit into the broader HR system and organizational strategy. In other words, the effectiveness of some HR practices may be contingent on the context (e.g., industry, culture) and the configuration of other HR practices that are part of a larger system.[19] In addition to adopting universal best practices, we recommend taking a **systems perspective,** which means considering how all of the pieces of the HR puzzle fit together and how HR fits within the broader organization. Research has shown that integrated systems of high-performance work practices outperform well-designed individual HR practices. Further, an investment in an HR system can lead to valued organizational outcomes, such as lower turnover, higher productivity, and higher financial performance.[20]

Without taking a systems perspective, it is unlikely that a system of HR practices will reach its full potential. For instance, imagine a company in which teamwork is integral for achieving a strategic objective. Accordingly, this company devised a selection tool to identify job applicants who are likely to be team players and an onboarding program to train new employees to work effectively in teams. Now imagine that the same company introduces a new compensation program that rewards only individual performance and not the performance of teams. Rather than interacting synergistically

High-performance work practices Bundles of HR universal best practices, such as promoting within the organization and offering training

Systems perspective The view of how all pieces of a system and its subsystems fit together

■ **FIGURE 2.4**   Pfeffer's Seven Practices of Successful Organizations

Pfeffer's practices are examples of high-performance work practices that are instrumental for developing human capital capabilities across different contexts.

1. *Create employment security* policies to encourage employee involvement and commitment.

2. *Selectively hire new employees* to create a highly qualified workforce that are a good fit.

3. *Organize employees into self-managed teams* to achieve higher-performing teams.

4. *Compensate employees based on performance* to attract, motivate, and retain talented employees.

5. *Train employees* to enhance the knowledge and skills necessary for high performance.

6. *Reduce status differences between employees* to leverage ideas, skills, and effort at all levels.

7. *Share information on strategy and performance* to motivate employees to contribute to the organization.

Source: Pfeffer, J. (1998). Seven practices of successful organizations. *California Management Review, 40,* 96–124.

TABLE 2.1   Factors Influencing the Effectiveness of HR Practices

FACTORS	DESCRIPTION
Internal Environment	
Business Strategy	Although research findings have been mixed, some evidence indicates differentiation strategies enhance the effectiveness of HR systems in relation to certain organizational outcomes, such as reducing turnover.
Culture	Most evidence to date indicates that a positive and supportive organizational culture enhances the effectiveness of HR systems in relation to organizational outcomes.
Manager Characteristics	Research has shown that having more senior managers and managers with stronger HR backgrounds enhances the effectiveness of HR systems.
External Environment	
Industry Characteristics	The type of industry an organization operates within can influence the effectiveness of HR systems. For example, the positive effects of HR systems on organizational outcomes tends to be stronger in manufacturing industries (as opposed to service industries).

Source: Adapted from Jackson, S. E., Schuler, R. S., & Jiang, K. (2014). An aspirational framework for strategic human resource management. *Academy of Management Annals, 8,* 1–56.

with the selection and training subsystems to improve team effectiveness, the compensation subsystem may thwart team effectiveness by focusing individuals' efforts toward their own individual achievement, as opposed to the achievement of their team. Table 2.1 provides examples of other factors that have been found to influence the effectiveness of HR practices.

Strategic HRM, Data-Driven Decision Making, and HR Analytics

LO 2.3   Demonstrate the use of data-driven decisions in realizing organizational strategy and contrasting different HR analytics competencies and levels of HR analytics.

Like the rest of the world, HR departments are faced with ever-increasing amounts of data and big decisions to make. This is due in part to technological advances that have made it easier to capture and store data via HR information systems and other platforms. Such data are only valuable to the extent HR departments actually use them, though. Moreover, HR departments must consider carefully which data to use and for what purposes. When decisions are informed by the analysis and interpretation of relevant, accurate, and timely data, we refer to these as **data-driven decisions**.

Above all, data-driven decisions should inform and support strategic HRM objectives. To that end, **human resource (HR) analytics** refers to the use of data to support and inform high-stakes decision making, to achieve strategic objectives, and to sustain a competitive advantage. In some organizations, HR analytics goes by other names, such as people analytics, human capital analytics, talent analytics, or workforce analytics. As a scientific process, HR analytics is a data-driven approach to designing and implementing HR systems, policies, and practices. That is, HR analytics requires organizational leaders and HR professionals to think like scientists—instead of relying solely on their gut instincts, or intuition. At the same time, they also need business acumen to make a strong case for using science-based HR practices to improve the organization.[21] An overarching goal of HR analytics should be to provide managers with actionable evidence-based practices that improve the management of people.

Earlier in the chapter, we described Tesla's mission and strategy. To realize its strategic objectives, Tesla has embraced HR analytics. Because Tesla requires a workforce filled with talented, motivated people to help the company realize its strategic objectives, its HR department uses data to acquire, manage, and retain talented people. For example, Tesla HR analysts mined data from the company's employee referral program and found that higher-performing employees referred higher-potential job candidates, midrange employees referred lower-performing job candidates, and lower-performing employees referred all levels of job candidates. Using these data-analytic findings, the team devised ways to improve its recruitment and selection practices to attract and attain high-potential people.[22]

Data-driven decisions Decisions that are made based on the analysis and interpretation of relevant, accurate, and timely data

Human resource (HR) analytics The process of collecting, analyzing, interpreting, and reporting people-related data for the purpose of improving decision making, achieving strategic objectives, and sustaining a competitive advantage

How Does a System of HR Practices Influence Organizational Outcomes?

Performance = Ability × Motivation × Opportunity

The *ability-motivation-opportunity model* proposes that a system of HR practices influences employee outcomes and, ultimately, operational and financial outcomes to the extent that the practices target three different elements: ability to perform, motivation to perform, and opportunity to perform. The first element—*ability* to perform—encapsulates employees' knowledge, skills, and abilities. In a sense, ability to perform can be thought of as what an employee *can do* on the job. The second element—*motivation* to perform—refers to the work-related effort that employees exert toward goal completion and captures what employees *will do* on the job. That is,

just because employees have the ability to do the work does not necessarily mean they have the motivation to do the work and vice versa. The third element—*opportunities* to perform—entails whether employees have the chance to perform on the job. Taken together, we can conceptualize employee performance as a function of their ability, motivation, and opportunity to perform. According to this model, if ability, motivation, or opportunity falls to zero, performance will be zero. We recommend using this conceptual formula to help you wrap your mind around how employees achieve high levels of performance in the workplace, as well as how different HR practices can be designed to target each of these three elements.[23]

Spotlight on Data and Analytics
ALIGNING ANALYTICS WITH STRATEGY

Business analytics, in general, has received a great deal of media attention, as evidenced by *New York Times* and *Wall Street Journal* headlines such as "Data-crunching is coming to help your boss manage your time"; "Big data, trying to build better workers"; and "The algorithm that tells the boss who might quit." Despite the media and organizational attention paid to analytics and big data, some argue that analytics is overhyped, misunderstood, or misused. In a recent article

by Ransbotham, Kiron, and Prentice (in collaboration with SAS Institute, Inc.) for the *MIT Sloan Management Review,* the authors concluded that the *idea* of analytics is now mainstream, but analytics is still not widely practiced. Further, based on the results of a survey of over 2,000 managers, the authors found that organizations with innovative analytics programs were much more likely to have an official strategy for analytics. Although awareness of analytics has increased

(Continued)

(Continued)

substantially in recent years, translating analytics into practice has remained an elusive goal in many organizations. As you will learn later in the chapter, most companies rely on a basic level of analytics called descriptive analytics. Essentially, this means that these companies have the capability to report what *has* happened in the past based on data but not to predict what *will* happen in the future. Although it is important to build analytics capabilities, particularly in the area of HR

analytics, companies also need to develop strategies for using analytics. That is, using analytics to achieve a competitive advantage depends on the development of a clear plan for integrating analytics into organizational decision making and for aligning analytics strategy with organizational strategy. In fact, some have even argued that a lack of alignment between HR analytics and strategy could have damaging effects on the organization and its employees.[24]

The Washington Post/Contributor

D. J. Patil, who has worked for eBay and LinkedIn, helped coin the term *data scientist*. He became the first chief data scientist in the U.S. Office of Science and Technology Policy.

The Value of HR Analytics

Given its large focus on data and scientific decision making, HR analytics has been referred to jokingly as "HR's nerdy best friend."[25] And many would argue that HR analytics has the potential to be HR's nerdy *and valuable* best friend. In general, HR analytics can provide evidence supporting the links among HR systems, policies, and practices and employee, operational, stakeholder, and financial outcomes. Advanced HR analytics can even provide prescriptive recommendations for the future.

The growth in HR analytics interest signals that more and more organizations are beginning to understand the importance of making data-driven decisions to achieve a competitive advantage. To that end, after reviewing survey responses and panel discussions, the Society for Human Resource Management (SHRM) Foundation concluded in a report that leveraging HR analytics to achieve a competitive advantage is an important area of growth for HRM.[26] The report concluded that talent shortages are on the rise and that HR must provide HR analytics to aid in strategic business decision making.

A number of organizations, including Chevron, T-Mobile, and Facebook, have expanded their internal HRM function by adding an HR analytics team. Further, companies like ADP, Inc. and SAP SuccessFactors now provide products and services for analyzing people data in addition to those related to data collection and storage. These changes reflect the findings of a 2015 Deloitte survey, which showed that, on average, executives rated HR analytics as important for their business but, at the same time, reported feeling only somewhat ready to respond to the need.[27] Further, only 4% of executives reported that their company was excellent at leveraging people data to predict performance and improvement. Many organizations and HR departments are in need of individuals who possess knowledge and skills related to HR analytics.

HR Analytics Competency Identification

Integrating HR analytics into the HRM function requires certain competencies that do not necessarily need to be held by a single individual. Ideally, HR analytics should be a team endeavor. Working as a team with diverse backgrounds and perspectives can facilitate sound judgments and good decision making, particularly when it comes to ethically or legally gray areas. While some HR analysts may have degrees in business or HRM, others may have backgrounds in industrial and organizational psychology, law, statistics, mathematics, data science, computer science, or information systems. Aside from educational differences among HR analysts, what matters most is that an HR analytics *team,* as a whole, is competent in the following seven areas: theory, business, data management, measurement, data analysis, employment law, and ethics (see Table 2.2).

A common complaint from data analysts is that managers do not understand or recognize the value of data analysis and data-driven findings, leading to frustration. Conversely, a common complaint among managers is that data analysts fail to provide *understandable* answers to the questions that managers *actually* need answered, also leading to frustration. In recognition of this communication issue, Tom Davenport, who is an independent senior advisor to Deloitte Analytics, wrote a blog post praising what he refers to as *light quants* or *analytical translators.*[28] Whereas a *heavy quant* would include the likes of a statistician, mathematician, or data scientist, a light quant is someone who knows enough about

TABLE 2.2   The Seven Competencies of Effective HR Analytics Teams

COMPETENCY	DESCRIPTION
Theory	Knowledge of psychological and social scientific theory is critical because findings from people data should be interpreted through the lens of human behavior, cognition, and emotion.
Business	Business knowledge and skills ensure that the activities of an HR analytics team are in the service of HR and organizational strategies and help the organization gain a competitive advantage.
Data Management	Data management knowledge and skills ensure that data are acquired, cleaned, manipulated, and stored in a way that facilitates subsequent analysis while maintaining data privacy and security.
Measurement	Measurement knowledge and skills provide a basis for developing sound HR metrics and measures that demonstrate sufficient reliability and validity.
Data Analysis	Knowledge and skills related to mathematics, statistics, and data analysis are critical, especially when it comes to identifying an appropriate analysis technique to address a given hypothesis or question.
Employment Law	Knowledge of employment law and HR legal issues separates an HR analytics team from a general business analytics team; teams lacking such knowledge might inadvertently violate laws when collecting data, analyze data that should not be analyzed, or use data in ways that may result in adverse consequences for protected groups.
Ethics	Knowledge of ethics helps the team navigate legally gray areas while also answering the question: "Just because we can, should we?"

mathematics, statistics, and data analysis to communicate with a heavy quant and who knows enough about the business to communicate with a manager. Davenport contends that many organizations with an analytics function would benefit from hiring or training individuals who qualify as light quants, as such individuals can help managers pose better questions for heavy quants to answer and, in turn, translate the findings of heavy quants into words and ideas that are understood by managers.

Understanding the Levels of HR Analytics

There are three levels of HR analytics: descriptive, predictive, and prescriptive. **Descriptive analytics** focuses on understanding what has happened, which implies a focus on the past. Typically, descriptive analytics includes summary statistics, such as sums, averages, and percentages, as well as commonly reported HR metrics, such as absence rate, turnover rate, cost per hire, and training return on investment. Descriptive analytics does not have to be complicated, and most involve simple arithmetic.

A more advanced form of analytics is **predictive analytics**, which focuses on what is likely to happen in the future based on available data and is more forward looking. Examples of predictive analytics include various statistical and computational models. A common type of statistical model is a regression model. Using regression, we can evaluate the extent to which scores on one or more predictor variables are associated with scores on a particular outcome variable. For instance, in the context of selection, we might test whether applicants' level of extraversion predicts their future level of sales performance. Note that we do not expect 100% accuracy in our predictive models, as human behavior is influenced by many factors that may not be captured in the regression model. However, we strive to forecast future events and outcomes with as much accuracy as we can. As described by a SHRM Foundation report, very few companies have reached the level of predictive analytics, as the vast majority relies on descriptive analytics and basic reporting for HRM.[29]

Finally, the most advanced form of analytics is prescriptive analytics, and at this point, relatively few companies effectively apply prescriptive analytics to HR decision making. **Prescriptive analytics** focuses on what actions should be taken based on what is likely to happen in the future. By definition, prescriptive analytics is forward-looking, just like predictive analytics, but prescriptive analytics builds on predictive analytics by taking predictions and translating them into prescriptive action.

HR Analytics and the Scientific Process

LO 2.4   Summarize the arguments for a scientific, ethical, and legally compliant approach to HR decision making.

Regardless of whether a company uses descriptive, predictive, or prescriptive analytics, we recommend that you envision HR analytics—and data-driven decision making, in general—as a scientific process. The **scientific process** offers a rigorous framework for guiding the way in which HR departments collect, analyze, and interpret data in service of HR and organizational strategies. In essence, the scientific process can be thought of as a rigorous and rational approach to problem solving and decision making. The scientific process consists of the six steps shown in Figure 2.5.

Descriptive analytics
Focuses on understanding what has already happened, which implies a focus on the past

Predictive analytics
Focuses on what is likely to happen in the future based on available data

Prescriptive analytics
Focuses on what actions should be taken based on what is likely to happen in the future

Scientific process A method used for systematic and rigorous problem solving that is predicated on the assumption that knowledge requires evidence

■ **FIGURE 2.5**   Steps in the Scientific Process

The scientific process can be thought of as a rigorous approach to problem solving and decision making.

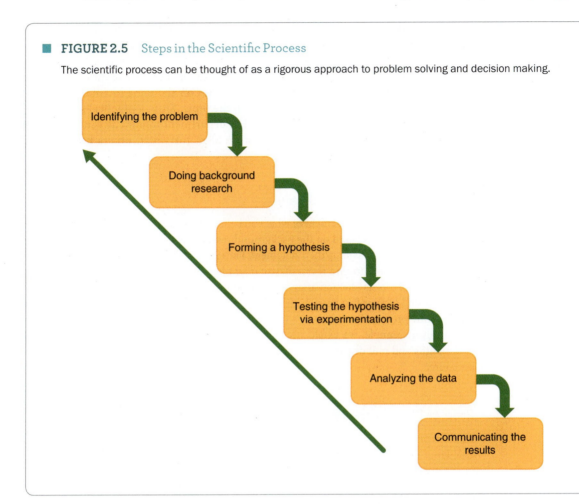

Step 1: Identifying the Problem

Like any problem-solving approach, the first step of the scientific process is to identify and define the problem. That is, what specifically will you try to describe, predict, explain, or understand using data? Imagine your organization has been facing a retention issue, in which employees are voluntarily leaving the organization at a concerning rate. In general, turnover is a major cost for organizations,[30] with some estimates suggesting that selecting and training a replacement employee can cost organizations between 50% and 200% of the first-year salary for each person who leaves the organization.[31] Given the cost of voluntary turnover and your organization's latest turnover rates (which represent a type of a descriptive analytics), you might define voluntary turnover as a problem for which you wish to find a solution.

Step 2: Doing Background Research

It is unlikely that the problem you identified is entirely unique to your organization. For example, others who came before you have investigated the problem of voluntary turnover. Universities and other academic institutions employ organizational scholars and researchers who have investigated countless organizational problems. As such, before starting from scratch, look to prior theory and research to help you understand the phenomenon you wish to investigate using the scientific process. If you were to look through scholarly journal articles on the topic of voluntary turnover, you would find thousands of articles on the topic. From a practical standpoint, doing background research can save your HR department money, as you will spend less time and energy on trying to solve a problem for which others have already found a viable solution.

Step 3: Forming a Hypothesis

A hypothesis is simply a statement of what you believe or predict to be true. In other words, it is an educated guess based on the background research you performed. We recommend stating the hypothesis as an if/then statement. For example, based on your identification of the problem and background research, you might hypothesize, "If new employees perceive a low degree of job satisfaction after 3 months on the job, then they will be more likely to quit by the end of their first year." Your hypothesis serves as a compass to guide you through the scientific process. For instance, a hypothesis informs what data you need to collect. In the turnover example, we would need to measure new sales employees' job satisfaction at 3 months and pull organizational turnover records for these same employees at 1-year post-hire.

Step 4: Testing the Hypothesis via Experimentation

A true experiment is one of the most rigorous research designs you can use to test a hypothesis. For a true experiment, employees must be randomly assigned to either a treatment or control group. For instance, imagine a scenario in which you developed a new training module aimed at increasing new sales employees' job satisfaction. Using a true experimental design, you could randomly assign half of new employees to a treatment group that receives the training and the other half to a control group that doesn't receive the training. At the end of the first year, you could evaluate whether fewer individuals quit when they received the job satisfaction training.

Under some circumstances, however, it may be impractical or inappropriate to conduct a true experiment. Instead, you might opt for an observational design in which you survey employees or record their behavior directly through observation or archival organizational records. For example, to test our turnover hypothesis, we might administer a survey in which employees respond to a job satisfaction measure and then gather their organizational turnover records 1-year post-hire. Regardless of how a hypothesis is tested, it is important to consider the types of data that will be collected, as the type of data informs the type of analysis.

Qualitative data Nonnumeric information that includes text or narrative data, such as interview transcripts

Qualitative Versus Quantitative Data

In general, there are two types of data: qualitative and quantitative (see Table 2.3). On one hand, **qualitative data** are nonnumeric and include text or narrative data, such as interview transcripts or responses to open-ended survey questions. Additional examples of qualitative data include videos and photos. Qualitative data can be quite rich, providing

TABLE 2.3   Example of Qualitative Versus Quantitative Data

This data table provides an example of a qualitative variable and quantitative variable. The performance description variable is qualitative because the associated data are nonnumeric and text. The performance rating variable is quantitative because the data are numeric.

EMPLOYEE ID	PERFORMANCE RATING	PERFORMANCE DESCRIPTION
9082625	2.65	Peter performed satisfactorily. He still struggles with his TPS reports and arrives late to work at least once a week. Nonetheless, he showed glimpses of potential from time to time.
9077854	4.99	Lisa's performance was exceptional this quarter. She went above and beyond on her grant proposals and showed great teamwork when she helped get a team member back up to speed who had been on maternity leave.

important information about context and processes. Qualitative data, however, are analyzed differently than quantitative data. For instance, qualitative interview data could be thematically analyzed such that the transcripts are coded for recurring themes.

On the other hand, **quantitative data** are numeric and can be counted or measured in some way. Employee age is an example of a continuous quantitative variable, whereas employee voluntary turnover—when coded in binary as 0 = stayed and 1 = quit—is an example of a categorical variable. Statistical models are created using quantitative data.

Big Data Versus Little Data

In addition to the qualitative versus quantitative distinction, we can distinguish between big data and little data. The term *big data* has received a lot of attention in the popular press in recent years, and companies like Amazon, Facebook, and Google have built enormous reputations and revenues from leveraging data to optimize business decision making. Amazon, for example, tracks huge volumes of consumer data and, using sophisticated algorithms, can predict what consumers will buy.

In the realm of HRM, HR analysts have begun to use big data to make better people decisions. Signaling the growth in big data in HRM, the Equal Employment Opportunity Commission met in 2016 to discuss big data and analytics from a legal perspective.[32] But exactly what are big data? **Big data** refer to large (or massive) amounts of unstructured, messy, and sometimes quickly streaming data—often from sources that we did not originally intend to leverage for analytical purposes (e.g., scraping or coding résumé data).

In contrast, **little data** are structured data that are gathered in smaller volumes, usually for a previously planned purpose. Consider an analogy involving a water fountain and a fire hydrant to illustrate the distinction between little data and big data. Working with little data is like drinking from a water fountain; the water flow is steady, clean, slow, predictable, and easy to manage. Alternatively, working with big data is like drinking from a fire hydrant spraying out untreated and unfiltered water; the water flow is voluminous, dirty,

Quantitative data Numeric data that can be counted or measured in some way

Big data Large amounts of unstructured, messy, and sometimes quickly streaming data, which can be described in terms of volume, variety, velocity, and veracity

Little data Structured data that are gathered in small volumes, usually for a previously planned purpose

fast, largely unpredictable, and difficult to manage. Working with big data requires a lot of upfront data management and restructuring, so much so that prepping big data for subsequent data analysis may require the expertise of a data scientist.

Data Collection and Measurement

Regardless of how or where data are collected, sound measurement is key. Think carefully about what is being measured and how it is being measured, and distinguish between two terms: concept and measure. A concept is theoretical, and job performance is a prime example. Performance on a given job entails a number of different behaviors. For instance, a sales position requires the enactment of customer service behaviors. Different measures can be used to assess the concept of job performance for a sales position. For instance, an

---

Spotlight on Legal Issues
LEGAL IMPLICATIONS OF BIG DATA

Organizations can benefit from big data and analytics when it comes to key HRM functions, such as recruitment and selection. For example, algorithmic systems and analytic tools, such as those based on machine learning, can provide more accurate predictions of future performance given a number of candidate attributes (e.g., personality, experiences).

Using an algorithm or an analytic tool, however, will not necessarily result in recruitment processes and selection decisions that meet legal scrutiny. To that end, a White House report from May 2016 addressed the legal implications of big data and analytics in a variety of areas, including access to credit, higher education, criminal justice, and employment. With regard to employment, the report recognized that modern algorithmic and automated recruitment and selection systems do, in fact, have the potential to reduce bias, but the report cautions that algorithms are designed by humans. As a result, bias can inevitably find its way into algorithms and models. In fact, algorithms and models can even magnify biases in the data. Nonetheless, the report contends that the use of data-driven approaches in hiring can reduce bias if designed properly.

The major challenge to using data-driven approaches is improving decision making while also adhering to legal guidelines. When building algorithms and models to predict employee behavior and outcomes, analysts must carefully consider whether it is appropriate to include variables that are directly or indirectly linked to the protected group status of individuals. This means that analysts should proceed with caution when including variables like age or race—or variables that are likely to be strongly correlated with such variables—in their algorithms and models, unless they have a clear and defensible rationale for doing so, such as identifying sources of bias or uncovering evidence of disparate impact. Further, it is important that analysts communicate data-analytic findings to managers in a manner that ensures appropriate and legally compliant actions are taken based on the findings.

As HRM continues to evolve, big data and analytics can provide a strategic advantage. However, without careful consideration, analytics can be susceptible to bias, potentially leading to poor decisions and legal issues.[33]

HR analyst might survey customers for feedback on their experiences working with specific salespeople. Or the analyst might observe and rate salespeople interacting with customers. Different measurement types and sources can be used to measure the same concept.

■ **FIGURE 2.6** Examples of Different Types of Data Visualizations

Data visualizations can take different forms, from simple text to bar graphs to geographic plots. Pick the visual that best represents the data and tells the most accurate story.

76% of the employees were **satisfied with their job** in March 2018, compared to 52% in 2017.

LOCATION	AVERAGE AGE	FEMALE
Redmond	33.4	42%
Portland	37.9	52%
Las Vegas	35.1	49%
San Jose	35.3	56%

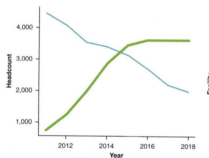

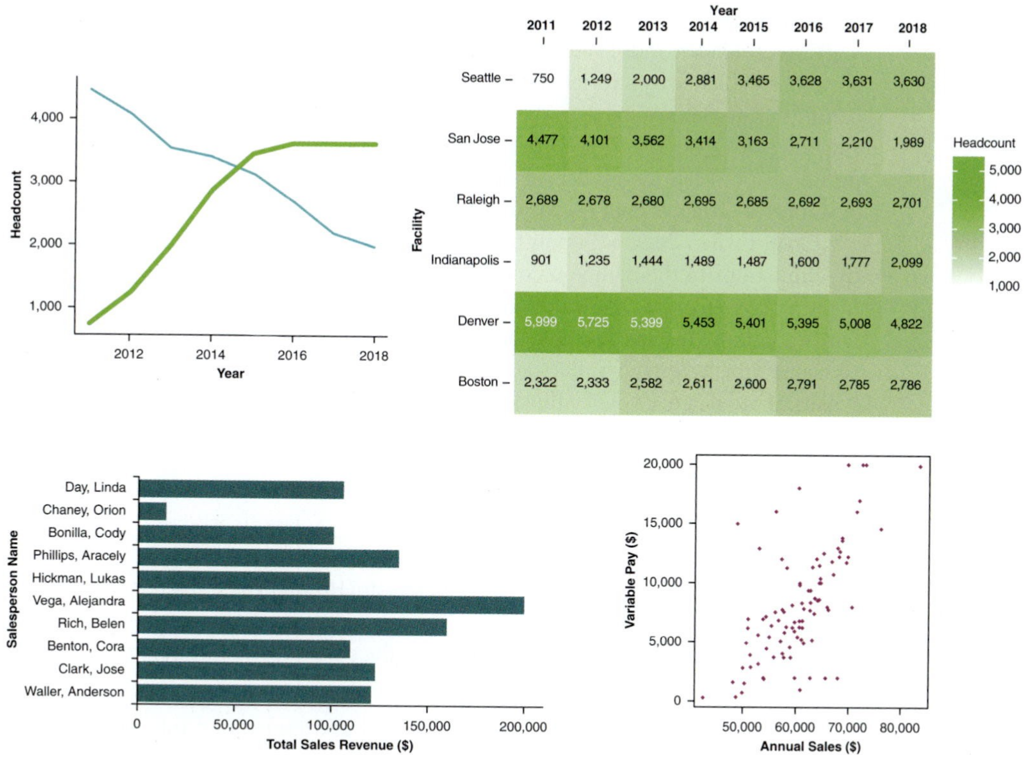

Facility	2011	2012	2013	2014	2015	2016	2017	2018
Seattle	750	1,249	2,000	2,881	3,465	3,628	3,631	3,630
San Jose	4,477	4,101	3,562	3,414	3,163	2,711	2,210	1,989
Raleigh	2,689	2,678	2,680	2,695	2,685	2,692	2,693	2,701
Indianapolis	901	1,235	1,444	1,489	1,487	1,600	1,777	2,099
Denver	5,999	5,725	5,399	5,453	5,401	5,395	5,008	4,822
Boston	2,322	2,333	2,582	2,611	2,600	2,791	2,785	2,786

Year (column header above)

Headcount
5,000
4,000
3,000
2,000
1,000

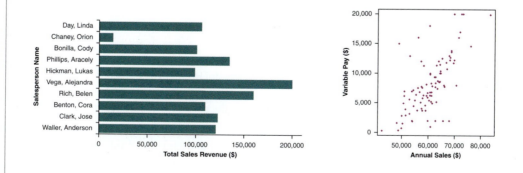

Step 5: Analyzing the Data

After testing your hypothesis through experimentation (or alternative research designs), you are ready to analyze the data to formally test your hypothesis. The way in which you analyze the data will differ based on whether you collected qualitative or quantitative data, and a full discussion of such distinctions is beyond the scope of this chapter. Once the data have been analyzed, the next step is to interpret the results. Remember, data do not "speak"; they are interpreted or evaluated. That is, the act of interpretation, like other aspects of the scientific process, requires sound judgment and decision making. This also means that interpretation is susceptible to bias and error, and steps should be taken to reduce bias and errors when measuring, analyzing, and interpreting data.

Step 6: Communicating the Results

The manner in which you communicate the results of the scientific process depends largely on where you work and the company culture. In academia, this refers to presenting a formal research paper at a conference or publishing the results in a peer-reviewed journal. In other types of organizations, it is common to communicate findings in internal presentations, technical reports, or even white papers. Amazon, for example, is known for communicating findings in technical reports that are read silently during the first part of meetings. Many other companies rely on PowerPoint presentations in which written and oral descriptions of results are provided.

In recent years, more value has been placed on creating easy-to-understand data visualizations, which are pictorial and graphic representations of data. Regardless of how you communicate the results, it is important to focus on the story you are telling. When storytelling with data, try to keep the story simple, be clear and concise, use repetition, and do not overburden the reader or viewer with too much information.[34] See Figure 2.6 for examples of different data visualizations.

Finally, when deciding upon the specific results you wish to communicate, recognize the limitations of the data you collected and the study design you employed to test your hypothesis. Remember, no study is perfect, and there will always be some level of uncertainty about the results. As such, take care not to overstate or exaggerate your findings. At the same time, try not to understate your findings, either. In general, when communicating results, try to balance your enthusiasm with a healthy level of skepticism.

HR Analytics Success

LO 2.5   Manage the components of a successful HR analytics function.

A sustainable HR analytics function requires the consideration of a number of important issues.

- First, HR analytics should be integrated and embedded into HR and organizational strategies, and this requires taking a systems perspective of the organization and its various subsystems. HR analytics can become an integral part of the HR strategic business partnership by leveraging people data to inform and support people decisions and strategy. In other words, the HR analytics function can provide data-driven recommendations regarding the design and implementation of HR practices to facilitate the organization's achievement of strategic objectives.

- Second, HR analytics should be integrated into the culture of HR and the organization. As we previously noted, many executives continue to make major decisions based on their gut instincts, or intuition. As such, developing an HR analytics function in some organizations may be difficult, especially if the culture does not value data and data-driven decisions. By gaining manager support and creating a culture that supports evidence-based practices, the HR analytics function will have a better chance of implementing changes.

- Third, and related to the second point, HR analytics must be paired with good change management, where change management refers to the "systematic process of applying knowledge, tools, and resources to transform organization from one state of affairs to another."[35] People have a natural tendency to resist change, and, in addition to creating a culture supportive of data-driven decision making, a culture of continuous change should be cultivated as well.

- Fourth, an HR analytics team must comprise the right people with the right mix of competencies. We recommended the following seven competencies earlier in the chapter: theory, business, data management, measurement, data analysis, employment law, and ethics. Deficiencies in any one of these competencies within a team may result in failure to make a contribution or, worse, may use HR analytics in ways that are illegal or unethical.

- Finally, we cannot overstate the importance of ethics. Today, new information technologies make it easier than ever to collect, manage, and analyze potentially sensitive people and organizational data, and with these new technologies come new ethical responsibilities. For example, some platforms allow us to systematically scrape data about our employees from social media sites. Before doing so, however, we must pause and ask this question: "Just because we can, should we?" For example, just because we can "scrape" employees' social media data from websites with ease and just because that data might be predictive of employee outcomes, should we do it? The same rigor that is applied to the scientific process should also be applied to decision making surrounding what data to use, how to use data, and whether to run certain analyses. A systems perspective reminds us that one decision—ethical or not—can result in a large ripple effect through the organization system and beyond.

CHAPTER SUMMARY

HRM has evolved immensely over the past century, with the development of strategic HRM, data-driven decision making, and HR analytics. Leading organizations leverage their HR function to inform and support organizational strategy; to realize employee, operational, stakeholder, and financial outcomes; and to achieve a competitive advantage. Data-driven decision making in the form of HR analytics plays an important role in strategy realization. An effective HR analytics function can be leveraged to improve the quality of decisions we make by informing the way an organization collects, manages, analyzes, and interprets its people data.

KEY TERMS

strategic human resource
management 26

strategy 26

mission 27

vision 28

values 28

stakeholders 29

strategy implementation 29

human capital 29

high-performance work
practices 32

systems perspective 32

data-driven decisions 34

human resource (HR)
analytics 34

descriptive analytics 38

predictive analytics 38

prescriptive analytics 38

scientific process 38

qualitative data 40

quantitative data 41

big data 41

little data 41

$SAGE edge™

Get the tools you need to sharpen your study skills. SAGE edge offers a robust online environment featuring an impressive array of free tools and resources.

Access practice quizzes, eFlashcards, video, and multimedia at **edge.sagepub.com/bauerbrief**

HR REASONING AND DECISION-MAKING EXERCISES

EXERCISE 2.1: ORGANIZATIONAL CULTURE AND THE SUCCESS OF HR ANALYTICS

Chapter 1 discussed the importance of organizational culture in relation to HRM. Specifically, the chapter reviewed a popular organizational culture typology called the Competing Values Framework, which characterizes different culture types by their emphasis on collaboration, creating, controlling, or competing. The culture types are as follows: clan, adhocracy, market, and hierarchy. Given what you learned in this chapter about HR analytics and data-driven people decisions, consider how the different culture types might influence an organization's acceptance of HR analytics.

Now, you decide.

Questions

1. For which organization culture type do you think HR analytics will best integrate? Is there an ideal culture type to support HR analytics? Why?

2. Which organization culture type will be least likely to accept HR analytics as a viable part of the organization's strategy? Why?

EXERCISE 2.2: BUILDING YOUR HR ANALYTICS TEAM

HR analytics is an interdisciplinary field, and as a result, HR analytics teams are often composed of individuals from different disciplines, specializations, and degree programs. Critical areas of expertise in any HR analytics team include the following: theory, business, data management, measurement, data analysis, employment law, and ethics. For this exercise, work in a group to determine how you would recruit, select, and train members of an effective HR analytics team.

Questions

1. As a group, create a series of jobs for which you will ultimately recruit and select new employees. A given job may cover more than one area of expertise, and multiple jobs may overlap in terms of some areas of expertise.

2. For each job created in Step 1, identify the competencies and educational/professional experiences that are necessary for success on each job.

3. Develop a brief recruitment and selection strategy for each job. In other words, where will you recruit individuals for these positions? Why? How and why will you select and hire individuals for these positions?

ETHICAL MATTERS EXERCISE: THE CASE OF THE BODY SHOP

The Body Shop is a global manufacturer and retailer of ethically made beauty and cosmetic products. When she founded The Body Shop in 1979, Anita Roddick believed that companies have the potential to do good and just things for the world, as evidenced by the company's *mission* statement: "To dedicate our business to the pursuit of social and environmental change." In other words, Roddick was an early supporter of *corporate social responsibility*. Roddick passed away in 2007 at 64 years of age, but her legacy lives on in the form of The Body Shop's following core *values:*

The Asahi Shimbun via Getty Images

- Against animal testing
- Support community fair trade
- Activate self-esteem
- Defend human rights
- Protect the planet

When the company was acquired by L'Oréal in 2006, the CEO of L'Oréal, Lindsay Owen-Jones, expressed his admiration for The Body Shop's mission, vision, and core values. He described how his company's expertise and knowledge of international markets could bring The Body Shop and its ethically made products to new customers.[36]

Questions

1. How might The Body Shop's ethical values influence its HRM policies?

2. If you were a manager for a competitor of The Body Shop, how would you go about investigating the implications of corporate social responsibility for a company's success?

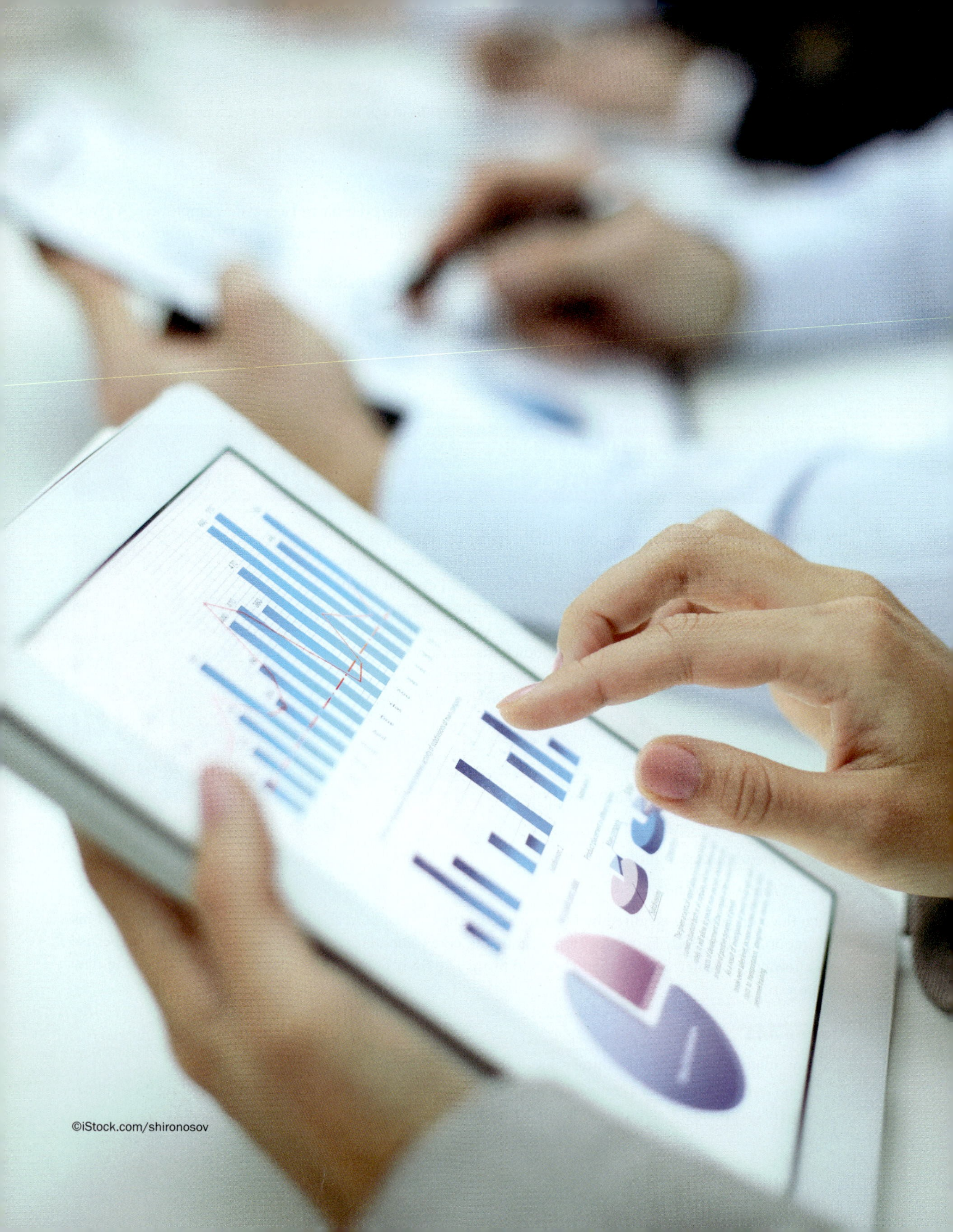

3

Data Management and Human Resource Information Systems

LEARNING OBJECTIVES

After reading and studying this chapter, you should be able to do the following:

3.1 Describe key aspects of data management.

3.2 Apply opportunities for data management and HRIS.

3.3 Identify and address challenges for data management and HRIS.

3.4 Describe basic technical aspects of developing an HRIS.

3.5 Address key points of the process of HRIS implementation.

HR in Action: The Case of Automatic Data Processing, Inc. (ADP)

Since 1949, Automatic Data Processing, Inc. (ADP) has developed a global reputation for payroll processing products and services. For a number of years, the company had the highest rating given (AAA credit rating) from both Moody's and Standard & Poor's. ADP has changed in several ways since its inception. ADP now provides various products and services that connect the HRM function to company strategy by using data analytics. In recent years, the company made headlines for developing an algorithm that predicts employees' risk of quitting based on several factors, such as employees' commuting distance and their income relative to neighbors' incomes.

Given the general decrease in the U.S. unemployment rate since 2009, there is a greater likelihood of increased turnover, as evidence indicates that individuals who are thinking about quitting will be more likely to do so when unemployment rates are lower. The United States has seen an uptick in turnover since 2012 as the unemployment rate has fallen. Because

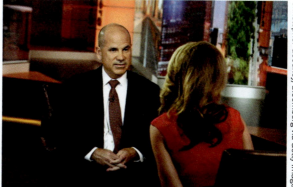

ADP chief executive officer Carlos Rodriguez

Christopher Goodney/Bloomberg via Getty Images

turnover—especially among high-performing employees—can be costly for organizations in terms of lost productivity and increased selection and training costs, adopting ADP's new algorithm as part of their HRM software packages may help organizations' bottom lines and help them reduce turnover.

There are legal and ethical implications associated with using employee data of this kind. The kind of personal data used in the algorithm, such as commute length and neighborhood income, could be representatives for other factors, such as socioeconomic status, race, and ethnicity.[1]

Case Discussion Questions

1. Do you think it is a good idea to gather non-work-related information on employees such as the ADP algorithm does? Why or why not?

2. Do you think that turnover is necessarily a "bad" thing? Defend your answer.

3. What are some ways that data and data management help organizations to be more effective?

After reading Chapters 1 and 2 of this book, you can see that our approach to covering HRM is based on the concepts and developments you will need to understand now and in the future of HR, organizations, business, and your own career. Among those concepts are the skills needed to make use of data to make sound HRM decisions. In today's business world, effective HRM requires that organizational members be knowledgeable about how data are managed, stored, retrieved, merged, analyzed, and reported to help with data-driven decision making. Even if they are not data analysts or experts in **human resource information systems (HRIS)**, all employees should be familiar with issues around data management and HRIS. Understanding these concepts will make you an effective consumer of data and its possibilities within your organization regardless of your position, functional area, or title.

Managing Data

Human resource information systems (HRIS) Systems used to collect, store, manage, analyze, retrieve, and report HR data and allow for the automation of some HR management functions

LO 3.1   Describe key aspects of data management.

The availability of people data has increased dramatically with advances in technology and data-gathering tools. *People data* refers to data associated with various groups of individuals, such as employees and other stakeholders, who might be integral for an organization's success. HR analytics has emerged as an approach to leveraging people data to make data-driven decisions to improve the flow of human capital into and through an organization. Because of this, strategic data management has become especially salient to HR professionals and HR analysts. HR has long since outgrown the days of employee records and data stored on paper and housed in filing cabinets. Before computer-based information systems became the norm, relatively small amounts of data were accessed with regularity, and merging data from different files was a cumbersome and time-consuming process. Today, with ever-accumulating amounts of people data and sometimes easier access to such data, we must think critically, ethically, and legally about how large volumes of data about individuals are stored and managed and how advances in information systems are used to facilitate this process. HR information systems and electronic HRM (e-HRM) represent two closely related HRM data management topics that play an important role in that regard. In many organizations, HR information systems and e-HRM are integrated into a larger cross-functional data management system called an enterprise resource planning system—all of which can be broadly classified as information systems.

Enterprise Resource Planning Systems

An **enterprise resource planning (ERP)** system refers to integrated business management software intended to coordinate and integrate processes and data across different functional areas of a company, such as accounting, sales, finance, operations, customer service, and HRM. For instance, an ERP might capture, track, and integrate data pertaining to payroll, inventory, production capacity, applicant tracking, and purchase orders, to name a few things. By integrating data cross-functionally, an ERP creates a robust data ecosystem, which enables organizational stakeholders to take a systems perspective when making important decisions. For example, imagine that customer service data residing within an ERP indicates that customer service representatives have been fielding increasingly more customer complaints having to do with faulty products. Using those data, a decision maker on the manufacturing floor might investigate where mistakes are being made in the production process. Ultimately, that decision maker might reach out to someone from the HR department with expertise in employee training to help design a new training program for manufacturing employees. A well-designed and well-integrated ERP has the potential to improve decision making across different functional areas, as the entire business can be viewed as an integrated system with separate yet related subsystems.

Human Resource Information Systems

Many organizations incorporate an HR information system within their broader ERP systems, such that HR processes and data are linked to and integrated with data from other business functions. An HR information system (HRIS) refers to a "system used to acquire, store, manipulate, analyze, retrieve, and distribute pertinent information about an organization's human resources,"[2] and the concept of HRIS can be nested within the broader concept of e-HRM. At its most basic, an HRIS is simply a system of the following: input → data management → output. Broadly speaking, **e-HRM** refers to Internet-based information systems and technology that span across organizational levels.[3] HRIS represents a blending of HRM and information technology, and when coupled with strategic HRM, HRIS offers a way to realize possibilities between and across different HR practices. It can provide a wealth of readily available data to provide organizational decision makers with accurate and timely information.

Enterprise resource planning (ERP) Integrated business management software intended to coordinate and integrate processes and data across different functional areas of a company

e-HRM Internet-based information systems and technology that span across organizational levels

Just like the broader ERP system, an organization can use its HRIS to integrate people data across different HR functions, such as recruitment, selection, training, performance management, compensation, and benefits. An HRIS can be designed to automate transactional HR activities, such as benefits enrollment or applicant tracking. After World War II, the payroll function was one of the first to be automated using early computers and information systems. As computer technology advanced in the following decades, organizations began to integrate web- and cloud-based services into their HRISs. An HRIS is a cost-saving tool, as it can reduce errors and increase efficiencies related to storing, accessing, and using data. Beyond efficiency, an HRIS, by definition, involves the complex collection, storage, and analysis of people data, providing an opportunity to analyze these data to make better people decisions.

The hallmarks of an advanced HRIS are consistency, accuracy, timely access to data, and integration. Rather than using a separate and insular information subsystem for each core HR function—such as selection, training, performance management, and retention—an advanced HRIS integrates people data across HR functions. And when integrated into a company's ERP, the comprehensiveness of the data becomes even more robust. Further, allowing subsystems to "speak" with one another means that analysts can retrieve and merge data from multiple subsystem functions for subsequent analysis and reporting. A number of vendors (e.g., Oracle, SAP) offer HRIS and ERP solutions, thereby facilitating data management and integration processes. In fact, many vendors now integrate data analytics solutions into their data management platforms. At the click of a button, the software can run and generate off-the-shelf analyses and reports.

Some vendors, like ADP, offer proprietary data analysis algorithms to predict important outcomes, such as employee retention. Because such algorithms are proprietary and considered intellectual property, the specific criteria used in the algorithmic models often remain locked in a "black box" where the contents are unknown. As such, HR professionals, and all organizational members, should do their due diligence to understand, to the best of their ability, what data are being used in such models and how to properly interpret output or results from such models.

Data Management and HRIS Opportunities

LO 3.2   Apply opportunities for data management and HRIS.

When it comes to data management and HRIS, there are a number of opportunities and challenges. Figure 3.1 illustrates several of these when it comes to developing, implementing, and maintaining an HRIS. Opportunities exist in the form of being able to track employees throughout their employment life cycles, automating HR functionality for employees, allowing data to be available for HR analytics, and storing and merging employee attitude surveys and other sources of people data over time. An example of HRIS in practice is Virginia Beach, Virginia (a town with more than 6,000 city employees and 45 city HRM professionals). In 2003, it embarked on what was considered an innovative approach to merging data from the city's HRIS, the Virginia Retirement System, and other data sources to enhance its workforce planning efforts. Managers can now use the system to understand projected retirement statistics, changing workforce demographics, and pending job vacancies, making the city more proactive and less reactive in terms of workforce planning.[4]

Track the Employee Life Cycle

Recall that HRM is *the constellation of decisions and actions associated with managing individuals through the employee life cycle to maximize employee and organizational effectiveness in attaining goals* (see Figure 3.2, next page). This includes a range of functions such as analyzing and designing jobs; managing diversity and complying with local, national, and global employee laws; recruiting individuals to apply for jobs; selecting individuals to join organizations; training and developing people while they are employed; helping manage their performance; rewarding and compensating employee performance while maintaining healthy labor relations and helping keep them safe; and managing their exit from the organization.

A major opportunity for an organization is to manage the valuable resources that are data in a manner that helps the organization not only describe its employees and predict their future movements throughout the organization but also prescribe what the ideal state of HR will be in the future. Effective data management and HRIS are critical to realizing this potential. One study of HR executives and managers working in diverse countries, including Argentina, Brazil, China, India, Latvia, and Slovakia, found that the presence of a global HRIS was related to higher staff retention of global IT service providers in emerging markets. This was especially helpful in decreasing turnover for employees assigned to other countries, as the support of a global HRIS for scheduling and training was cited as helpful for new employees and their managers alike.[5] It is clear that "the effective management of human resources in a firm to gain a competitive advantage requires *timely and accurate information* on current employees and potential employees in the labor market."[6]

■ **FIGURE 3.1**   Challenges and Opportunities of Data Management and HRIS

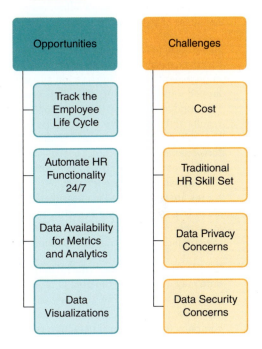

Spotlight on Data and Analytics

TALENT ANALYTICS FOR RETENTION

HR analytics has many uses, and companies have started leveraging data collected during and after hiring employees to predict and manage retention. Companies can link a wide variety of information at their disposal to employee turnover and determine the strongest drivers of turnover. Identifying employees at risk of turnover may then be used to develop targeted interventions for those employees. For example, the telecommunications company

(Continued)

(Continued)

Sprint found that employees who have not signed up for the company's retirement program are at risk of leaving shortly after being hired.

In addition to identifying predictors of turnover, many companies examine low work engagement and job satisfaction as early and lagged indicators of turnover. This means that conducting regular surveys and tracking results and metrics over time will be helpful. For example, JetBlue Airways created a "crewmember net promoter score," which asks employees their willingness to recommend the company as a place to work. Net promoter scores are usually used to measure customer satisfaction, but JetBlue asks this question to all new hires on their hire dates, which means the company can regularly track these data.

Simply tracking satisfaction and engagement data may not achieve the goal of reducing employee turnover: The company will need to intervene using these data. The food service company Sysco tracks satisfaction ratings of its delivery associates and intervenes when satisfaction drops below a certain point. Using this method, the company was able to increase its retention rate from 65% to 85%.

It is also possible to identify the specific employees who are at risk for turnover for intervention purposes. At Credit Suisse, once employees with high turnover risk were identified, internal recruiters called employees to notify them about internal openings. This method allowed the firm to retain employees who might have left the company otherwise. Preemptive intervention

©iStock.com/RiverNorthPhotography

is often a better strategy than providing a counteroffer to an employee who gets a job offer.

At the same time, companies will need to be careful in what type of data they use and how they intervene. It is technically possible for businesses to monitor how much time employees spend in networking sites such as LinkedIn or to use data from employee badges to see which employees may be interviewing at other locations within the company. Then the manager of the employee may have a conversation with at-risk employees about whether they are happy about their jobs. Although there is value in having career-related conversations with employees, this situation may quickly evolve into a "Big Brother is watching" scenario, violating employee feelings of trust, privacy, and fairness, depending on how the manager broaches the subject. Any intervention with individuals or groups of employees should reflect a genuine concern for employee well-being and career goals to be useful for turnover reduction.[7]

The Value of Automated, Employee-Centered HR Functionality

The trend in HRM is moving away from processing paperwork and more transactional interactions toward more strategic work. We have discussed the benefits of this approach in terms of time and cost savings as HR becomes more efficient. It also means better customer service for employees. Rather than waiting for HR to process paperwork, answer questions, or implement changes, employees now have access to their HR systems 24 hours a day, 7 days a week. Some questions are escalated to HR professionals, but many of their more routine questions can be answered anytime and anywhere. Research shows that the perceived ease of use and perceived usefulness of an HRIS are related to higher job satisfaction and lower turnover intentions.[8] Moving toward automated, employee-centered HR functionality meets two goals. First, it enables employees to access information more quickly and to verify the accuracy of the data, as they can view and detect inaccuracies more readily, which helps them feel more satisfied with their jobs.[9] Second, because HR data are increasingly accessible via the web or the cloud, data from across the organization can be retrieved and merged with greater ease, enabling timely and efficient analysis of the data for HR decision making.

■ **FIGURE 3.2**   HRM as a Linking Pin for Critical People Decisions

Data Availability for Metrics and Analytics

The theme of technology has played a revolutionary role in the evolution of HRM. Data must be accessible for people to make data-informed people decisions. As experts state, "Data are the lifeblood of an organization."[10] As the Society for Human Resource Management (SHRM) notes, trends such as the growth of social networking and the rise in data analytics and dashboards have fundamentally changed what HR needs.[11] Having a clear data management plan and having an effective HRIS in place are critical aspects to HR analytics success, and an HRIS update, upgrade, or reenvisioning is a great opportunity to fix problems and set up the organization for success for becoming more deeply data informed when making people decisions. These are important considerations in avoiding huge problems and generating solutions while there is time to plan.

Data Quality

An important point to remember when thinking about metrics and analytics is the importance of gathering high-quality data, which starts with sound measurement. A measure is a tool or method used to gather data about a concept. Without sound measurement, we cannot state with any confidence whether we consistently or accurately measured a

■ **FIGURE 3.3**   Garbage In, Garbage Out (GIGO) Phenomenon

Data

Analysis

Findings and
Interpretation

Image sources: © garyfox45114/Shutterstock; © Oleksandr Kostiuchenko/
Shutterstock

concept. With poor measurement techniques, we become susceptible to low-quality (e.g., unreliable) data—also known as "garbage data." When garbage data are collected, it does not matter how we analyze the data, as the findings and interpretations will be of low quality (e.g., invalid)—also known as "garbage findings." This phenomenon is referred to as "garbage in, garbage out," or GIGO (see Figure 3.3).

Data Structure and Storage

Databases are designed to store structured data, and a common approach to adding structure to data is to use tables, whereby the rows represent distinct entities (e.g., individual employees) and the columns represent unique fields or variables that characterize the entities (e.g., employee start date, address, job title). Databases and data warehouses were designed to deal with such data. With the rise of semistructured and unstructured data, new forms of storage are needed. Data lakes are a solution that many organizations are turning to, because unlike a data warehouse, a **data lake** stores a vast amount of raw data in its native format. Technology companies are meeting demand for data lakes such as with Microsoft's Azure and offerings by Amazon Web Services and IBM Analytics. Typically, these platforms allow users to use the open-source software framework called Apache Hadoop, which helps users process vast amounts of data across clustered computers. There are pros and cons to each storage approach, but at this point, consider what types of data you might have access to now and in the future, and plan data storage options accordingly and with the future in mind.

Data Visualizations

Although HRIS, HR metrics, and HR analytics are critical for making data-informed people decisions, effective data visualizations and storytelling with data can help facilitate the interpretation and communication of the findings. Today, HR professionals and managers use data visualizations to understand, predict, explain, and communicate their human capital challenges and opportunities based on available data. And data visualizations are useful tools for telling a compelling story about HR data.

Part of telling an effective story with data is knowing how to boil down the key points and communicate the most important findings. In other words, analyzing data can be quite complex, and a good storyteller understands how to craft a straightforward, simple, and comprehensible narrative. Doing so requires striking a careful balance between engaging the audience and remaining faithful to the analytical findings derived from the data.

Data lake Stores a vast amount of raw data in its native (and often unstructured) format

As the saying goes, "A picture is worth a thousand words." Effective data visualizations play an important role when interpreting and communicating data and data-analytic findings in a succinct way. In fact, research even shows that the way in which data are presented visually has an effect on how data are interpreted and which decisions are ultimately made. For example, adjusting the axis scaling of a scatterplot can give the impression that two variables are more strongly correlated than they actually are, as the figure on the right seems to show a stronger pattern than the one on the left.[12] As such, it is important to be cognizant of the ways in which data visualization displays can be unintentionally or intentionally manipulated to affect the interpretations of different audiences. This means that choosing how to display data should be coupled with careful consideration of the ethical implications.

How does one begin to think through how to create the most effective data visualizations? Following work by experts on storytelling and data visualizations,[13] keep the following six points in mind when creating data visualizations:

1. ***Understand the context.*** There are three key questions to ask at the highest level when thinking about storytelling. First, *what* do you want your audience to know after you are done? Second, *how* do you want them to feel? Finally, *what,* exactly, do you want them to do based on exposure to your presentation or report? In addition, it is important to determine the context, understand who your audience is, and determine the tone you want to take with them. For example, are you presenting in an informative, exploratory, or urgent way? It can be helpful to "boil down" your goal into a concise 2-minute story. If that is compelling, the presentation or written document stands a better chance of being clear and concise.

2. ***Choose an appropriate visual display.*** Regarding data visualizations, there are many kinds of elements for displaying data to choose from, including simple text, tables, bar graphs, line graphs, scatterplots, heat maps, and geographic charts. Certain display types are appropriate for communicating certain types of data or for communicating different messages. For example, if a few key numbers make a powerful statement, simple text might have the most impact. Alternatively, if you are interested in sharing a table full of numbers but want to emphasize patterns in the numbers, a heat map, as presented in Table 3.1, can be effective. Consider using one color for positive numbers and another for negative numbers. The key is to match your goals to an appropriate display.

3. ***Keep things simple.*** By removing clutter and focusing on your main points in the most efficient and succinct manner, you make it easier for your audience to focus because you are minimizing the energy they need to process the new information. In other words, you are decreasing their cognitive load. If anything in your visual is unnecessary, *eliminate it!* An example of this is to avoid gridlines, borders, and unnecessary shading on graphs.

4. ***Focus attention where you want it.*** Use color and shading strategically. The use of color and bolding of lines and figures can help people see trends more quickly and accurately. Effective emphasis using color and shading is a factor to consider

TABLE 3.1   Heat Map Table

Heat map table displaying headcount by year and facility, such that darker green values represent larger head counts.

FACILITY	2013	2014	2015	2016	2017	2018	2019	2020	Headcount
Seattle	750	1,249	2,000	2,881	3,465	3,628	3,631	3,630	
San Jose	4,477	4,101	3,562	3,414	3,163	2,711	2,210	1,989	5,000
Raleigh	2,689	2,678	2,680	2,695	2,685	2,692	2,693	2,701	4,000
Indianapolis	901	1,235	1,444	1,489	1,487	1,600	1,777	2,099	3,000 2,000
Denver	5,999	5,725	5,399	5,453	5,401	5,395	5,008	4,822	
Boston	2,322	2,333	2,582	2,611	2,600	2,791	2,785	2,786	1,000

when it comes to data visualizations. When it comes to color, less is more. Use it sparingly.

5. ***Think like a designer.*** You may have heard the phrase "form follows function." It is an important phrase for designers, as it helps them focus their work. In our case, the function is what we want the audience to do with the data, and the form is the visualization created to communicate this. Designers also focus on making things visually appealing, or attractive, which is a goal of design thinking.

6. ***Tell a persuasive story.*** Research tells us that one of the most effective ways to persuade individuals is through storytelling. As Cole Nussbaumer Knaflic writes, "At a fundamental level, a story expresses how and why life changes. Stories start with balance. Then something happens—an event that throws things out of balance."[14] This dramatic tension can feature data as the event that throws things off. Now you know something new, or a key point that you had not noticed has become salient. Stories have a beginning, a middle, and an end. Stories start by introducing the plot and building the context for the reader or audience. With the audience in mind, the introduction should address the "So what?" question and explain why

they should care about the topic at hand. The middle describes what could be possible, given more context and detail, and allows you to discuss potential solutions for the issues raised. The end should focus on a specific call to action so that the audience truly understands what it is expected to do after hearing your story.

These six points can help guide the generation of data visualizations. The availability of data rests on the quality of the HRIS of your organization and your ability to gather and merge the data necessary to tell your story.

Challenges for Data Management and HRIS

LO 3.3   Identify and address challenges for data management and HRIS.

Although there are a great number of potential opportunities for data management and HRIS, challenges also exist. Being aware of them can help organizations proactively assess needs and manage potential threats to successful implementation. The challenges include cost, the lack of analytics skills in traditional HR skill sets, and privacy concerns.

Cost

Typical HRIS costs include time, money, and/or opportunity costs. With respect to budgeting time, it is important to think about the skill sets available within your organization versus hiring a consultant to help implement a project. The cost of an HRIS varies by organization, its needs, and the salesforce of the software vendor. Note that a request for proposal (RFP) is a key part of the HRIS vendor selection process. Of course, another way to think about costs is to more fully consider the potentially large cost savings due to system automation. Such cost reductions might include time entry and attendance tracking, benefits administration, recruiting, training, payroll, and performance management, to name a few. For large organizations, conducting a formal return-on-investment (ROI) analysis is a good idea when dealing with projects this large. For smaller organizations, it may simply be a matter of finding a package or platform that meets their needs into the foreseeable future.

Traditional HR Skill Sets

In 2004, 80% of organizations had an HRIS, but fewer than 40% reported using it to generate data used in strategic decision making. By 2007, the use of HRIS in strategic decision making had increased, with some organizations creating a competitive advantage through their use of data-driven decision making.[15] That means that many HRIS projects stop short of their potential to enjoy greater efficiency and reduced costs. As organizations hire and train more and more individuals with critical thinking skills, data management skills, and data analytics skills, we anticipate that the HR departments will begin to collect and store more higher-quality data in their HRIS and will apply not only descriptive analytics but also more sophisticated predictive and prescriptive analytics to inform and support decisions that affect the strategic objectives. In general, we expect HR to become more scientific.

It takes an organization between 5 and 8 years to put all the necessary pieces together to become a data-driven culture using data to inform decisions about people. This includes having the right people, processes, and infrastructure (such as hardware and software) in place. Researchers report that 80% of surveyed HR directors who were relatively early adopters of HRIS reported that HRIS improved their levels of information usefulness and information sharing, and 90% felt that HRIS added value.[16] Aligning the skill sets of those in HRM with the new realities of data and analytics is necessary to realize the full potential for HRM via HRIS.

Data Privacy Concerns

With great amounts of data comes great responsibility. Because HRIS is a repository for personal data, safeguarding data and maintaining data privacy and security are foundational. To begin, **data privacy** refers to individuals' control over the collection, storage, access, and reporting of their personal data.[17] Research shows that individuals who are able to choose the types of HR systems they use report lower privacy concerns and higher satisfaction with the system. They are especially sensitive to medical data, which may be used for insurance purposes, for example, to be available to those within the organization who make decisions regarding their careers, such as managers.[18] In accordance with the Fair Labor Standards Act of 1938 and other legislation, U.S. companies are required to maintain basic employee data, such as name, Social Security number, address, pay, and hours worked. Understandably, many employees would prefer that their personal data remain private, especially their pay or Social Security numbers. Employees grow concerned about their company's HRIS and data privacy when[19]

- supervisors are able to access employee data;
- employee data are used in employment and administrative decisions, as opposed to just HR planning purposes; and
- employees are unable to verify the accuracy of their own data.

An effective HRIS must guard against unauthorized access and disclosure of employees' personal data yet also allow employees to verify the accuracy of their own data. The rise of social media and scraping tools has turned the Internet into an enormous repository of data, where scraping and crawling tools include programs designed to scour and pull data from websites and other electronic sources in a systematic manner. In fact, a survey by SHRM in 2015 revealed that 84% of surveyed organizations recruited applicants using social media websites.[20]

Recognizability of an Individual's Data

The extent to which individual employee records can be recognized is largely dependent on how the data were collected in the first place. Three terms describe data in terms of recognizability: anonymous, confidential, and personally identifiable data. **Anonymous data** refers to those pieces of information that cannot be linked to any information that might link those responses to an individual, thereby disclosing the individual's identity. To be truly anonymous, data should be gathered without IP addresses, GPS coordinates, e-mail addresses, and demographic questions—all of

Data privacy Individuals' control over the collection, storage, access, and reporting of their personal data

Anonymous data Pieces of information that cannot be linked to any information that might identify an individual, thereby disclosing the individual's identity

Spotlight on Legal Issues

SCRAPING DATA CAN LEAD TO BIG LEGAL TROUBLE

In 2010, a software engineer in Colorado named Pete Warden developed and deployed a program designed to "crawl" publicly available Facebook pages. In no time, he had gathered data from 500 million Facebook pages from 220 million Facebook users. The data gathered were identifiable, as they included names, locations, friends, and interests. In the interest of research, Mr. Warden created an anonymized version of the data set and offered it to others to use.

This was not the end of his story. As Mr. Warden is quoted as saying, "Big data? Cheap. Lawyers? Not so much." To try to avoid legal problems with Facebook, he deleted all copies of his data set and never made it public. Data scraped or crawled (automatically extracted using computer software programs) from websites are subject to three major legal claims against their collection, including copyright infringement, the Computer Fraud and Abuse Act, and terms-of-use violations, among others. Subsequent data privacy issues emerged when Cambridge Analytica gathered data from Facebook users. These breaches of trust led Facebook to rethink which data are gathered and how much control users have over what is shared about them.[21]

---

which can be used to narrow down the respondent. **Confidential data** refers to data for which individuals' identities are known by the researchers due to the linking of a name or code but are not generally disclosed or reported. This type of data is useful when dealing with sensitive issues such as salary, complaints, opinion survey responses, or exit interviews. In such cases, only those who need to know whose data they are have access to that information. **Personally identifiable data** refers to data that are readily linked to specific individuals.

Social Security Numbers

One particularly sensitive issue is the safeguarding of Social Security numbers.[22] The Federal Trade Commission estimates that more than 9 million Americans have their identities stolen each year, and because Social Security numbers are such valuable targets to identity thieves, steps must be taken to ensure their safekeeping. Such steps include keeping all Social Security number information in secured locations (both virtually and physically) and allowing access from authorized-access computer stations. Only individuals with legitimate business reasons should have access. Any documents released should be destroyed by shredding, and all state and federal laws should be followed regarding the collection, storage, and destruction of Social Security numbers.

Data Security Concerns

Like data privacy, data security is a primary concern of both employees and managers. **Data security** refers to protective measures taken to prevent unauthorized access to employee data and to preserve the confidentiality and integrity of the data.[23] **Cybersecurity** can be

Confidential data Information for which individuals' identities are known by the researchers due to the linking of a name or code but are not generally disclosed or reported

Personally identifiable data Data readily linked to specific individuals

Data security Protective measures taken to prevent unauthorized access to employee data and to preserve the confidentiality and integrity of the data

Cybersecurity Data security applied to information accessible through the Internet

thought of as data security applied to information accessible through the Internet. Data security can be threatened by a number of entities and for a variety of reasons. While data hacks, attacks, and viruses are real threats, human error is a huge risk when it comes to data security. An information system can have the most sophisticated password protection and security features, but an unintentional human error could still wreak havoc. Imagine a scenario in which you are logged into your company's HRIS while working on a company laptop in a coffee shop. You hear the barista announce your coffee order is ready and step away from your laptop for a moment, forgetting to log out. After picking up your order, you walk back to your table, and to your astonishment, your laptop is gone! An innocent human error and lapse of judgment on your part has put employees' personal data at risk. Unfortunately, human error is inevitable, but we can do our best to prevent these errors by training managers and employees on data security and providing rules and guidelines for protecting people data.

As a relatively recent example, the U.S. Office of Personnel Management (OPM), a federal agency that manages many of the federal government's human resources, suffered an attack. In the summer of 2015, hackers stole more than 20 million current and former federal employees' work and personal data, including birthdates, Social Security numbers, and fingerprint records.[24] In the year that followed, it came to light that OPM was using outdated information systems in need of serious improvements, thereby putting OPM at risk for the data breach. Since the data breach took place, the American Federation of Government Employees has filed a class-action suit against OPM. Beyond damages to its reputation and putting individuals' personal information at risk, the government stands to lose financially too. In addition, it is likely that federal employees lost trust in OPM's ability to secure their personal data, and if this is the case, OPM will need to regain the trust of its employees when it comes to data privacy and security.

Approaches for Maintaining Data Security

There are several common approaches for ensuring data security. Some are technological, including requiring strong passwords, training users, using two-step authentication, and applying blockchain technology. Other approaches have to do with proper training of the users of data.

Technological Security Measures. Increasingly complex passwords are something that we are all familiar with as we are creating and maintaining online accounts. As we now realize that human error is a large factor in many data breaches, it is important to realize that one of the ways these problems manifest themselves is via lack of password security, such as passwords being written down near computers, remembered by computers, or shared with others. In addition, as computing power increases, it becomes easier for computer programs to be able to decode passwords. It might be surprising to know that Mark Zuckerberg, founder of Facebook, has had his Pinterest, LinkedIn, and Twitter accounts hacked.[25] Although many websites allow only a few attempts before locking out users, it is still advisable to select strong passwords, not to reuse the same password across multiple accounts, and to change your passwords to important sources of information frequently.

An extra layer of security can be had in the form of **two-step authentication** (also known as **multifactor authentication**), an additional piece of information that only the user knows. For example, Apple computer, iPhone, or iPad users may be familiar with this authentication

Two-step authentication (multifactor authentication)
An extra layer of security that requires an additional piece of information that only the user would know

process when any new device is seeking to access Apple ID information. Of course, two-step authentication works well when you are in possession of your devices, but if a thief has access to both and they are not sufficiently password protected, that can be a bigger problem.

Technology has and will continue to shape the way HR is managed and implemented in a number of ways. *Forbes* declared 2018 to be the year that blockchain "establishes itself as the fastest-growing digital technology since the evolution of the Internet."[26] To that end, blockchain is poised to disrupt the current practice of HR. **Blockchain** is "a distributed incorruptible digital technology infrastructure which maintains a fully encoded database that serves as a ledger where all transactions are recorded and stored."[27] It has also been more simply described as an approach that "provides a decentralized and secure ledger that gives participating parties a way of validating the information related to a secure transaction."[28] Because it is more secure than other technology available today, it has the potential to be used in compensation, background checks, recruiting, and other HR functions in ways that we can only imagine at this point (and other ways that likely we cannot

Blockchain
A distributed incorruptible digital technology infrastructure that maintains a fully encoded database that serves as a ledger where all transactions are recorded and stored

---

⚙ Manager's Toolbox
TIPS FOR CREATING STRONG PASSWORDS

©iStock.com/designer491

Some of the tips for creating strong passwords are obvious, such as not writing down the password anywhere physically near your computer. The following are some key considerations when dealing with password management, including creating passwords:

- **Long.** The longer the better, with eight or more characters currently recommended.

- **Contain numbers, letters, and symbols.** There are only 26 letters in the alphabet and 10 numbers. So mixing them up and using symbols helps to create more powerful

passwords, which are exponentially more challenging to decode.

- **Include both upper- and lowercase letters.** Using both uppercase and lowercase letters creates more options for the user and makes it tougher for hackers to crack your password.

- **Unique.** Some of the most common passwords include 123456, qwerty, Password, starwars, and admin. It is estimated that 10% of people have used at least one of the worst (because they are commonly known) passwords on this list, with nearly 3% using 123456 alone.

- **Generated randomly.** There are random password generators available online. Although they make remembering passwords more challenging, they are more secure than using actual words. Using a password manager such as LastPass can help with that part, but such a treasure trove of information can be a highly attractive target for hackers, and even that company, LastPass, was hacked in 2015.

yet imagine). Although blockchain is relatively new and will continue to evolve rapidly in terms of its applications to business broadly and HR specifically, it is important to include it in our discussion of potential data security tools. Maintaining data security is especially consequential given that 1.4 billion data records were compromised in 2016.[29]

User Training. One of the major entry points for data security breaches is human error, which is the number-one cause of data breaches, especially for small- and medium-sized businesses.[30] It makes sense to consider training an essential part of a data security program. Training might include awareness of key security issues, ethics and compliance when dealing with sensitive data, and security training for new employees or those moving to more information-sensitive positions within the company. There are several steps to consider when training employees, starting with a needs assessment aligned with the desired outcomes of the training. Many organizations have developed and offer such training programs for organizations not wishing to develop programs themselves. The key is to make sure the right employees are taking the training and engaging in safe data management behaviors.

Developing a Human Resource Information System

LO 3.4   Describe basic technical aspects of developing an HRIS.

As you have seen so far in this chapter, a complex and comprehensive HRIS can be a costly and time-consuming undertaking for an organization. Before deciding whether to do so and how, organizations are well advised to systematically work through a step-by-step process for evaluating the needs and feasibility of implementing an HRIS (see Figure 3.4).[31] After that, it is important to outline the features needed in such a system, to select a vendor, and to engage in activities designed to control costs.

■ **FIGURE 3.4**   HRIS Decision Steps

Deciding which HRIS to use entails following several steps to ensure ultimate success.

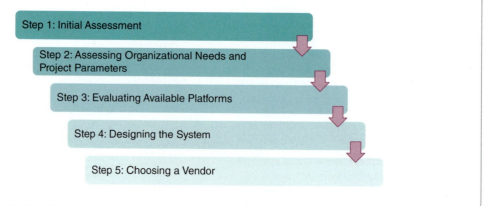

Conducting a Needs Assessment

The process of conducting a needs assessment for an HRIS ensures that you design the right program by conducting an analysis of what exists, what should change, and what factors might hinder successful implementation. The best plan can be developed to deal with potential setbacks and challenges during implementation, including identifying the key stakeholders who should be involved in the process.

Initial Assessment

In the initial assessment phase, a key question is whether the selection process is best led by internal HR individuals or whether engaging the services of an HRIS consultant to help with the process makes the most sense given time, experience, and cost factors. For example, if there seems to be a strong need for a new HRIS but the HR staff does not have a great deal of time or expertise in this area, it probably makes sense to bring in a consultant to help facilitate the process. During this phase, it is important to gain buy-in from management and key stakeholders by including them in the conversation; failure to do so may result in hurdles later on in the development and implementation process, as ultimately management and certain stakeholders may be gatekeepers to key resources.

Assess Organizational Needs

The next major activity is to assess organizational needs. The goal is to develop a system that meets all the current organizational needs as well as having room to expand in the future. Every organization will have a different set of needs, but all share some common goals with an HRIS, including the need to have a system that allows them to gather, organize, and securely maintain employee data. The system also has to allow for the generation of standardized compliance and strategic HR reports such as new hires or turnover. Beyond that, the goal of this step is to determine the needed features of a potential system versus the wanted features of the system.

Many systems allow for optional HR-relevant modules to be added, such as compensation, benefits, onboarding, and performance management modules. The needs of the specific organization's HR functions and strategy will determine the specific configuration. One thing to keep in mind is the need for system integration. It is one thing to "have" the data, and as many organizations find out, it is a very different thing to access, retrieve, and merge such data.

Having standalone modules within HR that do not have the capability to link data with other organizational systems is not optimal. Another key factor to consider in the needs assessment phase is various ways to handle the merging and joining of data from different databases. Finally, research consistently finds that understanding users' individual needs is a critical component of success when developing a new HRIS.[32]

Designing the System

After identifying a list of minimum requirements and additional "wish list" items, assessing project parameters comes next, including budgetary, technological, and time constraints. Being as explicit and honest about these at this stage allows organizations to focus on features that are both feasible and desirable. These will lead directly into the design of the HRIS.

■ FIGURE 3.5 Data Flow Diagram Excerpt

This excerpt from a data flow diagram depicts the logical design of a performance management system.

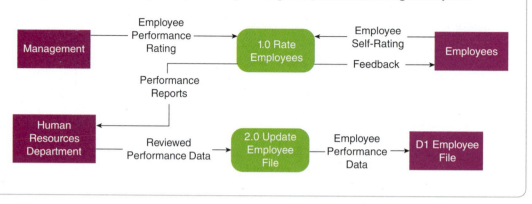

Two related but distinct factors are important to consider: logical design and physical design. On one hand, logical design refers to the translation of business requirements into improved business processes.[33] For example, HR might identify all of the steps in the recruitment process, as well as the types of data that will be exchanged and stored. Often **data flow diagrams,** such as the one pictured in Figure 3.5, are used to depict the old and/or new business processes. As the name implies, data flow diagrams show how data flow from one entity to the next, as well as how the data are processed.

On the other hand, physical design refers to determining the most effective way to translate business processes into the software and hardware solutions that make those processes a reality. For example, information technology experts might take the logical design of a recruitment system designed by HR and determine the software and hardware needed to bring the system to life and to integrate with other existing systems. As a general rule, the logical design (including process and data requirements) should precede the physical design (including both the associated hardware and software), as sometimes the logical design will reveal that the current physical design is actually fine, and just the process needs to be changed.

Selecting a Vendor

The first step in choosing a vendor is creating a list of what you want the HRIS to be able to accomplish. This list is included in a request for proposal (RFP), which is sent to several potential vendors. When writing an RFP, important considerations include the price and the configuration of the plan. For example, does the organization seek to purchase and install the hardware and software on internal machines staffed by internal staff? Or is the organization interested in software as a service so that a subscription to software makes sense and employees access the software via the Internet? There are, of course, pros and cons to either approach, so it is important to be clear regarding which of these options is desirable and viable when sending out the RFP. Small- to medium-sized companies find the

Data flow diagrams Depict the logical design of how data move from one entity to the next and how data are processed within an information system

software-as-a-service option to be particularly attractive, as software can be accessed via web browsers without having to install it on local computers and other devices, such as tablets and smartphones. Easy access to HR systems and information paves the way for useful employee self-service functions such as benefits enrollment, tax information, and updating employee contact information, as well as more sophisticated functions such as access to onboarding materials, training and development programs, and performance management systems.

Identifying references is also important when considering different vendors. As the SHRM toolkit on designing and managing an HRIS notes, any reputable developer or reseller should provide references from current clients of similar size with comparable business processes.[34]

SHRM recommends that HR professionals ask vendors' references questions like these:

- How has the system improved HR functions?

- What modules are you using?

- Has the system met your expectations? If not, what is it missing?

- Are end users satisfied with the system?

- Has the system been expanded or upgraded since the original purchase? If so, how did the upgrade affect customizations and other features?

- How has the vendor responded to any problems?

- What do you like best about the system? What do you like least?

- Has the system provided the expected ROI? Why or why not?

- What was the implementation experience like? Did the vendor deliver on budget and on schedule?

After reviewing the different proposals that the organization receives and checking with vendor references, the selection committee should invite two to three vendors to give a demonstration of the HRIS platform to stakeholders within the organization. Finally, taking into consideration all of the available information, one vendor should be selected and a contract finalized. Key points to consider in the contract are pricing, technical and maintenance support, and upgrades.

Implementing a Human Resource Information System

LO 3.5 Address key points of the process of HRIS implementation.

To this point, we have walked through the points to think about when considering, designing, and choosing a package. Next comes implementation. Although HRIS has the potential to transform organizations, and we covered several examples of HRIS successes, researchers note, "The available evidence suggests that in the vast majority of cases information technology (IT)–enabled HRIS have not helped produce a wholesale transformation of the HR function away from routine processing and compliance and towards the strategic business partner role that many were expecting."[35]

Managing Resistance to Change

Implementing a major HRIS or changing the way that data are gathered, stored, and retrieved can be a major change within an organization, and it can be challenging to handle effectively. It is not only about the software and hardware; it is also about the individuals whose work lives will be affected by the change in procedures, job descriptions, and access to information. It is an organizational change process that must be managed, and such processes are, at their heart, people management challenges as well as opportunities.

CHAPTER SUMMARY

Managing data is important to HR because all organizations need to be able to make decisions about people, and data-informed decisions can be more effective. HR information systems, or HRIS, provide both opportunities and challenges. Opportunities include the ability to track employees through their employment life cycles, employee-centered HR functionality, data availability for metrics and analytics, and the ability to create effective data visualizations. Challenges to consider include cost, the HR skill set, data privacy concerns, and data security concerns. In developing an HRIS, an organization conducts a needs assessment, creates a design, and considers choosing a vendor. Core information system concepts include the management of databases and users, as well as relational database concepts.

KEY TERMS

human resource information
  systems (HRIS)   50
enterprise resource planning
  (ERP)   51
e-HRM   51
data lake   56
data privacy   60

anonymous data   60
confidential data   61
personally identifiable data   61
data security   61
cybersecurity   61
two-step authentication   62
multifactor authentication   62

blockchain   63
data flow diagrams   66

HR REASONING AND DECISION-MAKING EXERCISES

EXERCISE 3.1: DETERMINING WHETHER TO CONTINUE HRIS CONSULTING

The Monday morning meeting is just starting. The room is full of individuals from the HR team. As the newest member and most well trained on statistics and HR analytics, you are looked to by staff to help them frame questions, conduct research to answer the questions, and help walk them through the implications.

John Bettle, a senior HR manager within your division, walks in. He starts the meeting off with several scenarios that the team has been asked to address. As the new HR analytics guru in your group, you've been asked to address key questions.

The organization has been spending a lot of money bringing in HRIS consultants and experts to help with understanding the HRIS needs of the organization. The VP of HR, Raja Sutton, has asked John to let him know if he thinks the investment in time and money is worth it. John's gut tells him it is, but he's not sure how best to make the business case for this. Given that the request came from "up high," John is asking for your help in how to address it.

Now, decide what you would do. Share your approach to how the team might best respond to this request from the VP of HR.

Questions

1. What specifically would you tell John to say to justify the continued investment in understanding the organization's HRIS needs?
2. Be specific, and outline your recommendations for John, being sure to include key points from this chapter.

EXERCISE 3.2: ORGANIZATIONAL ATTRACTIVENESS AUDIT

You work on a team with four other members of the customer service team at C-Zone, an auto-parts wholesaler. Your company has around 2,000 employees nationally. The company has low job acceptance rates of only 30%, which you suspect is too low, but since you do not work in HR, you have never mentioned anything about this. For a long time, you have believed that the high customer service turnover (75% each year) and low acceptance rates of jobs offered are related. It may be time for your team to think about what might be done about this. Your company recently implemented a new HRIS, which now makes it possible to get data on employees on request. You decide it is time for your five-person leadership team to start doing a little investigation.

Questions

1. Develop a plan to examine why employees are hesitant to join the organization and always seem to be leaving. How can you assess why employees turn down job offers? How might you assess why employees are leaving? After you choose your method of measurement (i.e., focus groups, survey, interviews), develop an instrument, along with the questions to be included. How would you analyze the data to identify the top reasons for employee departures?

2.   Let's assume that you found out the top three reasons for low job acceptance to your company are as follows:

(a)   Management is very authoritarian and not supportive of employees. When potential applicants read the comments on Glassdoor.com, it scares them off.

(b)   Compensation is below average compared with other similar organizations.

(c)   Employees feel they are working all the time with little downtime. This is especially true in the call center when calls can be stressful and plentiful at peak times.

3.   What would be your proposed action plan to deal with these issues? Be specific, and make sure that your recommendations focus on recruitment, selection, training, compensation, and any other stages of the employment cycle.

ETHICAL MATTERS EXERCISE: FITNESS TRACKERS AND DATA PRIVACY

Today, many organizations partner with vendors to address employee health and engagement. For example, with the goal of improving employee well-being for partnering organizations, Virgin Pulse provides employees with wearable devices and applications to track their sleep, stress, activity level, and other personal data. Companies like Virgin Pulse tout their commitment to data privacy, security, and compliance, thereby implying that employee data will not be shared in an unauthorized manner.

The surprising thing with data recognizability is understanding how seemingly anonymous data, such as a query into a search engine, can give enough unique information to track that person down. For example, an IP address is a unique online identifier that may be tracked when a form is filled out or an online survey is taken. Although not 100% accurate, IP addresses can be used to identify a person or pinpoint their location, especially over a period of time as individuals travel to the same places (e.g., from their homes to work and back).

If an organization decided to provide employees with wearable devices instead of working through a third-party vendor like Virgin Pulse, this could pose an ethical dilemma under certain circumstances. Namely, without proper data privacy and compliance restrictions in place, the data could be used in ways that would compromise individuals' privacy and other personal rights. Although perhaps not illegal, HR professionals may run dangerously close to committing discrimination under the Americans with Disabilities Act (ADA) if they use these data to make employment decisions. Poor or irregular sleep, for example, does not necessarily constitute a disability according to the ADA, but it could be an indicator of various physical diseases or psychiatric disorders, which are protected as disabilities under the ADA. Further, even if deemed legal, using employee health data in this manner could be construed as unethical, particularly if the data are used in a way that deviates from their intended use.[36]

Questions

1.   How does the use of a third-party vendor like Virgin Pulse make it more ethical to have employees wear monitoring devices than it would be if the employer did so directly?

2.   Do you think the use of monitoring devices should be optional for employees? How would you ensure that employees who opted out of using the device would not be penalized for nonparticipation?

4

Diversity, Inclusion, and Equal Employment Laws

LEARNING OBJECTIVES

After reading and studying this chapter, you should be able to do the following:

4.1 Describe the challenges and benefits of diversity and inclusion in the workplace.

4.2 Identify major U.S. laws pertaining to equal employment opportunity and how they apply to various kinds of employment decisions.

4.3 Discuss the impact of Title VII of the Civil Rights Act.

4.4 Identify additional antidiscrimination acts and protections in the workplace.

4.5 Recommend ways in which organizations can maintain legal compliance and address key analytical, legal, ethical, and global issues associated with diversity and inclusion in HRM.

HR in Action: The Case of Salesforce.com

Even when companies realize the benefits of having a diverse and inclusive workplace, getting there often takes a deliberate, comprehensive, and multipronged approach. Marc Benioff, the CEO of cloud-based software company Salesforce.com, summarizes this as "there is no finish line when it comes to equality." Benioff is among a growing cadre of tech CEOs tackling the lack of diversity and pay inequity in their companies.

In 2015, Salesforce.com spent $3 million to tackle gender imbalance in pay. The company examined the pay of men and women across the company, and in cases in which pay differences were not explainable by factors such as job function, location, or level, adjustments were made for both men and women and affected 6% of the workforce. A second global assessment in 2017 affected 11% of employees and again cost around $3 million.

©iStock.com/Bjorn Bakstad

CEO Marc Benioff sees addressing gender gaps in pay as only one piece of Salesforce.com's Women's Surge initiative. The company ensures that women are at least 30% of the attendees at every meeting, and their High Potential Leadership Program works to ensure fairness in advancement opportunities. Salesforce.com also started granting millions of dollars to the San Francisco school district in support of computer science and science, engineering, technology, and math (STEM) programming with the goal of increasing the diversity of kids exposed to computer science at an early age and possibly consider a career in STEM.[1]

Case Discussion Questions

1. Why do you think Salesforce.com decided to tackle pay inequity between men and women?

2. Why do you think pay inequity exists?

3. Why do you think organizations may benefit from having systematic programs in place to monitor and intervene with pay inequity?

A s a collective characteristic, **diversity** refers to real or perceived differences among people with respect to sex, race, ethnicity, age, physical and mental ability, sexual orientation, religion, and attributes that may affect their interactions with others.[2] By hiring, retaining, and supporting a diverse workforce, companies have the potential to achieve better business results and minimize the chances of costly lawsuits. This chapter discusses the basics of diversity management and the legal landscape relating to it.

Challenges and Benefits of Managing Diversity Effectively

LO 4.1   Describe the challenges and benefits of diversity and inclusion in the workplace.

In 2017, women constituted 47% of the workforce in the United States. White employees were 78%, Hispanics 17%, African Americans 12%, and Asian workers 6% of the labor force.[3] How organizations hire, manage, and retain a diverse workforce has implications for organizational effectiveness.

Diversity
Real or perceived differences among people with respect to sex, race, ethnicity, age, physical and mental ability, sexual orientation, religion, and attributes that may affect their interactions with others

Is Diversity Beneficial for Work Groups and Organizations?

When employees work in a diverse group, do they experience benefits? Studies show that diverse groups actually feel less cohesive, experience more conflict, misunderstand each other more, have higher rates of turnover, and have lower team performance. Similarly, individuals who work with others who are dissimilar to them feel less interpersonal attraction to their peers. In other words, simply diversifying a work group is no guarantee for immediate success. Instead, it may be a recipe for conflict and frustration.[4]

At the same time, diversity's potential is unlocked when diversity is accompanied by inclusion. **Inclusive environments** are organizations or groups in which individuals, regardless of their background, are treated with dignity and respect, are included in decision making, and are valued for who they are and what they bring to the group or organization. Inclusiveness allows individuals to be themselves. Everyone is valued not only for their performance but also as human beings. Employees have input in decision making, and everyone's ideas are heard. Research shows that when accompanied by inclusion, diversity has positive effects on groups in the form of lower conflict, and the negative effects on unit performance disappear. At the company level, inclusive climate was associated with more positive relationships within the company and lower turnover rate. Further, perceptions of equal access to opportunities and fair treatment are associated with positive outcomes for individuals. These findings underline the importance of jointly considering diversity and inclusion in HR-related decision making.[5]

Diversity and innovation are related such that the more diversity that exists within a group, the more innovative it tends to be.[6] Consider product design. Today, many products target a diverse set of customers. Yet when a product design team is homogeneous, members typically consider only their own experiences with the product and neglect to consider unique challenges users dissimilar to them may experience. As a case in point, facial recognition software ranging from Hewlett-Packard's (HP) motion-tracking webcams to Google Photos had difficulty recognizing darker skin tones, causing frustration for end users. Analysts raised the possibility that lack of diversity in design teams could be contributing to these problems.

Frank Polich/Bloomberg via Getty Images

Diversity also has effects on firm reputation and performance. Diversity at the highest levels of a company signals that the firm gives power to a diverse group of individuals. A study of *Fortune* 500 companies showed that the racial diversity of the board of directors was positively related to firm performance as measured by return on investment, because firms with diverse boards had a more positive reputation and greater investments in firm innovation as captured by investment in research and development (R&D).[8] However, in 2018, only 5% of *Fortune* 500 firms had female CEOs, and racial diversity was also lacking, with less than 1% of *Fortune* 500 companies being helmed by Black CEOs and 1% by Hispanic CEOs.[9]

The CEO of the financial firm TIAA Roger Ferguson leverages the power of diversity at work. He credits the firm's diversity at all levels for having pushed them to question the safety of investing in subprime mortgage market and thereby avoiding the worst effects of the 2008 economic crash.[7]

Why Are Diversity and Inclusion Still Challenging to Achieve?

Even though diversity and inclusion are important for competitiveness, there are still barriers. Prejudices and biases continue to exist, and they serve as barriers to hiring and retaining a diverse workforce. Many of the challenges to achieving diversity and inclusion reflect simple human tendencies, which make it extremely difficult to eradicate them. In many cases, being aware of them is a useful first step, but instead of trying to change human nature, organizations are starting to design systems that recognize that these biases exist and seek to prevent them from affecting HR decisions in the first place.

Inclusive environments
Organizations or groups in which individuals, regardless of their background, are treated with dignity and respect, included in decision making, and valued for who they are and what they bring to the group or organization

Similarity-Attraction

Perhaps the biggest challenge to having a diverse workforce and creating an inclusive work environment is the tendency of individuals to prefer others who are similar to them. Researchers name this tendency the **similarity-attraction hypothesis**. People tend to establish trust more quickly, show willingness to cooperate, and experience smoother communication with others who are similar to them. This attraction could be a barrier to hiring employees who are different from the existing employee pool. Often this tendency manifests itself as greater perceived chemistry, or a positive "gut feeling" signaling that one candidate is a better fit for the company or the team relative to the other candidates. Even when employees who are different from the majority are hired, feeling different could result in a sense of alienation and isolation. Research has shown that individuals who are demographically different from others they work with are at a higher turnover risk, particularly early in their tenure in the company.[10]

Similarity-attraction hypothesis
The theory that individuals prefer others who are similar to them

Stereotypes
Overly simplified and generalized assumptions about a particular group that may not reflect reality

Unconscious (or implicit) bias Stereotypes individuals hold that reside beyond their conscious awareness

Stereotypes and Unconscious Biases

Stereotypes cause problems during and after hiring. **Stereotypes** are simplified and generalized assumptions about a particular group. These assumptions may be implicit or explicit. If you believe that younger people are more technology savvy, and you are aware that this is a perception you have, then this is an example of an explicit stereotype. However, if you don't consciously think that, and yet you are taken aback when you interact with an extremely tech-savvy older person, then you may have an implicit, or unconscious, bias about how age affects technical acumen. **Unconscious (or implicit) bias** refers to stereotypes individuals hold that reside beyond their conscious awareness. To explore your own potential implicit biases, try the implicit association test developed by Harvard University researchers (https://implicit.harvard.edu/implicit/takeatest.html). By definition, implicit biases are unconscious, and a person may have difficulty identifying and eliminating them.

Becoming more aware of how hidden biases affect organizational decision making is the first step in dealing with them. For example, Google developed a program training its employees on unconscious bias, giving employees a common understanding of implicit bias and a common language to collectively confront its effects and hold each other accountable. Organizations are designing structures and systems that start with the assumption that human decision makers are biased but

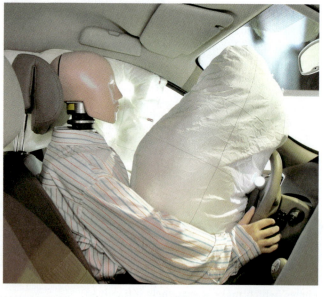

©iStock.com/uatp2

Since the 1970s, automotive manufacturers used crash test dummies that represented the average American male, resulting in 47% higher injury rates for women wearing seatbelts. The situation was resolved with a federal law in 2011 requiring manufacturers to use a smaller female dummy in their tests.[11]

prevent those biases from affecting decision making. One of the successful methods for dealing with lack of diversity in national orchestras has been to conduct auditions behind a screen, which has resulted in the admission of more female musicians to national orchestras even though they constituted only 5% of orchestra members in the 1970s.

An Overview of Equal Employment Opportunity Laws

LO 4.2   Identify major U.S. laws pertaining to equal employment opportunity and how they apply to various kinds of employment decisions.

Legal compliance is the first step in diversity management. Discrimination lawsuits are costly both in terms of legal fees and penalties and because of their costs to firm reputation. The legal landscape is dynamic and constantly changing. HR professionals need to continually keep up with new developments in the legal field. States and municipalities have their own laws and, presidential **executive orders**, which carry the force of law, may be applicable to HR issues.

In the United States, federal law prohibits discrimination in employment decisions based on protected characteristics. These laws are referred to as Equal Employment Opportunity (EEO) laws. Most EEO laws pertaining to private, government, and state institutions are monitored and enforced by the **Equal Employment Opportunity Commission (EEOC)**, an independent federal agency that ensures compliance with the law and provides outreach activities designed to prevent discrimination from occurring in the first place. In addition to the EEOC, the **Office of Federal Contract Compliance Programs (OFCCP)**, a division of the Department of Labor, monitors EEO compliance of federal contractors.[12]

Most EEO laws apply to organizations with 15 or more employees. EEO laws cover businesses, private employers, government agencies, employment agencies, and labor unions. These laws aim to prevent discrimination against employees, job applicants, and participants in training and apprenticeship programs.

Excluding the Equal Pay Act, EEO laws require applicants or employees to file a complaint with the EEOC as the first step. Even though illegal discrimination may have occurred, individuals do not have the ability to file a lawsuit without filing a charge with the EEOC first.[13] The laws require employees or job applicants to file their complaint within a specific number of days. Once a charge is filed, the EEOC investigates claims of discrimination and seeks to help parties reach a settlement. The EEOC is authorized to file lawsuits when there is evidence of bias. If the EEOC finds evidence of discrimination but decides not to pursue a lawsuit, it issues a "right to sue" letter, allowing the individual to file a lawsuit on their own.[14]

Equal Pay Act of 1963 (EPA)

Pay equity between men and women remains a concern, with women being paid an average of 83 cents for every dollar men made in 2014.[15] Reasons for this gap include segregation of sexes across different occupations with different pay averages, résumé gaps due to child-rearing responsibilities, or sex discrimination. One piece of legislation aimed at

Executive orders
Presidential orders that carry the force of law

Equal Employment Opportunity Commission (EEOC) An independent federal agency that ensures compliance with the law and provides outreach activities designed to prevent discrimination

Office of Federal Contract Compliance Programs (OFCCP) A division of the Department of Labor; monitors EEO compliance of federal contractors

closing the gap is the Equal Pay Act of 1963. This law applies to "employers engaged in commerce or production of goods," which means virtually all businesses. According to this law, when employees perform similar jobs requiring similar skills and under similar conditions, employees cannot be paid differently based on their sex. To make a claim, the employee would need to show the following:

a. they and an employee of the other sex are doing equal work, *and*

b. they are paid differently for the same work.

As a defense, the employer would need to show that there is a reason other than sex for the pay difference, such as seniority, merit, or quality or quantity of production. Note that the individual does not need to prove that the organization acted intentionally when paying sexes differently; rather, simply showing that the difference exists is sufficient. The law covers all aspects of employee compensation and rewards, including salaries, benefits, commissions, stock options, and allowances. Even though job titles may be different, if the job is essentially the same, then the pay of men and women is expected to be the same.

Title VII of the Civil Rights Act

LO 4.3 Discuss the impact of Title VII of the Civil Rights Act.

Title VII is the most comprehensive federal legislation relating to equal employment opportunities. The law applies to all employers with 15 or more employees and prohibits employment decisions based on sex, race, color, national origin, and religion. The law prohibits both intentional discrimination based on these protected characteristics and seemingly neutral decision criteria that have a discriminatory effect on different groups. The law includes harassment as part of discriminatory practices. Title VII applies to all groups equally. Discriminating against men as well as women, employees of all races, all religions, color, and national origin is against the law, regardless of who is the victim of discriminatory action.

Disparate treatment
Treating different groups of applicants or employees differently because of their race, color, religion, sex, or national origin

Disparate (or adverse) impact
When employers use seemingly neutral criteria that have a discriminatory effect on a protected group

What Is Discrimination Under Title VII?

Title VII prohibits two types of discrimination: **disparate treatment** and **disparate (or adverse) impact**. Disparate treatment refers to treating different groups of applicants or employees differently because of their race, color, religion, sex, or national origin. Using different tests, questions, and/or hiring and promotion procedures for different groups are examples of disparate treatment. Hiring or refusing to hire employees into a particular position based on these protected characteristics (such as giving preference to men for warehouse positions or giving preference to women for sales jobs in a store) is also illegal. In contrast, disparate impact involves using seemingly neutral criteria that have a discriminatory effect on a protected group. For example, a workplace policy prohibiting head coverings may seem neutral on the surface, but it is likely to have a more negative impact on Muslim, Sikh, and Orthodox Jewish employees.

Disparate Treatment

Despite the decades that have passed after the passage of Title VII in 1964, disparate treatment discrimination still occurs and continues to be costly. In 2010, Walmart agreed to pay more than $11 million in back pay and compensatory damages because for 7 years, it had excluded women from warehouse positions and only hired men between ages 18 and 25 for these jobs, violating the law.[16] It is allowable for organizations to have physical ability requirements for particular positions, but they may not have policies segregating employees of different sexes or other protected characteristics into different positions.

Here is how a disparate treatment case is handled: Imagine that an applicant applies for a job at a retail store. She wears a hijab, a veil traditionally worn by Muslim women. She is qualified for the job. The interviewer asks questions about her need to wear a hijab and her religion. After the interview, the applicant learns that she did not get the job. Instead, the company hires someone who has less experience in retail. The applicant would have prima facie evidence (at first glance, or preliminary evidence) that discrimination may have happened because

a. the person applied for a job for which she was qualified;

b. she was rejected, and someone with similar or less qualifications was hired; and

c. there is circumstantial evidence indicating that religion, a protected characteristic, may have been a factor.

After prima facie evidence has been established, the burden of proof shifts to the employer. Now the employer will need to demonstrate that there was a nondiscriminatory reason for the decision. For example, if the candidate lacked critical skills or the person who was hired was chosen for a nondiscriminatory reason, such as a specific expertise, this would be the employer's defense. If there is strong evidence that religion was the reason for not hiring this applicant (e.g., e-mails come to light that display religious prejudice), then the employment decision would be deemed illegal.

If the employer can present a nondiscriminatory reason, the burden of proof once again shifts to the applicant. Now the applicant would need to show that the reason provided by the employer is an excuse and not the real reason. This can be shown if the employer's reason is factually incorrect or there is some evidence that it was not the true reason.

What Should Organizations Do to Proactively Defend Themselves Against Disparate Treatment Claims?

In Title VII disparate treatment cases, the employer may present two kinds of defense. First, they may show that there was a nondiscriminatory reason for the action against the applicant or employee. To do that, employers would need to be aware of the law and must avoid using legally protected characteristics in their employment decisions. In addition, they must keep careful records of all applicants following interviews and document all employment decisions to be able to defend them when necessary.

A second defense of the organization could be to show that the protected characteristic in this particular case is a **bona fide occupational qualification (BFOQ)**, or an

Bona fide occupational qualification (BFOQ)
A particular instance where a normally legally protected characteristic (such as age or gender) is an essential necessity of a job

Manager's Toolbox

AVOIDING ILLEGAL INTERVIEW QUESTIONS AND EMPLOYMENT PRACTICES

Consider the following interview questions and employment practices and why they may be potentially illegal.[17]

Are you married?	This question may violate state laws prohibiting marital status discrimination. If only asked to women, it may be an example of sex discrimination under Title VII. The organization may be trying to screen out female applicants who are likely to become pregnant, violating pregnancy discrimination.
How old are your children?	If this is a question only asked to women, it would be an example of sex discrimination. Given its irrelevance to the hiring process and potential discriminatory effects, this question is best avoided.
You have an interesting accent. Where did you grow up?	This question could reveal the national origin of the applicant, which is a protected category.
Have you ever been arrested?	Statistically, Hispanic and Black men are more likely to have been arrested, and arrest record is not a reliable indicator of crime. The use of this criterion could have a disparate impact.
Using a thick accent as a reason not to hire	If the accent does not seriously interfere with one's performance at work, using someone's accent as a reason not to hire them may be discrimination based on national origin.
Using English-only rules	A policy forbidding the use of one language (e.g., no Spanish) would be illegal due to national origin discrimination. English-only rules may be legal as long as they are dictated by business necessity and job requirements. For this reason, implementing such rules during breaks will be suspect.
Using a language test as part of hiring	Even when communication in English is essential for the job, requiring language skills that go beyond what is needed during the regular performance of the job could be a violation of Title VII.
Do you have a disability that requires an accommodation? What impairments do you have?	Even with good intent, it is best to avoid this question. If the employee has a disability, the accommodation request should come from the employee. It is acceptable to ask whether the individual is able to perform the major functions of the job.

essential necessity of the job. BFOQ is a very narrow defense, and any claims that a characteristic is important for the business in question because of customer preferences typically fail. Instead, successful uses of the BFOQ defense involve customers' privacy concerns. As a case in point, Beth Israel Medical Center was able to successfully defend itself in a lawsuit brought by a male OB/GYN. The doctor claimed the hospital was discriminating against him because it was accommodating female patients who expressed a preference for female doctors. In this case, the court found gender to be a BFOQ due to patients' privacy concerns.[18]

Disparate Impact

According to Title VII, discrimination does not necessarily involve discriminatory intent. Instead, employers may sometimes use seemingly neutral criteria that have a discriminatory effect on a protected group. This type of discrimination is termed *disparate impact* (or adverse impact). For example, organizations often use tests that may lead to greater hiring of one group than others. The City of Chicago used a physical performance test to hire paramedics between 2000 and 2014. During this period, 98% of all men and 60% of all women who took the test passed. The court sided with the female paramedics who brought the lawsuit.[19] Even though it is a seemingly neutral criterion, the test had different effects on male and female candidates. When a test or decision criterion has different effects on different groups, the company will need to demonstrate that there is a business necessity to use that specific test. If there is no compelling reason, then its use may be illegal under Title VII.

Disparate impact claims do not necessitate showing evidence that discrimination was intentional. In a claim involving disparate impact, prima facie evidence can be demonstrated by showing that the selection criterion or employment policy has a differential effect on different groups. This requires a statistical analysis to assess the effects of the selection criterion. In 1978, the EEOC, the Department of Labor, and the Department of Justice adopted the **Uniform Guidelines on Employee Selection Procedures**, which outline how selection systems can be designed to comply with EEO laws. According to the *Uniform Guidelines,* a simple way of establishing whether disparate impact occurred is to use the **4/5ths (or 80%) rule**. According to this rule, one group's selection ratio may not be less than 80% of the majority group's ratio. In the example of the City of Chicago's paramedics, the male paramedic selection ratio was 98%, whereas for women, it was 60%. But is this gap large enough to show that female applicants were negatively affected? To answer this question, multiply 98 by 80%, which is 78.4%. Given that female applicants had a selection ratio of 60%, which is less than 78.4%, there is prima facie evidence that the test was discriminatory. Alternatively, divide 60% by 98%, which is 61%. Because this is smaller than 80%, there is prima facie evidence that disparate impact exists. The 4/5ths rule is criticized because it is prone to giving false positives (shows discrimination when none exists). Instead, organizations may use more rigorous statistical tests such as a chi-square test, particularly if they have a large sample.

Once prima facie evidence is established, the burden of proof shifts to the employer. Now they would need to demonstrate that the test is job related and is consistent with business necessity. If the person challenging the selection procedure can demonstrate that there

Uniform Guidelines on Employee Selection Procedures Guidelines adopted by the EEOC, the Department of Labor, and the Department of Justice, which outline how selection systems can be designed to comply with EEO laws

4/5ths (or 80%) rule According to this rule, a protected group's selection ratio may not be less than 80% of the majority group's ratio

are other, nondiscriminatory alternatives to the test in question, then the employer may need to abandon their use of this criterion. The *Uniform Guidelines* (http://uniformguide lines.com/uniformguidelines.html#20) include information regarding how to validate selection tests and ensure that they comply with Title VII. In other words, an organization may continue to use a specific test if its validity can be established. However, often organizations have difficulty defending themselves because the requirements of selection tests may not reflect the reality of the jobs. For example, in manual jobs, the physical agility or ability requirements expected of job applicants may be harsher than what the job actually entails, leading to the conclusion that the test unnecessarily discriminates.

What Should Organizations Do to Proactively Defend Themselves Against Disparate Impact Claims?

When it comes to disparate impact cases, the employer's defense is to establish that the test being used is job related and that there is a business necessity. To establish job relatedness, organizations need to be ready to defend the validity of their tests. The cutoffs used in selection tests should be reasonable and aligned with normal expectations in the day-to-day

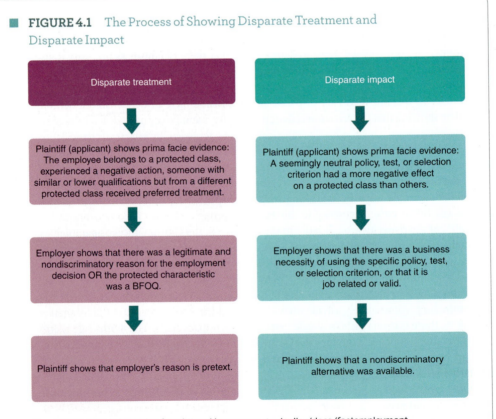

■ FIGURE 4.1   The Process of Showing Disparate Treatment and Disparate Impact

Disparate treatment	Disparate impact
Plaintiff (applicant) shows prima facie evidence: The employee belongs to a protected class, experienced a negative action, someone with similar or lower qualifications but from a different protected class received preferred treatment.	Plaintiff (applicant) shows prima facie evidence: A seemingly neutral policy, test, or selection criterion had a more negative effect on a protected class than others.
Employer shows that there was a legitimate and nondiscriminatory reason for the employment decision OR the protected characteristic was a BFOQ.	Employer shows that there was a business necessity of using the specific policy, test, or selection criterion, or that it is job related or valid.
Plaintiff shows that employer's reason is pretext.	Plaintiff shows that a nondiscriminatory alternative was available.

Source: Based on information from https://www.eeoc.gov/policy/docs/factemployment_procedures.html

performance of the job. The *Uniform Guidelines* is an important source for HR profession-als in charge of selecting tests and setting decision criteria used to screen out and make employment decisions about employees and applicants. Figure 4.1 summarizes the two processes for showing disparate treatment and disparate impact.

Title VII and Harassment

In addition to prohibiting discrimination based on disparate impact and disparate treat-ment, Title VII has prohibitions around harassment. **Harassment** involves unwelcome behaviors based on sex, race, religion, national origin, and other protected characteristics. Under Title VII, harassment that would be offensive to a reasonable person and that occurs on a frequent basis so that it creates a hostile work environment is illegal. Harassment may include name-calling; offensive jokes, pictures, or other explicit materials; and insults or mockery, among others.

Sexual harassment, which includes unwanted advances and other harassment that are sexual in nature, is also prohibited. The victim of sexual harassment may be male or female, and the victim and the perpetrator do not need to be of opposite sexes. The EEOC defines two forms of sexual harassment. **Quid pro quo harassment** involves making employment decisions contingent on sexual favors. A manager hinting that a promotion or a raise depends on the employee providing a sexual favor or punishing an employee for refusing to fulfill a sexual request are examples of quid pro quo harassment. In other words, the use of sexual favors as a bargaining tool is prohibited. Alternatively, sexual harassment may be in the form of creating a **hostile work environment**, or conduct sexual in nature that contributes to an environment that a reasonable person would find offensive.

Because claims against organizations are more likely to be successful if the company had known and yet failed to act on the information, businesses should establish safeguards by training their managers and employees, ensuring that there are clear and safe mechanisms for employees to voice complaints, and any such complaints are taken seriously and resolved promptly. Retaliating against complainants or resolving the issue in a way that punishes the victim (such as transferring the victim to a less desirable job) increase the company's liability.

Title VII and Special Considerations Regarding Sex Discrimination

Title VII prohibits the use of one's sex in employment-related decisions. Organizations may not classify jobs as "men's jobs" and "women's jobs" unless there is a strong reason to believe that sex is a BFOQ. Making assumptions about one's sex and using those stereotypes in employment decisions is also illegal. For example, an employer may not restrict jobs with physical demands to men with the assumption that men have greater physical endurance.

Title VII and the Equal Pay Act (EPA) both provide protections, even though the EPA is solely concerned with pay differentials, whereas Title VII includes all types of employment decisions. A plaintiff concerned about pay discrimination can technically use either or both laws, but there are important differences. When filing a claim based on EPA, plaintiffs are not required to go through the EEOC. This means they can initiate a lawsuit themselves. Further, the EPA applies to businesses of all sizes, but Title VII only applies to businesses with 15 or more employees. EPA claims may be filed within a longer period of time, and the

Harassment
Unwelcome behaviors based on sex, race, religion, national origin, and other protected characteristics

Sexual harassment
Unwanted advances and other harassment that are sexual in nature

Quid pro quo harassment
Involves making employment decisions contingent on sexual favors

Hostile work environment
Behavior that contributes to an environment a reasonable person would find offensive

prima facie evidence is simpler to establish. One main advantage of Title VII for plaintiffs is that it allows them to recover more money at the end of the lawsuit.[20]

Title VII, Race, and Color

Title VII prohibits discrimination in employment based on race. Restricting certain positions to a particular race is a violation of the law. Treating employees of different races differently is also a violation. As a case in point, in 2016, a sheet metal union agreed to a $1.6 million settlement because the EEOC's analysis showed that African American and Hispanic workers received fewer hours and lower wages. Organizations are advised to examine their employment practices to ensure that there are job-related and defensible reasons for decisions that lead to differences in pay, hiring, promotion, and advancement of employees.[21] Finally, harassment based on one's race is also illegal.

Title VII and Religion

In addition to prohibiting discrimination based on religion, Title VII requires organizations to provide **reasonable accommodation**. Simple nondiscrimination is insufficient by itself, and in fact, uniform application of organizational rules with rigidity may be a cause for discrimination claims. Organizations are asked to make allowances for an employee for their religion unless doing so imposes an undue hardship on the employer. When the employer's dress code policy, schedules, breaks, and time-off periods clash with employee religious needs, employers are expected to make a good-faith effort to accommodate them.

The law defines a religion as one's sincerely held beliefs, which includes those practiced by a small minority. Title VII also protects individuals from being discriminated against because they have no religious beliefs. Finally, the expectation that the employee would need to be accommodated due to their religion may not be a reason to discriminate against an employee.

Training managers is a key first step of legal compliance. An important issue is to avoid asking questions about religion during job interviews. If it becomes clear that the employee needs a religious accommodation, the organization must consider whether a reasonable accommodation is possible. This is a high bar: If the employer chooses not to accommodate, it must show that accommodation would have been unsafe or extremely costly or would significantly affect other employees. If an HR manager observes or hears that someone is being harassed because of their religion (or due to other reasons), immediate action should be taken.

Title VII and National Origin

Reasonable accommodation
An accommodation provided to employees to help them perform their jobs that is reasonable given a firm's resources

Title VII has protections against national origin discrimination. Taking adverse action against someone due to their nationality or due to the nationality of someone they are related to (e.g., married to) is prohibited under this law. Harassment of others based on nationality is also prohibited. Seeking to hire U.S. citizens, unless necessitated by a government contract or other special reason, is prohibited, given that U.S. citizenship is not necessary to be legally employed in the United States. Discriminating based on accent is prohibited under Title VII, and instituting English-only rules, unless there is a business necessity such as safety of others, is a practice that should be used cautiously. It is also important for businesses to disregard nationality-related information in employment decisions. For example, the consulting firm Accenture was faced with a class-action lawsuit claiming that it paid software engineers from India (who were working in the United States) significantly less than what American engineers were being paid, forcing the company to settle the case for $500,000.[22]

Additional Antidiscrimination Acts and Protections

LO 4.4   Identify additional antidiscrimination acts and protections in the workplace.

Along with Title VII of the Civil Rights Act, additional acts and amendments have been put in place by states and municipalities to protect employees. We cover some of the major ones in this section.

Pregnancy Discrimination Act (PDA) of 1978

This law amends Title VII and prohibits employers from discriminating against employees due to a pregnancy or related conditions. An individual's pregnancy or assumptions about pregnant individuals may not be used in hiring decisions as long as the person is capable of performing the major functions of the job. When the employee seeks leave, the employer may not treat a pregnancy-related leave any differently than leave granted to employees due to other reasons.[23]

A 2015 Supreme Court decision reaffirms the importance of treating pregnancy-related requests similarly to other medical requests. In the legal case *Young v. UPS,* following her doctor's advice, a UPS driver sought to take on lighter duties with lower weight-lifting requirements during her pregnancy. UPS did not accommodate this request, stating that its policy was to treat pregnancies similarly to an off-the-job injury, which meant that the employee was not entitled to special accommodations. The employee was instead put on unpaid leave, resulting in the loss of her medical insurance. However, employees injured on the job, employees with other disabilities, and those employees who had lost their Department of Transportation credentials were routinely accommodated through lighter duties, suggesting that temporarily accommodating employees was not an undue hardship for the business, and UPS was unable

The Pregnancy Discrimination Act protects employees during and after a pregnancy. Failing to give the employee the same or a similar job upon return to work may be a violation of the PDA.

©iStock.com/Yuri-Arcurs

to present a nondiscriminatory reason for why employees could not be accommodated for a pregnancy-related condition but other classes of employees could be accommodated for other temporary disabilities. The Supreme Court decision suggests that employers should treat a pregnancy as a form of temporary disability and react to it similarly.[24]

The PDA is not the only legislation relating to pregnancy and related conditions. Pregnancy-related complications are protected under the Americans with Disabilities Act (ADA), discussed later in this chapter. The Family and Medical Leave Act (FMLA) covers leave employees are entitled to take, including for childbirth and adoptions. The Affordable Care Act (ACA) has provisions requiring some employers to accommodate the needs of new mothers by giving them sufficient break time to pump breast milk and a private space to do so.

Age Discrimination in Employment Act of 1967 (ADEA)

The Age Discrimination in Employment Act (ADEA) applies to employers with 20 or more workers and prohibits employers from discriminating against an applicant or employee due to their age. The ADEA protects only individuals 40 years of age or older and only applies when old age is used as a rationale to exclude an individual from opportunities. When an older worker is preferred over a younger one, even when age was a factor used in decision making, the decision is not necessarily illegal under ADEA. Harassment due to one's age from managers, coworkers, or customers is also prohibited, and age-based comments and teasing that are frequent enough to create a hostile work environment would be illegal.[25] While the law provides protections, age discrimination is challenging to prove. The Supreme Court decision of *Gross v. FBL Financial Services* in 2009 suggests that plaintiffs have the burden of proof that age was the primary reason for the adverse employment decision (as opposed to the employer having to prove that it would have taken that action regardless of age).[26] One important first step to defend a business against ADEA claims is to avoid asking questions about the employee's age, which surprisingly still happens. Similarly, the organization should avoid using age or age-related stereotypes in employment-related decisions. Having a legitimate and non-discriminatory reason for all business decisions and application of all HR decisions consistently across age groups is particularly important.

Americans with Disabilities Act (ADA) of 1990

The ADA prohibits discrimination against individuals with disabilities who are able to perform the major functions of the job with or without accommodations. The act was amended in 2008 (Americans with Disabilities Act Amendment Act—ADAAA). The act applies to organizations with 15 or more employees and defines a disability as a physical or mental impairment that affects one's major life activities. ADAAA provides a list of major life activities in consideration of a disability and includes activities such as

- Walking
- Reading
- Communicating

- Major bodily functions
  - Immune system
  - Respiratory
  - Reproductive
  - Neurological

Having a history of a specific ailment and being perceived as disabled are two additional forms of protected disabilities.

Each job has essential functions that every incumbent needs to perform, as well as marginal functions that can be assigned to others. Essential functions are core tasks that are expected of all incumbents and are important for effective and safe performance of the job. If the person is not capable of performing the essential functions even with accommodations, the employer is not required to hire or retain the individual. However, if the disability is preventing the person from performing the marginal functions, these functions may be reassigned to others, and the disability may not be a factor in decision making. Finally, the law uses the term *reasonable accommodations* to indicate that as long as accommodating the person does not cause undue hardship on the business, the employer is expected to provide accommodations.

To be able to accommodate the individual, the organization needs to know about the specific disability and the need for an accommodation. Unless a disability is obvious, the request needs to originate from the employee, and once a request is made, the employer and employee are expected to arrive at a mutual resolution. Organizations are allowed to set maximum limits on how much leave employees are entitled to take, but they may need to make exceptions in the case of disability-related leave, as long as doing so does not create an undue hardship for the business.[27]

ADA compliance requires careful planning. The organization would benefit from having updated job descriptions that clearly delineate essential job functions and marginal duties. When a request for accommodation is received, it is essential for managers and HR to be open to ideas and work with the individual to arrive at solutions. Just because an accommodation is unusual is not a reason to dismiss it.[28]

Genetic Information Nondiscrimination Act (GINA) of 2008

The Genetic Information Nondiscrimination Act (GINA) of 2008 is a federal law that prohibits organizations from discriminating against applicants or employees in employment decisions (and in health insurance) based on genetic information. Genetic information is defined as the results of genetic tests, as well as family health history. Employers covered by GINA are prohibited from using an employee's family history and other genetic information when making decisions. The law covers organizations with 15 and more employees. According to EEOC rules, employees may not offer employees incentives to disclose genetic information, with the exception of wellness programs. Genetic disclosures as part of wellness programs are regulated as well, with upper limits to how much incentive employers may provide to encourage participation in wellness programs and requirements to avoid discrimination based on this information.[29] GINA is a recent law, and complaints based on GINA are still rare but growing. GINA complaints usually result from requiring applicants or employees to submit data on their family history.[30]

Lilly Ledbetter Fair Pay Act of 2009

This law is an amendment to Title VII, ADEA, and ADA and specifically relates to pay discrimination. Prior to the passage of this law, a pay discrimination decision under these acts had to be filed within 180 days after discriminatory acts. This was highly impractical, because employees often do not become aware of discrimination until months or years after the fact. This was the situation for Lilly Ledbetter, who worked as a supervisor for Goodyear Tire until her retirement. Over time, her pay lagged behind that of her male peers, even those with less seniority. Ledbetter did not find out about the situation until she had worked there for 19 years and it was not possible for her to file a claim within 180 days. She filed a lawsuit, but the Supreme Court (*Ledbetter v. Goodyear Tire & Rubber Co.*, 2007) held that she should have filed the suit within 180 days. Under the Lilly Ledbetter Fair Pay Act (2009), the 180-day clock restarts with each paycheck, allowing employees to file a claim after they find out that discrimination occurred.[31]

Protections for LGBTQ Workers

Individuals may have gender identity or expression that differs from their biological sex, and they may be sexually or romantically attracted to the opposite sex, the same sex, both, or neither. Studies suggest that between 15% and 43% of homosexual individuals experienced discrimination, and 90% of transgender individuals experienced harassment and mistreatment at work. As of 2019, 21 states, as well as the District of Columbia, Guam, and Puerto Rico, have laws prohibiting discrimination based on both sexual orientation and gender identity in private and public sectors. Additional states provide protections for sexual orientation but not gender identity, and some states provide protections in public but not private employment.[32]

The EEOC regards gender identity and sexual orientation as part of Title VII's sex discrimination clause, taking the view that Title VII provides protections to LGBTQ workers. However, the U.S. Department of Justice does not endorse this view as of this writing.[33] In a growing number of court cases, the EEOC interpretation was upheld, but in other cases, the EEOC interpretation was challenged.[34] The issue is controversial because Congress has repeatedly failed to pass specific legislation to prohibit discrimination based on sexual orientation. In fact, a bill called the Employment Non-Discrimination Act (ENDA) has been regularly introduced in Congress since 1994 but has not passed. Some courts took this to mean that Title VII sex discrimination was not intended as protection for LGBTQ workers.[35]

There is general consensus that Title VII prohibits sexual harassment regardless of the sex of perpetrator and victim, including same-sex harassment. Further, based on precedent, Title VII allows for a stronger case to be made for protections of transgender applicants and workers. Title VII's prohibitions against sex discrimination and gender stereotyping suggest that discriminating against an employee because they violate expectations of how a man or woman should act is considered discrimination. Courts have often interpreted claims by transgender individuals who did not conform to traditional gender notions as examples of sex discrimination. In a landmark Supreme Court case from 1989 (*Price Waterhouse v. Hopkins*), a female employee was denied partnership in the firm because she was considered to be "too macho"; she was told to go to "charm school" and learn how to "dress and walk like a woman." Although this case did not involve a transgender employee, it established the framework that discriminating against individuals because they do not conform to stereotypes about their biological sex is prohibited. Examples of successful cases involving transgender workers include occasions in which an employee was fired or was discriminated against after the employer found out about employee plans for transitioning, harassing a transgender employee by intentionally calling them by their former name, and disciplining them for failure to comply with the company dress code. Courts are split on whether employees are required to provide access to restrooms that match the employee's gender identity or whether failure to provide such access constitutes unlawful discrimination.[36]

In 2015, the EEOC issued a ruling for the first time that it regards sexual orientation discrimination to be a form of sex discrimination and is covered under Title VII and filed lawsuits based on this rationale. The rationale is simple: Sexual orientation is intricately linked to sex. In the example provided by the EEOC, if an employer takes adverse action against a female employee for displaying a picture of her female spouse but does not take similar action against a male employee displaying a picture of his female spouse, the female employee would have been discriminated against due to her sex. Whether this argument will be successful in cases against private employers remains to be seen. In cases in which the legal argument was based around a person not fitting the gender stereotype (e.g., looking and acting feminine or masculine), courts decided that Title VII protections applied.[37]

A 2016 Supreme Court case (*EEOC v. R.G. & G.R. Harris Funeral Homes*) may be considered a step back for LGBTQ worker protections. In the case of a funeral home employee fired for transitioning from male to female, the court upheld the employer's right to fire the employee due to the funeral home's argument that accommodating the employee would violate the employer's sincerely held religious beliefs. In the case of closely held businesses, employers' religious beliefs may shield employers from damages, at least according to the way the legal landscape stood as of this writing.[38]

Fear of disclosing one's gender identity and sexual orientation is associated with negative outcomes, whereas openness and the ability to be open and authentic about oneself have benefits for workplace outcomes, including job attitudes, stress, and workplace adjustment.[39] Organizations are advised to be proactive with respect to adding protections for LGBTQ workers. Providing training for employees and managers, making allowances in the dress code for transitioning employees, using the correct names and gender pronouns, respecting confidentiality of employee plans to transition, and treating applicants and employees with dignity and respect regardless of their specific gender identity and sexual orientation are among the ways organizations may create an inclusive and respectful environment.[40]

Alan Joyce, CEO of the Australian Qantas airlines, was named the most powerful LGBT executive in the world in 2017. He credits the inclusive culture of Qantas for the turnaround of the company and recording the highest profits in its 95-year history.[41]

Brendon Thorne/Bloomberg via Getty Images

Diversity and Inclusion in the Age of HR Analytics

LO 4.5   Recommend ways in which organizations can maintain legal compliance and address key analytical, legal, ethical, and global issues associated with diversity and inclusion in HRM.

Up to this point, we have discussed the importance of diversity and inclusion and covered the legal terrain affecting diversity in the workplace. Now we address initiatives and methods companies are using to manage diversity effectively.

Should Companies Use Affirmative Action?

Affirmative Action Plans (AAPs) aim to increase hiring and labor participation of groups that suffered from past discrimination. Some companies are legally required to have AAPs. For example, under Executive Order 11246, businesses with at least 50 employees *and* government contracts exceeding $50,000 are legally required to develop AAPs for hiring women and minorities. Federal contractors with more than $10,000 worth of business are required to have AAPs for hiring of workers with disabilities. Those with contracts exceeding $100,000 and having at least 50 employees also need to establish written AAPs for hiring veterans. Finally, courts may order a company to temporarily institute an AAP to rectify past discrimination. Employers are permitted to institute AAPs to rectify significant imbalances, but these need to be narrow in scope and temporary.[42]

Spotlight on Legal Issues
GIG WORKERS

EEO laws cover applicants and employees, but they do not apply to independent contractors. Who is an employee? This issue is becoming less straightforward with the rise of the gig economy. Today, many individuals hold temporary positions and perform specific tasks. Technology vendors bring together those willing to perform tasks for others and consumers seeking to fill a need. For example, Uber and Lyft match travelers and those who are willing to drive. TaskRabbit and Bellhops allow consumers to hire someone for specific errands. These companies rely on the assumption that individuals performing the services are contractors and not employees.

The distinction between who is an employee and who is an independent contractor is a fine line, and it has little to do with the title assigned to the individual. The more control a company exercises over workers, the more likely those individuals are regarded as employees from a legal perspective. Lawsuits brought against companies such as Uber and other technology providers allege that the independent contractor classification was a misnomer. In 2015, FedEx reached a settlement for $240 million with its drivers, who were misclassified as contractors. In 2016, Uber agreed to a settlement for up to $100 million in a lawsuit claiming that it misclassified workers (later rejected at federal court for being inadequate).

EEO laws apply to employees, but organizations need to understand the legal definition of *employee* to understand their legal obligations.[43]

Two myths about affirmative action in employment are that (a) affirmative action requires using quotas and (b) affirmative action permits or even requires hiring a less-qualified individual. Both are *false*. Simply hiring someone because they are from an under-represented minority, even though someone else is more qualified, is an example of illegal discrimination according to Title VII—regardless of whether the organization has an AAP in place. Further, race or sex quotas would violate Title VII. Organizations may not have different selection criteria or different cutoff scores to encourage hiring of different groups of individuals.

The Office of Federal Contract Compliance Programs (OFCCP) provides guidelines and sample AAPs. Part of affirmative action is to conduct a workforce analysis to identify barriers to hiring minorities, disabled workers, and women. When these roadblocks are identified, the organization is expected to take steps. A sample AAP is available from OFCCP's website (https://www.dol.gov/ofccp).

Research suggests that AAP beneficiaries experience stigma regarding their competence and likeability, which affects their effectiveness at work. Broadly publicizing qualifications of AAP targets is a useful method to counteract some of these effects.[44] The backlash against AAP and the association of AAPs with quotas and lowering the bar (even though both are actually illegal) has led to the relative unpopularity of AAP programs. Today, many businesses shy away from AAPs and focus on diversity management and inclusion initiatives.[45]

How to Comply With EEO Regulations

EEOC and OFCCP have specific expectations of businesses. Organizations need to adopt precautions to remain on the right side of the law:

- **Training decision makers** to understand their legal obligations is an essential first step in legal compliance.

- **Creating policies** around legally protected areas, such as family and disability-related leave, harassment, and nonretaliation, is vital.

- **Meeting documentation requirements set by EEOC** is important. For example, all private employers covered by Title VII that also have 100 or more employees and federal contractors with 50 or more employees are required to annually file an EEO-1 report with the EEOC and OFCCP. This form requires the organization to count all full-time and part-time employees for each major job category and break them down by ethnicity, race, and sex.

Internal Complaint Mechanisms

Supreme Court decisions such as *Burlington Industries v. Ellerth* (1998) found that organizations are liable for unlawful harassment by supervisors. However, organizations may protect their employees and limit legal liability by establishing internal complaint procedures and promptly investigating and taking action against discrimination and harassment.[46] Establishing policies and procedures explaining what discrimination and harassment are and giving employees mechanisms through which they can file a complaint with HR may ensure that employees are protected in a timely fashion. This information should be included in the employee handbook and communicated to all employees clearly. Ignoring employee complaints and failing to take prompt action will increase the liability of the organization.

Diversity Initiatives

Many organizations have diversity initiatives aimed at increasing inclusion. Having a chief diversity officer, having support for employee resource groups, and having mentoring programs that ensure that employees are matched to a mentor are among the methods in use in many companies to facilitate an inclusive culture. Simply having policies and practices is no guarantee that the organization actually has built an inclusive culture. According to studies, the presence of these programs may create the illusion that the organization is fair and inclusive in the eyes of White and male employees without actually achieving their intended outcomes.[47]

One of the popular initiatives in diversity and inclusion is unconscious bias training.[48] On a day-to-day basis, unconscious biases have implications for micro-inequities. If we feel closer to those of our own sex, we may be warmer, more helpful, or kinder toward them; perhaps smile at them more frequently; or initiate conversations more often. None of these actions are illegal or problematic if done once or twice, but when they constitute patterns of behavior, they affect how inclusive the workplace is. Google and Pinterest are examples of companies that have implemented programs to raise awareness of unconscious bias.

There is debate around whether diversity training initiatives actually work and add value. Unfortunately, hard data on this issue are difficult to come by. Not surprisingly, if managers and employees view diversity training as motivated by minimizing the likelihood of lawsuits and do not personally feel accountable and engaged by diversity initiatives, these are less likely to be successful.[49] Goal setting, tracking diversity metrics, and sharing diversity data are regarded as more promising approaches.[50]

In 2015, Intel announced double referral bonuses for women, minorities, and veterans and committed $300 million to combat their underrepresentation.[51]

Big Data as a Pathway to Increasing Diversity and Inclusion

Organizations may leverage analytics as a pathway to build more diverse and inclusive organizations. Paradigm is a firm that uses HR analytics to examine the effects on diversity of various selection and recruitment methods. Today's organizations can also reach a diverse base of customers through targeted advertisements, as companies like Google and Facebook analyze data on consumer demographics and tailor advertisements to the audience. When organizations are able to purchase ad space to reach a more diverse applicant base, they diversify their recruitment pool.[52]

Organizations can use HR analytics to prevent biases from entering into the decision-making process. Selection tools such as GapJumpers and Unitive allow organizations to blind themselves to applicant demographic characteristics, socioeconomic background, and other factors that could be sources of bias.[53] GapJumpers uses software that acts like a blind audition for businesses. Applicants solve skill-based challenges and their background information is hidden so that applicants are given a fair chance to demonstrate their skills.

People analytics can also help with managing existing employees. A Chicago-based accounting firm used a proprietary analytics tool that gathers information from the HR information system and creates a dashboard. The tool revealed an increase in turnover of women in the fifth to sixth year of their employment in the company. This information allowed the firm to investigate the phenomenon and identify data-driven solutions.[54]

Internal Audits

Organizations can ensure compliance with EEO laws by conducting internal audits to identify problems and correct them proactively instead of risking a costly lawsuit. In particular, pay audits that examine gender differences in pay are often valuable in enabling the organization to take corrective action.

Even though it is straightforward to group jobs that are similar to each other and conduct a statistical difference test based on sex (or other protected characteristics), HR is strongly cautioned against conducting this analysis without top-management commitment. The results of a pay audit are "discoverable" as part of legal proceedings. If the pay audit reveals that there were unexplainable differences between men and women, and if these differences are not corrected, the results of the audit become evidence for potential discrimination and increase the company's liability. If the audit finds differences, it is essential to promptly correct them, which will require resources and top-management commitment to the issue. Working with legal counsel during this audit and ensuring that the audit findings are protected by attorney–client privilege is important. HR still plays a key role as part of diversity audits, ensuring that jobs are classified and grouped correctly, and reasons for pay differences across employees are well documented.[55] There may be many legitimate differences for observed pay differences, including number of years of experience, tenure within the organization, and managerial responsibilities, among others. During the pay audit, these differences would be statistically controlled for.

Big Data and Legal Compliance

One of the key uses of predictive analytics is in employee selection. The idea to automate hiring using algorithms, or at least identifying criteria that are most likely to predict desired outcomes using big samples, is appealing due to potential cost savings and the desire to make more objective selection decisions. HR technology vendors such as Cornerstone

Spotlight on Data and Analytics
DIVERSITY INITIATIVE AT KIMBERLY-CLARK

©iStock.com/jfmdesign

In 2009, Kimberly-Clark, maker of products such as Huggies, Kleenex, and Kotex, came to the realization that although its customer base was 83% female, its leadership consisted mostly of men. Making diversity and inclusion a key initiative became an important business priority, and Kimberly-Clark tackled this question using data analytics. The analytics team analyzed data on which employees were promoted, derailed, and left the company and used the results to make specific changes.

One realization was that women were not applying for open internal positions unless they met most or all of the criteria, whereas men were more likely to apply if they met half the desired criteria. Some jobs required work experience that was unusual for women (e.g., mill experience), so the company moved to a comparable-experience approach rather than looking for narrow types of experience.

Despite the benefits of analytics, the company credits top-management support as the key for the success of the initiative, which resulted in an 82% increase in women in high-level positions in 4 years, as well as helping create a more inclusive, creative, and innovative workplace.[56]

OnDemand provide software that helps companies use predictive analytics using publicly available information, test scores, and biometric data. What are the legal consequences of these approaches?

Data scientists and industrial/organizational psychologists caution that big data may not always be better data.[57] Depending on how they were formulated, these algorithms may codify and perpetuate past systematic discrimination or potentially result in disparate impact. Certain metrics picked up by algorithms as predictive of performance may be proxies for age, sex, race, or other protected categories. Suppose the algorithm discovers that those with a short commute to work are more likely to stay longer and be more effective at work and recommends not hiring those with a long commute. This may make the selection pool less diverse due to the exclusion of some geographic areas if such areas differ in their level of diversity, which they often do. In other words, equating big data with more objective and unbiased data can be a mistake, and overreliance on historical data may result in biased decision making.

There are currently many unknowns regarding how organizations may benefit from predictive data analytics while also ensuring compliance with EEO laws. Selection decisions based on big data may be challenged based on the disparate impact theory, and future court decisions are important to follow to understand the best practices.[58]

CHAPTER SUMMARY

Diversity has advantages for businesses, ranging from increased innovation to higher firm performance, but the benefits of diversity necessitate having an inclusive work environment. Diversity management has its challenges, particularly because individuals are more likely to be interpersonally attracted to similar others and the existence of biases that may serve as barriers to employment and advancement. Numerous federal and state laws, executive orders, and local ordinances aim to prevent discrimination based on sex, race, color, religion, national origin, age, disability status, pregnancy, and genetic information. Although HR analytics may be a crucial tool, the legal implications of big data in employee selection and talent management are still uncharted territory, which means HR professionals should pay attention to this rapidly evolving field.

KEY TERMS

diversity   74
inclusive environments   75
similarity-attraction
    hypothesis   76
stereotypes   76
unconscious (or implicit) bias   76
executive orders   77
Equal Employment Opportunity
    Commission (EEOC)   77

Office of Federal Contract
    Compliance Programs
    (OFCCP)   77
disparate treatment   78
disparate (or adverse) impact   78
bona fide occupational
    qualification (BFOQ)   79
Uniform Guidelines on Employ-
    ee Selection Procedures   81

4/5ths (or 80% rule)   81
harassment   83
sexual harassment   83
quid pro quo harassment   83
hostile work environment   83
reasonable accommodation   84

$SAGE edge™

Get the tools you need to sharpen your study skills. SAGE edge offers a robust online environment featuring an impressive array of free tools and resources.

Access practice quizzes, eFlashcards, video, and multimedia at **edge.sagepub.com/bauerbrief**

HR REASONING AND DECISION-MAKING EXERCISES

EXERCISE 4.1: WORKPLACE DIVERSITY DILEMMAS

Imagine that you are working at a medium-sized business as an HR professional. You are faced with the following dilemmas. Decide how you would handle each issue in the short term and long term. What additional information would help you decide? What changes seem necessary to the company given these dilemmas, if any?

Questions

1. An African American job applicant has just been offered a position as a customer service representative in the company's call center. The job does not have any face-to-face customer contact. The manager who conducted the interview just told the applicant that her hair, which is in dreadlocks, violates the company's dress code, which requires "professional" hairstyles. The manager asked the employee to cut her hair. The applicant refused. The manager is considering revoking the job offer to the employee. What would you do?

2. An applicant for your janitorial services is hearing impaired and is unable to speak. He was invited for a job interview. However, when contacted, the applicant informed management that he would need a sign language interpreter for the interview, and he can bring his sister as an interpreter. The hiring manager cancelled the job interview. What would you do?

3. An employee in your department sent you an e-mail stating that he examined the salaries of more than 100 employees working in the call center and found that male employees seemed to be paid more than female employees. What would you do?

EXERCISE 4.2: ASSESSING DISPARATE IMPACT

Recently, your organization advertised openings for sales associates. The selection process includes gathering and evaluating information on a personality test and in-person interview.

Here is a breakdown of who applied and who was hired:

	APPLIED	HIRED
Men	150	15
Women	90	15
White	100	10
Asian American	50	10
African American	30	5
Hispanic	60	5

Questions

1. Using the 4/5ths rule, do you have prima facie evidence that disparate impact may have occurred? Explain your rationale.

2. If there is prima facie evidence for disparate impact, what information can you use as defense? What would be your action plan for the future?

ETHICAL MATTERS EXERCISE: APPLICANTS WITH CRIMINAL HISTORIES

Should an organization avoid hiring individuals with a criminal background? There is no federal law prohibiting discrimination against former inmates. Yet having blanket policies excluding those with criminal backgrounds has an ethical dimension. There are certainly legitimate reasons for not hiring someone with a criminal record, particularly when public health and safety are a concern. If the ex-convict commits a crime and harms a coworker or customer, the organization may be responsible for negligent hiring. At the same time, the rehabilitation of ex-convicts depends on finding employment. Depending on when the crime occurred and what it was, the risks to the business may be minimal. In some cases, individuals choose to plead guilty instead of fighting a conviction, which helps them avoid incarceration but results in a criminal record.

Businesses such as Seattle-based Mod Pizza and Oregon-based Dave's Killer Bread are committed to giving those with criminal backgrounds a second chance, and they benefit from a qualified and highly motivated workforce. There is also a movement ("ban the box") for states and jurisdictions to pass laws banning the question, "Have you been convicted of a crime?" on employment applications. These laws typically do not prevent companies from using criminal history as part of the hiring process, but they require the employer to wait until a job offer is made before a criminal background check is conducted; the offer may then be revoked if needed. There are no easy answers, but whether and how criminal records should be used in employment decisions is an ethical dilemma.[59]

Questions

1. As a manager, suppose you need to decide whether to hire a candidate with excellent qualifications for the position but with a felony conviction in his or her background. What factors would you take into consideration to decide whether to hire this candidate?

2. Think of a case, or find one in the literature, of a company that encountered legal trouble as a result of hiring an employee with a criminal record. What could have been done differently? What did the company do right?

5

The Analysis and Design of Work

LEARNING OBJECTIVES

After reading and studying this chapter, you should be able to do the following:

5.1 Define job analysis and competency models and describe their purposes in organizations.

5.2 Demonstrate the use of different ways of collecting job analysis information.

5.3 Differentiate between job analysis and competency modeling and evaluate the advantages of each approach.

5.4 Explain how job design can be used to increase employee motivation, job attitudes, and performance.

5.5 Describe how flexible work environments affect employee well-being.

HR in Action: The Case of Using HRM to Understand the Nature of Work

A clear definition of what workers do on the job, and which employee traits are needed to do them, is central for effective HRM. Defining job behaviors and the needed employee characteristics is a focus of many organizations. This is done within specific professions as well. This process is called job analysis.

The U.S. Office of Personnel Management (OPM) is the federal agency that manages many of the HR functions for U.S. government agencies such as recruitment, hiring, retention, and compensation. OPM's HR practices affect millions of government employees. OPM provides detailed guidelines to federal agencies about how to define what workers do on the job. OPM also helps federal agencies use job analysis data to develop selection procedures such as structured interviews.[1] Other organizations analyze work through a similar process called competency modeling. IBM has developed a comprehensive competency model that defines what traits and behaviors are required for all its professional workers.[2]

These types of analyses are also done for professions like health care. The National Council of State Boards of Nursing, Inc. (NCSBN) conducted a detailed analysis for the job of nurse aide. And the National Council for Therapeutic Recreation Certification (NCTRC) developed a job analysis for Certified Therapeutic Recreation

Specialists, including a survey of thousands of job experts. The Society for Human Resource Management (SHRM) systematically developed a competency model that defines the competencies required for success in the HR profession across a range of different types of HR jobs.[3]

Case Discussion Questions

1. Suppose you are working in the HR department of a small city. If you were asked to do a job analysis for firefighter, what are some ways you would use to learn about the job?

2. Describe three ways that a city might use this job analysis information about the firefighter job.

3. Why do you think that job analyses are done for specific professions? How could this information then be used by employers and by the workers themselves?

To develop effective HR systems, organizations conduct a **job analysis**, which is *the analysis of work and the employee characteristics needed to perform the work successfully.* Organizations must understand how individual jobs help achieve organizational goals and how the design of jobs can help employees do their jobs well. In this chapter, we describe the science and best practices regarding how to analyze jobs and work processes. We also discuss how the job is experienced from the employees' standpoint and why this is important.

The Analysis of Work and Its Critical Role in HR Practice

LO 5.1 Define job analysis and competency models and describe their purposes in organizations.

Successful organizations must consider what work they do at the organizational level and which employee responsibilities and job requirements are needed to carry this work out. Organizations must understand their broader goals. This is so they can know what workers in different roles actually do and what skills and abilities workers need to perform successfully.

This analysis of work and the employee characteristics needed to perform the work successfully is called *job analysis*. Job analysis is an essential HR function that forms the basis for all other HR functions, including recruitment, selection, promotion and succession planning, performance management, training and development, and pay and rewards.[4] For example, consider the job of firefighter. When developing legally acceptable procedures to recruit and hire people who fit this job, an understanding of the job is needed: What tasks do firefighters perform, and what skills and abilities do they need to perform them? In fact, city governments frequently conduct job analyses for their public safety jobs, such as firefighters and police officers, to develop hiring criteria and selection procedures. As noted

Job analysis The analysis of work and the employee characteristics needed to perform the work successfully

in the opening case, the U.S. Office of Personnel Management has guidelines about how to conduct job analyses.[5] In the private sector, many organizations either conduct detailed job analyses or use the related process of competency modeling to better understand the different jobs in their companies and how they fit together to achieve organizational goals.[6] In short, employers that do job analyses have an advantage in terms of managing their human capital. Although you may or may not ever actually conduct a job analysis yourself, you have probably benefited from a job analysis. This is because job analysis helps determine selection procedures, pay, and promotion considerations.

©iStock.com/rocketegg

It is commonplace for governments to maintain job analyses of their public safety jobs such as firefighter, a job that requires a number of specialized technical skills that are not familiar to members of the general public.

Technical Terms Used in Job Analysis and Competency Modeling

In this section, we define some terms used in job analysis and competency modeling. First, **tasks** are the elements of a job analysis that are typically used to describe the job itself. They usually contain an action verb followed by an object and then clarify how the work is performed (e.g., under what conditions, using what equipment, and for what purpose). In the case of a barista's job, a task might be "Makes (action verb) espresso drinks (object) using espresso maker and other coffee equipment to serve customer needs (clarification of conditions, equipment, and purpose)."

Second, knowledge, skills, abilities, and other characteristics (**KSAOs**) are used to describe the characteristics workers need to carry out their work effectively.

- *Knowledge* is generally something a person could learn from a book (e.g., knowledge of laws pertinent to the HR profession).

- A *skill* is something an employee can learn how to do (e.g., skill in the use of fire equipment).

- An *ability* is a relatively innate talent or aptitude (e.g., spatial relationships ability).

- *Other characteristics* refers to personality traits such as extraversion or integrity.

Third, the people who provide information about the job are called **subject matter experts (SMEs)**. Usually, an SME is an employee who performs the job or a supervisor. Both employees and supervisors each give unique information about what the job involves.[7]

Over the past few decades, organizations have increasingly begun to use the related processes of competency modeling in addition to job analysis. The goals of **competency modeling** are to understand what types of employee characteristics and behaviors are required for a group of jobs, perhaps over an entire organization. (We will discuss competency modeling in greater detail later in the chapter.) The primary pieces of a competency model are the employee competencies that are needed to perform the job, such as "competency in working with team members." For simplicity's sake, in this chapter, the term *job analysis* refers to either job analysis or competency modeling.

Tasks The elements of a job analysis that are typically used to describe the job itself

KSAOs Knowledge, skills, abilities, and other characteristics employees need to have to do their work most effectively

Subject matter experts (SMEs) People (e.g., employees, supervisors) who provide information about the job

Competency modeling A type of job analysis with the goal of understanding what types of attributes and behaviors are required for a group of jobs, perhaps over an entire organization

Job (job classification) A group of related duties within an organization

Position Duties that can be carried out by one person

Job descriptions Job descriptions provide the title and purpose of the job, as well as a general overview of the essential tasks, duties, and responsibilities (i.e., observable actions) associated with the job

Job specifications Job specifications focus on the characteristics of an employee who does the job

In addition, it is important to distinguish between the concept of a **job** (or **job classification**) in an organization versus a **position**. A job classification is a group of related duties within an organization, whereas a position is the duties that can be carried out by one person. For example, a city government may have the job classification of "police officer," but there might be hundreds of individual police officers (positions) in that job classification.

It is also useful to distinguish between job analysis and the terms **job descriptions** and **job specifications**. A job analysis results in a very detailed document that allows a person who is unfamiliar with the job to get a good idea of what the job involves. In fact, a detailed job analysis might list hundreds of tasks and dozens of KSAOs. In contrast, both job descriptions and job specifications are usually shorter documents, maybe only one page long. It can be useful to have a relatively short document like this to show job applicants and current employees what their job involves. Table 5.1 is a brief example of a job description and a job specification for a hypothetical administrative assistant position.

Job descriptions provide the title and purpose of the job, as well as a general overview of the essential tasks, duties, and responsibilities (i.e., observable actions) associated with the job. The material in job descriptions can be used in recruitment materials for attracting new employees, for job ads, and for postings so that applicants know what the job involves and given to employees so that they understand their job. In contrast, job specifications focus on the characteristics of an employee who does the job, such as the KSAOs and any physical or emotional requirements. Job specifications are essential to consider when recruiting and hiring. Maintaining and documenting job descriptions and job specifications are a key role of HR departments.[8]

TABLE 5.1   Sample Brief Job Description and Job Specifications for an Administrative Assistant

Administrative Assistant Job Description

Overview and Purpose

The purpose of the administrative assistant position is to provide support to other workers (e.g., managers) in carrying out their job tasks.

Duties

The administrative assistant carries out a range of duties in support of organizational functions, including scheduling meetings and appointments and answering phone calls. Includes providing assistance in preparing reports and developing and implementing filing systems. May also include taking notes and minutes.

Major Tasks and Responsibilities

- Plan and organize meetings, including developing a meeting agenda and taking notes and minutes as needed.
- Coordinate with others within and outside of the organization, including other administrative assistants, as needed.

- Make appointments for other staff within the business unit.
- Answer phone calls in support of the work unit.
- Develop filing systems for work unit and implement.
- Order supplies as needed.
- Plan meetings and trips of office visitors, providing needed support.
- Develop office policies and procedures.
- Support simple bookkeeping functions within the unit such as reimbursements and paying of vendors.

Administrative Assistant Job Specifications

Job Requirements

- Organizational skills
- Interpersonal skills necessary for working with coworkers and outside clients
- Ability to prioritize work
- Knowledge of basic office practices and procedures
- Basic knowledge of office equipment, including simple troubleshooting
- Oral and written communication skills
- Good attention to detail

Minimum Qualifications

- High school diploma (required); some college or college degree (desirable)
- Office experience, including at least 6 months working as an administrative assistant
- Demonstrated proficiency with typical office software

Manager's Toolbox
SOME BASICS OF JOB DESCRIPTIONS

Writing and updating job descriptions are some of the most basic functions of an HR department, because these descriptions are useful for many HR activities. For example, job descriptions are

- used to develop recruitment materials to attract job applicants and give them an idea about what the job involves,

- shared with job applicants during the selection process to provide a realistic preview of what the job is, and

- given to new and existing employees so that they know what is expected of them.

One of the challenges in organizations is keeping job descriptions up to date, and this is especially true in situations where jobs change quickly. There are some ways that HR practitioners can keep an eye on this issue:

- One practice is to update job descriptions every year. This is especially true in quickly changing industries and organizations.

- Reviewing an employee's job description can happen during performance appraisal meetings between supervisors and employees. Employees can tell their supervisor if the job has changed.

■ **FIGURE 5.1**   Summary of the Relationship Between Job Analysis and Other HR Functions

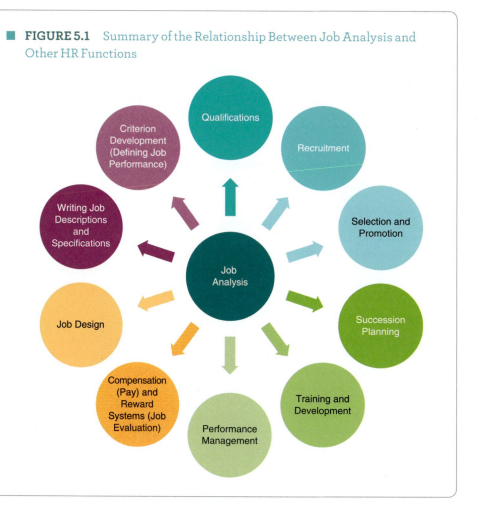

Why Do a Job Analysis?

Job analysis is often considered the cornerstone of other HR functions, and good HR practice is based on a robust job analysis. Figure 5.1 shows the many HR functions that are dependent on a job analysis.

A job analysis is important for deciding the minimum qualifications for a job, including education and experience. It is also used for recruitment to develop recruitment strategies and materials. For example, in hiring a software engineer, it is essential to understand the minimum qualifications of the job, such as the KSAOs and the amount of education and work experience needed. Job analysis is necessary for developing selection procedures. This includes the basic requirements of the job (e.g., experience) and types of tests and assessments that should be used to decide a job applicant's fit with the job, including the KSAOs they should measure. U.S. employment law requires that selection procedures be based on a job analysis.

Spotlight on Legal Issues
JOB ANALYSIS AND LEGAL DEFENSIBILITY OF HR SYSTEMS

Job analysis is critical to other HR functions because it is key to their legal defensibility. This is perhaps best illustrated in the area of hiring.

For example, the U.S. federal government's *Uniform Guidelines on Employee Selection Procedures* (1978) state that with few exceptions, a job analysis is required to demonstrate the validity of selection procedures (i.e., that they predict future job performance).[9] The validity of selection procedures is core to their legal defensibility.

In addition, job analysis plays a critical role in implementation of the Americans with Disabilities Act (ADA, 1990). That is because a key aspect of complying with ADA is that employers identify essential functions of the job and document them in their job descriptions. An employer who makes a hiring decision based on requiring a nonessential function of the job or a marginal function that could be assigned to other workers could face legal challenges.[10]

An analysis of jobs and how they relate to each other is necessary for good succession planning. Succession planning (or succession management) involves taking stock of which employees are qualified to fill positions that are likely to be vacated soon. For example, a manufacturing company may realize that its plant manager will be retiring in 2 years. A job analysis would identify which KSAOs are required for the plant manager's job so that other employees can be identified to take on the plant manager's job.

Job analysis is also necessary for developing the most effective training and development programs as well as performance standards to be used in performance management systems to assess employees' current skill and performance levels.

Job analysis is needed to set pay scales that are both fair to employees and competitive with the current employment market. This type of job analysis, used to set pay in organizations, is called job evaluation. Further, job analysis is important for designing jobs that will motivate employees in their work (discussed later in this chapter). Job analyses are used for writing job descriptions and job specifications. Finally, job analyses are used in developing criterion measures—that is, the specific measures organizations use to evaluate the effectiveness of HR systems, such as whether they are successfully hiring the best people and training them correctly.[11] In short, a well-produced job analysis can provide a strong basis for the success of an HR system, while a poor (or nonexistent) job analysis can decrease the effectiveness of an HR system.

Seeing the Big Picture: Workflow Analysis

Most of this chapter is focused on the analysis of jobs and individual positions. However, before moving into a discussion of how to analyze individual jobs, it is important to step back and consider how work is accomplished at the organizational level. This broad, organization-level focus on work within the organization and within organizational units is known as **workflow analysis**. It is often useful to think of this process in reverse order: Begin with the desired final output, then define the tasks necessary to create this output, and go on to identify the organizational resources, equipment, and human capital necessary to carry out these tasks. This helps managers think critically about organizational processes and how they might be carried out more efficiently. This might also allow organizations to adjust to changes in the economic or technological environments. For example, online retailers such as Amazon and Walmart are constantly examining their workflow for ways to optimize it, as they must frequently adapt to changing conditions, including supply, inventory, and delivery of goods.[12]

As an example, a restaurant's managers might decide to analyze their operations.

- The restaurant's output is the production of food and drinks. They need to determine how they would measure this output, including measures of both the quantity and the quality of the food and drinks.

Workflow analysis A broad, organization-level focus on work within the organization and within organizational units and the input needed

- From there they could decide what tasks need to be performed to produce this output, including tasks performed by the chef (e.g., preparing menus, cooking food) and those performed by others in the shop, such as the people operating the cash register (e.g., interacting effectively with customers, making change).

- Then they could determine the resources (e.g., chicken, lettuce, milk), equipment (e.g., oven, mixer, grill), and KSAOs (e.g., knowledge of recipes, skill at using equipment) that are needed to create the output.

Spotlight on Data and Analytics

ANALYZING AND ADVANCING THE DATA SCIENCE PROFESSION

©iStock.com/Rawpixel

It is harder to develop a job analysis or competency model when the job or profession is new or changing. The job of data scientist within the field of data analytics and big data is an example. The EDISON Project (http://edison-project.eu/), funded by the European Commission's Horizon 2020 research and innovation program, is an initiative that undertakes this challenge with the specific goal of supporting the development of the data science profession. The EDISON Data Science Framework (EDSF) includes a number of freely available documents that define the data science profession in terms of the skills and competencies that make up the profession. These documents were developed to assist not only educators but also data scientists themselves and the organizations that employee them. They also help define the education needed for data scientists.[13]

Collecting Job Analysis Data

LO 5.2   Demonstrate the use of different ways of collecting job analysis information.

There are many ways to collect job analysis data.

- First, *interviewing* SMEs is the most common method. The job analyst (typically an HR staff member) might discuss with SMEs (employees and supervisors) the job tasks they perform, the KSAOs needed to do the job, and critical job situations they might face.

- For more technical jobs, it may be necessary to *observe* people doing the work. For example, to understand the highly specialized equipment used by firefighters, it would be good to see how they use that equipment in their work.

- When there are large numbers of job incumbents and supervisors, it is common to conduct *surveys* of SMEs instead of interviews. Note that software is available from a number of vendors to help with collecting and processing of job analysis data.

Often it is not necessary to carry out a job analysis from scratch. Existing job analysis materials may be available from professional organizations (e.g., a job analysis for engineers from an engineering professional association). In addition, a source of some basic information about jobs is the O*NET, published by the U.S. Department of Labor. The O*NET is discussed later in this chapter.[14]

Specific Job Analysis Methods and Approaches

LO 5.3   Differentiate between job analysis and competency modeling and evaluate the advantages of each approach.

There are a number of different approaches for collecting job analysis data. Each produces a slightly different job analysis product and is best for purposes. In this section, we provide some common examples.[15]

Task–KSAO Analysis

Task–KSAO analysis is a job analysis method that carefully defines the tasks that make up the job, as well as the KSAOs needed to do those tasks (see Figure 5.2). First, the job analyst determines an initial list of tasks that make up the job as well as the KSAOs that are needed to complete them. A task includes an action verb, object, and purpose and equipment used. For example, Figure 5.3 shows that one task for the job of administrative assistant might be *contacts* (action verb) *client* (object) *to coordinate meetings using e-mail or telephone* (purpose and equipment). Second, the job analyst documents that these tasks and KSAOs are critical to performing the job. Noncritical tasks and KSAOs are eliminated. Third, the final list of KSAOs is reviewed by the SMEs to be sure that the

KSAOs on the list really are needed to do the critical job tasks. Note that task–KSAO analysis provides great detail about one or relatively few jobs. Frequently, this results in a list of dozens or even hundreds of tasks. This detail involved in task–KSAO analysis means that it is a more difficult method to use to analyze many jobs at one time. This can be a problem if the goal is to compare several jobs. However, task–KSAO analysis is a good method when trying to understand job details, such as when developing job-specific technical training. We also refer the reader to other sources that provide more information about how to carry out a task–KSAO analysis.[16]

Critical Incidents Technique

Critical incidents technique
A technique that involves asking SMEs to describe critical job situations that they frequently encounter on the job

The **critical incidents technique** involves asking SMEs to describe critical situations that they frequently encounter on the job. SMEs are then asked to generate examples of good and poor employee responses to these critical incidents. This might include responses that they have seen other employees give or ways that they themselves responded to a critical job situation very well or very poorly.[17] As an example, a customer service representative could report that a common critical incident they must face is an angry customer. A positive response might be to figure out what the customer is angry about and come up with solutions that work well both for the customer and the organization. A negative response might be to become angry with the customer, which would only make matters worse. In Figure 5.4, we show some examples of

■ **FIGURE 5.2**   The Steps in a Task–KSAO Analysis

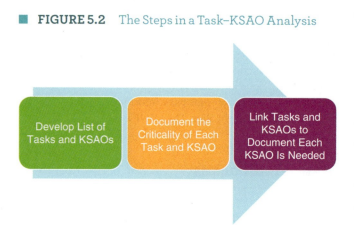

Develop List of Tasks and KSAOs

Document the Criticality of Each Task and KSAO

Link Tasks and KSAOs to Document Each KSAO Is Needed

■ **FIGURE 5.3**   Example of a Task Statement for Administrative Assistant

Contacts (action verb)

client (object)

to coordinate meetings using e-mail or telephone (purpose and equipment)

©iStock.com/BrianAJackson; ©iStock.com/vgajic; ©iStock.com/Szepy

■ **FIGURE 5.4**   Critical Incidents for the Job of Barista

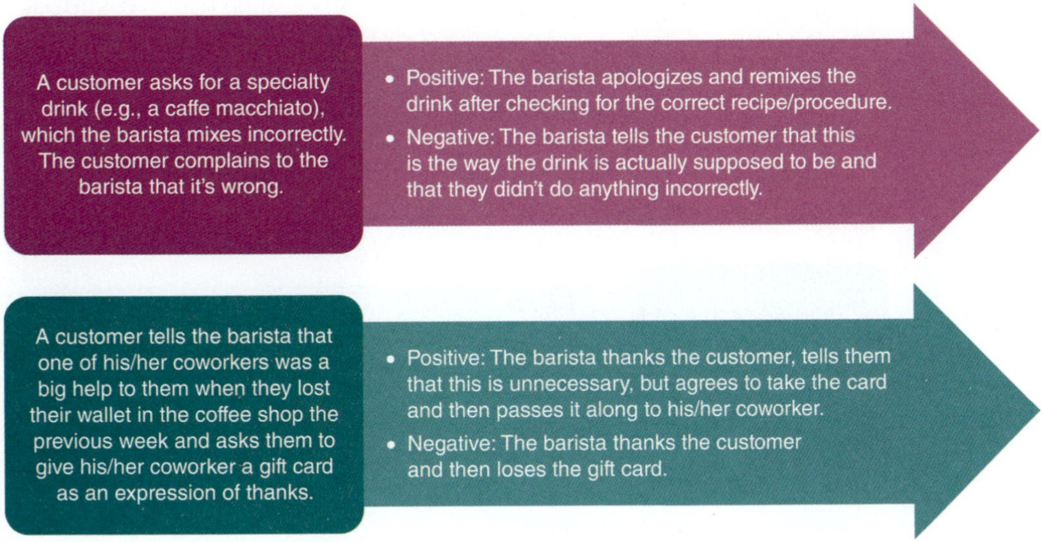

A customer asks for a specialty drink (e.g., a caffe macchiato), which the barista mixes incorrectly. The customer complains to the barista that it's wrong.

- Positive: The barista apologizes and remixes the drink after checking for the correct recipe/procedure.
- Negative: The barista tells the customer that this is the way the drink is actually supposed to be and that they didn't do anything incorrectly.

A customer tells the barista that one of his/her coworkers was a big help to them when they lost their wallet in the coffee shop the previous week and asks them to give his/her coworker a gift card as an expression of thanks.

- Positive: The barista thanks the customer, tells them that this is unnecessary, but agrees to take the card and then passes it along to his/her coworker.
- Negative: The barista thanks the customer and then loses the gift card.

critical incidents for the job of barista. The critical incidents technique gives valuable information for developing job-related interview questions for hiring employees, developing training content, and developing performance management systems.

Position Analysis Questionnaire

The Position Analysis Questionnaire (PAQ) is an "off-the-shelf" job analysis survey that is purchased from its publisher. The PAQ consists of 195 generic statements describing what characteristics a worker needs to possess.[18] For instance, a job analyst might interview SMEs about their job, complete the PAQ survey based on the interviews, and then have the PAQ data scored online. The resulting report from PAQ can give recommendations for what types of selection procedures might be used for a job with this profile or what the pay should be relative to other jobs. The advantages of the PAQ are that it requires less work by the job analyst and is less expensive than the task–KSAO analysis. Also, its generic items and rich database of jobs allow for comparisons with other jobs. On the other hand, it does not provide as rich detail as other job analysis methods, and it must be completed by a job analyst who has been trained in its use.[19]

Occupational Information Network (O*NET)

The Occupational Information Network, or O*NET, published by the U.S. Department of Labor, is a handy source of job analysis data about a range of occupations, and it can provide a useful start to the job analysis process. Figure 5.5 provides a summary of the

■ **FIGURE 5.5**   The O*NET Job Analysis Framework

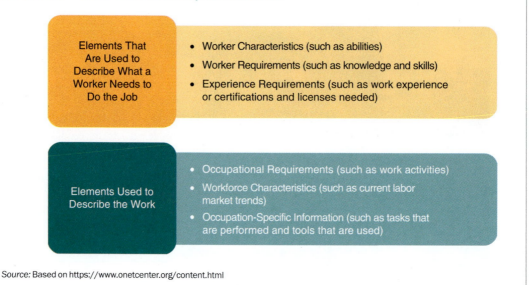

Elements That Are Used to Describe What a Worker Needs to Do the Job
- Worker Characteristics (such as abilities)
- Worker Requirements (such as knowledge and skills)
- Experience Requirements (such as work experience or certifications and licenses needed)

Elements Used to Describe the Work
- Occupational Requirements (such as work activities)
- Workforce Characteristics (such as current labor market trends)
- Occupation-Specific Information (such as tasks that are performed and tools that are used)

Source: Based on https://www.onetcenter.org/content.html

O*NET framework, which includes elements used to describe what a worker needs to do a particular job (such as abilities, knowledge, skills, and work experience), as well as a job itself (such as tasks, general work activities, and labor market trends). An exercise at the end of this chapter gives some information about using O*NET. Additional detail and documentation about O*NET can be found at the O*NET website (https://www.onetonline .org/). If you check out the O*NET website and enter a job title, you will see the significant amount of data provided by the website. For instance, just type in *data scientist*—or any job title that may be of interest to you—to get an idea of the typical tasks and KSAOs that are part of the job.[20]

Competency Modeling

Competency modeling began to emerge in the 1990s as an approach to analyzing jobs, and its use has increased steadily since then. The focus of competency modeling is similar to that of other job analysis methods. It involves understanding what KSAOs are needed for doing a job and how these KSAOs—or competencies—are manifested on the job in terms of behaviors. However, competency modeling differs from traditional job analysis in several ways, and this is why competency models have grown in popularity.

Perhaps the biggest difference between competency modeling and most job analysis methods is the comprehensive nature of competency models. Competency models are usually broad enough that they can describe a range of jobs within an organization and do so across multiple levels in the organization. For this reason, competency modeling is beneficial to organizations wanting to understand similarities and differences across jobs. It is also why SHRM chose to use a competency modeling approach to capture a range of HR job types. Similarly, IBM developed a competency model to understand the wide range of training needs of different jobs across a very large, global organization. Other large organizations such as Boeing and Microsoft have also taken a competency modeling approach.[21]

In addition, competency models typically allow organizations to communicate their goals and values. For example, an organization that wanted to include a "Value for Diversity" across all of their jobs—and make sure that all employees realize the importance of this value for success in the organization—might include a "Value for Diversity" competency. SHRM's competency model explicitly included the value of "Integrity" because of its desire to articulate the importance of integrity in HR work.[22]

Courtesy of Alexander Alonso

Designing Jobs to Enhance Motivation, Attitudes, Well-Being, and Performance

LO 5.4   Explain how job design can be used to increase employee motivation, job attitudes, and performance.

Alexander Alonso, PhD, SHRM-SCP, is the Society for Human Resource Management's (SHRM's) chief knowledge officer leading operations for SHRM's Certified Professional and Senior Certified Professional certifications, research functions, and the SHRM Knowledge Advisor service. He is responsible for all research activities, including the development of the SHRM Competency Model and SHRM credentials.

So far, our focus has been on how to analyze jobs to understand what a worker does on the job and the worker characteristics needed to do the job. This is to have a deep understanding of what the job involves, which helps to develop HR functions such as selection, pay, or training, among others. However, employers need to consider **job design** in terms of how jobs are *experienced* by workers. Designing or redesigning jobs based on how workers experience their work (e.g., stressful, boring, meaningful) is important because it can affect worker motivation, job attitudes, well-being, and job performance. In this section, we examine some of the approaches that have been taken to design jobs for workers and the job characteristics that have been shown to be important in redesigning jobs. Later in this book, we will discuss how designing the physical aspects of jobs, such as from an ergonomic perspective, can help improve worker safety and health.

Some concepts are important in discussing job design.[23]

- First, **job enlargement** involves the addition of more responsibilities to a job to make it less boring and more motivating for workers. This might include adding some challenges that can make the job more interesting or allow workers to gain more skills. For example, having a worker take on a new project that is different from the ones she has taken on before could be a form of job enlargement.

- Second, **job enrichment** involves allowing workers to have greater decision-making power. For example, a team of workers in a high-tech manufacturing firm might be allowed to manage themselves rather than only being managed by the

Job design
The process of identifying how a job's characteristics are experienced from the employee's perspective to enhance well-being and performance

Job enlargement
The addition of more responsibilities to a job so that it is less boring and more motivating for workers

Job enrichment
Allowing workers to have greater decision-making power

supervisor or team leader. Although job enlargement and job enrichment are both considered important for reducing boredom and improving employee motivation and performance, it is important to keep in mind that not all employees will do well with enriched or enlarged jobs: Some employees may prefer not to take on additional responsibilities, while others may not perform well with such responsibilities.

- Finally, **job rotation** includes rotating employees from one job to another, not only making their work less boring but also allowing them to learn new skills.

Job Design Considerations

Job rotation Rotating employees from one job to another, allowing them to learn new skills

Job Characteristics Model (JCM) The first complete model of job design, explaining which job characteristics are the most important to increasing worker motivation and productivity

In the early 20th century, the Scientific Management approach advocated for the simplification of jobs, so jobs were often designed in ways that ignored worker boredom and social needs. But later, the Tavistock Mining Institute Studies, conducted in England in the mid-20th century, showed the importance of designing jobs with people in mind—people who can become bored and need social interaction. These studies found that a highly "logical" redesign of coal mining jobs during World War II—with, for example, a decreased emphasis on the intact teams that had previously functioned to make this uncomfortable and dangerous work less stressful—had resulted in serious decreases in productivity. Many consider this to be the beginning of job design.[24]

Hackman and Oldham's **Job Characteristics Model (JCM)**, developed in the 1960s, was the first complete model of job design, explaining which characteristics are the most important to increasing worker motivation and productivity. Most of the subsequent job design models are largely based on it. Figure 5.6 shows the basics of the JCM and the process by which job characteristics are said to affect worker outcomes. The model proposes that enhancing the characteristics of the job leads to improved psychological states, which leads

■ **FIGURE 5.6**   Hackman and Oldham's Job Characteristics Model

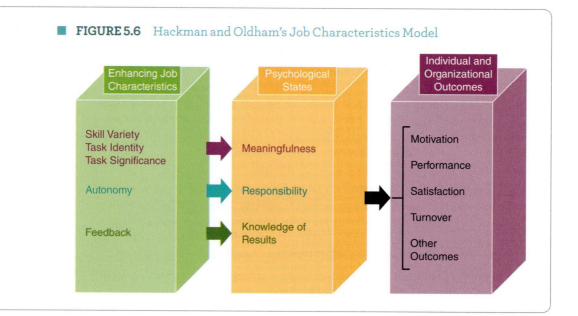

to improved individual and organizational outcomes. Specifically, the characteristics of skill variety (applying a range of skills on the job), task identity (completing a complete piece of work on the jobs), and task significance (doing work that is important, for example, affects others) lead to experienced meaningfulness of work; autonomy (freedom in how the work gets done) leads to experienced responsibility; and feedback (the degree to which the job gives you feedback about performance) leads to knowledge of results. These three psychological states—meaningfulness, responsibility, and knowledge of results—all in turn lead to improved outcomes such as motivation and performance.[25]

Later models of job design take a slightly different approach from the JCM, with a focus on understanding how workers' experiences might affect outcomes such as stress. For example, the **Job Demands-Resources Model (JDR**; see Figure 5.7) emphasizes that job demands, such as workload and time pressure, can be counteracted by characteristics such as job control, participation, and supervisor support.[26] In fact, research suggests that providing factors like supervisor support can improve employee motivation and even health.

In the early 21st century, Morgeson and Humphrey developed a more comprehensive model of job design, which takes into account the dimensions from these previous job design models (see Figure 5.8). The model includes 18 types of job characteristics falling into four broad categories: task characteristics, knowledge characteristics, social characteristics, and the work context (which includes more physical aspects of the job). In other words, according

Job Demands-Resources Model (JDR) This model emphasizes that job demands, such as workload and time pressure, can be counteracted by characteristics such as job control, participation, and supervisor support

■ **FIGURE 5.7**   The Job Demands-Resources Model (JDR)

Job Demands Examples:
• Physical Workload
• Time Pressure
• Physical Environment
• Shift Work

Job Resources Examples:
• Feedback
• Rewards
• Job Control
• Participation
• Job Security
• Supervisor Support

■ **FIGURE 5.8**   Morgeson and Humphrey's Comprehensive Job Design Model

Task Characteristics
• Autonomy
• Task Variety
• Task Significance
• Task Identity
• Feedback From the Job

Knowledge Characteristics
• Job Complexity
• Information Processing
• Problem Solving
• Skill Variety
• Specialization

Social Characteristics
• Social Support
• Interdependence
• Interaction Outside the Organization
• Feedback From Others

Work Context
• Ergonomics
• Physical Demands
• Work Conditions
• Equipment Use

Source: Adapted from Morgeson, F. P., & Humphrey, S. E. (2006). The Work Design Questionnaire (WDQ): Developing and validating a comprehensive measure for assessing job design and the nature of work. *Journal of Applied Psychology, 91,* 1321–1399.

to this model, many job characteristics can enhance workers' jobs to increase motivation, satisfaction, and performance.[27]

How Effective Are Job Design Considerations for Predicting Employee Outcomes?

Does improving the psychological characteristics of work actually pay off for organizations? A large meta-analysis of 259 studies and more than 200,000 workers suggests that it does. For example, autonomy, task variety, and task significance among workers were positively related to increased job performance. Greater autonomy and task significance were negatively related to employee burnout. Increased support from coworkers was negatively related to intention to quit the job. And higher levels of most of the job characteristics were positively associated with greater job satisfaction.[28]

It is important to know that some employees will value enriched jobs more than others. As one example, researchers have recently argued that the age of the employee may determine which job characteristics employees want and need in their work.[29] For instance, younger employees may especially need job characteristics like task variety that allow them to gain the experience they need to advance in their careers, whereas older employees may benefit from being allowed to apply the wide range of skills that they have already acquired throughout their careers. The empirical research does in fact suggest that older and younger workers may benefit from different job characteristics.[30] For example, one recent study showed that increasing autonomy led to increased job satisfaction and mental health of older construction workers compared to their younger counterparts.[31] However, many other factors, such as the particular type of job and industry, likely play a role as well.[32]

Job Crafting

It has also been recognized that workers may be capable of **job crafting**—redesigning their own jobs to fit their needs and personalities—provided they stay within the guidelines of the organization. Job crafting can lead to significant improvements in worker morale and performance.[33] For example, an employee may decide to take on additional challenges that could be helpful in gaining the work experiences that they need to advance in their career. You may have done some job crafting in your own work. Other employees may decide to craft their job as they gain expertise, or late-career employees may adapt their jobs to fit their changing needs.

In one early study of job crafting, researchers examined how cleaning crew workers in a hospital, a fairly low-skills job, experienced their work. In conducting interviews with these workers, the researchers found that some workers experienced their jobs as rather boring and repetitive and without much meaning—just as you might expect. In contrast, other workers found their jobs to be quite meaningful. The difference was that these latter workers often performed tasks that were not in their original job descriptions, such as talking to patients. While the first group simply did their jobs as described, the latter group molded their jobs in ways that made their jobs more meaningful to them.[34]

Job crafting
Redesigning one's own job to fit one's needs (e.g., abilities, interests, personality)

Not surprisingly, the willingness and ability of workers to craft their jobs have often been associated with the personality characteristic of proactivity, as crafting requires an active role on the part of workers.[35] A recent meta-analysis of more than 120 studies and 35,000 workers confirmed this: Job crafting behaviors were related to proactive personality and employee engagement, meaning that more proactive and engaged employees reported they did more job crafting. Job crafting seems to benefit the organization as well.[36] And research also suggests that job crafting can also be taught to employees.[37] In any case, for job crafting to be successful, organizations need to give employees sufficient freedom to craft their jobs.

Flexible Work Arrangements

LO 5.5   Describe how flexible work environments affect employee well-being.

Organizations can design work in other ways to support employees. Many organizations offer flexible work arrangements to workers to help them balance work and life needs. One type of work arrangement is **flextime**, in which workers can choose from a number of work schedules. For example, some workers in an organization may choose to work from 7:00 a.m. to 3:00 p.m., while others may choose to work from 9:00 a.m. to 5:00 p.m. Other examples include the possibility of working four 10-hour days each week. Some organizations allow workers to change their work schedules from day to day, while others require that workers choose a set time that they are at work. Of course, many of these flexible work schedules are not suitable for all kinds of work. For example, medical personnel would need to ensure that hospitals are always sufficiently staffed.

Many organizations have now taken this idea of flexible work schedules a step further, implementing flexible times and telecommuting. **Telecommuting**, or remote work, is when an employee is not physically at an office or other location but instead works much of the time away from the office. For example, an employee might choose to work from home and only come in to work 2 days per week or even 2 days per month. Such flexibility can allow workers to better manage their nonwork lives and save commuting time. In fact, many organizations such as Dell, Xerox, and Aetna have adopted telecommuting with the goal of reducing energy consumption.[38]

But what does the research indicate about whether telecommuting actually benefits organizations and employees? The answer is generally favorable, but with some exceptions. A meta-analysis of 46 employee samples comprising more than 12,000 employees showed that telecommuting was negatively related to work–family conflict, turnover intentions, and role stress for employees and also was positively associated with better job satisfaction and performance. However, heavy telecommuting (more than 2.5 days per week) led to more negative relationships with coworkers. Another concern with telecommuting is that it can be hard to manage relationships at work. There is also value in working face to face with coworkers. For these reasons, some companies like IBM, HP, and Bank of America decided in the early 2000s to pull the plug on telecommuting.[39] In summary, although telecommuting has many advantages, it is not universally beneficial for all types of work.

Contingent Employees

Contingent employees are those who are hired for a limited, fixed amount of time such as a short-term contract or a project consulting contract. The use of contingent employees has been expanded, with some sources citing that 40% of U.S. workers hold contingent types of

Flextime A work arrangement in which workers can choose from a number of work schedules

Telecommuting A work arrangement in which an employee is not physically at an office or other location but instead works a substantial amount of time away from the office

Contingent employees Individuals who are hired for a limited, fixed term such as a short-term contract or a project consulting contract jobs.[40] The idea is that employers would only hire workers when they are needed. Using contingent workers also allows employers to "try out" employees before making the commitment of hiring them permanently (temp-to-permanent). The *gig economy* is a type of contingent work in which highly skilled workers to link up with organizations using a digital platform.

Although there has been significant growth in contingent jobs, these work arrangements are not without their downsides to employees and to organizations. For example, gig economy jobs have been criticized because they leave workers vulnerable to job insecurity and wage theft. Contingent workers are also more likely than permanent workers to have lower pay, higher poverty rates, and decreased access to health insurance. And some argue that hiring contingent workers does not necessarily lead to cost savings. In summary, it is important for organizations not to simply assume that the use of contingent workers is always cost-effective. For that reason, organizations should carefully consider the advantages and disadvantages of using contingent workers, both for the workers themselves and for the organization.[41]

CHAPTER SUMMARY

Job analysis is the basis for most HR functions, including recruitment, selection, training, performance management, and pay. It is also used to develop job descriptions and job specifications. Methods used to collect job analysis data include interviews, observations, surveys, and government data (the O*NET). Different job analysis approaches—such as task analysis, the critical incidents technique, and competency modeling—each have their own advantages and disadvantages. Understanding how work is experienced from the employee's perspective is also important because it can be used to increase worker engagement, satisfaction, well-being, and performance. Flexible work arrangements such as flextime, telecommuting, and contingent work are increasingly common, although organizational decision makers should consider them carefully in terms of their advantages and disadvantages.

KEY TERMS

job analysis   100
tasks   101
KSAOs   101
subject matter
    experts (SMEs)   101
competency modeling   101
job (job classification)   102
position   102
job descriptions   102

job specifications   102
workflow analysis   106
critical incidents
    technique   108
job design   111
job enlargement   111
job enrichment   111
job rotation   112

Job Characteristics
    Model (JCM)   112
Job Demands-Resources
    Model (JDR)   113
job crafting   114
flextime   115
telecommuting   115
contingent employees   115

$SAGE edge™

Get the tools you need to sharpen your study skills. SAGE edge offers a robust online environment featuring an impressive array of free tools and resources.

Access practice quizzes, eFlashcards, video, and multimedia at **edge.sagepub.com/bauerbrief**

HR REASONING AND DECISION-MAKING EXERCISES

EXERCISE 5.1: JOB ANALYSIS AND KSAO RATINGS

The city of Jasper has conducted a job analysis of its firefighters. The job being analyzed is a fire apparatus operator/driver (FAOD). In addition to conducting regular firefighting activities, FAODs also drive the fire equipment and apparatus to the fire incident. They also have a deep knowledge about operating the equipment.

Jasper has collected data from 35 FAODs and 10 of their supervisors, all of whom served as subject matter experts (SMEs). These 45 SMEs then completed a survey where they rated how critical (important) each KSAO is for the job on a scale of 1 to 5. The following table lists the means and standard deviations of the KSAO criticality ratings in terms of importance. The goal is to identify the KSAOs that are (1) critical (important) and that (2) most SMEs agree are critical, that is, those KSAOs that have a high mean and low standard deviation.

MEANS AND STANDARD DEVIATIONS FOR THE CRITICALITY (IMPORTANCE) RATINGS OF EACH KSAO		
FIRE APPARATUS OPERATOR/DRIVER (FAOD) KSAOS	**MEAN (1–5 SCALE)**	**STANDARD DEVIATION**
A. Ability to work within a team	4.9	0.2
B. Mechanical ability	4.8	0.3
C. Upper body strength	4.5	0.3
D. Ability to read maps (both paper and online) and to memorize all city streets	3.1	1.7
E. Knowledge of fire equipment functions and capacity	4.8	0.1
F. Ability to supervise crew	3.2	1.6
G. Knowledge of fire suppression principles related to residential buildings	3.6	1.5
H. Knowledge of fire suppression principles related to commercial/high-rise buildings	4.8	.3
I. Critical thinking/decision making	4.7	.2

Questions

1. Based on your review of the mean criticality (importance) ratings for each KSAO, which KSAOs would you consider dropping from the job analysis? Explain why.

2. You know that a key role of this job is driving fire equipment (e.g., fire trucks) to the fire scene. But KSAO D has a fairly low mean and a high standard deviation. Why might this be? Rather than tossing out this KSAO, do you see any problem with the way that the KSAO is currently written and how it might be rewritten?

3. You learn that the city of Jasper collected most of the data for this job analysis from SMEs who are located in urban areas of the city rather than in the more suburban areas. Knowing this, would it affect any of your decisions about which KSAOs to remove from the job analysis? How might the city approach future data collections like this differently?

EXERCISE 5.2: USING O*NET

As discussed earlier in the chapter, O*NET was developed by the U.S. government to provide a general job analysis system to help employers conduct their job and work analyses. Please go to the O*NET website at https://www .onetonline.org/ to answer the following.

Questions

1. Search for a job with which you are familiar. Were you able to find the job quickly, with the same job title you were using, or did O*NET use a slightly different job title? Or did it suggest multiple possible job titles? If so, why do you think this is?

2. Now look at the tasks, knowledge, skills, and abilities that O*NET notes as associated with that job. Do these match your impression of the job? Why might there be some differences between the job title you used and the job title in the O*NET database?

3. Sometimes no single O*NET job title captures the job for which you are searching. In your case, did it require piecing together the information from two or more jobs listed in the O*NET database to adequately describe the job you're looking for? If so, can you explain why this may have happened?

4. For most jobs you will search for, the O*NET job titles will not be a perfect fit for a particular job in a particular organization. More important, the content listed in the O*NET may not be a perfect match, either. Given these challenges, what do you see as the value to HR professionals using the O*NET when conducting job analyses?

ETHICAL MATTERS EXERCISE: DESIGNING ETHICS AND INTEGRITY INTO WORK

Throughout this book, we show the importance of ethics and integrity to the practice of HR. A key factor is to make ethical behavior an explicit part of the job analysis, competency model, and job description. In other words, the essential role of job analysis and competency modeling makes them important for communicating the values of ethics and integrity to the organization's employees. Putting ethics and integrity explicitly into a job analysis (e.g., including a KSAO related to ethics; including a competency on integrity) also lets people know that these are needed to get ahead in the organization. In this way, the value of ethical behavior will be echoed throughout the other HR functions, including recruitment, selection, training, and performance management.

There are a number of examples of how ethics can be incorporated into the job analysis process. For example, the O*NET framework published by the U.S. Department of Labor includes integrity as one of its work styles. SHRM's competency model includes ethical practice as one of its core competencies; these also include integrity, courage, and professionalism. Including employee ethics in describing the job requirements should increase the odds of recruiting and hiring ethical workers, as well as rewarding ethical behavior.[42]

Questions

1. Do you see ethics and integrity as personal qualities of an employee, or can they also be characteristics of an organization?

2. Give an example of how would you define ethics as a KSAO in a job analysis.

3. Give some examples of events in the news involving ethics or integrity in an organization.

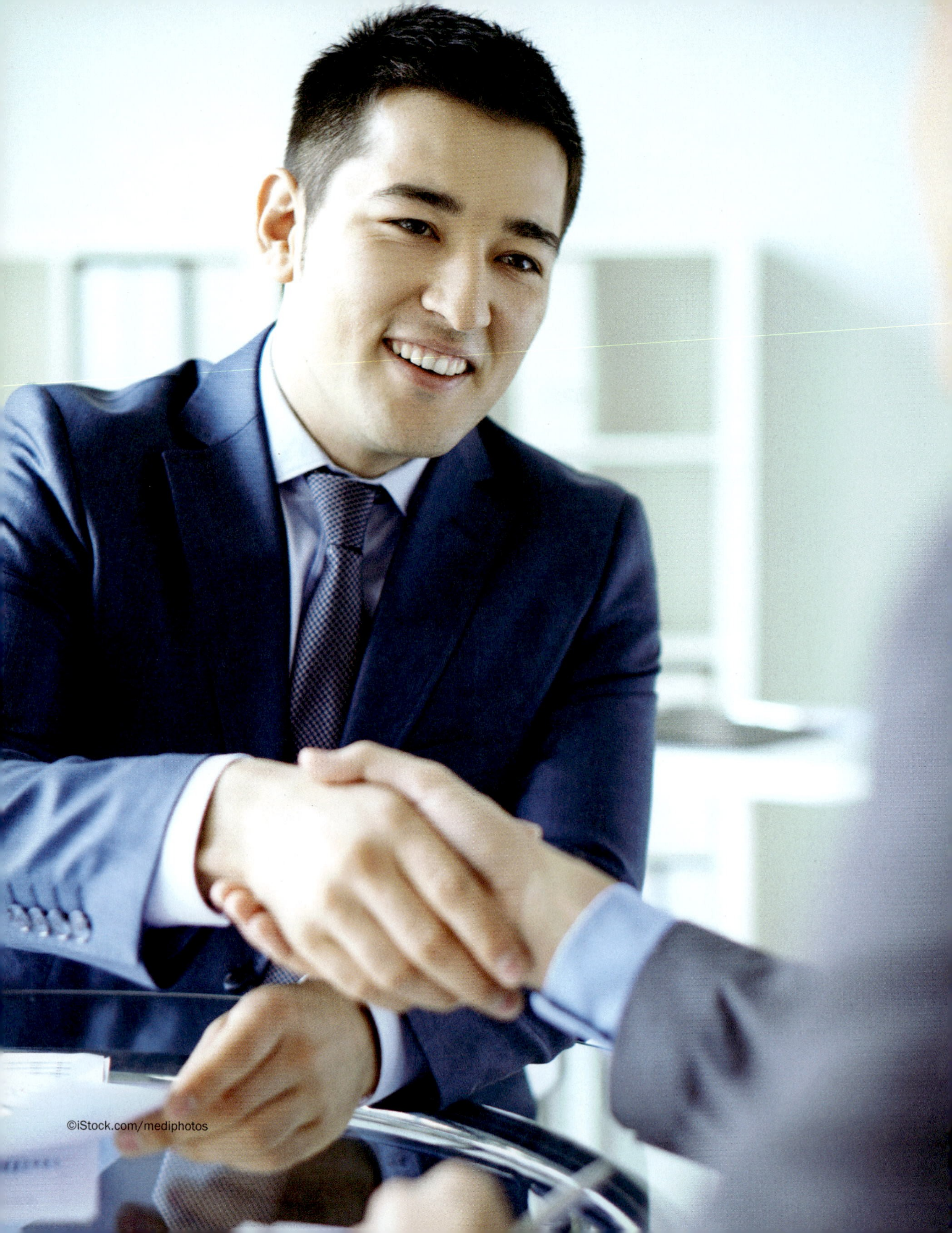

6

Workforce Planning and Recruitment

LEARNING OBJECTIVES

After reading and studying this chapter, you should be able to do the following:

6.1 Describe workforce planning and its role in HR.

6.2 Identify what recruiting is and its key components.

6.3 Describe the three stages of recruitment and what takes place in them.

6.4 Explain the various aspects of diversity in recruiting.

6.5 Understand recruitment results (both positive and negative).

HR in Action: The Case of Labor Shortages for Basic Services

You may not reflect on all the steps that the water you drink goes through before it comes out of your kitchen faucet. However, water treatment plant and system operators do. They monitor operating conditions, meters, and gauges among several other things at water treatment plants to make sure what you drink is safe. The job requires a high school diploma or equivalent and a license.

Job growth is brisk, with 7,000 new job openings expected by 2024. With that said, local and state governments around the United States are worried about whether they will be able to successfully fill water infrastructure positions, as a labor shortage is projected in this field. In fact, water treatment worker is one of the jobs most at risk in terms of not having enough qualified candidates, according to an employment report by the Conference Board. Websites seeking to attract applicants for the water treatment industry boast that such jobs require no college degree, offer good opportunities for advancement as well as great pay and benefits, are resistant to recessions, and provide the ability to benefit society. It remains unclear whether or not increased automation may be able to help employers meet demands with fewer workers.

©iStock.com/Avatar_023

Other basic services jobs also have challenges. For example, the electric power industry is plagued by staggering estimates of 30% to 40%

of its entire 400,000-person workforce being eligible to retire. The nursing profession has similar issues, with job openings continuing to grow due to the aging population in the United States but new nurses not entering the profession quickly enough to keep up with demand.[1]

Case Discussion Questions

1. What might employers do to help recruit more individuals into professions with potential labor shortages?

2. Local governments employ large numbers of people. What do you see as the potential pros and cons of working in a government job?

3. What do you see as a bigger problem, labor shortages (fewer applicants than jobs) or labor surpluses (more applicants than jobs)? Explain your answer.

This chapter discusses the basics of workforce planning and recruitment. By hiring, retaining, and supporting a workforce diverse in terms of KSAs, gender, race, religion, age, sexual orientation, physical abilities, and other characteristics, employers can achieve better business results and, if done correctly, minimize the chances of costly lawsuits. Having diverse employees and creating a culture of inclusion are good for business. Studying this chapter will give you the knowledge and tools to engage in effective recruitment.

Understanding the Labor Landscape

LO 6.1   Describe workforce planning and its role in HR.

Workforce planning and forecasting are important parts of effective human resource management. To survive in both good and tough times, organizations that successfully plan for future needs can navigate challenging times and avoid some of the labor-related surprises that are likely to occur over time. Engaging in the process of workforce planning can help eliminate (or at least decrease) surprises, smooth out business cycles, identify problems early, prevent problems, and take advantage of opportunities.[2] While no amount of planning can be 100% effective, planning and forecasting can help organizations avoid some obvious challenges out on the horizon. Plus, solving a talent problem that is years away from happening is much easier than trying to respond to one that is immediate. So what exactly is workforce planning and how is it done?

Workforce planning The process of determining what work needs to be done in both the short and long term and coming up with a strategy regarding how positions will be filled

Workforce Planning

Workforce planning refers to the process of determining what work needs to be done in both the short and long term and coming up with a strategy regarding how positions will be filled (Figure 6.1). Workforce planning is linked to strategic goals in many ways. If the organization is considering entering a new industry sector, it will need to understand what skills are necessary to be successful in the new industry. For example, when Future Mobility Corp (a Chinese start-up backed by Tencent Holdings) decided to enter the electric vehicle

■ **FIGURE 6.1**   Workforce Planning and Recruitment Process Steps

Each step of the planning process is important for long-term recruitment success.

Forecast → Set recruitment goals → Develop the recruitment process → Implement the recruitment process → Evaluate the recruitment process

market, it needed new expertise. It decided to acquire expertise in this area by hiring the entire electric vehicle development team from BMW.[3] Whether this decision was effective remains to be seen, but it is an illustration of a strategic acquisition decision.

This chapter is especially focused on the role of recruitment in workforce planning, and a key step in this process is forecasting. **Forecasting** refers to the act of determining estimates regarding what specific positions need to be filled and how to fill them. This analysis includes understanding internal and external talent supply and demand, labor costs, company growth rates, and revenue. The forecast can be as detailed or general as makes sense for the organization depending on how volatile or stable the organization, industry, or economy is at a given point in time. However, even positions that have historically been easy to fill may become challenging to fill over time as the workforce ages, unemployment rates decrease, or positions change in terms of how attractive they are to potential applicants.

The next step after engaging in a thorough forecast is to set recruitment-specific goals that are aligned with the organization's strategic plans. The overarching goal is to identify and attract qualified applicants while avoiding problems associated with labor shortages or surpluses. Many questions should be answered (Figure 6.2). For example, what skills are needed? How many of those skills exist already within the organization and how many are new? What are the forecasted attrition rates during recruitment and selection as well as turnover rates, and how might they affect recruiting goals? The next step is to develop recruitment processes to achieve these goals. This is followed by implementation and, finally, evaluating the recruitment process for ways to improve or alter it for the future.

Forecasting The act of determining estimates during workforce planning regarding what specific positions need to be filled and how to fill them

Succession planning Taking stock of which employees are qualified to fill positions that are likely to be vacated soon

Leadership development The formal and informal opportunities for employees to expand their KSAOs

Succession Planning and Leadership Development

Succession planning refers to the active forecasting of leadership needs and the strategies for filling them over time. **Leadership development** refers to the formal and informal opportunities for employees to expand

■ **FIGURE 6.2**   Sample Questions for Workforce Planning

Workforce planning requires asking and answering key questions.

What skills do we have internally? Which do we need to hire?	• How will this change over time?
How do our jobs compare to competitors'?	• How tight is the labor market?
Where will we find our applicants?	• Who is eligible to retire? When are they eligible? Who will replace them?
What metrics should we use to evaluate recruiting?	• How many new positions do we need to fill?

their KSAOs. It is important to recognize that both recruitment and retention are tied to whether potential employees and existing employees perceive that there are developmental opportunities in the form of training and promotion. It is important to consider succession planning in terms of what KSAOs an employer will need, when they will need them, and how to develop employees so that transitions in leadership occur smoothly. Doing so is part of effective workplace planning. At a minimum, organizations need replacement planning to identify a minimal plan of individuals to take over top leadership roles over time. Succession planning involves both the identification and training of individuals who might serve as replacements of top leaders within the organization. Finally, **succession management** refers to identifying and developing successors at all levels of the organization.[4]

Labor Market Conditions

Labor market conditions refers to the number of jobs available compared to the number of individuals available with the required KSAOs to do those jobs. Earlier chapters referred to various Bureau of Labor Statistics (BLS) analyses, findings, and projections. The U.S. Department of Labor oversees the BLS, which is "the principal Federal agency responsible for measuring labor market activity, working conditions, and price changes in the economy. Its mission is to collect, analyze, and disseminate essential economic information to support public and private decision-making."[5] One of the important functions provided by this research arm of the Department of Labor is to help organizations understand labor market conditions, as this is a fundamental aspect of workforce planning and recruitment strategies.

Workforce Labor Shortages

Workforce characteristics may influence recruitment in various ways, including through labor shortages and surpluses. A **workforce labor shortage** refers to labor market conditions in which there are more jobs available than workers to fill them. When there is a labor shortage, there is a "tight labor market," with recruiters consistently reporting that finding skilled job candidates is harder. For example, organizations seeking to hire women in the computer sciences face serious recruiting efforts, as women accounted for only 18% of college graduates with this degree, down from 37% in 1984.[6] A decreasing unemployment rate is one signal that labor market conditions may become more challenging for employers. The United States, Canada, Germany, and Japan have been experiencing falling unemployment rates, which can signal employment challenges.[7] In 2016, 69% of recruiters surveyed within the United States reported a lack of skilled candidates in the labor market as the largest obstacle to hiring. Labor shortages may change what applicants are offered. Surveys of recruiters indicate that job candidates are more willing to ask for higher salaries—especially in the technology and health care sectors. In response, 68% of companies have increased the average salary offer made to job candidates in 2016 compared to 2015.[8] It is important to keep in mind that although the overall employment rate is one indication of labor availability, there can be dramatic differences between jobs, industries, and even locations depending on the requirements of the jobs. For example, when Amazon announced plans to add 100,000 new jobs over 18 months, it was good news for those looking for a job, but it was a situation that put added pressure on the labor market where the company was hiring.[9]

Succession management The process of identifying and developing successors at all levels of the organization

Labor market conditions The number of jobs available compared to the number of individuals available with the required KSAOs to do those jobs

Workforce labor shortages Labor market conditions in which there are more jobs available than workers to fill them

Workforce Labor Surpluses

Workforce labor surplus (slack) refers to labor market conditions in which there is more available labor than organizations need. Such a situation can result in high unemployment rates and make finding a job tough for individuals. This can be nationwide, or it can happen within specific regions or areas. For example, the logging industry was greatly curtailed in the Pacific Northwestern United States in the 1980s. Similarly, manufacturing jobs available have decreased in America's Midwestern states. Under such labor market conditions, the challenge becomes matching the skills needed to do the jobs with those in need of employment. Programs such as job retraining and educational reimbursements represent some ways that organizations and, at times, the government can seek to align skills in the local labor market more with local labor demands. Organizations facing a workforce labor surplus in their area or industry have an easier time finding employees to fill their positions. However, organizations must often compete for those with key skills.

Talent Analysis

A **talent analysis** refers to actively gathering data to determine potential talent gaps, or the difference between an organization's talent demand and its available talent supply (Figure 6.3). The talent supply, more often called a **talent pool,** is a group of individuals (employees or potential applicants) who possess the KSAOs to fill a particular role. As you can imagine, determining the needed KSAOs comes from job analysis information. Understanding the current and future talent needs is an important aspect of this analysis, as is understanding the current internal labor pool (those who already work for an organization) and future external labor pool (those who do not currently work for an organization but who might be

Workforce labor surplus (slack) Labor market conditions in which there is more available labor than organizations need

Talent analysis The process of gathering data to determine potential talent gaps, or the difference between an organization's talent demand and the available talent supply

Talent pool A group of individuals (employees or potential applicants) who possess the KSAOs to fill a particular role

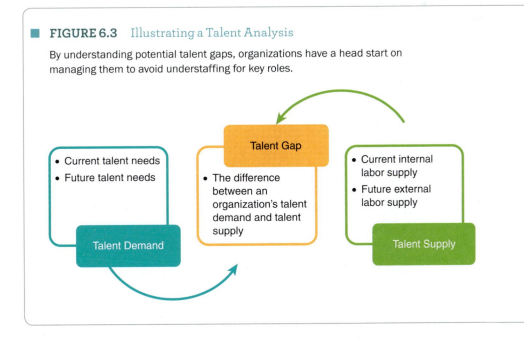

■ **FIGURE 6.3**   Illustrating a Talent Analysis

By understanding potential talent gaps, organizations have a head start on managing them to avoid understaffing for key roles.

- Current talent needs
- Future talent needs

Talent Demand

Talent Gap

- The difference between an organization's talent demand and talent supply

- Current internal labor supply
- Future external labor supply

Talent Supply

hired in the future). For example, Boeing uses predictive workforce modeling techniques to predict and fill talent gaps before they develop. It considers several factors such as business trends, associated workforce skill needs, internal workforce demographics such as skill populations, job levels, age and retirement eligibility, economic trends, and expected employee life cycles.[10]

One way that the talent pool can be increased is via immigrants to the United States. Data show that more than 26 million individuals who were born outside of the United States were legally employed in 2015.[11] Immigrants serve as a major talent supply if they possess skills that are in demand.

The Recruiting Process

LO 6.2   Identify what recruiting is and its key components.

Recruitment is the process of identifying and working to attract individuals interested in and capable of filling identified organizational roles. These individuals may be from either the external or internal labor markets. When it comes to recruitment, both quantity and quality matter. It is a mutual decision-making process on the part of both employers and individuals, with organizational representatives considering such factors as needs, costs, and timing and individuals considering factors such as their reactions to the recruitment process, location of the job, and organizational reputation.

Why Recruitment Matters

Effective recruitment is a critical aspect of organizational success. Reasons for this include innovation, firm performance, and organizational culture.[12] In fact, recruitment has consistently been identified as one of the most impactful HR functions.[13] As you may recall, HRM is defined as *the decisions and actions associated with managing individuals throughout the employee life cycle to maximize employee and organizational effectiveness.* Recruitment is the start of the employee life cycle and the source of human capital within an organization.

Recruitment Strategy

A recruitment strategy is the formalization of the recruitment process at a given organization. It includes recruitment objectives, strategy development, recruitment activities, recruitment results, and understanding the intervening job applicant variables, which may influence any of these factors.

Recruitment The process of identifying a group of individuals (employees or potential applicants) who possess the KSAOs to fill a particular role

Recruitment Objectives

Identifying recruitment objectives, or goals, at the start of the recruitment process sets the stage for the next steps. Objectives might include the number and qualifications and characteristics of applicants, time frame for recruitment, and how effective recruitment will be determined.

Strategy Development

There are many elements of a recruitment strategy, but overall, this is where needs are articulated, including whom to recruit, where to find them, how to reach them, who will interact with them, and what they will be offered to join the organization. Recruitment need refers to the results of the workforce planning process in terms of what KSAOs are needed within the organization as well as when they will be needed. Placement refers to two aspects of strategy development. First, where do we need the talent to be placed? Where in the organization are employees needed? Second, where will they be found? Will these be internal or external hires? Is the talent pool sufficient, or do steps need to be taken to develop the necessary talent?

Recruitment Activities

Recruitment activities include which methods will be used, what information about the job will be conveyed, and the details of the strategy developed in the previous step. One opportunity to make recruitment more effective is to closely align the recruitment process to selection and onboarding. Many organizations focus so much time and attention on recruiting that they forget how important it is to have everyone on the same page regarding what the job entails, what is expected of new employees, and what they can expect when they enter the organization. Research shows that the more highly these are aligned, the more effectively new employees adjust to their jobs.[14]

The Role of Recruiters in the Recruitment Process

Recruiters are an important part of the recruitment process. In addition, a **hiring manager** is defined as the person who asked for the role to be filled and/or whom the new hire will be reporting to as his or her manager. Recruiters and hiring managers are the gatekeepers of the hiring process and, in the best case, are working as partners during the recruitment process. The goal of the selection process is to obtain large pools of qualified applicants. However, recruiters and hiring managers can become inundated with large numbers of applications, overburdening hiring personnel with more applications than they can process. This can result in nonstrategic, suboptimal decision making as, in general, decisions made under tight timelines are more likely to result in little thought on the part of decision makers, and research has shown that placing increased information-processing burdens on decision makers allows biases to enter the decision-making process.[15]

Further, recruitment decision makers need to feel confident that they can rely on the assessment solutions (e.g., employment tests, interviews) that they are using in the hiring process to help them find the best candidates possible. Assessment solutions need to be valid predictors and legally defensible. In other words, recruiters need assessment systems that can provide large numbers of qualified applicants but that can effectively and efficiently determine who the best applicants are. Addressing these issues for recruiters will do much to increase the cost–benefit analysis of the hiring process.[16]

Considering the role of recruiters is important to understanding organizational effectiveness at attracting talent. Overall, the job of recruiter is seen as a desirable one. Corporate recruiter has been listed as one of the 50 best jobs in the United States based on salary, job openings, job score, and job satisfaction ratings.[17] But recruiters are human, which means that their effectiveness is subject to their strengths and weaknesses pertaining to their attitudes, decision making, and other behaviors. For example, have you ever wondered how

Hiring manager The person who asked for the role to be filled and/or to whom the new hire will be reporting as their manager

the use of photos in social media affects the recruiting process? Photos can send positive or negative signals to recruiters, 41% of whom say that seeing a picture of a job candidate before they meet in person influences their first impression.[18] Even more potentially damaging are photos focused on alcohol and a perception by a majority of recruiters that "oversharing" on social media sites counts against an applicant. Impressions do not end there. Researchers in Belgium studied the influence of attractive profile photos on Facebook and found that candidates with more attractive photos obtained 38% more job interview invitations than those with less attractive photos.[19] Recent recruiter surveys indicate that typos, drug use, body odor, and dressing too casually for interviews negatively affect hiring decisions.[20] Factors that led to favorable impressions included applicant enthusiasm, command of job requirements and skills, culture fit, and strong conversation skills.[21]

Stages of Recruitment

LO 6.3   Describe the three stages of recruitment and what takes place in them.

The stages of recruitment move through a recruitment funnel (see Figure 6.4) in which the number of participants gets smaller the further down the funnel the applicant goes. It is important to understand how critical this recruitment funnel is. This is because only those individuals who become applicants can ultimately be hired, so the initial applicant yield ratio (how many ultimately hired compared to those who applied) is important. The goal is to get a large number of qualified applicants from which the employer can choose. Further, any applicants who remove themselves from the process cannot be selected, so keeping applicants' interest so that they do not drop out is important. Understanding this concept is helpful as we discuss the recruiting process.

At its most basic level, the idea behind the recruitment funnel is that the number of applicants needed at the start of the selection process is much larger than the ultimate number of hires made (see Figure 6.4). While every organization will identify its own ratios for success based on its workforce planning and actual number of hires per applicants, it is clear that as applicants move through the selection process and the best applicants are identified at each selection hurdle, fewer and fewer applicants are considered further. How wide or narrow the recruitment funnel is depends on the number of employees needed and the level of skills needed to perform the job. For example, when hiring a retail employee to help customers and ring up sales, there are often fewer requirements than when hiring a mechanic to fix cars. That is because retail employees can be more easily and quickly trained compared to mechanics, who take years to perfect their craft.

There are three fundamental stages of recruitment:

1. Identify and generate applicants.

2. Maintain applicant interest and participation as they continue through the assessment process. During recruitment, the organization is trying both to assess and to attract the best job applicants.

3. Influence job choice so that desired applicants are willing to accept offers made to them.

■ **FIGURE 6.4**   The Recruitment Funnel in Relation to the Stages of Recruitment

The recruitment funnel narrows the number of candidates considered from the time of recruitment through hire, leaving the very best candidates to hire.

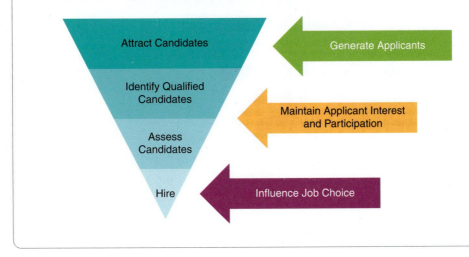

Generating Applicants

Generating applicants is an important first step to the recruitment process. It is one that has also garnered a great deal of well-deserved attention, as it represents a substantial investment of both time and money on the part of the recruiting organization (see Figure 6.5). Generating applicants determines the talent pool that will be considered for positions within an organization. Following are some important considerations, starting with applicant quantity and quality.

Applicant Quantity and Quality

It is important to understand that there are two major goals within the first stage of the recruitment process.[22] The first goal is quantity: Generating a sufficient number of applicants during the first stage of the recruitment process is important for several reasons, including that the effectiveness of the selection process depends on having a large enough talent pool that has the skills needed to do the job and meets other strategic needs such as diversity and succession planning. We know that lower selection ratios—and how "choosy" the employer can be—are achieved by attracting large numbers of applicants. It is not clear whether the relationship is causal. It may be that well-run and profitable organizations are more attractive than other organizations. Nonetheless, this does highlight the importance of having sufficient numbers of applicants.

The second goal is quality. Quality relates to applicants having the requisite skills needed as well as representing a diverse pool of applicants. Research shows that low selection ratios are associated with positive organizations' financial performance.[23] As such, in addition to applicant quantity, applicant quality is important.

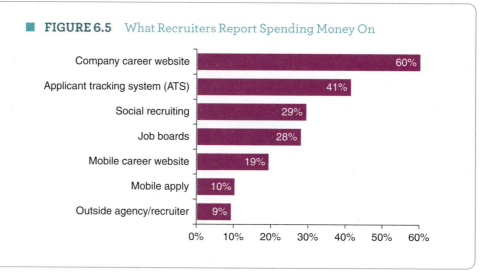

■ **FIGURE 6.5**　What Recruiters Report Spending Money On

Realistic Job Previews

One important function of the recruitment process is to attract individuals to apply for jobs and be inclined to take a job if offered one. High turnover rates can create recruitment challenges, as the organization needs to constantly recruit and hire new employees. An important consideration is to attract individuals to the job and organization while also being realistic enough that once they begin the job, they will not be disappointed and quit. One way in which organizations and researchers address these concerns is the **realistic job preview (RJP)**, which offers potential applicants a realistic, and sometimes unappealing, view of the actual job.

For example, the Indiana Department of Child Services created a 35-minute video that frankly outlines the challenges and frustrations along with the rewards and joys of the job of child services caseworker. It starts with a warning that "due to mature subject matter, viewer discretion is advised." It includes references to the job being "rewarding, complex, stressful, and sometimes a bit frightening."[24] On a lighter note, the Walt Disney Company shows job candidates a film depicting what it is like to work at Disney and outlines its employment policies and conditions. Some candidates self-select out of the recruitment process based on viewing this film, deciding it is not a good fit for them.[25] Research regarding RJPs has been mixed, with some studies finding support and others finding no appreciable differences between those who experience RJPs during recruitment and those who do not.[26]

One innovative example of an RJP is used by Zappos. It offers a financial incentive for new employees to quit after going through the training program, because it is only at that point that they can fully understand what the job would entail. Zappos effectively pays a new employee to quit if the employee doesn't feel they are a good fit. Specifically, Zappos pays for time invested in training, plus $4,000 if the person doesn't think it is the right position or company them. About 2% to 3% of employees take the offer.[27]

Realistic job preview (RJP) Offers potential applicants a realistic view of the actual job, including both positive and negative information

Recruitment Sources

Perhaps no single aspect of recruitment has received more time and attention than recruitment sources. Deciding exactly how to reach potential applicants is both a strategic and a financial decision. Recruitment sources can be divided into two main categories: passive recruitment and active recruitment (see Figure 6.6).

Although research has been conducted around the globe in the hopes of identifying which recruitment sources are the most effective, what is effective for one organization may be less effective for another due to the differences in their recruitment strategies, brands, and industries. In addition, organizations may choose to focus on the recruitment of internal candidates or look for talent outside of the organization. A recent SHRM survey found that 25% of organizations filled positions with current internal employees and 75% with external hires.[28]

■ **FIGURE 6.6**   Recruitment Sources May Be Passive or Active for Organizations and Applicants

Internal Recruiting Sources

Steve Kerr, senior advisor and former chief learning officer at Goldman Sachs, is quoted as saying, "It's very odd to me. The assets walk home at night. If people are your most important asset, you ought to develop them. It is Goldman's philosophy that not only do people have to be developed, it ends up being a huge competitive advantage." He further argues that development can help with "recruitment as well as retention."[29] As noted earlier, succession planning is an important piece of workforce planning. Another benefit of recruiting for positions internally is that advancement and development opportunities can be attractive to current employees and help with retention. If you are able to redeploy talent throughout the organization rather than losing it, the organization is able to retain valuable organizational knowledge.

External Recruitment Sources

External recruitment refers to an employer's actions that are intended to bring a job opening to the attention of potential job candidates outside of the organization and, in turn, influence their intention to pursue the opportunity. A key aspect to external recruitment is to identify the most effective external recruitment sources. Types of sources include external services such as search firms, employment agencies, on-demand recruiting services, alumni employees, and military transition services, as well as job postings such as those in newspapers, on social media, and on career sites. In addition, some organizations find that cultivating an employee pipeline to keep up with anticipated talent demands is useful.

External recruitment An employer's actions that are intended to bring a job opening to the attention of potential job candidates outside of the organization and, in turn, influence their intention to pursue the opportunity

Spotlight on Data and Analytics

INTERNAL RECRUITING AT CREDIT SUISSE

©iStock.com/stockwerk

In the age of big data and analytics, it is not unheard of for an organization to identify who might be likely to quit. What is new is how accurate such estimates have become.

Credit Suisse, a multinational financial services holding company headquartered in Zurich, is using this information to identify employees who might benefit from internal recruitment efforts. In 2014, Credit Suisse began asking recruiters to contact such employees to alert them to internal job opportunities. They report that the program served to reduce turnover and prompted 300 employees to find new positions within the firm. They estimate that the program saved $75 million to $100 million in rehiring and training costs. This is a good example of pairing internal data, analytics, and an internal recruitment strategy to avoid unwanted attrition.[30]

Many attend college job fairs, work with college placement offices, and use internship programs. Another option is to consider non-U.S. citizens for hard-to-fill positions. This might include offshoring or visa sponsorship issues. Each of these sources has potential benefits and drawbacks that should be considered as part of an organization's recruitment strategy.

Webpages

For most organizations, the webpage is a vital part of recruitment because it sends signals regarding what the organization is like and because it contains employment information. Public webpages may serve as recruitment sources for both internal and external applicants. Internal webpages, which are accessible by only current employees, are another important source.

Unadvertised Jobs

Although the following sections outline both internal and external recruiting sources, another key recruitment source is word-of-mouth listings. About 50% of positions are actually filled via informal channels and may never have been formally advertised or listed.[31] As a best practice, we recommend making a recruitment pool as large as possible; however, there may be times when informal channels yield unique talent acquisition opportunities for an organization. It is important to consider the pros and cons of hidden job listings and informal hiring, although very little research has been conducted in that regard. However, hiring those one knows can lead to lower diversity in terms of approaches and ideas, can be perceived by others as unfair, and might run afoul of federal guidelines.

Internal Transfers and Promotions

Firms report filling positions with internal transfers and promotions a little more than 37% of the time.[32] A key aspect of managing internal transfers and promotions is the use of an internal **applicant tracking system (ATS)**, which offers a centralized way to house employee and applicant data in a single repository. This repository of data can then be linked with other HR information systems like that of retention and performance management to analyze the effectiveness of applicants from different recruitment sources, for example. It can also be used to track employee transfers and promotions over time.

Internal Job Boards

Internal job boards allow organizations to post available positions internally before the rest of the potential talent pool sees them. When internal candidates are given early consideration for positions, it can be good for morale and for mobility within the organization. In fact, some organizations invest a considerable amount to help existing employees find new opportunities within the organization because this may serve to help boost retention rates and retain top talent.

Alumni Employees

More and more organizations are considering rehiring former employees. The practice of employing "boomerang employees" who return to the organization is common in accounting and consulting firms. In fact, Deloitte conducted a study of alumni rehires and found that rehires saved them $3.8 million in search fees alone.[33] For National Basketball Association (NBA) players, for example, research revealed that for players who left a team and later returned, success was related to leaving on good terms initially, being successful while they were away, and the terms of their reemployment.[34] In general, research shows that rehires are less likely to quit and have an easier time onboarding back into the organization.[35] Overall, nearly 7% of hires are former employees.[36] Organizations can cultivate effective alumni networks in several ways, including by creating a website with a directory of members, job boards, and information about networking events and professional development.[37] Microsoft traditionally has hired around 5% alumni employees each year. It launched the Microsoft Alumni Network in 1995, which currently has thousands of members.[38]

Employee Referrals

An employee referral is a specific recruitment method that taps existing employees for potential applicant suggestions. Some firms such as Google pay existing employees a bonus for a successful referral. The average bonus reported is between $1,000 and $2,499.[39] Other incentives might include a paid day off, gifts, or recognition at a staff meeting. Employers may give rewards immediately when referred employees are hired or after a set number of days of successful employment. They further work to ensure that current employees find the process pleasant by ensuring that referred individuals are contacted within 48 hours.[40] This can be an effective way to recruit, because existing employees understand the organizational culture and job demands and are in a good position to suggest potential candidates they feel would be successful. When surveyed, 78% of recruiters reported that employee referrals helped them find their best candidates. Referrals account for more than 22% of applicants.[41]

Applicant tracking system (ATS) An internal system that offers a centralized way to house applicant and employee data and to enable electronic business processes related to recruitment

To help ensure that referral programs do not result in unfair hiring practices, SHRM recommends the following. SHRM also has an available online toolkit to help with designing referral programs.[42]

- *Reread legal recruitment guidelines.* This helps ensure that you are not unintentionally creating a system that is not consistent with existing laws.

- *Use a variety of recruiting methods when advertising job openings.* This will help keep the applicant pool more diverse.

- *Make employee referral programs open to the entire organization, not limiting them to specific employee groups, departments, or divisions.*

- *Evaluate all candidates—including employee-referred candidates—using the same qualification criteria.*

- *Conduct ongoing analyses of the workforce and the applicant pool to ensure that the employee referral program is effective and is yielding the intended results.* Included in the analyses should be diversity categories, the quality of hire, and resulting tenure from referrals. If the program is not meeting its intended goals and is negatively affecting workforce diversity, reevaluate it.

Search Firms

Search firms are paid to find candidates to help organizations fill roles. Executive search firms focus on the upper levels of an organization. Some organizations use search firms to fill all their positions. Others use them rarely. Time Warner, Inc. hired thousands of senior-level employees from 2005 and 2012 but used an executive-search firm only once.[43] Some industries, such as higher education, tend to use search firms to generate candidates for key positions like university president, provost, or dean. Search firms can also be used to fill open positions quickly in areas in which the organization does not have an established recruitment process or brand. For example, Apple hired a search firm to help it quickly staff its retail stores in China.[44] Regardless of who is responsible for the actual recruitment, it is imperative that job expectations and qualifications are clear and accurate. Not doing so can lead to higher levels of turnover and frustration for those hired and organizations.

University Relationships

New college hires often originate from recruitment strategies aimed at leveraging university relationships such as targeting specific universities, attending university job fairs, and developing internship programs. Some schools even host "virtual" job fairs so that a wider number of hiring organizations and students can attend at a lower cost.[45] Research shows that job fairs have a significant impact on student perceptions of organizations.[46] Such relationships work for current students but can be effective for university alumni relations as well.

Located in the 30,000-person rural town of Bozeman, Montana, RightNow Technologies, Inc. struggled to find enough qualified software engineers and marketing professionals. To aid recruitment efforts, the company turned to Montana State University, figuring that former students would be aware of the livability of Bozeman and might be interested in returning if offered the right opportunity. This led RightNow to purchase a list of alumni from the school to recruit directly, which yielded such success that other firms in the area have adopted similar practices.[47]

Rosetta, a marketing and advertising company, created a campus ambassador program in which past interns interested in staying involved with Rosetta were trained on the company's recruiting process and recruitment message. It provided them with giveaways to help promote Rosetta's brand and asked ambassadors to engage in specific programs such as conducting information sessions, participating in Rosetta's campus visits, and providing referrals. In 2015, 26% of its past interns participated, and applications were up 7% that year.[48]

Internship Programs

Internships can be an important tool for both organizations and students. For students, research shows that they almost double the chance of full-time job offers when they graduate. This makes sense, as many interns are eventually offered full-time employment. Further, those who have had internships earn more than those who do not, have lower turnover, and are more likely to report that their college degrees helped prepare them for their careers.[49]

Research shows that organizations that want to hire interns tend to be more open to their creativity, which helps to attract interns who are interested in full-time jobs after graduation.[50] In a 2015 recruiter survey, 55% of respondents reported that intern-to-hire programs led to their best hires.[51] Some organizations invest heavily in their internship programs (see Table 6.1).

Internships are also very successful recruitment tools for small- and medium-sized businesses. Resources for setting up internship programs can be found on the National Association of Colleges and Employers (NACE) website (http://www.naceweb.org/intern ships/15-best-practices.aspx).

Best practices include

- providing interns with meaningful work assignments,

- holding orientations,

- providing a handbook or relevant website for addressing rules and frequently asked questions, and

- conducting exit interviews at the end of the internship experience to learn how it went and ways to improve future internship experiences.

External Job Boards

External job boards have made advertising jobs much easier than it has been in the past. They have largely replaced the

TABLE 6.1   Which Organizations Have the Most Prestigious Internships?

Vault.com surveyed 13,000 current and former interns and asked them to rate the prestige of companies on a 1-to-10 scale. The research methodology used to compile this list included only large companies.

Here are the results for 2019:

1. Google	6. Goldman Sachs
2. Apple, Inc.	7. Amazon
3. Microsoft Corporation	8. J.P. Morgan
4. Tesla	9. SpaceX
5. Facebook	10. The Walt Disney Company

Source: Vault. (2019). Most prestigious internships. https://www.vault.com/best-internships-rankings-search/most-prestigious-internships

idea of placing help-wanted ads in the newspaper. Online job boards allow organizations to post for current and potential jobs, direct applicants where to apply, and provide specific information to help applicants narrow down potential positions via a number of search parameters such as location, job requirements, or pay. Types of job boards range from those with jobs in all categories such as Monster.com (one of the oldest job boards), Glassdoor .com, and Indeed.com to more specific job boards such as AllRetailJobs.com or www .truckerswanted.ca, the latter of which is specific to the trucking industry in North America and free for both drivers and companies to use. ZipRecruiter.com allows organizations to post to more than 200 job boards at once. In the United States, nearly 10% of hires were found via job boards.[52] Globally, perhaps the largest job board is China's job51.com website, which reports having 81 million registered individuals, with 72 million résumés contained within its database.[53]

Social Networking Sites

Each day, millions of people spend time on social media. These sites allow organizations to dramatically widen their reach when it comes to recruiting. Social networking sites such as Instagram, Twitter, Facebook, and Snapchat vary in the degree to which they have traditionally been considered recruitment sources. It is hard to ignore the trend toward social networking sites being an important source for potential talent and networking. These sites are large and continue to add members. For example, LinkedIn reports having 530 million members.[54] On average, upward of 60,000 jobs are posted on Twitter daily.[55]

Using social media can help pinpoint specific skills and more narrow needs. For example, PepsiCo shares job openings and responds to candidate questions on Twitter.[56] Innovis Health runs specialty clinics in Minnesota and North Dakota. To help with physician recruitment, this company loads videos to YouTube to show potential recruits what the facilities look like and how they operate.[57] In China, Marriott launched a promotional campaign to help staff 20,000 positions in its new hotels. Marriott found that videos featured on its website as well as launching a social game online to allow users to virtually manage their own restaurants as a way of exposing them to Marriott's customer service principles were helpful.[58]

Employment Agencies

Employment agencies vary a great deal in terms of the services they offer and roles they perform. For example, they might engage in roles such as information provider, matchmaker, or administrator. Employment agencies also provide employers with flexible workers. Flexible workers include contract, contingent, and part-time workers, who account for a little more than 16% of hires.[59] Further, within the United States, 81% of organizations report using flexible workers.[60] Staffing firms, also known as temporary employment agencies, can help organizations fulfill workforce needs and handle the administration of employees needed for only a short period of time. However, it is important to remember that those employers considering working with agencies should follow guidelines to ensure they work only with reputable firms, document any agreement with the agency with a written contract, and ensure that the staffing agency controls all aspects of the working relationships such as setting hours, paying their employees, and complying with employment laws.[61] Some organizations such as T-Mobile have turned to temporary workers to fill permanent positions such as engineers and technicians.[62] Regardless, organizations should continue to work to make sure all employment decisions comply with all antidiscrimination and similar laws even for temporary workers hired by staffing firms.

Freelance Employees

The gig economy is growing every year. As more and more individuals are choosing freelance work as their primary form of employment or as side employment, gig workers have become a viable source for organizations to find desired skills. Although previous chapters describe the pros and cons associated with hiring freelance employees, it is becoming easier and easier for employers to locate them using online marketplaces for work outsourcing. Sites such as Elance.com for business and engineering services, FlexJobs.com, Guru.com (which boasts 1 million jobs completed to date and 3 million freelancers), and GetAFreelancer.com help organizations locate the skills they need.[63]

Walk-Ins

Only a negligible 1% of new hires come from applicants applying in person at stores or facilities.[64] With that said, depending on the type of job, walk-ins may be an important form of recruitment source. For example, in retail and hospitality sectors, walk-ins occur with greater frequency. Typically, individuals apply in person at local companies when seeking part-time work. The formula is simple: Organizations receptive to walk-ins should be prepared with job application forms. Depending on how strong the need is, some organizations give managers the freedom to interview prospective employees on the spot. One obvious and low-tech way to indicate that you are interested in walk-ins is to post a "help wanted" sign in the window of the business.

Recruiting for Diversity

LO 6.4   Explain the various aspects of diversity in recruiting.

Recruitment is covered by several laws designed to protect individuals from discrimination on the basis of their sex, race, age, or differential abilities. Laws such as Title VII of the Civil Rights Act, the Americans with Disabilities Act, and the Age Discrimination in Employment Act all serve to protect individuals. In addition to wanting to comply with legal requirements, organizations often also want to attract members of protected groups to leverage the positive aspects of having a more diverse workforce. In its survey of college employers, NACE found that 56% of respondents indicated that they have a formal diversity recruitment effort.[65] In reviewing specific issues and research findings associated with different groups, we also recognize that individuals vary a great deal in the degree to which they identify with each group as well as how their specific constellation of demographics and beliefs influences their reactions to recruitment and organizational attraction.

One thing that organizations can do to ensure stronger diversity within the organization is to treat their existing employees well and to invest in their career development once they are hired into the organization. If your organization does a reasonable job of attracting a diverse workforce but is not able to retain such individuals, it might be time to examine other factors such as the organization's culture and perceptions of how it is to work there from those on the frontlines. It can also be illuminating to do an analysis of who is leaving to see if the numbers are equally distributed across different groups. For example, ride-sharing company Uber found out that ignoring such issues can lead to decreases in a diverse workforce as well as create a public relations problem, thereby affecting the bottom line.[66]

David Dee Delgado/Stringer

In 2019, the U.S. Military Academy at West Point graduated a record 34 Black women graduates.

Gender Diversity

Some industries have a more challenging time recruiting and maintaining women than others. The high-tech industry has had an especially tough time with recruiting and retaining women for many reasons. Research shows that women are less likely to engage in persistent job-search behaviors. This is consistent with findings regarding promotions within organization such as for Google, wherein women were less likely to put themselves up for promotions and less likely to persist if passed over the first time they applied.[67] Nevertheless, organizations can enact key activities to attract and retain women at all ranks of the organization, including the creation of a united front in which the message and behavior are clear regarding how women are to be treated within the organization, the spreading of a wide recruitment net, the development of a female-friendly benefits program, the serious treatment of sexual harassment and gender discrimination, and the placement of women in positions of power.[68]

Recruitment is a process in which unconscious biases of both applicants and organizational decision makers may play a role, limiting diversity. This is particularly challenging because it is unconscious, meaning that employers may not be aware of how their recruitment efforts are not attracting a wide range of applicants. Conscious effort may be needed to reverse the effects. Research has shown that there are differences in how male- and female-dominated occupations advertise these positions, with traditionally male-dominated occupations using words such as *competitive* and *dominant* in position descriptions. Textio is a Seattle-based start-up that develops software to get around this problem by analyzing the text of job postings to make postings attractive to a diverse pool of applicants.[69]

The recruitment of greater numbers of individuals for jobs with labor shortages such as nursing has led to the ongoing need for the recruitment of men as well as women. At this point, men represent only 9% of the 3.5 million nurses in the United States.[70] When it comes to gender diversity, it is not solely a male or female issue. The key is to give everyone access to the same positions for which they are qualified. It is important that applicants are able to pass key selection criteria such as the ability to lift a certain amount of weight or to drag heavy hoses in the case of firefighters if those tasks are job related. Diversity management is an ongoing process. These examples highlight the importance of considering diversity along a number of key dimensions.

Racial Diversity

Strategic ad placement can be an effective way to attract a more diverse applicant pool.[71] In addition to where ads are placed, the content of those ads may influence applicant attraction as well. Research found that African American applicants were more attracted to organizations indicating that they emphasize a commitment to equal opportunity, access to training, and to recruiting applicants of color.[72] Studies show that recruitment materials matter a great deal for applicants. For example, recruitment materials depicting employees of color have been found to attract African Americans and Latinos without negatively affecting Caucasian applicants.[73] Further, when photos illustrated minorities in supervisory roles, positive effects were even stronger.[74] An important consideration is to firmly align the recruitment message with the organizational reality. It makes no sense to recruit individuals with false promises of an organization that does not exist, because this results in an *unreal*-*istic* job preview. Doing so creates a costly situation for both individuals and organizations and can serve to undermine diversity recruitment and retention in the long run.

Age Diversity

By 2030, 20% or more of the U.S. population will be aged 65 or older. People are working longer due to longer life spans, and people of different ages will be working side by side as never before.[75] This has implications for recruitment as more and more individuals are choosing to continue working and may go for "encore" careers. Research shows that there are few differences between the performance of older and younger workers. In fact, older workers are more likely to engage in organizational citizenship behaviors and have fewer unexcused absences.[76] In a study examining common age stereotypes, researchers found that across all available data, few of the older worker stereotypes are true: There was no evidence that older workers were less motivated, more resistant to change, less trusting, less healthy, or more vulnerable to work–family imbalance, although they may be less interested in training and career-development activities.[77] Additionally, given their extensive experience, older workers can be seen as bringing important human capital to an organization.[78] Attracting more seasoned employees is becoming more attractive to many companies. Organizations are beginning to take notice. For example, Walmart approached AARP (previously known as the American Association of Retired Persons) in the hopes of recruiting older workers.[79] Organizations would benefit from considering how the recruitment methods they use affect the diversity of their applicant pool. For example, the exclusive use of college recruiting programs may exclude older applicants and violate the Age Discrimination in Employment Act (ADEA). Similarly, using wording such as *new college graduate* and *digital native* may repel older applicants and may run afoul of ADEA.[80] Further, recruiters play a key role, and they should be aware of their own biases against both younger and older applicants when making hiring decisions.

Veterans

There are approximately 22 million military veterans in the United States, making up 9% of the adult population. Once service members leave active duty and enter the civilian job market, they represent another potential source of recruitment. Matching the KSAOs of military positions to civilian positions, however, can pose a challenge within civilian organizations, because the job titles, duties, and requirements may differ greatly. In fact, in a SHRM survey, 60% of respondents indicated that they had experienced challenges related to the hiring of veterans for this very reason. Some companies see hiring veterans as an expression of goodwill.[81] Others see it as a win-win to close their talent gap.

For example, Raytheon Company hires thousands of engineers each year. As part of the U.S. Army's Partnership for Youth Success (PaYS) program, which connects new recruits with postservice jobs, Raytheon can hire qualified employees and get them security clearance, which is timely and can be expensive. Raytheon states, "Military professionals come to us with security clearances, and in many cases they've used our products, so they're familiar with the company and our processes. That's a big timesaver and cost-saver."[82]

Researchers suggest several strategies for success when considering veterans as a recruitment source, including[83]

- understanding (and modifying as needed) beliefs about veterans,

- hiring and training knowledgeable decision makers to work on recruitment,

- increasing the organization's knowledge of military job-related tasks and KSAOs, and

- socializing veterans in the role requirements and norms of civilian organizations.

Spotlight on Legal Issues

GENERAL GUIDELINES FOR RECRUITMENT

The information here should not be considered a substitute for legal advice. The application and impact of laws vary based on the specifics of the case, and laws may change over time. We encourage readers to seek out legal advice if unsure of the legality of specific programs or actions.

When it comes to recruitment, legal issues are an important consideration. As the EEOC's compliance manual says, "*Who* ultimately receives employment opportunities is highly dependent on how and where the employer looks for candidates." For instance, disparate racial impact occurs when a recruitment practice produces a significant difference in hiring for protected racial groups. It does not necessarily matter whether such differential impact is intentional—just that it occurred.[84]

Here are some questions to ask about your recruiting practices to help avert or curtail potential problems. Ideally, you will be able to answer yes to the following:

- Do you have standardized recruiting practices?

- Have you ruled out that your recruiting practices indicate possible disparate impact?

- Can you provide evidence that each of your recruiting practices is consistent with business necessity and is job related?

- Are you casting a wide net in your recruiting sources by using a variety of sources accessible to everyone?

- Are recruiters and agencies you work with familiar with discrimination laws and how to comply with them?

Differently Abled Individuals

The Americans with Disabilities Act (ADA) (1990) prohibits discrimination against a qualified applicant or employee with a disability. Determining who is qualified to perform the major functions of the job with or without accommodations is based on a job analysis. The ADA applies to organizations with 15 or more employees and defines a disability as a physical or mental impairment that affects one's major life functions. The key point to understand is that the ADA includes both applicants and employees, so it is in full force during recruitment efforts, and if requested, reasonable accommodations must be made in terms of all aspects of recruitment and selection. For example, an organization would need to make sure that the recruitment methods it uses do not exclude applicants with disabilities. If recruitment activities are conducted on a college campus or at a job fair, the location needs to be accessible. If online sources are used, it is important to ensure that applicants with visual and hearing impairments can complete the application process.

Recruitment Results: Evaluating Effectiveness and Metrics

LO 6.5 Understand recruitment results (both positive and negative).

Up to this point, this chapter has focused on various aspects of recruitment. Let's now consider some broader issues, including how to evaluate the effectiveness of recruitment efforts, how to keep applicants interested and motivated throughout the process, and how to choose the right job for the right applicant.

When it comes to measuring the quality of their college hires, the energy corporation Chevron says it looks at ethnic and gender diversity, schools attended, campus interview assessment scores, total internships the employee had, internships with Chevron, performance ratings, promotions, and turnover. As one of Chevron's recruiters says, "Being able to see what you're doing right and what needs attention is critical to the long-term health of your organization."[85] Five principles to keep in mind when it comes to strategic workforce measures are as follows:

1. *Don't start with the measures.* While measures can be an important tool, they should not be the goal of strategic workforce planning and implementation.

2. *Don't rely on benchmarking.* By definition, benchmarking means matching what others do. Doing so will not generate competitive advantages to your organization.

3. *Don't expect measurement alone to fix problems.* While measurement can identify areas of strength and weakness in your recruitment processes, simply gathering the data is not enough to fix potential problems.

4. *Focus on the strategic impact of the workforce.* Not all individuals, teams, or divisions within an organization have the same impact on the organization's success on key goals. Focus on the places where it matters most.

5. *Measure both levels and relationships between workforce measures.* Some measures may go down when others go up. Understanding how they work together is important for getting a full picture of organizational functioning.

The key to implementing strategic recruitment is to think of these measures as a starting point rather than the goal. That is because such measures may serve to incentivize the wrong behaviors or mask important relationships with strategic implications. For example, time to hire and cost per hire are common metrics used in recruiting, and research shows a positive relationship between these metrics and firm performance. However, as Becker and colleagues note, it is important to pay attention to the outcome of measuring behavior. For example, potential efforts to later work to minimize measures might serve to encourage

Manager's Toolbox
COMMON RECRUITMENT KEY PERFORMANCE INDICATOR (KPI) METRICS

A variety of potential workforce metrics may be used to assess recruitment effectiveness. We list several of these metrics below within their recruitment stage.

Generating Applicants

- *Application completion rate percentage* (number of applicants who complete the application process/number of applicants who start the application process)
- *Qualified candidates* (those moving past the phone screen stage)
- *Source of hire* (tracking, surveys)

Maintaining Applicant Participation

- *Applicants per hire* (number of applicants hired/number of applicants who start the application process)
- *Candidate experience* (survey)
- *Time to hire* (number of days between when a person applies and accepts an offer)
- *Yield ratio* (number of applicants who move from one recruitment hurdle to the next)

Job Acceptance

- *Acceptance rate* (number of accepted offers/total number of offers)
- *Open vacancies versus positions filled*
- *Time to fill* (number of days a job is open)

After New Employee Organizational Entry

- *Cost per hire* ([internal costs + external costs]/number of hires)
- *Diversity* (qualitative and quantitative approaches)
- *Hiring manager satisfaction* (survey)
- *New hire satisfaction* (survey)
- *Performance* (track performance ratings)
- *Turnover/retention rate percentage* ([number of employees employed after 1 year/number of employees hired 1 year ago] × 100)
- *Quality of fill* (a combination of metrics such as new employee satisfaction, performance, promotion, high potential ratings, and retention).

recruiters to engage in lowering how select they are when choosing recruitment channels or actual applicants. They argue that a better idea would be to focus on other metrics such as the quality of hires. And only 23% of organizations report that their organization measures quality of hire.[86] That could mask or create a problem. For example, if recruiters are given bonuses for hiring 20% of those who apply, they could increase their percentage by making offers to applicants with fewer alternatives. Although this could help them earn a bonus, it would hurt the organization overall because weaker employees are hired. All of these measures indicate the need for an effective tracking system to gather information, and adding new information such as new hire surveys is another way to tap into key metrics such as new hire satisfaction levels. Similarly, the only way to address hiring manager satisfaction is to ask managers how they feel.

Maintaining Applicant Interest and Participation

A major consideration when it comes to the recruitment process and associated activities related to effectiveness is maintaining applicant interest and participation.[87] If an applicant withdraws from the process or goes through the process without much enthusiasm for the organization and, ultimately, turns down a job offer, recruitment has not been effective. With this in mind, we cover some key factors related to the maintenance of applicant interest and participation.

Treatment During Recruitment

Research finds that recruiter behaviors such as how personable, competent, and informative they are matter. These behaviors are related to applicant perceptions of job attributes and how they feel about the organization and job, as well as the likelihood of accepting a job offer.[88] Timing and communication are fundamentally important factors when it comes to maintaining applicant interest and participation. Research shows that, overall, job applicants like to hear back quickly and have regular status updates. Not surprisingly, the *best* applicants have the most alternatives and are also the most likely to withdraw from the hiring process if they feel they are not being treated well.[89] Firms report greater success when they begin their recruiting process earlier. To help applicants understand where they stand in the recruitment process, Disney created a hiring dashboard through which applicants can track the status of their application.[90]

Interviews

There are two types of interviews to consider. The first is the **informational interview,** which is defined as the exchange of information with the goal of learning more about the organization and its industry. If you have ever had an informal discussion with a recruiter at a job fair or interviewed an organizational insider about his or her job, you have already conducted an informational interview. The purpose of such interviews is to begin the process of getting to know more about the organization and industry and potential career opportunities in general. Even though such interviews are informal, they may still serve to influence the reactions that applicants have to that organization. Imagine you are a supply and logistics student looking to find out more about the packaging and distribution industry. You reach out to three organizations, requesting an informational interview, but only one replies. You have a great time at the interview and learn a lot. Although you are not

Informational interview The exchange of information between an individual and an organizational representative with the goal of learning more about the organization and its industry

looking for a job right now, imagine if you would be more or less likely to pursue a job with the two companies that never got back to you versus the one that did.

The other type of interview is the **selection interview,** which is what we traditionally think of as a job interview. Even though the selection interview puts the applicant "on the spot," it is also important to approach it as a two-way process. While the employee is being evaluated, he or she is also gaining insights into what it would be like to work for the interviewing organization. And the organization is also still trying to attract the applicant to the job and the organization to increase the chances that the applicant accepts a potential offer. In these ways, selection interviews also serve a recruitment purpose.

Site Visits

One important part of the recruitment and selection process for both organizations and individuals is the site visit. On a **site visit,** the job applicant physically goes to the organization's location to meet with and to be interviewed by its representatives. Site visits serve many important functions, including presenting a chance for applicants to meet key organizational members, compare their expectations to the realities encountered during the visit, and allow for them to have a more substantial set of interactions. Research shows that applicants report several benefits related to site visits, including opportunities to meet current employees, high-level organizational members, and those with similar backgrounds. In terms of site visit logistics, they report being positively influenced by being treated professionally, having a likeable site visit host, quality hotels, and the site visit being well orchestrated.[91]

Selection interview
A traditional job interview

Site visit When a job applicant agrees to physically go to the organization's location to meet with and to be interviewed by its representatives

■ **FIGURE 6.7**   Job Choice Involves Weighing Features in Terms of Attractiveness

Many factors influence an individual's job choice as they weigh a number of pros and cons associated with a given job. Examples of features are given below.

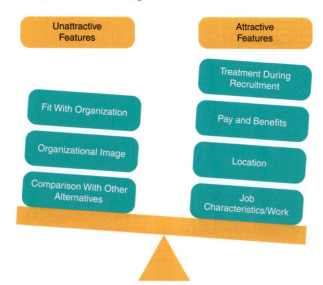

Factors Influencing Job Choice

As seen in the previous section on maintaining applicant interest and participation, poor treatment at any stage of the recruitment process can lead job applicants to withdraw. In addition, organizational and individual considerations influence job choice (see Figure 6.7).[92]

Organizational Image, Brand, and Reputation

NACE routinely surveys companies and finds that branding continues to be a key focus for university recruiting programs, and research supports the idea that organizational image affects applicants.[93] Slogans like "Work hard. Change the World," used at Amazon, help organizations signal important aspects of their culture. Being a well-regarded brand is a good problem to have, but it can make keeping up with the number of applications challenging. For example, Google receives millions of résumés each year. In 2014 alone, it received more than 3 million résumés.[94] Worried that it might alienate its brand if it relied on algorithms to decide who made the cut or not, Google modified its hiring process to ensure that human eyes look at every one of those millions of résumés.[95] And the importance of maintaining a company's brand is likely to continue. For example, the Conference Board surveyed CEOs and asked them to identify key challenges they anticipated in the coming years. At the top of the list was a need to use decision-making tools like data analytics to understand what is attractive about their brands and social media that reinforces a positive brand image.[96] Social media can also present opportunities and challenges for employment brands. The Twitter account of the Wendy's fast food chain got a great deal of attention based on online exchanges. In fact, the team who manages this account even has a publicist.[97] Research has shown that word-of-mouth opinions regarding the hiring process affect whether or not an applicant will choose a job.[98]

Organizational Fit

Research shows that applicants who highly identify with an organization are more likely to pursue jobs and to accept them if offered.[99] Organizational cultures vary a great deal, and they are not equally attractive to everyone. For example, someone attracted to a clan culture (e.g., Costco or Southwest Airlines) might be less attracted to a hierarchical culture (e.g., Walmart or Boeing). Research has found that specific values such as an organization's social and environmental responsibility are related to how attractive the company's is to job applicants.[100] Organizational fit is another consideration that job candidates take into consideration when deciding whether to accept a job.[101]

Job Features

Pay and benefits are also important considerations for decision makers. For instance, 78% of Jobvite recruiter respondents say that medical/dental coverage is the most effective perk to attract new candidates, and 65% report that offering a 401(k) plan is also helpful, followed by 44% indicating that flexible schedules and a casual dress code are also attractive to potential employees. In addition to financial aspects of employment, the actual work that will be done and how it will be done (or job characteristics) also can serve to influence decision makers. In general, people tend to prefer work that affords them autonomy, is seen as meaningful, and allows them to receive feedback.

Alternative Offers

Finally, the process of individual decision making involves comparing potential alternatives. If a job candidate has multiple offers, they may simply decide that one offer is more attractive overall than another one. The best applicants tend to have the most job alternatives. Organizations wanting to hire such individuals should consider putting their best offer forward as much as it can to attract them.

CHAPTER SUMMARY

Understanding the labor landscape makes it possible to follow the steps in the workplace planning and forecasting process, including succession planning, leadership development, assessing labor market conditions, and talent analysis. Effective recruitment begins with setting objectives to develop a strategy.

Its advantages for organizations range from increased hiring success to higher firm performance to the ability to attract a diverse set of applicants. Recruitment stages include generating applicants, assessing the quantity and quality of applicants, and accessing sources of recruitment—both internal and external. Hiring for diversity means attending to multiple kinds of diversity, including gender, race, age, veteran status, and differently abled individuals. In the process of recruitment, organizations need to comply with various laws and policies. Organizations strive to maintain applicant interest and participation so that the best applicants accept job offers. Global considerations also come into play in attracting talent. Measuring effective recruitment using metrics and analytics is also an important part of recruitment.

KEY TERMS

workforce planning   122
forecasting   123
succession planning   123
leadership development   123
succession management   124
labor market conditions   124
workforce labor shortages   124

workforce labor surplus
 (slack)   125
talent analysis   125
talent pool   125
recruitment   126
hiring manager   127
realistic job preview (RJP)   130

external recruitment   131
applicant tracking system
 (ATS)   133
informational interview   143
selection interview   144
site visit   144

$SAGE edge™

Get the tools you need to sharpen your study skills. SAGE edge offers a robust online environment featuring an impressive array of free tools and resources.

Access practice quizzes, eFlashcards, video, and multimedia at **edge.sagepub.com/bauerbrief**

HR REASONING AND DECISION-MAKING EXERCISES

EXERCISE 6.1: EMPLOYEE TURNOVER RATE

You have been with your large high-tech organization for 3 years, having joined right after earning your college degree in business. You enjoy working in human resource management on the recruitment side of things. Lately you have noticed that even though you are doing a good job at attracting applicants—you are able to keep them interested in the selection process and have established a strong acceptance rate among applicants—there is a problem. The turnover rate for employees within 18 months of being hired is at 34%. Although that isn't the highest rate in the industry, it certainly is higher than you'd like to see, and it is higher than it used to be.

You have done some initial analyses and determined that part of the issue seems to be that recruiters tell potential employees things to attract them to the organization, but the reality once they join is quite different. And especially for top performers, other options at other organizations quickly become attractive.

You have spoken with your boss, the vice president of HR, and she has authorized you to create a task force to investigate the issue further and develop a strategy to solve the root causes of the problem. She suspects that the turnover rate is a symptom of bigger problems rather than the main problem.

Questions

1. Whom do you think you need to involve in this decision? Why?
2. How should you begin to tackle this problem in terms of your approach and sources of information?
3. What data should you gather?
4. Are there experiments you might do to test potential causes and to identify different solutions?

EXERCISE 6.2: RECRUITMENT AND BEYOND

Imagine that you and a small team of two to five colleagues are working with a medium-sized retail company that is expanding internationally. Although the headquarters will remain in Columbus, Ohio, the firm is opening a second office in Japan. They want to know what your team recommends in terms of recruiting for this new 30-person office. Your team's job is to decide how to handle recruiting in the short term and long term.

Questions

1. Should your company hire locally, hire expatriate employees, use a search firm, start developing a college recruiting program in Japan, or use a different recruiting approach? Explain the advantages and disadvantages of each of these approaches.
2. What additional information would help your team decide?
3. Where will your team begin its recruitment efforts?

ETHICAL MATTERS EXERCISE: APPLICANT INFORMATION PRIVACY

Job boards have become popular with organizations and job applicants. However, one major ethical concern has to do with information privacy. Two considerations seem especially important to consider.

First, who "owns" the data that applicants input into job board systems? Although online information privacy laws vary by country, with the European Union having stricter laws than the United States, the answer to this question is not clear. Imagine a scenario in which an online job board company tracks all your job application information and personal information and then sells this research about you. This is not as far-fetched as it sounds; there are documented accounts of job boards selling résumés and e-mail addresses.

A second concern is information security. Even if an organization does not plan to share your information with others, it is possible that cybercrime could lead to your information being stolen. For example, more than 1 million Monster.com subscribers had their information stolen. This is a serious concern, given how sensitive personal information such as Social Security numbers can be for identity theft. In response, Monster.com now allows users to make their résumés completely private so that employers cannot search for you but you can still search job listings and send out résumés and applications yourself.[102]

Questions

1. How would you discuss these ethical issues with the decision makers in your organization? Are there specific policies or practices you would recommend?

2. Beyond the issues described here, what other ethical questions might you ask about online job boards? Think of them from the perspective of the job applicant, the recruiting organization, the tech company that operates the board, and any other stakeholders.

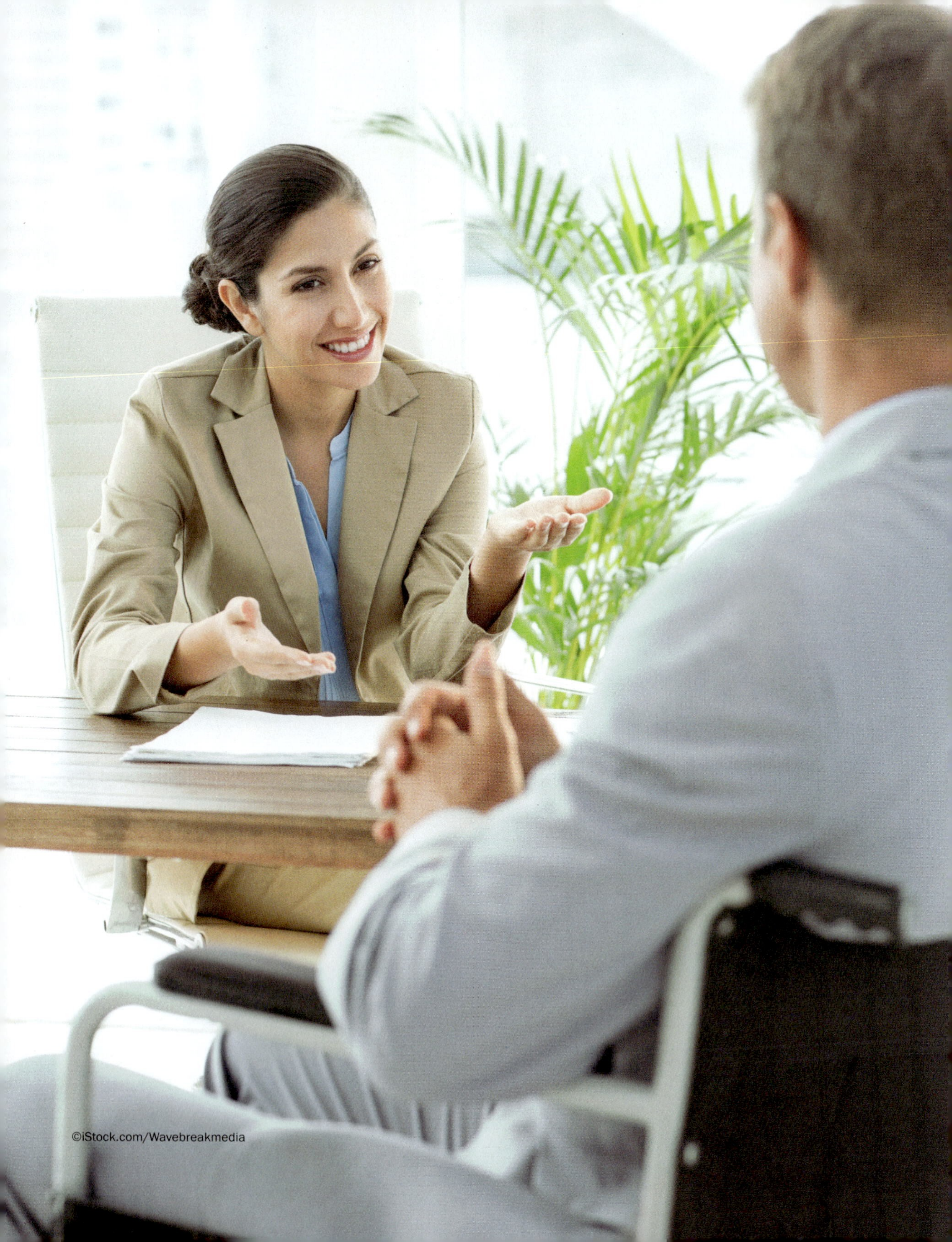

7 Selection Processes and Procedures

LEARNING OBJECTIVES

After reading and studying this chapter, you should be able to do the following:

7.1 Explain how job analysis and legal issues apply to recruitment and selection.

7.2 Describe the concepts of reliability, validity, and selection utility.

7.3 Identify the different selection procedures available for making hiring decisions and their advantages and disadvantages.

7.4 Recognize and explain key analytical, legal, ethical, and global issues associated with personnel selection.

7.5 Describe the importance of applicant reactions to selection processes and how to deploy selection procedures within organizations.

7.6 Explain how to deploy selection procedures within organizations to enhance job performance.

HR in Action: The Case of Leveraging Interviews for Hiring

One of the most common personnel selection tools is the interview. Most supervisors want to get to know job candidates and their skills prior to making a hiring decision, and most applicants expect an interview and have a positive reaction to it. But research has shown that some interview formats are better than others for predicting later job performance. As we will see in this chapter, unstructured interviews, which are simply an informal conversation between the job applicant and the employer, are not the best selection method because they are susceptible to a number of biases and are not necessarily job related.

In contrast, research shows that structured interviews, where all applicants are asked the same job-related questions, are a good selection tool. Structured interviews have grown in popularity due to the science that consistently supports them. For example, the U.S. Office of Personnel Management (OPM, which provides the U.S. government's HR functions) provides guidance for how government agencies can develop and deploy structured interviews to make good hiring decisions. In the private sector, behavioral interviews (a type of structured interview where applicants are asked how they have handled past situations) are a standard part of Google's selection procedures.[1] HRM plays an important role by guiding supervisors and managers as to how to use structured interviews to get the best talent.

Case Discussion Questions

1. What is an example of a structured interview question you would use to hire a supervisor for a customer service job?

2. What types of biases might occur when using an unstructured interview?

3. Do you think that job applicants would prefer structured or unstructured interviews? Why?

People are arguably an organization's most precious resources. They can determine an organization's success. Luckily, there is a robust science on how to choose the employees who best fit the job and the organization and how to do so in a fair, legally defensible way that aligns with an organization's strategy. This chapter reviews the science of employee selection, including established data-analytic techniques for enhancing the quality of hiring decisions. It also discusses the wide variety of selection procedures that are available to support hiring decisions and talent acquisition.

Well-developed selection systems bring talented individuals into the organization, who in turn can help the organization realize strategic objectives. In fact, Jeff Bezos, CEO of Amazon.com, is quoted as saying, "I'd rather interview 50 people and not hire anyone than hire the wrong person."[2] And the Mayo Clinic takes 3 years before it decides if a doctor has what it takes to remain there.[3]

There are many choices when it comes to selection methods, including personality tests, background checks, and interviews—to name a few. But how useful are each of these methods, and which are the best? What are the ethical and legal issues surrounding the use of these methods?

Setting the Stage for Selection: Job Analysis, Recruitment, and Legal Issues

LO 7.1 Explain how job analysis and legal issues apply to recruitment and selection.

Job Analysis

As noted in Chapter 5, job analysis and competency modeling involve the identification of the tasks that make up a job and the KSAOs that are required for the job. Job analysis is important for choosing selection procedures because different selection procedures capture certain KSAOs more effectively than others. To give a simple example, if you determined that a product-design job required engineering skills and teamwork, you would want to use hiring procedures that reflect these requirements. You might consider a personality test that reflects a person's abilities to work well as part of a team, and you might include relevant engineering and teamwork questions in the job interview. As an example, PepsiCo and Starwood Hotels and Resorts are using analytics to understand the profile of their most successful current employees to which selection procedures to use for screening future candidates.[4] Keep in mind that some sort of job analysis is also legally required for selection procedures, and it is also recommended by professional guidelines.[5]

Using Recruitment to Enhance Hiring Decisions

Chapter 6 discussed recruitment as a key way of increasing the odds of hiring the best employees. (As a reminder, see the recruitment funnel in Figure 7.1.) The goal is to increase the *size* of the applicant pool to increase the odds of selecting the best employees. For example, all things being equal, being able to choose from among 10 job candidates will increase a company's odds of hiring the best person, as opposed to being able to choose from only one candidate. But a second key goal of recruitment is to increase the number of *qualified* applicants. This is why it is so important during recruitment to focus on both getting a large number of people to apply *and* making sure that they are the best qualified applicants.[6] The recruitment and selection funnel decreases the number of candidates considered from the time of initial recruitment through the final hiring process, leaving only the very best candidates to hire.

Legal and Ethical Issues in Hiring

Chapter 4 discussed the importance of legal issues to HR decision making. Perhaps the area in which legal issues are most evident is in selection. As a result of Title VII of the Civil Rights Act of 1964 and the later court cases interpreting it (referred to as "case law"), a significant body of laws and legal guidelines has developed to guide employers in choosing, developing, and administering hiring procedures. To help employers make sense of this large, often complex set of laws and court cases, the EEOC, Department of Justice, and Department of Labor developed the *Uniform Guidelines on Employee Selection Procedures* (1978). Although the *Uniform Guidelines* are not technically laws in themselves, they do summarize the laws up until that time and are typically treated by the courts as if they were law. As described in Chapter 4, the *Uniform Guidelines* provide substantial legal guidance to employers on the implementation of recruitment programs and the determination of whether a test has adverse impact against protected groups, for example, by using the 4/5ths or 80% rule in terms of hiring ratios. We encourage you to review the material in Chapter 4 on adverse impact and how to calculate it, as it is a critical issue in understanding the implementation of selection procedures. In addition, the *Uniform Guidelines* set legal standards on a broad range of selection-related issues such as establishing the technical adequacy of selection procedures, setting cutoff scores, promoting diversity in organizations, and monitoring the diversity of an employer's applicant flow and workforce. Note that in addition to these laws and government guidelines, there are also professional guidelines on the development and administration of selection procedures, published by the Society for Industrial and Organizational Psychology (SIOP's *Principles for the Validation and Use of Personnel Selection Procedures*, 2018).[7]

■ **FIGURE 7.1**   The Recruitment and Selection Funnel

The recruitment and selection funnel decreases the number of candidates considered from the time of recruitment through hiring, leaving only the very best candidates to hire.

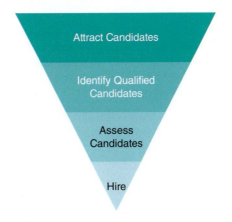

Attract Candidates

Identify Qualified Candidates

Assess Candidates

Hire

Data-Driven Decision Criteria for Choosing Selection Procedures: Reliability, Validity, and Utility

LO 7.2   Describe the concepts of reliability, validity, and selection utility.

Selection procedures based only on the "gut" impressions of hiring managers can be a legal liability for employers. And research shows that this approach generally results in poor hiring decisions.[8] However, selection procedures based on systematic data collection and analysis not only can result in more legally defensible hiring procedures but also lead to better hiring decisions. This requires attention to the reliability, validity, and utility (dollar value) of selection procedures.

Ensuring the Quality of Selection Measures: Reliability and Validity

Some selection procedures are of higher quality than others. Two concepts come into play in determining this.

Reliability
The consistency of measurement

Validity
The accuracy of a measure, or the degree to which an assessment measures what it is supposed to measure

- **Reliability** is how consistent or dependable selection procedures are in measuring something, such as a skill or ability.

- **Validity** is the accuracy of a measure and the degree to which it measures what it is supposed to measure. Within the selection context, this is generally how well the selection procedure can predict actual job performance (see Figure 7.2).[9] Legal and technical guidelines for assessing validity are described in the *Uniform Guidelines on Employee Selection Procedures* (see Chapter 4) as well as in professional guidelines (SIOP *Principles*).[10]

Spotlight on Legal Issues
UNDERSTANDING REASONABLE ACCOMMODATION

Question. If an applicant has a disability and will need an accommodation for the job interview, does the Americans with Disabilities Act (ADA) require an employer to provide them with one?

Answer. Employers are required to provide "reasonable accommodation" (appropriate changes and adjustments) to enable applicants to be considered for a job opening. Reasonable accommodation may also be required to enable them to perform a job,

gain access to the workplace, and enjoy the "benefits and privileges" of employment available to employees without disabilities. *An employer cannot refuse to consider an applicant because the person requires a reasonable accommodation to compete for or perform a job.*

Question. Can an employer refuse to provide an applicant with an accommodation because it is too difficult or too expensive?

Answer. An employer does not have to provide a specific accommodation if it would cause an "undue hardship" that would require significant difficulty or expense. *If the requested accommodation causes an undue hardship, the employer still would be required to provide another accommodation that does not.*

Question. What are some examples of "reasonable accommodations" that may be needed during the hiring process?

Answer. Reasonable accommodation can take many forms, such as

- providing written materials in large print, braille, or audiotape;

- providing readers or sign language interpreters; and

- ensuring that recruitment, interviews, tests, and other components of the application process are held in accessible locations.

Question. When does an applicant have to tell an employer that they need an accommodation for the hiring process?

Answer. It is best for applicants to *let an employer know as soon as they realize that they will need a reasonable accommodation* for some aspect of the hiring process.

Question. How do applicants request a reasonable accommodation?

Answer. They must inform the employer that they need some sort of change or adjustment to the application/interviewing process because of their medical condition.

Source: Modified from material developed by the U.S. Equal Employment Opportunity Commission. (n.d.). Job applicants and the Americans with Disabilities Act. https://www.eeoc.gov/facts/jobapplicant.html

The validity of personnel selection procedures is one of the most important metrics used in HR decision making. Organizations that understand and ensure validity of selection procedures through analytics have a competitive advantage. Specifically, if organizations choose selection procedures that are highly predictive of job performance, they are more likely to make good hires. Being able to show a test's validity is also key to its legal defensibility.

Selection Utility

Another factor to consider when hiring is the **utility** of selection decisions, or the monetary value of using a selection procedure. Which factors affect utility?

- One of the most important ways to increase selection utility is to be sure that selection procedures are valid. If selection procedures are not valid, it is not worth taking the time and money to use them.

- Second, the selection ratio, or the number of job vacancies relevant to the number of applicants, also affects the utility of selection procedures. Suppose you had two job vacancies and only two job applicants. It may not be worth the trouble to use any selection procedure other than to be sure that the applicants were minimally qualified and not a risk to the organization, because you know that you will need to hire both of these applicants to fill the two vacancies. Rather, when there are

Utility
The monetary value of an HR function (e.g., a selection procedure)

■ **FIGURE 7.2**   Reliability and Validity

Reliability
Consistency or dependability of measurement; a necessary condition for validity

Validity
The degree to which a test or other selection procedure measures what it is supposed to measure

more applicants relative to the number of vacancies, it is worth taking the time and money to use a selection procedure to select the best candidate.

- Third is the cost of the selection procedure. All other things being equal, there is greater utility in using a cheaper selection procedure than one that is more expensive.

- Finally, if the job is of high value to the organization, the utility of using good selection procedures increases even further. For instance, a city government might decide that a test for emergency dispatchers

has high utility because it could save lives. For example, the CritiCall test, which is used by many public-sector organizations to hire emergency dispatchers, was found in a study of the Florida Highway Patrol to predict the performance of dispatchers.[11]

Selection Procedures

LO 7.3   Identify the different selection procedures available for making hiring decisions and their advantages and disadvantages.

Many selection procedures are available to employers. Each of these selection procedures has advantages and disadvantages in terms of validity (how well it predicts job performance), utility (its cost), and its likelihood to cause adverse impact and thus affect the diversity of the organization. Keep in mind that there is no best selection procedure for choosing applicants. Also, some combination of selection procedures will usually provide the best prediction of job candidates. Throughout this section, you will want to refer to the summary of selection procedures in Table 7.1.

Interviews

The interview is the most commonly used selection procedure. Due to the popularity of interviews and their long history, a large amount of research has examined the effectiveness of interviews in selection. Furthermore, there are a number of recommended best practices for enhancing the validity of selection interviews.

Unstructured interview
When the interviewer has a conversation with a job applicant with no fixed set of questions for each applicant

Unstructured Interviews

The interview format that has been used for hiring employees for the longest time is the **unstructured interview**, in which the interviewer (e.g., a hiring manager or supervisor) has a conversation with the job applicant. There is no fixed set of questions for each applicant. In fact, different applicants are likely to be asked different questions, and the questions may not necessarily be particularly job related. Not surprisingly, the unstructured interview

TABLE 7.1 A Summary of Selection Procedures, Their Validity, and Practical Considerations for Their Use

SELECTION PROCEDURE	VALIDITY (AVERAGE CORRELATION WITH JOB PERFORMANCE)	APPLICANT REACTIONS[a]	PRACTICAL CONSIDERATIONS FOR USING THEM
Structured interviews	Large (.44–.51)[b]	***	Behavioral interviews ("What have you done in the past?") may predict job performance slightly better than situational interviews ("What would you do in this situation?").[c]
Unstructured interviews	Medium (.33–.38)[d]	***	The ability of unstructured interviews to predict job performance may vary because of inconsistency across applicants and interviewer biases.
Personality tests	Small (.11–.25)[e]	**	Although personality tests have been criticized for having low validity, they are low-cost assessments with low adverse impact. Validity can be enhanced by telling the applicant to think about how they are "at work" when responding.
Integrity tests	Medium (.26–.47)[f]	*	Solid predictors of counterproductive work behavior. Inexpensive, with fairly low adverse impact.
General cognitive ability	Large (.51)[g]	**	One of the most consistently valid predictors of job performance. Low cost. However, they can have adverse impact against certain ethnic groups.
Specific cognitive abilities (e.g., clerical ability, mechanical ability)	Varies	**	Validity varies by the specific type of cognitive ability assessed. Certain cognitive ability tests may have adverse impact (e.g., mechanical ability and women).
Work samples	Large (.54)[h]	***	Work samples are highly correlated with job performance and preferred by applicants. Due to high administrative costs, work samples may be administered as a final hurdle to a smaller group of finalists rather than to all applicants.

(Continued)

(Continued)

Situational judgment tests (SJTs)	Small to medium (.19–.43)[j]	***	Solid validity and appealing to applicants.
Assessment centers	Medium (.45)[j]	***	Work samples are often used to assess manager candidates for promotion. Although they are expensive to administer, they may serve not only as a predictor of job performance but as a training and development tool as well.
Biographical data	Medium to large (.37–.52)[k]	**	Practical method for predicting job performance for large numbers of applicants. Primary costs are in the initial research and development for a particular company or industry.

Notes: Correlations between .10 and .29 are considered small compared to correlations between .30 and .49, which are considered medium, and those between .50 and above, which are considered large. Most preferred by applicants = ***; preferred by applicants = **; least preferred by applicants = *.

[a]Anderson, N., Salgado, J. F., & Hülsheger, U. R. (2010). Applicant reactions in selection: Comprehensive meta-analysis into reaction generalization versus situational specificity. *International Journal of Selection and Assessment, 18,* 291–304; Hausknecht, J. P., Day, D. V., & Thomas, S. C. (2004). Applicant reactions to selection procedures: An updated model and meta-analysis. *Personnel Psychology, 57,* 639–683.

[b]McDaniel, M. A., Whetzel, D. L., Schmidt, F. L., & Maurer, S. D. (1994). The validity of employment interviews: A comprehensive review and meta-analysis. *Journal of Applied Psychology, 79,* 599–616; Schmidt, F. L., & Hunter, J. E. (1998). The validity and utility of selection methods in personnel psychology: Practical and theoretical implications of 85 years of research findings. *Psychological Bulletin, 124,* 262–274.

[c]Levashina, J., Hartwell, C. J., Morgeson, F. P., & Campion, M. A. (2014). The structured employment interview: Narrative and quantitative review of the research literature. *Personnel Psychology, 67,* 241–293.

[d]McDaniel, M. A., Whetzel, D. L., Schmidt, F. L., & Maurer, S. D. (1994). The validity of employment interviews: A comprehensive review and meta-analysis. *Journal of Applied Psychology, 79,* 599–616; Schmidt, F. L., & Hunter, J. E. (1998). The validity and utility of selection methods in personnel psychology: Practical and theoretical implications of 85 years of research findings. *Psychological Bulletin, 124,* 262–274.

[e]Shaffer, J. A., & Postlethwaite, B. E. (2012). A matter of context: A meta-analytic investigation of the relative validity of contextualized and noncontextualized personality measures. *Personnel Psychology, 65,* 445–493.

[f]Ones, D. S., Viswesvaran, C., & Schmidt, F. L. (1993). Comprehensive meta-analysis of integrity test validities: Findings and implications for personnel selection and theories of job performance. *Journal of Applied Psychology, 78,* 679–703; Van Iddekinge, C. H., Roth, P. L., Raymark, P. H., & Odle-Dusseau, H. N. (2012). The criterion-related validity of integrity tests: An updated meta-analysis. *Journal of Applied Psychology, 97,* 499–530.

[g]Schmidt, F. L., & Hunter, J. E. (1998). The validity and utility of selection methods in personnel psychology: Practical and theoretical implications of 85 years of research findings. *Psychological Bulletin, 124,* 262–274.

[h]Hunter, J. E., & Hunter, R. F. (1984). Validity and utility of alternative predictors of job performance. *Psychological Bulletin, 96,* 72–98; Schmidt, F. L., & Hunter, J. E. (1998). The validity and utility of selection methods in personnel psychology: Practical and theoretical implications of 85 years of research findings. *Psychological Bulletin, 124,* 262–274.

[i]Christian, M. S., Edwards, B. D., & Bradley, J. C. (2010). Situational judgment tests: Constructs assessed and a meta-analysis of their criterion-related validities. *Personnel Psychology, 63,* 83–117.

[j]Arthur, W., Day, E. A., McNelly, T. L., & Edens, P. S. (2003). A meta-analysis of the criterion-related validity of assessment center dimensions. *Personnel Psychology, 56,* 125–153.

[k]Hunter, J. E., & Hunter, R. F. (1984). Validity and utility of alternative predictors of job performance. *Psychological Bulletin, 96,* 72–98; Vinchur, A. J., Schippmann, J. S., Switzer, F. S., III, & Roth, P. L. (1998). A meta-analytic review of predictors of job performance for salespeople. *Journal of Applied Psychology, 83,* 586–597.

has relatively low validity in terms of predicting job performance. And because different job applicants may be asked different questions, it is hard to compare the responses of different applicants, and there is a definite risk of applicants being treated unfairly or introducing interviewer biases. For these reasons, the unstructured interview has largely fallen out of favor regarding selection, at least in terms of being the primary basis for hiring decisions.

That said, unstructured interviews are likely to continue to be part of most hiring decisions, and this is not necessarily a bad thing as long as they are used wisely. It is hard to imagine a situation in which a hiring manager or supervisor would not want to have the opportunity to have a casual conversation with a job applicant prior to hiring them. And unstructured interviews may be helpful to sell the applicant on the job, to give the applicant a realistic job preview (see Chapter 6), and to make an impression regarding the specific job and the organization.[12] Unstructured interviews may also be a good way to assess interpersonal skills and some personality traits. In fact, it has been argued that unstructured interviews are simply measuring different characteristics than structured interviews. These structured interviews are much more focused on job-related behaviors and skills.[13]

Structured Interviews

HR researchers and practitioners began to think of different ways to approach selection interviewing, with all job applicants asked the same, job-related questions. This approach, known as the **structured interview**, has been found to have good validity in making hiring decisions (see Table 7.2).[14]

There are two main types of structured interviews:

- In the **situational interview**, job applicants are asked what they would do in a hypothetical work-related situation. For example, applicants for a supervisory role might be asked, "What would you do if you had an employee whose performance suddenly decreased? How would you handle the situation?" This approach might be more appropriate when job applicants have little work experience.

- In the **behavioral interview**, applicants are asked how they handled a work-related situation in the past. As we noted in our opening case, Google is a leader in the selection space, and behavioral interviews are part of its selection procedures.[15] For the supervisor position, applicants might be asked, "What have you done when you had an employee whose performance suddenly decreased? How did you handle the situation?"

In the Manager's Toolbox that follows, we give some advice on how to use structured interviews to make good hiring decisions.

Structured interview
An interview in which all job applicants are asked the same, job-related questions

Situational interview
A type of structured interview in which job applicants are asked what they would do in a hypothetical work-related situation

Behavioral interview
A type of structured selection interview that uses questions about how applicants handled a work-related situation in the past

©iStock.com/BraunS

Interviews are the most commonly used selection procedure, and there is a long history of research on how to make them most effective. Perhaps the most important finding of this research is that increasing the structure of the interview—such as asking all candidates the same job-related questions—can significantly increase the validity of the interview in predicting job performance.

TABLE 7.2   Structured Interview Questions With Rating Scales

You and a coworker are collaborating on a project that is due in 10 days. You are beginning to fall behind because your coworker is not working quickly enough. How would you handle this?

Rating scale:

1—Candidate either ignores the issue completely or handles it in way that makes things worse (e.g., confronts the worker in a negative way).

2

3—Candidate recognizes the problem, but they develop a suboptimal solution, such as telling their boss.

4

5—Candidate develops a constructive solution, such as speaking with the worker to find out what may be wrong, what he or she themselves may be doing to slow things down, or what they can do to help develop a solution.

Tell us about a time when you were dealing with a difficult customer. How did you handle the situation?

1—Candidate describes that they did something to make the situation worse, such as ignoring the customer or being rude back.

2

3—Candidate chooses a suboptimal solution such as passing the customer on to their supervisor.

4

5—Candidate worked with the customer to figure out what the problem is and to come up with a mutually acceptable solution.

Manager's Toolbox
HOW TO ADD MORE INTERVIEW STRUCTURE

Interview "structure" means asking the same questions of all interviewees. But what else is meant by "structure"? The following best practices identified in the research make selection interviews more structured and thus more likely to lead to good hiring decisions.

1. *Develop job-related questions that are asked to all applicants.* This is one of the most important ways to increase interview validity. Consider what behaviors are performed on the job and what KSAOs are needed to perform them. These behaviors and skills can be derived from a job analysis or competency model as well as critical incidents faced by employees on the job.

2. *Treat all interviewees consistently.* To the extent that all job candidates are interviewed under the same conditions—for example, in the same place and by the same interviewers—better information can be gained to compare job applicants.

3. *Train interviewers.* Train interviewers on how to interview applicants, and be sure that all interviewers use the same procedures when interviewing and evaluating job candidates.

4. *Have more than one interviewer interview each applicant for consistency.*

5. *Have interviewers take notes.* This allows interviewers to check back as they compare different candidates, and it allows interviewers to compare their ratings with each other.

6. *Develop rating scales for each interview question.* Providing rating scales can be one of the most important ways to increase the validity of interviews. (Refer to Table 7.2, which shows rating scale examples for structured interview questions.) Robust rating scales also provide interviewers with a consistent framework for rating job candidates.[16]

Finally, here are a couple of current issues that come up when using interviews for selection:

- Online interviews using video are becoming increasingly common. However, research has suggested that interviewer ratings may be lower in technology-mediated interviews and that applicant reactions to the process may be lower for interviews that are not done in person.[17]

- The "group interview," in which multiple candidates are interviewed at one time, has seen increased use by organizations. Little empirical research on the validity of this approach has emerged in the literature, however, and we suggest caution in terms of having multiple interviewees compete within the same interview unless such competition is part of the job.[18]

Personality Tests

Five-Factor Model (FFM) or the "Big Five"

Since the early 1990s, there has been a growing interest in personality tests for use in selection, with 62% of employers recently reporting that they use personality tests in hiring.[19]

TABLE 7.3   Example of Big Five Items

Openness to Experience	Conscientiousness	Extraversion
Have a rich vocabulary.	Am always prepared.	Am the life of the party.
Have a vivid imagination.	Pay attention to details.	Feel comfortable around people.
Have excellent ideas.	Get chores done right away.	Start conversations.
Am quick to understand things.	Like order.	Talk to a lot of different people at parties.
Use difficult words.	Follow a schedule.	Don't mind being the center of attention.
Spend time reflecting on things.	Am exacting in my work.	
Am full of ideas.		

(Continued)

TABLE 7.3   (Continued)

Agreeableness	Neuroticism
Am interested in people.	Get stressed out easily.
Sympathize with others' feelings.	Worry about things.
Have a soft heart.	Am easily disturbed.
Take time out for others.	Get upset easily.
Feel others' emotions.	Change my mood a lot.
Make people feel at ease.	Have frequent mood swings.
	Get irritated easily.
	Often feel blue.

Note: 1–5 response scale, from "very inaccurate" to "very accurate"; the person would respond about how they perceive themselves to be.[20]

Much of this interest has been focused on the five-factor model of personality. The five dimensions of the **five-factor model (FFM)** ("Big Five") of personality are related to a number of job performance dimensions. The Big Five are best remembered by the acronym *OCEAN*: Openness to Experience, Conscientiousness, Extraversion, Agreeableness, and Neuroticism. Openness to Experience has to do with a person's inquisitiveness and willingness to learn new things and relates to employees' performance in training programs. Conscientiousness includes traits such as dependability and achievement orientation and relates to job performance across most jobs. Extraversion, which includes traits such as sociability, relates to jobs such as sales and management. Agreeableness is the degree to which the person is kind, is sensitive, and pays attention to others' feelings. Finally, Neuroticism (or its opposite, emotional stability) relates to anxiety and worry.[21] Table 7.3 shows sample items for each of the Big Five dimensions. Numerous tests of the Big Five are available.[22]

Interest in the use of personality tests in selection has grown because most are relatively easy, quick, and inexpensive to administer, and they have generally been found to have lower adverse impact than other selection tests such as cognitive ability tests (i.e., they are less likely to have a negative impact on an organization's diversity). However, their validity is not as high as some other selection procedures such as structured interviews.[23] Note that for legal reasons, personality tests developed to make clinical diagnoses—that is, those not focused on normal adult personality like the FFM—should not be used for hiring except under very specific, limited circumstances.

In addition to the Big Five, other personality variables that have been found to be useful in selection include proactive personality; proactive people tend to recognize and act on opportunities at work. Research has shown, for instance, that proactive personality is a good predictor of performance of real estate agents, over and above conscientiousness and extraversion.[24] Another personality variable that has gained research attention as a selection procedure is adaptability, which has to do with a person's ability to adjust

Five-factor model (FFM)
A model of normal adult personality that includes the dimensions of Openness to Experience, Conscientiousness, Extraversion, Agreeableness, and Neuroticism

to new situations.[25] Although the use of adaptability in selection research is still early, interest in this personality variable for selection is expected to grow given the dynamic nature of work today.

Integrity Tests

The use of polygraph (lie detector) tests was generally outlawed in the 1980s except for very limited circumstances, such as for certain job applicants in security service firms and pharmaceutical manufacturers.[26] Instead, employers are screening out applicants who are at the highest risk of exhibiting these negative behaviors on the job by using self-report **integrity tests**.

Some personality variables can be useful for predicting job performance in certain, specific jobs. For example, proactive personality has been shown to predict the job performance of real estate agents over and above conscientiousness and extraversion.

There are two primary types of integrity test formats: personality-based integrity tests and overt integrity tests (see Table 7.4). Personality-based integrity tests are more subtle in their wording, and the "correct answer" may not be obvious to test takers. Most personality-based integrity tests are considered a function of conscientiousness, neuroticism, and agreeableness, plus an additional personality dimension referred to as "honesty-humility."[27] Overt integrity tests, in contrast, ask the test taker to give their opinions

Integrity test
A test specifically developed to assess applicants' tendency toward counterproductive and antisocial behavior

TABLE 7.4   Examples of Overt and Personality-Based Integrity Test Items

SAMPLE INTEGRITY TEST ITEMS	
OVERT INTEGRITY TEST ITEMS	**PERSONALITY-BASED (COVERT) INTEGRITY TEST ITEMS**
I have used illegal drugs at work.	It's OK to make some mistakes when you work quickly.
It's OK to hit a coworker if they yell at you.	You need to take risks sometimes if you want to get the job done.
I have stolen money from my employer.	I am always seeking excitement and thrills in my life.
If a coworker is rude to me, I would do something to his car.	I don't get along with other people because I always stand up for my rights.

about negative behaviors at work (e.g., theft), whether such behaviors are acceptable, and whether they have engaged in these behaviors themselves.

There have been a number of meta-analyses on the topic of integrity tests, and the findings are that these tests correlate .47 with a number of negative work behaviors such as violence and theft.[28] Although there is still some difference of opinion among testing experts on just how valid these tests are for predicting performance, the research generally shows that integrity tests are valid, can pass legal muster, and provide value to employers trying to screen out job applicants who pose a risk to the organization and employees.[29] Integrity tests seem to exhibit low adverse impact.[30] Integrity tests are perhaps best considered in combination with other selection procedures to screen out job applicants who are most likely to be difficult employees at work.

Cognitive Ability Tests

Cognitive ability tests have a long history in personnel selection, going back into the early 20th century. Here we define a **cognitive ability test** as an assessment of the ability to "perceive, process, evaluate, compare, create, understand, manipulate, or generally think about information and ideas."[31] On the positive side, cognitive ability tests have been demonstrated to be one of the best predictors of job performance across a range of job types, with a correlation with job performance as high as .51.[32] They are also fairly inexpensive.

On the negative side, cognitive ability tests are prone to lead to adverse impact, with the mean score of certain groups (e.g., Blacks, Hispanics) being significantly lower than the mean score of other groups (e.g., Whites, Asians), even if there is still substantial overlap between the scores of these different subgroups. As a result, many employers prefer to avoid the use of cognitive ability tests, for reasons of diversity and the possibility of legal challenges.[33]

Employers use a few different types of cognitive ability tests. First are tests of general cognitive ability, sometimes referred to as "*g*" by psychologists.[34] One test of general cognitive ability that has a long history in personnel selection is the Wonderlic Personnel Test. The Wonderlic is a 50-item, 12-minute test that includes items such as math reasoning and verbal tasks.[35] For example, Subway requires that prospective Subway franchisees take and get a certain score on the Wonderlic Personnel Test.[36]

Cognitive ability test A measure of the ability to perceive, process, evaluate, compare, create, understand, manipulate, or generally think about information and ideas

In addition to tests of general cognitive ability, tests of specific cognitive abilities, such as tests of mechanical ability and clerical ability, have been designed for use with specific job types in which these abilities have been found to be important through a job analysis. The adverse impact issue with these tests of specific cognitive abilities varies by the type of test. For example, tests of mechanical ability have been found to have some adverse impact against women.[37]

Emotional intelligence (EI) One's ability to recognize and appraise emotions in oneself and others and behave accordingly

Finally, tests of **emotional intelligence (EI)** have recently gained attention as predictors of job performance. EI is defined as one's ability to recognize and appraise emotions in oneself and others and behave accordingly.[38] Research has found that EI tests are better predictors of job performance when jobs are high in emotional labor. Research also suggests that certain types of EI tests do not predict job performance over and above traditional tests like personality and cognitive ability; in other words, this research suggests that the concept of EI is nothing new.[39]

Spotlight on Data and Analytics
GAMIFICATION OF PERSONNEL SELECTION PROCEDURES

Gamification, or the transformation of an ordinary activity into a game-like activity to increase engagement, motivation, and competition, including scoring, has taken hold in a variety of fields from advertising to eLearning.

Gamification of personnel selection procedures is now drawing increased interest from employers. For example, conventional hiring procedures might require job applicants to take tests of cognitive ability or personality. In gamified selection procedures, applicants might participate

in a game activity to assess factors such as cognitive processing speed or risk tolerance. The idea is that such gamified assessments could attract job applicants who might not otherwise take conventional selection tests.

Gamification of selection procedures is still fairly new, and more research is needed. The validity of gamified assessments for predicting job performance relative to traditional selection tests is still relatively unknown, and some applicants may not like gamified selection procedures.[40]

Work Samples, Situational Judgment Tests (SJTs), and Assessment Centers

In this section, we describe three different "families" of selection procedures that directly sample a person's potential job performance and their fit for the job: work samples, assessment centers, and situational judgment tests (SJTs).

Work Samples

A **work sample** is what the name implies: a sample or example of the work produced by an applicant. Suppose an organization needs to hire a computer programmer. The hiring manager might meet with each applicant and give them a short coding task to see how well they do. The hiring manager then has SMEs (current programmers) evaluate how well the applicants perform on the coding task. For example, Google uses coding exercises as part of its selection procedures when hiring engineers.[41] As another example, JetBlue Airways used a job analysis to identify the key skills employees in its call center needed, and once it identified the desired KSAOs, it developed a call simulation test to use in the hiring process. With the use of this selection procedure, turnover decreased by 25%.[42]

Work samples have good validity.[43] The research shows that they are correlated about .54 with work performance. And applicants tend to like work samples, seeing them as very fair because they are obviously job related. However, one drawback of work samples is that they are more expensive than other methods, usually requiring that one person at a time go through the assessment. Given the cost of work samples—in terms of their individual administration and scoring—they are usually placed at the end of a series of cheaper selection hurdles.

Work sample
A sample or example of the work produced by a job applicant

Situational Judgment Tests (SJTs)

The value of work samples in terms of their validity and attractiveness to applicants led HR researchers to consider cheaper alternatives. This is where the concept of **situational judgment tests**, or **SJTs**, comes into play. SJTs capture some of the realism of work sample tests but in a format that can be used more easily with large numbers of applicants. An SJT might present the applicant with a scenario, in either paper or video format, and then ask the respondent to choose a series of alternatives. While many SJTs use a written, multiple-choice format, others ask candidates to choose which video response seems most appropriate, and others use an open-ended format that must be scored later.[44] Additional examples of SJT items are given in Table 7.5. Because of their relatively low administration costs, SJTs have gained popularity. In fact, you may have taken an SJT when you applied for a job. In addition, they have solid validity, with correlations with job performance of .19 to .43. For instance, one SJT focused on medical school applicants' predicted work performance years later.[45]

Situational judgment tests (SJTs)

A test that captures some of the realism of work sample tests but in a format (e.g., multiple-choice) that can be used more easily with large numbers of applicants

Assessment Centers

So far, we have described work-sample types of assessments that can be used for a large number of job types. In addition, a specific type of work sample, known as an **assessment center**, was developed to assess management skills. Assessment centers were first pioneered

Assessment center

A specific type of work sample, often used for manager selection

---

TABLE 7.5   Situational Judgment Test (SJT) Items for a Retail Clothing Job

You are helping a customer choose a tie. Another customer approaches you and interrupts your conversation. What would be the best thing to do?

  a. Ignore the customer who interrupted you.

  b. Tell the customer who interrupted you that you are busy and that he should not interrupt a conversation.

  c. Kindly tell the second person that you would be glad to help him in a few minutes.

  d. Explain to the first customer that you have given him all the time you can and you need to help others.

You have a friend who admires the clothing in the store where you work. She tells you that, although she doesn't have much money, she would really like to have a blouse from the store. Which of the following would be the best thing for you to do?

  a. Tell your friend when you see a sale on the kind of blouse she likes.

  b. Ask your boss if there are any extra blouses in the store so you can give one to your friend.

  c. Take one of the blouses and give it to your friend.

A customer comes in to return a piece of clothing that is obviously defective. He is very angry about the failure of the item. Which of the following would be the best thing to do?

  a. Tell the customer that this is not your fault personally, and so he should not be mean to you.

  b. Tell the customer that you can replace the item and also give him a free gift card to make up for the inconvenience.

  c. Try to calm down the customer by asking him to explain what happened and then work with him to find a solution.

in U.S. businesses in the 1960s at AT&T, and their popularity has grown considerably over the years as a means of promoting people into management positions. Note that an assessment center is not an actual place maintained by the company. Rather, center assessments are typically carried out over a series of days at a remote site provided by the organization, such as a hotel.

A common type of assessment center exercise includes the role-play, in which candidates might be asked to handle a situation with an actor or one of the assessors. For example, the candidate might be told that they will need to interact with an employee whose performance has declined in recent months, getting to the bottom of what the problem is and developing a solution. Another common assessment center exercise is the in-basket or inbox, in which a candidate is told to provide responses to a series of e-mails that they have received that morning. Generally, assessment center exercises are evaluated by at least two raters, typically expert managers or trained psychologists.

Not surprisingly, assessment centers are good predictors, correlating .37 to .45 with job performance.[46] And not only can they be used to make promotion decisions, but they are also good for training and development purposes, so that management candidates can see their strengths and weaknesses and determine where further development is needed. On the other hand, assessment centers are expensive, as they require the development of detailed, realistic materials and the use of teams of trained experts.[47]

Doug Reynolds, PhD, is executive vice president at Development Dimensions International (DDI), where he directs the product development and technology functions. His department develops and implements software-based assessment centers, testing, and learning products for *Fortune* 500 companies. His consulting work focuses on the implementation of assessments in organizations, and he publishes on topics related to the intersection of I-O psychology and technology. Dr. Reynolds is a past president of the Society for Industrial and Organizational Psychology (2012–2013).[48]

Biographical Data and Related Data Collection Methods

In addition, employers can also collect useful information about job applicants' backgrounds to make selection decisions.

Training and Experience Forms

One way of collecting applicant background information is training and experience (T&E) forms, which ask applicants about their work-related education, training, and experience. Applicants' training and experience are then tabulated and scored based on job analysis information and input from SMEs. T&E forms have a long history in personnel selection, especially for government jobs. There is considerable variability in their validity in predicting job performance: The correlation between T&E scores and job performance ranges from .11 to .45.[49]

Biodata

Employers can also use **biographical data (biodata)** as a predictor of job performance. Typically, organizations that use biodata items have done empirical research to determine that the items are statistically related to job performance. This method assumes that past

Biographical data (biodata)
Information about a job applicant based on their personal history that can be used to make selection decisions

behavior—whether at work or even outside of work—is the best predictor of future behavior. For instance, a retail employer might be concerned that the high turnover rate for certain jobs is causing serious financial losses for the company. For this reason, they may ask applicants about how many jobs they have held in the past 3 years. They would then examine the relationship between the number of jobs a person has held and how long they remain on the job. Through this research, the company discovers that people who have held more than four jobs in the past 3 years are likely to quit in fewer than 6 months. In other words, this question allows employers to decide which applicants are the best risk for staying with the organization.

In addition, some biodata items focus on nonwork experiences as predictors of work performance. As an early example of the use of biodata, in World War II, the U.S. military found that one item—whether someone played with model airplanes when growing up—was a good predictor of how well they performed in flight training. The idea was that an applicant who played with model airplanes was interested in flying and a good bet for succeeding in flight school.

Moving to recent times, a sports equipment retailer might find, through research, that people who participated in a range of different sports during their school years are the best at helping customers. This might be because these applicants are knowledgeable about a range of different sports and sports equipment. This knowledge would allow them to help customers make good decisions in their purchases. In short, employers can research a number of different types of background questions that they suspect will predict job performance. They can then choose those questions that stand out as the best predictors of job performance.[50] The key is for employers not to ask questions that might be unfair or have adverse impact, such as in which part of town job applicants live. In addition, biodata items have solid validity, correlating about .35 with job performance.[51]

Résumés

Another commonly used selection screening method is the résumé, in which job applicants describe their job-relevant education and work experience. The résumé is often used as an initial screening method, allowing a hiring manager, supervisor, or HR recruiter to narrow down the applicant pool to a more manageable size. Because résumés are used so much, one might think that they are well researched and have good validity. However, this is not necessarily the case. One of the biggest problems with résumés is that there is not a single format that all applicants use, and different job applicants report their education and experience differently. And some applicants are better at putting together a résumé than others. For this reason, résumés from different applicants are difficult to compare, limiting their value as a screening device. In addition, because so many résumés are received by organizations, they may overwhelm the recruiter. This may result in less-than-satisfactory decisions because recruiters may need to quickly sort through hundreds of résumés in a short period of time.[52]

With these concerns, why do résumés remain popular? We see two reasons. First, résumés are now an expected, customary part of many job application processes. Second, some applicants may like the résumé because it allows them to show their education and experience.[53] The good news is that there is an increased use of structured résumés, which have a standardized structure. Further, algorithms can now "read" these résumés to rank applicants based on job requirements—and perhaps avoid some cognitive biases of overwhelmed recruiters.

References and Background Checks

A number of employers also use references from past employers, typically obtained through letters of reference, as another screening device. However, obtaining accurate data about an applicant in this way can be challenging. First, applicants tend to provide only the names of people they know who will give a positive recommendation. Second, many employers have policies that only allow them to say whether a person worked for them and will not provide an assessment of the quality of that person's work. These two factors alone limit the amount of information that can typically be obtained through references. On the other hand, such references continue to be used by employers to screen out applicants who would be a high risk either to coworkers or to the company.[54]

Related to this, many employers, especially those hiring for high-security jobs (e.g., police officer, jobs working with children), may require some sort of background check (e.g., through legal databases) to ensure that the applicant is not a risk to others.[55] However, the use of criminal background checks is beginning to decline for many jobs and in certain U.S. states due to "ban the box" laws, described in Chapter 4. In 2016, companies such as American Airlines, Starbucks, and Xerox were among many organizations pledging to voluntarily remove the box from their applications. Google banned the box in 2011, and Unilever claims to be one of the first companies to do so.[56]

Physical Ability Tests

Physical ability tests are often used for physically demanding jobs such as police officer or firefighter to test for physical requirements of the job (e.g., upper body strength for firefighters). Because some physical ability tests can have adverse impact against women, employers need to ensure that the ability measures are truly job related (e.g., based on a job analysis, correlated with job performance) to ensure their legal defensibility. For example, recently the City of Chicago was successfully sued and required to pay millions of dollars for including a test of strength that was not considered job related and had adverse impact against women.[57] Note that the use of physical requirements such as height generally has been discontinued as these may have adverse impact against some ethnic groups and women, while not tapping into whether applicants can actually do the job.[58]

Physical ability tests are often used as part of the selection procedure for physically demanding jobs such as police officer or firefighter. Which physical abilities do you think are especially important for most law enforcement jobs or firefighting? Are tests for these physical abilities likely to have adverse impact?

©iStock.com/shaunl

Emerging Issues in Selection

LO 7.4   Recognize and explain key analytical, legal, ethical, and global issues associated with personnel selection.

Social media are often used by employers in the recruitment process. In addition, there has been some interest in using applicant information obtained from social media to make hiring decisions as well. However, we recommend against employers using such information for making actual hiring decisions for a number of reasons. First, different applicants provide different types and amounts of information on their social media pages. This makes it difficult to compare different job applicants fairly. Research has also shown that the information provided by social networking sites may not lead to good hiring decisions. In one study, researchers found that recruiters' ratings of students' Facebook pages were not predictive of later work performance. They also found that decisions made on the basis of this information favored White and female applicants, suggesting that such decisions would have systematic biases.[59] Of course, because some employers may use information from social networking sites, we suggest that job applicants remain cautious about what they post about themselves on these sites.

In addition, there has been some interest among employers in using credit history as an applicant screening method. The assumption among some employers is that a poor credit history may be a sign of other problems such as low conscientiousness.[60] However, there are a number of reasons to caution against using credit histories in selection, and their use appears to be on the decline among employers for the following reasons.

- First, many people may have a poor credit score due to factors that are not their fault, such as being laid off from their job.
- Second, the relationship between credit scores, personality, and performance is not at all clear. For example, one study showed that a poor credit score is not associated with workplace deviance and that a good score is actually associated with poor agreeableness.
- Third, there is also evidence that credit scores may show adverse impact.

Applicant Reactions to Selection Methods and Procedures

LO 7.5   Describe the importance of applicant reactions to selection processes and how to deploy selection procedures within organizations.

There is also a growing realization that job applicants' perspective on selection, or **applicant reactions**, matters as well. Research has shown that how applicants perceive the hiring process, including how fairly they believe that they were treated, can affect important outcomes such as their willingness to buy the company's products or even whether they accept a job offer.[61] In other words, organizations would do well to consider the **candidate experience** (the term for applicant reactions often used by employers) when using hiring procedures, and many now do.

Applicant reactions
A job applicant's perspective regarding the selection procedures they encounter and the employer that uses them

Candidate experience
A term for applicant reactions often used by employers

Many employers are concerned that a bad candidate experience could cause the best applicants to look for jobs elsewhere, and this may in fact be true. The British cable and mobile provider Virgin Media found that a significant number of job candidates who had had a negative interview experience (e.g., a rude interviewer) switched providers as a result, costing the company the equivalent of $5.4 million per year. To attack this issue, Virgin developed an intensive program to train interviewers on how to treat applicants with respect.[62]

An extensive body of research has examined what applicants want in a selection system. Applicants want to be treated fairly during hiring, and this perceived fairness in turn affects their attitudes and behaviors.[63] Applicants prefer selection methods that appear to be related to the job. As an example, applicants tend to prefer job interviews that ask clearly job-related questions rather than abstract questions with no obvious relationship to the job. In addition, applicants value feedback and communication from employers during the hiring process, and they also like methods that treat all applicants the same way. Finally, applicants want to be treated with respect: A cold or unfriendly person signals to the applicant that cold relationships prevail in the organization. These results have been found across countries and cultures, having been found in North America, Europe, South America, and Asia.[64] A summary of some of the key factors that affect job applicants' perceptions is presented in Table 7.6.

TABLE 7.6 Characteristics of Selection Systems That Have Been Found to Affect Applicant Perceptions and Behaviors

SELECTION PROCEDURE CHARACTERISTICS	DEFINITION
Job-relatedness	The selection procedure is either obviously related to the job (e.g., a work sample) or the applicant understands that it is important to the job (e.g., a test of agreeableness and extraversion for a customer service job).
Opportunity to perform	The selection procedure gives the applicants a feeling that they can "show what they know" or "show what they can do" relative to what is required for the job.
Interpersonal treatment	The applicant is treated with respect by people from the organization. This might include respect in communications with the applicant, both written and in person, and letting the applicant know the final outcome (e.g., the employer lets the applicant know if they got the job rather than simply saying nothing).
Feedback timeliness	Applicants are given the results of the application process in a timely manner.
Consistency	Applicants are all treated in a consistent manner.

Sources: Based on information contained in Bauer, T. N., Truxillo, D. M., Sanchez, R. J., Craig, J., Ferrara, P., & Campion, M. A. (2001). Applicant reactions to selection: Development of the Selection Procedural Justice Scale (SPJS). *Personnel Psychology, 54,* 387–419; Gilliland, S. W. (1993). The perceived fairness of selection systems: An organizational justice perspective. *Academy of Management Review, 18,* 694–734; Hausknecht, J. P., Day, D. V., & Thomas, S. C. (2004). Applicant reactions to selection procedures: An updated model and meta-analysis. *Personnel Psychology, 57,* 639–683.

■ **FIGURE 7.3**   Selection Procedures Preferred by Job Applicants

Most Preferred	Favorable Evaluation	Least Preferred
• Work Samples	• Résumés	• Honesty Tests
• Interviews	• Cognitive Tests	• Personal Contacts
	• References	• Graphology (handwriting analysis)
	• Biodata	
	• Personality Tests	

Sources: Anderson, N., Salgado, J. F., & Hülsheger, U. R. (2010). Applicant reactions in selection: Comprehensive meta-analysis into reaction generalization versus situational specificity. *International Journal of Selection and Assessment, 18*, 291–304; Hausknecht, J. P., Day, D. V., & Thomas, S. C. (2004). Applicant reactions to selection procedures: An updated model and meta-analysis. *Personnel Psychology, 57,* 639–683.

This all leads to the question regarding which selection procedures applicants prefer (see Figure 7.3). Not surprisingly, they tend to prefer procedures that are obviously job related such as work samples, assessment centers, and job interviews; feel less positively toward more abstract selection procedures such as résumés, biodata, personality tests, cognitive tests, and references; and feel least positively toward graphology (handwriting analysis), the use of personal contacts to get a job, and integrity tests, which may seem the least job related.[65]

One challenge for employers is that some of the methods applicants like most are not always the most cost-effective to administer. For example, work samples are valid predictors, but they can be quite expensive to administer. Research has also suggested that providing explanations to job applicants—for example, how a test that does not appear to be obviously job related actually has been carefully developed and researched to be quite valid—can help to alleviate applicant concerns.[66]

The candidate experience is so important that the Talent Board, an organization that focuses on understanding the candidate experience, gives awards to organizations each year. In 2018, companies such Southwest Airlines, New Balance Athletics, Intel, Marriott International, and Pratt & Whitney were among the winners recognized by the Talent Board.[67] In short, in addition to considering the validity, utility, and legality of selection procedures, employers should consider applicants' perceptions of these procedures.

Deployment of Selection Procedures

LO 7.6   Explain how to deploy selection procedures within organizations to enhance job performance.

Suppose an employer has decided to use a personality test, an integrity test, and a structured interview to hire its programmers. There are approximately 10 vacancies, and the company expects to have 100 strong applicants due to a successful recruitment effort. One simple

■ **FIGURE 7.4**   Example of the Multiple-Hurdle Selection Process

This is an example of a multiple-hurdle approach in which the least expensive selection procedures are put first with the full applicant pool, and the most expensive selection procedures are put last with fewer applicants to save on administration costs.

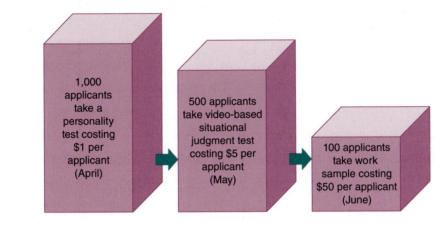

approach would be to administer all of the selection procedures at one time. So an applicant might come in to visit the organization and take the personality and integrity tests and then go to the interview all in one day. However, there are some problems with this approach: There are 100 applicants, and interviewing all 100 of them would be costly. Instead, the company might decide to administer these selection procedures sequentially in what is called a **multiple-hurdle approach** (see Figure 7.4). Typically, the less expensive selection procedures—in this case, the tests of personality and integrity—are put first. Only those applicants who score high enough on these two tests would then be put through the more costly structured interview.[68] However, making applicants wait too long between selection hurdles can give applicants a negative impression of the company and may cause employers to lose the best talent to other employers who are willing to move more quickly. In other words, using selection hurdles rather than administering all selection procedures at once makes a lot of practical sense, as long as the delays between hurdles are not too lengthy.

Multiple-hurdle approach
When a series of selection procedures is administered sequentially and applicants must pass each hurdle to move to the next one

CHAPTER SUMMARY

Obtaining the best talent gives an organization a competitive advantage and is the main goal of selection. Understanding reliability, validity, and selection utility enables organizations to choose the best predictors for a given hiring situation. A range of selection procedures is available to organizations, and these should be used according to their relative validity, practicality, and effects on workforce diversity. Practical issues such as the timing and sequencing of selection procedures to ensure cost-effectiveness need to be considered along with the candidate experience.

KEY TERMS

reliability   154
validity   154
utility   155
unstructured interview   156
structured interview   159
situational interview   159
behavioral interview   159
five-factor model (FFM)   162

integrity test   163
cognitive ability
    test   164
emotional intelligence (EI)   164
work sample   165
situational judgment
    tests (SJT)   166
assessment center   166

biographical data (biodata)   167
applicant reactions   170
candidate experience   170
multiple-hurdle approach   173

$SAGE edge™

Get the tools you need to sharpen your study skills. SAGE edge offers a robust online environment featuring an impressive array of free tools and resources.

Access practice quizzes, eFlashcards, video, and multimedia at **edge.sagepub.com/bauerbrief**

HR REASONING AND DECISION-MAKING EXERCISES

EXERCISE 7.1: SELECTION SYSTEMS FOR HIRING

You are working for a regional coffee chain, Al Bar. Currently, the company has 900 employees, but it is expanding. The CEO would like to be more systematic in the approach to hiring new baristas. Al Bar also needs a valid but practical and cost-effective approach given the large number of new hires expected in the coming years.

A glance at the O*NET database shows the following sorts of skills are typically required of baristas:

- Take orders from customers and give orders to coworkers for preparation.
- Prepare beverages such as espresso drinks, coffee, and tea.
- Clean work area and equipment.
- Describe items on the menu to customers and suggest menu items that they might like.
- Take customer payments.

You have been asked to propose a new selection system for hiring baristas.

Questions

1. Which selection procedures would make the most sense for hiring baristas? Weigh each of your suggested selection procedures in terms of (a) validity, (b) enhancing workforce diversity, (c) utility, and (d) applicant reactions.
2. Once you have chosen your selection procedures, in what order would you administer the selection procedures? Would you administer them in person or online (or some combination)? Explain why.
3. Assuming that you would use an interview at some point in the process, what would be some good interview questions? Would you use an unstructured interview, a behavioral interview, a situational interview, or some combination? Explain why.
4. Which selection procedures would you definitely not use for the barista job?

EXERCISE 7.2: ASSESSING THE VALIDITY OF A NEW TEST FOR HIRING EMPLOYEES

A test vendor has approached the vice president of HR in your company with a new test of conscientiousness. The test vendor claims that the new conscientiousness test is at least as valid as the old test that your company is currently using—but the new test is half the price! As a result, the vice president of HR has asked you to determine whether the company should use this new test of conscientiousness or stick with the old test. This is important, because having a valid test affects hiring decisions regarding hundreds of new employees.

You have decided to examine the validity of the new test and the old test by looking at how well test scores correlate with job performance. This approach, referred to as *criterion-related validity,* is based on whether there is a significant correlation between a test and job performance.

You have been able to give the new conscientiousness test and the old conscientiousness test to 200 current employees. You also have supervisor job performance ratings on file for each employee regarding their job performance. In other words, you have a lot of what you need to begin to assess the validity of the new test of conscientiousness in terms of predicting job performance.

The correlations among these different tests and measures are presented in Table 7.7. Note that statistically significant relationships are indicated by an asterisk (*).

Take a few minutes to orient yourself to this correlation matrix.

TABLE 7.7   Correlations Among Tests and Job Performance

	1	2	3	4	5	6
1. New Conscientiousness Test Time 1	–					
2. New Conscientiousness Test Time 2	.97*	–				
3. Old Conscientiousness Test	.92*	.90*	–			
4. Achievement Striving Test	.62*	.65*	.58*	–		
5. Verbal Skills Test	.11	.12	.12		–	
6. Job Performance: Supervisor Ratings of Organizational Citizenship	.35*	.33*	.32*	.25*	.15*	–

Questions

1. What do you think about the validity of the new conscientiousness test?
2. What do you think about the validity of the old conscientiousness test?
3. Would you recommend using the new test or the old test of conscientiousness for hiring workers? Why?

ETHICAL MATTERS EXERCISE: KEEPING APPLICANT AND EMPLOYEE DATA SECURE

Applicant information privacy is a major ethical issue faced by employers. We mentioned the issue of keeping applicant information secure—something that is more easily said than done due to the risks inherent in both human error and the ingenuity of cyber-criminals.

In 2014, McDonald's Canada's job website was hacked, which put the personal data of as many as 95,000 job applicants at risk of being stolen; the data included their home addresses, e-mail addresses, and phone numbers. As another example, a laptop theft at Coca-Cola involved the private data of more than 74,000 employees, contractors, and suppliers. These cases are likely to happen more and more frequently as employers seek to use mobile-optimized application portals. Often, the cause of such data breaches is simple human error—errors that result from behaviors that many of us engage in on a regular basis.

How does an employer protect applicant data? It is recommended that HR work closely with IT staff. Employees should be asked to share their ideas for protecting data security. Employers should conduct a risk assessment of where things might go wrong. And employers should train employees in the basics of keeping data secure.[69]

Questions

1. What practices should you follow to keep personal data secure? Consider yourself and others such as job applicants at your workplace or university.

2. Look up the McDonald's or Coca-Cola data breach and read the details of what happened, how, and why. What could have been done differently? How did the employer respond once the breach happened?

©iStock.com/SDI Productions

8 Training, Development, and Careers

LEARNING OBJECTIVES

After reading and studying this chapter, you should be able to do the following:

8.1 Describe the steps to a training needs assessment, including the purpose of each, and how they are used to develop training goals.

8.2 List the characteristics of the employee and the organizational context that can be leveraged to enhance training effectiveness.

8.3 Describe some of the most important training methods and media used by organizations and list their respective advantages and disadvantages.

8.4 Identify the major categories of criteria for assessing training effectiveness.

8.5 Analyze the factors associated with effective career development and management.

HR in Action: The Case of Tying Training Data to Performance

Research shows that organizational training improves performance of both employees and organizations. Analytics provides a good opportunity for companies to research the effectiveness of their training programs in terms of productivity, sales, attitudes, and worker well-being. These sorts of analytics can give an advantage to organizations that want to improve their training functions to achieve the best organizational results. Analytics can also show where a training program may need to be tweaked to improve it.

Analytics requires measures of training effectiveness, and the challenge is finding practical ways to measure training effectiveness. As we will discuss in this chapter, we know that training outcomes can be broken down into four categories: (1) trainee reactions to the training, (2) whether trainees actually learned, (3) trainees' behavior back on the job, and (4) organizational results (e.g., financial improvements for the company). But collecting these types of data in organizations is not always easy.

©iStock.com/cnythzl

Some organizations are addressing the challenges of measuring the effectiveness of their training. Allstate Insurance developed a single set of standardized training performance measures. This allowed Allstate to compare training performance in different business units across the company.[1]

Case Discussion Questions

1. Give an example of a performance measure that you think could be used across a single company for different types of jobs.

2. What are some factors—in addition to the training itself—that could affect how well people do in training?

3. If you were a manager, what would you want to know about a training program to determine if it is effective?

As we have said in the earlier chapters, an organization's employees are its greatest asset. For this reason, organizations invest a lot in training their employees. Some sources estimate global expenditures on training at $362 billion.[2] But for this investment to pay off, the training must address the needs of both the organization's objectives and the needs of employees. And organizational decision makers need to know whether the training worked.

This chapter describes the process for building a training program and showing its value to the organization. As shown in Figure 8.1, this process involves conducting a training needs assessment, considering the characteristics of the worker and the organization, choosing the right training methods, and evaluating the program's effectiveness.

Most of you will be involved in organizational training and development activities at some point in your lives as a trainee. But you may also have to decide whether to undertake a training program for yourself, your team, or even for an organization. The

■ **FIGURE 8.1**   The Process for Developing, Implementing, and Evaluating an Organizational Training Program

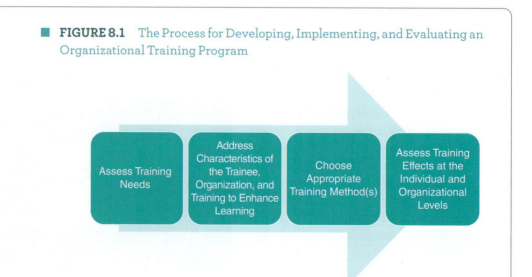

Assess Training Needs

Address Characteristics of the Trainee, Organization, and Training to Enhance Learning

Choose Appropriate Training Method(s)

Assess Training Effects at the Individual and Organizational Levels

principles described in this chapter will help you make informed decisions about training in your workplace.

Training Needs Assessment

LO 8.1 Describe the steps to a training needs assessment, including the purpose of each, and how they are used to develop training goals.

Before spending the capital needed to train employees, it is wise to get a better understanding of what the organization's training needs actually are through some sort of a needs assessment. Training **needs assessment** is a systematic evaluation of the organization, the jobs, and the employees to determine where and what type of training is needed. Training needs assessment is a key part of developing training goals that fit the organizational strategy. Training needs assessment also helps in understanding how to develop and implement the training program in the best way.[3] In fact, it may be the most important step in developing an effective training program. This process has three components: organizational analysis, job analysis, and person analysis (see Figure 8.2).

Needs assessment
A systematic evaluation of the organization, the jobs, and the employees to determine where training is most needed and what type of training is needed

Organizational Analysis

Organizational analysis involves getting to know the organization at a broader level so a training program can be developed to fit the organization. Organizational analysis could involve interviews with management and employees, review of company records, or surveys.

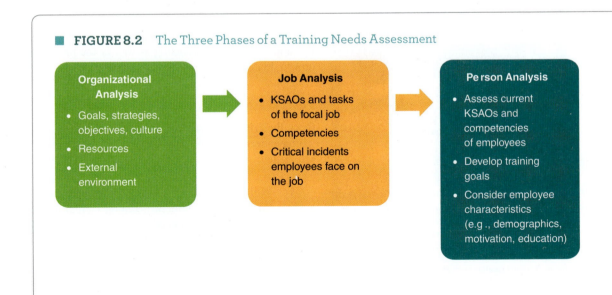

■ **FIGURE 8.2** The Three Phases of a Training Needs Assessment

Organizational Analysis
- Goals, strategies, objectives, culture
- Resources
- External environment

Job Analysis
- KSAOs and tasks of the focal job
- Competencies
- Critical incidents employees face on the job

Person Analysis
- Assess current KSAOs and competencies of employees
- Develop training goals
- Consider employee characteristics (e.g., demographics, motivation, education)

Organizational analysis includes understanding issues such as the following:

- The organization's *goals and strategies,* which should be aligned with the training program. Imagine that an organization's focus is to gain market share over the next 5 years. In this case, it may be worthwhile to consider training efforts focused on the salesforce to develop the market share.

- The organization's *culture*—the shared beliefs that employees have about accepted behavioral norms—is key to implementing an effective training program. For example, if a company's culture values nonconfrontational interpersonal relationships, developing a training program focused on promoting an assertive, confrontational interpersonal style would not be appropriate. Or if managers show little support for training, that would probably have a negative impact on the training program. In short, the culture is an important factor in determining training effectiveness.

- The *resources* that the organization can devote to training are important to know from the start. This includes issues such as the available budget, facilities, equipment, and personnel.

- The organization's *external environment* such as laws and regulations are important to understand when developing training. This might include requirements for safety training or for training about equal employment opportunity laws among hiring managers.

Both administrative assistants and airline customer service agents have to deal with tricky interpersonal situations. These circumstances can be quite different in terms of whom the assistants and agents are dealing with, the levels of anger and anxiety involved in the interactions, and the mode of communication such as in-person, by phone, or by e-mail. What kind of interpersonal skills training content would you recommend for each type of job?

©iStock.com/PeopleImages

©iStock.com/Xavier Arnau

Job Analysis

Once an organizational analysis has been conducted, the next step in a training needs assessment is to conduct a job analysis. A job analysis helps determine which KSAOs, tasks, and competencies are associated with a job, as well as the critical incidents that employees face on the job, to develop an effective training program. In Chapter 5, we discussed the range of options for job analysis and competency modeling as well as the basics of how to do them (e.g., interviews, surveys).

Person Analysis

Once the critical competencies, KSAOs, and tasks of a job have been identified, two types of information still are needed:

1. Which specific KSAOs or competencies need further development among employees? Which employees need this training most?

2. Which characteristics of the employees (referred to as demographics) need to be considered to develop the most effective training program?

Spotlight on Legal Issues

FAIRNESS AND COMPLIANCE

Legal issues are relevant to the training function in organizations. First, consider the *Uniform Guidelines on Employee Selection Procedures* (discussed in Chapters 4 and 7). Although training may not be a selection procedure per se, to the extent that a training program affects which employees are retained or promoted, the training program is part of selection decisions. For example, if success in a training program for new supervisors is necessary for an employee to keep a supervisory job, the training program is being used as a selection procedure. The organization needs to be sure that the training is job related and that employees have fair access to training programs that are used as the basis for hiring and promotion.

Second, certain kinds of training programs are required by employers to remain compliant with current government guidelines and to avoid legal liability. Such compliance training is focused on regulations, laws, and policies related to employees' daily work. These might include providing supervisors with the skills training they need to be effective; safety training, particularly for workers in safety-sensitive jobs; and diversity and sexual harassment training to protect all employees and provide a safe work environment. If employees are not sufficiently trained, and if their actions then result in injury to themselves or to others, the company may be held liable for *negligent training*. In short, training programs should be examined with an eye to legal issues from their inception.[4]

Identifying KSAOs and Candidates for Development

One approach an organization might take is to train employees on every KSAO that is required for the job. But this would assume that employees are weak on all of the KSAOs, which is unlikely to be the case. Also, some employees are more likely to need training more than others do. A person analysis helps you to determine KSAOs that need to be trained and which employees need this training the most.

A number of methods are available for obtaining person analysis data, and there is no one "correct" method. The options include examining objective production or sales data, customer survey data, and performance appraisals. Employees can be surveyed regarding their training needs. Or employees might take tests or go through job performance simulations. The most appropriate method depends largely on which KSAOs are being assessed as well as on the practicality and cost.

Finally, it is important simply to understand some basic employee demographics that might help with training system design. For example, employees' education level or age might affect the training methods the organization chooses to use. Or a group of employees with little exposure to computer technology may not be good candidates for an eLearning approach.

Developing Training Goals

Once the job analysis and person analysis data have been collected, the gap between what the job requires and what KSAOs the trainees currently possess should be examined. The goals of the training should then be developed based on this gap (see Figure 8.3). Two groups of people will

■ **FIGURE 8.3**   Developing Training Goals Based on the Gap Between Job Requirements and Current Employee Abilities

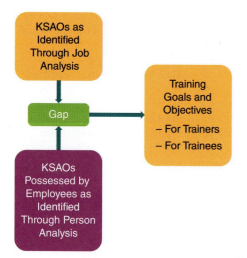

use this information about training goals. Training developers will use the goals as the basis for their training programs. Trainees need to be given their training goals to help in their learning the material. (We will discuss the importance of goal setting for learning later in this chapter.) And to the extent possible, training goals should be expressed in specific, behavioral terms. For example, a weak training goal might be, "By the end of training, the employee can assemble equipment." In contrast, a stronger, more useful training goal for training developers and trainees would be, "By the end of training, an employee can assemble two pieces of equipment per hour."

As a final point about training needs assessment, it is important to remember that it is not always necessary to perform a training needs assessment with the exact steps and stages described here. In fact, many organizations approach the needs assessment process a bit differently. The important thing is to keep the goals of each stage of needs assessment in mind and to stay focused on organization, job, and persons as much as possible prior to designing a training program.[5]

Enhancing Learning

LO 8.2   List the characteristics of the employee and the organizational context that can be leveraged to enhance training effectiveness.

Once the training needs assessment is complete, the next step is to consider ways to enhance learning. Learning can be defined as the acquisition of new knowledge, skills, and behaviors and can occur either within or outside of the training context.[6] Effective training programs take into account trainee characteristics and characteristics of the organization.[7]

Trainee Characteristics

A number of trainee characteristics may affect the success of a training program and should be taken into account to enhance the effectiveness of the training system.

- **Self-efficacy**, or a person's belief that they can accomplish a task, is one of the most important predictors of training effectiveness. If a person does not believe that they can master the material in a training course, they will not do so well in training. This is because people who don't feel they can master a particular skill will put less effort into learning it. One of the most effective approaches to address low self-efficacy among learners is to teach the training material in small "bites" that allow people to feel a sense of accomplishment.

Self-efficacy
A person's belief that they can accomplish a task

- **Trainee motivation** also predicts training success. In other words, learners have to be motived to learn for the training to be effective. Part of this means that trainees have to believe that the training is relevant to them and to their work. In addition, perhaps the most practical motivation theory for the training context is goal-setting theory. According to this theory, it is important to make the training goals specific but achievable and to clearly communicate training goals to the learner. The theory also emphasizes the importance of providing feedback to learners.

- **Metacognitive skill** is the person's ability to step back and assess their own performance—are they doing well in training? Are there some topics that they find harder than others and that they need to brush up on? Some people are better at assessing their own performance than others, and this ability can affect whether they learn.[8] As a solution, training programs can give learners frequent feedback about their actual performance levels and even remind them to step back and think about how well they are learning.

- Personality and cognitive ability can affect a person's learning. For example, proactive personality, conscientiousness, openness to experience, and extraversion have all been shown to be related to training performance. And cognitive ability is related to a person's learning speed. One way to address these personality and cognitive differences among learners is to devise training systems that allow people to learn at their own pace. For example, a training program could be made up of three modules. More proficient learners could move through the three modules quickly, while less proficient learners could go more slowly.

Organizational Context: Enhancing Transfer

Perhaps one of the most important issues in training is **training transfer**, or whether the training results in changes in performance on the job. A training program may create increased knowledge among employees, but if performance is not affected, the training is not helping the organization.

A number of factors can affect whether training results in transfer.

- First, is there support for training in the organization? For example, a bank may implement a training program to improve interactions with customers. In fact, the trainees may show strong improvement in their interpersonal skills while in the training environment. But when they return to work, the bank managers tell them that the training is nonsense and that there is no time to interact with customers in this way. In other words, despite the strength of the training, training knowledge and skills are unlikely to transfer due to an unsupportive climate.

- Training is more likely to transfer to the extent that the training environment is similar to the work environment. Consider employee training focused on the use of a new software system. Company A gives its employees training on the system using computer equipment that is the same system that employees will use on

Trainee motivation The sustained motivation of employees during the training process, which is a predictor of training success

Metacognitive skill A person's ability to step back and assess their own skill, performance, or learning

Training transfer Whether the training results in changes in job performance

the job. Company B simply gives a lecture describing the new software and how to use it. In this case, Company B's training approach is not much like the work environment and is not likely to lead to good results.

- Training employees on the principles behind the training content helps transfer. Consider a situation in which customer service workers are being trained on how to handle customer complaints. Company A trains its employees on the issues involved—addressing customer complaints by balancing fairness and customer satisfaction. Company B, however, only tells the trainees to apologize to customers if there is a complaint. Clearly, the employees in Company A will be better able to handle a range of customer service complaints and also handle them in a way that results in customer satisfaction.[9]

Training Methods

LO 8.3   Describe some of the most important training methods and media used by organizations and list their respective advantages and disadvantages.

As with many HR practices, there is no one best way to train employees. Instead, it may be best to think about choosing the best combination of methods for training. For example, rather than choosing between lectures and on-the-job training, an organization may use a combination of both to get the strongest effect at a reasonable cost. In this section, we present some of the most common training methods, as well as their advantages and disadvantages.

On-the-Job Training

Perhaps the most commonly used training method is on-the-job training (OJT), in which a more senior employee works with a new employee to teach him or her how to perform the job tasks. In fact, you may have experienced some form of OJT. In theory, OJT could be the most effective type of training: The training and transfer situations are the same, ensuring a high potential for transfer. However, in practice, the advantages of OJT are sometimes not maximized. Often the employee doing the training is not given much support and must continue doing their job, with the extra burden of training a new employee. Also, to do OJT well, the "trainer" employee should be given some training themselves on how best to do OJT, not just be told, "Go train this person." Still, mixed with other training methods such as lectures or online training, OJT can be a powerful training tool if done correctly.[10]

Lectures

Lectures are training events in which a trainer speaks to a group of workers to explain and impart knowledge. Lectures have a bit of a bad reputation in terms of being boring and not very engaging. Although the lecture method does have some drawbacks, it also has some definite strengths. Lectures can be great for getting information to a large number of people quickly. Lectures can also be much more engaging and useful if they involve interaction between the lecturer and trainees, not just one-way communication. Lectures are also excellent supplements for other training methods. And despite lectures' negative reputation, meta-analytic research suggests that they can provide significant value in terms of training many types of tasks and skills.[11]

Simulators

We know that OJT is a potentially effective training method. But it can be very dangerous to conduct OJT with certain types of jobs such as commercial airline pilots. For these types of jobs, simulators are used for training. As just one example, at its Aircrew Training Center in Atlanta, Delta Airlines has multiple flight simulators reflecting its different types of aircraft.[12] Simulations attempt to balance the limitations of OJT by providing a safe environment to train employees. In addition, simulators can allow the trainer to expose the trainee to some important but rarely occurring conditions. For airline pilots, this might include dangerous but rare weather conditions that a pilot would need to be able to act on safely. The simulator experience is often followed up by a debriefing to discuss what happened during the training session. The drawback of many types of simulators, including pilot simulators, is their cost, and they are often only used for very specific types of jobs in which safety is important.[13]

Programmed Instruction

Programmed instruction involves presenting the learner with a set of learning modules or steps. After each module, the learner takes a quiz to demonstrate that they have mastered the material. If they pass the quiz, they can go on to the next module. If not, they must repeat the module until they can demonstrate that they have mastered the material. Programmed instruction has been around since at least the mid-20th century, with modules and quizzes presented in paper form. Today, however, programmed instruction is typically delivered online.

Programmed instruction provides a number of advantages. It gives learners feedback on whether they are mastering the material—and we know that feedback enhances training effectiveness. Programmed instruction also allows learners to go at their own pace. It may also be helpful for those with poor metacognitive skills to gauge whether they understand the training material. And once the upfront development costs are invested, programmed instruction can be cost-effective. In fact, organizations do not necessarily have to develop their own programmed instruction training—it is available from many vendors and eLearning platforms. However, programmed instruction may sometimes lead to disengaged trainees, especially if the modules are little more than a series of PowerPoint slides. With that said, programmed instruction can be a great way to teach certain types of skills and can be used in combination with other training methods.[14]

eLearning

eLearning, or training that is delivered through an online platform via computers or mobile devices, is quickly increasing in popularity. Although online and computer-based training has been around for years, investment in learning technology has grown substantially over the past few years.[15] The flexibility and variety of eLearning means that companies have access to tens of thousands of eLearning modules, which can be tailored for specific

eLearning
Training that is delivered through an online platform via computers or mobile devices

eLearning platforms are sold by a number of online vendors, and the size of the course offerings is growing rapidly. One example is SAP's learning hub, which provides access to training 24 hours per day, 7 days per week.[19]

skills within their particular industry. It also means that employers can provide standardized training to their employees, regardless of location.

At the same time, eLearning should not be seen as a solution for all training issues. Rather, it should be seen as a training method that fits into a larger training system that includes multiple training methods.[16] Also, online learning approaches that provide guidance to learners may prove most effective. As a positive point, a meta-analysis showed that online training can be as effective as classroom training for teaching simple knowledge types of material, and it can be highly effective if it allows some learner control and provides learners with feedback.[17] In short, eLearning and other types of online systems hold promise for tailoring to individual workers' needs but are not the only solution for delivering training.[18]

Behavioral Modeling Training

Behavioral modeling training (BMT) usually involves a trainee observing a person (model) performing a behavior (either live or in a video), practicing it, and then receiving feedback about their own performance. BMT is based on the idea that people can learn from observing others and then can practice that skill themselves and receive feedback about their own performance. BMT is often used to train interpersonal types of skills and is a popular type of training for supervisors, who need to develop strong skills for dealing with subordinates and providing them with feedback. Meta-analytic studies show that BMT is a powerful training tool and that its results last over time. Interestingly, BMT is more likely to result in good training transfer if learners are provided with both positive models (what to do) and negative models (what not to do).[20]

Diversity Training

Workplace diversity is increasing due to increasing diversity in the U.S. population. Work teams also comprise individuals from different cultural backgrounds working together remotely from around the world. One way that organizations seek to manage this diversity and have it work in their favor is the introduction of diversity training. Although the question of how to conduct diversity training is far from settled, some conclusions can be drawn at this point.[21]

- Meta-analytic research suggests that diversity training does have a positive effect on affective (attitudes), cognitive (beliefs), and skill-based (behavioral) outcomes.

- Diversity training seems to have greater effects when conducted face to face over time rather than in a single session.

- More research is needed on how training can target unconscious processes, that is, not only focusing on bias that participants are aware of. Google has begun to implement training to address unconscious bias in its gender diversity program.

- Others have noted that organizations will get better effects from diversity training if they frame it in positive terms to employees such as by making training voluntary, engaging employees, and increasing contact among workers from different backgrounds.

Training to Increase Team Effectiveness

The workplace has become more oriented toward teamwork, and companies sometimes focus their training not only on individuals but on work teams as well. This could involve team members taking on each other's jobs or learning how to better communicate and coordinate among themselves. The research suggests that these approaches work. For example, a meta-analysis found that team training can positively affect team performance. Another study found that cross-training could help teams develop a shared "mental model"—or conceptualization—of their work, an important issue for team coordination.[22]

Training for Managers and Leaders

Many of the training methods described so far can also be used to train managers. There are also additional options for training managers.

- In **role-plays**, trainees act in managerial situations such as counseling a difficult subordinate.

- In **case studies**, participants analyze a difficult business case.

- In **games and simulations**, teams challenge each other as if they were businesses in competition.

- *Assessment centers,* which Chapter 7 discusses in terms of their use for selecting managers, can do double duty as training and development exercises, providing feedback to managers.

- **Executive coaching** has grown in popularity as a way to provide individual advice and counseling to managers regarding their work and careers.

- Specific *job assignments* are sometimes provided to managers as a developmental experience. For example, a member of the sales team might be given a series of supervisory and managerial assignments in different geographical locations as preparation for a middle management role.[24]

Role-plays
When trainees act in managerial situations such as counseling a difficult subordinate

Case studies
A managerial training method wherein participants analyze and discuss a difficult business case

Games and simulations
A type of managerial training in which teams challenge each other as if they were businesses in competition

Cindy McCauley, PhD, is a senior fellow at the Center for Creative Leadership (CCL) in Greensboro, North Carolina. During her 30 years at CCL, much of her work has focused on using leadership assessments and stretch assignments in the development of leaders. One of her projects helps groups improve their leadership processes by examining the critical outcomes of those processes: agreement on direction, aligned work, and mutual commitment to the group.[23]

Current Workplace Training Issues

A number of new types of training methods and approaches are emerging. The first of these is **mindfulness training**. Mindfulness is a state in which a person allows themselves to be in the present moment and also learns to notice things around them in a nonjudgmental way. Initial research shows that mindfulness training can lead to important outcomes like reduced employee stress and better sleep.[25] According to some estimates, 22% of large employers offer mindfulness training to their employees, including Target, General Mills, and Google.[26]

A second recent training issue is gamification. **Gamification** might include training that is made into a game or simply competition among employees in terms of scores on their training performance (e.g., earning badges, test scores after training). The assumption is that it can increase trainee motivation and engagement. Although the number of vendors selling gamified training solutions is increasing quickly, the published research on gamified training is very limited, and the results do not lend themselves to simple recommendations for implementing gamified training in organizations. For example, employees with a lot of gaming experience (e.g., video games) may prefer gamified training, while others may not. Although gamification of training may hold promise, more research is needed about how and when to implement it and for whom it is most effective.[27]

Onboarding New Employees

Onboarding (or **organizational socialization**) is the process of helping new employees adjust to their new organizations by imparting to them the knowledge, skills, behaviors, culture, and attitudes required to successfully function within the organization. Good onboarding can lead to positive outcomes for both organizations and individuals such as better new employee role clarity, feelings of connectedness with coworkers, confidence in their new role, higher performance, better job attitudes, and higher retention.[28] The goal of onboarding is to make sure that new employees have the information, orientation, training, and support they need to be successful.

Effective Organizational Onboarding

Organizations can follow several onboarding best practices to set the stage for new employees' success. One way to think about how organizations can best direct their onboarding efforts is to focus on how to *welcome, inform,* and *guide* new employees.[29] It is important for new employees to receive resources such as websites, internal discussion boards, materials, on-the-job training, and additional training programs to help them learn what is expected of them and how to do their job well.

The **orientation program**, a specific type of training designed to help welcome, inform, and guide new employees, is a great way to give new employees the information they need in a short amount of time. However, a key problem with orientation programs can be that they impart *too much* information all at once. To solve this, Zappos spread the process out over 5 weeks. And at the Ritz-Carlton Hotel Company, employees spend 2 days with management and dine in the hotel's finest restaurant. They are introduced to the company's intensive service standards, team orientation, and its own language.[30] Organizations such as Microsoft, NASA, and PwC think of onboarding as lasting 1 year and beyond.[31]

Organizations may assign a "buddy" or peer to help a new employee with answers to questions, a tour of the facilities, and someone who checks in with the new employee on an ongoing

---

Executive coaching Individual advice and counseling to managers regarding their work and careers

Mindfulness training Teaches a person to be present in the moment and to notice things around them in a nonjudgmental way

Gamification Training that is made into a game or competition among employees in terms of scores on their training performance

Onboarding (organizational socialization) The process of helping new employees adjust to their new organizations by imparting to them the knowledge, skills, behaviors, culture, and attitudes required to successfully function within the organization

Orientation program A specific type of training designed to help welcome, inform, and guide new employees

Manager's Toolbox

WHAT CAN MANAGERS DO TO MAXIMIZE ONBOARDING SUCCESS?

- Make the first day on the job special.
- Implement formal orientation programs.
- Develop a written onboarding plan for every new employee.
- Consistently implement onboarding.
- Monitor and update onboarding programs over time.

- Use technology to help facilitate but not hinder the process.
- Engage organizational stakeholders in planning.
- Develop onboarding milestones and timelines.

Source: Information summarized based on research by Talya Bauer.

basis. Other programs might be to assign mentors to newcomers. New employees who receive guidance from organizational insiders such as their coworkers, managers, and mentors are more successful than those who are left to find their own guidance. Research has also consistently shown that organizational insiders are important for helping new employees adjust.[32]

What Can Newcomers Do? Effective Newcomer Onboarding Behaviors

Newcomers may feel overwhelmed during the adjustment process, but the good news is that much of their success is in their own hands. Seeking feedback and information, socializing with coworkers, networking, seeking to build relationships with managers, and framing things positively to themselves all help newcomers adjust (see Table 8.1).[33] Research shows that newcomers who actively seek out information not only receive more of it but also get more ongoing attention from their managers.[34]

TABLE 8.1   What Can New Employees Do to Maximize Onboarding Success?

- Gather information
- Manage first impressions
- Invest in relationship development
- Seek feedback
- Show success early on

Source: Information summarized based on research by Talya Bauer.

Evaluating the Effectiveness of Training Programs

LO 8.4   Identify the major categories of criteria for assessing training effectiveness.

There is a lot of pressure for HR departments to demonstrate the effectiveness of training programs. Evaluating a training program can show where the program may be falling short and how it can be adjusted or improved to better meet an organization's needs. Organizations that do evaluations—and do them well—not only can justify the use of organizational resources for training but also can improve their current program to make it even more effective. The increasing use of data analytics in organizations provides a number of advantages for quickly getting metrics regarding the success of a training program.

Measures of Training Effectiveness

The dominant framework for classifying different measures of training effectiveness is the Kirkpatrick framework. Kirkpatrick's model classifies training outcomes into four categories of training evaluation criteria: reactions, learning, behavior, and results. The criteria can be conceptualized as existing on four levels, from the lowest and most basic (reactions) to the highest and most robust (results) (see Figure 8.4).

Reactions criteria have to do with assessing how trainees react to the training, namely, whether they liked it. For example, an organization may send a survey to trainees after they have completed the training program, asking them whether they enjoyed the training, thought the training was interesting, or liked the trainer. College course evaluations that ask students what they thought about the course, the instructor, or the materials are reactions criteria that you are probably very familiar with. One important point, of course, is that while training reactions can be important to training effectiveness, they do not necessarily indicate whether the training actually increased employee knowledge or, even more important, whether the training actually transferred to the workplace in terms of increased performance. However, trainees' beliefs that the training was actually relevant and useful to their jobs have been shown to be related to transfer.[35]

The next level in the framework is **learning criteria**, or whether the trainee actually gained some sort of knowledge or skill while in training. For example, a company may train its employees on the use of a new software system to track the delivery of its product to customers. To evaluate the training, the company might give the employees a test at the end of the training in which the employees show that they can use the software effectively. Note that this is a major step up from simply asking whether the trainees liked the training or thought it was effective.

Still, just because the trainees have gained knowledge or skill as the result of training does not in itself indicate the training is beneficial to the organization. For example, a company may provide training about safety practices on the job, and the employees may be able to pass a test about safe practices as a result of the training. But maybe the types of practices described in the training are not relevant to the employees' jobs. Or maybe the training will not transfer into actual safety behavior back at work because supervisors are not supportive of it. This is where the next level in Kirkpatrick's model, behavior, comes in. **Behavior/behavior criteria** refers to actual behavior on the job, perhaps as measured by the supervisor.

Reactions criteria The assessment of how trainees react to training such as whether they thought it was valuable

Learning criteria Measures of whether the trainee actually gained some sort of knowledge or skill while in training

Behavior/ behavior criteria Actual behavior on the job that is an outcome of training

■ **FIGURE 8.4** Kirkpatrick's Four Levels of Training Outcomes

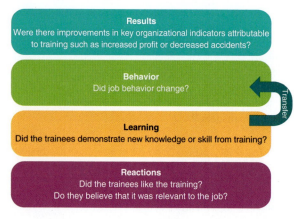

Sources: Goldstein, I. L., & Ford, J. K. (2002). *Training in organizations: Needs assessment, development, and evaluation* (4th ed.). Belmont, CA: Wadsworth Cengage Learning; Kirkpatrick, D. L., & Kirkpatrick, J. D. (2006). *Evaluating training programs: The four levels.* San Francisco, CA: Berrett-Kohler.

Spotlight on Data and Analytics
HARNESSING ANALYTICS TO ENHANCE AND EVALUATE TRAINING

The development of more high-tech analytics in recent years has led to significant opportunities for organizations to more effectively manage and evaluate their training. First, the measurement of training outcomes in organizations has become more easily accessible to organizational decision makers. As an example, Xerox evaluates its training in terms of efficiency (e.g., number of trainees completing a training program; program cost), effectiveness (e.g., knowledge assessment scores), outcomes (e.g., whether the learner is engaging with the training program, such as website visits), and alignment (e.g., the training function's net promoter scores within the organization). These types of outcomes can help organizational managers make more informed decisions about what people are learning and how training can be improved. A key here is to make these outcome measures relatively easy and affordable for the organization to collect.

Similarly, automation resulting from the use of artificial intelligence (AI) in organizations may also enhance training functions. AI can be used to follow up with learners to reinforce certain key learning points, or it can be used to survey learners to assess their knowledge retention. In short, AI may become a significant tool for enhancing learning in organizations.[36]

The final and highest level of Kirkpatrick's training criteria is **results criteria**, or whether the training actually translates into improvements in organizational outcomes such as profits and performance. Using the safety example presented here, the company may be able to demonstrate that, as a result of the training program, accidents actually decreased company-wide and employee injuries and medical claims as a result of injuries decreased.

One of the most challenging aspects of training evaluation is demonstrating that the training outcomes are actually tied back to business objectives—that is, to results criteria. The use of analytics in organizations can be particularly helpful in this regard, allowing decision makers and managers to see whether training is affecting training outcomes, such as learning, and how these are impacting business outcomes, such as performance. The key is to be able to measure these training outcomes accurately—not just quickly and cheaply. For example, an organization may implement a two-part training program, finding that the training increases employee skill levels and sales but does not increase quality. Armed with this information, decision makers can determine how to tweak the program to provide better results. For example, Bloomingdale's tracks its sales associates' knowledge acquisition, retention, and application. It can track this by employee and by store. Bloomingdale's can also analyze employee knowledge and tie it back to employee behavior and results.[37] In short, the linkage between training and organizational performance can be clearly illustrated in ways that can aid in organizational decision making—an approach used by Allstate Insurance and discussed in the opening case.

Results criteria Whether the training actually translates into improved organizational outcomes

Career Development and Management

LO 8.5   Analyze the factors associated with effective career development and management.

Another important aspect of development relates to one's career. **Career management** is the continual process of setting career-related goals and planning a route to achieve those goals.[38] Understanding career management in the context of training and development is important because the needs of employees change over time.

Career Management Activities

Three categories of career management activities include work performed, personal relationships, and education. First, work performed includes job rotation, which refers to employees who work on different assigned jobs within the same organization. Job rotation allows employees to develop a variety of skills and helps them to be more informed about various aspects of the business and to be exposed to different individuals, teams, and departments across the organization. At Raytheon, its multiyear job rotation program is a leadership development program that helps employees gain valuable leadership skills across a variety of settings within the organization.[39] Second, organizations can give people challenging or stretch assignments. Specifically, employees are given a task, project, or responsibility that is outside their current KSAOs. Challenging assignments can groom employees for management positions. The key is not to stretch employees so far that they fail.

Second, personal relationships at work are important. Relationships with managers can help make or break an employee's career. In addition, other organizational members or even someone outside of the organization may be helpful in mentoring employees to achieve positive career outcomes. Research consistently shows that having a mentor can help employees' career outcomes such as compensation, promotions, and career satisfaction.[40] Third, employees may seek additional education to help them develop skills either at their own expense or via reimbursement from their organization.

Career Movements

Sometimes an employee's career path is defined, and redefined, by promotions, transfers, and even demotions. A promotion, when an employee is given a greater amount of responsibility within their job, is often accompanied by a pay increase because of the additional level of work. A transfer refers to an employee making a lateral move to part of the organization (domestic or international) without a major change in job duties, responsibilities, or compensation. Transfers can be helpful both for the organization (the better use of employees) and to address employee needs.

Career management
The continual process of setting career-related goals and planning a route to achieve those goals

Are Managers or Employees Responsible for Career Management?

Both organizations and individuals play an important role in career management. For example, strong career management pays off at Genentech, one of *Fortune*'s "100 Best

TABLE 8.2   Career Development and Management Best Practices

BEST INDIVIDUAL PRACTICES FOR CAREER DEVELOPMENT AND MANAGEMENT	BEST ORGANIZATIONAL PRACTICES FOR CAREER DEVELOPMENT AND MANAGEMENT
• Build relationships.	• Invest in career development.
• Seek mentors, including peer-to-peer mentors.	• Career development is aligned with employees' personal goals as well as corporate objectives.
• Develop self-awareness of your own strengths and weaknesses.	• Develop a culture that values, supports, and rewards learning.
• Set career goals and review them on a regular basis.	• Managers are given training on how to help employees with career development.
• Create a plan for developmental activities aligned with your career goals.	• Accountability for career development exists.
• Take on challenging assignments in areas related to your career goals.	• Employees are provided with the processes, information, tools, and resources they need to develop their careers.

Sources: Based on information contained in Berkeley Human Resources. (n.d.). Career planning: Career development action plan. http://hr.berkeley.edu/development/career-development/career-management/planning/action-plan; Lam, N., Dyke, L., & Duxbury, L. (2006). Career development in best-practice organizations: Critical success factors. *Optimum, The Journal of Public Sector Management, 29,* 22–30.

Companies to Work For." Genentech invested heavily in one-on-one career consulting, webinars, mentoring programs and support, career assessments, and short online video clips to help employees think about their careers in new ways. All of this led to an employee turnover rate of nearly 6% versus the industry average of 11%, and in 1 year alone, it helped retain 76 high-potential employees.[41] For individuals, career management strategies include seeking mentoring relationships, understanding your own strengths and weaknesses, setting career goals, and taking on challenging assignments. Some best practices for both individuals and organizations are noted in Table 8.2.

CHAPTER SUMMARY

Organizations invest significant resources in training and development, and this investment can lead to increased performance. The best practices described in this chapter include conducting a training needs assessment, considering trainee and organizational characteristics when developing a training program,

TABLE 8.3   Key Questions Human Resource Executives, Chief Learning Officers, and Business Leaders Should Ask About Training

For training in general throughout the organization or business unit:

- Have we *invested* sufficiently and wisely in training- and learning-related activities in our organization? How do we know?
- How have we determined and *prioritized* our most important training needs?
- How clear are we about the *competencies* we will need to compete successfully? How clear are we about where the gaps exist?
- What have we done to diagnose our organization's *learning environment?*
- What are we doing to make our organization more conducive to learning?
- What do you need me to do to send the *right signals* to our employees about the importance of training and learning in our organization?
- How will we know that our overall efforts in training and development have an impact? What *evidence* do we expect to see?

Source: Reproduced from Salas, E., Tannenbaum, S. I., Kraiger, K., & Smith-Jentsch, K. A. (2012). The science of training and development in organizations: What matters in practice. *Psychological Science in the Public Interest, 13,* 74–101.

choosing the appropriate training methods for the situation, and measuring training outcomes that are tied to organizational objectives. Guidelines for how to actually implement these best practices in organizations are summarized in Table 8.3. When done well, training forms part of overall career development, which benefits both the employee and the organization.

KEY TERMS

needs assessment   181
self-efficacy   184
trainee motivation   185
metacognitive skill   185
training transfer   185
eLearning   187
role-plays   189

case studies   189
games and simulations   189
executive coaching   189
mindfulness training   190
gamification   190
onboarding (organizational socialization)   190

orientation program   190
reactions criteria   192
learning criteria   192
behavior/behavior criteria   192
results criteria   193
career management   194

⑤SAGE edge™

Get the tools you need to sharpen your study skills. SAGE edge offers a robust online environment featuring an impressive array of free tools and resources.

Access practice quizzes, eFlashcards, video, and multimedia at **edge.sagepub.com/bauerbrief**

HR REASONING AND DECISION-MAKING EXERCISES

EXERCISE 8.1: EVALUATING TRAINING PROGRAMS

The Kehoe Company, which specializes in the sales of medical office software, has decided to provide training for its salespeople. The training includes live role-plays and online training about the products themselves.

To evaluate the program, the company assessed sales performance and product knowledge in the year before and after the training. The company compared employees in two regions, Atlanta (the trained group) and Houston (who were not trained). The two groups were considered equivalent in terms of their performance and demographics. All metrics are on a 10-point scale.

The following table shows the results of the training evaluation for the two offices. The metric used to evaluate the training is a composite of sales volume and a measure of employees' product knowledge.

OFFICE	PRETRAINING COMPOSITE (AVERAGE) OF SALES PERFORMANCE AND PRODUCT KNOWLEDGE	POSTTRAINING COMPOSITE (AVERAGE) OF SALES PERFORMANCE AND PRODUCT KNOWLEDGE	SAMPLE SIZE
Atlanta (trained)	8.4	9.2	449
Houston (untrained/control)	8.5	8.7	398

Questions

1. Overall, based on these numbers, how effective would you say the training program is?

Next, the company decided to evaluate the effects of the training program on the two metrics separately. The first table shows a measure of average employee sales performance for the two offices pre- and posttraining. The second table shows a measure of product knowledge for the two offices pre- and posttraining.

OFFICE	PRETRAINING JOB PERFORMANCE (SALES)	POSTTRAINING JOB PERFORMANCE (SALES)	SAMPLE SIZE
Atlanta (trained)	8.0	9.4	452
Houston (untrained/control)	8.5	8.6	398

OFFICE	PRETRAINING PRODUCT KNOWLEDGE TEST	POSTTRAINING PRODUCT KNOWLEDGE TEST	SAMPLE SIZE
Atlanta (trained)	8.8	8.9	449
Houston (untrained/control)	8.5	8.8	403

2. Based on these numbers, what would you say is the effectiveness of the training program with regard to each of the training outcomes?

3. If the company wanted to adjust the training program, what would you recommend?

4. A colleague argues that sales numbers seem to be up as a result of the training program, so it doesn't matter whether employees showed an increase in product knowledge. What would be your response to that argument?

EXERCISE 8.2: INTERPRETING TRAINING AND SAFETY KNOWLEDGE ANALYTICS

The following table shows the average knowledge of safety practices related to chemical leak emergencies at a chemical plant, based on a sample of 221 chemical plant employees.

The employees were given a knowledge test at the time they were hired. They were then given the test again at multiple time points after their original hire date. They were trained on safety procedures at 3 months posthire.

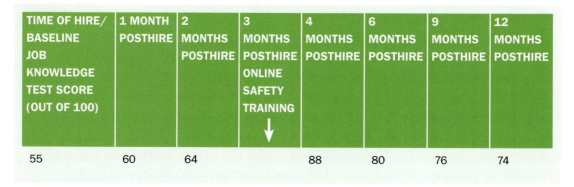

TIME OF HIRE/ BASELINE JOB KNOWLEDGE TEST SCORE (OUT OF 100)	1 MONTH POSTHIRE	2 MONTHS POSTHIRE	3 MONTHS POSTHIRE ONLINE SAFETY TRAINING	4 MONTHS POSTHIRE	6 MONTHS POSTHIRE	9 MONTHS POSTHIRE	12 MONTHS POSTHIRE
55	60	64		88	80	76	74

The data presented here are sometimes called a *time-series quasi-experimental design* that can be used in evaluating the safety training program.

Questions

1. These data indicate a slight increase in the employees' mean performance on the emergency safety procedures knowledge test at baseline and for the first 2 months after they are hired (prior to the online safety training). What are some possible reasons for this effect?

2.   There is a "bump" in the employees' performance on the knowledge test immediately after they are trained. However, their knowledge then begins to decline over the next several months. What are some possible reasons for this effect?

3.   Why would employees' knowledge in this particular domain decline, even though they are on the job? Put differently, wouldn't their working on the job continue to maintain their knowledge of emergency safety procedures? Why or why not?

4.   Safety is a top priority in companies such as this one. If you were a manager, what could you do to remedy this decline in knowledge level among employees posttraining?

ETHICAL MATTERS EXERCISE: THE TRAINING OF ETHICS IN ORGANIZATIONS

We discussed the fact that ethics have been integrated into SHRM's competency model as a key competency. It's not surprising, then, that many organizations have integrated the training of ethics into their training curricula. This might include training in more general ethical issues such as diversity training. Or it might be more specific to certain types of jobs, such as how to handle monetary transactions, gifts from clients, or conflicts of interest. There have been recent discussions about the ethical issues faced by those working in the high-tech industry and how what they do can affect millions of lives. (Critics say that this sort of ethical training is not discussed enough within the high-tech industry, much less trained.) Still, other organizations do provide explicit training focused on ethics. For example, the National Institutes of Health (NIH) offers annual ethics training for its employees on understanding rules and issues such as those for gifts and financial conflicts of interest.[42]

Questions

1.   Do you think people violate ethics because they lack training (i.e., they don't know what is ethical and unethical) or see some advantage to their unethical behavior? Give examples to support your opinion.

2.   Find an example in the news or in the HR literature of an organization charged with ethics violations. What did the organization do right? What could the organization have done differently?

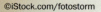

9 Performance Management

LEARNING OBJECTIVES

After reading and studying this chapter, you should be able to do the following:

9.1 Differentiate between performance management and performance appraisals.

9.2 Compare the design features of different types of appraisals with respect to their benefits and downsides.

9.3 Identify best practices for making performance reviews fair and unbiased.

9.4 Explain how to implement performance management for maximum effectiveness.

9.5 Describe how teaching managers how to be good coaches helps improve performance management.

HR in Action: The Case of Accenture Transforming Performance Management

With more than 400,000 employees worldwide, the global consulting and professional services company Accenture has a large number of employees receiving performance reviews every year. When Accenture realized that employees were not receiving the feedback they needed, the company started a global effort to transform its performance management process.

Much of this work was shouldered by Ellyn Shook, the firm's chief leadership and human resources officer. The effort began by gathering input about what employees and managers needed. Employees expressed a need for real-time feedback, personalized career training, and more transparency from the company.

As a result of the input gathered, Accenture decided to abandon the use of annual reviews, instead adopting a system to identify each employee's strengths and build on them. Key pieces of the transformation include an in-house app that enables employees to share their priorities with their team and

Slaven Vlasic/Getty Images for Advertising Week New York

seek feedback. After testing the system on 20,000 employees, Accenture released it worldwide. As of 2017, the company also was in the process of training its managers in effective coaching of employees. The resulting improvements will mean that managers and employees will spend more time managing performance, but they will find more value in the process.

It is important to note what Accenture *added* after it dropped the annual review. It is still early to tell if the transformation met its goals, but it is clear that this was an effort at transforming the organization's performance culture rather than simply changing an appraisal system.[1]

Case Discussion Questions

1. Which aspects of the change did you find most useful? Which aspects seemed least useful?

2. What are your thoughts on reviewing performance once a year?

3. What do you think about using apps to deliver real-time feedback to employees? Are there downsides to this approach?

Employees need to know how well they are performing and how they can improve their performance. Companies often base pay and promotion decisions on employee performance. They need ways of measuring, capturing, and comparing performance levels of different employees. For all these purposes, companies need accurate performance measures.

What Is Performance Management?

LO 9.1   Differentiate between performance management and performance appraisals.

Performance management is the process of measuring, communicating, and managing employee performance. If we unpack this definition, it will be easier to see the critical components of a performance management system. First, performance management involves measuring employee performance, or **performance appraisal**. Second, performance management systems involve giving feedback to employees regarding where they stand. Third, the ultimate goal behind performance measurement systems is the management of performance. When successful, performance management systems help with employee engagement, retention, and the achievement of organizational objectives.

In practice, organizations have traditionally treated performance management and once-a-year performance appraisals synonymously. The problem with this is that feedback relegated to a once-a-year meeting is not useful to employees because it is too infrequent. These ratings are often not regarded as fair or accurate, because managers may be biased and do things such as give high ratings to reward an employee they like. It is not surprising that a SHRM study found that only 2% of the surveyed firms gave the performance

Performance management
The process of measuring, communicating, and managing employee performance

Performance appraisal
A measurement of employee performance

management practices of their organization an A grade.[2] To solve these problems, companies have started experimenting with different formats, and companies abandoned formal, end-of-year assessments altogether.

Purposes of Performance Appraisals

Following are five critical reasons why organizations are interested in measuring employee performance in the workplace.

Giving Employees Feedback

To increase their performance, employees need to know their current performance level. Regular formal performance reviews serve as tools to communicate to employees what they are doing well and what they can do better and to document their progress. In fact, companies such as education start-ups Quizlet and CareerFoundry found that once their company size reached 50 employees, workers started demanding a formal performance review system that gives them feedback about where they stand and documents their performance.[3]

Development and Problem Solving

Measuring performance is an important step before taking corrective actions. Performance reviews identify employee strengths and deficiencies and develop ways to improve performance. This may include employee training, additional coaching, or putting the poor-performing employee into a performance improvement plan.

Decision Making

Organizations may make some decisions using performance metrics. When individual pay, incentives, and bonuses are based on employee performance, employees find their pay more fair. Companies may use performance data to decide who is next in line for managerial positions and to identify employees who are not meeting job expectations.

Spotlight on Data and Analytics
USING PERFORMANCE METRICS IN SCREENING JOB APPLICANTS

In addition to their use in managing the performance of existing employees, predictive analytics can also be used in screening job applicants. Specifically, predictive analytics can identify factors that differentiate job applicants who will end up being high performers from those who are likely to fall behind.

For example, the commercial airline JetBlue developed predictive analytics for use in screening applicants for flight attendant and customer service agent positions. Using the services of a data analytics vendor, the Houston, Texas–based retail chain Mattress Firm administered an online assessment to its job applicants, measuring 39 traits. The profiles of applicants were compared to the profiles of the strongest performers among Mattress Firm's employees when making the selection. The ability of a firm to use these data-driven approaches relies on the availability of reliable, valid, and objective performance data.[4]

Data Analytics

The ability of a firm to benefit from data analytics depends on the availability of high-quality performance data. For example, suppose a company is considering using a personality test in employee selection. It may administer the test to all applicants and hire without using the test scores. Then they can examine the relationship between personality test scores and job performance metrics 6 months after hiring. A high correlation would be good evidence for the predictive validity of the personality test in employee selection.

Unfortunately, in many organizations, performance management systems do not produce high-quality, objective, and fair performance metrics that can be reliably used in data analytics efforts. The notable exception is when objective metrics such as call completion time, sales volume, or other productivity metrics are available. However, as this chapter later demonstrates, objective metrics have their own problems. Performance management systems have the potential to produce data that can be predicted and managed using data-analytic tools, but often the subjective and biased nature of these systems results in data that are not useful for analytics purposes.

Legal Purposes

Accurate performance metrics may be useful in defending organizations against costly lawsuits. Even though organizations have a lot of freedom in how they manage their workforces, there are several *non*permissible decisions they may make, such as using sex, age, disability status, religion, or other protected characteristics to make decisions about employees.

Imagine an organization that fires an employee due to poor performance. However, the employee files a complaint stating that he believes that his religion was the reason for the firing. The organization's main defense is to show that the firing decision was due to the employee's poor performance. This requires records and documentation of the employee's performance over time.

Challenges of Conducting Fair and Objective Performance Appraisals

Performance appraisals provide important information to organizations that can be used to make critical HR decisions. At the same time, this chapter began by pointing out that performance appraisal systems are often disliked and regarded as unfair and that their accuracy and objectivity are often questioned. The challenge, then, is to design a system that is fair, relevant, and accurate.

The classical view of performance appraisals is that they are a measurement tool. Prior to the 1980s, scientists and practitioners experimented with different rating formats that would make it easier to eliminate unconscious biases from performance reviews. They also created systems and developed rater training programs that would increase managers' accuracy.[5]

Decades of research now show that this is a limited view of performance appraisals. It is naive to regard performance appraisals as simply a measurement tool. Managers have multiple motives when evaluating the performance of their employees. Simply stated, managers are not always motivated to rate employee performance accurately. Instead, they may be trying to preserve their relationship with the employee, send a strong signal to employees regarding "who's the boss," avoid an unpleasant confrontation, or make themselves look good to upper management. In other words, performance appraisals are both a political tool and a measurement tool. This means that HR departments need to understand that user buy-in and rater motivation are necessary to have fair and accurate appraisals.

Characteristics of Effective Performance Appraisal Systems

Performance appraisal systems, or the way performance is measured in organizations, are expected to meet certain criteria for effectiveness. As shown in Figure 9.1, these include alignment with organizational strategy, perceived fairness, accuracy, and practicality.

Strategic Alignment

The most effective performance appraisal systems are aligned with corporate strategy. They motivate employees to demonstrate behaviors that are consistent with the strategic direction of the company. For example, the online retailer Zappos had a performance appraisal system focusing on metrics such as meeting deadlines and being punctual. They realized that the system lacked strategic alignment. So they switched to a system where they measure how well employees demonstrate Zappos's 10 core values such as showing humility and "wow" levels of customer service.[6]

Perceived Fairness

If employees do not perceive their rating and the system to be fair, they will not be motivated to improve their performance. Fairness usually involves three characteristics.[7] First, employees should be evaluated using standards that were clearly communicated to them in advance. Second, a formal meeting should be used to explain why and how a particular rating was decided. Third, performance standards should be administered consistently across all employees, and the ratings should be free from personal biases and prejudice.

Accuracy

Accuracy is difficult to achieve because it is difficult to measure. It is often impossible to know whether performance ratings are accurate, given that "true scores" are not known. Still, accurate measurement is a good goal to have. When measures are perceived as inaccurate, they are problematic.[8] Accuracy has a lot to do with reliability and validity of ratings. When the criteria used to assess performance are not reliable or valid, employees will be frustrated and demotivated.[9]

Practicality

When the users of the system find it too time-consuming and burdensome, their motivation to embrace the system will be low. As a result, perceived practicality will affect how motivated managers are to rate employees accurately and how engaged employees and managers are with the system.

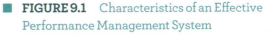

■ **FIGURE 9.1**   Characteristics of an Effective Performance Management System

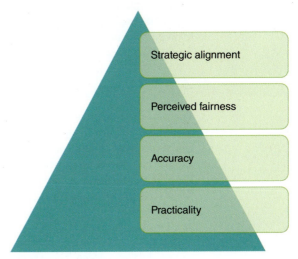

Strategic alignment

Perceived fairness

Accuracy

Practicality

Design Features of Performance Management Systems

LO 9.2   Compare the design features of different types of appraisals with respect to their benefits and downsides.

A number of decisions need to be made when designing performance management systems, including the following:

- Determining the purposes and desired outcomes of the performance appraisals
- Defining performance
- Determining specific performance criteria
- Choosing the rating method
- Choosing the source of performance information
- Deciding how closely performance ratings should be tied to compensation

Determining the Purposes and Desired Outcomes of Performance Appraisals

Organizations may have different reasons for why they conduct performance appraisals. Some may be using them for developmental purposes, which means they are primarily interested in providing employees feedback on performance. Others may use performance appraisals for administrative purposes, which means that they are used to make decisions such as assigning merit pay and bonuses or determining which employees will be sent to training or promoted. Typically, organizations use one performance appraisal for multiple purposes. Different purposes may be addressed via different types of appraisals. For example, if the goal is to assign bonuses and promotions, the system needs to meaningfully differentiate between employees. This means that the system will probably have to assign numerical ratings to employees. In contrast, if the primary goal is to give feedback, assigning a numerical rating to performance may not add a lot of value and may detract from the main purpose of the appraisal, which is to give feedback. These organizations may benefit from a narrative review with open-ended questions.

Defining Performance

There are three different approaches to measurement of performance: traits, behaviors, and results. Each has important strengths and limitations. Regardless of which is used, the specific dimensions should come from a strong job analysis and job description. The criteria and metrics used to assess performance should be directly aligned with corporate strategy. For example, focusing on short-term sales volume may be inconsistent with an organizational strategy that emphasizes customer loyalty and customer service.

Trait Appraisals

Trait appraisals measure employees' different attributes such as dependability, helpfulness, and product knowledge. These systems define performance as characteristics the employee has (rather than how they actually use or display these characteristics). The key advantage of traits is their simplicity of use. This approach does not necessitate identifying behaviors that constitute high performance, so developing a trait-based appraisal is usually a simple and cost-effective process.

At the same time, trait appraisals have serious limitations. First, trait appraisals are associated with a greater number of rater errors and suffer from lack of accuracy in ratings. This is because they are vague and open to interpretation. In fact, when trait appraisals are used, agreement between different raters, such as self and managers, tends to be lower, suggesting poor reliability.[10] This may contribute to a sense of unfairness. Second, trait appraisals describe the person and not the behavior. They increase the likelihood that any negative feedback will be regarded as an attack on the employee's personality.

Behavioral Appraisals

Behavioral appraisals assess the frequency with which employees demonstrate specific behaviors at work. For example, an organization that expects employees to approach customers about its extended warranty program may have a performance appraisal behavioral dimension related to how well the employee explains the warranty program to customers.

Behavioral appraisals are useful for feedback purposes. Behaviors are observable and under the control of the employee. As a result, they will give the employee the greatest amount of useful feedback. At the same time, behavioral appraisals assume that there is a set, predetermined way in which performance can be accomplished. In reality, it may not be possible to create a list of behaviors that capture high performance in all jobs, and in fact, the use of behaviors for employees who have a lot of expertise may alienate the employees and reduce their perceived autonomy. Consequently, using behaviors for new employees rather than more experienced employees may be meaningful. The use of behavioral appraisals may also be more appropriate when employees are expected to always display a specific set of behaviors, such as greeting customers, making product recommendations, and offering to open a store credit card.

Results-Based Appraisals

Results-based appraisals define performance in terms of the outcomes of a job. Sales figures, number of mistakes, number of reservations taken, number of new clients, and minutes taken to complete a phone call may all be important metrics that describe an employee's performance. Their key advantage resides in their objectivity. Unlike behaviors and traits, results are naturally occurring outcomes of performance at work, and their measurement usually does not necessitate one person rating another. Therefore, these metrics are less subjective.

At the same time, results-based assessments bring their own unique problems. They are not always under the control of employees. For example, sales volume may depend on the territory assigned to the individual, quality of products, and availability of competition. If employees feel that the metrics are not under their control, they will develop a sense of helplessness and will not be motivated. Second, some important aspects of performance may not have metrics. Sales volume, for instance, is easier to track compared to quality of customer interactions. As a result, employees may neglect other important aspects of their performance. Individual metrics may also have negative effects on cooperation if only individual performance is tracked and rewarded. Finally, metrics can be misleading. For example, the best salespeople may be assigned the more problematic customers because they are the only ones who can handle them. This means that simply looking at metrics may not provide an accurate picture of performance.

Goal Setting

Goal setting is one of the best methods available for increasing performance, making it a useful performance management tool.[11] Goal setting is a key part of **management by objectives (MBO)**, a management strategy in which organizational goals are translated into department goals, which in turn are converted into individual-level goals to ensure that individual and company goals and objectives are fully aligned. First, company-level performance metrics are identified. Then, these are translated into individual-level goals for employees, as discussed between the employee and the manager.

Goals that have the greatest motivational value are **SMART goals**:

- Specific
- Measurable
- Aggressive
- Realistic
- Time bound

This means that the most effective goals are quantifiable, difficult enough to motivate the employee although remaining reachable, relevant to the performance of the employee's job and aligned with corporate strategy, and accomplished within a specific period of time. A goal such as "increase the fee income from service contracts by 10% by December of the calendar year" is an example of a SMART goal. As long as employees have abilities to reach the goal and are committed to the goal, having SMART goals is associated with higher levels of performance.

Perhaps the biggest concern with respect to goal setting is the possibility of ethics violations, such as cutting corners or using ethically questionable means to meet the goal. Further, goals narrow the focus of employees, leading to focusing on one or two dimensions of performance at the exclusion of others. Goals can also result in reduced motivation to learn new things and may lead to the creation of a culture of competition. All these downsides suggest that the use of SMART goals should be accompanied by careful monitoring and ensuring that *how* the goals are attained is not disregarded in the process.[12]

Management by objectives (MBO)
A management strategy in which organizational goals are translated into department- and individual-level goals

SMART goals
Goals that are specific, measurable, aggressive, realistic, and time bound

Choosing the Rating Method

Performance may be assessed using absolute ratings or relative rankings. Absolute ratings compare employee behaviors or outcomes to performance criteria, whereas relative rankings involve comparing employees to each other. Both approaches involve quantifying performance in some way. In addition, some highly visible organizations have opted to abandon the tradition of assigning numbers to employee performance, switching to more qualitative approaches. Which approach to use should be motivated by the purpose of the performance assessment. Figure 9.2 summarizes advantages and disadvantages of each method.

■ **FIGURE 9.2**   Summary of Strengths and Limitations of Different Approaches to Performance Ratings

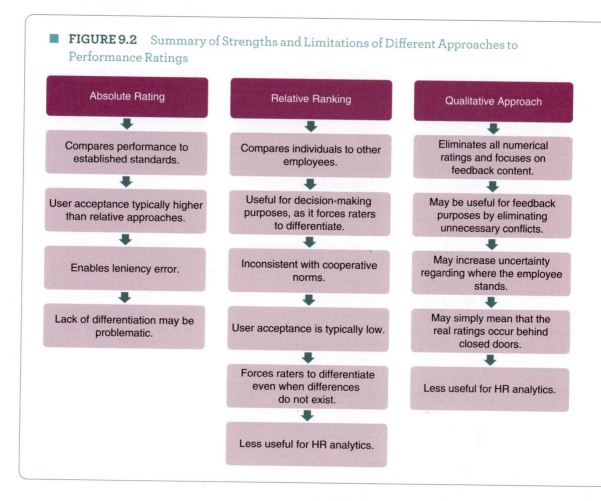

Absolute Ratings

These systems involve a comparison of the employee's performance to predetermined criteria. In these systems, all employees can technically be rated as "exceptional," or all employees may be rated as "needs improvement." One employee's rating does not influence ratings given to other employees. The rater is expected to gather data about each employee's performance, compare performance to agreed-on criteria, and then rate each employee. Systems that use absolute ratings may take the form of graphic rating scales, behaviorally anchored rating scales (BARS), and behavioral observation scale (BOS), as shown in Figure 9.3.

Relative Rankings

These systems involve comparison of each employee's performance to that of coworkers. Most commonly, it takes the form of **forced distribution**, commonly known as "stack rankings," which involves placing a specific percentage of employees under the exceptional,

Forced distribution Also known as stack rankings; involves the rater placing a specific percentage of employees into categories such as exceptional, adequate, and poor

adequate, and poor performer categories. Forced distribution was popularized by GE (but later abandoned by the firm in 2015, as well as by other early adopters such as Amazon and Microsoft) and is still in use in companies including Intel and Cisco.[13]

Relative rankings have some limitations compared to absolute ratings (see Figure 9.2). First, rankings discourage cooperation, given that for some employees to be rated as exceptional, others will have to be rated as average or below average. Second, employee performance in organizations does not necessarily follow a normal distribution, violating a key assumption behind these systems.[14] As a result, trying to force employee performance into a bell-curve distribution seems problematic. Finally, managers and employees dislike these systems, given the necessity to differentiate between employees even when differences in performance are not large enough to be meaningful.

On a more positive note, though, these systems force the rater to differentiate among followers. Lack of differentiation in ratings can be a problem, so using rankings may yield results that are more useful for decision-making purposes such as distributing bonuses, providing merit pay increases, and making decisions relating to promotions.

Qualitative Assessment

Some performance assessments do not use quantitative ratings. Instead, these systems rely on qualitative assessment, or describing the areas of strengths and limitations for feedback purposes, without assigning a numerical rating to each employee. An example of this approach is the **critical incident method**, through which managers identify examples of exceptionally high and low incidents of performance and document them in narrative form.

Critical incident method A method through which managers identify examples of exceptionally high and low incidents of performance and document them in narrative form

In recent years, companies such as GE and Adobe have eliminated numerical ratings, replacing them with frequent check-ins and informal conversations. Such companies may choose not to quantify performance reviews because their primary purpose is developmental. In the absence of ratings, employees may more easily have a conversation around performance with their managers.

There is emerging evidence that eliminating ratings because employees do not like them and expecting that frequent feedback could replace them may be shortsighted. The elimination of ratings may simply mean that the company continues to rate employees behind closed doors but stops sharing ratings with employees. When ratings are abandoned in performance reviews, managers may still rate employees to determine pay raises and promotions, but the main change is that employees do not see or influence the ratings.[16] This lack of transparency will contribute to employee dissatisfaction.

©iStock.com/4kodiak

The world's largest chip maker, Intel, conducted an internal experiment where they gave employees feedback but no performance scores for 2 years. Eventually, they went back to using ratings, believing that ratings increase healthy competition among employees.[15]

■ **FIGURE 9.3**   Descriptions of Different Absolute Rating Scale Formats

Graphic Rating Scale

Raters are presented with attributes and behavioral descriptions and are asked to rate the individual using an established scale.

Circle the number that describes the employee's

Quality of work

1	2	3	4	5
Unacceptable	Below Average	Average	Good	Exceptional

Quantity of work

1	2	3	4	5
Unacceptable	Below Average	Average	Good	Exceptional

Behaviorally Anchored Rating Scale (BARS)

Employee's behavior is measured on a scale that describes specific examples of behaviors that could occur for different levels of performance. These scales are developed following identification of critical incidents for high, moderate, and low performance levels. The purpose of the examples is to give all raters a common frame of reference and increase accuracy. These scales are useful as feedback tools, but could be challenging and costly to develop for all dimensions of performance.

Use the specific descriptions to rate the employee's customer service performance.

5 – Answers customer questions on the same day. Could be expected to investigate queries even when not directly within his/her line of responsibility.

3 – Answers customer questions respectfully and within a week.

1 – Treats customers with disrespect; customer inquiries are often ignored.

Behavioral Observation Scale

The rater assesses the frequency with which the employee displays the behaviors in question.

	Never	Rarely	Often	Usually	Always
Answers customer queries within the same day.	1	2	3	4	5
Greets customers within 60 seconds of them entering the store.	1	2	3	4	5

Choosing the Source of Performance Information

Due to the nature of their jobs and responsibility for employee performance, managers are typically the primary raters in performance appraisals and serve the role of a major coach and source of feedback for employees. At the same time, information from managers may be supplemented with feedback from coworkers, subordinates, customers, and self. Using **360-degree feedback**, or multiple-rater systems, presents employees with feedback from different stakeholders and has the potential to provide useful, rich information. At the same time, different sources have different limitations that need to be considered.

Managers

Because the role of a manager includes managing the performance of employees, managers are naturally involved in performance management. Managers are often the most knowledgeable source in the assessment of employee performance, and they can collect more information if needed. They may provide higher-quality data to the performance assessment compared to other sources.

Relying solely on a single manager as the rater could be problematic. In some contexts, managers know little about the employee's performance. For example, this could occur if the employee is working in a field setting, when the manager is supervising a large number of employees and has limited interactions with each employee, or if the manager only recently started working with the employee. Further, the nature of the relationship the manager has with the employee will affect the rating and the interactions during performance reviews, potentially resulting in skepticism among some employees that the appraisal process is biased. Adding multiple perspectives makes a lot of sense to ensure that ratings reflect diverse perspectives and capture the full picture of how the employee performs at work.

Coworkers

The involvement of coworkers in performance assessments introduces a rating source that potentially has more interactions with the focal employee. Because coworkers have the ability to rate certain aspects of performance (such as contributions to the team) more effectively, the introduction of coworkers as raters could increase perceived fairness of ratings. At the same time, coworker ratings may show bias toward the employee due to liking, similar to supervisor ratings.[17] Companies often use coworker ratings for developmental purposes rather than for reward or other administrative decisions. When coworker ratings are used, managers are typically also involved to ensure that the coworker raters remain anonymous and the feedback from multiple sources is combined. For example, at Facebook, employees nominate three to five peers to evaluate them. This is followed by managers writing the review.[18]

Direct Reports

When the employee to be evaluated is a manager, the direct reports, or subordinates of the manager, are a relevant and important source of information. Feedback from the manager's direct reports could provide useful information and help the manager develop leadership skills. At the same time, anonymity of this feedback is essential to maintain the quality of subordinate feedback. In fact, research shows that when the source of subordinate feedback is known, raters have a tendency to inflate their assessments, resulting in distorted and unrealistic feedback.[19] This means that subordinates will be more useful as a source of feedback in large groups in which anonymity can be maintained. Further, similar to coworker

360-degree feedback
Multiple-rater systems, which present employees with feedback from different stakeholders and have the potential to provide rich information

ratings, feedback provided by subordinates also shows more evidence of a leniency bias as a result of liking, compared to assessments managers provide for their employees.

Customers

Internal and external customers provide a unique perspective to performance measurement. Internal customers are users of an employee's output within the same firm, whereas external customers are outside the organization. Feedback collected from customers is relevant and oftentimes is one of the more important indicators of performance. Seeking feedback from customers also signals to customers that their opinions matter, which may contribute to organizational reputation and customer relationships. A primary challenge will be to gather these data, as often customers are reluctant or uninterested in giving feedback unless they have complaints. Further, customers have little accountability and motivation to provide fair feedback, and they have little training to do so. As a result, their ratings may suffer from biases. In fact, research has shown that customer satisfaction ratings suffer from bias against women and minorities.[20]

Self-Assessment

Self-assessments have only moderate overlap with manager and coworker ratings. You may assume that self-assessments that are part of a performance appraisal system will be inflated, but research actually shows that rating inflation is more likely to occur if the information will be used for decision-making purposes (as opposed to developmental purposes), and the leniency of these appraisals is reduced when individuals are told that their appraisals will be verified through other methods. Self-ratings seem to be most useful for developmental purposes, as a way of getting employees to think about their strengths and weaknesses, and to have two-way dialogue during performance-related conversations, coaching sessions, and performance review meetings. Using self-assessments ensures that the employee is part of the conversation, has a chance to highlight their greatest contributions, and learns what their manager sees as their greatest strengths.[21]

360-Degree Feedback

The 360-degree feedback approach is a method in which performance is evaluated from multiple perspectives all around the focal person, typically including manager, coworkers, and subordinates in the process. Different raters are better at evaluating different performance criteria. As a result, there is value in conducting 360-degree feedback to improve the quality of feedback available to the employee. At the same time, simply providing this feedback in raw form will not necessarily be useful for improving performance. For example, multisource feedback is perceived as more useful when feedback is accompanied by a facilitator or coach who helps interpret the feedback and turn it into action.[22] A 360-degree feedback system requires significant trust on the part of employees, as rating one's coworkers and managers can be a sensitive issue. In this sense, organizations may want to carefully develop and roll out a 360-degree feedback system should they choose to go this route and include features such as ways to protect the anonymity of raters.

Choosing the Ratee

So far, we have assumed that organizations are interested in measuring and managing individual performance. In reality, though, focusing on individual performance has a number of limitations. For example, with the increasing use of teams in organizational settings, treating individual performance as if each individual performs independently may not be realistic. Further, in many instances, individuals are expected to cooperate while performing their jobs. For example, a team of employees may make the sales, with input from each employee. Identifying which employee was responsible for making this sale may be challenging and inconsistent with the ultimate goal of cooperation.

Some organizations face the limitations of individual metrics by using **team appraisals** rather than individual-based measures. In these systems, goals and performance metrics may be at the team level. For example, banks often use "net promoter score" (a score that measures customers' likelihood to recommend the bank to others) to capture the performance of each branch. This is an important metric for banks, but it is unclear which employees have the most influence over a customer's likelihood to recommend the bank. Using team-based metrics may focus employee attention on the unit's goals and encourage them to cooperate. In these organizations, individuals may receive team bonuses and team incentives depending on team performance metrics or on whether their team meets specific targets.

A challenge of team-based appraisals is the possibility that employees might not pull their weight because they are not individually accountable. To tackle this problem, the organization may assess the degree to which the individual supports the team and complements coworker efforts.

Deciding How Closely to Link Performance Ratings to Compensation

Pay for performance, particularly in the form of bonuses, has established effects on future performance.[23] Research shows that employees who feel that they are treated fairly by the organization have stronger engagement and other positive job attitudes. Part of achieving fairness is ensuring that employees are rewarded and recognized in line with their contributions to the organization.[24]

When performance metrics are objective and reflect results that naturally follow employee performance (such as sales volume), tying pay to performance is more straightforward and less subject to bias. One concern with more subjective assessments is that the knowledge that performance ratings will be tied to performance may affect the rating managers give employees. Such knowledge may result in inflated performance ratings so that more employees receive raises or deflated ratings because the organization has a limited merit pay or bonus budget. Unfortunately, both of these approaches to performance reviews will result in a disconnect between the actual performance of the employee and the rating given.

Companies adopt different approaches to how they manage the link between pay and performance ratings. For example, Facebook uses a formula that minimizes manager influence over the compensation decision. A key benefit Facebook sees in this approach is that managers spend their time rating the employee, and once ratings are determined, compensation decisions are straightforward.[25] The difficulty of ensuring that performance appraisal ratings are error free is leading some organizations to disconnect performance reviews from compensation, with the belief that linking pay to reviews diminishes their developmental value. However, motivation experts caution that this may lead to a situation in which the basis for bonuses is less transparent. Instead, some companies introduce several check-ins throughout the year but reserve one annual review for compensation-related decisions to ensure that employees know where they stand.[26]

Team appraisals
A team evaluation in which goals and performance are evaluated at the team level

Conducting Fair Performance Reviews

LO 9.3   Identify best practices for making performance reviews fair and unbiased.

Once the performance appraisal system is designed, implementation depends on the motivation and ability of raters to use the system in a fair and consistent manner. The rater is expected to work with the employees on a day-to-day basis, give regular feedback, and provide coaching and support throughout the evaluation period. When the time comes to give a performance review, the rater will have to look back on the employee's performance and provide an assessment. Although raters may have every intention of being fair and accurate, a number of errors can affect the rating process.

Factors Leading to Rating Errors

Performance assessment requires raters to collect information about performance through observation and data gathering and then rate performance. Because this is a perceptual process, ratings oftentimes suffer from errors. Errors may include **leniency error** (the tendency of a rater to rate most employees highly), **severity error** (the tendency to rate most employees closer to the lower end of the scale), **central tendency error** (the tendency to rate almost all employees in the middle category), and **halo error** (basing performance ratings on one or two performance dimensions, with one prominent dimension positively affecting how the employee is perceived on other dimensions). Another issue in performance appraisals is the **recency error**, wherein a rater will focus on the most recent employee behaviors they have observed rather than focusing on the entire rating period. Manager awareness of factors that cause rating errors helps HR departments design training programs or other interventions for raters that will minimize the harmful effects of rater errors.

Impression Management

Employees are not passive recipients of performance ratings. In fact, they have the ability to influence the ratings managers give them through the use of impression management tactics. Impression management consists of behaviors individuals demonstrate to portray a specific image. Research shows that impression management tactics that are particularly effective in positively influencing performance ratings are supervisor-focused tactics, such as offering to do favors for the manager, complimenting the manager, and taking an interest in the manager's life.[27] It is easy to see that when managers fall prey to impression management tactics of employees who are perceived as poor performers by their coworkers, employees will likely question the validity of performance assessment and be concerned about favoritism.

Personal Characteristics of Raters and Ratees

There is some evidence that performance ratings are affected by ratees' personal characteristics. For example, rater–ratee race similarity is positively related to ratings, even though these effects are small. Attractiveness of the ratee seems to be an advantage for ratings of nonmanagerial women, is a disadvantage for managerial women, and has no effects for men.[28] Other personal characteristics that can influence ratings include age, gender,

Leniency error The tendency of a rater to rate most employees highly

Severity error The tendency to rate almost all ratees low

Central tendency error The tendency to rate most employees in the middle category

Halo error Basing performance ratings on one or two performance dimensions, with one prominent dimension positively affecting how the employee is perceived on other dimensions

Recency error When a rater focuses on the most recent employee behaviors they have observed rather than focusing on the entire rating period

Spotlight on Legal Issues

SEX DISCRIMINATION CLAIMS AT QUALCOMM

Performance appraisals can play an important role in employment discrimination lawsuits. Sometimes they provide key evidence supporting the organization's argument that a decision taken against an employee was due to poor performance as opposed to illegal discrimination. At other times, the absence of a legally defensible performance review serves to support claims of discrimination. One example of the latter is the case of Qualcomm, a San Diego–based chip designer with more than 30,000 employees worldwide.

In 2016, Qualcomm faced a sex discrimination lawsuit alleging discrimination against women engineers in pay and promotions. Instead of fighting the lawsuit in court, Qualcomm chose to settle it for $19.5 million and promised to make meaningful changes in its reward and promotion systems. Part of the

discrimination claim was that the firm used performance ratings to allocate raises and bonuses. In Qualcomm's system, managers rated performance with little guidance, and there was a lack of clear, quantifiable criteria to capture job performance. The rating rubric focused on qualitative criteria, and in this male-dominated environment, female employees routinely received lower performance evaluations relative to their male counterparts.

The use of subjective and vague criteria in performance reviews makes it harder to defend the legality argument. Although it is unclear how the Qualcomm lawsuit would have been resolved had it not been settled out of court, this case underlines the importance of reliable performance assessments for legal purposes.[29]

pregnancy, religion, racial or ethnic background, and disability—all factors for which employment discrimination is illegal.

Rater personality also plays a role: Studies show that raters who are agreeable, emotionally stable, and extraverted rated their employees more highly, suggesting that raters' own personality could affect how lenient or harsh the rating is.[30] In other words, rater and ratee personalities have the potential to lead to unconscious biases that may affect the fairness, accuracy, and eventual acceptance of performance reviews and feedback received based on these reviews.

Liking

One other possible source of rating distortion is liking, or favorable attitudes toward the ratee. Liking an employee may result in unintentional biases such as giving the employee the benefit of the doubt for low performance or giving more credit for high performance. Alternatively, managers may knowingly distort their ratings when they like an employee in an effort to preserve the relationship quality. Even though it seems plausible that liking an employee should be a major source of bias in performance ratings, research supporting this argument is limited. In fact, there is some evidence that liking may be a function of the performance level of the employee. If this is the case, then liking would not be a biasing factor in performance assessments and in fact could be a good indicator of how well the employee is performing.[31] Further, research indicates that the role of liking in the performance review process depends on system characteristics. For example, liking seems to lead to inflated ratings when raters are coworkers or subordinates. Further, trait appraisal formats, as opposed to more results-based metrics or behavioral appraisals, are more strongly affected by liking.[32]

Rater Motivation

Whether the rating actually reflects the employee's true performance level is also a function of how motivated the rater is to provide an accurate evaluation. Raters are thought to consider the advantages and downsides of rating the employee accurately versus inaccurately and how likely they are to get caught (or be called out for poor behavior). If the rater feels that giving the employee an inflated score is more advantageous and is likely to yield more positive outcomes for the rater, then the rating will be biased. This means that understanding why raters feel that inaccurate ratings are more beneficial will be helpful in counteracting this biasing factor. For example, rater discomfort with performance appraisals is known to yield overly positive ratings, presumably because raters are more highly motivated to avoid confrontation as opposed to providing high-quality feedback.[33] Retraining raters to alleviate discomfort helps increase rater motivation.

Improving the Effectiveness of Performance Management

LO 9.4   Explain how to implement performance management for maximum effectiveness.

Companies can improve the effectiveness of their performance management systems in a number of ways. Much like other HR systems, it is important to frequently explore improvement opportunities and ensure that the system in place continues to meet organizational needs over time.

Training Managers and Employees

Even though performance management is a key part of managers' roles, skills involved in effective performance management are often lacking. For example, a study by an HR consulting firm on 223 companies around the world revealed that only 45% of participants believed that managers had the skills to build actionable development plans, and 44% had the skills to provide high-quality feedback and coaching.[34]

Interestingly, research indicates that teaching raters about the different types of rating errors such as halo effect, leniency, and severity does not lead to more accurate ratings, and in fact, it reduces rater accuracy. As a result, rating error awareness training does not have much support with respect to its usefulness. However, a specific type of training, **frame of reference (FOR) training**, has benefits. FOR training involves having raters observe specific instances of performance through videotapes or vignettes and then telling them the "true score" and why raters should rate in a particular way so that different raters are on the same page and pay attention to similar aspects of performance. The purpose of

Frame of reference (FOR) training Training that involves raters observing specific instances of performance through videotapes or vignettes and then telling them the "true score" and why raters should rate in a particular way

©iStock.com/JHVEPhoto

What happens in calibration meetings reflects the core values of a company's culture. The law firm retained to conduct a culture audit at Uber recommended it drop the process of calibration of performance ratings. Calibration at Uber consisted of enforcing a strict curve, potentially making the ratings more subjective.[37]

this training is to ensure that all raters evaluating similar types of employees share a common conceptualization of performance. FOR training has been shown to reduce rating errors and increase accuracy.[35] Other types of training that could be useful include training managers in confronting performance problems and delivering positive and negative feedback. Such training is likely to increase rater confidence and motivation to provide high-quality feedback, which can yield significant improvements in the quality of feedback employees receive.

Increasing Rater Accountability

Organizations use three primary means to increase rater accountability. First, managers' effectiveness in giving feedback and conducting appraisals may be a performance dimension in their own evaluations. This approach would communicate the expectation that effective managers take performance reviews seriously. Second, the manager's supervisor may have to sign off on the appraisals, introducing accountability to a higher-level manager. Third, organizations including Google and Intel use **calibration meetings**, where groups of managers come together and discuss the ratings they will give their employees before ratings are finalized.[36] This approach makes managers accountable to each other by requiring them to justify their ratings and the distribution of their ratings to their peers. This method has its downsides, such as ratings being dependent on a manager's communication and negotiation abilities. Even though systematic information about the benefits of these methods is slow to emerge, it is important to know that these methods exist and are used with the hope that rater accountability improves ratee reactions to performance appraisals.

Calibration meeting
A meeting in which groups of managers come together and discuss the ratings they will give their employees before ratings are finalized

Having Raters Keep Records of Employee Performance

Rating performance periodically, even when it occurs regularly and frequently, such as on a quarterly basis, will require the rater to recall past performance for each employee reporting to them. As a result, raters would benefit from help in recalling performance information. Keeping records of employee performance has been shown to improve rating accuracy by enabling raters to recall specific information about their employees. Keeping a log of critical performance incidents could be helpful, even though managers may find it cumbersome. This method allows the manager to remember and recognize important milestones and provide feedback rich in detail.[38]

Auditing the System

One of the best practices of performance management is to periodically audit the system. An audit might reveal if raters are serious about evaluations, whether employees are satisfied with the quality of the feedback, and if they feel that their efforts are fairly rewarded and recognized. Performance reviews may not always work the way they were intended. For example, the system may have low user acceptance. Managers' lack of skills in confronting performance problems may lead to unproductive conversations. In some instances, the performance review criteria may become outdated as jobs change and evolve. Auditing the system periodically will help uncover and address these and other problems. As a case in point, Facebook has a team of analysts that go through reviews to identify potential evidence of bias. For example, they examine whether managers describe their male and female subordinates using similar language—the more frequent use of the word *abrasive* to describe female employees may capture unconscious biases, which may be worth further investigation to ensure that performance reviews and the resulting compensation are not biased.[39]

Teaching Managers How to Be Good Coaches and Build Trust

LO 9.5 Describe how teaching managers how to be good coaches helps improve performance management.

In companies that do the best job in performance management, managers serve as coaches to employees and give frequent feedback and support. Coaching is an important skill for a manager to have. Coaches ask the right questions and model the right behaviors. They show employees how to complete difficult tasks, offer specific advice regarding how to tackle problems, and provide support.[40] As you can see, behaviors coaches perform are important for performance improvements.

Further, it is important to remember that the ongoing professional relationship between managers and employees and the trust that exists in this relationship provide the context in which feedback is delivered and performance is reviewed. As a result, thinking of performance reviews and feedback delivery in isolation from the relationship quality is a mistake. Performance feedback is delivered to employees who have a history with the manager. Even though providing the right tools can help, in the absence of trust, feedback may not reach its potential and measurement may not be viewed as fair. For example, the same level of employee participation in the appraisal interview does not give employees the sense that they have voice in the process when trust in the manager is low.[41] This suggests that anything organizations can do to ensure that managers are trained in leading and that trust exists between management and employees should go a long way in improving the quality of performance management that takes place in the organization.

Manager's Toolbox
FEEDBACK DELIVERY BEST PRACTICES

Feedback delivery is a skill that is useful to managers throughout their careers. Giving feedback allows a manager to recognize exemplary behaviors and confront performance that would benefit from improvement. Following are some best practices in feedback delivery that managers can apply in their organizations.[42]

Recognize contributions.

Many managers assume that feedback is delivered only when something is wrong. This may mean that high performance and "extra mile" contributions go unrecognized. It is important to recognize positive behaviors using specific language. You may consider describing what you saw, explaining why this was a good behavior to demonstrate, and thanking the employee for doing it.

Conduct regular one-on-one meetings.

These meetings are among the most helpful tools for ensuring that you will give the employee regular feedback and have opportunities to coach and develop the employee.

Be a role model for feedback.

Your direct reports and coworkers will feel more comfortable receiving feedback from you if you take feedback seriously, seek it frequently, and display an openness to learn about your own blind spots.

Focus on actual behaviors or results, not personality.

When feedback targets an individual's personality, it may be perceived as unfair and taken personally. Instead, consider focusing on actual behaviors the employee may successfully change. For example, instead of telling someone, "You seem low in energy," you could say, "You did not contribute any ideas in the past five meetings," which is more behavioral and concrete and less likely to put the employee on the defensive.

Use the "start–stop–continue" model.

One way of structuring your feedback is to specify what the employee should start doing, stop doing, and continue doing. This framework ensures that you will focus on both positive and negative behaviors.

Developing a Feedback Culture

Feedback culture
A culture in which employees and managers feel comfortable giving and receiving feedback

In a **feedback culture**, employees and managers feel comfortable giving and receiving feedback. The characteristics of an organization that has a supportive feedback environment can be seen in Figure 9.4. Top management support, role modeling for feedback, and training managers to realize the importance of feedback as a tool for performance improvement are among the steps companies may take to help create a feedback culture. Organizations are realizing that annual or semiannual reviews are inadequate to provide useful feedback to employees. Goldman Sachs and J. P. Morgan are among companies that rolled

■ **FIGURE 9.4**   Characteristics of a High-Quality Feedback Environment

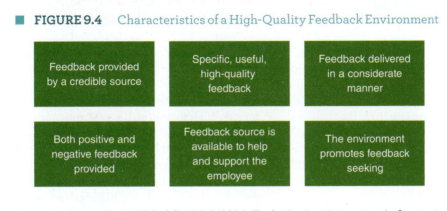

Feedback provided by a credible source	Specific, useful, high-quality feedback	Feedback delivered in a considerate manner
Both positive and negative feedback provided	Feedback source is available to help and support the employee	The environment promotes feedback seeking

Source: Steelman, L. A., Levy, P. E., & Snell, A. F. (2004). The feedback environment scale: Construct definition, measurement, and validation. *Educational and Psychological Measurement, 64,* 165–184.

out tools accessible from smartphones to facilitate such feedback seeking any time during the year.[43] Such tools by themselves will not be useful unless there is a feedback culture in which employees feel comfortable and psychologically safe to seek and give feedback.

Establishing Performance Improvement Plans (PIPs)

When employees' performances do not meet established performance standards, tying performance reviews to a **performance improvement plan (PIP)** could make these systems more developmental. Performance improvement plans keep poor performers accountable and give them a chance to improve. The plan starts with documentation of poor performance using specific language. Then a collaborative process is used to establish an action plan. Using SMART goals as part of the action plan ensures that it is clear whether the struggling employee meets the expectations at the end of the agreed-on period. Having a third party such as HR or the manager's own supervisor review the plan would be helpful to ensure that the plan is fair and free from tense emotions.

After a meeting between the manager and employee in which a plan is established, the manager and employee meet regularly to review improvements and roadblocks are removed along the way. The PIP concludes when the employee's performance improves and reaches the established goals. If performance does not improve, actions such as transfer or termination may be taken.[44]

PIP is a tool to ensure that poor performers are given a fair chance to improve their performance. PIPs contribute to an overall sense of fairness in the organization and serve to protect the organization from costly lawsuits by showing that employees are treated fairly and given the benefit of the doubt. These plans emphasize the role management has to work with employees to improve performance rather than simply rating employees to make decisions about them.

Performance improvement plan (PIP) Plan aimed at helping poor performers be accountable to meeting performance standards

CHAPTER SUMMARY

Performance management takes the form of measuring and documenting employee performance. Companies need to assess the validity and reliability of data collected and analyzed if it is to lead to good performance management practices. The traditional annual performance appraisal is too infrequent to be useful for daily feedback. Consequently, performance appraisals need to be combined with other feedback, such as one-on-one meetings or tools that allow employees to seek and receive feedback in shorter intervals. Performance appraisals may measure traits, behaviors, or results, and performance information may be derived from multiple sources, including managers, coworkers, subordinates, and customers. Because performance appraisals often involve subjectivity, many errors may occur as part of the evaluation process, resulting in nonperformance factors affecting performance ratings. Ultimately, the effectiveness of a performance management system depends on user acceptance, so involving users in designing the system, ensuring that managers and employees are trained in giving and receiving feedback, and helping develop a strong culture of feedback are among the steps organizations may take to strengthen performance management systems.

KEY TERMS

performance management   202
performance appraisal   202
management by objectives
   (MBO)   208
SMART goals   208
forced distribution   209
critical incident method   210

360-degree feedback   212
team appraisals   214
leniency error   215
severity error   215
central tendency error   215
halo error   215
recency error   215

frame of reference (FOR)
   training   217
calibration meeting   218
feedback culture   220
performance improvement
   plan (PIP)   221

⑤SAGE edge™

Get the tools you need to sharpen your study skills. SAGE edge offers a robust online environment featuring an impressive array of free tools and resources.

Access practice quizzes, eFlashcards, video, and multimedia at **edge.sagepub.com/bauerbrief**

HR REASONING AND DECISION-MAKING EXERCISES

EXERCISE 9.1: UNFAIR PERFORMANCE REVIEWS

You are the HR manager of a professional services firm with 300 employees. Your company uses annual reviews along with frequent check-in meetings throughout the year as part of performance management. Employees are evaluated on a number of questions assessing customer service quality and sales volume (results of a customer satisfaction survey and actual sales metrics, weighted at 60%) and demonstrating corporate values in day-to-day activities (mentoring others, driving change, and creativity, weighted at 40%).

The annual reviews have just been completed, and you heard from Orlando Nicholson, an employee who has been with the firm for 2 years. Orlando has a cordial but distant relationship with his manager. He asked for a meeting with you and revealed that he feels the most recent performance review he received is unfair. Orlando feels that his customer satisfaction scores are modest, but this is due to being assigned some of the most difficult clients the company has. In addition, the manager rated him as average in mentoring others, discounting the fact that he was heavily involved in the onboarding of two new employees 8 months ago. Orlando also feels that his relatively quiet and shy personality is being held against him. He feels that he heavily influences organizational change, but this happens informally and not in big meetings. In fact, there have been several times when he feels that other people took credit for his ideas.

Questions

1. What would you advise Orlando to do in this meeting?
2. What would you tell his manager, if anything?
3. Are there any systemic changes you could think of that may help prevent instances like these from happening in the future?

EXERCISE 9.2: DESIGNING A PERFORMANCE MANAGEMENT SYSTEM

You are in the process of developing a performance review system for Grimard Groceries, a regional retail chain with 80 stores. The job description of hourly employees includes

- Preparing sandwiches
- Baking bread and cookies
- Making sure that shelves and displays are organized and attractive
- Working at the cash register
- Assisting customers with their questions about merchandise
- Providing efficient service
- Helping customers during checkout

Employees are expected to be helpful, friendly, and fun. The company emphasizes good-quality customer service to build customer loyalty.

If you were designing a performance management system for this company, what would it look like? Assuming that the company is interested in providing feedback to employees on a regular basis but also in tying pay to performance, propose a performance management system for the company. Please make sure that your answer includes specific details such as the forms to be used and the criteria with which performance will be measured.

ETHICAL MATTERS EXERCISE: A GOAL-SETTING SCANDAL AT WELLS FARGO

Goal setting is one of the most effective and promising ways of motivating employees and aligning individual effort with department and organizational strategy. At the same time, goal setting can have a serious side effect that suggests the organizations using this strategy should take steps to avoid harmful consequences. In an aggressive culture that emphasizes ends and disregards means, goal setting may be a tool that corrupts employees and harms the company reputation.

Wells Fargo's experience with goal setting offers a cautionary tale. The company made headlines with the revelation that it had opened hundreds of thousands of unauthorized accounts for its customers, leading to charging of fees for accounts customers did not realize they had. The company agreed to pay $185 million in fines; its CEO at the time, John Stumpf (pictured here), resigned, and more than 5,000 employees were fired as a result.

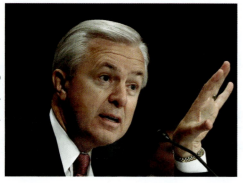

Win McNamee/Getty Images

The way goal setting was used at Wells Fargo illustrates some of the worst practices of goal setting and its consequences. Employees were required to reach impossible daily sales goals to keep their jobs. Managers did not seem to care *how* employees met the goals as long as they were met. In fact, in some cases, managers encouraged employees to cheat, such as by opening up accounts for friends and family members or even opening accounts for customers without their knowledge and apologizing afterward if the customer realized it. District managers pressured branches by discussing goal achievement four times a day. The company eventually replaced sales goals with a bonus structure emphasizing customer satisfaction.[45]

Questions

1. How would you advise your organization if top management proposed an aggressive goal-setting policy for employee performance? How might the organization reap the benefits of goal setting while avoiding negative consequences?

2. In your own work, how do you set goals for yourself and measure your progress in attaining them? What have you learned that might help you to gain more benefits from goal setting?

10 Managing Employee Separations and Retention

LEARNING OBJECTIVES

After reading and studying this chapter, you should be able to do the following:

10.1 Describe multiple aspects of managing employee retention and separations.

10.2 Explain the costs of voluntary turnover to an organization.

10.3 Identify the steps organizations should take to manage employee retention.

10.4 Indicate the costs of employee dismissals to an organization.

10.5 Estimate the cost of employee layoffs to an organization.

HR in Action: The Case of Employee Retention at Mars, Inc.

Mars, Inc. is a private, global corporation, owning many familiar brands such as Wrigley's, Dove, M&Ms, Mars, and Twix. Mars is more than 100 years old, is still a family-owned business, operates in 73 countries, and boasts a low turnover rate: around 5%. What is the secret to such high loyalty and retention?

The company is old-fashioned in many ways. All employees, including the president, have to clock in and out every day; their pay will be docked if they are late. There is no free food, although there are free candy-dispensing machines. The focus is on investing in people. Mars provides high levels of opportunities for mobility and advancement. Employees may find their true home after working in several different departments, and additional skills and education are rewarded and used with advancement and increased responsibilities. Formal rotation programs are used to help employees build new skills. Many employees also get a mentor to help them chart their path. The company shares financials with employees, and employees receive significant bonuses

©iStock.com/Ekaterina79

based on their team's performance. Managers are available and accessible, with a workplace climate emphasizing collaboration and camaraderie.

The company also takes care of its employees. Benefits include a pension plan, 401(k) plans with Mars matching up to 6% of the employee's salary, paid time off for volunteer work, maternity and paternity leave, and generous health care coverage.

Mars focuses on doing good and helping employees follow their passions. The Mars Ambassador Program allows employees to work in one of the company's partner organizations (e.g., World Wildlife Foundation) for up to 6 weeks to share their expertise. It seems that when an organization invests in its people, treats them with dignity and respect, and shows consideration, employees are loyal and engaged.[1]

Case Discussion Questions

1. Which of the tools mentioned in the case would be useful for employee retention in most companies?

2. What are other ways that companies can invest in their people?

3. What is the role of supporting employee volunteer activities for employee retention?

Voluntary turnover
A departure initiated by an employee

Involuntary turnover
An employee terminated by the organization against their own wishes

Dismissal
Employment termination because the worker fails to meet organizational expectations

Layoffs
Organizationally initiated termination of employment due to economic or strategic reasons

Employees may decide to leave their jobs because they are unhappy, have better alternatives, are retiring, are quitting the workforce to become a student or full-time caregiver, or are relocating. In other cases, organizations initiate the separation through layoffs or dismissals. It is also important for line managers and HR professionals to know how to manage employee separations and retention to ensure that the organization has the right talent to get work done.

Understanding and Managing Employee Separations

LO 10.1   Describe multiple aspects of managing employee retention and separations.

Employee separations may take several different forms. **Voluntary turnover** is a departure initiated by an employee, and it typically happens because of the availability of better alternatives or unhappiness with current work. A specific type of voluntary turnover is retirement. Even though retirements are also voluntary, we discuss it separately because why people retire is distinct from other forms of voluntary separations. **Involuntary turnover** is a discharge initiated by the organization. This may take the form of a **dismissal**, or employment termination, because the worker failed to meet organizational expectations. Alternatively, it may be in the form of **layoffs**, which involve separation due to economic or strategic reasons.

Voluntary Turnover

LO 10.2　Explain the costs of voluntary turnover to an organization.

Voluntary turnover occurs when employees quit their jobs. Quitting one's job may be regarded as the final stage of employee withdrawal at work. Employees, in fact, may withdraw from their jobs without actually quitting: Other forms of withdrawal include **tardiness,** or being late to work without giving advance notice, and **absenteeism,** or unscheduled absences from work. Absenteeism and tardiness may be warning signs that the employee is withdrawing from work.

You may calculate an organization's turnover rate using the formula below.[2] This formula can be modified to calculate voluntary turnover (employee initiated), involuntary turnover (employer initiated), and overall turnover (employee + employer initiated). Simply adjust the numerator accordingly.

$$\text{Turnover rate} = \frac{\text{Number of departures during the year}}{\text{Average number of employees during the year}} \times 100.$$

For example, if a company had 10 departures every month during the year and had an average of 1,000 employees during the year, its annual turnover rate would be 12% $(10 \times 12/1{,}000) \times 100$. Is a turnover rate of 12% high? If other firms in the same industry are averaging 30%, our example company is doing relatively well. Further, the unemployment rate will affect turnover rates: When the unemployment rate is high, employees may feel lucky to have a job and are more likely to stay put.

Another helpful formula helps calculate the retention rate. This is somewhat different from the turnover rate. This is because an organization may have a few positions for which it is difficult to hold on to employees, inflating the turnover rate. For example, let's assume that a company has 10 employees. One leaves, and then the position is filled by four consecutive new hires who all quit during the year. Turnover rate for this company will be $5/10 \times 100 = 50\%$. However, using the following formula,[3] in the same company, the retention rate will be $9/10 \times 100 = 90\%$.

$$\text{Retention rate} = \frac{\text{Number of employees who stayed during the entire period}}{\text{Number of employees at the beginning of the period}} \times 100.$$

This means that 90% of the people who were with the company at the beginning of the year are still there at the end of the year. Both metrics are useful, complement each other, and are helpful in spotting trends and identifying patterns.

Costs of Voluntary Turnover

Replacing an employee who leaves may cost anywhere between 90% and 200% of the annual salary of the departing employee.[4] Voluntary turnover is problematic for company performance for three key reasons. First, when employees leave, there are direct costs involved in

Tardiness
Being late to work without giving advance notice

Absenteeism
Unscheduled absences from work

replacing, onboarding, and training the replacements. Second, employees build expertise and organization-specific knowledge over time, and when employees quit, the company loses access to this expertise. Third, turnover involves the loss of interpersonal connections employees have developed with coworkers, managers, and clients. For example, a key client who enjoys interacting with a particular employee may take their business elsewhere when that employee leaves, whereas coworkers may find that they no longer have someone to go to for information or advice.

Of course, not all turnover is harmful. Sometimes, a particular employee's departure may be regarded as an opportunity to hire a better replacement. Still, research shows that excessive turnover is problematic for company performance, and such negative effects on performance are stronger for long-term than short-term performance.[5] In other words, many of the harmful effects of turnover may be hidden and become easier to observe over time.

Causes of Voluntary Turnover

Why do employees quit their jobs? Voluntary turnover is a function of desire to leave and ease of movement (see Figure 10.1). According to this view, employees desire to leave for

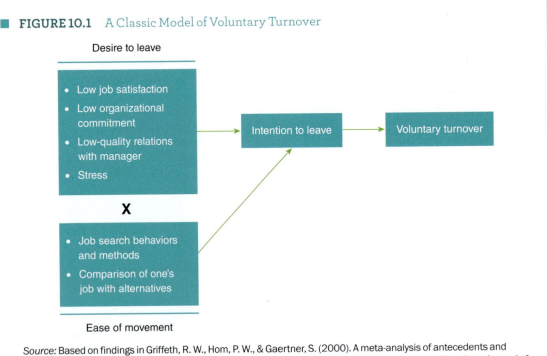

■ **FIGURE 10.1**   A Classic Model of Voluntary Turnover

Desire to leave

- Low job satisfaction
- Low organizational commitment
- Low-quality relations with manager
- Stress

X

- Job search behaviors and methods
- Comparison of one's job with alternatives

Ease of movement

Intention to leave → Voluntary turnover

Source: Based on findings in Griffeth, R. W., Hom, P. W., & Gaertner, S. (2000). A meta-analysis of antecedents and correlates of employee turnover: Update, moderator tests, and research implications for the next millennium. *Journal of Management, 26,* 463–488.

the following reasons: dissatisfaction with different aspects of their job, lacking commitment to the organization, poor supervision, and experiencing stress due to lack of role clarity or the presence of role conflict (including work–life conflict).[6] A meta-analysis showed that average job satisfaction level within the organization (the degree to which employees report feeling satisfied with their jobs) and average job engagement level (involvement and enthusiasm for work) were both related to overall turnover rates.[7]

On the ease-of-movement side, employees consider the job market, examine the availability of alternative jobs, and think about the likelihood of finding a job that is at least as good as their current job. Even if they have no other alternatives lined up, assessing how the job market is doing at the moment, how quickly coworkers with similar qualifications found jobs, and how high the demand is for their skills will give them ideas about the ease of movement. The outcome of this decision-making process is voluntary turnover. Social media platforms like LinkedIn have made it easier for employees and employers to find each other, providing employees with more information about the job market and the demand for certain skills.

Interestingly, happiness at work is not a guarantee for employee retention, and turnover decisions do not require a prior steady decline in happiness. Researchers identified an **unfolding model of turnover** to describe exceptions to the classic model.[8] This model recognizes that employees often leave without lining up a new job. Sometimes they leave even though they have happily worked in that firm for years. The model explains the turnover decision as a result of "shocks" to the system. The employee experiences a critical event, which shakes them out of their comfort zone and gets them to start thinking about leaving. The shock could be at work (e.g., the company was acquired by a larger firm with a poor reputation), in one's career (e.g., receiving an unsolicited invitation to interview elsewhere), or at home (e.g., the employee finds out that they are going to be a parent, motivating them to reassess career goals). Once a shock occurs, the employee may quit without lining up a new job, may start looking for a new job, or may decide that staying is better than leaving after all. The unfolding model suggests that shocks are more common predictors of turnover as opposed to simply feeling unhappy at work. The "shocks" that result in turnover may sometimes be psychological, rather than specific events. For example, job search activity increases around work anniversaries, milestone birthdays, and class reunions.[9]

Turnover literature also examines why people stay.[10] The **job embeddedness model** explains that employees stay because of their links to others and fit with the context at work and in their communities and how much they would have to sacrifice by leaving their work and communities, as illustrated in Table 10.1. According to this model, both on- and off-the-job embeddedness are negatively related to turnover. Note that the table lists only some examples of links, fits, and losses. To illustrate, a high-level employee who worked for a highly reputable firm for a decade may find it challenging to leave due to high embeddedness. Changing jobs may mean relocation, which comes with leaving one's current life, house, city, friendships, proximity to a beloved vacation spot, or any other number of off-the-job sacrifices along with leaving coworkers, managers, one's job, and social network at work.

Unfolding model of turnover A model that recognizes that employees often leave without lining up a new job and that turnover is often a result of "shocks" to the system

Job embeddedness model A model that explains that employees stay because of their links to others and fit with the context at work and in their communities, and how much they would have to sacrifice by leaving their work and communities

TABLE 10.1   Job Embeddedness Model Explains Why Employees Stay

	WORK	COMMUNITY
Links	• Relations with manager • Relations with coworkers	• Membership in clubs and organizations • Spouse's work • Children's school and friends • Friends, neighbors
Fit	• Fit with organizational values • Fit with job	• Fit with community • Fit with city
Losses (what must be forfeited when leaving the job)	• Ability to negotiate parts of job • Nonportable benefits • Job stability and security • Social network • Pride of organizational membership	• Short commute • Familiarity with neighborhood

Source: Based on information contained in Mitchell, T. R., & Lee, T. W. (2001). The unfolding model of voluntary turnover and job embeddedness: Foundations for a comprehensive theory of attachment. *Research in Organizational Behavior, 23,* 189–246.

Managing Employee Retention

LO 10.3   Identify the steps organizations should take to manage employee retention.

Many factors play key roles in retention of employees, including upper management's level of support for retention, the use of employee surveys and interviews, effective hiring and onboarding practices, investment in high-commitment HR practices, and attention to predictors of turnover.

Gain Upper-Management Support

An important aspect of increasing employee retention is to have upper management care about the turnover rate. For this, HR will need to calculate the rate of turnover, provide industry-level turnover rates for benchmarking, and demonstrate the cost of turnover for the organization. By calculating these numbers, it is easier to combat dismissive attitudes from upper management.[11]

Leverage Engagement and Attitude Surveys

With the advent of predictive analytics, organizations have important tools at their disposal to predict with greater confidence which employees will stay and which will leave. One of the best predictors of voluntary turnover is reported intentions to leave. Asking questions

Spotlight on Data and Analytics
USING SENTIMENT ANALYSIS FOR ENGAGEMENT

Sentiment analysis is the analysis of text and natural language to extract the mood of the conversation. Employers have access to employee speech and conversations in the form of e-mails, texts, and written feedback to open-ended questions in employee surveys. These exchanges are treasure troves of data, but it is impossible for one or more experts to analyze them manually.

As technology that can conduct text analysis advances, organizations are increasingly capable of identifying the mood of their employees and intervene early. For example, when IBM used text analysis on employee survey feedback, it noted a pattern indicating that employees were frustrated about the available choices for computers in the workplace. This led to offering more choices,

including Apple computers. The company also analyzes comments employees leave in the internal social networking platform (Connections) to identify patterns.

This technology is not perfect. Among other shortcomings, it may give false alarms. For example, "I hate my boss" may be too similar to "I hated my boss" (referring to one's former job) for the software to distinguish. In addition, it is unclear how employees will react to having their text messages, e-mails, and online conversations monitored. Companies can and do monitor these conversations, but structuring and formalizing this monitoring may create feelings of mistrust. Ultimately, the usefulness of these technologies will depend on how and for what purposes businesses use them.[12]

about how much someone agrees with statements such as "I intend to leave my job in the next year" or "I intend to stay in this company for more than a year" is useful.

Companies may also use **pulse surveys**, which are short, frequent surveys. These surveys do not necessarily replace the rich and detailed information that can be obtained via annual surveys but could be used to predict and manage turnover and to even detect "shocks" like those discussed earlier in the chapter. The media marketing company HubSpot, Inc. uses an outside vendor to send a single, anonymous question to employees every week. A sample question is "How happy are you working here on a scale of 1 to 10?" If an employee leaves written feedback, the manager of the employee can respond directly to feedback, ask additional questions, and retain anonymity, which helps identify problems and resolve conflicts.[13]

Use Exit Interviews

Companies may learn why a particular employee is leaving by conducting exit interviews. These interviews are opportunities to learn why employees are leaving and make changes in the organization to increase retention. For exit interviews to be useful, organizations need to conduct them regularly, analyze the data, and disseminate the data among decision makers who can enact changes. Many employees will be reluctant to share the reason for their departure, as they may worry that being honest will cost them a positive reference, or they simply may have little motivation to share their reasons. Companies may use exit

Pulse surveys Short, frequent surveys

interviews to understand which HR practices and departmental, managerial, and organizational factors contribute to departure and make systematic changes. Experts recommend the following[14]:

- Exit interviews may be conducted by HR, but having a manager higher than the employee's own manager conduct the interviews has benefits, as they will have power to make actual changes.

- It is beneficial to make exit interviews mandatory for some positions.

- The interview may be face to face or via telephone. Either method provides rich information, although face-to-face interviews could be more helpful to build rapport.

- Information obtained in these interviews should be collated, analyzed, and shared among decision makers.

- When changes are made, it is useful to let other employees know that the changes came about from exit interview information so that employees see value in exit interviews—which could make them more forthcoming when they themselves leave.

Hire for Fit

Employees often leave because they are not a good fit with what the organization needs and provides. Therefore, hiring for skills, values, preferences, and personalities that will maximize happiness and engagement at work in the specific company is an essential tool for retention. Also, it is important to give employees a realistic job preview (RJP) to ensure that employees can assess their own level of fit.

Structure Onboarding Experiences

In a Korn Ferry survey of 1,817 executives, more than half of respondents noted that 10% to 25% of newly hired employees leave within their first 6 months. Successful onboarding can help increase the retention of new employees. Onboarding teaches newcomers about the company culture, welcomes them to the organization, connects them to others, and sets them off to a good start.

Invest in High-Commitment HR Practices

HR practices that indicate investment in long-term and high-quality management–employee relationships reduce employee turnover.[15] Specifically, HR practices that indicate commitment to employees, such as providing internal mobility opportunities and advancement possibilities, employee participation initiatives, and engaging in selective hiring, are among the HR practices useful for retention. In contrast, HR and employment practices that signal strict short-term performance expectations and practices that reduce employee empowerment such as electronic monitoring of employees and routinization of work are associated with higher levels of turnover rates at the firm level.

Some HR practices that develop employee skills may create a high-quality relationship between the employee and the employer and could increase retention. However, they may also increase the ability of the employee to find an alternative job and leave. Tuition reimbursement programs are a good example of this. Companies such as Chipotle, Starbucks, Walmart, and UPS pay for partial or full tuition for eligible employees.[16] While these programs contribute to retention during the employees' educational studies, their overall effects on retention are more complicated. One study in a high-tech firm showed that when employees completed graduate degrees, they were more likely to leave, whereas obtaining an undergraduate degree or course enrollment without obtaining a degree did not contribute to turnover. These findings show that simply investing in human capital will not generate high engagement and loyalty to the company; the organization will need to provide a job that uses the employee's newly acquired qualifications as well.[17]

Focus on Turnover Predictors

We know from research that important predictors of turnover include job satisfaction, work engagement, organizational commitment, manager–employee relationship quality, and stress. This means that by focusing on these factors, organizations may make progress in reducing turnover. Figure 10.2 outlines factors that are most strongly related to work engagement. Companies that are deliberate about designing jobs and working conditions that satisfy employee needs and desires will find it easier to attract and retain workers. For example, Facebook provides an environment in which employees take initiative, work on meaningful projects, and learn and grow on the job through feedback and coaching.[18]

Stress is another reason employees quit their jobs. Difficulty balancing work with other obligations such as school and child and elder care responsibilities cost businesses

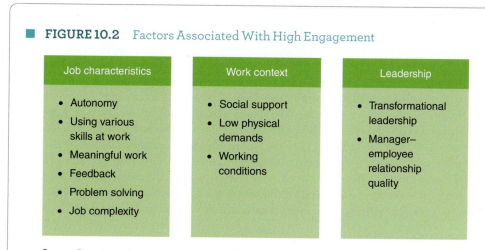

■ **FIGURE 10.2**   Factors Associated With High Engagement

Job characteristics	Work context	Leadership
• Autonomy • Using various skills at work • Meaningful work • Feedback • Problem solving • Job complexity	• Social support • Low physical demands • Working conditions	• Transformational leadership • Manager–employee relationship quality

Source: Based on information contained in Christian, M. S., Garza, A. S., & Slaughter, J. E. (2011). Work engagement: A quantitative review and test of its relations with task and contextual performance. *Personnel Psychology, 64,* 89–136.

in the form of turnover. Taking steps, such as introducing flexibility to schedules, allowing employees to work remotely as needed, and facilitating access to quality care facilities, are among the benefits organizations may provide that would reduce stress. Similarly, ensuring that each department is adequately staffed and employees are not working long hours is beneficial.

Finally, building a trust-based relationship with employees is a key driver of employee retention. By recognizing employee contributions, ensuring that employee jobs provide sufficient challenge and meaning to employees, and providing development opportunities, eliminating unnecessary stressors, and providing social support, effective managers make a big difference in whether employees are attached to the organization and interested in leaving and how long they stay.

Managing Relations With Former Employees

Former employees may provide key benefits to organizations even after they leave. A company's former employees (or alumni) may be a source of referrals for future employees, provide useful business intelligence, serve as brand ambassadors, and even become customers.[19] Some companies deliberately invest in alumni relations and stay in touch with them.

For example, McKinsey & Company provides a well-developed alumni network with a members-only website. It organizes events for members and employs an alumni engagement person at each site. Being part of this exclusive alumni network is a selling point in McKinsey recruitment efforts, and alumni bring significant business to McKinsey. It is important to recognize that although turnover may conclude the employer and employee relationship, the two parties may still cross paths.

Sometimes former employees decide to come back to the organization, becoming **boomerang employees**. Even though some businesses refuse to hire former employees to encourage loyalty of current workers, those who choose to consider hiring them experience possible benefits. Hiring former employees requires less time investment, given the mutual experience. Onboarding takes less time for these employees. Finally, employees who choose to go back make the organization look good from a reputational perspective.[20]

Departing employees are more likely to come back if they left for personal reasons (such as a relocation, family obligations), as opposed to leaving because they were unhappy with their work. Also, alumni are more likely to come back if they stayed away for a relatively short period of time, if they had chosen to stay in the same industry, or if they had a career break.[21] Finally, not all boomerang employees will have high performance when they return. A study conducted on National Basketball Association players is informative: Boomerang employees' performance after they return depended on their performance before departure and whether they stayed away long enough to acquire new skills, but not too long.[22] In other words, organizations may want to follow a selective strategy for boomerang employees, considering their prior performance and the conditions under which they left.

Boomerang employees
Former employees who rejoin an organization

Retirements

Retirements are normally a type of voluntary turnover (except in rare cases when it is legally mandated), but it is worthwhile to consider them separately. Retirement is a type of

Manager's Toolbox
RETAINING TOP TALENT

Every organization will have "star employees" whose voluntary turnover would constitute a major loss. How can an organization be proactive in retaining these employees? Top performers stay when they do meaningful work and have the opportunity to perform at their top level. To retain top talent, organizations may engage in the following targeted actions:[23]

Identify top performers. The first step in retaining top performers is to know who they are. Performance reviews, or simply asking managers to identify top performers, could serve this purpose.

Track retention data for top performers. Companies would benefit from calculating their top performer turnover rate. Although the company may have an incentive to tackle overall turnover, knowing how serious the issue of top talent retention is would be helpful to generate targeted interventions.

Be aware of their job attitudes. The organization may break down the results of their engagement or attitude surveys by performance level to see what factors are systematic problems for high performers. In addition, having one-on-one conversations with them to understand their frustrations would be helpful.

Identify risk factors. Organizations may use data analytics to identify factors most strongly related to voluntary departure of high-performing employees. Knowing the risk factors would allow the organization to identify who are at greater risk of leaving in the near future.

Rerecruit and reenergize. Having "stay interviews" with these employees to find out why they stay and to give them reasons to stay are helpful tools. These meetings can be helpful in redefining their job to keep employees motivated and challenged. Further, the organization should make sure that over time, the employment conditions remain competitive with the market.

Counteroffer or let them go? There will be instances when the employee decides to leave. Should the organization present a counteroffer? Keeping an unhappy worker by paying them more may not make sense. If there is a way to reengage them and deal with problems that motivated them to leave, having that conversation could be helpful.

work withdrawal where the employee chooses to finish working activities, replacing work with other life activities or perhaps pursuing a different career. When employees retire, the organization may experience some benefits in the form of the ability to hire lower-paid employees who may bring a fresh perspective to the job and organization. At the same time, retirement costs organizations in the form of lost expertise.[24] Particularly with the mass retirement of baby boomers, organizations are faced with the possibility of losing critical expertise in a short period of time.

Retirement may be due to personal and work-related reasons. Among personal factors, the worker's age and health play key roles. Among work-related factors, performing jobs with high physical and psychological demands, dissatisfaction with work, and feeling "tired of work" are noteworthy. Further, those who have a strong attachment to their careers

©iStock.com/spooh

Retirements may cause labor shortages, such as the one expected in the aviation industry where commercial airline pilots have a mandatory retirement age of 65. In June 2017, Horizon Air announced cancellation of 300 flights scheduled between August and September due to pilot shortages.[26]

and those who see work as central to their identities are less likely to retire, whereas commitment to leisure activities contributes to the decision to retire. Finally, research examined the role of age-related stereotypes and negative treatment of older workers as potential factors contributing to retirement decisions.[25]

Organizations may consider providing an "age-friendly workplace," allowing workers to switch to part-time roles, offering flexibility, ensuring that tasks still match employee capabilities, paying attention to workplace ergonomics, and building a workplace culture that supports age diversity. Many older workers are embracing **bridge employment** in the form of reducing one's hours or job demands within the same or a different organization (and often reducing one's pay as well) instead of exiting the workforce. In the United States, bridge employment before full retirement is common, with around 60% choosing this option.[27]

Are there ways for organizations to encourage employees to retire? Because employees close to retirement are usually highly paid, sometimes organizations see value in encouraging them to retire early. These moves have legal consequences. The organization may design an early retirement incentive plan for employees who meet particular criteria with respect to age, department, or position, offering them incentives such as continued health insurance coverage, severance pay (pay typically provided to dismissed employees), or access to pension benefits if they retire within a given window.

However, it is important to ensure that these programs remain voluntary, as forcing employees to retire is illegal under the Age Discrimination in Employment Act. Mandatory retirement due to age exists in only a small number of jobs such as law enforcement, air traffic controllers, and judges in some states. As a result, the organization needs to ensure that there is no coercion involved in these programs.[28] Organizations considering using early retirement programs are advised to seek legal counsel. It is essential to conduct careful analyses before implementing such programs, because a larger number of employees than expected may take advantage of them, leaving the organization short staffed.

Bridge employment
Reducing one's hours or reducing job demands within the same or a different organization in preparation for full retirement

Involuntary Turnover: Dismissals

LO 10.4   Indicate the costs of employee dismissals to an organization.

The employment relationship typically starts optimistically. However, sometime after organizational entry, it may become clear that an employee was a poor fit for the job. An employee's performance may fall short of expectations due to reasons such as poor person–job fit, poor work ethic, or behavioral problems. Consequently, the organization may decide to terminate the employment relationship.

Costs of Dismissals

Terminating a poorly performing or disruptive employee has costs. Even when problems are so severe that it is obvious to everyone that the employee should be fired, there are risks to the organization. For example, the employee may say negative things about the company in person or online. The employee may sue the company, which will cost time and energy to defend against even if the organization ultimately prevails. The terminated employee may engage in acts of sabotage or aggression. In some cases, the organization needs to continue to have a professional relationship with the dismissed employee; for example, a dismissed employee may be hired by a client organization and put in charge of the organization's account, essentially becoming a client to be pleased. All of these are not reasons to avoid dismissing an employee, but they indicate that a dismissal decision is not one that should be made in anger or impulsively. Developing fair procedures around how to dismiss employees, being systematic, treating employees consistently over time, and being respectful to the employee at every step of the process are helpful in minimizing these costs. In fact, research shows that when faced with a negative outcome, employees are most likely to retaliate when they are treated unfairly.[29]

Although dismissals are costly, *not* dismissing some employees has its own costs, and in fact the organization may be considered guilty of negligence. For example, research shows that a "toxic worker" costs a team more than $12,000 by causing their coworkers to leave.[30] Employees who harass, intimidate, or simply do not pull their weight may poison the group's atmosphere or cause other employees' performance to suffer.

When to Dismiss an Employee

When deciding whether to dismiss an employee, there are a few questions to answer:

- *Did you investigate the root cause of performance problems?* Is this a case of an employee mismatched with the current role but who could be valuable in a different role? In some cases, the investigation may show that the solution is retraining or referring them to an Employee Assistance Program (EAP).

- *Did you give the employee feedback and opportunities to improve?* Ideally, before you reach the termination decision, the employee should be given feedback and ample opportunities to improve.

- *Did you follow organizational procedures?* To ensure that termination decisions are systematic and fair, many organizations embrace a **progressive discipline** system. As shown in Figure 10.3, these systems aim to ensure that employees have a chance to correct their behavior and are given multiple chances.

- *Did you consider the timing of your decision?* Firing the employee at the wrong time may open the company up for a discrimination lawsuit or cause other

Progressive discipline The process of using increasingly severe steps to correct a performance problem

■ **FIGURE 10.3**   Stages of Progressive Discipline

difficulties. For example, terminating an employee shortly after the employee files a discrimination complaint will appear like retaliation, even when this is not the intent. (Note that firing an employee in retaliation for filing an EEOC complaint *is* illegal.)

The Legal Side of Dismissals

In the United States, with some exceptions, **employment at will** prevails. This means that organizations have the right to terminate the employment of anyone at any time, and employees have the right to quit at any time. In fact, even though it is polite, providing a 2-week notice before quitting is not a legal requirement.

At the same time, there are numerous exceptions to at-will employment. A dismissal that violates the law is termed **wrongful dismissal**. For example, employees who are covered by a *collective bargaining agreement* are subject to the contract negotiated between the union and the employer regarding when and how to terminate employment. There may also be an *employment contract* between the employer and employee with respect to terms and duration of employment and conditions for termination (such as one that may exist for teachers). If a contract is in place, the organization needs to follow it rather than assume that employment is at will. Sometimes, there may be an *implied contract* between the employee and the organization. For example, if the organization verbally mentioned that employees in this organization are not fired without a reason, this may constitute a legally binding verbal contract, an exception to employment at will. *Public policy exception* suggests that the employee may not be fired in a way that violates public interest, such as firing an employee for performing jury duty or reporting illegal behavior of the organization. *Statutory exceptions* refer to myriad federal and state laws that prohibit discrimination based on specific actions or protected characteristics. Finally, some states endorse the principle of *covenant of good faith*. This means that in these states, it is illegal to dismiss the employee in a malicious way. An example of this is the dismissal of an employee to avoid paying them their earned sales commissions. Organizations benefit from being familiar with state and federal laws that limit their ability to dismiss employees.[31]

The Dismissal Interview

Experts agree that there are right and wrong ways of conducting the termination interview. Following are some recommendations to facilitate a less negative interview.

- *Be there.* Ultimately, it is the responsibility of the dismissed employee's manager to communicate the news. A representative from HR may be a part of the dismissal

Employment at will When organizations have the right to terminate the employment of anyone at any time, and employees have the right to quit at any time

Wrongful dismissal A dismissal that violates the law

meeting. Instead of expecting HR to do the talking, it is reasonable to expect that HR play a supportive role.

- *Be straightforward.* Although thanking the employee for their contributions is a good idea, discussing how difficult this decision was for the manager or mentioning the strengths of the employee may appear patronizing.[32]

- *Do not lie.* Telling the employee that their position is being eliminated to spare their feelings is sure to backfire when you are looking for a replacement. Such behavior erodes the company's credibility and is also likely to increase its legal exposure.[33]

- *"It is not me, it is you."* When communicating difficult news, a natural tendency is to apologize, mention the employee's good qualities, and place the blame on the situation. Experts warn that this strategy is undesirable, may cause the employee to blame the organization, and may increase legal liability. A quick summary of the steps that happened before you got to this point is warranted.[34]

- *Clarify the timeline.* This meeting is also a good opportunity to discuss what happens next. When is the employee's last day? Is the employee eligible for severance pay? (See more details later in this chapter.) What happens to unused vacation time and insurance?

Spotlight on Legal Issues

WRONGFUL TERMINATION AT UNITED AIRLINES

In 2013, United Airlines fired two flight attendants who had served the company a combined total of 70 years and 30,000 flight hours. The employees had exemplary records and had never been disciplined or received complaints. In fact, they had received multiple awards for service and dedication over their careers. They were fired when a supervisor observed them watching an iPad for 15 minutes during a flight and noticed that they did not wear their aprons while serving customers. They were notified about the termination decision and were offered the option to retire instead.

The flight attendants filed a lawsuit in which they claimed that the real reason for the termination decision was age. The case was decided in favor of the plaintiffs, and they were awarded $800,000 for back pay and damages.

The cost of the case is estimated to be around $1.5 million.

Organizations are advised to ensure that termination decisions are not made lightly. Organizations can take several steps to stay on the right side of the law, such as

- Being sure that employees are not terminated for illegal reasons

- Ensuring that the organization establishes and follows consistent procedures for termination decisions

- Having strong documentation of past performance. It is not permissible to go back and create a paper trail for past offenses. Instead, managers need to document problem behavior along the way, communicate with the employee, and ensure compliance.[35]

Explaining the Decision to the Team

When an employee is dismissed, it is important to communicate the decision to the remaining employees. There will be speculation about what happened. Employees will also wonder whether something similar could happen to them. It is important to protect the privacy of the employee being dismissed but also to reassure the team that the decision was fair. Firing an employee in an unfair manner may lead to loss of trust on the part of the dismissed employee's coworkers.[36]

Involuntary Turnover: Layoffs

LO 10.5   Estimate the cost of employee layoffs to an organization.

When organizations are faced with pressures to contain and reduce costs, reducing the number of employees is one method available to them. Layoffs refer to involuntary turnover of employees due to organizational restructuring, downsizing, or other strategic or economic reasons. Unlike dismissals, layoffs involve discharge of employees through no fault of their own.

Layoffs typically involve discharge of multiple employees, often reaching hundreds or even thousands. For example, in 2008, Citigroup cut 50,000 jobs during the credit crisis.[37] Layoffs are painful for employees being let go and their coworkers and managers, as well as families. As the numbers get larger, the effects may spread throughout the community in which the business is located.

Costs of Layoffs

The literature and the popular press treat layoffs as traumatizing events with good reason. Those directly affected by layoffs are sometimes termed "victims" of a layoff, whereas employees who escape the layoff are "survivors." Of course, this view is overly simplistic. In any layoff, there will be some employees who would prefer to be (and sometimes volunteer to be) among those who are being laid off; some employees may have been looking for an exit anyway, and the accompanying financial packages, such as a generous severance pay, may seem an attractive way of leaving an organization they were not committed to. Alternatively, among those who are laid off, there will be some who look at it as a blessing in disguise: an opportunity to pursue a different career, job, or life change that they were hesitant to take while employed. At the same time, layoffs have numerous significant and negative effects and costs to employees, business outcomes, communities, customer relations, and the reputation of a business.

When organizations engage in downsizing, it is often perceived as a violation of one's psychological contract with the organization. Employee justice perceptions, job involvement, loyalty, trust, creativity, and job performance suffer following downsizing.[38] In fact, research shows that these effects are not limited to feelings of injustice and anger toward the organization they are leaving. Layoff victims have lower trust in their next employer, express cynicism about the intentions of the new employer, and even worry that they will be mistreated by the new organization.[39] Further, an individual's layoff history has been linked to voluntary turnover in jobs following the layoff. This is partially because employees are more likely to be underemployed or hold poor-quality jobs following layoffs but also because layoffs become part of an individual's personal history, preventing them from forming strong attachments to their next employer.[40] In other words, layoffs are traumatic in the sense that they erode trust in employers in general and lead to a sense that organizations are not trustworthy.

Interestingly, whether layoffs ultimately improve organizational performance is controversial. Organizational downsizing is not always the result of a well-thought-out plan to benefit the organization: Sometimes it occurs because organizations imitate each other. Research shows that downsizing may result in some reductions in labor costs, but it also disrupts organizational relations, erodes the skill base of the organization, and harms the business, with several studies suggesting a negative relationship between downsizing and organizational performance. In cases in which studies identified positive effects on organizational performance, these were realized several years after downsizing, suggesting that any positive effects typically happen in the long term.[41]

Layoffs also have some direct financial costs. **Unemployment insurance** is payment made to unemployed individuals. Unemployment insurance is a federal program providing income continuation to employees who lost their jobs through no fault of their own. The program is administered by individual states, so the amount and conditions vary by the state. This tax rate goes up as the organization lays off more employees and those employees end up drawing funds from the unemployment insurance. To manage these costs, organizations may consider alternatives to layoffs such as retraining employees to use them elsewhere and speed up the process of finding a new job for laid-off employees through referrals, providing leads, and other forms of assistance in finding a new job.

Benefits of Job Security

Job insecurity, or the feeling and worry that individuals may suddenly lose their jobs, is an important stressor, with consequences for employee well-being and job attitudes. Although feelings of job insecurity may originate from individual factors such as personality and qualifications, having gone through layoffs and other adverse organizational changes in the past play an important role in generating feelings of job insecurity.[42]

Unemployment insurance
Payment made to unemployed individuals

To avoid the negative consequences of layoffs and the resulting job insecurity, some organizations make efforts to avoid layoffs. For example, Southwest Airlines and the San Diego, California–based Scripps Health have policies around avoiding layoffs and instead invest in retraining employees.[44] Companies that pursue zero-layoff policies aim to build long-term relations with their employees and seek alternative ways of managing their payroll expenses.

HR can minimize the need for layoffs through effective workforce planning. If an organization is in the habit of laying off employees regularly in response to seasonal fluctuations in demand and rehiring employees because key talent is lost after layoffs, these may be indications that this process is not being managed well. For example, in the United

Lincoln Electric, a manufacturer of welding products founded in 1895, follows a no-layoffs policy for its workforce of over 10,000.[43]

©iStock.com/Phonix_a

Kingdom, the Department for Work and Pensions was criticized when it announced plans to hire 3,000 employees on fixed-term contracts a few weeks after thousands of employees were laid off through a volunteer process. Instead, organizations may take a long-term view to layoffs by considering alternatives to layoffs and regarding layoffs as a last resort.

Deciding Layoff Criteria

As long as the layoff criteria are not illegal (i.e., choosing employees based on their age, disability status, sex, or race), organizations are allowed to set the criteria to fit their business needs. Layoffs may be seniority based and performance based. When layoffs are based on seniority, the organization retains the most senior workers and lets go of the newer workers. Even though this may lead to the loss of newly acquired key talent, this method has the advantage of ease of implementation. Employees are simply let go based on their hire date, and the implementation is likely to be systematic. When performance is used as the layoff criterion, the organization will be able to retain higher performers. In practice, however, any biases and subjectivity inherent in performance measurement systems will affect layoff decisions, which may lead to feelings of unfairness.

Regardless of the criteria to be used, organizations are advised to keep good records of what criteria were used to implement layoffs and to ensure that the implementation is systematic.[45] Further, it is important to conduct an adverse-impact analysis to identify the effects on diversity. In many organizations, women and minorities may be clustered in staff functions and may have less tenure. As a result, a seemingly neutral layoff criterion like seniority may wipe out one demographic group from the department. Understanding how different criteria will affect the level of diversity within the organization may motivate the organization to consider multiple criteria and to ensure that the criteria being used are fair and defensible.[46]

The Legal Side of Layoffs

When an organization is planning a layoff, an important federal law to be familiar with is the Worker Adjustment and Retraining Notification (WARN) Act. This act covers employers with at least 100 full-time employees or employers with at least 100 part-time and full-time employees who work a combined total of 4,000 hours per week. Federal, state, and local government employees are *not* covered by this law. Further, when calculating the size of a business, employees who had been employed for fewer than 6 months in the past 12 months are excluded. Covered organizations who intend to do one of the following are required to provide 60-day written advance notice to employees:

a. close a plant or facility and lay off at least 50 employees within a single site for a period of 6 months or more, or

b. conduct a mass layoff in which the organization lays off 50 to 499 employees within a single site within a 30-day period, and that number is at least 33% of the organization's workforce, or

c. the organization will lay off 500 or more employees within a 30-day period.

Even when a single layoff may not reach one of these thresholds, the organization may still be covered by the WARN Act if the organization lays off two or more groups of employees, with the total reaching one of these thresholds within a 90-day period. Further, in addition to laying off employees, if the organization is planning to reduce the hours of employees by more than 50% for 6 months, the WARN Act's notification requirements are triggered. If the organization fails to provide advance notice, the organization is responsible for back pay and benefits up to 60 days.

Some organizations choose not to provide written advance notice, instead opting to provide 60 days' pay and benefits instead of notice and lay off employees immediately. This is technically a violation of the WARN Act, but this approach means that the organization has satisfied its WARN Act obligations by paying the penalty for violating the act.[47] In addition to the federal WARN Act, state laws often extend the advance notice requirements for businesses engaged in layoffs. For example, states such as California, Illinois, New Hampshire, and New York have their own WARN Acts.[48]

The layoff decision needs to be compliant with the EEOC laws. When layoff criteria used by the organization intentionally or unintentionally discriminate against a protected group, the layoff decision may violate the law. For this reason, as well as to maintain the fairness of the decisions, experts recommend that layoff decisions are based on objective criteria that can easily be verified, such as possessing multiple skills, seniority, and experience, as opposed to subjective criteria such as "attitude" or "initiative."[49]

Delivering the Message

How the layoff victims are treated matters not only because fair treatment is the right thing to do but also because it affects the job attitudes, performance, and retention of layoff survivors. Poor treatment of layoff victims may harm the company's reputation. Social media and websites such as Glassdoor.com, where current and former employees leave comments about their treatment by a company, make it easier for tales of unfair treatment to spread to potential job applicants and clients. In contrast, in a study on highly educated layoff victims, workers who were treated fairly during layoffs were more likely to recommend their former employer to others and report that they would return to work in that organization if given the chance.[50]

Delivering layoff news is stressful for managers, who may experience feelings such as guilt, worry about employees' reactions, anger at the organization's decision, and doubt regarding their self-image as an effective manager. Managers need to be trained in how to structure the layoff interview to ensure that the bad news is delivered in a professional way and to ensure that the process teaches managers to be fair. Researchers showed in a series of two laboratory studies that a training program that followed this structure was successful in ensuring that layoff news was communicated in a fairer manner, and the negative emotions reported by managers delivering the news were lower when trained. Unfortunately, such training is not common because layoffs are a relatively infrequent event, but managers need to learn how to deliver bad news in general, particularly when it comes to layoff news.[51]

Severance Pay

Severance pay refers to payments made to departing employees during organizationally initiated turnover. It is important to note that severance pay is not a federal legal requirement in the United States. However, many organizations choose to provide severance pay, and when severance pay is promised in an employee handbook or employment contract, it becomes a legally binding obligation. According to a study by the Institute of Management and Administration (IOMA), more than 70% of study participants working in organizations with at least 2,500 employees provided severance pay to all terminated employees, whereas only 15% of businesses with fewer than 50 employees did so. Further, it was most common to provide severance based on the length of the employee's service.[52]

Severance packages often include 1 or 2 weeks of pay for each year the employee has been employed by the organization. They may include additional benefits, such as an extension of employee health insurance for a period of time. Even though severance may be provided for both dismissals and layoffs, organizations may choose not to provide severance when an employee is terminated for cause (such as stealing money, violating company policy, or willfully behaving in a way damaging to the company), whereas organizations with severance policies typically provide them to all laid-off employees.

Employers may want to provide a generous severance pay during layoffs to soften the blow and help out displaced workers. Even in the best-case scenario, employees may find themselves unemployed for several months, and providing a generous severance package helps deal with the financial stress. Severance packages also play a protective role: Organizations usually provide severance pay in exchange for a waiver of one's right to sue the company for reasons of discrimination. In practice, signing a severance agreement and receiving severance payment do not automatically prevent an employee from suing for discrimination; the court may still decide that the waiver is not valid. However, this waiver is usually valid if the departing employee signed it willingly and understood what it meant upon signing.[53]

Outplacement Assistance

In addition to providing laid-off employees with severance pay, some organizations also provide services that assist laid-off workers to find reemployment quicker. A study of more than 1,000 organizations showed that such programs benefit organizations by reducing unwanted turnover of employees and increasing survivor job satisfaction after layoffs. Helping employees find new employment is part of showing concern for them.[54]

Outplacement services are typically provided by outside companies contracted by the organization. Ideally, the program will be individualized and tailored to the person. For example, key elements of these programs include having a one-on-one meeting with a counselor who helps the person cope with the emotions arising from the layoff, a comprehensive assessment of the employee's skills and an analysis of how the person may fit with the job market, and providing training to help the employee brush up on their job search, interviewing, and negotiation skills.[55]

Severance pay
Payments made to departing employees during organizationally initiated turnover

Managing Survivors

An important aspect of managing layoffs is to have a plan for how the layoffs will be communicated to layoff survivors (or those employees who are not being laid off) and how these remaining employees will be reengaged and motivated. A strong communication plan may mitigate some of the negative effects of layoffs on survivors. Communication by management and ethical treatment of layoff victims were found to mitigate some of the harmful effects of layoffs on survivor work satisfaction, fairness, and empowerment.[56] Organizations have an incentive to clearly communicate the reasons and consequences of layoffs for the remaining workforce, as well as to provide the necessary reassurances if they are able. For example, if the layoffs were to be a one-time event and no other layoffs are expected or planned in the near future, communicating this information is beneficial. However, management needs to be honest: If layoffs are going to occur in the near future, providing reassurances may comfort employees in the short run but is bound to break trust when promises are not kept.[57]

CHAPTER SUMMARY

Employee turnover may take the form of voluntary turnover such as quitting and retiring and involuntary turnover such as dismissals and layoffs. Because turnover is costly, it is important for HR professionals to understand how to manage employee retention. Retention is influenced by many factors, including upper management's level of support for retention, the use of employee surveys and interviews, effective hiring and onboarding practices, investment in high-commitment HR practices, and attention to predictors of turnover. Although some forms of turnover may have benefits for organizations in the short and long term, organizations need to be deliberate in managing employee separations to ensure that they have access to the talent they need to reach organizational goals. Effective HR practices may aid in turnover management, but ultimately managers play a key role in motivating employees to quit their jobs or retire, as well as how employee dismissals and layoffs are handled in the organization. So, managing employee separation requires a true partnership between HR departments and line managers.

KEY TERMS

voluntary turnover   228
involuntary turnover   228
dismissal   228
layoffs   228
tardiness   229
absenteeism   229

unfolding model of
   turnover   231
job embeddedness model   231
pulse surveys   233
boomerang employees   236
bridge employment   238

progressive discipline   239
employment at will   240
wrongful dismissal   240
unemployment insurance   243
severance pay   246

$SAGE edge™

Get the tools you need to sharpen your study skills. SAGE edge offers a robust online environment featuring an impressive array of free tools and resources.

Access practice quizzes, eFlashcards, video, and multimedia at **edge.sagepub.com/bauerbrief**

HR REASONING AND DECISION-MAKING EXERCISES

EXERCISE 10.1: DISMISSING AN EMPLOYEE

You work for the HR department of a manufacturing firm. The company has 500 employees, a significant portion of whom have long tenure in the company.

Eric Jenkins, a department manager who was hired 2 years ago, contacted you, saying that he is interested in dismissing Laura Harrison. Laura has been with the company for the past 25 years. He is concerned that Laura is not adapting well to the new technological changes over the past year. Plus, she is always debating every point with Eric, trying to argue "this is not how we do things around here." Eric feels that Laura's knowledge of the business is stale, and she is displaying strong resistance to change and innovation. He also feels that she is not respecting him because she is much older than he is. They have had performance conversations in the past, but Laura does not seem interested in improving. Eric gave Laura a 3 out of 5 (meets expectations) in her last performance review, which was about a year ago.

Your company is not unionized and does not have a formal discipline procedure.

Questions

1. What would you advise Eric to do? Should Eric dismiss Laura? Explain your rationale. What would be the consequences of dismissing and not dismissing Laura?
2. What additional information would be helpful to you in making your recommendation about this case?
3. Let's say you decided not to dismiss Laura in the short run. What would be your recommended action plan to solve this problem?
4. What type of procedures would be helpful to have in this company? Provide your recommendations for structural changes so that cases such as these are more easily resolved.

EXERCISE 10.2: CREATING A RETENTION MANAGEMENT SYSTEM

You are working at Shek, Inc., an organization providing private and group surfing and scuba diving lessons, adventure tours, and rental services to tourists in Hawaii. Your company has around 200 employees consisting of instructors, sales, marketing, and office personnel. The company has an annual turnover rate of 80%, which you suspect is too high.

Questions

1. How would you assess why employees are leaving? After you choose your method of measurement (survey, interviews), develop questions to include in your instrument. How would you analyze the data to identify the top reasons for employee departures?
2. Let's assume that you found out the following top three reasons for turnover in this company:
    a.   Management is very authoritarian and not supportive of employees.
    b.   Employee schedules vary a lot and often are announced with very short notice.
    c.   Employees feel they are working all the time with little downtime.

What would be your proposed action plan to deal with these issues? Be specific, and make sure that your recommendations focus on recruitment, selection, training, compensation, and any other stages of the employment cycle.

ETHICAL MATTERS EXERCISE: COMPASSIONATE DELIVERY OF LAYOFF NEWS

Even though not every layoff "victim" may feel like a victim, learning about one's impending layoff may be met with anger, humiliation, and a feeling that one is disposable. In some companies, the news is delivered in an unnecessarily careless and humiliating way. Ideally, layoff news should be delivered by showing compassion and respect to the employees. Here are some examples that miss the mark on this issue.

Escorted by security. It is common for organizations to have security presence during mass layoffs or when retaliation and aggression are expected, but should escorting employees to the exit be routine practice? Organizations need to strike a balance between ensuring safety and showing compassion. A senior executive who was a long-time employee shared his experience: "I had to go down, grab some things quickly, and there was some security guards waiting. And then I got marched out of the building. And I thought that was so demeaning. . . . And the thing that I did find humiliating, I had to ring up and ask permission to come back and collect all my stuff."[58]

Learning about it last. One employee reports that his company was conducting layoff meetings while outgoing voicemails of departing employees were being changed. An employee's wife found out about the layoff of her husband from a voicemail message stating that the employee no longer worked there.[59]

Mass announcements. Companies sometimes find it cumbersome to conduct one-on-one meetings with employees to be laid off and resort to mass announcements. Although this method is efficient, employees often find it disrespectful and unfair, especially when the announcement is not made in a face-to-face meeting. In one case, a Ford assembly plant in Chicago notified laid-off employees via an automated phone call on Halloween. Many employees thought it was a prank and showed up to work the next day, only to find that their ID badges had been disabled.[60]

Can you come back and teach us what you do? An employee who performed a task vital to the company's operations was laid off. A few days later, she received a call from HR. Apparently, no one had realized how important her job was to the operations until after she was laid off. Would she consider coming back for a few days and teaching what she did to someone still employed in the company?[61]

Questions

1. What reasons can you think of to explain why employers chose to use what can be perceived as insensitive layoff announcements like those described here?
2. Find an example in the news or in the HR literature of a layoff that was handled with respect and compassion for the workers. Were there any problems nevertheless? What did the company do right, and what could have been done better?

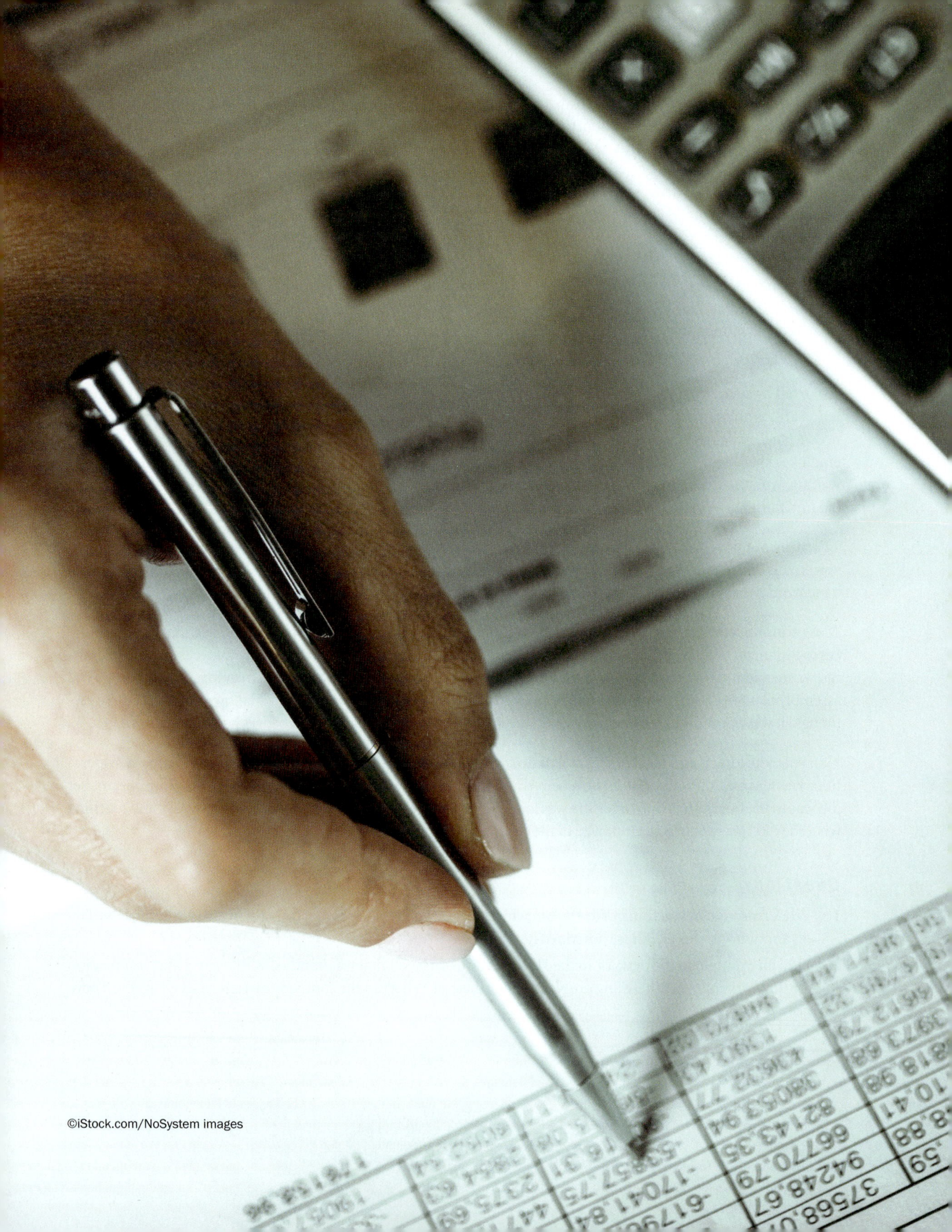

11 Rewarding Employees

LEARNING OBJECTIVES

After reading and studying this chapter, you should be able to do the following:

11.1 Explain the conceptual foundation of compensation and reward systems.

11.2 Describe how to develop internally, externally, and individually equitable and legally compliant pay structures.

11.3 Describe the motivating potential of pay and other rewards.

11.4 Describe common individual and group pay-for-performance programs.

11.5 Assess common challenges and opportunities of reward systems.

HR in Action: The Case of Gravity Payments

In 2015, Dan Price—the CEO of a small company called Gravity Payments, which offers credit card processing—announced that all employees' annual pay would be raised to a minimum of $70,000 per year and that his $1 million in annual pay would be temporarily lowered to $70,000 to help cover the increased labor costs associated with the initiative. Price's inspiration for the change stemmed from a confrontation with an employee regarding pay and from a study by Kahneman and Deaton. In that study, the researchers found that emotional well-being increased steadily along with increased pay until an annual income of about $75,000 was reached, at which point additional pay did not result in higher emotional well-being.

Dan Price, CEO of Gravity Payments

In the days that followed, Price's announcement was met with a mixture of praise, consternation, and criticism. On one hand, Gravity Payments received an influx of résumés, interest from business scholars, and praise from some clients and even an elected official. On the other hand, the company faced criticism from clients who feared that the price of Gravity Payments' services would increase, from current employees who were concerned about the potential internal inequity of having positions of different worth being compensated at similar rates, and from members of the general public who thought the announcement was nothing but a publicity stunt.

Six months later, only two employees had left the company, alleviating potential concerns by some of a mass exodus due to perceived pay inequity. Around 18 months later, the company had seen a 67% increase in new clients and a 75% increase in revenues, and by about 2 years later, 10% of Gravity Payments' employees had purchased a home or planned to do so in the near future—a purchase that previously had seemed out of reach for many. In the end, what began as an initiative to improve the emotional well-being of those who earned less than $70,000 ended up helping the company's bottom line.[1]

Case Discussion Questions

1. If you were a Gravity Payments' employee who made $50,000 per year, how would you have reacted to the new $70,000 per year pay minimum? What if you were an employee who made $90,000 per year?

2. Were you surprised by the different reactions of employees and of the general public? If so, how?

3. To improve the perceptions of employees and the general public, what could the Gravity Payments' CEO have done differently when communicating the new pay policy?

A **pay structure** is an important part of an organization's compensation and reward systems, and it refers to the way in which an organization applies pay rates and financial rewards to different jobs, skills, or competencies. Further, a well-designed pay structure is important for attracting and retaining talented individuals, as well as for motivating existing workers to achieve higher levels of performance. A pay structure should align with an organization's strategic goals, distribute pay fairly, compete with the pay practices of other organizations, and abide by federal, state, and local employment and labor laws.

Pay as a Reward

LO 11.1   Explain the conceptual foundation of compensation and reward systems.

Pay structure
The way in which an organization applies pay rates and financial rewards to different jobs, skills, or competencies

When thinking about rewarding employees, pay is likely the first thing that comes to mind—and for good reason. Pay, which includes wages and salaries, often accounts for nearly 70% of a total compensation package's overall value. The remainder of a total compensation package may also include benefits and other employment offerings such as health care and paid time off.[2] Managers and employees often view the role of pay differently. For managers, pay is often viewed as a major cost. For employees, pay often represents an entitlement offered in exchange for work. This chapter focuses on how to develop an effective pay structure that addresses the concerns of both managers and employees.

Although workers often emphasize the importance of pay when deciding to accept a job offer, pay is not the only reason workers gravitate to certain organizations. A 2017 survey by Korn Ferry revealed that only 4% of professionals ranked pay as the #1 reason for choosing one organization over another.[3] Accumulated research has revealed only a small correlation between employees' pay and their overall job satisfaction, meaning that employees who are paid more are only slightly more likely to be satisfied with their jobs.[4] Why might this be the case? Other factors, such as individuals' interactions and relationships with coworkers and supervisors, characteristics and conditions of work, HR practices, and even their own personalities, play important roles in employees' overall job satisfaction.[5]

Reward Systems

Before focusing on pay, specifically, it is important to understand how pay fits into a reward system. A **reward system** refers to the policies, procedures, and practices used by an organization to determine the amount and types of returns individuals, teams, and the organization receive in exchange for their organizational membership and contributions.

A reward system should be designed to attract, motivate, and retain individuals who directly or indirectly can contribute to the development, sale, or provision of the organization's products or services. For best results, a reward system should be integrated with other HR systems. First, even the most effective recruitment and selection processes can fail to attract qualified individuals if the rewards offered are not competitive with offers made by other organizations. Second, without a competitive rewards package and financial incentives, an organization may struggle to motivate existing employees to use and apply their KSAOs. Third, an organization may struggle to retain workers when other organizations offer more attractive rewards packages or when workers are not rewarded fairly with respect to their contributions or position.

Next, we distinguish between two broad categories of rewards: relational returns and total compensation.[6]

Relational Returns

Relational returns include nonmonetary incentives and rewards, such as new learning and developmental opportunities, enriched and challenging work, job security, and recognition. As an example, Google offered a "20% time" policy in which employees were encouraged to spend 20% of their time working on personal projects of their own choosing that had the potential to benefit the company. This served not only as an enriching activity for employees but also as a source of potentially valuable new products and services, such as Gmail and Google News.[7]

Total Compensation

Total compensation subsumes compensation and benefits, which are often referred to as direct pay and indirect pay, respectively. **Compensation** includes base pay and forms of variable pay (e.g., sales commission), and **benefits** include health, life, and disability insurance; retirement programs; and work–life balance programs.

Reward system The policies, procedures, and practices used by an organization to determine the amount and types of returns individuals, teams, and the organization receive in exchange for their membership and contributions

Relational returns Nonmonetary incentives and rewards, such as new learning and developmental opportunities, enriched and challenging work, job security, and recognition

Total compensation Package of compensation and benefits that employees receive

Compensation Employee reward that includes base pay and variable pay and is sometimes referred to as direct pay

Benefits Employee rewards that are sometimes referred to as indirect pay and include health, life, and disability insurance; retirement programs; and work–life balance programs

Developing a Pay Structure

LO 11.2   Describe how to develop internally, externally, and individually equitable and legally compliant pay structures.

As a component of a reward system, a pay structure refers to the way an organization applies pay rates to different jobs. When developing a pay structure, an overarching objective should be to ensure that its resulting policies adhere to the principles of fairness and equity. Specifically, steps should be taken to ensure individual employees are paid equitably relative to other employees in the organization and relative to employees at other organizations performing similar work. Further, a pay structure should abide by prevailing employment and labor laws. In sum, when developing and administering a pay structure and associated policies, an organization should strive for the following goals: (a) internal equity, (b) external equity, (c) individual equity, and (d) legal compliance (see Figure 11.1).

Internal equity The fairness of pay rates across jobs within an organization

Ensuring Internal Equity

Internal equity (sometimes called *internal alignment* or *internal consistency*) refers to the fairness of pay rates across jobs *within* an organization.[8] In other words, internal equity has

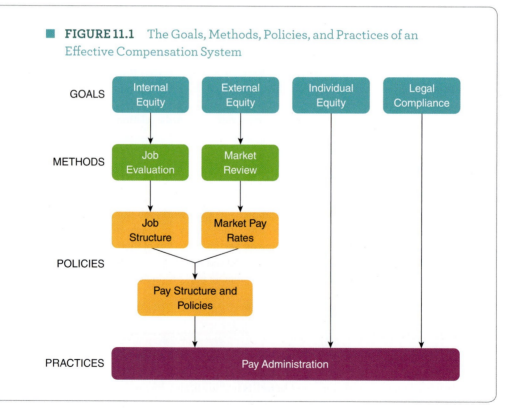

■ **FIGURE 11.1**   The Goals, Methods, Policies, and Practices of an Effective Compensation System

to do with whether jobs of greater worth to an organization are compensated at a higher level.

Job Structure

Creating a fair job structure is an important step toward an internally equitable pay structure. A job structure—sometimes called a *job hierarchy*—refers to the ranking of jobs based on their respective worth.

Job Evaluation

Job evaluation is used to create a fair job structure. Job evaluation refers to a process in which subject matter experts (SMEs), such as incumbents, supervisors of job incumbents, and/or internal or external compensation experts, determine the relative worth of jobs within an organization. In a job evaluation, SMEs determine the relative worth of each job based on how much each job contributes (relatively speaking) to the organization's attainment of strategic objectives. Prior to doing so, however, a rigorous, up-to-date job analysis should be conducted for all jobs that will be evaluated in the job evaluation. The reason for this is that it is critical to identify the core tasks, KSAOs, and/or competencies associated with each job to systematically evaluate the relative worth of each job. In addition, a job analysis yields job descriptions and specifications that feed into the job evaluation and ultimately serve as the foundation of the job structure (as shown in Figure 11.2).

The **point-factor method** is a common job evaluation approach in organizations given its rigor and relative objectivity.[9] Like other approaches, the point-factor method requires a team of SMEs, preferably including at least one person who is an internal or external compensation expert.

Point-factor method
A job evaluation approach in which a team of subject matter experts systematically identifies compensable factors and develops and applies scales and weights for compensable factors, ultimately resulting in points being assigned to different jobs to describe their relative worth

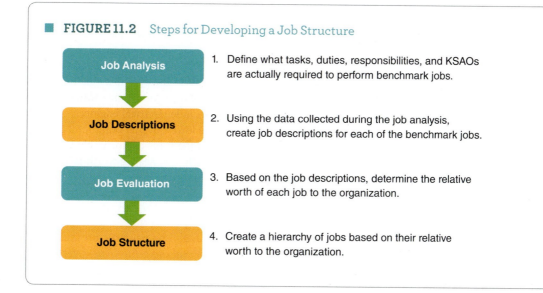

■ **FIGURE 11.2** Steps for Developing a Job Structure

Job Analysis
1. Define what tasks, duties, responsibilities, and KSAOs are actually required to perform benchmark jobs.

Job Descriptions
2. Using the data collected during the job analysis, create job descriptions for each of the benchmark jobs.

Job Evaluation
3. Based on the job descriptions, determine the relative worth of each job to the organization.

Job Structure
4. Create a hierarchy of jobs based on their relative worth to the organization.

Spotlight on Data and Analytics

PAY AND HUMAN RESOURCE INFORMATION SYSTEMS

To design a competitive, externally equitable pay structure, an organization must obtain or access information about other organizations' pay practices. Traditionally, a consortium of organizations would subscribe to a third-party market survey and submit pay data confidentially, and in return, the organizations would receive a hard copy or an electronic copy of the survey results.

Today, some enterprise resource planning and HR information system vendors offer integrative solutions that reveal how well an organization is paying certain benchmark jobs in relation to similar jobs at other organizations. Both ADP and PayScale provide cloud-based software that facilitates the process by which organizations participate in market surveys, as well as off-the-shelf analytics and data visualizations for decision-making purposes. For example, ADP leverages existing client pay information across different jobs to provide automated data analytics and visualizations, including information about pay equity related to race and sex.[10]

The point-factor method requires SMEs to identify and apply compensable factors to determine the relative worth of different jobs. **Compensable factors** are the common dimensions by which jobs vary in terms of their worth to the organization. Examples of compensable factors might include the levels of experience and education needed to do the job, the level of complexity inherent to the job, or even the level of danger and risk involved in performing the job. For instance, a job that requires an advanced degree and significant experience will pay more than an entry-level job requiring a high school degree, assuming education and experience are compensable factors.

For a given job, the point-factor method earns its name by resulting in a specific point value for each compensable factor based on the extent to which the job embodies each compensable factor. Further, this approach yields an overall point total for each job, such that the point total of one job can be compared to the point total of another job. As a result, this method clearly shows the relative worth of each job to the organization. Table 11.1 shows three benchmark jobs, where **benchmark jobs** are key jobs that are common across different organizations. Examples of benchmark jobs include electrical engineer, psychiatrist, and customer service representative. Job 1 has the lowest overall point total and Job 3 has the highest. Look at the columns associated with the three compensable factors of experience, education, and complexity, and note that each job's relative worth is based on the level of each compensable factor required for performing the job.

Ensuring External Equity

In addition to internal equity, organizations should also establish a pay structure that is high in external equity. **External equity** (also known as *external competitiveness*) refers to the extent to which the pay for a particular job is competitive and fair relative to the pay of the same or similar jobs at other organizations. In other words, external equity has to do with

Compensable factors The common dimensions by which jobs vary in terms of worth to the organization

Benchmark job A key job that is common across different organizations in terms of its job description

External equity The extent to which the pay for a particular job is competitive and fair relative to the pay of the same or similar jobs at other organizations

TABLE 11.1   Example of Calculated Points for Benchmark Jobs Using the Point-Factor Method

BENCHMARK JOBS	COMPENSABLE FACTORS			
	EXPERIENCE	EDUCATION	COMPLEXITY	TOTAL
Job 1	200	60	200	460
Job 2	200	180	400	780
Job 3	200	300	500	1,000

how well an organization compensates benchmark jobs compared to how well competitor organizations compensate them.

In an ideal world, an organization would pay whatever it takes to attract, motivate, and retain top talent for each position. In reality, such an approach would quickly exceed an organization's compensation budget. Consequently, compensation experts must carefully consider the labor supply and labor demand for benchmark jobs, and how much to pay those working benchmark jobs relative to competitors. For instance, if the labor demand exceeds the labor supply for a particular job, then the organization may need to pay more to attract, motivate, and retain qualified individuals.

By conducting a market review, an organization can determine if it is lagging, matching, or leading the market in terms of pay, which encourages data-informed decisions regarding pay. A **market review** is the process of collecting pay data for benchmark jobs from other organizations. Ultimately, the data collected by reviewing benchmark jobs can be combined with an organization's job structure data to create a pay structure that includes benchmark and nonbenchmark jobs alike. Often, a market review is conducted with the help of a third-party survey company that collects pay data confidentially from employers or employees; sometimes these are referred to as *salary surveys* or *market surveys*. These surveys typically include important pay information, such as the mean or median pay level for a particular benchmark job.

Integrating Internal Equity and External Equity

So far, we have discussed internal equity and external equity separately. However, when integrated, internal equity and external equity can provide the foundation for an effective pay structure. Specifically, by integrating the job structure data gathered from a job evaluation (internal equity) and the market pay data gathered from a market review (external equity), an organization can set the pay levels for all benchmark and non-benchmark jobs.

There are different ways to integrate job evaluation and market review data, and research has shown that compensation decision makers often place a greater emphasis on market review data as compared to job evaluation data; in other words, they tend to attribute more importance to external equity than to internal equity.[11] In fact, some organizations base

Market review The process of collecting pay data for benchmark jobs from other organizations

their pay levels and pay structure directly on their competitors' pay levels, a process called *market pricing*.[12]

For a balanced approach, an organization can use the point-factor method of job evaluation combined with market review data to determine how much a single point is worth in dollars. This information can be used to establish a market pay line and a pay policy line for both benchmark and nonbenchmark jobs.

Market Pay Line

A market pay line reflects the relationship between the internal job structure of the organization for benchmark jobs—which is often represented in terms of job evaluation points—and the external pay practices of other organizations gathered from a market review. Table 11.2 contains the names of nursing family benchmark jobs, their job evaluation points, and the corresponding market pay rates. The market pay line shown in Figure 11.3 was estimated using the data from Table 11.2. In Figure 11.3, the solid black line represents the market pay line, the x-axis contains the jobs from the nursing job family (e.g., RN = registered nurse) and their respective job evaluation points, the y-axis contains the median monthly base pay rates, and the blue diamonds represent the observed data points used to estimate the market pay line.

To estimate this market pay line, we used regression analysis. Regression analysis results in a line of best fit, and in this context, the line of best fit represents the market pay line. The line of best fit can also be written out as an equation:

$$\text{Monthly base pay (\$)} = -8{,}988.99 + 19.71 \times \text{job evaluation points}$$

In Figure 11.3, note that nearly all of the blue diamonds fall very closely to the black line, which suggests that the estimated market pay line fits the observed data closely. In other words, the internal job structure for these benchmark jobs appears to align closely with the pay practices of other organizations. Employees would likely perceive such a pay structure to be high in both internal and external equity.

TABLE 11.2　Job Titles of Benchmark Jobs, Job Evaluation Points, and Market Pay Rates

JOB TITLE	JOB EVALUATION POINTS	MARKET PAY RATES
Certified Nursing Assistant (CNA)	570	$2,590
Licensed Practical Nurse (LPN)	670	$3,938
Registered Nurse (RN)	760	$5,952
Charge Nurse (CN)	810	$7,072
Nurse Practitioner (NP)	920	$8,759
Nursing Manager (NM)	940	$8,947
Nursing Director (ND)	1000	$11,567

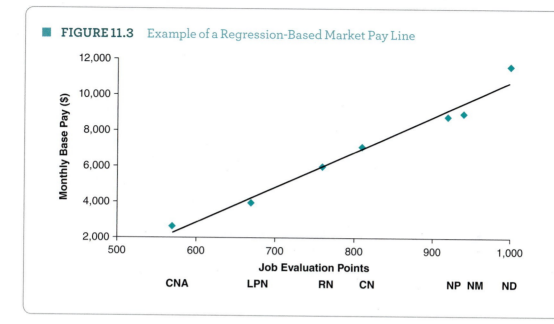

■ **FIGURE 11.3** Example of a Regression-Based Market Pay Line

Pay Policy Line

Using the market pay line as a foundation, a pay policy line translates information about the internal job structure and external pay rates of competitors into actionable pay practices (see Figure 11.4). To do so, an organization specifies—depending on its market strategy—whether it wants to lag, match, or lead the market pay line for specific jobs—or across all jobs. If a decision were made to match the market across all jobs, then the market pay line would likely become the pay policy line without any adjustment. If, however, a decision were made to lead the market by 5%, then the market pay line would need to be adjusted upwardly.

Pay Grades

A common practice is to establish pay grades based on the pay policy line. A pay grade represents a group of jobs with similar job evaluation point values that are then assigned common pay midpoint, minimum, and maximum values. Pay grades allow an organization to differentiate between employees holding the same job or similar jobs but who have different levels of performance, experience, or seniority. To create a pay grade, jobs with relatively similar job evaluation points are typically grouped together. For example, the nurse practitioner and nursing manager jobs received 920 and 940 job evaluation points, respectively (as shown in Table 11.2), and can be grouped together in a common pay grade.

To establish the minimum and maximum values for the pay grade, market review data pertaining to the 25th and 75th percentiles for these two jobs can be used to set a floor and ceiling. Figure 11.4 shows five pay grades for the nursing job family, along with which jobs belong to which pay grade. Note how the pay policy line crosses the midpoint of each pay grade, as well as how different pay grades have different pay ranges, which reflects differences in their respective market-based minimum and maximum values.

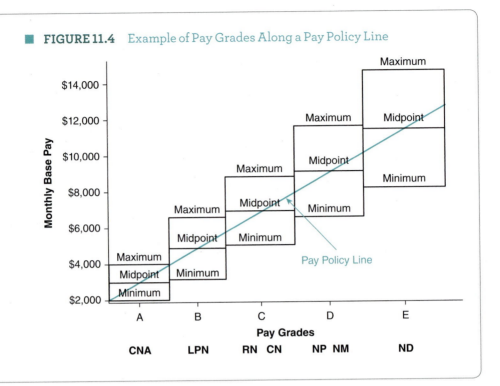

■ **FIGURE 11.4** Example of Pay Grades Along a Pay Policy Line

Ensuring Individual Equity

Once the pay structure and pay policies are in place, it is time to ensure that individual equity exists. **Individual equity** refers to the fairness of how pay is administered and distributed to individual employees working similar jobs within the same organization. For individual equity to exist, such differences in pay rates should be attributable to differences in performance, seniority, and/or experience, as opposed to other factors that are not job related (e.g., race, sex, national origin). Using the minimum and maximum values of a pay grade as upper and lower limits, compensation analysts and/or managers can determine how much to compensate each individual employee. Individual equity will be higher when high-performing, more-senior, and more-experienced employees in a given pay grade are compensated at a higher rate than low-performing, less-senior, and less-experienced employees in the same pay grade.

Individual equity The fairness of how pay is administered and distributed to individual employees working similar jobs within the same organization

Ensuring Legal Compliance

In addition to ensuring internal, external, and individual equity, a pay structure and the resulting pay policies, procedures, and practices should comply with federal, state, and local guidelines. In most cases, federal legislation is overseen and enforced by the Equal Employment Opportunity Commission (EEOC) or Office of Federal Contract Compliance Programs (OFCCP). Over the years, congressional legislation and executive orders have shaped the pay landscape in the United States. In the following sections, we cover the Fair Labor Standards Act and Internal Revenue Code.

Fair Labor Standards Act

Enacted in 1938, the **Fair Labor Standards Act (FLSA)** introduced major provisions aimed at regulating overtime pay, minimum wage, hours worked, and recordkeeping. The FLSA covers nonexempt employees who work for organizations in which the annual gross volume of sales or business meets or exceeds $500,000 or those who are engaged in interstate commerce or in the production of goods for commerce. Hospitals, businesses providing nursing or medical services, schools, preschools, and government agencies are also covered by the law. Some exceptions to FLSA coverage include workers with disabilities, those who work in tipped employment, and student learners.[13]

An important component of the FLSA is the distinction between exempt and nonexempt employees. The term *exempt* refers to those employees who do not fall under the purview of the minimum wage and overtime provisions. In contrast, the term *nonexempt* refers to those employees who are directly affected by the provisions. As it currently stands, to be classified as exempt, an employee must typically meet all three of the following tests:

- Earn $455 or more per week (which equals $23,660 per year)
- Receive a salary or charge a fee (and not an hourly wage)
- Perform job duties classified as exempt (e.g., performance of nonmanual work related to management)[14]

The overtime provision of the FLSA mandates that organizations pay at least 1.5 times a nonexempt worker's regular pay for time worked beyond 40 hours in a week.[15] Those workers classified as exempt are not eligible for overtime. Some cities and states have passed legislation to augment the federal minimum.

The minimum wage provision of the FLSA establishes an income floor, which provides some protection to workers in terms of unfair pay practices. As of 2019, the federally mandated minimum wage was $7.25/hour,[16] but certain worker populations have higher minimum wages. For example, in 2015, Executive Order 13658 introduced a $10.10/hour minimum wage for individuals working on federal contracts. Further, some cities and states have passed legislation to increase the minimum wage in their regions.

The FLSA also defines what constitutes hours worked for nonexempt employees as well as what information is required for recordkeeping purposes. Regarding hours worked, the FLSA defines a number of key concepts relevant for determining how hours are counted and tracked, such as waiting time, on-call time, rest and meal periods, and travel time.[17] As for recordkeeping, the FLSA requires that employers keep a record of nonexempt employees' names, addresses, birth dates (if younger than 19), sex, occupation, hours worked each day, regular hourly pay rate, overtime earnings, and other information relevant to pay.[18]

Internal Revenue Code

In addition to complying with antidiscrimination and fair-pay practices laws, employers and employees must also adhere to tax laws. The Internal Revenue Code of 1986 stipulates income and payroll tax regulations.[19] On one hand, taxpayers, which include individual employees and business entities, must pay income taxes, which are based on the amount of

Fair Labor Standards Act (FLSA) Enacted in 1938, this act introduced major provisions aimed at regulating overtime pay, minimum wage, hours worked, and recordkeeping

Spotlight on Legal Issues

ACCUSATIONS OF DISCRIMINATION AT THE U.S. SECRET SERVICE AGENCY

The U.S. Secret Service is a federal law enforcement agency tasked with protecting the president, the vice president, and their family members. It also investigates financial, cyber, terrorism, and child-exploitation crimes. In 2000, a small group of African American Secret Service agents filed a lawsuit against the agency, alleging racial discrimination in various employment practices, including performance evaluations and bonus pay. In 2008, a senior Secret Service inspector acknowledged that documents related to the lawsuit had been destroyed. Later, a federal judge ruled that the agency "made a mockery" of the law by refusing to provide documents requested by the African American plaintiffs during the discovery process and defying court orders, among other things. The number of plaintiffs eventually increased to include more than 100 African American agents, and the case became a class action.

In 2017, the U.S. Secret Service agreed to settle the lawsuit by paying $24 million to the group of African American agents, which could include lump-sum payments of $300,000 for each agent. Upon the announcement of the settlement agreement and resolution, Secretary of Homeland Security Jeh C. Johnson issued an official statement, which concluded, "This settlement is also, simply, the right thing to do."[20]

---

income or profits earned. On the other hand, employers must pay payroll taxes, which are based on how much employers pay their employees. Additional income and payroll taxes may be imposed by local and state governments.

Pay as a Motivator

LO 11.3   Describe the motivating potential of pay and other rewards.

So far in this chapter, we have focused on rewarding employees based on the job they perform. Many employers, however, also use financial rewards to motivate employees to perform their job at a higher level and to attain key goals. These two approaches to rewarding performance are referred to as traditional-pay programs and pay-for-performance programs, respectively.

Traditional-pay programs
A payment program that is based on the content of employees' job descriptions, job titles, and/ or organizational levels

Traditional-pay programs reward employees based on the content of their job description, title, or level. They usually correspond to the relatively stable and fixed base-pay component of individual employees' compensation package. Think of traditional-pay programs as being a wage or salary guarantee; in exchange for organizational membership and holding a particular job, employees receive a base pay amount that depends on the relative worth of the job they were hired to perform. As long as employees hold onto their jobs, they receive their base pay, regardless of how well they perform.

In contrast, **pay-for-performance programs** reward employees for the behaviors they *actually* exhibit at work and for the results or goals they *actually* achieve. That is, pay is distributed as a reward for demonstrating a certain level of performance. Compared to traditional-pay programs, pay-for-performance programs are more strongly linked to on-the-job motivation. By attaching financial incentives to the enactment of certain behaviors and fulfillment of certain goals, employees are encouraged to align their behaviors with the objectives considered most critical for companywide success.[21] Moreover, pay-for-performance programs not only motivate individuals to perform at a higher level on the job but also serve as a tool to attract high-potential applicants and to retain high-performing incumbents.[22] Later in the chapter, we cover pay-for-performance programs in more detail, but first it is important to understand what motivation entails.

Understanding Motivation

Employee motivation is an anticipated outcome of a well-designed pay-for-performance program. Motivation is a psychological force that propels an individual to enact certain behaviors or to strive for a goal or result. We can distinguish between two broad types of motivation: extrinsic and intrinsic.

Extrinsic motivation is a force that is external to an individual, and this force drives the individual to action.[23] Often, we use the term *extrinsic motivator* when referring to an external source of extrinsic motivation. The classic example of an extrinsic motivator is pay, particularly when it is pay for performance. Other extrinsic motivators include nonmonetary awards and recognition such as praise or validation from a supervisor. With extrinsic motivators, individuals are not necessarily enacting certain behaviors or pursuing certain goals because they have the internal desire to do so but rather because they receive some kind of compensation, reward, or award. If deployed strategically and tied to particular behaviors or goals, pay can signal to employees the types of behaviors or goals they should spend their time and effort pursuing.

Unlike extrinsic motivation, *intrinsic motivation* is an internal force that drives the individual to action because the action itself is perceived as meaningful, challenging, or enjoyable.[24] For example, in the workplace, some people might feel intrinsically motivated to write code for a computer program because they simply enjoy the process of building something new and challenging. Others might find writing code to be unpleasant and tedious. The point is people vary in terms of what they consider to be intrinsically motivating.

Both extrinsic and intrinsic motivation are important for performance, but accumulated research indicates that they influence different aspects of performance.[25] Higher extrinsic motivation is associated with higher *quantity* of performance—or rather, *how much* an individual produces, completes, or provides in terms of products and services. In contrast, intrinsic motivation is more strongly linked to the *quality* of performance—or rather, *how well* an individual produces, completes, or provides products and services. Thus, even though this chapter focuses mostly on extrinsic motivation (and specifically on pay), ultimately both forms of motivation are important for employee performance.

Pay-for-performance programs Compensation programs that reward employees based on the behaviors they actually exhibit at work and the results or goals they actually achieve

■ **FIGURE 11.5**   Expectancy Theory

Expectancy theory proposes that motivation consists of three components: expectancy, instrumentality, and valence. Expectancy refers to the perception that effort will lead to performance, instrumentality refers to the perception that performance will lead to a reward, and valence refers to the perception that a reward is valuable.

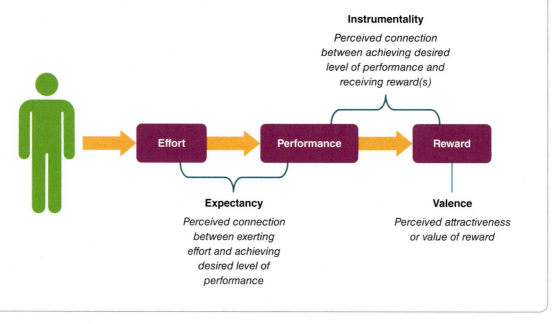

Expectancy Theory

From a motivational perspective, **expectancy theory** can help us get the most out of our pay-for-performance program. The theory offers a powerful framework that can be used when designing a pay-for-performance program or when diagnosing why such a program is not working as designed. Expectancy theory frames motivation in terms of the following psychological concepts: expectancy, instrumentality, and valence (see Figure 11.5).[26]

Expectancy refers to an individual's perceived connection between their effort and their performance. An individual will perceive higher expectancy when they *expect* that exerting more effort will lead to higher performance. Imagine that your supervisor assigns you the following performance goal: *Sell 100 software licenses by the end of the month.* If you possess the knowledge of the software product and skills to sell it, then you will likely perceive that applying effort will help you accomplish the sales goal. You will feel more motivated because you perceive higher expectancy.

Instrumentality refers to an individual's perception that performing at a high enough level will lead to rewards. In other words, an individual will perceive more instrumentality when they perceive that performance is *instrumental* for earning rewards. As an example, if your organization communicates that selling 100 software licenses will result in a bonus,

Expectancy theory A theory that suggests that if a person sees that their efforts will lead to greater performance, and if they believe that performance will lead to an outcome that they value, they will be more motivated

then you will perceive higher instrumentality (and higher motivation), especially if, in the past, you saw the same or similar reward schemes work as communicated. You will feel more motivated because you perceive higher instrumentality.

In the context of pay-for-performance programs, specifically, instrumentality often reflects the quality of the respective performance management and reward systems, as well as the degree to which they are integrated effectively. For instance, if performance is not tracked and measured accurately, then employees may perceive the rewards to be arbitrary

---

Manager's Toolbox

EVALUATING PAY-FOR-PERFORMANCE PROGRAMS USING EXPECTANCY THEORY

Without thoughtful communication and consideration of employee perceptions, a pay-for-performance program may fail to improve employee motivation and performance. Managers can apply expectancy theory to determine why the pay-for-performance program does not lead to higher motivation and performance.

1. **Expectancy.** If employees do not perceive a link between their effort and attaining a performance goal, then a manager should consider the following:

   - *Do employees have the requisite KSAOs necessary to meet the goal?* If not, the employees may need training.

   - *If a group pay-for-performance program is in place, do employees understand their role in the group and how they can contribute to the group's attainment of the goal?* If not, the manager should explain to employees how their efforts contribute to the group's success.

2. **Instrumentality.** If employees do not perceive a link between attaining a performance goal and receiving a reward, then the manager should consider the following:

   - *Do employees understand how the pay-for-performance program works?* If not, the manager should explain the program

and, in particular, how rewards are determined and why they are distributed.

   - *Is performance measured consistently, accurately, and fairly?* If not, the performance management system may need to be improved by enhancing the measurement tools, training users on how to use the measurement tools, or addressing office politics that influence the way performance is measured.

   - *Is the reward distributed in a timely manner after the goal is attained?* If not, the manager should work to ensure that the reward is distributed soon after the goal is met.

3. **Valence.** If employees do not perceive the reward to be attractive or of value, then the manager should consider the following:

   - *Is the size of the reward commensurate with the amount of effort and the level of performance it takes to earn the reward?* If not, the amount of the reward or the type of reward may need to be changed.

   - *Do employees want a monetary reward?* If not, the manager should ask employees what nonmonetary rewards they might find valuable (e.g., praise, challenging work, flexible work schedule).

or unpredictable. These can result in lower levels of perceived instrumentality and, consequently, lower motivation.

Valence refers to the extent to which an individual perceives a reward as attractive or important. It refers to the value an individual attaches to a particular reward. For example, you will likely perceive higher valence if the month-end reward for selling 100 software licenses is $1,000 as opposed to $5; consequently, you will be more motivated to apply effort toward demonstrating the level of performance necessary for attaining the reward when the reward itself is more highly valued.

Pay-for-Performance Programs

LO 11.4   Describe common individual and group pay-for-performance programs.

Pay-for-performance programs can be designed to reward individuals or groups. In terms of time orientation, they can be attached to short- or long-term goals. The following sections address some of the more common types of pay-for-performance programs.

Individual Pay-for-Performance Programs

In the United States, employees generally prefer individual pay-for-performance programs over group pay-for-performance programs.[27] Pay-for-performance programs aimed at rewarding individuals can be broadly organized using the categories of merit pay and variable pay. Variable-pay programs may include bonuses, spot awards, and individual incentives.

Merit Pay

Pay distributed to employees based on the ratings or feedback they receive on a performance evaluation measure is known as merit pay. By being integrated into an employee's base pay, merit pay results in the pay increase carrying forward to subsequent pay periods. Of those organizations with a formal performance management system and performance evaluation process, 87% tie merit-pay increases to performance ratings or rankings, according to a WorldatWork survey.[28]

Bonuses and Spot Awards

Unlike merit pay, bonuses are a form of variable pay, which means that they are not integrated into an individual's base pay. Instead, bonuses are distributed as a one-time payout in recognition of performance after the fact; they may be attached to a performance rating or to a completed goal. Bonuses can be distributed in recognition of individual performance, but they can also be distributed in recognition of team, unit, facility, or organizational performance. Because bonuses are not integrated permanently into employees' base pay, they can be less expensive for the employer than distributing pay in the form of merit pay.[29] Similar to a bonus, a spot award is another type of after-the-fact recognition that is often reserved for exceptional levels of performance. As shown in Figure 11.6, new information system solutions have made it easier for organizations to track and administer awards.

■ **FIGURE 11.6**   Reward and Recognition Functionality in SAP SuccessFactors Compensation Solution

New information system solutions, like this one created by SAP SuccessFactors, facilitate the process of determining and awarding various forms of variable pay such as spot awards.[30]

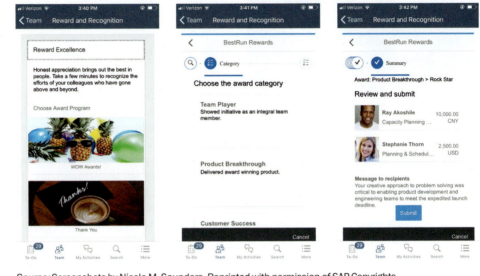

Source: Screenshots by Nicole M. Saunders. Reprinted with permission of SAP Copyrights.

Individual Incentives

As a type of variable pay, research has shown that individual incentive programs generally have a positive effect on performance outcomes.[31] Individual incentives refer to the distribution of pay in response to the attainment of certain predetermined and objective levels of performance. In general, they are nondiscretionary, which means managers do not have much say when it comes to who receives individual incentives and the amount of the distributed rewards.

A common example of an individual incentive program is the piecework plan. In a piecework plan, employees are compensated based on their respective production levels. For example, imagine that Cheryl works for a medical device company, and her main task is to assemble feeding tubes that will ultimately be used for patient care. A portion of her total compensation is variable and is distributed in accordance with a piecework plan. According to the plan, Cheryl earns $0.25 for every feeding tube she assembles within a pay period. Thus, if Cheryl assembles 2,000 feeding tubes in a pay period, she will receive $500 in variable pay (2,000 × $0.25 = $500).

Sales Commissions

Those who have worked in sales are likely familiar with sales commissions, which reward the sale of a product or service as opposed to the production of a product or provision of a service. Workers who sell products and services such as cars, real estate, stocks, consumer

Sales commission programs are common at car dealerships where salespeople may earn a percentage of the revenue of each car they sell.

packaged goods, medical devices, software, telecommunications, and insurance are commonly paid in commissions or a combination of base pay plus commissions. Typically, the amount of a sales commission is based on the percentage of the revenue or profit associated with each sale, overall sales volume, or customer satisfaction.

Group Pay-for-Performance Programs

Many organizations distribute rewards for group performance. In fact, some argue that deploying pay-for-performance programs only at the individual level may discourage collaboration and effective teamwork.[32] The strategic deployment of group pay-for-performance programs— generically called *success-sharing* plans—can improve group performance under certain circumstances, and group performance can be used to motivate a team, unit, facility, or entire organization.[33] Research has shown that group incentives tend to be more effective when the group in question is relatively small, such as a team, rather than the organization as a whole.[34]

Team Rewards

Just like individual programs, an organization can use financial rewards to motivate teams to achieve goals and reach specified performance levels. For instance, an organization might provide a year-end bonus for the manufacturing team that reduces waste the most during the manufacturing process. As an example, in 2004, Google introduced its Founders' Awards, given to teams that made outstanding accomplishments on a project.[35] In the inaugural year, $12 million in stock was given to two project teams in recognition of their accomplishments. One of the award-winning teams created a process whereby Google users would be presented with advertisements that would be most relevant to them—an online experience that is ubiquitous today but was groundbreaking at the time. This team award motivated teams to continue pursuing excellence and maximize their contributions to the company. In addition to the financial reward, winning teams received accolades and recognition.

Gainsharing

Gainsharing is a type of group pay-for-performance program that rewards a group of employees—often a unit or facility—for achieving certain milestones. As the name implies, individual employees share in the success of the overall *gains* of their group, such as those related to productivity, quality, and customer service. As an example, between 2006 and 2009, the Beth Israel Medical Center in New York City implemented a gainsharing program aimed at decreasing costs at the hospital level.[36] In total, 184 physicians participated in the gainsharing program, and through their involvement and participation, the 1,000-bed teaching hospital reduced costs by $25.1 million, while measures of patient care quality remained unchanged. Individual physicians shared in the hospital gains by receiving a portion of cost savings that was relative to their individual performance. In doing so, the Beth Israel Medical Center managed to recognize individual contributions to hospital-level gains, thereby providing physicians with a clearer indication of how much they uniquely contributed to the hospital's success.

Profit Sharing

As the name implies, profit sharing refers to pay-for-performance programs in which employees share in their organization's profits (e.g., return on assets). Profit-sharing rewards may be distributed as cash or placed in a retirement fund. Under profit-sharing programs, the organization shares profits with its employees when targets are met or exceeded. In many cases, organizations use a formula for determining how much each individual employee receives as part of the profit sharing; however, in other cases, the amount received by each employee may be discretionary in nature.[37]

Stock Options

Stock options are a type of group pay for performance that makes employees partial owners of the organization. Such programs allow employees to purchase a certain number of stock shares at a fixed price in a given time frame. Stock options are a long-term incentive because an employee may begin exercising these options only after a vesting period. Exercising stock options means that they may sell their stock options at a price that is higher than the fixed price when they purchased the stocks originally, resulting in a financial gain. However, if the company stock shares fail to exceed the original fixed price at which they were purchased, then the employee gains nothing. Thus, employees may perceive stock option programs as risky, and organizations may find it difficult to attract and retain high-performing employees if stock prices follow a downward trend.

Employee Stock Ownership Plans

Like stock options, employee stock ownership plans (ESOPs) reward employees when company stock shares increase in value and can only be used after a vesting period. ESOPs are also a type of defined-contribution retirement plan. Under these plans, the organization provides employees with stock shares and places these shares in an account. Employees never actually have possession of the shares while employed at the organization; rather, the organization disseminates the stock shares when an employee retires, dies, becomes disabled, or is fired by the organization. ESOPs position employees as owners of their company, which may lead employees to feel more invested in their company and more motivated to participate in organizational decisions, especially when they are dissatisfied with the state of their company.[38]

Bob's Red Mill Natural Foods is a grain company based in Oregon. The company uses an employee stock ownership plan (ESOP), which makes its employees owners of the company.[39]

Challenges and Opportunities of Reward Systems

LO 11.5   Assess common challenges and opportunities of reward systems.

Once designed, an organization must determine how to implement and administer its reward system. When it comes to pay administration, there are a number of issues to consider, and here the chapter focuses on the following issues: pay compression, adherence to pay policies, labor costs, and unintended behavioral consequences.

Pay Compression

Pay compression can occur when a pay structure is strongly influenced by prevailing market pay practices. It tends to occur when growth in the external market pay practices outpaces growth in an organization's internal pay practices. **Pay compression** refers to one of two situations within a single organization: (a) a more recently hired employee with less experience earns nearly as much or the same as a more experienced, longer-tenured employee in the same job, or (b) an employee in a lower-level job earns nearly as much or the same as another employee in a higher-level job, the latter of whom might even be the supervisor of the employee performing the lower-level job.[40] Relatedly, *pay inversion* constitutes a more severe form of compression and occurs when a newer, less-experienced employee in a given job earns (a) *more* than another, more-experienced employee in the same job, or (b) *more* than another employee in a higher-level job. Understandably, widespread compression and inversion may negatively affect employees' perceptions of pay-system fairness and especially individual equity.

Adherence to Pay Policies

Over time, an organization's enacted pay practices may begin to drift away from its espoused pay structure and policies. An HR metric called the compa-ratio can be a useful source of information when evaluating an organization's adherence to its pay policies and pay structure. The **compa-ratio** reflects how much employees are actually paid for a given job or pay grade compared to the espoused pay structure and policies, and it can be used to assess whether systematic compression or inversion is occurring.[41] To calculate the compa-ratio for a group of employees, simply divide the average pay for employees in a given job or pay grade by the pay range or grade.

$$\text{Compa-ratio for a group of employees} = \frac{\text{Average actual pay of employees}}{\text{Midpoint of pay range or grade}}$$

A compa-ratio value of 1.00 indicates that employees are paid, on average, at the midpoint of their pay range or grade, which reflects that pay practices generally adhere to pay policies. A value that is greater than 1.00 indicates that, on average, employees are paid more than the midpoint of their pay range or grade. Conversely, a value that is less than 1.00 indicates that, on average, employees are paid less than the midpoint of their pay range or grade.

Pay compression
Occurs when more recently hired employees with less experience earn nearly as much or the same as more experienced, longer-tenured employees in the same job or when employees in a lower-level job earn nearly as much or the same as employees in a higher-level job

Compa-ratio
A ratio that reflects how much employees are actually paid for a given job or pay grade compared to the espoused pay structure and policies, and it can be used to assess whether systematic compression or inversion is occurring

A compa-ratio can also be calculated for individual employees by dividing the individual's pay by the midpoint of the pay range or grade to which they belong.

$$\text{Compa-ratio for one employee} = \frac{\text{Actual pay of employee}}{\text{Midpoint of pay range or grade}}$$

Calculating the compa-ratios for individual employees can be a useful practice for detecting pay compression, especially when information about employee tenure is taken into consideration. For example, consider the scatterplot presented in Figure 11.7 in which individual employees' compa-ratios are plotted in relation to their tenure. Note that compa-ratio is on the *x*-axis, tenure is on the *y*-axis, and each circle represents a single employee. If the organization's espoused policy is to pay more-tenured employees at higher rates than less-tenured employees, then the scatterplot reveals that the organization's actual enacted pay practices depart dramatically from that espoused policy. In this example, employees with the shortest tenure tend to have the highest compa-ratios. This indicates that newcomers to the organization earn notably higher wages than the midpoint of their pay range, whereas the opposite appears to be true for longer-tenured employees.

■ **FIGURE 11.7**   Scatterplot of the Compa-Ratios and Years of Tenure for a Group of Employees

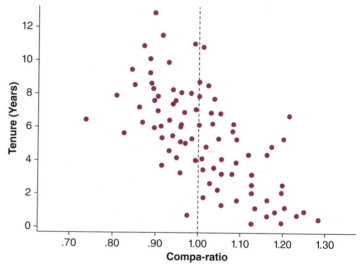

Labor Costs

Labor costs associated with reward systems can account for 70% of an organization's total costs, which means that they should be invested wisely, monitored closely, and forecasted accurately.[42] As external market pay rates rise, an organization may find it challenging to acquire, motivate, and retain talented individuals unless it also increases the pay rates associated with its internal traditional-pay and pay-for-performance programs.

Further, pay-for-performance programs make it particularly challenging to predict future labor costs, especially when the number of employees earning such rewards varies over time. To plan for anticipated labor costs associated with pay-for-performance programs, statistical modeling can be applied. Statistical modeling allows an organization to use prior evidence (e.g., performance, pay, and other factors potentially influencing performance and pay) to project how much money should be set aside to cover future labor costs. However, it is important to remember that a statistical model contains uncertainty, making it unlikely to predict a future event perfectly.

Unintended Behavioral Consequences

Pay-for-performance programs can lead to unintended behavioral consequences, particularly when management fails to monitor employee behavior. In general, when earning a reward is contingent on achievement of a certain level of performance, individuals are more likely to enact behaviors that help them reach that level of performance—even if some (or all) of those behaviors are unethical. Thus, not surprisingly, research has shown that rewarding individuals for engaging in unethical behavior leads to even more unethical behavior.[43] Interestingly, pay-for-performance programs can also encourage unethical behavior even when unethical behavior is not directly or intentionally incentivized.

As an example, Wells Fargo made major news headlines in 2016 after it was revealed that employees opened and closed unauthorized bank accounts for customers, which is not only unethical and discourteous but also illegal.[44] Employees engaged in this unethical behavior because they received financial incentives based on meeting their sales goals, which were contingent on how many customer accounts they opened. Perceiving the instrumentality of opening accounts and receiving rewards, some employees took advantage of the pay-for-performance program by opening accounts for customers without their knowledge or consent. Wells Fargo leadership was somewhat sluggish in its attempts to investigate the unethical behavior and allowed it to remain unchecked for some time.[45] In the aftermath, Wells Fargo was fined $185 million, and it terminated the jobs of thousands of employees who engaged in these unethical and illegal behaviors.

CHAPTER SUMMARY

Pay, or compensation, represents one type of formal reward. A reward system encompasses relational returns (e.g., recognition, challenging work) and total compensation, where the latter includes compensation (e.g., base pay, variable pay) and benefits (e.g., health insurance, income protection). An effective pay structure requires fairness in the form of internal, external, and individual equity, as well as legal compliance. Many organizations integrate pay-for-performance programs into their reward system to motivate employees to enact certain behaviors or achieve certain results. Finally, organizations often face various challenges and opportunities when implementing and administering reward systems. For instance, organizations should be proactive in addressing issues related to pay compression, adherence to pay policies, labor costs, and unintended behavioral consequences.

KEY TERMS

pay structure   252
reward system   253
relational returns   253
total compensation   253

compensation   253
benefits   253
internal equity   254
point-factor method   255

compensable factors   256
benchmark job   256
external equity   256
market review   257

$SAGE edge™

Get the tools you need to sharpen your study skills. SAGE edge offers a robust online environment featuring an impressive array of free tools and resources.

Access practice quizzes, eFlashcards, video, and multimedia at **edge.sagepub.com/bauerbrief**

HR REASONING AND DECISION-MAKING EXERCISES

EXERCISE 11.1: APPLYING EXPECTANCY THEORY TO UNDERSTAND PAY FOR PERFORMANCE

Three years ago, a large clothing retailer called La Ropa de Moda developed and implemented a new pay-for-performance program targeted at sales associates. The relatively new program is a sales performance incentive fund (SPIF) that provides a bonus for selling certain items of clothing. La Ropa de Moda learned that one of its competitors used SPIFs to sell old inventory to great effect. Because La Ropa de Moda has been having issues selling clothes from prior seasons, the company decided to implement a similar program. Unfortunately, La Ropa de Moda has found that even when a SPIF is attached to certain items of clothing, much of the old inventory sits on sales floors across the company's many locations, and to date, the SPIF program has been largely ineffective when it comes to motivating employees to sell old inventory.

Sales associates' base hourly wage ranges from $14 to $19, and differences in hourly wage are attributable to years of experience in retail, seniority, and merit-based pay increases. SPIFs are attached to specific clothing items from prior seasons and range in value from $1 to $5. In addition to the SPIF program, sales associates receive a 7% commission on each article of clothing they sell. For example, if a sales associate sells a $100 pair of jeans, then the associate will earn a commission of $7. The average cost of an article of clothing in the store is $50, and on a typical 8-hour day, the average salesperson will sell $600 worth of clothing. The average salesperson works 33 hours per week.

On one hand, the base wage and commissions earned by sales associates each pay period are distributed in a biweekly paycheck. On the other hand, the annual SPIFs earned by a single sales associate are paid out in one year-end lump-sum bonus, so SPIFs are not included in the paycheck corresponding to the pay period in which they were earned.

Apply the principles of expectancy theory to understand why the pay-for-performance program at La Ropa de Moda is failing to motivate sales associates to sell old inventory.

Questions

1. Based on the information provided, do you think that low perceived *expectancy* among sales associates explains the lack of motivation to sell old items with SPIFs attached? Why?

2. Do you think that sales associates' perceptions of *instrumentality* explain the lack of motivation to sell items with SPIFs? Why?

3. Do you think that sales associates' perceptions of *valence* explain the lack of motivation to sell items with SPIF? Why?

EXERCISE 11.2: CONDUCTING A MARKET REVIEW

A video game company named Zenyah with 8,000 employees recently hired your consulting firm to develop a more externally equitable pay structure. Zenyah began as a start-up 10 years ago and has grown very rapidly ever since. Lately, the company has been having difficulty recruiting and selecting talented candidates for key software development, marketing, and sales jobs, which is likely due to the external labor shortage for individuals qualified for those jobs. As such, Zenyah has asked your consulting firm to conduct a market review for the following benchmark jobs:

- Computer programmer
- Systems software developer
- Applications software developer
- Market research analyst
- Marketing manager
- Advertising sales agent
- Advertising and promotions manager
- Sales representative

As part of the contract, Zenyah has requested that your consulting firm conduct new job analyses on the benchmark jobs, as it suspects that the job descriptions are out of date and inaccurate. As a starting point, you decide to use O*NET (ONETonline.org) to draft initial job description summaries that you can use to compare to the job description summaries that appear in the market review sources.

Questions

1. Using O*NET, write three- to five-sentence job description summaries for each benchmark job.
2. Using Salary.com and CareerOneStop.com as free market review sources, gather pay data for as many of the benchmark jobs as you can, and enter the data into a table. Be sure to match the job description summaries you created for Zenyah with the job description summaries in the market review sources to ensure you are making an appropriate comparison.

ETHICAL MATTERS EXERCISE: MERIT PAY FOR TEACHERS

Implementing merit pay for teachers has been a contentious issue, particularly in the United States. Supporters contend that merit pay motivates teachers to do a better job, leading to better outcomes for students in terms of academic achievement and eventual employment success. Critics, on the other hand, contend that the ways in which teacher performance is evaluated can lack transparency and may be beyond teachers' direct control.

Selecting key performance indicators for teachers can be particularly challenging given that teachers can be evaluated based on their own behavior or on the behavior of their students and that student behavior can be influenced by many factors other than the teachers' classroom performance. That is, teachers may exert some degree of influence over students' behavior, including test scores, but students also arrive in a classroom with their own personal histories and unique circumstances that may affect how receptive and prepared to learn they are. Some critics argue that it can be unethical to base a substantial portion of teachers' take-home pay on their students' performance, particularly if performance is defined based on their students' success on standardized tests.

In the United States, the push for pay-for-performance programs in educational settings gained traction in the 1980s and early 1990s. At about that time, a statistician named William Sanders began advising Tennessee lawmakers on a method for evaluating teachers based on the extent to which they improved their students' standardized test scores, referred to as the *value-added approach*. The value-added approach takes into account the historical trends in students' test scores, such as whether they improved, stayed the same, or declined, and determines whether a teacher improved their students' test scores more than would be expected given that history.

Critics argue that the value-added approach is unfair, as a number of factors outside of teachers' direct control can affect their value-added scores. Moreover, some teachers teach subjects that do not have an associated standardized test, which can make it difficult to evaluate them in the same manner as their peers. Analytical software companies like SAS Institute have developed algorithms to calculate the value-added scores of teachers. Some teachers and administrators have complained that these algorithms are difficult for nonstatisticians to understand, and due to the often proprietary nature of the algorithms, there can be a lack of transparency when it comes to communicating how the value-added scores are computed. Supporters of the value-added approach point to evidence that students of high value-added teachers are more likely to attend college and to go on to earn higher salaries than other students.

In terms of empirical research on the topics, research has shown that incentivizing teachers with merit pay does not always lead to higher teacher motivation or better student outcomes. In fact, the empirical findings are mixed. Some evidence indicates that merit pay leads to higher student scores in math, science, and reading, whereas other evidence suggests that merit pay may have some effect on students' math scores but not on reading scores and that teachers do not find merit-pay programs to be motivating. As a way forward, some education reform advocates contend that rewarding teacher performance should not necessarily be thrown out; rather, the structure and organization of the schools themselves should also be taken into consideration when recognizing teacher performance.[46]

Questions

1. Given the risk that low-performing teachers may do a poor job of preparing their students for eventual career success, do you think it is ethical to pay teachers without taking into account their performance? Why or why not?

2. Do you think it is ethical to base teacher pay on key performance indicators that may be, to some extent, beyond teacher control? Why or why not? Give some examples to support your opinion.

12 Managing Benefits

LEARNING OBJECTIVES

After reading and studying this chapter, you should be able to do the following:

12.1 Understand how benefits act as rewards and support organizational strategy.

12.2 Identify the different types of legally required benefits.

12.3 Describe the different types of voluntary benefits.

12.4 Assess the common challenges and opportunities associated with administering benefits programs.

12.5 Assess the common challenges and opportunities associated with communicating benefits programs.

HR in Action: The Case of Providing Benefits to Gig Workers at Care.com

A gig refers to a single project or task that an individual completes for pay, and individuals who complete gigs are often referred to as gig workers. Examples of gigs range from driving for Uber and Lyft to performing assignments for TaskRabbit and Postmates. Estimates suggest that more than 23 million Americans work in the gig economy, and a 2017 MetLife survey indicated that 51% of workers expressed interest in gig work instead of a full-time, salaried position at a single organization. Because many gig workers earn most of their income through part-time employment or independent contracts, they typically do not have access to the employer-sponsored benefits that full-time employees have. As such, a common complaint among gig workers is the lack of certain voluntary benefits—something that an organization called Care.com has sought to change.

Founded in 2007, Care.com is the world's largest online marketplace aimed at connecting families with caregivers, babysitters, and nannies. The company's over-arching objective is "to improve the lives of families and caregivers by helping them connect in a reliable and easy way." Care.com's online marketplace connects millions of families with gig workers who provide care services. Amid calls for added protections and benefits for gig workers, in 2016, Care.com unveiled an initiative to contribute up to $500 per year to each care provider for health care, educational, and transportation expenses—a benefit that is relatively unheard of among gig workers.[1]

Case Discussion Questions

1. Have you (or someone you have known) ever performed gig work? If so, what was your experience (or the experience of the person you have known), and did you receive any nonmonetary benefits?

2. In addition to financial support toward health care, educational, and transportation expenses, what other benefits might gig workers value?

3. Should federal, state, or local governments pass legislation that requires organizations to offer voluntary benefits to their gig workers? Why or why not?

B enefits are an important component of an organization's broader reward system and constitute an important part of an employee's total compensation package. In 2018, the U.S. Bureau of Labor Statistics (BLS) reported that benefits, on average, accounted for 32% of organizations' total compensation costs.[2] Benefits include programs, services, and perquisites related to health care, retirement, work–life balance, and income protection. In many companies, HR plays a big role in administering and, sometimes, even selecting which benefits will be offered. In addition, HR professionals often play key roles in communicating what the benefit plan offering(s) entail(s), particularly if the organization will be contributing financially to employees' plans in some way.

Benefits as Rewards

LO 12.1 Understand how benefits act as rewards and support organizational strategy.

In the United States, some benefits are legally required, whereas others are voluntary (see Figure 12.1). Just like other rewards, voluntary benefits can be used as tools to attract, motivate, and retain workers. And just like other rewards, benefits have the potential to support organizational strategy and play an important role in achieving a competitive advantage, particularly when properly aligned with strategic objectives. In fact, SHRM reported in 2018 that over the prior year, 34% of surveyed employers reported expanding their voluntary benefits offerings over the previous year, signaling their strategic value. Perhaps not surprisingly, in a SHRM report from 2017, employers that leveraged benefits strategically to boost recruitment and retention efforts reported higher organizational performance and higher-than-average recruitment and retention effectiveness.[3]

Legally Required Benefits

LO 12.2 Identify the different types of legally required benefits.

In the United States, some legally required benefits are referred to as social insurance programs, as they address societal problems that many or all individuals face and provide a minimum income floor. Among civilian workers in the United States, legally required

■ **FIGURE 12.1**   Legally Required Versus Voluntary Benefits

In the United States, employers must provide certain legally required benefits, whereas employers may offer other voluntary benefits at their own discretion.

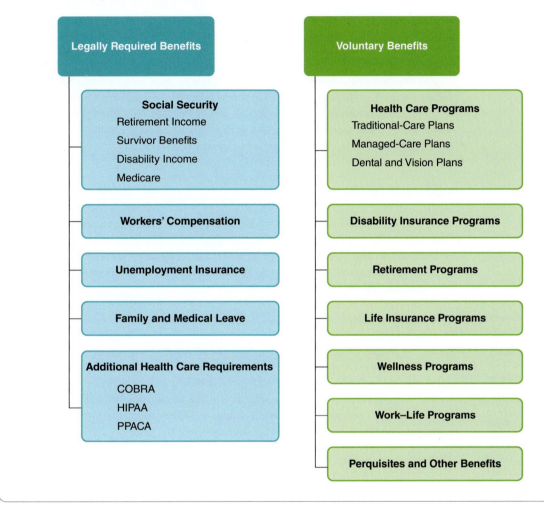

benefits account for, on average, 23% of employers' total benefits costs, and payroll tax contributions to such programs are a significant expense for most employees (as well as their employer).[4] The following sections describe the legally required benefits of Social Security, workers' compensation, unemployment insurance, and family and medical leave, as well as legally required health care programs.

Social Security

In 1935, the U.S. Congress passed the **Social Security Act**. The act is designed to provide economic security for those who are older, mothers and children, those with disabilities, those who are unemployed, and those whose family members have died. Approximately 20% of Americans receive some type of Social Security benefit, which ensures that they are provided with a minimum floor of income and supplements other sources of income.[5]

Social Security benefits are funded through a tax based on the amount of a worker's income (with a few exceptions). This tax is called the **Federal Insurance Contributions Act (FICA)** and is deducted from payroll, and both the employee and the employer contribute a set percentage of the employee's earnings to FICA; self-employed individuals are responsible for paying both the employee and the employer tax.[6]

To determine whether an individual is eligible to draw upon certain Social Security benefits, a work credits system is used, wherein each person must earn a particular number of work credits to become eligible to receive certain benefits at different points in their life. These work credits accrue throughout a person's life based on the amount of income they generate working each year. The amount of benefit an individual receives is dependent, in part, on the average income they earned during their life.

Retirement Income

Retirement income is one of the primary benefits provided through Social Security. At the earliest, an eligible individual can begin receiving benefits at 62 years but will receive a permanently reduced benefit, as 62 years is not considered full retirement age. The current full retirement age ranges from 66 to 67 years, and the exact age depends on an individual's year of birth. An individual may maximize the benefit amount by delaying receipt of benefits after reaching full retirement age.[7]

Survivor Benefits

If an individual who is eligible for Social Security benefits dies, some family members may be eligible to receive survivor benefits. For example, a surviving spouse can receive a one-time $255 payment and potentially recurring monthly benefits; under certain conditions, surviving children, parents, or even a divorced spouse may be eligible for monthly benefits as well.[8] Any monthly benefit received by a surviving family member will be contingent on the deceased person's average lifetime earnings as well as the age of the surviving family member(s) and their relationship to the deceased person.

Disability Income

Social Security disability income was created to support those who develop or face a disability that inhibits their ability to participate in the workforce. Eligibility for disability income depends on an individual's current age, the age at which they first experienced the disability, and their accrued work credits. The benefit may also extend to a worker's spouse or child under certain circumstances. The benefit also provides incentives and assistance aimed at helping individuals transition back to the workforce.[9]

Medicare

As another Social Security benefit, Medicare is a government-funded health insurance program designed for those who are 65 years or older. In addition, Medicare is available for those who are under the age of 65 and have qualifying conditions (e.g., disabilities, permanent kidney failure). Medicare is designed to cover some but not all health care costs.[10]

Social Security Act Passed by the U.S. Congress in 1935 as part of the New Deal to help the United States recover from the Great Depression by providing economic security for old-age individuals and, later, additional programs for mothers and children in need, individuals with disabilities, the unemployed, and those whose family members have died

Federal Insurance Contributions Act (FICA) A federal payroll tax paid by both employees and employers that funds current Social Security beneficiaries

Workers' Compensation

One program funded entirely by the employer in the form of payroll taxes is called **workers' compensation.** It typically provides medical coverage, including rehabilitation services and income replacement, for an individual who was injured or fell ill due to accidents or hazards at work.[11] In addition, workers' compensation programs often provide benefits to an individual's family members in the event the individual dies due to an injury or illness sustained from work. It is important to point out that such programs are not the same as Social Security disability insurance programs. Nearly all states mandate that employers offer workers' compensation programs to employees. Many private employers purchase workers' compensation coverage through insurance companies, whereas public employers provide coverage through government programs. The amount of payroll taxes an employer must contribute to workers' compensation programs varies by industry; industries with higher rates of injuries and illnesses typically contribute more.

Unemployment Insurance

The U.S. federal–state unemployment insurance program provides income replacement and job-search services to individuals who become unemployed through no fault of their own yet are still able to work and available for work, assuming they meet certain eligibility requirements. The unemployment insurance program is funded through payroll taxes contributed by employers and is overseen and administered by the U.S. Department of Labor.[12] The weekly benefit distributed to eligible individuals through unemployment insurance is a function of past income, with the amount of benefits received limited by certain minimums and maximums.

Family and Medical Leave

The U.S. **Family and Medical Leave Act (FMLA)** was introduced in 1993 to protect employees' job security when they need to take unpaid leave due to certain family or medical issues (e.g., serious health issue, giving birth, adopting a child). Eligible employees may use up to 12 weeks of unpaid leave in a year, during which their job and health care benefits remain protected. A spouse or family member of a service member may use up to 26 weeks of FMLA in a year to care for the individual. Importantly, employees can take FMLA all at once or intermittently. FMLA covers virtually all public and private employers with 50 or more employees. To be eligible to take leave under FMLA, an employee must have worked at least 1,250 hours for their employer for at least 12 months and must have worked at an employer's location (e.g., campus, facility) that has at least 50 employees working within a 75-mile radius.[13]

Additional Health Care Requirements

Many U.S. employers must abide by other important health care laws. For example, the **Employee Retirement Income Security Act (ERISA)** of 1974 and subsequent amendments established minimum standards for many private employers' health care plans and did so as a means of protecting employees.[14] (ERISA also provides protections for employees and guidelines for private-sector voluntary retirement plans.) Two amendments to

Workers' compensation
Program funded entirely by the employer in the form of payroll taxes that provides medical coverage and income replacement for an individual who is injured or becomes ill on the job due to an accident or hazard

Family and Medical Leave Act (FMLA)
Introduced in 1993 to protect employees' job security when they need to take unpaid leave due to family or medical issues

Employee Retirement Income Security Act (ERISA)
Introduced in 1974 to establish minimum standards for many private employers' health care plans to protect employees

ERISA have implications for many employers and their health care coverage: Consolidated Omnibus Budget Reconciliation Act (COBRA) and Health Insurance Portability and Accountability Act (HIPAA).

The **Consolidated Omnibus Budget Reconciliation Act (COBRA)** of 1985 protects employees' (and their beneficiaries') health care coverage for a designated amount of time in the event of voluntary or involuntary job loss, work-hour reductions, or another major occurrence (e.g., death, divorce).[15] COBRA protections apply to employers with 20 or more employees that offer group health insurance plans. It allows individuals to continue their health care coverage even after the aforementioned major job and life events. COBRA protection can last for a maximum of 36 months, and the specific length of coverage is dependent on the type of qualifying job or life event that the individual experienced. An eligible employee may have to pay for the entire cost of the plan and a 2% administrative fee.

The **Health Insurance Portability and Accountability Act (HIPAA)** of 1996 adds protections to the portability of employees' health care coverage as well as protections to ensure the privacy and security of employees' health care data.[16] More specifically, HIPAA put into place certain protections for preexisting health conditions, where previously a health insurer might exclude individuals with certain conditions (e.g., genetic predispositions) or a prior claim history. In addition, HIPAA protects individuals against discrimination in which they are targeted for their general health condition or specific illnesses or injuries.

The **Patient Protection and Affordable Care Act** of 2010 offers rights and protections associated with access to health care coverage. The act is commonly known as the Affordable Care Act or the **ACA,** and because the law was signed into law by President Barack Obama, some refer to the ACA as "Obamacare." The ACA provides a number of benefits and protections to individuals, including the following:

- Insurance providers are required to eliminate exclusions on the basis of preexisting conditions as well as other discriminatory practices.

- Tax credits are provided to individuals and their families, which they can use to purchase coverage through a government-operated marketplace.

- All marketplace plans (and many other plans) are required to cover preventive medical services.

- Children and other dependents are allowed to remain on their parents' insurance plan until they reach 26 years of age.

- Lifetime and certain annual benefits limits are eliminated.

- As of 2019, employers must offer affordable health care plans to full-time employees or potentially pay a fee.[17]

Voluntary Benefits

LO 12.3 Describe the different types of voluntary benefits.

In addition to those that are legally required, many organizations voluntarily provide benefits to employees. Voluntary benefits can add value by helping to attract, motivate, and retain talent. Yet at the same time, many of these benefits have substantial financial

---

Consolidated Omnibus Budget Reconciliation Act (COBRA)
Introduced in 1985 to protect employees' and their beneficiaries' health care coverage for a designated amount of time in the event of job loss, work-hour reductions, or another major occurrence

Health Insurance Portability and Accountability Act (HIPAA)
Introduced in 1996 to add protections to the portability of employees' health care coverage and ensure the privacy and security of employees' health care data

Patient Protection and Affordable Care Act (ACA)
Introduced in 2010 to provide rights and protections associated with access to health care coverage

costs for both the organization and its employees. For example, many organizations contribute to employees' health insurance plans by subsidizing the cost of monthly premiums. Consequently, each organization must weigh the potential short- and long-term advantages and disadvantages of offering such benefits. Some of the most common employer-sponsored voluntary benefits include health care, retirement, life insurance, and work–life programs.

Health Care Programs

In general, health care programs provide employees with access to health care providers and services to prevent and treat medical, dental, and vision conditions. The Manager's Toolbox provides an overview of key terminology and concepts, such as premiums, deductibles, and coinsurance.

Medical Plans

Medical plans provide health care and treatment opportunities for those who are plan members. It is not uncommon for employers to offer employees more than one medical plan from which to choose, each with different associated costs. In the following sections, we review some common types of medical plans as well as health savings options.

Traditional-Care Plans. Also called *conventional-indemnity plans*, *traditional-care plans* allow participants to select any provider of their choosing without affecting how they are reimbursed, and participants' expenses are reimbursed as they are incurred. Over the past century, true traditional-care plans have become increasingly rare, as more organizations opt for managed-care plans.

Managed-Care Plans. Designed to provide wide-ranging health care services to insurance plan participants, *managed-care plans* are preferable to traditional plans when it comes to meeting cost-containment goals and managing the quality and use of services. A common theme among managed-care plans is that participants incur lower cost sharing when they use in-network providers and services. In-network refers to providers and services that are members of the managed-care plan, and out-of-network refers to providers that are not members. Table 12.1 describes some of the most common managed-care plans.

Health Savings Options. In the United States, there are various health savings options. In Table 12.2, we review the following three health savings options recognized by the Internal Revenue Service: health flexible spending arrangement, health reimbursement arrangement, and health savings account. These programs offer tax advantages aimed at reducing overall out-of-pocket health care expenses for individuals.[18]

Dental and Vision Plans

Insurance plans for dental care and vision care may be offered as a supplement to medical plans or as standalone plans. With regard to dental plans specifically, many plans provide coverage for routine preventive and maintenance services like X-rays, cleanings, and fillings. Dental plans often differ in terms of how much a plan will cover when it comes to more costly procedures such as root canals or orthodontics.

Manager's Toolbox
HEALTH CARE TERMINOLOGY AND CONCEPTS

Employees often ask their managers for help understanding their benefits. Health care programs, in particular, involve several terms and concepts that a manager may need to define and explain.

- **Participant:** an individual who is enrolled in a plan during a coverage period, allowing them to have access to the plan benefits.
- **Cost sharing:** a reimbursement model in which a participant is reimbursed for qualified services and procedures at a specified rate, subject to certain exceptions and limitations.
- **Premium:** a fee for a plan coverage period, which may be paid by any or all of the following entities: employer, employee, or union.
- **Deductible:** a set amount that a participant must pay during a coverage period for services rendered before the insurance provider begins contributing payments for expenses.
- **Coinsurance:** a cost sharing between the insurance provider and the participant, wherein the participant pays a percentage of expenses and the insurance reimburses the rest; typically comes into effect when a participant reaches the deductible for the coverage period (or if there was no deductible in the first place).
- **Copayment (or copay):** a fee charged when a participant receives a particular

service or visits a particular provider; may be as little as $5 for preventive care such as an annual physical.

- **Maximum out-of-pocket expense:** an upper limit for how much the participant will pay for a coverage period after reaching the deductible (if applicable); once reached, the insurance provider typically covers subsequent expenses.
- **Maximum plan limit:** an upper limit of how much an insurance provider will pay to cover a participant's expenses for a coverage period or during the participant's lifetime; the Patient Protection and Affordable Care Act prohibits annual and lifetime limits, except when applied to certain services that are not considered essential.
- **Primary care physician:** a physician who provides most routine and preventive services (known in the past as a general practitioner or family doctor) and who serves as the main contact for the participant; may also be a gatekeeper who must authorize referrals to specialists and nonemergency hospital visits; some medical plans require participants to select a primary care physician.
- **Specialist:** a health care provider who provides less-routine or highly specialized services, such as the services provided by a dermatologist, obstetrician-gynecologist, neurologist, oncologist, or cardiologist.

Disability Insurance Programs

In addition to legally required workers' compensation and Social Security disability insurance, employers may also offer voluntary benefits in the form of short- and long-term disability insurance plans through private providers. Unlike workers' compensation, employees may be eligible to draw on disability insurance benefits even if their disability originated outside of work. Both short- and long-term disability insurance plans provide

TABLE 12.1   Common Managed-Care Plans and Health Savings Options

MANAGED-CARE PLANS	CHARACTERISTICS
Health maintenance organization (HMO)	*Definition:* a plan in which out-of-network, nonemergency services are not covered, and plan participants select an in-network primary care physician who acts as a gatekeeper for in-network specialists. • Provides a comprehensive array of health care providers and services, ranging from generalists to specialists, as well as physical therapists and mental health providers. • Most require lower out-of-pocket costs for plan participants and sometimes even lack a deductible. • May not cover physician and specialist visits that are deemed out of network.
Preferred-provider organization (PPO)	*Definition:* a plan in which participants incur lower cost sharing for in-network service providers, and seeing a primary care physician is not required prior to seeing a specialist.[a] • Unlike an HMO, PPO participants may see providers outside of their network; however, going out of network will result in higher cost sharing by participants. • Unlike an HMO, PPO participants are not typically required to select a primary care physician.
Exclusive-provider organization (EPO)	*Definition:* a specific type of PPO in which participants are only covered when they seek services from in-network providers, except in the event of an emergency.
Point-of-service (POS)	*Definition:* a plan that is essentially a hybrid between an HMO and a PPO.[b] • Like an HMO, participants must select an in-network primary care physician who typically serves as the gatekeeper for referrals to specialists. • Like a PPO, participants may go out of network to find service providers at higher cost sharing. • In some plans, visiting a primary care physician and receiving preventive services do not contribute to the deductible, which reduces the out-of-pocket costs for routine care and treatment.
High-deductible health plan (HDHP)	*Definition:* a plan with a high deductible (and often higher out-of-pocket maximums than other plans). • According to the Internal Revenue Service, as of 2018, a plan becomes an HDHP when the annual deductible meets or exceeds $1,350 for an individual or $2,700 for a family. • Technically, an HDHP may be a special type of HMO, PPO, or POS that includes a high deductible. • Typically, an HDHP offers more affordable plan premiums than other plans and incentivizes participants to think carefully about which service providers they visit and which treatments they pursue.
Consumer-driven health plan (CDHP)	*Definition:* an HDHP that is combined with a health reimbursement arrangement (HRA) or health savings account (HSA), resulting in certain tax advantages.[c]

[a]The Kaiser Family Foundation and Health Research & Educational Trust. (2017). *Employer health benefits.* Menlo Park, CA: Henry J. Kaiser Family Foundation.

[b]The Kaiser Family Foundation and Health Research & Educational Trust. (2017). *Employer health benefits.* Menlo Park, CA: Henry J. Kaiser Family Foundation.

[c]Song, G. Y. (2010, October 25). Consumer-driven health care: What is it, and what does it mean for employees and employers. U.S. Bureau of Labor Statistics. https://www.bls.gov/opub/mlr/cwc/consumer-driven-health-care-what-is-it-and-what-does-it-mean-for-employees-and-employers.pdf

TABLE 12.2   Common Health Savings Options

HEALTH SAVINGS OPTIONS	CHARACTERISTICS
Health flexible spending arrangement (health FSA)	*Definition:* an option that offers tax advantages for individuals who are enrolled in some employer-sponsored health care plans.[a] • Permits employees (and optionally employers) to set aside funds into an untaxed account, which means employees do not pay taxes on the money within a health FSA. • Imposes certain limitations regarding how the funds can be used. For example, funds cannot be used to pay premiums but can be used to pay deductibles, copayments, prescription medication, and medical equipment, as well as other qualified medical and dental expenses. • With some exceptions, participants cannot roll the entirety of account funds forward to the subsequent year in the event they do not use all of the funds.
Health reimbursement arrangement (HRA)	*Definition:* an option that allows an employer (and not the employee) to contribute unlimited funds to an account, such that the account reimburses the employee on a tax-free basis for qualified medical costs.[b] • For each coverage period, there is an upper limit on how much tax-free reimbursement a participant can apply toward qualified medical costs. • At the end of the year, any remaining funds can be rolled forward to the subsequent year. • Because the employer owns the HRA, the employer retains control of the funds should the employee leave the organization, so some view the HRA as an employee retention inducement.
Health savings account (HSA)	*Definition:* an option that permits participants to contribute a portion of pretax income to an account that can be used to pay for services. • Contributed funds are not taxed. • Funds can accumulate tax-deferred interest. • At the end of the year, any remaining funds can be rolled forward to the subsequent year.

[a]U.S. Internal Revenue Service. (2013, September 30). Internal Revenue Bulletin: 2013-40. https://www.irs.gov/irb/2013-40_IRB
[b]U.S. Internal Revenue Service. (2013, September 30). Internal Revenue Bulletin: 2013-40. https://www.irs.gov/irb/2013-40_IRB; U.S. Internal Revenue Service. (2018). Health reimbursement arrangements (HRAs). https://taxmap·irs.gov/taxmap/pubs/p969-003.htm

Short-term disability insurance
A form of income protection for employees who temporarily become unable to work as a result of illness or injury

income protection to plan participants, and with the exception of some states, employers may voluntarily contribute fully or partially to employees' disability insurance.

Short-term disability insurance is a form of income protection for employees who temporarily become unable to work as a result of an illness or injury, whether sustained at work or during their personal time. In most organizations, employees first draw on accrued paid time off prior to accessing any short-term disability benefits covered through their plan. For the majority of short-term disability insurance plans, employees may receive their income protection benefit for 90 to 180 days, and the income protection benefit usually covers 60% to 75% of their base pay.[19]

Long-term disability insurance is similar to short-term disability insurance, except that it offers longer-term benefits that activate once short-term disability insurance benefits expire. Although long-term disability insurance also provides income protection benefits, the percentage of overall base pay is sometimes lower than the percentage afforded by short-term disability insurance benefits. Some plans stipulate a maximum time period for receiving income protection benefits, whereas other plans allow individuals to continue receiving the benefits through retirement.[20]

Retirement Programs

An employer may offer employees a variety of different retirement plans, which might include defined-benefit and defined-contribution plans, as well as plans designed to contribute to employees' individual retirement plans. In fact, a 2018 SHRM report indicated that 95% of employers offered at least one type of retirement plan to their employees.[21]

Defined-Benefit Plans

In a **defined-benefit plan**, the employer provides retirement plan participants with a pre-established benefit that, upon retirement, is paid out over a fixed time period. A defined-benefit plan is also known as a *traditional pension plan*. Sometimes a defined-benefit plan may stipulate an exact amount to be distributed, such as $3,000 per month at retirement. The funding for these plans sometimes differs between the public and private sectors. Often, both the employee and the employer are required to contribute to defined-benefit plans in public organizations, whereas in many cases, only the employer contributes to such plans in private organizations.[22] Compared to other retirement programs, defined-benefit plans allow employers to contribute more. Plus, by definition, defined-benefit plans offer predictable benefit amounts that can be accrued relatively quickly, which may be appealing to many employees, particularly those who have a discomfort for incurring risk. Although still offered by many companies, defined-benefit plans are becoming less common as more companies opt for defined-contribution plans.

Defined-Contribution Plans

Unlike a defined-benefit plan, a **defined-contribution plan** does not provide a preestablished, fixed benefit for the employee. Instead, a defined-contribution plan is built on employee and/or employer contributions to an investment fund and any investment gains or losses of that fund.[23] Typically, such plans permit certain contribution amounts from the employee or employer and enforce a maximum contribution level for the year. Employee contributions are typically tax deferred. This means that the taxable income an employee contributes to a plan will not be taxed until a later date, often when the earnings are distributed during retirement. Because plan contributions are placed in an investment fund, employees take on investment risk. In fact, investment gains or losses can have a significant effect on the amount of earnings distributed upon retirement (or termination).[24] Common types of defined-contribution plans include 401(k), 403(b), profit-sharing, employee stock ownership, and money-purchase pension plans.

401(k) and 403(b) Plans. Both 401(k) and 403(b) plans are types of defined-contribution plans. Both typically allow employees to direct their own investments, and employees

Long-term disability insurance A form of income protection for employees that is similar to short-term disability insurance, except it offers longer-term benefits activated once short-term disability insurance benefits expire

Defined-benefit plan Also known as a traditional pension plan, a type of retirement plan in which the employer provides plan participants with a preestablished benefit to be paid out over a fixed time period

Defined-contribution plan A type of retirement plan in which the employee and/or employer contributes to an investment fund

are often allowed to transport their plan balance to another employer's plan should they switch jobs.

An employee enrolled in a 401(k) plan makes contributions to an individual account in the form of deferred income, and depending on the parameters of a particular plan, the employer may also be able to contribute to the employee's plan. In fact, some plans require the employer to make plan contributions. As long as employer contributions fall under Section 404 of the IRS code, employers may deduct the contributions on their federal tax returns.[25] Some plans allow employees to make contributions on a before-tax basis, whereas other plans require employees to make contributions on an after-tax basis.[26] Further, some plans allow employees to withdraw benefits prior to retirement, such as in the event of personal hardship or loans.

A 403(b) plan is sometimes referred to as a tax-sheltered annuity plan. A 403(b) plan is very similar to a 401(k) plan, but a notable difference between the two is that 403(b) plans are reserved for public schools and universities, religious organizations, and certain tax-exempt organizations such as charities.[27] Similar to a 401(k), the employee (and sometimes the employer) contributes to an individual account using deferred income. A 403(b) plan typically allows employee income to be deferred on a before-tax basis.[28]

Profit-Sharing Program. A profit-sharing program is one type of pay-for-performance program that can double as a retirement plan. Employees earn rewards by sharing in their organization's profits (e.g., return on assets), and rewards may be distributed as cash or placed in a retirement plan. Employers typically use a formula for determining how much each individual employee receives as part of the profit sharing. When designed for retirement, a profit-sharing program can be considered a type of defined-contribution plan and may even include a 401(k) option.[29] Under a profit-sharing program, employers are under no legal obligation to make certain levels of contributions or to contribute every year. Finally, stock bonus plans are similar to a profit-sharing program; however, under stock bonus plans, employers contribute stock as opposed to cash.

Employee Stock Ownership Plan (ESOP). Like profit-sharing programs, an employee stock ownership plan can double as a pay-for-performance program and a retirement program. Specifically, an employee stock ownership plan (ESOP) rewards employees when company stock shares increase in value and can only be used after a vesting period. As an employee benefit, ESOPs are defined by the U.S. Internal Revenue Service as a defined-contribution plan, wherein the bulk of contributions is invested in an employer's stock.[30] ESOPs are different from stock options and stock purchase plans in that ESOPs typically allow an organization's employees to own a substantially larger portion of the organization (and sometimes even own the organization outright). Further, only employees are eligible to participate in ESOPs, so when employees separate from their organization, they are required to cash out of their ESOPs.[31] Those who participate in ESOPs stand to benefit should their organization perform well throughout their tenure.

Money-Purchase Plan. In a money-purchase plan, employers simply contribute a specified amount to each plan participant's account. Compared to some of the other plans, these plans are relatively straightforward and simple to communicate to employees. The amount specified for each employee can be a percentage of annual compensation, and up to 25% of the amount of a participant's annual compensation can be contributed to their plan. Like other defined-contribution plans, contributions to money-purchase plans are placed into an investment fund. Consequently, the amount of an employee's fund at retirement will be a function of all employer contributions to the fund as well as the investment gains or losses of the fund over time.[32] For example, imagine that Jorge's company contributes 8% of each employee's pay to a money-purchase plan. Because Jorge earns $65,000 a year, his company will contribute $5,200 ($65,000 × 0.08 = $5,200) to his money-purchase plan at the end of the year. Over time, investment gains or losses will affect the fund value.

Individual Retirement Plans

Plans that allow individuals to make tax-deferred investments for retirement are called individual retirement plans or individual retirement arrangements (IRAs). Although individual retirement plans can be employer sponsored, they need not be. Any individual who earns income or is compensated, whether as an employee or through self-employment, may be eligible to contribute to an individual retirement plan—subject to some restrictions.[33] Individual retirement plans may be especially beneficial for those who are self-employed or lack access to employer-sponsored retirement plans. Examples of individual retirement plans include traditional individual retirement accounts or annuities (traditional IRAs) and Roth IRAs, both of which offer tax advantages and impose restrictions on the overall amount of contributions made each year.

Life Insurance Programs

As another common voluntary benefit, **life insurance programs** provide financial compensation for designated beneficiaries when the insured individual dies, which can be distributed in the form of a lump-sum payment.[34] More than half of full-time employees are enrolled in plans in which the benefit is paid out as a fixed multiple of employees' respective annual earnings, whereas the remainder is enrolled mostly in plans in which the benefit is paid out as a flat dollar amount.[35]

Life insurance program
Provides financial compensation for designated beneficiaries when the insured individual dies

Wellness Programs

Wellness programs refer to a wide array of employer-sponsored initiatives aimed at promoting healthy behaviors. More than half of surveyed organizations in a 2017 Kaiser Family Foundation report indicated that they provide wellness programs, such as smoking cessation, weight management, and behavioral and lifestyle coaching programs.[36] In fact, some employers even provide employees with financial incentives for participating in wellness programs. Accumulated evidence indicates that, in general, wellness programs are associated with positive employee health and work outcomes, as well as positive organizational financial outcomes.[37]

©iStock.com/ Sezeryadigar

To promote healthy behaviors, 37% of organizations offer smoking cessation as a wellness program.[38]

Work–Life Programs

Work–life programs are intended to help employees navigate the demands of their work and nonwork lives. As we describe in the following sections, common work–life programs include payment for time not worked, compensatory time off, child and elder care, flextime and telecommuting, college savings plans, educational-assistance programs, and legal services and identity-theft benefits.

Payment for Time Not Worked

Employees require time away from work for a variety of legitimate reasons, and many employers voluntarily provide payment for time not worked. At the federal level, the Fair Labor Standards Act of 1938 does not require employers to pay employees for time away from work due to sickness, vacations, holidays, or other circumstances.[39] However, some state and local laws do require payment for time not worked under certain circumstances.

Paid Time Off (PTO). When an employer compensates employees for time away from work, it is most often under a **paid time off (PTO)** program. Approved reasons for using PTO often include vacation, holidays, non–work-related illness or injury, and personal days. In addition, some employers offer PTO for jury duty, military duty, or other unforeseen circumstances or absences. It is becoming more common for employers to treat PTO as an inclusive program in which there is little or no distinction regarding the reason an employee takes time away from work. In many organizations, employees accrue PTO based on the number of hours worked and years of service, and the PTO accumulates into a pool until the employee decides to use some or all of it. Some employers place restrictions on how PTO can be used, such as limiting how many PTO days can be used for vacation versus sickness, whereas other employers allow employees to use PTO as needed without a specific reason.[40]

Sick Time. When an employee takes time off from work due to a foreseen or unforeseen personal health issue or an immediate family member's health issue, it is referred to as sick time or sick leave. As an example, if an employee takes time away from work due to the flu, this could be considered sick time. In many organizations, sick time is accrued each year based on the cumulative time worked.

Holiday Pay. When employees take time off from work on a recognized federal, state, or local holiday, employers use holiday pay to compensate workers. Examples of recognized U.S. federal holidays include Martin Luther King Jr. Day, Independence Day, and Thanksgiving Day.

Vacation Pay. A great many employers provide vacation pay, which is compensation for taking time away from work for planned reasons, such as for relaxation or travel. Typically, an employee must schedule vacation time in advance and receive approval from a supervisor. In many organizations, paid vacation time is accrued based on cumulative time worked per year.

Personal Leave. Often used as a catch-all for any foreseen or unforeseen time away from work, personal leave is a benefit employers use to supplement their vacation and sick time offerings. Employers may offer personal leave as paid or unpaid. Personal leave is

Paid time off (PTO) A program that provides employees with compensation when they take time away from work, subject to employer approval

distinguishable from leaves of absence covered under the Family Medical and Leave Act (FMLA) or the Uniformed Services Employment and Reemployment Rights Act.

Compensatory Time Off

When a nonexempt employee works overtime hours and receives paid time off rather than earning time-and-a-half pay for the extra hours worked, it is known as compensatory time off or, more commonly, comp time. In the United States, comp time is currently only permitted for employees who work in the public sector, although some HR professionals have encouraged the U.S. Congress to introduce legislation that would require private employers to offer comp time.[41]

Child and Elder Care

Today, many workers require child or elder care when they are at work.[42] From a financial perspective, accessing or providing such care can be costly. For example, the Care Index estimates that the U.S. national average for at-home child care is $28,354 per year, and for in-center child care, the national average is $9,589 per year.[43] Employer-sponsored or subsidized child and elder care can help workers cope with the challenges of balancing work and caring for loved ones. Some employers provide child care services on site. As an example, The Home Depot offers the Little Apron Academy at a location in Atlanta. This center provides affordable on-site child care and educational services for employees' children aged 6 weeks to 5 years.[44]

Flextime and Telecommuting

Allocating time for family and nonwork responsibilities and commuting to work can be challenging for many workers. To cope with such demands, many employees seek flexible work schedules and arrangements. Flextime and telecommuting have emerged as two prominent forms of flexible work arrangements. Flextime occurs when an employer permits employees to adjust their work schedule to meet family and nonwork demands while also meeting their overall work-hours requirement. In contrast, telecommuting occurs when an employee works from home or another remote location, such as from a coffee shop.

College Savings Plans

To help employees save for future college expenses, employers can contribute to or offer college savings plans. One plan, called the 529 College Savings Plan (529 Plan), even offers certain tax advantages.[45] Many states allow for tax credit or deduction after payments have been made to a 529 Plan. Further, 529 Plan funds can be withdrawn for qualified higher-educational expenses without being subject to state or federal income taxes. Although individuals can open their own 529 Plans, some employers administer 529 Plans as a voluntary benefit, which enables employees to apply after-tax income directly to their plan.[46]

Educational-Assistance Programs

In addition to administering and/or contributing to college savings plans, employers can also offer direct financial assistance for educational expenses. An **educational-assistance program** refers to an employee benefit program wherein the employer provides financial assistance for employee educational expenses, which may come in the form of tuition

Educational-assistance program
A program whereby the employer provides financial assistance for employee educational expenses

©iStock.com/ Wavebreakmedia

Companies in the high-tech industry have been leaders in employee perks. Some offer on-site massage treatments gratis or at a discounted rate.

assistance, payment toward qualified educational expenses, or employer-sponsored scholarship programs. Under certain circumstances, an employer can apply these financial contributions as a tax deduction, and under the American Taxpayer Relief Act of 2012, employees do not have to pay income tax on their employer's contributions if the contributions are $5,250 or less per year.[47]

Legal-Services and Identity-Theft Benefits

Legal costs and identity theft can impose heavy demands on employees' time and finances. These demands not only disrupt their family and nonwork lives but also have the potential to disrupt their work lives. Common reasons for legal services include divorce, bankruptcy, lawsuits, wills or trusts, and traffic violations. Some employers sponsor legal services to help employees through legal difficulties and to support their physical presence and psychological focus at work. Alternatively, employers may also opt to provide a referral service—possibly through an employee-assistance program—wherein employees are referred to outside legal resources.[48] Finally, with identity theft on the rise, more individuals are facing the inconvenience and difficulties that come when identities are stolen.[49] In response, some employers offer identity-theft benefits to help employees protect their personal information.

Perquisites

Nonmonetary services or benefits that an employer provides to its employees are referred to as **perquisites**, or **perks**. Essentially, the term *perks* is a catch-all for any voluntary benefit that does not fit neatly into one of the classic programs previously covered in this chapter. Typical examples of company perks include a designated parking space or an office with a view. Famously, Google provides employees with free food via small displays, kitchen areas, and cafeterias; in fact, to encourage healthy eating choices, Google places the healthiest free-food options closer to eye level and less-healthy options in places that are harder to see and reach.[50] Google also offers on-site hair salons, dry cleaning, and bike repair as conveniences, although employees must pay for those.[51]

Administering Benefits Programs

LO 12.4   Assess the common challenges and opportunities associated with administering benefits programs.

Perquisites (perks)
Nonmonetary services or benefits provided by an employer

If benefits are selected and deployed in house, internal HR professionals must possess the knowledge and skills necessary to administer legally required and voluntary benefits programs. In fact, larger organizations often have a team of individuals who work as dedicated benefits specialists. In the following sections, we describe some common challenges and opportunities associated with benefits administration.

Flexible Benefits Plans

Some employers choose to administer flexible benefits plans. As the name implies, employer- sponsored **flexible benefits plans** offer employees some degree of choice when it comes to the voluntary benefits they select and the benefits they are able to receive on a pretax basis. Employees typically make contributions to flexible benefits plans as paycheck deductions, and the employer also pays a portion of the costs. The plan might provide employees with credits, which they can use to purchase the benefits that best suit their needs. For example, using their allotted credits, employees might choose from various medical, life insurance, and retirement plans, and they may be entitled to cash out a portion of their unused credits.

Flexible benefits plans go by other names, such as flex plans or cafeteria plans—the latter name communicates how these plans work: Employees may choose from a variety of benefit offerings as though they were walking through a cafeteria line and choosing from a variety of food options. In addition, these plans are also referred to as Section 125 plans—a label that references the applicable section of the U.S. Internal Revenue Code.[52] Section 125 permits flexible benefits plan participants to select two or more benefits, where at least one benefit is taxable and at least one benefit is qualified. Under Section 125, taxable benefits include cash payments that are taxed upon receipt. In contrast, qualified benefits plans offer several potential tax advantages for the employer and employee: employer tax deduction, employee pretax payroll contribution, and tax-free investment returns. Qualified benefits include the following approved benefits that are received on a pretax basis (with certain limitations):

- employer-sponsored accident and health plans;
- group life insurance plans;
- child, elder, and other dependent care plans;
- adoption assistance programs; and
- health savings accounts (HSAs).

Taxes and Accounting

Different laws and taxes must be considered when administering benefits. Moreover, different benefits often have different sets of rules, regulations, reporting standards, and taxes. Accordingly, successful benefits administration entails partnering with individuals, departments, or consulting firms with expertise in taxes and accounting. A comprehensive review of all pertinent tax and accounting forms and statements (e.g., Statement of Financial Accounting Standards 106) is beyond the scope of this textbook. However, we encourage interested readers to review documentation provided by government and professional organizations, such as the Internal Revenue Service (www.irs.gov) and the Financial Accounting Standards Board (www.fasb.org).

Discrimination

As with other HR functions, benefits should not be administered in a manner that intentionally or unintentionally discriminates against different legally protected groups.

Flexible benefits plans Offer employees some degree of choice for the employer-sponsored voluntary benefits they select and the benefits they are able to receive on a pretax basis

Spotlight on Legal Issues
SAME-SEX MARRIAGE AND SPOUSAL BENEFITS

In June 2015, the U.S. Supreme Court ruled that the Constitution guarantees the right to same-sex marriage. In the years leading up to the Court's decision, 37 states and the District of Columbia had already ruled in favor of same-sex marriage. Nonetheless, this landmark case guaranteed the right to same-sex marriage and spousal benefits at the federal level and across all states, in the process becoming the law of the land. Two years prior, the Supreme Court voted to strike down a federal law that denied spousal benefits to married same-sex couples; however, the Social Security Administration continued to deny same-sex spousal benefits for some individuals in states where same-sex marriage was not yet recognized. As such, the subsequent 2015 ruling provided blanket protections across the 50 states and the District of Columbia, and in the case of the Social Security Administration, spousal Social Security benefits for married same-sex couples became guaranteed.[53]

Consistent with the following pieces of U.S. legislation (covered in Chapter 4), benefits administration should not discriminate on the basis of race, color, religion, sex, national origin, age, pregnancy and associated medical conditions, disability, and genetic information: Title VII of the Civil Rights Act of 1964, Age Discrimination in Employment Act of 1967, Pregnancy Discrimination Act of 1978, Americans with Disabilities Act of 1990, and Genetic Information Nondiscrimination Act of 2008. In addition, benefits should not discriminate in favor of highly compensated employees. For example, for a benefit to be classified as qualified, an employer must demonstrate that all employees, regardless of their compensation levels, have access to the benefit and are helped by the benefit in similar ways.

Selecting Benefits

When selecting which voluntary benefits to offer, organizational decision makers should determine (a) the benefits employees want and (b) the benefits competitors offer. Regarding the first objective, as shown in Figure 12.2, a variety of data-gathering methods can be used to identify the most desirable benefits. In particular, employee surveys represent a relatively efficient data-gathering method because a large number of surveys can be sent out quickly (or even instantaneously). High survey response rates from all departments or units can help ensure that employees' responses are representative of all employees in the organization. Although potentially less efficient than surveys, employee focus groups offer an opportunity to gather rich, in-depth information regarding the most sought-after benefits. With respect to the second objective, competitor benchmarking based on market reviews remains one of the best approaches for determining what benefits other organizations offer.

■ FIGURE 12.2 Methods Used to Determine Employees' Most Desired Voluntary Benefits

Results from SHRM's 2016 Strategic Benefits Survey provide a glimpse into the methods employers use to determine the voluntary benefits employees most desire.

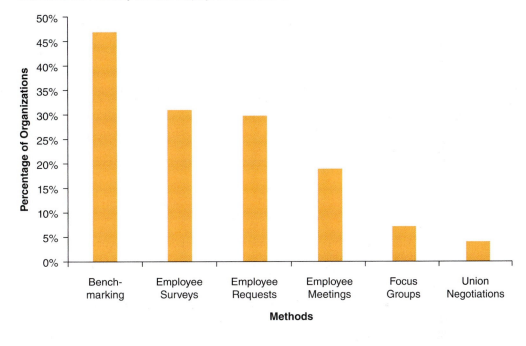

Source: Adapted from "Strategic Benefits Survey—Assessment and Communication of Benefits" (2016) with permission of the Society for Human Resource Management (SHRM). © SHRM 2016.

Spotlight on Data and Analytics

EVALUATING BENEFITS OFFERINGS

Offering voluntary benefits to employees has the potential to add value for both employees and the organization. Analytics can be used as a decision-making tool (a) to determine which voluntary benefits to offer and (b) to evaluate the extent to which employees utilize different voluntary benefits. In fact, data analysis may reveal differences between the benefits employees say they want and the benefits they actually use.

To determine if any new voluntary benefits should be offered, HR professionals can gather data on employee needs and wants. One of the most efficient ways to collect data from a large number of employees across the organization

(Continued)

(Continued)

is to use an employee opinion survey. The survey should include items (i.e., questions or prompts) aimed at measuring employees' attitudes and behaviors toward existing benefits and potential benefits offerings. For example, to gauge employees' overall level of satisfaction with current benefits offerings, you might ask employees to rate the extent to which they agree with the following survey item, using a 1-to-5 scale (1 = *strongly disagree*, 5 = *strongly agree*): "Overall, I am satisfied with the company's current employee benefits offerings."

To evaluate benefits utilization, HR professionals can use existing data. For instance, using data that are perhaps already captured in the HR information system, an organization can analyze the number of employees enrolled in each benefit and the frequency with which employees access or utilize each benefit. In addition, using statistical analyses like regression, HR professionals can investigate whether the enrollment in or use of certain benefits is associated with important outcomes such as turnover and performance.[54]

Communicating Benefits Programs

LO 12.5   Assess the common challenges and opportunities associated with communicating benefits programs.

The importance of effectively communicating benefits programs to (prospective) employees cannot be overstated, which includes communicating program details and communicating the value of benefits. Some evidence has shown that employees' awareness of their benefits offerings can be enhanced by providing them with informational materials about available benefits and by meeting with employees to discuss the available benefits.[55] Findings from a 2017 SHRM survey indicated that HR professionals generally perceived face-to-face communication methods like one-on-one communications and orientations as being effective.[56] As for virtual communication methods, approximately one third of the surveyed HR professionals thought online benefits portals were effective.

In addition, HR professionals should make an effort to communicate the *value* of benefits programs. Employee benefits represent a major cost for organizations, and evidence indicates that employees tend to underestimate the amount their employer contributes to their benefits.[57] In fact, many individuals may be unaware of how much benefits are worth. For example, differences in benefits offerings may ultimately lead a job applicant to accept a job offer from one organization over another. Thus, it is important to provide applicants and employees with an accurate summary of benefits offerings, including their worth.

CHAPTER SUMMARY

Benefits are part of the organization's broader rewards system, and like other rewards, strategic deployment and administration of benefits can have important implications for attracting, motivating, and retaining

workers. In the United States, legally required benefits include Social Security benefits, workers' compensation, federal and state unemployment insurance, and certain health care benefits. Voluntary benefits are discretionary in nature; employers must think carefully and strategically to decide which benefits they will offer. They must also monitor the extent to which employees are using already available benefits. Examples of voluntary benefits include various forms of medical, dental, vision, life, and retirement insurance, as well as wellness and work–life programs and perquisites. Finally, employers often face certain challenges and opportunities when administering and communicating benefits.

KEY TERMS

Social Security Act   281

Federal Insurance Contributions Act (FICA)   282

workers' compensation   283

Family and Medical Leave Act (FMLA)   283

Employee Retirement Income Security Act (ERISA)   283

Consolidated Omnibus Budget Reconciliation Act (COBRA)   284

Health Insurance Portability and Accountability Act (HIPAA)   284

Patient Protection and Affordable Care Act (ACA)   284

short-term disability insurance   288

long-term disability insurance   289

defined-benefit plan   289

defined-contribution plan   289

life insurance program   291

paid time off (PTO)   292

educational-assistance program   293

perquisites (perks)   294

flexible benefits plans   295

$SAGE edge™

Get the tools you need to sharpen your study skills. SAGE edge offers a robust online environment featuring an impressive array of free tools and resources.

Access practice quizzes, eFlashcards, video, and multimedia at **edge.sagepub.com/bauerbrief**

HR REASONING AND DECISION-MAKING EXERCISES

EXERCISE 12.1: COMMUNICATING THE VALUE OF BENEFITS

Trident Health System has been experiencing difficulties attracting and retaining registered nurses (RNs) at its central hospital. Based on data from follow-up surveys with former applicants and from exit interviews conducted with former employees who voluntarily left the organization, HR leaders have concluded that a large number of individuals have been lured to a local competitor called Advantage Health. In particular, a number of former applicants and employees have reported that their primary reason for leaving was because Advantage Health paid RNs higher hourly wages as well as higher night and weekend pay differentials.

The HR leadership at Trident Health System acknowledges that they pay RNs lower wages than Advantage Health. However, based on market review data, they have reason to believe that Trident Health System offers one of the most generous benefits packages of any similar-sized health care organization in the region. Specifically, they offer generous employer cost-sharing contributions to employee medical, dental, and vision plans, as well as on-site subsidized child care services and a free employee cafeteria. Despite their generous benefits package, HR leaders are concerned that perhaps they are not doing a good enough job communicating information about their benefits to job candidates and current employees. At this time, job candidates and current employees can access information about benefits via the company's benefits webpage, and current employees can also look at their benefits deductions presented in their biweekly pay stub.

Questions

1. What can Trident Health System do to improve how it communicates benefits to job candidates? What about current employees?
2. What methods would you recommend that Trident Health System use to communicate the value of its benefits offerings? Why?
3. What data-collection method(s) can the HR leaders use to determine which benefits employees (a) say they want and (b) actually utilize?

EXERCISE 12.2: PAID PARENTAL LEAVE AT JEMBE BANKS

Jembe Banks is a regional bank that is headquartered in Detroit, Michigan, and has branches throughout Michigan, Indiana, Wisconsin, and Illinois. The bank currently employs nearly 350 employees at its headquarters and more than 2,300 employees at its various branches.

Each year, the HR team at Jembe Banks conducts a benefits survey designed to measure employees' preferences and attitudes regarding different benefits, as well as which benefits they plan to enroll in during the next fiscal year. At the end of each year's survey, the HR team provides the following open-ended question: "Is there a benefit that you would like for Jembe to offer in the future? Explain why." After reviewing responses from last year's survey, the HR team discovered that 121 employees out of the 899 who completed the survey stated that they wanted Jembe to offer paid parental leave.

Questions

1. If the company decides to provide paid parental leave, how many weeks of paid leave should the company provide? Why?

2. Should the company provide the same amount of paid parental leave to mothers and fathers alike? Why or why not?

3. Should a mother and father who are both employed by Jembe be allowed to take their paid leave concurrently? Why or why not?

ETHICAL MATTERS EXERCISE: MAKING CHANGES TO HEALTH INSURANCE PLANS

It is not unusual for employers to change health insurance plans. For example, an employer may switch to a plan with lower monthly premiums and a higher deductible or may switch from offering a preferred-provider organization (PPO) to a health maintenance organization (HMO). Employers may make such changes to achieve cost savings over the previous plan, or they may do so in an attempt to improve employee coverage or benefits utilization. Many health insurance plans are inherently complex and nuanced, such that employers and employees alike may experience unintended positive or negative consequences when changes are made. Given this uncertainty, it is important for organizational decision makers, particularly benefits experts, to do their due diligence when determining what changes to make to a plan; due diligence might include performing a benefits utilization analysis, employee opinion survey, or cost-benefit analysis.

Consider an organization that originally used a three-tiered employer cost-sharing system. Employees who earned the least income were placed in the first income tier and employees who earned the most were placed in the third income tier. Employers in the lowest tier received the highest cost-sharing contributions to monthly insurance premiums from the organization, whereas those in the highest tier received the lowest. In an attempt to refine the cost-sharing tier system, decision makers subsequently designed and implemented a five-tier system based on the same cost-sharing principle.

The decision makers in this scenario hoped that this change would make benefits administration fairer. Unfortunately, there was an unintended consequence that adversely affected some of the most vulnerable employees. Specifically, some employees who were originally in the first tier subsequently moved to the second tier based on this change. This resulted in higher monthly premiums for those individuals, leaving them with lower take-home pay after the benefits were deducted from their paychecks. Some of these individuals ended up leaving the organization.

If the organization had applied data analytics to model the potential effects prior to making the decision to implement the new five-tiered system, they might have anticipated the negative impact on certain employees. This example illustrates why it is an organization's ethical responsibility to identify potential unintended consequences of changes to benefits. By leveraging the available data, an organization can avoid an unfortunate outcome.[58]

Questions

1. In your opinion, to what extent are organizational decision makers ethically obligated to provide employer-sponsored health insurance for their workers? Give examples to support your answer.

2. In the scenario described, how might the company's HR administrators have intervened *after* the new five-tiered system was implemented to prevent employees from leaving due to reduced take-home pay?

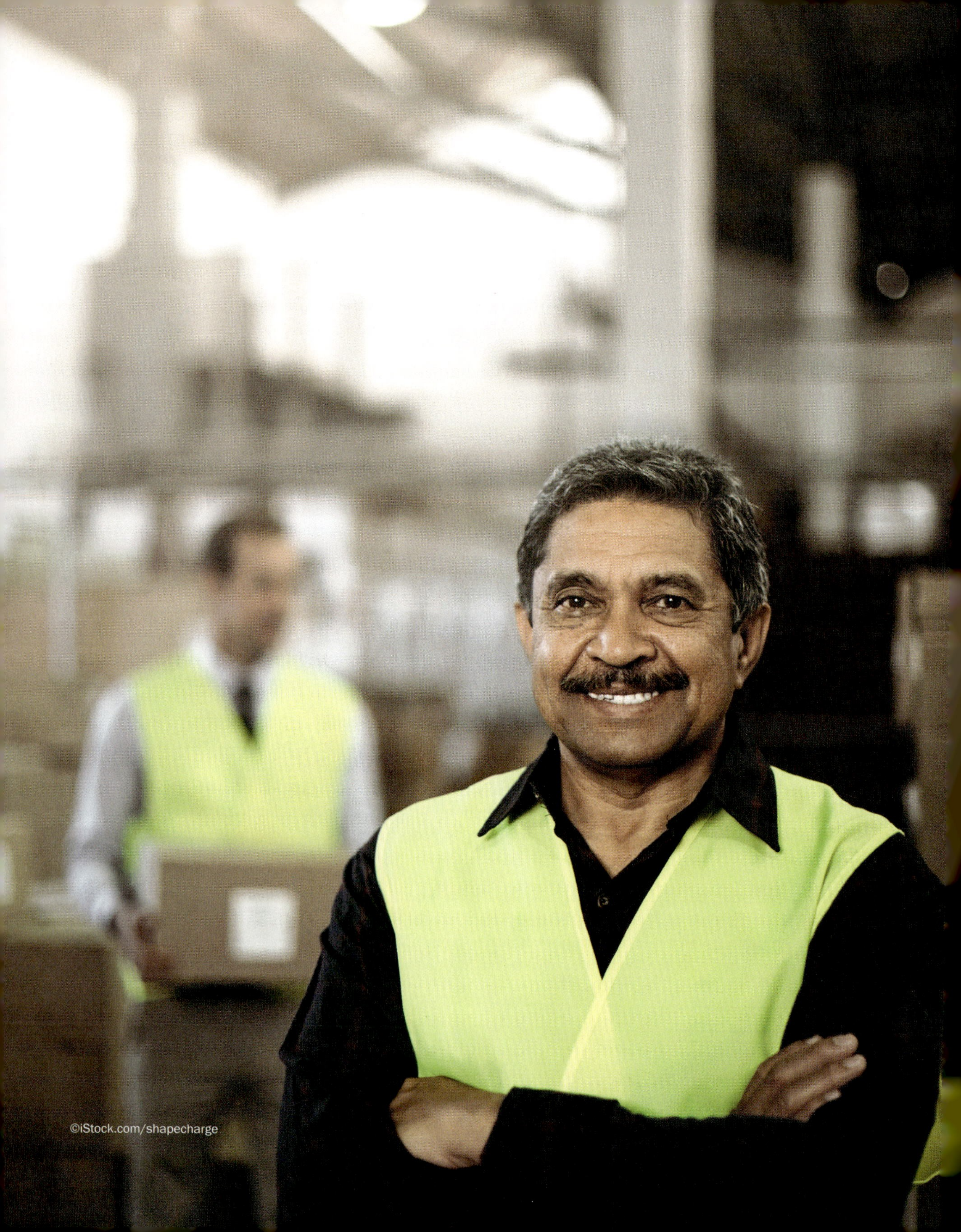

©iStock.com/shapecharge

13

Employee and Labor Relations

LEARNING OBJECTIVES

After reading and studying this chapter, you should be able to do the following:

13.1 Define *employee and labor relations*.

13.2 Compare different types of organizational policies and procedures.

13.3 Recognize the role that the labor movement plays globally.

13.4 Briefly outline the collective bargaining process.

13.5 Evaluate the possible courses of action when negotiating parties fail to reach an agreement.

HR in Action: The Case of Kaiser Permanente Unions

The Kaiser-Permanente/coalition agreement represents the largest, longest-lasting labor–management partnership in the United States.[1] The Coalition of Kaiser Permanente Unions, AFL-CIO, is a federation of 32 local unions associated with health care in California. This coalition includes 11 international unions and represents 120,000 health care workers.

This partnership has a history going back to the early 1990s. At that time, in response to increasingly strained labor relations, the coalition was formalized in 1996. It sought to adopt new policies, including a new constitution and bylaws. It also proposed a "new" idea to work with Kaiser Permanente to develop a partnership that included participation in decision making throughout the organization and to "have a say in how to deliver affordable, high-quality care." The key was that coalition members were involved in the development of ideas rather than just talking about them after the organization had proposals already developed.

This partnership has been lauded as an effective example of how working together can be more powerful in long-term win-win solutions than against one another. In fact, both its San Diego and San Rafael, California, medical centers have been featured in case studies at Cornell University titled "How Labor–Management Partnerships Improve Patient Care, Cost Control, and Labor Relations."[2] Of course, having such a partnership does not always mean that labor

©iStock.com/ shapecharge

relations go smoothly. In 2017, Kaiser Permanente reached a collective bargaining agreement with 1,200 registered nurses at the Los Angeles Medical Center after 17 months of heated contract negotiations and two short-term strikes.[3]

Case Discussion Questions

1. What experience(s), if any, have you had with unions?

2. Do you think that the collective agreement with Kaiser is a positive or negative thing for patients? Kaiser? Its employees?

3. How might positive employee relations help avoid negative consequences for organizations and employees? Please think of a few examples to share.

Factors Influencing Employee Relations

LO 13.1   Define *employee and labor relations*.

Employee relations refers to the collective relationships between different employees as well as between employees and management in an organization. Much of employee relations is tied to an organization's HR policies and procedures. In addition, organizations must adhere to formal labor laws such as terms of employment and particularly labor laws relating to unions and collective bargaining, referred to as **labor relations**. Employee relations and labor relations are related to a wide range of HRM topics you have already learned about in this book such as rewards, benefits, training, and job security.

This chapter explores the key components of both employee relations and labor relations from both a historical and a modern organizational perspective and begins by delving into the definition of employee relations and factors related to this concept. Then the chapter shifts to organizational policies and procedures, employee rights and responsibilities, and grievance procedures, which are also aspects of employee and labor relations. The labor movement and issues associated with union formation, functioning, and dispute management are covered. And finally, the chapter includes a short outline of the collective bargaining process and the alternative methods of resolving negotiations when an agreement cannot be reached.

Many factors influence employee relations. If you have taken an organizational behavior or principles of management course, you are probably familiar with such factors, as entire chapters are devoted to many of them; this textbook has touched on several of these issues as well. Here the focus is on these five important factors that might influence employee relations: culture, fair treatment, working conditions, employment laws, and unions (see Figure 13.1).

Employee relations The collective relationships between different employees as well as between employees and management in an organization

Labor relations Managing in response to labor laws relating to unions and collective bargaining

Culture

Culture is defined as the shared assumptions that members of an organization have, which affect how they act, think, and perceive their environment. Therefore, the culture that evolves within an organization can exhibit a major positive or negative effect on employee relations. It is also important to keep in mind that subcultures may also develop within organizations such that different groups may have different perceptions or experiences that influence their employee relations. One major factor that affects culture and employee relations is how individuals are treated in terms of both procedures and outcomes. In fact, employment law attorney Aaron Zandy says the key to avoiding employment lawsuits is to do three things: *be fair, be consistent,* and *do not surprise employees.*[4] Thus, the next point addresses how fair (or unfair) treatment may affect employee relations.

■ **FIGURE 13.1**   Factors Influencing Employee Relations

Employee relations are influenced by several aspects of organizations, including those depicted here.

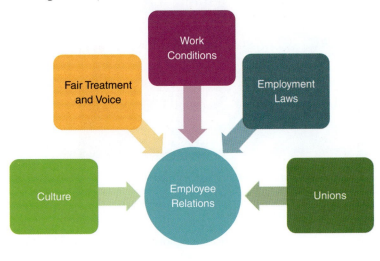

Fair Treatment and Voice

Fair treatment is so important for employee relations that SHRM's Code of Ethics includes Fairness and Justice. Specifically, it reads, "As human resource professionals, we are ethically responsible for promoting and fostering fairness and justice for all employees and their organizations." This includes cultivating an environment of inclusiveness, developing and administering policies that are fair and consistent, and respecting individuals. When individuals feel that they are not being treated fairly, they tend to have lower job attitudes, have poorer performance and greater withdrawal behaviors, and are more likely to join a union.[5] Thus, organizations wishing to develop and maintain positive employee–employer relations should keep fairness in mind when interacting with employees and applicants, to gather feedback from employees regularly to see what issues and improvements might be addressed, and to keep fairness and justice in mind when making decisions that affect employees. Even better, research finds that when employees have more voice in how organizations function due to programs like profit sharing, worker ownership, or worker participation in decision making, higher productivity is found as well.[6]

Working Conditions

When referring to working conditions, many possible aspects of work relate to employee relations. For example, rewards and benefits are aspects of work that are often reasons for employees to passively withdraw or actively look for employment elsewhere. Similarly, working in unsafe conditions can be a major concern and has been related to strained employee relations. In other instances, the actual workplace might be physically safe but create stress due to shift work, overtime, or a lack of flexibility in how or when work gets

Not complying with employment labor laws can be costly. For example, in 2002, Starbucks paid $18 million in a dispute regarding overtime pay, and in 2008, it paid $105 million in a dispute over tips, to settle lawsuits in California.

done. Changes to benefits can lead to strained employment relations and union activity. Some companies such as Costco are known as leaders in their industry in terms of wages and benefits even in the low-margin world of groceries and retail. The company is known for promoting from within, like Craig Jelinek, a 30-year veteran who took over as CEO in 2012. In fact, 98% of store managers have been promoted from within stores. Costco also pays well, with an average of $22/hour versus the average of $13.38/hour at Walmart, a store offering similar items, or the national average of around $11/hour for retail employees. In 2018, Amazon began offering $15/hour for all U.S. employees, including seasonal, temporary, and part-time workers. Some saw this as a reaction to increasing criticism about its labor practices.[7] Employees also receive full health benefits, a 401(k) retirement plan with stock options after 1 year, and generous vacation and family leave policies.[8]

Employment Laws

In the United States, employment laws are a major factor in the practice of HR. Understanding how they influence and regulate employee relations is important. Employment laws matter for the practice of HRM and for what employees expect in terms of employment relations with organizational members and the organization as a whole.

Unions

The mere possibility of an organization's workforce joining a labor union (referred to as "unionization") may influence employee relations. However, once a union is in place, employee relations become formalized in specific and prescribed ways. Much of this chapter focuses on understanding the history of labor unions, trends in unionization, how they are formed, and how they function. Also covered are organizational policies and procedures, which exist regardless of whether a union is in place. Keep in mind, however, that unions are tasked to bargain over policies as well, so at times, they are deeply involved in forming, informing, and monitoring organizational policies and procedures.

Organizational Policies and Procedures

LO 13.2   Compare different types of organizational policies and procedures.

Designing, implementing, and enforcing organizational policies and procedures are often managed by HR departments. When unions are in place, these policies are negotiated, as we will see in greater detail in the sections that follow. However, it is important to understand how organizational policies and procedures are communicated and what they typically entail regardless of how they came to be.

Employee Handbooks

Organizational policies and procedures outline the rules and expectations for both employees and employers. Although laws require employers to inform their employees about their specific workplace rights, it is not a legal mandate to have an actual employee handbook. However, many organizations do create handbooks including such information because they are useful for employees and managers to understand what is expected of them. Some handbooks are long and read like legal documents. Others are short and written simply. However, it is critical that employees of all levels understand that handbooks are part of the HR compliance process, so what is written in the handbook provides an answer if disputes occur between managers and employees. Thus, it is important that what is included is accurate, consistently enforced, and understood by everyone within the organization. Not doing so can put organizations at risk should an employee complaint be filed.

Normally, new employees receive their handbooks as part of the onboarding process of orientation and compliance. Handbooks can make for pretty dry reading, and it might be tempting to skip reading it while trying to adjust to one's new job. Some companies such as The Motley Fool, which has appeared on Glassdoor.com's Best Places to Work list, have created fully interactive onboarding experiences, which include a video introduction from the CEO, specific company policies and procedures, and a list of key terms for employees. Zappos.com's employee handbook is written in a comic book style and features a story of a grandmother explaining Zappos's culture, policies, and procedures.[9] Regardless of how entertaining the information is, all new employees should take the time to read and understand the handbook given what an important document it is as the basis for the employment relationship.

Organizational Policies

Organizations vary in how many policies they include in their employee handbook depending on a number of factors, including the organization's industry, size, age, and culture, as well as state and local requirements. Rather than review all the potential policies that might be included, the focus is on five different types of policies that might be included: legally required information, code of conduct, leaves, appearance, and social media policies.

Legally Required Information

Although employee handbooks are not legally required, they are often included since policies that must be addressed by law are important to outline and share with employees. These include workers' compensation policies, family medical leave policies, and EEOC nondiscrimination policies as required by the U.S. Department of Labor. Requirements change over time, so the suggestion to review the content shared with new employees is an ongoing task.

Code of Conduct

The code of conduct might include information about expectations for workplace behaviors such as respect, confidentiality, EEO compliance, and unacceptable behaviors such as discrimination or sexual harassment. It is important that organizations communicate their expectations regarding what constitutes a *conflict of interest* that might unduly influence decisions or have the appearance of doing so. Such policies should include definitions of conflicts of interest and what to do if such conflicts exist. Some organizations include code-of-conduct training that all employees must complete. Often employees will be asked to sign that they have read, understand, and agree to the code of conduct.

Leave Policy

Beyond the Family Medical Leave Act considerations, some organizations prescribe and strictly enforce how sick days, personal days, and/or vacation days are to be taken. Other organizations such as GrubHub, LinkedIn, Kronos, and Netflix have no limit on the amount of leave that can be taken.[10] Instead, they trust employees to behave responsibly and only take as much time as they need while keeping up with their responsibilities. Regardless of where a company is on this continuum, it is important to be clear about what the policy is and how employees should schedule days off to avoid confusion or resentment.

Appearance

Many aspects of employee appearance may or may not be outlined in an employee handbook. For example, dress codes, personal hygiene, facial hair, and body art and piercings may be addressed. Dress codes range from business formal, such as wearing a specific uniform, to casual. The type of dress code often depends on a number of factors such as the type of industry the organization is in, the type of work an employee does, whether special dress or equipment is needed for safety such as when working in construction sites, geography, or the organizational culture. Personal hygiene issues range from a safety requirement at work, such as a restaurant employee washing their hands before returning to work, to the uncomfortable topic of body odor. Managers and employees need guidance in how to handle such matters with sensitivity, and SHRM reminds us that odors may be caused by many factors outside of an employee's control such as a medical condition or a specific diet. Such issues must be addressed appropriately to avoid violating the Americans with Disabilities Act or triggering other claims of discrimination.[11] Including guidelines on what is expected and whether perfumes and colognes are allowed in the workplace can be helpful for employees and those who work around them to deal with the issues professionally and discreetly. Overall, the thing to keep in mind is that organizations have the legal right to adopt whatever dress codes and grooming requirements they desire to fit their culture and/or promote a particular brand or look as long as they do not discriminate on the basis of a protected class. The policies they choose to enact will most likely have an influence on employee relations.

Social Media

Nordstrom is known for a unique approach to employee relations for having a handbook that fits on a 5 × 8 card. The "handbook" includes the following:

> Our number one goal is to provide outstanding customer service. Set both your personal and professional goals high. We have great confidence in your ability to achieve them, so our employee handbook is very simple. We have only one rule. . . .
> Our one rule: Use best judgment in all situations. There will be no additional rules.

Spotlight on Legal Issues
TATTOOS IN THE WORKPLACE

©iStock.com/gpointstudio

In the United States, more than 20% of adults and nearly 40% of millennials aged 18 to 29 have at least one tattoo, according to a study by Pew Research, and research finds that men with tattoos are actually slightly more likely to have jobs than other men.[12] Of course, this varies by industry. But, in general, employers have the right to choose not to hire someone, or to fire them, for tattoos. An exception to this is when tattoos are due to religious reasons. In one case, Red Robin restaurant fired a server for having tattoos that were part of his religious practice. Red Robin lost its case for termination in court and paid the server $150,000.[13] This is relatively rare in terms of outcomes for such court cases—especially those simply dealing with personal-expression or freedom-of-speech arguments. Another way employers can get into trouble, however, is if they discriminate against some types of tattoos but not others. The key for organizations is to be consistent and fair in applying their dress code and grooming standards across all employees.

The First Amendment of the U.S. Constitution protects the rights of individuals to free speech, and this includes the display of tattoos. But that does not mean that employers in the private sector have to allow them. A survey found that 60% of HR professionals felt that visible tattoos would negatively affect an applicant's chances of securing employment, and 74% felt that way about facial piercings. It is not clear how these negative reactions may evolve over time given the growing number of individuals with tattoos in the United States. The key for organizations is to be consistent and fair in applying the dress code and grooming standards across all employees.

That, however, is not the end of Nordstrom's workplace policies. For example, Nordstrom's social media guidelines point to 10 guidelines as an offshoot of its original rule, stating, "If you use social media accounts to connect and share about Nordstrom, we ask that you use good judgment and follow these additional guidelines."[14] Keep in mind that policies should follow employment laws like those related to the right of employees to discuss working conditions, as this is behavior protected by the National Labor Relations Board (NLRB) laws. For example, an ambulance company, American Medical Response of Connecticut, fired an employee for criticizing her supervisor on Facebook, and the NLRB filed a complaint that this violated worker rights.[15] Organizations should clearly delineate their policies regarding social media both during and outside of work hours, as this has become an increasingly controversial issue.

The Labor Movement

LO 13.3   Recognize the role that the labor movement plays globally.

The history of the labor movement and the growth of labor unions can be traced back to fundamental changes in the workplace. In the early 1900s, factories began to set up procedures to address concerns regarding employee wages and additional labor concerns. However, following the Great Depression in the 1930s and then World War II, a surge in union membership took place through the 1950s. Union membership has been on a steady decline in the United States in recent decades. The decision to organize or join a union is a personal one for each employee, but there are some common reasons why employees pursue unionization in their workplaces. There are also a number of different types of unions.[16]

Reasons Employees Unionize

Employees unionize for a variety of reasons, including job dissatisfaction, working conditions, and employee disengagement. We start with job dissatisfaction.

Job Dissatisfaction

Dissatisfaction with one's job is a major reason employees organize and join unions. This makes sense, because when an individual is unhappy about a situation at work, they may engage in a number of behaviors in response. Different reactions to job dissatisfaction are illustrated using the exit–voice–loyalty–neglect framework, which argues that employee behavioral reactions range in terms of how active and constructive workers are. Behaviors directed toward withdrawing from the organization include employee lateness, absenteeism, and turnover and are termed *exit*. Active and constructive responses to dissatisfying working conditions include *voice*, through which employees attempt to improve conditions. *Neglect* and *loyalty* are passive and refer to allowing the conditions to worsen or hoping they will get better. Figure 13.2 illustrates these four possible reactions in terms of these factors. Attempts to organize and unionize represent one potential form of voice behavior.

■ **FIGURE 13.2**   Four Possible Reactions to Job Dissatisfaction

Employees may respond to dissatisfaction through exit, voice, neglect, or loyalty.

Working Conditions

So what specific things might employees be dissatisfied about? A number of reasons related to working conditions may affect whether employees are motivated to organize or join a union. These include concerns regarding working conditions such as pay, benefits, safety, job security, hours, the working environment, and treatment. In other words, employees interested in voting for a union believe that the union will help them get more of the financial and nonfinancial working conditions they value.[17]

One study found that membership in a labor union was related to better coping and lower stress for individuals working in a chemical plant.[19] Although union membership has been declining, the inequality in hourly wages has been increasing, indicating that unions do influence wages.[20] In support of the argument that union workers enjoy greater levels of compensation, on average, union members earn more and enjoy better benefits (e.g., health insurance and retirement accounts) than their nonunionized

Underwood Archives/Getty Images

The 40-hour workweek and the concept of the "weekend" did not come into existence in the United States until 1937 with the passage of the Fair Labor Standards Act at the urging of unions, leading to the union slogan "Labor Unions: The folks who brought you the weekend."[18]

counterparts across the United States within the same occupations.[21] For example, across all industries, union workers earn a median weekly pay rate of $1,004 versus $802 for non-union workers in 2016.[22] Bus drivers for Facebook received $9-per-hour raises after their union negotiated for higher wages, better benefits, additional pay for shift work, and the establishment of grievance procedures. Google and Apple increased the hourly pay and benefits for their own shuttle drivers shortly after Facebook's agreement with its employees represented by Teamsters Local 853.[23]

Employee Disengagement

How engaged employees are at work is also related to whether employees are interested in unionizing. Employees who report not being engaged with their work also reported being more likely to vote yes to a union and to become union members.[24]

Employees who are disengaged or dissatisfied or feel unfairly treated can work with organizations toward improvement. But organizations need tools to do so. One such tool is the administration of an annual employee opinion survey to gauge employee attitudes and to identify problems and potential problems within the organization. Such surveys are big undertakings in terms of employee time to respond as well as the effort to create, administer, and analyze the results. Although large organizations such as Disney, Walmart, and Ford Motor Company already administer such surveys, more and more organizations are also beginning to administer smaller surveys more frequently.

Why Do Some Organizations Resist Unionization?

Not all organizations resist unionization, but it is common for organizations to work to avoid it for a number of reasons, including profit concerns and decreased autonomy. We discuss each of these in the section that follows.

Profit Concerns

It makes sense that organizations might be concerned that if they pay workers more in terms of wages or increase worker benefits and programs, they will become less profitable. However, that is only true if there are no financial benefits to workers being satisfied, such as stronger productivity or innovation. There is a great deal of debate regarding whether belonging to a union makes employees more or less satisfied overall.[25] Similarly, it is not clear if organizations with unions are more or less profitable than their nonunionized counterparts, as it depends on a variety of factors.[26] For example, a meta-analysis of 73 global studies examining the relationship between productivity and unions found that, in the United Kingdom, there was a negative association. For the United States, however, there was a positive association in general, as well as for within U.S. manufacturing.[27] Even though the reality for a given organization within a given country or industry is unclear in terms of profit, it is clear that unions do decrease an organization's autonomy to make decisions that affect employees.

Decreased Autonomy

As you will see in the pages that follow, when an organization's workforce is unionized or has a union in place, it serves to decrease how much discretion the organization has to alter wages and benefits and to set policies that affect employees. Rather than having full autonomy to make changes as long as they are legal, organizations with union members must consider the contract in place. This can make them less able to respond quickly to changes in the market or to changing conditions. This can be a concern for organizations. In fact, research shows that the worse the market conditions are, the more likely executives of a firm are to choose union-avoidance strategies rather than union–labor cooperation strategies.[28] Business and labor do not have to have an adversarial relationship. In countries such as Denmark, unions and employers work together closely, and Denmark is considered one of the easiest countries in the world in which to conduct business. It is ranked behind New Zealand and Singapore according to the World Bank (the United States was ranked sixth).[29]

Unions and Laws

To really understand the context of labor movements, it is important to trace the series of laws associated with their growth and regulation from the 1930s through today. First and foremost, unions exist in a legal context. Now that we have covered some of the reasons modern employees join unions as well as types of unions, we will move to a discussion of the different laws that set the legal context for work and workers. While many laws relate to employees and unions, we will highlight some of the most important acts related to HR practices, starting with the Norris-LaGuardia Act.

Norris-LaGuardia Act (1932)

This act was a critical step toward changing national labor relations. It outlawed the ability of federal courts to stop union activities such as pickets or strikes. It also outlawed agreements from employees to employers that they would not form or join a union. The passage of this act signaled a new era of support for unions and their activities. Although not a comprehensive act in itself, it is regarded as being important in laying the foundation of changing attitudes toward supporting labor movements in the United States.

National Labor Relations (or Wagner) Act (1935)

Building on the legislative momentum of the Norris-LaGuardia Act, the **National Labor Relations (or Wagner) Act** regulated national labor relations by granting unions fundamental rights and powers. These included important provisions such as the right to collective bargaining and the definition of **unfair labor practices**; importantly, it established penalties for companies that violated these rights. The act describes five key unfair labor practices that include the right to self-organization; to form, join, or assist labor unions; to bargain collectively through representatives of their own choosing; and to engage in other concerted activities for the purpose of collective bargaining or other mutual aid or protection, and shall also have the right to refrain from any or all such activities.

These rights, however, do not extend to the railway or airline industries. Finally, the act established the **National Labor Relations Board (NLRB)**. As an independent U.S. governmental agency, the NLRB is tasked with supervising union elections and is empowered to investigate suspected unfair labor practices. The NLRB consists of a five-person board, and general counsel is appointed by the president of the United States with Senate consent. In 2017, the NLRB handled nearly 19,000 unfair practice charges (see Figure 13.3). For example, the NLRB argued that the following provisions within T-Mobile's employee handbook violated the Wagner Act: maintaining a positive work environment, not arguing or fighting, failing to be respectful or to demonstrate appropriate teamwork, outlawing all photography and audio or video recording in the workplace, and barring access to electronic information by individuals not approved. The court ruled that these handbook items did not violate the act and that "a reasonable employee would be fully capable of engaging in debate over union activity or working conditions, even vigorous or heated debate, without inappropriately arguing or fighting, or failing to treat others with respect."[30]

Labor Management Relations Act (1947)

The **Labor Management Relations Act (1947)**, also known as the Taft-Hartley Act, amended and limited the National Labor Relations Act in key ways. For example, it added additional unfair labor practices employees might engage in rather than limiting such unfair acts to companies. In essence, the act was designed to limit the power of unions and to limit the ability of labor to strike. Specifically, it prohibited jurisdictional strikes so that only unions directly related to the work of a targeted business could participate, prohibited

■ **FIGURE 13.3** Disposition of Unfair Labor Practice Charges in 2017

A majority of unfair labor practice charges end in settlements, adjustments, or by being withdrawn.

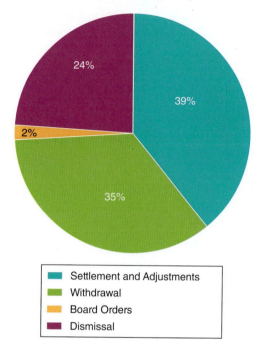

- Settlement and Adjustments
- Withdrawal
- Board Orders
- Dismissal

Source: National Labor Relations Board. (2017). Disposition of unfair labor practice charges in FY17. https://www.nlrb.gov/news-outreach/graphs-data/charges-and-complaints/disposition-unfair-labor-practice-charges

National Labor Relations Act Stipulates that employees protected under the act have a right to discuss pay as part of activities related to collective bargaining and protection, thereby providing an avenue through which employees may uncover pay discrimination

unions and corporations from making independent expenditures for federal candidates, outlawed closed shops that required employers to only hire union members, allowed states to pass right-to-work laws, required unions and employers to give 80 days' advance notice before striking, gave the president of the United States the power to stop strikes if they might create a national emergency, allowed employers to terminate supervisors for supporting union activity, and gave employers the right to oppose unions. Finally, the act gave federal court jurisdiction to enforce collective bargaining agreements. We will cover the details of such agreements later on in this chapter.

Labor–Management Reporting and Disclosure Act (LMRDA) (1959)

The **Labor–Management Reporting and Disclosure Act (LMRDA) (1959)**, also known as the Landrum-Griffin Act, deals with the relationship between a union and its members by prescribing how unions are internally regulated. The act protects union funds and was established to promote union democracy and fair elections. It requires labor organizations to file annual financial reports and reports on labor relations practices and established standards for the election of union officers as well as a Bill of Rights for union members. The act is administered by the Office of Labor–Management Standards.[31]

Right-to-Work Laws

A highly political topic involves who is covered and required to financially participate in unionized settings. A shift in terms of this has taken the form of state **right-to-work state laws**. Such laws, if enacted, mean that no one within that state may be compelled to join a union to obtain or keep their job. In states without this law, employees who benefit from union activities such as collective bargaining, even if they choose not to join it, may be compelled to pay their "fair share" of union dues. The National Labor Relations Act (also known as the Taft-Hartley Act), Section 13(b), grants the right of states to enact such laws. The first two states to enact this were Arkansas and Florida in 1944. As of 2017, 26 additional states had joined them. In 2018, the Supreme Court ruled that nonunion workers cannot be forced to pay fees to public-sector unions, which overruled a 40-year-old ruling that led to fair-share fees.

Trends in Union Membership

The Great Depression began in 1929 in the United States, and although unemployment was at record-high levels, union membership grew by 300%. Unions had fewer than 3 million members in 1933 and more than 10 million by 1941.[32] That trend has reversed itself in the past 35 years, and union membership has been on the decline in the United States, with 13.6 million workers belonging to a union in 2016, down from a high of 17.7 million workers in 1983.

Union Membership in the United States

Union membership has decreased by nearly half since the 1980s, with 20% of all workers belonging to a union in 1983 and only 10.5% belonging to unions in 2018, according to the Bureau of Labor Statistics (Figure 13.4). Some of this is due to the changing nature of work. Unions tend to be highly concentrated within certain industries such as transportation and utilities, construction, manufacturing, education and health services, wholesale and retail trade, and public-service employees.[33] However, even in many of those

---

Unfair labor practices Defined in the United States as actions taken by either unions or employers that violate the National Labor Relations Act or other legislation. Such acts are investigated by the National Labor Relations Board.

National Labor Relations Board (NLRB) An independent U.S. governmental agency, the NLRB is tasked with supervising union elections and is empowered to investigate suspected unfair labor practices

Labor Management Relations Act (1947) Also known as the Taft-Hartley Act; amended the National Labor Relations Act and restricts the activities and power of labor unions

Right-to-work state laws Vary from state to state but generally prohibit requiring employees to join a union or pay regular or fair-share union dues to obtain or keep a job

■ **FIGURE 13.4**   Union Membership, 1983–2018

This chart illustrates how union membership (as a percentage of employed workers in the United States) continued to decrease. We have seen a high of 20.1% in 1983 to 11.6% in 2018.

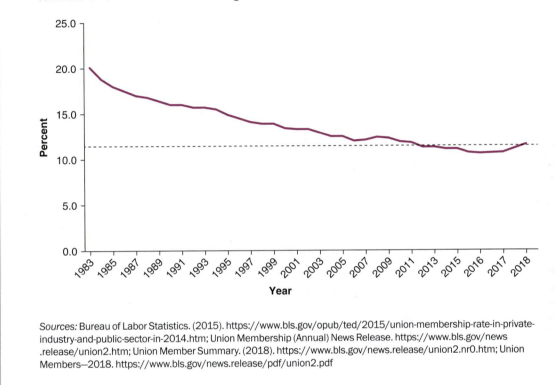

Sources: Bureau of Labor Statistics. (2015). https://www.bls.gov/opub/ted/2015/union-membership-rate-in-private-industry-and-public-sector-in-2014.htm; Union Membership (Annual) News Release. https://www.bls.gov/news.release/union2.htm; Union Member Summary. (2018). https://www.bls.gov/news.release/union2.nr0.htm; Union Members—2018. https://www.bls.gov/news.release/pdf/union2.pdf

industries, membership has been declining. It is interesting that unions are actually winning more workplace elections (i.e., elections that would allow them to form a union in their workplaces), with 72% of the elections conducted by the National Labor Relations Board in 2016. Additionally, 61% of adults generally support labor unions during this period of decline, but fewer elections are being held.[34]

Global Unionization

The global landscape stands in sharp contrast with the trend in the United States. For example, 92% of workers in Iceland belong to a union. In contrast, Figure 13.4 shows that the United States has a relatively low percentage of unionized workers. For multinational corporations, which must deal with different labor laws and norms in different countries, it is important to understand the concept of *works councils*. These comprise elected employee representatives who work alongside management to help make decisions regarding working conditions. Work councils are mandated by law for organizations operating in European Union (EU) countries if they exceed certain sizes.[35] In Norway, the Working Environment Act regulates key provisions for employment relationships: Employees work 37.5

hours per week; flexible hours are encouraged; employees get 5 weeks of holidays per year, with employees more than 60 years old getting an additional week of vacation; 43 weeks of paid parental leave are available for employees working for at least 6 months; and employers have obligations to provide systematic training on health and safety issues.[36] It can be challenging for companies to navigate the different union rules and cultures, as they vary from country to country. For example, Amazon faced strong opposition in Germany from warehouse workers who wanted to organize toward a union. Resistance to such activities might be common within the United States, but in Germany, "that's virtually unheard-of."[37]

Union Formation and Dissolution

Even though union membership is in decline in the United States, it is still important to understand how unions are formed and dissolved, as 14.7 million workers is still a sizable number of individuals, and the potential for unionizing exists in most industries even if it is not traditionally a union industry. For example, digital news media have seen a surge of unionization, with 220 Huffington Post staffers joining the Writers Guild of America and East becoming the largest digital news company to become unionized.[38] Further, social media technology such as Unionbase by Larry Williams Jr. is making it easier than ever for labor to connect with unions.[39]

Steps to Forming a Union

The first step to the formation of a union is to conduct an organizing campaign. Formation is dependent on the union organizers getting at least 30% of the employees in the bargaining unit to sign an authorization card to prompt a union election. To secure those signatures, organizers normally need to have identified key issues that might motivate employees to want a union. This is because employees who are satisfied and feel they are treated fairly are less likely to join a union.

If the union organizers are successful in gathering 30% to 50% of the required signatures, they can file an election petition and conduct a union election online or via paper ballots.[40] It is important for managers and their employers to understand what is possible and not possible to do during an organizing campaign (see Table 13.1).

Achieving more than 50% of signed authorization cards may lead to the union organizers requesting that the company voluntarily recognize the union. If the employer does, the National Labor Relations Board is asked to certify the union. If the employer does not recognize the union, things can become more complicated. If the union wins the election, officers are elected, and they or a designated team begin negotiations with the employer on their membership's behalf.

Decertifying Unions

The Labor Management Relations Act (Taft-Hartley Act), discussed earlier in this chapter, laid out employees' rights to elect union leaders of their own choosing. In much the same way in which unions are formed, they can also be disbanded or decertified. This may happen for a number of reasons, such as if employees do not think the union is doing a good job of representing them or if they prefer a different union. The process is parallel to union formation, with at least 30% of the workers in the bargaining unit needing to sign the petition to vote to decertify the union. However, the timing of union decertification is important. A decertification election may not take place when a contract is in place or

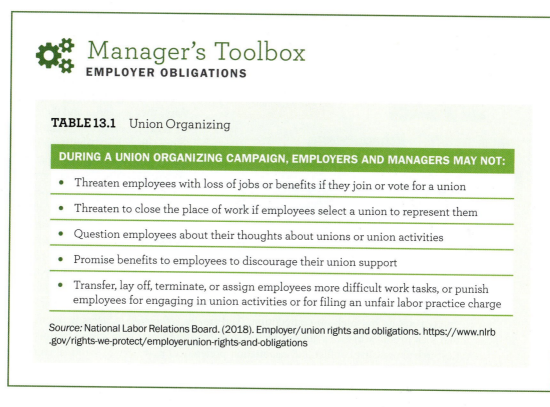

Manager's Toolbox
EMPLOYER OBLIGATIONS

TABLE 13.1 Union Organizing

DURING A UNION ORGANIZING CAMPAIGN, EMPLOYERS AND MANAGERS MAY NOT:
• Threaten employees with loss of jobs or benefits if they join or vote for a union
• Threaten to close the place of work if employees select a union to represent them
• Question employees about their thoughts about unions or union activities
• Promise benefits to employees to discourage their union support
• Transfer, lay off, terminate, or assign employees more difficult work tasks, or punish employees for engaging in union activities or for filing an unfair labor practice charge

Source: National Labor Relations Board. (2018). Employer/union rights and obligations. https://www.nlrb.gov/rights-we-protect/employerunion-rights-and-obligations

within 1 year following a union's certification by the National Labor Relations Board.[41] In the 4 years between 2012 and 2016, unions lost 596 of 970 decertification elections.[42]

The Collective Bargaining Process

LO 13.4 Briefly outline the collective bargaining process.

If a union is in place, it is responsible for negotiating with the employer on behalf of its members. This is one of the major functions of a union. The final agreement addresses details outlining wages, hours, and working conditions for employees. The process of negotiating in good faith toward agreed terms on wages, hours, and working conditions is called **collective bargaining**. In other words, the union and employer engage in negotiations on behalf of the employees/union members. Engaging in effective negotiations includes having a conflict management approach, which we discuss in the following section.

Conflict Management Approaches

Although negotiations are not necessarily conflicts, they can sometimes be perceived or become that way. This is especially true in high-stakes negotiations between unions and management. Thus, it is helpful to recognize and understand that individuals and groups

Collective bargaining The process of negotiating in good faith toward agreed terms on wages, hours, and working conditions

■ **FIGURE 13.5**   Different Approaches to Conflict Influence the Negotiation Process and Outcomes

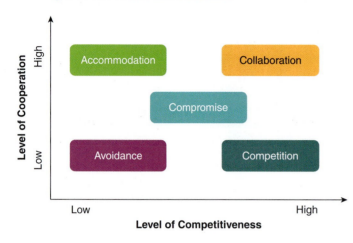

differ in their approach to conflict management. This includes the level of cooperation (focusing on both parties keeping conflict limited) as well as the level of competition (focusing on getting what they want) they engage in and their preferences for each approach. These approaches are summarized in Figure 13.5 and include avoidance, accommodation, compromise, competition, and collaboration. *Avoidance* refers to low cooperation and competitiveness. *Accommodation* refers to low competitiveness but high levels of cooperation. *Compromise* refers to an approach predominantly in the middle range of cooperative and competitive approaches. *Competition* refers to an approach that is low on cooperation but high on competition. And finally, *collaboration* refers to approaches that seek to find win-win solutions by being high on both cooperation and competition. Research shows that conflict and negotiation preferences may vary by national culture.[43] But generally, labor relations should be better when win-win collaboration strategies are sought because both parties will see their needs met at least partially. In a study of unionized manufacturing facilities, areas with more collaborative labor relations had lower costs, less scrap, higher productivity, and a higher return on direct labor hours than those characterized as more adversarial.[44] In another study of 305 branches of a large unionized bank in Australia, cooperative labor relations were related to better information sharing and pursuing win-win solutions as well as higher productivity and customer service.[45]

Failure to Reach an Agreement

LO 13.5   Evaluate the possible courses of action when negotiating parties fail to reach an agreement.

Unfortunately, research shows that negotiators who fail to reach an agreement may become less willing to work together in the future, share information, or behave cooperatively. So, having negotiators with experience and confidence in their negotiating abilities can be effective in helping to buffer these negative effects of impasse.[46] In addition, helping negotiators reach an agreement can be important for labor relations.

Alternative dispute resolution
Methods of resolving disputes that do not involve litigation

Alternative Dispute Resolution

When two parties fail to reach an agreement, alternative dispute resolution may be entered into either voluntarily or involuntarily. **Alternative dispute resolution** is defined as any method of resolving disputes that does not involve litigation. There are several different types of alternatives, including mediation, fact finders, and arbitration, which we discuss next.

Mediation

In mediation, the two parties are still in control of reaching a mutually acceptable agreement. The mediator is an impartial, third-party individual who helps the parties communicate more effectively and may be helpful when the ongoing relationship is important to preserve, such as in the case of collective bargaining. However, if one or both of the parties are unwilling to cooperate, mediation may not result in a resolution of the disputed contract terms.

Fact Finders

With fact finding, an impartial third party listens to the evidence and makes specific non-binding recommendations to both parties. Fact finders gather and assess the information presented to them and also collect new information via investigation and consultation with experts. Their goal is to evaluate the facts of the case objectively to propose resolutions.

Arbitration

An arbitrator is an impartial third party who hears the facts of the case and then decides the outcome of the disputed contract terms. Arbitration may be *binding,* meaning that both parties agree to abide by the arbitrator's decision and not seek other options to resolve the dispute. A *nonbinding* resolution means parties may pursue a trial if they do not accept the recommended outcome.

Strikes and Work Stoppages

The history of HR was powerfully affected when workers organized and began to demand better treatment. In fact, it was following a bitter strike in 1901 that the first human resource department was established by the National Cash Register Company. Thus, it is clear that the failure to reach an agreement can end in a strike or work stoppage (see Figure 13.6). A *strike* is defined as a type of work stoppage as the result of a concerted refusal of employees to work. The number of strikes in the United States has been decreasing since the 1940s. At the same time, in China, strikes are becoming increasingly common, with 2,726 strikes in 2015 compared to only 185 in 2011.[47] In 2016 in the United States, a total of 15 work stoppages involved nearly 100,000 employees.[48] Another type of work stoppage is a *lockout,* defined by the Bureau of Labor Statistics as "a temporary withholding or denial of employment during a labor dispute in order to enforce terms of employment upon a group of employees."[49] Lockouts are initiated by the management of an organization.

Disputes and Grievances

As you might imagine, even with an accepted labor agreement or following a successfully completed strike, labor relations may remain strained, which may result in employees feeling unfairly treated. For this reason, unions are responsible for ensuring that the terms of the contract are followed. If a member feels that the agreement is being violated, they may file a grievance, or a formal complaint. For example, if a unionized construction employee feels they have been required to perform practices that are unsafe and not in their job description,

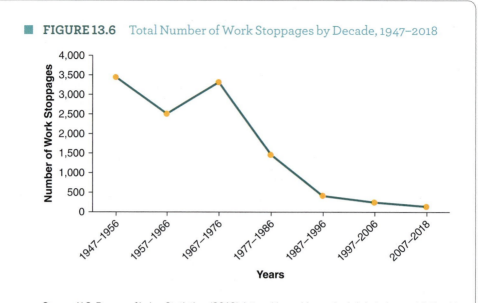

■ **FIGURE 13.6**   Total Number of Work Stoppages by Decade, 1947–2018

Source: U.S. Bureau of Labor Statistics. (2019). https://www.bls.gov/web/wkstp/annual-listing.htm

they may file a grievance against the company. How grievances are handled is normally specified in the labor agreement. Typically, the *grievance procedure* consists of four steps.[50]

Step 1: Inform
The first step in a grievance procedure is normally to inform one's supervisor formally or informally. Often a grievance form must be completed.

Step 2: Evaluate
After the first step, three things may happen. First, it may be determined by the supervisor and the union representative that the grievance is not valid. If this occurs, the process ends. Second, the grievance may be resolved to the satisfaction of the employee. If so, the process stops at this step. Finally, if the grievance is not resolved to the employee's satisfaction, it moves to the next step.

Step 3: Escalation
In Step 3, the grievance is escalated to the next level in the organizational hierarchy. If the grievance is resolved at this level, the grievance process stops here. If this grievance is not resolved, the next step typically involves moving outside of the organization.

Step 4: External Resolution
In Step 4, an outside arbitrator may be called on to help reach a resolution. And ultimately, if the grievance remains an ongoing concern, either the employee or the union may end up pursuing litigation. One reason that organizations have grievance procedures in place is to avoid such public resolutions of disputes within their organization.

Spotlight on Data and Analytics

TRACKING GRIEVANCE-RELATED METRICS

Organizations without unions often have grievance procedures in place to give employees a process to share concerns. Although not necessarily a common HR practice, it is recommended that organizations track metrics related to employee grievances. This becomes more and more important the larger the organization becomes because it is more challenging to know what employees are thinking as the number of employees grows. As data are gathered, summarized, and monitored, individuals within the organization can use these data to gain a better understanding of what is working in terms of employee relations and where there is room for improvement before small problems become large ones. Understanding the causes for grievances may require a combination of analytics in terms of numbers such as the following as well as qualitatively examining themes that emerge.

To get started, recommended metrics include

- The number of grievances per month, quarter, and year by number of employees

- A calculation of the cost of grievances, including the time spent by managers, HR, lawyers, and other organizational members to handle the complaints

- A determination of the root cause of grievances so that corrections may be made

- Average time to close or complete the grievance and make a decision

- Return on investment, which can be calculated as revenue or profit per employee before and after changes to employee grievance procedures

As Missildine-Martin, formerly of Dovetail Software, says, "Data leads to insights; insights lead to action."[51]

CHAPTER SUMMARY

Employee relations can be influenced by many different factors such as culture, fair treatment, working conditions, employment laws, and unions. Employee relations are managed through organizational policies and procedures. The types of policies an employer has will set the tone for the employee experience in that organization. Businesses use employee handbooks to ensure that workers know what is expected of them, including code of conduct, rules or guidelines for appearance, and the use of social media. The labor movement can be a major issue in the workplace. Reasons employees may seek to organize or unionize include job dissatisfaction, working conditions, and employee disengagement. Conversely, employers may resist unions based on concerns about profit and loss of autonomy for the business. HR professionals need to know about types of unions, laws pertaining to labor relations, and procedures to form and dissolve a union. The collective bargaining process includes conflict management approaches, negotiation phases, and what alternatives are available if an agreement cannot be reached. Proactively managing employee relations in a way that helps keep employees satisfied is a key component to promoting and ensuring more positive employee–employer relations.

KEY TERMS

employee relations   304

labor relations   304

National Labor Relations Act (1935)   313

unfair labor practices   313

National Labor Relations Board (NLRB)   313

Labor Management Relations Act (1947)   313

Labor–Management Reporting and Disclosure Act (LMRDA) (1959)   314

right-to-work laws   314

collective bargaining   317

alternative dispute resolution   318

$SAGE edge™

Get the tools you need to sharpen your study skills. SAGE edge offers a robust online environment featuring an impressive array of free tools and resources.

Access practice quizzes, eFlashcards, video, and multimedia at **edge.sagepub.com/bauerbrief**

HR REASONING AND DECISION-MAKING EXERCISES

EXERCISE 13.1: GROWING PAINS

You are a manager at a small firm with 85 employees. Not long ago, your firm had just 15 employees, and it felt like a big family more than a workplace. But as you've grown, the "family feeling" has dissipated. You just heard from your good friend Robert that employees are starting to complain about management not listening to them or caring about them. He has even heard some talk about interest in considering a union to make sure that they are heard.

Given the highly competitive market your firm competes in and how slim the profit margins are, you are worried that the potential move to a union would be devastating and result in people actually losing their jobs if the firm couldn't afford to give everyone raises and instead had to lay people off. When you talk to your boss, Kelvin, he says that you are 100% right. There is no way that the firm would survive becoming a union shop, and you must do everything you can to stop the employees from unionizing. You keep thinking back to your HRM course from 7 years ago and have a lingering concern that this may not be legal, but you aren't sure. You want to do what is best for the firm and the employees, but you aren't sure what that is.

Questions

1. What kind of actions are you legally able to take in this situation?
2. What would you tell your boss, Kelvin, if anything?
3. How common or unique do you think this situation is? In other words, how likely is it that dealing with this type of situation might happen to someone taking an HRM course at some point in their career? Please discuss your rationale.
4. Are there any systemic changes you could think of that might help prevent more concerns like these from happening in the future?

EXERCISE 13.2: A TALE OF TWO TRAINING PROGRAMS

You are in the business of developing training and development materials and programs for work organizations. Your company is currently in the process of developing new training products. As someone who oversees a large 30-person team that develops, sells, and administers different workplace training programs, you have always made money each year, and how much profit you have to reinvest in developing new programs is directly tied to the number of trainings held each year. Your team recently came up with a new training program that is in big demand. Each session is selling out quickly, and you need to add more and more training days to meet demand. On the other hand, one of your other training products that helped build the company and has been taught for the past 20 years is seeing decreasing demand. The two programs are very different. There are five individuals who are solely dedicated to the older program but only three to the new one. Unfortunately, the five employees working on the more established but less attractive training program can't teach the new ones, as they do not have the right expertise. Your company is small, and the trends are clear that demand is growing for the new program and dwindling for the older one. If the trend continues, pretty soon the company will be paying five employees to conduct fewer than one training per week, whereas the other three are giving three and four trainings per week. If you cancel the older program, you will have to let these five employees go. You don't see any way around these issues, but you want to let the group make recommendations.

Questions

1. Given the current trends you have observed, what do you think your training team should recommend to address this growing problem?
2. What do you think they will recommend?
3. How might you guide them?

ETHICAL MATTERS EXERCISE: THE 2007–2008 WRITERS GUILD OF AMERICA STRIKE

Charley Gallay/Getty Images

The Guild has engaged in three major strikes, including one in 1959 that lasted nearly 6 months and one in 1988 that lasted 155 days. On May 1, 2017, members voted to strike, but an agreement was reached in the early-morning hours of May 2, 2017, narrowly averting a repeat of this 8- to 10-year cycle. Balancing the ethical implications of studio owners paying writers fairly versus the fiscal implications of strikes continues to be a challenging dilemma.[52]

In November 2007, 12,000 screenwriters for film, TV, and radio represented by the Writers Guild of America went on strike over what they perceived as an unfair portion of profits made by studios on the shows compared to writers of those shows. The fundamental issues revolved around DVD residuals (a type of pay), new media such as Internet download and streaming videos (another issue of pay), and whether reality and animation shows should be covered by the Writers Guild. These writers worked for 397 entertainment companies, including CBS, NBCUniversal, News Corp./Fox, Walt Disney Company, and Warner Bros., among others. They were joined by members of the Screen Actors Guild, including actor Katherine Heigl, pictured here, of the TV show *Grey's Anatomy* at the time. The strike went on for 100 days. It is estimated that the strike cost $2.1 to $3 billion and shut down more than 60 TV shows. The final agreement was ratified, with nearly 94% of members voting in favor.

Questions

1. Examine this question from the workers' point of view and from the employer's point of view. What do you see as the ethical aspects of going on strike?
2. Some categories of workers in the United States are legally prohibited from striking. Are there potential ethical challenges related to such laws (both for or against)?

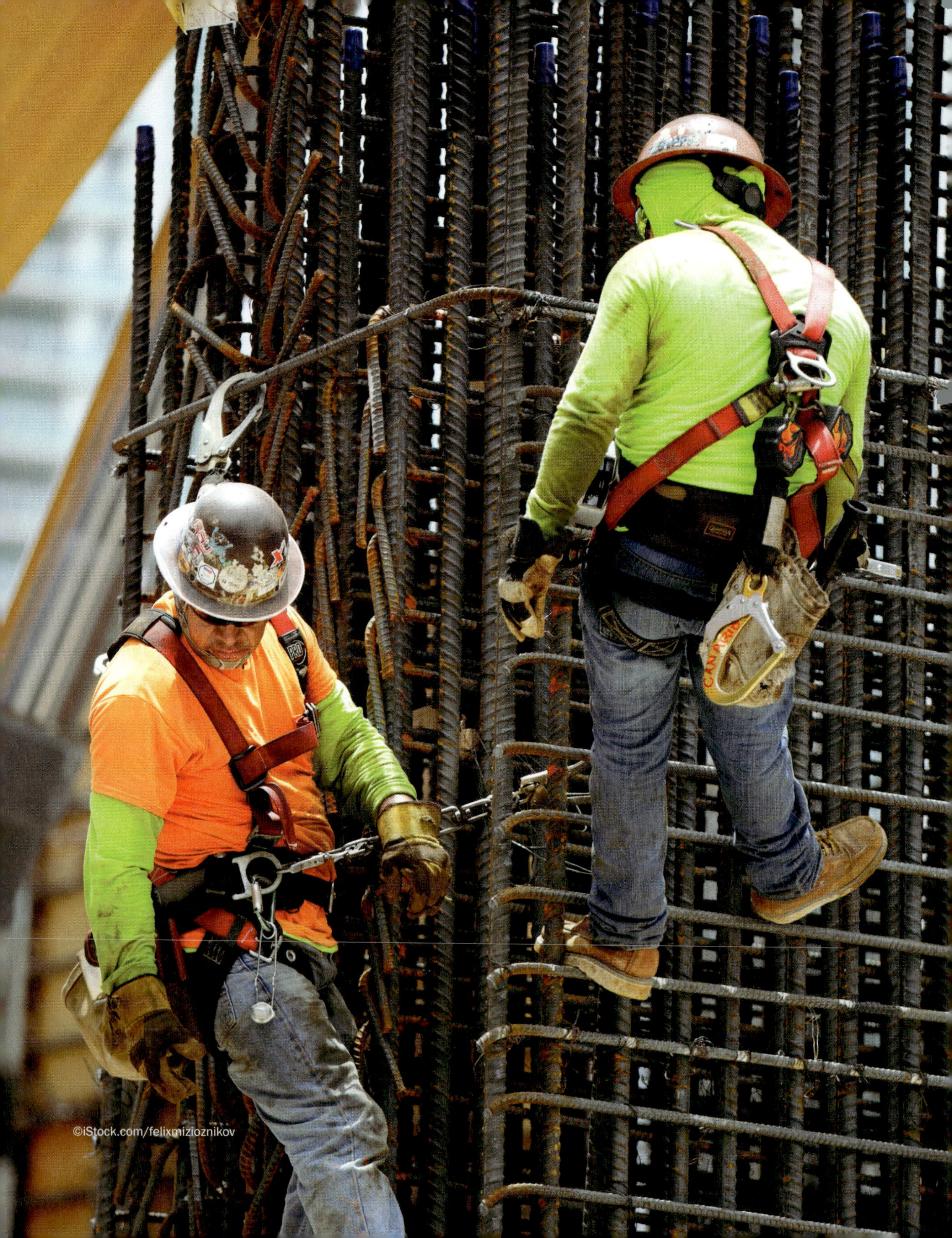

©iStock.com/felixmizioznikov

14

Employee Safety, Well-Being, and Wellness

LEARNING OBJECTIVES

After reading and studying this chapter, you should be able to do the following:

14.1 Give reasons why workplace well-being is important for employers and regulatory agencies.

14.2 Describe the main workplace safety outcomes measured by organizations and what organizations can do to promote safety.

14.3 Summarize issues around workplace stress and well-being.

14.4 Identify the characteristics of the variety of workplace wellness programs that are offered by employers.

14.5 Explain what is meant by an integrated Total Worker Health™ approach.

HR in Action: The Case of an Employee Wellness Program at Johnson & Johnson

Employee wellness programs have grown in popularity in recent years. One challenge is to determine which programs are most effective and most beneficial to specific employees.

Johnson & Johnson takes an evidence-based view of wellness and health, using the following approach:

1. Assess factors that might influence a person's health behavior (e.g., smoking, exercise). This happens through an annual employee survey.

2. Apply evidence-based science on behavior change to improve that health behavior.

3. Measure the impact of programs.

4. Use data analytics to measure program effectiveness and to gain insights about potential improvements to the process.

Another key component is that Johnson & Johnson promotes a culture of health for all workers, from the manufacturing floor to the boardroom. The program is multifaceted, including a range of factors such as making healthy foods available on site, encouraging

©iStock.com/jfmdesign

Johnson & Johnson, the U.S.-based multinational focused on pharmaceuticals and medical devices, is a recognized leader in the area of employee wellness.

workers to get up from their desks, and making exercise available to workers.

Does Johnson & Johnson's wellness program work? As reported by the company, the general answer is yes. Smoking has decreased among Johnson & Johnson's employees. Heart disease and hypertension among its employees are lower than national U.S. standards. Health care costs have gone down per employee per year. But Johnson & Johnson does not focus just on medical cost savings. Rather, the company sees wellness as a factor supporting employee and company performance more broadly. In short, Johnson & Johnson reports that its wellness program has resulted in a good return on investment, is linked to company market performance, and has improved employee health outcomes.[1]

Case Discussion Questions

1. What responsibility does an employer have for their employees' health and well-being? Explain the reasons for your answer.

2. Choose one type of job or profession. What do you think are the main sources of work stress for these employees? How would you address these sources of employee stress?

3. What do you think is the relationship among employee safety, stress, and health? Give examples of how these might be related.

The Role of HRM in Worker Safety and Health

LO 14.1   Give reasons why workplace well-being is important for employers and regulatory agencies.

Well-being
A worker's well-being is composed of their safety, health, satisfaction, and engagement

HRM plays a key role in attracting, hiring, developing, and rewarding employees to serve the strategic goals of the organization. Given this investment in talent, organizations also have an interest in the safety, health, and well-being of their employees. This includes developing a culture of safety; providing a healthy, safe, and secure work environment; and actively supporting the health of employees through wellness programs. All of these can help retain the best talent, reduce health care costs, improve performance, and reduce legal liability. They also make for a better work environment for employees. We begin the chapter by reviewing the importance of well-being in organizations.

The Case for Employee Well-Being

Many organizations feel an ethical obligation to keep their workers safe, healthy, and happy. And these concepts are not separate; they are intertwined. Consider railway accidents. (See Appendix A for greater detail.) The causes of some railways accidents have been attributed to a worker health issue: obesity, which can lead to sleep apnea, which causes train engineers to fall asleep during the day, which results in accidents. In addition, train accidents may be the result of a physical work environment that does not include safeguards (e.g., speed monitoring systems) to prevent accidents and perhaps a weak safety climate.[2] In other words, health and safety in the workplace are interrelated systems, and that is how we will approach these questions in this chapter. Taken together, the concepts of the safety, health, satisfaction, and engagement of employees are often referred to as worker **well-being**.[3]

Organizations also have a stake in worker well-being because it affects organizational effectiveness. For example, workplace safety is an important goal in itself, and violating safety regulations can lead to fines and to legal liability. An unhealthy workforce can lead to high medical costs. And employee stress can lead to turnover and to distractions that cause accidents and injuries. But maintaining workplace safety and health is an ongoing challenge. For example, there was an uptick in deaths due to on-the-job injuries in 2016, with more than 5,100 worker deaths (see Figure 14.1). This is an increase of 7% from 2015 and the highest number of worker fatalities since 2008.

On the positive side, a healthy and safe workplace can be an excellent recruitment tool. Decreasing employee stress can lead to improved performance. Providing a safe, healthy environment can increase employee retention. And many organizational leaders see worker well-being as a goal in itself. It is not surprising, then, that many successful organizations treat workplace safety and health as an important goal and collect measures to assess employees' safety, stress, and health.

The Legal Backdrop for Well-Being

In the United States, a number of government agencies regulate the area of workplace well-being. The **Occupational Safety and Health Administration (OSHA)** was established through the Occupational Safety and Health Act of 1970. Under the U.S. Department of Labor, OSHA's purpose is to ensure safe and healthy working conditions for employees by setting and enforcing safety and health standards. It also provides training and outreach, education, and assistance to both employers and employees. For example, OSHA provides a number of materials to help employers monitor safety conditions in their organizations. In addition to OSHA, 26 states, Puerto Rico, and the Virgin Islands have their own equivalent to OSHA, which provides additional workplace safety oversight.[4] Further, the National Institute for Occupational Safety and Health (NIOSH) is the federal agency that supports research on workplace safety and

Occupational Safety and Health Administration (OSHA) Under the U.S. Department of Labor, OSHA's purpose is to ensure safe and healthy working conditions for employees by setting and enforcing safety and health standards

■ **FIGURE 14.1** Number of Workplace Fatalities by Event Type, 2015–2016

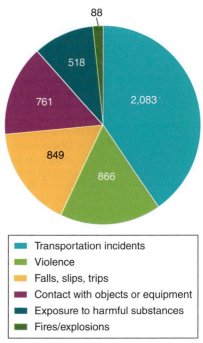

- Transportation incidents
- Violence
- Falls, slips, trips
- Contact with objects or equipment
- Exposure to harmful substances
- Fires/explosions

Sources: Bureau of Labor Statistics. (2017, December 19). https://www.bls.gov/news. release/pdf/cfoi.pdf; "Tragic trend": On-the-job deaths at highest level since 2008, BLS reports. (2017). http://www.safetyandhealthmagazine. com/articles/16544-tragic-trend-on-the-job-deaths-at-highest-level-since-2008-bls-reports

health and makes recommendations to employers. As part of its mission, NIOSH also can provide recommendations to employers regarding interventions and other initiatives that can help improve worker well-being.[5] We discuss the implications of specific OSHA regulations for employers throughout this chapter.

Workplace Safety

LO 14.2   Describe the main workplace safety outcomes measured by organizations and what organizations can do to promote safety.

Workplace illness, injury, and mortality are important because of their effects on workers and families. In addition, medical costs associated with work-related injury and disease are estimated at $67 billion, with indirect costs of $183 billion based on one estimate.[6] Not surprisingly, reducing work-related accidents and injuries is a major focus of most organizations. HR takes a central role in implementing such safety-related programs. For example, semiconductor manufacturer Texas Instruments has a strong safety program it is proud of, with a lost-time injury rate that is a fraction of the industry average. Part of its approach includes the collection and analysis of data that can help managers understand the causes of injuries in order to prevent them.[7] This section is concerned with the antecedents of workplace accidents and injuries and the regulatory environment for worker safety in the United States.

Workplace Safety Outcomes and Their Antecedents

Many types of safety and health outcomes are important to organizations and government agencies. These can be tracked, measured, and analyzed by organizations. These include workplace accidents, such as spilling a hazardous chemical. More dramatic would be workplace injuries, with the most extreme and rare being workplace fatalities; these might include workers being injured or killed by a chemical exposure.

In addition to these major safety outcomes, it is important for organizations to keep an eye on the much more frequent issues that lead to actual accidents and injuries. One of these is **near misses**. This is when an accident could have occurred but did not. As an example of a near miss, an electrician working on wiring an office in a new building forgot to turn off the electrical current before proceeding to install a section of the heating system, but a coworker noticed the problem and turned off the power just in time. In this example, there was no accident or injury because the coworker acted in time. In fact, the workers and the employer might think that there was nothing to report or to discuss. But if the coworker had not intervened, the electrician could have been seriously injured or killed. Analyzing near misses is important to understanding potential causes of accidents. Near misses are typically measured by worker self-reports or uncovered in team discussions. They can provide an essential part of understanding why accidents and injuries occur and how to prevent them.[8]

One challenge for organizations trying to prevent serious and fatal injuries is knowing which data to collect to understand their causes. It is estimated that only a relatively small percentage of the standard "recordable events" required by OSHA reporting leads to fatalities. One way to uncover these important data is to speak with workers out in the field to better understand specific situations where no one was injured but could

Near misses
Situations in which an accident almost occurred but did not

have been. For example, if an employee working on a tall building were to slip on a wet surface, it might not lead to an injury if they righted themselves in time. But understanding what led to that slip—that may otherwise have led to a fatal accident—is key to injury prevention.[9]

Another factor that is important to understanding the causes of safety outcomes is employees' safety behavior.[10] Safety behavior is work behavior that employees exhibit with regard to safety. The research has generally identified two different types of safety behavior.

Safety compliance behavior is the extent to which workers follow the safety rules and regulations, such as wearing personal protective equipment (PPE) to protect them from the workplace hazards. In the electrician's example, safety compliance behavior might include always following the rules about checking that a power source is turned off before performing electrical installations.

Safety participation behavior refers to employees' willingness to support safety among their coworkers. This might include explaining the safety rules to new workers or mentioning a safety problem that they have seen (e.g., broken safety equipment) to a supervisor so it can be taken care of. In the electrician example, the fact that a second employee noticed that her teammate had not turned off the power source and did it herself before any injury could happen is an example of safety participation behavior.

One challenge with measuring and preventing the most costly and catastrophic safety problems is the low-base-rate problem. That is, serious accidents and injuries are relatively rare—although they can have an enormous human and economic toll. One way to consider this problem is through a diagram referred to as Heinrich's triangle, shown in Figure 14.2. This shows that thousands of unsafe behaviors and near misses usually occur before a serious accident or injury. The triangle also shows the value of examining the behaviors that lead up to accidents and injury before they occur.

A key goal of HRM is to uncover the factors that may lead to serious accidents such as poor safety behaviors and near misses. This helps to identify and prevent safety problems. In fact, larger employers might use data analytics to identify high-risk areas of the organization, such as those with large numbers of safety violations, near misses, or unsafe behaviors that can lead to injuries, health risks, and legal liability. Sensors and wearable technology can also be used to monitor hazardous conditions (e.g., combustible dust and gases, hazardous sound levels) and the safe use of equipment (e.g., ladders, motorized equipment) in real time.[12]

Safety compliance behavior The extent to which workers follow the safety rules and regulations

Safety participation behavior Employees' willingness to support safety among their coworkers

Keystone/Getty Images

On March 25, 1911, in New York City, 145 garment workers died in the Triangle Shirtwaist factory fire. The factory was located on Floors 8–10 of the building. Because the exit doors had been locked, the workers were trapped and died of smoke inhalation, the fire itself, or jumping or falling to their deaths. One of the deadliest industrial disasters in U.S. history, the fire served as an impetus for the development of early workplace safety regulations.[11]

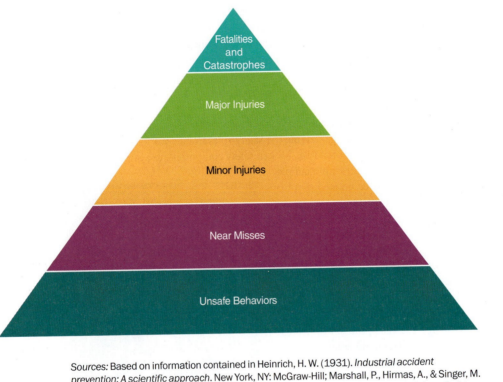

■ **FIGURE 14.2**   Heinrich's Triangle

A summary of Heinrich's triangle, which suggests that fatalities and catastrophes, although relatively rare, are a function of much more frequent problems like unsafe behaviors.

Sources: Based on information contained in Heinrich, H. W. (1931). *Industrial accident prevention: A scientific approach.* New York, NY: McGraw-Hill; Marshall, P., Hirmas, A., & Singer, M. (2018). Heinrich's pyramid and occupational safety: A statistical validation methodology. *Safety Science, 101,* 180–189; Martin, D. K., & Black, A. A. (2015, September). Preventing serious injuries and fatalities. *Professional Safety,* pp. 35–43.

Safety knowledge
Workers' understanding of how to protect themselves and others on the job

Safety motivation
Workers' perceived value for safety and desire to perform safely on the job

Many factors can lead to accidents and injuries (see Figure 14.3). First, **safety knowledge**, or workers' understanding of how to protect themselves and others on the job, is a key antecedent of accidents and injuries. Organizations can train workers to increase safety knowledge, such as how to handle dangerous equipment. This is why OSHA requires employers to conduct safety training and even requires specific types of training for certain jobs and industries.

Second, **safety motivation**, or the worker's value for safety and desire to perform safely on the job, is important for safe behaviors. The organization needs to be sure to reward safe behaviors (such as following safe procedures) and not reward unsafe behaviors (such as ignoring safe procedures due to pressure to work too quickly).

Third, **safety climate**, or the shared understanding that workers have about the importance of safety, is a key part of the workplace environment. Research has consistently shown that a strong safety climate, within the team and in the organization overall, is one of the most important predictors of safe behavior at work.[14] Management plays a big role in promoting and supporting the safety climate by showing that they take safety seriously, such as by

©iStock.com/DragonImages

- Modeling and rewarding safe behaviors

- Encouraging workers to speak up and identify any safety concerns that they observe. For instance, one study of a heavy manufacturing company showed that improved supervisor–employee communications improved safety climate as well as safety behavior and safety audit scores.[15]

Hotel workers face the workplace hazard of sexual harassment and assault from hotel guests. This issue came to light most dramatically in the high-profile case of Dominique Strauss-Kahn, the head of the International Monetary Fund, who was accused of sexual assault by a hotel housekeeper in 2012 in New York City. As a result of this issue, some cities are now requiring that hotels provide "panic buttons" and similar devices for their workers to alert security when they are concerned for their safety.[13]

- Training managers and workers on the importance of safety

Safety climate
The shared understanding that workers have about the importance of safety

Another employee well-being concern is workplace aggression, including verbal abuse, harassment, intimidation, and physical assaults.[16] Workplace aggression seriously hinders

■ **FIGURE 14.3**   Safety Climate and Individual Characteristics

Both the safety climate and characteristics of the individual worker play critical roles in safety performance and workplace accidents.

Source: Christian, M. S., Bradley, J. C., Wallace, J. C., & Burke, M. J. (2009). Workplace safety: A meta-analysis of the roles of person and situation factors. *Journal of Applied Psychology, 94,* 1103–1127.

workplace functioning. Aggression from supervisors, coworkers, and outsiders can affect job attitudes (e.g., job satisfaction), behavior (e.g., work performance), and health (e.g., depression).[17] Workers in certain types of jobs face a higher risk of aggression than others. For example, health care workers face nearly as many violent attacks as workers in all other industries combined—even though health care workers make up only 9% of the workforce. OSHA recognizes the violence faced by health care workers. It recommends that employers work with employees to identify hazards, examine incidents to learn why a specific violent attack occurred, and train supervisors and managers to spot dangerous situations in advance.[18]

Other Antecedents of Workplace Safety

Although workers and supervisors play a role in maintaining safety, there are other factors as well.

- The physical environment plays a role in worker safety. For example, one factor that can help reduce train accidents is a device to warn the engineers about possible hazards.[19]

- Another factor is worker health. For example, as noted earlier, obesity and sleep apnea have been linked to fatal train accidents.[20] Similar concerns about the role of sleep apnea have been noted among long-haul truck drivers.[21]

- Work **stressors,** such as work–life balance issues, can lead to distractions and to errors and accidents as well.[22]

To address these issues, many organizations appoint a **safety officer** to examine these and other workplace safety and health issues. Or there may be a **safety committee** that provides employees with a voice and an opportunity to participate in safety-related decisions in the organization. In any case, HR plays a central role in analyzing the causes of possible safety and health issues and developing an effective safety program to address them. This process can be enhanced by the measurement of safety-related variables and, where possible, the use of analytics to better understand how to prevent accidents and protect employee health.[23] What is key is to view safety as a systemic issue with multiple antecedents, such as worker motivation, safety climate, the physical environment, worker health, and stress.

OSHA Safety Regulations and Compliance

Compliance with OSHA safety regulations is a serious matter for employers. Employers with more than 10 employees must maintain safety records about OSHA "recordable events" such as work-related fatalities, injuries, and illnesses (including days away from work). Note that OSHA provides significant support to employers in terms of answering questions about workplace safety and health and how to comply with OSHA regulations for organizations of all sizes. (See Table 14.1 about complying with OSHA regulations.) In addition, OSHA provides guidelines and advice for organizations on how to develop emergency preparedness and response plans, such as to natural disasters, chemical spills, or even security threats (e.g., dangerous intruders and active shooters).[24] Further, employers must

Stressors
Demands in the environment to which a person must respond

Safety officer
An individual who is assigned to support safety and health issues in the workplace such as the promotion of safe practices and compliance with safety policies and rules

Safety committee
Provides employees with a voice and an opportunity to participate in safety-related decisions in the organization

TABLE 14.1 What Are the OSHA Requirements for Your Organization?

It's important to determine which safety regulations and requirements apply to your particular organization. For example, some industries are considered at least partially exempt (e.g., finance, real estate, retail). Other industries have specific OSHA regulations and guidelines. Here are some suggestions for determining what the safety requirements are for a particular organization.

1. **Determine the industry code for the organization.** OSHA organizes its data by specific industries to better analyze and report its statistics. Knowing this code also tells the organization which industry standards it must comply with.

2. **Comply with the General Duty Clause,** which requires that employers provide a safe and healthy workplace.

3. **Adhere to poster requirements from the U.S. government as well as local state government (if there is one).** For example, employers need to provide a poster explaining workers' rights in terms of workplace safety. (One of the most important of these posters published by OSHA is available at https://www.osha.gov/Publications/osha3165.pdf.)

4. **Determine the requirements for recording and reporting workers' injuries.** Note that organizations with 10 or more employees must maintain certain OSHA forms.

5. **Take care of electronic reporting requirements.** Note that organizations with 250 employees or more, or in certain high-risk industries, must also turn in electronic reports.

6. **Determine and follow OSHA training requirements.** These may vary by the particular industry.

Source: Based on Society for Human Resource Management. (2017, December 1). How to determine regulatory requirements for safety. https://www.shrm.org/resourcesandtools/tools-and-samples/how-to-guides/pages/determiningregulatoryrequirements.aspx

provide training to employees so that they can do their work safely. Note that OSHA may conduct workplace inspections, typically without advance notice to employers and when there is a specific reason. Figure 14.4 describes some of the safety and health issues that are covered by OSHA regulations.[25]

OSHA also spells out the rights of workers, providing them with guidance and assistance if they are facing a workplace hazard. For example, OSHA will take complaints from workers who believe that they are facing an unsafe or unhealthy workplace and will conduct an inspection if a worker believes there is a serious hazard or OSHA violation. OSHA also provides protection for workers in situations when an employer has retaliated against a worker. OSHA also can provide a worker with an inspection history of their employer if a worker is concerned that the employer has a history of violations.[26]

Ergonomics and Office Design

An important workplace well-being issue is fitting the person to the physical aspects of the job, often referred to as **ergonomic design**. The goal of ergonomic design is to reduce musculoskeletal disorders such as muscle strain, back injury, or carpal tunnel

Ergonomic design Fitting the physical aspects of the job to the human body

■ **FIGURE 14.4**   Workplace Issues Covered by OSHA

Drinking water, restroom use, and sanitation	Hazardous chemicals	Indoor air quality, temperature, and weather-related issues	Personal protective equipment (PPE)
Industry-specific rules and regulations	Wages, hours worked, and workers' compensation	Working alone	Workplace violence
Training	Employer responsibilities and assistance	Employee rights	Monitoring and reporting of accidents and injuries

Source: OSHA frequently asked questions. (n.d.). https://www.osha.gov/OSHA_FAQs.html#!employerassist

Spotlight on Legal Issues

SAFETY, HEALTH, AND OSHA COMPLIANCE

OSHA provides a number of resources for organizations of all sizes and across industries. The goal is to provide a healthy and safe working conditions to employees. OSHA requirements ensure the following:

- Workers should feel free to report unsafe or hazardous working conditions to their employers without fear of retaliation. Retaliation on the part of employers is, in fact, illegal. For instance, OSHA recently fined an employer $105,000 for terminating an employee who had reported a workplace mold issue.

- Workers should receive training about job hazards, including training about hazardous substances on their jobs.

- Workers can confidentially report any employer violations to OSHA and have legal "whistleblower" protections from employer retribution.

- Employers must post the OSHA poster "Job Safety and Health: It's the Law" in a prominent place. (See https://www.osha .gov/Publications/osha3165.pdf.)

What are the most typical types of OSHA violations? In 2017, some of the most common violations had to do with

- Failure to protect workers from falls

- Unsafe scaffolding

- Unsafe ladders

- Inadequate lockout-tagout procedures (e.g., being sure that equipment that is being serviced cannot accidentally be turned back on again)

- Inadequate respiratory protection[27]

syndrome.[28] For example, L. L. Bean, Maine's iconic outdoor equipment company, recently initiated a redesign of its warehouse. This included the use of machines rather than people for heavy lifting.[29]

Office design may also affect health. One issue is the effects of office natural lighting on worker health. One recent study found that people working in windowless offices had poorer sleep (i.e., shorter sleep duration, poorer sleep quality) and less physical activity than workers exposed to natural light.[31] Another recent trend in office design is the idea of **open offices**, where employees work in open spaces, without cubicles, with the idea that such work arrangements would lead to greater creativity and sharing of ideas. So far, however, the research on open offices suggests that they may lead to decreased satisfaction and greater stress due to less privacy and more chaotic work environments.[32]

Sit-stand desks provide the user to alternate between sitting and standing while doing desk work, which allows for increased blood circulation. As an ergonomic solution, the use of sit-stand desks may reduce back pain and also the chances of obesity and cardiovascular disease.[30]

©iStock.com/zoranm

Cybersecurity and Safety

Within the topic of workplace safety, it is important to also examine the issue of cybersecurity. Cybersecurity is an evolving issue that involves HRM for several reasons. Much of the private information used in organizations is stored, analyzed, and reported by HR personnel, including everything from Social Security numbers to health issues and even some day-to-day work activities. HR professionals are responsible for maintaining the security of other employees' data as well as that of clients. And employees can do considerable damage in the area of cybersecurity, either by mistake or on purpose. For example, in a recent U.K. court case, an unhappy employee of Morrisons Supermarket published the personal information of about 100,000 employees on the Internet. Morrisons was successfully sued by the employees who were affected, even though it had done all it could to protect against breaches.[33] Also, human error is considered one of the greatest organizational vulnerabilities. For example, an employee might fall for a phishing scam and threaten the security of the entire system. Employee training is seen as one of the most useful solutions to this vulnerability.

Another emerging issue is employee monitoring by employers to ensure that employees are not mishandling personal or sensitive data. New software solutions continue to develop to facilitate monitoring. However, organizations should consider such monitoring carefully before undertaking it. Employee monitoring can erode employee trust. Also, there are laws around employee monitoring. In addition, employee monitoring laws vary by state, and employees may need to give legal consent to be monitored.[34] Finally, it is important to realize that employee privacy issues differ around the world, with European rules being much more focused on protecting the workers' rights.

Open offices An office arrangement in which employees work in open spaces

Workplace Stress

LO 14.3   Summarize issues around workplace stress and well-being.

Consider the following issues regarding workplace stress:

- A recent survey by the American Psychological Association found that 37% of working Americans experience work stress, whereas another poll by CareerCast found that almost three in four workers were experiencing stress.[35] A Gallup poll found that stress was workers' number one complaint about their jobs.[36]

- In addition to the human cost of work stress, there are other reasons stress is important. For example, it may also lead workers to be distracted and thus lead to workplace accidents.[37]

- Stress can affect the health of an organization's workforce, even to the point of being deadly. One study examined the deaths of more than 2,363 workers in their 60s in high-demand (stressful) jobs. But the researchers found that if workers had high control at work, they had a 34% lower death risk. Low control combined with high demands was associated with a higher body mass index (BMI). The researchers noted that one solution is for organizations to give employees greater input and control in their work.[38]

- Stress can have negative effects on productivity and retention. Top stressors may include relationships with the boss or coworkers, work overload, and poor work–life balance.[39]

In short, worker stress can have serious implications for organizational competitiveness. At the same time, HRM can play a significant strategic role in reducing stress at work.

In discussing stress issues, it is important to differentiate the terms *stressors* and *strain*.

- Stressors are demands in the environment to which a person must respond, like dangerous work conditions, a difficult boss, ambiguity in a person's work role, or a heavy workload. Table 14.2 shows some common work stressors as identified by employees.

- **Strain** is a person's reaction to stressors, such as heart disease, burnout, or depression, or behavioral outcomes such as low performance and turnover. Other reactions to stress include expressions of anger, aggression, and violence by employees, as well as excessive alcohol consumption.[40] These strains in turn can lead to lower productivity and increased health care costs.

Strain
A person's reaction to stressors, such as heart disease, burnout, or depression, or behavioral outcomes such as low performance and turnover

In Chapter 5, we introduced the Job Demands-Resources (JDR) model of work design. The JDR model also provides some sources of stress. As a recap, the JDR model describes a number of work demands that can negatively affect work engagement and performance. These demands include the physical workload, time pressure, physical environment, and shift work. The job demands that can act as negative stressors include

TABLE 14.2 Results of a Survey of the Leading Stressors at Work

A SURVEY OF MORE THAN 1,000 RESPONDENTS IDENTIFIED THE FOLLOWING ISSUES AS THE LEADING CAUSES OF WORKER STRESS.	
ISSUE	**PERCENTAGE OF RESPONDENTS**
1. Deadlines	30%
2. Life of another at risk	17%
3. Competitiveness	10%
4. Physical demands	8%
5. Working in the public eye	8%
6. Lack of growth	7%
7. Life at risk	7%
8. Hazards	5%
9. Meeting the public	4%
10. Travel	3%

Sources: CareerCast. (2017). 2017 stressful jobs reader survey. http://www.careercast.com/career-news/2017-stressful-jobs-reader-survey; Wilkie, D. (2017, March 2). No. 1 stressor at work: Deadlines. https://www.shrm.org/resourcesandtools/hr-topics/employee-relations/pages/workplace-stress.aspx

- role conflict (having conflicting roles at work);
- role ambiguity (a lack of clarity about what your role and responsibilities are in the organization and how your job fits in with other jobs);
- interpersonal conflicts with a boss or coworkers;
- risks, hazards, and poor work conditions;
- work–life conflict;
- emotionally demanding work;
- job insecurity (worry that you may lose your job); and
- performance demands.

On the other hand, the JDR model also discusses resources that can reduce stress such as supervisor support, control over your work, job security, participation, and feedback (see Figure 14.5).

Here are some examples of how employers can reduce stress with improved resources.

■ **FIGURE 14.5**   Some Common Sources of Workplace Stress and Factors That Mitigate Them

Potential Sources of Stress in Organizations	Factors Organizations Can Use to Reduce Stress
• Role conflict • Role ambiguity • Interpersonal conflicts • Risks, hazards, and poor work conditions • Work–life conflict • Emotionally demanding work	• Supervisor support • Flexibility and control over work • Job security • Participation • Constructive feedback

Sources: Based on Demerouti, E., Bakker, A. B., Nachreiner, F., & Schaufeli, W. B. (2001). The Job Demands-Resources model of burnout. *Journal of Applied Psychology, 86,* 499–512; Schaufeli, W. B., & Taris, T. W. (2014). A critical review of the Job Demands-Resources model: Implications for improving work and health. In G. F. Bauer & O. Hämmig (Eds.), *Bridging occupational, organizational and public health* (pp. 43–68). Dordrecht: Springer Netherlands.

Physicians have their own stress issues, with high burnout rates and high levels of emotional exhaustion and feelings of depersonalization (feeling disengaged from one's surroundings).

- If employees are unsure about what their roles are, the organization can provide greater clarity through developing and updating job descriptions.

- Supervisors might be trained to give workers support in dealing with emotionally demanding jobs.

- If employees are experiencing high work–life conflict due to lack of schedule control, the organization can provide greater control over work schedules to the extent possible.[41]

- Perhaps the best approach is for organizations to analyze the sources of stress so that they can most effectively address the situation or the challenges of a particular profession. As one example, poor patient care is a serious outcome of physician stress. Physicians also have double the suicide rates of other professions. The causes of physician stress include high patient loads, time pressures, and dealing with patients' emotional difficulties.[42]

Work–Life Balance

A recent Gallup poll found that the standard "40-hour workweek" is not a reality for many U.S. workers, who work on average 47 hours per week. Many employees—especially salaried workers—put in upward of 60-hour weeks, which means that they are either working 12-hour days, working on weekends, or both.[43] This can lead to stress for workers in terms of burnout and work–life balance. This translates into less time for nonwork activities such as caring for children or aging parents, personal life, or outside interests. Always being connected by e-mail after work and on weekends is another challenge facing workers trying to balance their work and nonwork lives, with some countries even passing legislation to control e-mail.[44]

The issue of balancing work and nonwork time can be thought of in two ways:

- **Work-to-family conflict** is when work interferes with nonwork responsibilities.
- **Family-to-work conflict** is when nonwork responsibilities interfere with work responsibilities.[45]

Work-to-family conflict can lead to decreased job satisfaction and performance, increased turnover, and depression. Some solutions include employer policies focused on providing increased flexibility and support for employees balancing work and nonwork demands. Examples of workplace policies include

- Flexible work hours and compressed workweeks (e.g., fewer than 5 days per week as well as flexible work locations)
- Flexible location and teleworking to provide caregiving control over work time
- Breaks, sabbaticals, and other types of employee leave

HRM plays a central role in implementing these types of workplace policies and programs, such as ensuring that the work gets done and defining the roles of both managers and employees in carrying out such policies.[46] But it can have a big payoff. For example, SAS, a North Carolina–based business analytics software company, provides a cafeteria, on-site medical care, and a 35-hour workweek for many employees. Not surprisingly, SAS has one of the lowest turnover rates in the industry and a frequent spot on "best places to work" lists.[47]

Ways for Organizations to Reduce Stress

In addition to working to help employees with work–life balance, there are some other ways for organizations to help reduce some of the more toxic types of stress faced by employees.

Determine the Sources of Employee Stress

The most successful organizations will do research to find the sources of stress. For example, Hackensack University Medical Center regularly surveys its staff and benchmarks their results against a national database.[48]

Eliminate the Root Causes of Employee Stress Before Looking for Fixes

Stress management programs intended for individual employees can be effective, but organizations should first see whether the primary sources of stress can be addressed.[49] For example, **workplace bullying**, either by supervisors or by coworkers, as well as an employee culture or climate that supports bullying, is a serious source of employee stress and dissatisfaction with work.[50] If employees perceive that there is a problem with difficult supervisors, removing or training those supervisors would be in order rather than training

Work-to-family conflict When work interferes with nonwork responsibilities

Family-to-work conflict When nonwork responsibilities interfere with work responsibilities

Workplace bullying Consistent mistreatment by others in the workplace

employees how to deal with it. Or if there is a technical aspect of the job that is disruptive to employees, address that first. For example, when a Starbucks employee work-scheduling algorithm was found to be disrupting employees' personal lives with constant last-minute changes, the company revamped it.[51]

Provide Training Programs

A range of training programs can be used to support employees, such as training supervisors or employees on how to reduce stress.

Encourage and Allow for Employee Recovery Experiences

Employers can support recovery experiences among their employees:

- Detaching from work can lead to higher energy levels at work.[52] For example, accounting firm PwC provides a 4-week sabbatical to employees who have been with the organization for 5 to 7 years.[53]

- Employers can encourage workers to take vacation days. Many employees, especially in the United States, might let their vacation days—and thus an opportunity for recovery—go to waste.

- Some organizations may encourage employees to take short naps at work, as naps can increase performance, and the value of naps during the workday is recognized by companies such as Uber, Google, and Zappos.[54]

- Providing personal days, either paid or unpaid, can allow employees to take care of personal needs off the job and to manage their work–life balance.

Consider How to Redesign Work and Work Areas to Fit Employee Needs

This includes quiet areas where employees might be able to take a break. Or it could be more extensive, such as BMW's overhaul of some of its manufacturing facilities to address its aging workforce, introducing features like wood floors (that are easier on joints), seated assembly work, and easier grips. BMW found a 7% increase in productivity with the introduction of these changes.[55]

Support the "Corporate Athlete"

Remaining in the stressful corporate world requires that employees take care of themselves in the same way that athletes would in terms of healthy behaviors, such as exercise and recovery. Organizations can play a role in supporting their "corporate athletes" to build and sustain their physical, emotional, mental, and spiritual capacities.[56]

Employee Wellness Programs

Employee wellness programs
Organizational initiatives that promote the health, fitness, and well-being of workers

LO 14.4 Identify the characteristics of the variety of workplace wellness programs that are offered by employers.

What can organizations can do to actively promote employee health and well-being? **Employee wellness programs** are organizational initiatives that promote the health, fitness, and well-being of workers.[57] These programs have been increasing in popularity, with an estimate of $6 billion spent on them each year.[58] In addition, more than half of employers typically offer wellness programs, and the percentage is even higher for large employers.[59] HRM practitioners are centrally involved in the most effective, strategic implementation of wellness programs.

Wellness programs can take many forms, given the needs and resources of organizations, employees, and the industry. They include everything from helping employees manage illnesses (e.g., diabetes), increase exercise, or quit smoking to providing onsite medical screenings and care or improving their financial knowledge. For example, Cisco Systems, a multinational technology company, offers a wide range of options in its wellness program, including disease management programs, onsite health care, fitness, child care facilities, mindfulness training, and generous parental leave policies.[60] The key is to offer the program that is the best fit for the employee and their situation.

Benefits of Wellness Programs

A survey by *The Economist* Intelligence Unit surveyed 255 U.S. senior executives and 630 workers employed at organizations that have wellness programs.[61] Seventy percent of executives said that they considered the programs to be cost-effective because they see the wellness program as part of a progressive HR strategy that benefits the employer in other ways, such as attracting the best talent. One of the challenges of getting a good payoff from a wellness program is getting employees to participate in it. Both the executives and employees identified two leading factors that could reduce employee participation: Employees do not have the time to participate, and employees worry that their information may not remain confidential.

That said, there may be a good payoff for certain types of wellness programs, taking into account short-term versus long-term return on investment (ROI). A Rand study showed that disease management programs, which focus on helping workers with certain specific illnesses, seem to have the greatest short-term benefit in terms of saving money on health care costs, generating as much as $136 in savings per person and a 30% reduction in hospital admissions.[63] For example, a program that supports workers with heart disease could lead to a reduction in heart attacks. Lifestyle management programs, which focus on issues like exercise and better eating habits, might lead to long-term benefits like reduced rates of cancer or hypertension. Other reviews of the payoff from wellness

Mark Bertolini is the CEO of Aetna, a *Fortune* 500 health benefits company. Bertolini emphasizes the need to go beyond assessing return on investment (ROI) when determining the value of a wellness program and to focus instead on how the program affects the organization's people and their well-being.[62]

Cindy Ord/Getty Images for Yahoo

programs cite lower medical costs and decreased absenteeism and presenteeism (working while having health problems).[64] Finally, some people argue that given the value of worker well-being to increased engagement, performance, morale, and retention, an overly strong focus on ROI alone misses the point.[65]

Types of Wellness Programs

Wellness programs can include a range of elements (see Figure 14.6). Here are some common examples. Most organizations would select the types of wellness products that best fit their employees[66]:

- **Fitness club memberships and centers.** These can involve an on-site gym or special rates, discounts, or reimbursements at local fitness centers.

■ **FIGURE 14.6** Examples of Workplace Wellness Programs

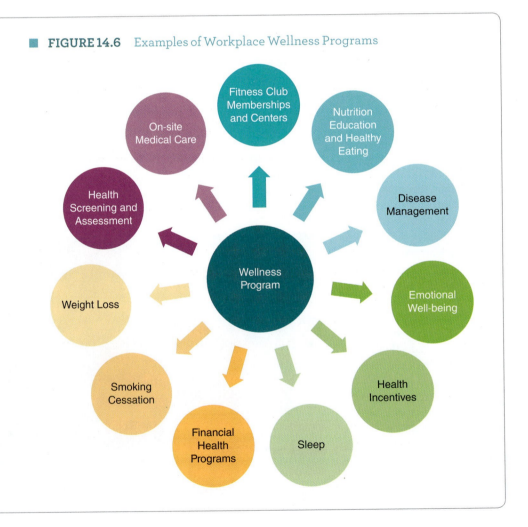

- **Nutrition education and healthy eating.** These programs provide instructions for employees on eating well. Some include making healthful food and snacks available on site or even an on-site farmers market.

- **Disease management.** Disease management programs include providing help, support, and guidance for employees who know that they have chronic conditions, such as heart disease or diabetes, so that they can better manage their diseases. These are better researched than some other types of wellness programs, and they appear to be good at reducing medical costs and employee mortality.

- **Emotional well-being.** With a focus on things like yoga instruction, mindfulness, and other ways to control employee stress, these programs have become more popular since the days of early wellness programs, which had a greater focus on physical health. As an example, Vancouver-based Mobify offers twice-weekly yoga classes to its employees.

- **Health incentives.** An organization may choose to reward any number of health behaviors such as smoking cessation, weight loss, or number of steps. The key is for workers to feel engaged, not coerced.

- **Sleep.** These programs may focus on anything from sleep hygiene education (explaining the value of sleep and how to develop good sleep habits) to workplace naps. For example, Asana offers its employees "nap rooms" where they can take a quick nap during work hours. And at LinkedIn, a recent focus of its wellness program was sleep health, including a "sleep fair."[67]

- **Financial health programs.** Employer-sponsored financial programs range from financial education and advice to paying student loans.

- **Smoking cessation.** Smoking cessation programs support people trying to quit.

- **Weight loss.** Weight loss programs are often included as part of healthy eating and exercise programs and may also include Weight Watchers meetings and weight loss competitions.

- **Health screening and assessment.** Offering employees the chance to get some basic health screening might uncover if they have particular medical needs (the privacy of which would also need to be protected).

- **On-site medical care.** Given that employees are sometimes pressed for time and do not get around to taking care of their personal health needs, some companies offer these on-site medical services to employees.

Employee Assistance Programs (EAPs)

Employee assistance programs (or EAPs) are in some ways the predecessors of wellness programs, but with a decidedly different approach. EAPs are focused on identifying employees' personal problems that may be affecting their work and helping them with these existing problems. The problems that they often address include alcohol and substance abuse, emotional challenges, and financial problems. The services offered by EAPs include providing basic legal assistance, counseling, advice on child or elder care services, and/or nursing advice by telephone. Typically paid for by the employer, EAP services generally support not only the employee but their family as well.[68] One classic example is the EAP offered by Accenture, which includes confidential support for issues such as anxiety, depression, and substance abuse, as well as support for financial issues.[69]

EAPs vary considerably from one organization to the next in what types of specific services they offer. Most medium- and large-sized organizations provide some type of EAP services to their employees. Many EAPs also require

- the development of consistent EAP rules and guidelines with input from employees and, in unionized organizations, from unions;

- legal guidance on the appropriateness of EAP rules and procedures;

- procedures for maintaining employee confidentiality;

- training for supervisors on appropriate methods for identifying employee performance problems that might be appropriate for referral to EAP;

- consultation services for supervisors dealing with a possible employee EAP issue; and

- a system for monitoring and follow-up.[70]

What is the role of HRM in EAPs? One issue is to ensure employee privacy and the security of employee information. In addition, most employers outsource EAP services given the highly specialized nature of the work, such as counseling and substance abuse treatment. HR personnel are heavily involved in selecting EAP vendors, developing EAP policies, and explaining to employees which EAP services are available.[71] This last issue is important because many employees are unaware of EAP services that are offered by their employer. By one estimate, although 97% of large companies have EAPs, only about 40% of employees know whether their employer offers these services.[72]

Best Practices for Implementing Wellness Programs and the Role of HRM

Given the costs of wellness programs, their careful implementation is essential to providing value to the organization. It is here that HRM plays a central role by ensuring that the program fits employees' needs as well as those of the organization.[73]

- **Needs assessment.** As with all other HR functions, the wellness program should be designed to fit what employees want and to address organizational concerns. A program that does not fit a need felt on the part of employees is of little value.

- **Engagement of leadership.** Research has shown that like so many other organizational initiatives, buy-in at all levels is necessary to ensure support and the success of the program.

- **Communication.** Another central role for HR is to ensure that employees know about the wellness services available to them. This means clear, consistent, and frequent messaging.

- **Ensure that the program is easy for employees to use.** Examples might include the decision to provide on-site child care or on-site health care services so that employees are more likely to use these services.

- **Evaluation.** We have noted that the payoff on wellness programs may not be as tangible as return on investment (ROI)—although sometimes it is. In any case, whether it is reduced health costs, absenteeism, employee satisfaction and morale, or better retention, some evaluation of the program should be included to illustrate its value. For example, measurement and evaluation are a standard part of Johnson & Johnson's wellness program.

- **Ensure integrity of private employee data.** Part of having rich data to evaluate wellness programs is the ethical responsibility to protect these data.

- **Consider the use of incentives.** There are many ways to encourage adoption of wellness programs. One way is to provide financial incentives for employee participation in wellness programs. Such incentives may work better for certain types of health behaviors (e.g., eating more fruits and vegetables) than others (e.g., stopping smoking). Incentives should be seen as fair by employees and not coercive. The Manager's Toolbox (p. 349) presents a number of suggestions for ensuring the success of a wellness program in organizations.

Spotlight on Data and Analytics
WEARABLE TECHNOLOGY IN THE WORKPLACE

One of the biggest sources of data for workplace safety and health analytics is wearable technology ("wearables") worn by employees. This can take a number of forms, such as fitness trackers or employee badges that monitor employee movements and their proximity to each other.

For example, a wearable allows employees not only to see their own steps in a day but also to become aware of dysfunctional behaviors that they are not aware of or to see where they might make simple changes to improve their health. Similarly, wearables can allow employers to set up incentives for employees to increase their activity or allow them to tailor health programs to fit the needs of an individual employee.

Wearables can be used in the realm of employee safety as well. For example, some wearable solutions alert employees operating heavy equipment when they are too close to other employees.

Workplace wearables are not without their challenges, however. Collecting such data about employees raises the issue of who will have access to the data and how the employer will protect the data from third parties. In addition, monitoring employees in such personal ways may actually increase worker stress because workers feel that they are always "on." Further, monitoring by their employers may not be to the liking of many workers. A recent news story indicated that wearables can also lead to serious security issues, such as when the wearables used by U.S. soldiers gave away their locations—which were not supposed to be revealed.

In short, workplace wearables can provide a tremendous opportunity if implemented with awareness of the pitfalls and with considerable planning.[74]

Workplace Interventions: Solutions to Address Specific Well-Being Issues

Sometimes, employers uncover the need to focus on a very specific issue (e.g., poor safety climate), or they may want to focus on the needs of their employee population (e.g., truckers). In these cases, they may choose to apply a more narrowly focused workplace intervention as a solution to address their needs. Examples of these types of proven workplace interventions include those focused on work–life balance issues, improving safety by increasing communications between leaders and employees, and addressing the needs of specific occupations such as truck drivers.[75]

Total Worker Health™: An Integrated Approach to Worker Well-Being

LO 14.5   Explain what is meant by an integrated Total Worker Health™ approach.

As we noted at the beginning of the chapter, workplace safety, stress, well-being, and wellness are all linked. An employer concerned with worker safety will also be concerned with worker well-being and will develop wellness programs to address these issues. These issues are also all intertwined. The result is that workers with health problems are involved in accidents that cause injury to themselves and to the public.

There is a growing recognition of the value of integrating wellness programs with traditional workplace safety and health programs. This is because such integration can bring about systemic change within the organization. The National Institute for Occupational Safety and Health (NIOSH) refers to these integrated safety, well-being, and wellness programs as **Total Worker Health™ (TWH™)** programs (see Figure 14.7).[76] As one example, Dow Chemical, which has 54,000 employees in 49 countries, adopted a TWH™ approach that integrates three distinct elements: healthy people, healthy workplace, and healthy culture. These are all part of Dow's integrated strategy to address the complex issues around protecting the safety, health, and well-being of its workers, and TWH™ is an explicit part of its 2025 Sustainability Goals.[77] Although the research on these integrated programs is still in the early stages, an initial review of 17 TWH™ interventions found they may have more long-term impact on worker safety and health than narrower, piecemeal approaches.[78] Further, seeing worker safety, health, and well-being through this integrated lens can help organizations identify underlying causes of safety and health issues. For example, through the use of data analytics, a company may be able to identify the relationship between costly outcomes (e.g., employee medical costs; accidents) that are associated with an underlying cause (e.g., safety climate) that could be addressed by specific management practices (e.g., top management support, supervisor training).

Total Worker Health™ (TWH™) An integrated approach to safety, well-being, and wellness

■ **FIGURE 14.7**   The Broad Range of Systemic Factors Associated With TWH™ Approaches to Managing Safety, Health, and Well-Being

Control Hazards and Exposures (e.g., chemicals)	Organization of Work (e.g., stress prevention, safe staffing)	Built Environment (e.g., access to healthy food, accommodation of worker diversity)
Leadership (e.g., commitment to safety and well-being; worker recognition)	Compensation and Benefits (e.g., work–life programs, disease management)	Changing Workforce Demographics (e.g., multigenerational and diverse workforce)
Policy Issues (e.g., worker privacy, reducing bullying)	Community Design (e.g., easy access to health care in the community)	New Employment Patterns (e.g., contingent workforce)

Source: Based on recommendations from NIOSH. (2015). Total worker health frequently asked questions. https://www.cdc.gov/niosh/twh/pdfs/faq-for-total-worker-health_2015-03-01-trademark-amended-for-download.pdf

---

Manager's Toolbox
TIPS FOR IMPLEMENTING AN EFFECTIVE WELLNESS PROGRAM

Here are some ideas to keep in mind when implementing a wellness program.

1. **Find out what employees actually want and need.** A program that allows some flexibility to address the different needs of different workers is also beneficial.

2. **Think about how to encourage participation** and that different employees will be motivated to participate for different reasons.

3. **Consider the marketing angle.** This might be as simple as providing sufficient knowledge of the program.

4. **Make participation convenient for employees.** An unused program is an unwise investment, so make it easy for employees to use.

5. **Leverage technology.** Technology can help with wellness programs in numerous ways, such as apps that help employees with meeting their health goals, attending webinars, or scheduling medical appointments.[79]

CHAPTER SUMMARY

HRM plays a central role in workplace safety, well-being, and wellness. HR professionals need to know the government agencies and resources devoted to safety and the safety regulations with which employers must comply. Proactive HRM will work to uncover workers' safety and health issues and their causes. HRM will also take steps to identify and implement appropriate solutions, including employee wellness programs and more specific interventions and integrated Total Worker Health™ approaches. Organizations with a culture of safety communicate the importance of safety and health to both managers and employees. Looking at the big picture of safety and health across the organization is a key strategy in supporting employee health and well-being and organizational success.

KEY TERMS

well-being   329
Occupational Safety and Health
    Administration (OSHA)   329
near misses   330
safety compliance behavior   331
safety participation
    behavior   331
safety knowledge   332

safety motivation   332
safety climate   332
stressors   334
safety officer   334
safety committee   334
ergonomic design   335
open offices   337
strain   338

work-to-family conflict   341
family-to-work conflict   341
workplace bullying   341
employee wellness
    programs   342
Total Worker Health™
    (TWH™)   348

⑤SAGE edge™

Get the tools you need to sharpen your study skills. SAGE edge offers a robust online environment featuring an impressive array of free tools and resources.

Access practice quizzes, eFlashcards, video, and multimedia at **edge.sagepub.com/bauerbrief**

HR REASONING AND DECISION-MAKING EXERCISES

EXERCISE 14.1: SAFETY FOR ALL

You are working for a construction company specializing in interior and exterior painting of newly built homes. You are the sole safety officer in this small company of 50 employees. The company is fairly young—5 years old— but it is growing rapidly with the high rate of construction in your metropolitan area. And so far, things are going well from a safety perspective, with no severe accidents or injuries yet reported. The company posts the required publications about employee rights and employer responsibilities. In addition, the company encourages you to provide safety training to employees.

However, you notice that the owner and the three lead supervisors in the company see safety as your role, not theirs. For example, the owner of the company rarely follows the company's own rules regarding safety, especially with regard to the handling of chemicals (e.g., solvents) that are used in painting work. He and the three supervisors are very much focused on company growth and encourage workers to work quickly; this is sometimes at the expense of safety. You have noticed that when employees voice a concern or suggestion about a safety problem, the suggestion is not welcomed by your supervisors—at least not in terms of their body language. You are trying to decide on your next steps in managing the safety function in the company.

Questions

1. What concerns do you have with the safety climate of this company? In what ways might these issues have a negative impact on worker safety?
2. What steps could you take in your role as safety officer to illustrate to management the safety issues that you are observing in this company?
3. What arguments could you make to these top managers about the importance of safety climate and the role they play in it? What suggestions would you make to them as to how they might foster a positive safety climate?

EXERCISE 14.2: ASSESSING THE VALUE OF A WELLNESS PROGRAM

A manufacturing company is preparing to implement a company wellness program within its East Coast, Southeastern, and West Coast locations. These locations employ about 1,800 workers in total.

The proposed wellness program would involve five possible components:

- on-site exercise equipment,
- smoking cessation program,
- mindfulness training,
- free mental health counseling, and
- financial education.

The company's CEO is supportive of a wellness program. But she also wants to justify the program in terms of its costs and benefits. So, she would like to know which of these proposed components of the program the company should consider undertaking.

Questions

1. How would you research the possible value of each of these components prior to implementation?
2. What types of company data would you use to determine if each of these components is needed?
3. Should you roll out the entire program at once, or should each component be rolled out separately? What would be the advantages and disadvantages of each approach? Consider whether the three company locations might be used differently for the rollout.
4. Assuming that the program is implemented by the company, what types of data—from objective data to employee attitudes—should the company collect to evaluate whether each component is effective?
5. Are there any "intangible" outcomes that might be considered in assessing the value of the wellness program?

ETHICAL MATTERS EXERCISE: PRIVACY, TECHNOLOGY, AND HUMAN ERROR

The large amount of highly personal data available to employers provides an opportunity to better understand employee behavior. These safety and health data can help uncover ways to support employees' well-being. However, they also present ethical concerns and challenges about employees' privacy. Employers must maintain the security of data. If the data were released, it could be damaging to employees, job applicants, or customers.

One recent example was the data breach at Uber, in which the private accounts of 57 million drivers and customers were stolen, and the company paid the hackers $100,000 to delete the data. (Uber also covered up the breach for several months, leading to the firing of its chief security officer and harming its reputation.)

Some security issues can be addressed by technological solutions like ensuring that the data cannot be hacked by outsiders. But other security issues are the result of human error. A single employee might mistakenly give out their login credentials in a phishing attack and make the entire database of all employees and customers visible.

The ethical issue of maintaining the security of private data is one that will continue to evolve with technological advances. But an organization is ethically responsible for maintaining the safety and security of its employees' and clients' personal information.[80]

Questions

1. People working in HR have access to private information about employees. What kind of training content should an employer provide for its HR employees so that they would know their ethical responsibilities for maintaining these private data?
2. Describe some everyday situations in which an employee in HR or another area could accidentally compromise employees' private data. How can workers prevent or contain the damage if this were to happen?

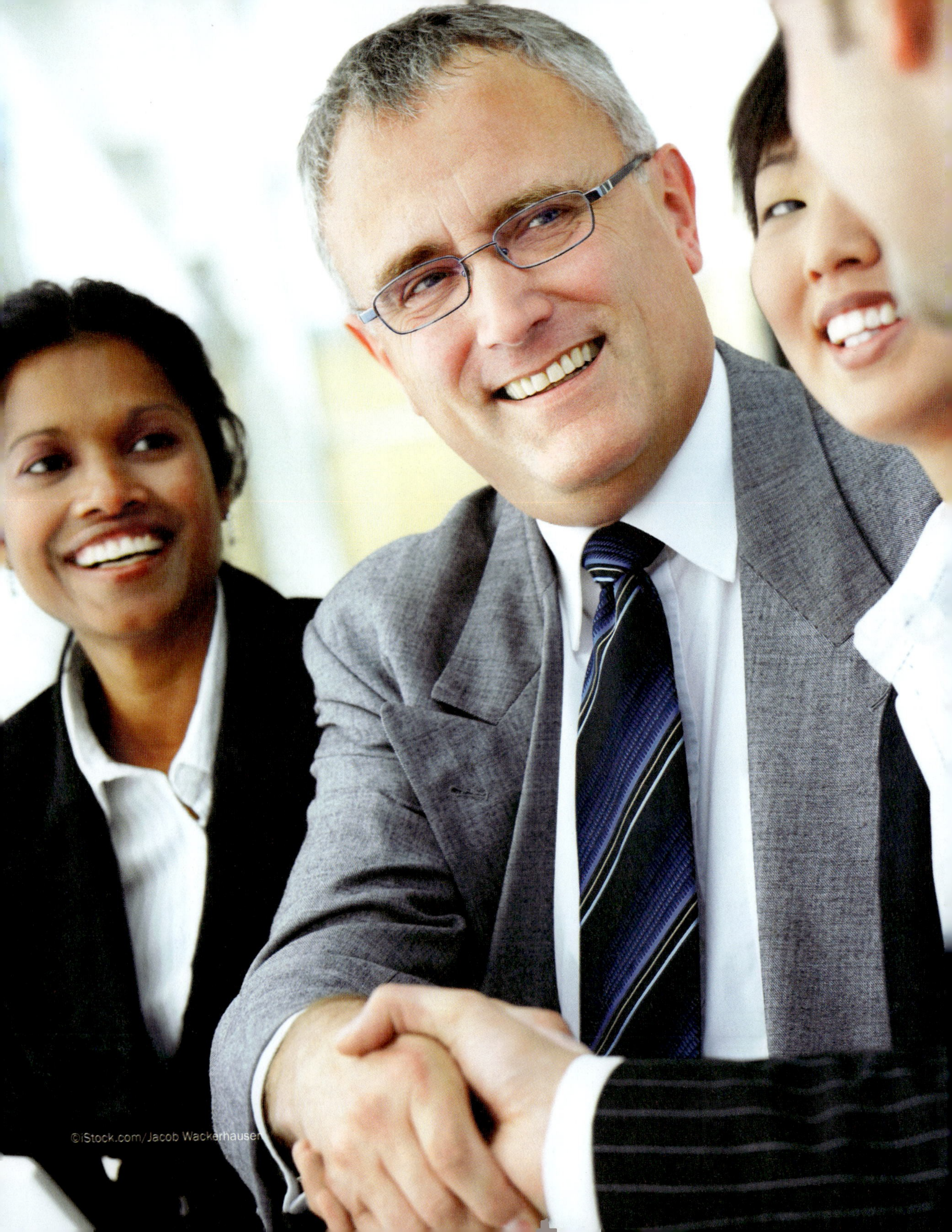

15 Opportunities and Challenges in International HRM

LEARNING OBJECTIVES

After reading and studying this chapter, you should be able to do the following:

15.1 Describe the advantages and disadvantages to standardizing HR practices in different locations of a business and barriers to standardization.

15.2 Examine the considerations an organization should make when expanding its business practices across borders such as cultural differences, unionization rates, and legal context.

15.3 Identify HRM practices that would benefit from local adjustments and those that would benefit from standardization across borders.

15.4 Summarize the forces affecting adjustment of expatriates to their overseas assignments and identify ways in which organizations can prepare expatriates for successful assignments.

15.5 Identify alternatives to long-term relocation assignments.

HR in Action: The Case of Leveraging Culture for Success at L'Oréal

Based in France and operating in 140 countries, L'Oréal is a global corporate giant. It employs more than 89,000 workers and owns brands such as Maybelline, Ralph Lauren, and Lancôme among its offerings. What makes a cosmetic product appealing in a particular geography varies greatly, requiring any company operating in multiple geographies to master cultural differences. In this arena, L'Oréal has important lessons to offer.

What makes the difference in the international success of L'Oréal is the deliberate efforts to infuse multiculturalism into its product development teams. The company brings experienced employees from subsidiaries, recruits from competitors, and new hires from top international business schools to its product development operations. Candidates receive a yearlong training in Rio de Janeiro, Singapore, Paris, or New York, then take

©iStock.com/Joel Carillet

part in a management development program before being placed in their teams in the Paris headquarters. After a while, these employees are placed back in its home-country operations as director-level employees. Using this method, the company ensures that it develops a pool of talented and multicultural managers who are involved in product development and then take charge in subsidiary operations. This approach allows the company to develop future leaders who can create products that fit the local environment while embracing the company's core values.

Despite all efforts to embrace multiculturalism, L'Oréal does not always adopt local norms. For example, the headquarters culture embraces the values of confrontation and disagreement, which is not a good fit in subsidiaries where harmony is valued. The company offers a program called "Managing Confrontation" to train employees. Even when it goes against employee instincts, the program underlines what the company values are and teaches employees the importance of effectively handling disagreements.[1]

Case Discussion Questions

1. Why is it important for L'Oréal to embrace multiculturalism? Which aspects of the company's operations would benefit the most from multiculturalism?

2. How should an organization decide whether to follow the values of the headquarters or the subsidiary?

3. What are the advantages and downsides of L'Oréal's approach to training local talent?

For businesses, national boundaries have been losing their relevance. Many iconic "all-American" brands established in the United States such as Budweiser, 7-Eleven, and IBM now have non-U.S.-based owners. Companies including Intel, Nike, GE, and McDonald's receive more than half their revenue from their overseas sales and operations. HR professionals are increasingly operating in a world in which they need to go outside of the local talent pool for recruitment, learn how to train and manage a global workforce, and ensure that they create HR systems that explicitly consider the global context.

Global markets often represent an important growth opportunity for businesses. Having access to a global talent pool may make companies more competitive. Moving production to a different country may provide advantages from a cost perspective. Regardless of its reasons, doing business globally is becoming the norm.

Global Transfer of HR Practices

International companies
Companies that export or import, but their investments are within one home country

LO 15.1   Describe the advantages and disadvantages to standardizing HR practices in different locations of a business and barriers to standardization.

Organizations vary in their degree of internationalization. For example, **international companies** export and import, but their investments are within one home country. Most large firms these days are international given that they source at least some materials from overseas. **Multinational companies** operate in multiple countries but with clearly designated headquarters in their home country. The headquarters typically set the standards for how host-country or subsidiary operations will function. Examples include Ikea (based in Sweden) and Amazon (based in the United States). **Transnational companies** have operations in multiple countries. However, they act like a borderless company and do not consider any one country as the center of operations. These businesses are more decentralized and adapt their operations following the best practices that may emerge from different operations. Examples include Nestlé and Unilever.

An important trend resulting in internationalization of businesses is **offshoring**. Companies often find that producing physical goods or performing some of their operations overseas has cost advantages. As a result, they may move some of their operations to an overseas location. Offshoring may help companies to deal with talent shortages in local markets as well, such as the shortage in engineering and sciences graduates in the United States. Offshoring is different from **outsourcing**. Outsourcing refers to moving some operations of the company to a different company. For example, a company may decide to stop handling its own payroll operations and instead contract another company to provide this service. Outsourcing does not necessarily involve an international operation: A firm may outsource to another company in the same country or region. Offshoring may be combined with outsourcing, such as Apple's use of Taiwanese manufacturer Foxconn to produce its iPhones and iPads.

In a global organization, a key decision that needs to be made with respect to HR practices is striking a balance between **global integration** and **local differentiation**: Should the organization standardize its HR practices around the world? Or should it vary its practices in consideration of the local environment? There are clear advantages to having all units use the same selection, training, performance management, and reward systems so that operations are more consistent and coherent. Global integration ensures that the company establishes a common corporate culture and common ways of doing business, which could be helpful in achieving fairness across different operations.

At the same time, there are good reasons not to transfer all or even some HR practices and instead follow a local differentiation strategy. For example, headquarter HR practices might not fit with the regulatory or cultural context of subsidiaries. Subsidiaries may sometimes develop their own HR practices that the company could be interested in disseminating to other overseas operations. Trying to centralize HR operations might prevent these opportunities from taking place.

When considering the question of global integration versus local differentiation, it is important to remember that this is not an "all or nothing" proposition; it is a matter of degree. Companies may choose to standardize some HR practices, whereas other practices may be subject to localization. Further, it is important to distinguish between HR philosophy and HR practices. The company may have HR practices that are adapted to each locality but may also have a centralized HR philosophy guiding HR-related decisions. As long as there is shared understanding about the company's fundamental values with respect to workforce management, the company may differentiate its HR practices yet manage to coordinate effectively across business units.

Multinational companies Companies operating in multiple countries but with clearly designated headquarters in their home country

Transnational companies Companies that have operations in multiple countries and do not view themselves as belonging to any one country

Offshoring When companies produce physical goods or perform some of their operations overseas

Outsourcing Moving some operations of the organization to a different organization

Global integration When a company standardizes its HR practices around the world

Local differentiation When organizations vary their HR practices in consideration of the local environment

Important Considerations When Transferring HR Practices Across Borders

LO 15.2 Examine the considerations an organization should make when expanding its business practices across borders such as cultural differences, unionization rates, and legal context.

When a multinational organization is interested in transferring particular HR practices across borders, it may run into difficulties. Cultural differences, unionization rates, the legal context, and the reason behind internationalization are four of the many reasons businesses may find that their best practices in one country may not be possible or desirable in other countries.

Legal Context

Businesses in the United States have a lot of freedom regarding talent management. In contrast, in Europe, the commonly held assumption is that businesses need to be monitored, controlled, and constrained so that they do not harm employees. There are simply more protections for employees that constrain the autonomy of European businesses. For example, terminating an employee in Europe for any reason requires following specific procedures, giving employees advance notice, and providing generous severance pay. Most other countries around the world mandate paid time off for employees and new parents. In France, the workweek is limited to 35 hours, and employees have the "right to disconnect," or have the right to hours during which they are not required to check or answer e-mail.[2]

Unionization Rates

Union membership has been in decline in the United States. This rate was over 90% in Iceland, 55% in Belgium, 26% in Canada, and 13% in Mexico as of 2017.[3] Further, European Union law requires most companies to establish employee representation committees. When operating in countries with a strong tradition of unions, businesses need to involve union representatives in their decision-making process and follow more participatory approaches to management.

Cultural Differences

HR practices that work well in one context may be difficult to transfer to other contexts due to differences in culture. A Dutch researcher, Geert Hofstede, conceptualized national culture as consisting of four dimensions (later versions added more dimensions), as shown in Table 15.1. Note that countries are not homogeneous with respect to cultural values: Some cities, regions, or different segments of the population will show variability. Still, the differences across countries with respect to average cultural values are important to consider.

Cultural differences may serve as a barrier to transferring HR practices. For example, overall, the United States is a highly individualistic, relatively highly masculine culture, with moderately low values in power distance and uncertainty avoidance. (Definitions of these

TABLE 15.1   Dimensions of Culture Based on Hofstede's Framework

DIMENSION	DEFINITION	EXAMPLE OF COUNTRIES HIGH AND LOW ON THIS DIMENSION
Individualism versus collectivism	The degree to which individuals define themselves as individuals as opposed to through their relationships. Collectivists emphasize loyalty to the group, face saving, and cooperation within the in-group.	Highly individualistic: Australia, United States, United Kingdom Highly collectivistic: Ecuador, Guatemala, West Africa
Power distance	The degree to which the society accepts power in the society is distributed unequally and hierarchy is naturally accepted.	High power distance: Guatemala, Panama, Philippines, Romania, Slovakia Low power distance: Austria, Denmark, Israel
Uncertainty avoidance	The degree to which the society feels uncomfortable with uncertainty and risk and emphasizes procedures or traditions to deal with it.	High uncertainty avoidance: Australia, Greece, Guatemala, Portugal, Uruguay Low uncertainty avoidance: Denmark, Jamaica, Singapore
Masculinity versus femininity	Masculine cultures are those that embrace values such as achievement and materialism. Feminine cultures emphasize modesty, caring for the weak, and quality of life.	Highly masculine cultures: Japan, Slovakia Highly feminine cultures: Costa Rica, Netherlands, Norway, Sweden

Sources: Retrieved from https://www.hofstede-insights.com/models/national-culture/ on June 3, 2018; Retrieved from https://harzing.com/download/hgindices.xls on June 3, 2018.

values are in Table 15.1.) Let's say that a U.S.-based multinational is doing business in Colombia. Colombian culture is highly collectivistic, which would make it difficult to transfer reward systems that pit individuals against each other such as in individual sales competitions.

Some countries have specific traditions around particular HR practices, and multinationals will have to adopt these local practices. For example, in many countries in Asia, major companies hire a cohort of new graduates and subject them to specific and pre-planned developmental experiences, preparing them for future managerial roles. Job applicants will expect major firms to follow this practice, and failing to adopt this practice may serve as a disadvantage in hiring.[4]

Management practices may also be interpreted differently in different cultural contexts. For example, a flat organizational structure, absence of managerial supervision, and having a lot of autonomy over one's work may be regarded as empowering in cultures that emphasize low power distance. However, in cultures that emphasize high power distance such as India, the same practices may be disappointing to workers because they afford fewer opportunities for promotions and career growth. Japanese employees may react negatively to telecommuting and work-from-home arrangements because in their culture, work is expected to happen at the office, and Japanese homes are traditionally small, leaving little room for a home office to be set up.

Even though culture matters, it is important not to overestimate the effects of national culture as a reason particular HR practices may not work in a given context. Differences in legal context, unemployment rates, and economic conditions may be more important than culture as the reasons why particular practices fail. For example, the reason employees may react negatively to pay-for-performance programs such as bonuses in some contexts may not be a fundamental difference in cultural values but rather the uncertainty introduced by economic factors, leading employees to believe that their effort will not lead to higher performance.[5]

Causes and Forms of Internationalization

The reason a company chooses to internationalize is a key consideration in whether the organization chooses global integration in favor of local adaptations.[6] In some organizations, subsidiaries require close coordination with the parent company. Examples of this are Ford or General Motors, which offshore manufacturing to take advantage of lower labor costs overseas. Because the cars are manufactured for the global market, ensuring that subsidiaries around the world are closely coordinated with headquarters is important. In other cases, the reason subsidiaries exist is to reach overseas markets, as in the case of global food and beverage companies like Kellogg's and Kraft. Because local responsiveness in product design and marketing is important, the companies may give greater autonomy to subsidiaries and make greater efforts to ensure that HR practices fit the needs of each locality.

Managing HR Globally

LO 15.3 Identify HRM practices that would benefit from local adjustments and those that would benefit from standardization across borders.

Organizations need to design their HR practices to leverage the advantages of operating in multiple geographies, such as access to a wider talent pool and the ability to transfer expertise across locations. They face challenges such as understanding the fundamental cultural, legal, and economic differences and adapting practices accordingly. There are also some practices that companies could benefit from replicating. For example, researchers contend that giving newcomers an orientation, arriving at pay decisions using systematic analyses, and using salary surveys are among the best practices that may be standardized across operations.[7] In this section, we discuss individual HR practices and important adaptations that often take place when operating globally.

Recruitment and Selection

Operating overseas necessitates hiring employees in diverse national contexts. A key decision that needs to be made is to determine the proper mix of parent country nationals, host-country nationals, and third-country nationals to be employed in a specific overseas operation.

The degree to which the local labor market meets the multinational's needs will vary by industry and geography, and there are costs and benefits associated with different mixes.

Multinational firms often find that they have to compete with other multinational and local firms for the best talent. A well-known multinational company may have an advantage in recruiting local employees, but it also needs to provide a work environment and resources that are competitive to attract talent. As IBM's loss of talent to local firms such as Infosys in India shows, companies should not assume that being well known globally will be sufficient for recruiting the best talent. Alternatively, a firm well known in its country of origin may have little name recognition in the subsidiary location, which may limit the ability to attract talent. Sometimes, the country of origin may serve as a barrier to recruitment. For example, some Indian multinationals operating in industrialized country contexts report difficulties attracting managerial employees and having to rely on sending expatriates instead of localizing their management team due to negative perceptions of Indian firms as employers and concerns regarding some corporate policies being a poor fit to the local environments.[8] Organizations will need to invest in developing their brand as an employer and building a good reputation in the markets in which they operate.

Finding the necessary talent is also made difficult in markets in which demand for skilled talent exceeds local availability. Organizations may need to provide in-house training to employees to make them ready for employment. At the same time, providing training introduces the problem of poaching by other organizations.[9]

Understanding how local employees expect to find job openings and their expectations for fair compensation will increase the competitiveness of the firm. For example, when educational technology company Blackboard tried to hire employees in the Netherlands, it was surprised by the low response rate its job posting generated, only to realize that in that market and for that job category, hiring was done through staffing agencies—a recruiting approach it hadn't used.[10]

Motivating, Rewarding, and Managing Expatriates

LO 15.4 Summarize the forces affecting adjustment of expatriates to their overseas assignments and identify ways in which organizations can prepare expatriates for successful assignments.

©iStock.com/Tramino

In Europe, Asia, the Middle East, and South America, a company car is often a critical recruitment and retention tool and is intended to meet business and status needs. Determining who is eligible, whether to provide the car or a car allowance, and what make and model to allocate to different job levels requires careful consideration of each local market.[11]

Multinational companies often differentiate their reward systems and benefits around the world to fit the national context. To begin with, businesses need to be aware of differences in legal requirements that affect compensation practices. In many parts of the world, companies are mandated to provide 13th- or 14th-month bonuses (e.g., Brazil, Costa Rica, and Ecuador). In other countries, providing these bonuses is customary (e.g., Austria and Japan). Typically, these amount to 1/12 of the employee's pay. Different countries will have different requirements relating to who is eligible for 13th- or 14th-month bonuses, and payment schedules vary.[12]

Having extrinsic rewards that fit a given context is essential for attracting and retaining talent. In addition to cultural differences, workforce demographics may necessitate regional adaptation. For example, some countries have aging populations: Japan and Germany have populations with a median age of 47, whereas India, Ecuador, and South Africa have a median age of 27.[13] Such differences will inevitably affect benefits packages and workplace conditions employees find desirable.

Spotlight on Legal Issues
THE LEGAL SIDE OF WORKING INTERNATIONALLY

When managing an international workforce, legal compliance is complicated due to the need to reconcile multiple legal frameworks. Here are a few important considerations:[14]

- When moving an employee overseas either as an expatriate or in short-term operations, the employee will likely need to acquire a work permit or visa.

- When an employee is staying in a different country for 6 months or more, the stay may trigger tax implications for the employer. This means that monitoring short-term assignments is important.

- EEOC laws cover all employees of a U.S. employer working in the United States. For example, a Chinese citizen working in a U.S. firm is covered by EEOC laws. Host-country employees of U.S. firms are not subject to EEOC laws (e.g., Japanese employees of a U.S.-based multinational in Japan are not covered), but a U.S. citizen expatriate sent to work in the Japanese operations of a U.S.-based multinational is covered.

- When two laws clash, companies are required to follow the laws of the countries they operate in, even if this means violating the U.S. law.

Educating employees on local laws is important to protect employees. Toyota found this out the hard way: An American executive moving to Japan was arrested and imprisoned for 20 days on suspicion of illegally importing a prescription painkiller.

Employee Separations

Organizations that operate in multiple countries need to be aware of differences in how separations are handled, given the differences in labor law. For example, in Europe, employment is regarded as a fundamental right, and taking away that right may not be done in an arbitrary fashion. Given the high levels of unionization and works councils (similar to unions) in Europe, organizations need to work with labor representatives in setting up procedures for terminating employees. Approaching the termination process systematically and respectfully, creating strong employment contracts, and specifying how performance and absenteeism are to be handled are essential for success.[15]

Handling of Personal Data

European Union countries have implemented General Data Protection Regulation (GDPR), which overhauls how businesses store, safeguard, and use personal data. This law gives more power to individuals and has clear implications for human resource functions that routinely retain, access, and use data about current and former employees as well as job applicants. For example, according to the law, companies need to have consent to store unsuccessful job candidates' details. If they fail to secure consent, companies must remove the data from their records. Employees have the right to access their own personal data with a required maximum turnaround time of 1 month. Companies may be required to designate a data-protection officer depending on the scope of data they handle. Faced with steep penalties for failures in compliance, companies need to make structural changes in collecting, storing, and using employee data.[16]

Management of Expatriates

When doing business internationally, a critically important HR issue relates to the management of expatriates. An **expatriate** (or expat) is a person who is living and working in a different country than their country of origin. Expatriate assignments typically describe a move overseas that is longer than 6 months. In multinational enterprises, expatriates are **organizationally assigned**, or sent by the organization for a predetermined time to work in an overseas operation. Alternatively, a **self-initiated expatriate** is a skilled professional who moves to a different country for a specific period of time with the intention of gaining overseas work experience. Although much can be learned from self-initiated expatriates, this chapter focuses on organizationally assigned expatriates.

Expatriate
A person who is living and working in a different country than their country of origin

Organizationally assigned expatriate
When an expat is sent by the organization for a predetermined time to work in an overseas operation

Self-initiated expatriate
A skilled professional who moves to a different country for a specific period of time with the intention of gaining overseas work experience

Benefits and Downsides of Using Expatriates

Expatriate assignments provide a variety of benefits to organizations and individuals. By moving talented employees overseas, companies aim to meet specific business needs and close skill gaps. Moving employees overseas ensures that they gain skills in global management. Completing an overseas assignment successfully may be a boon to the career of the expatriate, helping them develop unique skills and achieve visibility. Expatriates can facilitate direct knowledge sharing across units and indirect knowledge sharing by linking home- and host-country operations.[18]

At the same time, there are potential downsides to the use of expatriates. First, from the organization's perspective, overreliance on expatriates or using expatriates for the wrong types of

©iStock.com/Pere_Rubi

Employees in sales and marketing at Adidas may apply for the company's Talent Carousel program, allowing them to work in a different country for 2 years, which may be followed by another round of overseas assignment or returning home. The company is planning to open this talent development program to other departments.[17]

positions may backfire. The use of expatriates is a way of transferring home-country practices overseas, and using expatriates may make it difficult to use regional knowledge. In other words, the organization should carefully consider whether a local employee is not in fact a better candidate for a given position. Second, expatriate assignments run the risk of failure and necessitate careful planning. Moving to a different country and taking on a new role is stressful, and poor adjustment results in low job satisfaction, low effectiveness, and premature return from the assignment.[19] Finally, expatriate assignments are costly: It is estimated that each international posting may cost as much as twice the salary of the employee, and even higher in the case of failed assignments.[20]

Expatriate Adjustment

Cultural adjustment
Adjusting to the new culture one is now living in, including factors such as transportation, entertainment, health system, education, and general living conditions

Expatriate adjustment refers to the degree of comfort and lack of stress associated with being an expatriate. Research shows that three forms of adjustment matter for expatriates. **Cultural adjustment** refers to adjusting to the new culture one is now living in, including factors such as transportation, entertainment, health system, education, and general living conditions. **Work adjustment** involves feeling comfortable at work and with one's new tasks. **Interactional adjustment** is the comfort felt with interacting with local individuals inside or outside work. Being successful as an expatriate relies not only on feeling comfortable at work but also on achieving comfort with interpersonal interactions and with general living conditions. Although work adjustment has the strongest effect on expatriate job satisfaction, simply mastering one's job will not be sufficient for a successful expatriate assignment. Key factors that affect the pace of adjustment and the degree of adjustment success are shown in Figure 15.1.[21]

Work adjustment
Feeling comfortable at work and with one's new tasks

Spouse Adjustment

Interactional adjustment
The comfort felt with interacting with local individuals inside or outside work

Research shows that the biggest influence over an expatriate's cultural adjustment is the adjustment of the spouse. When spouses have difficulty adjusting to the culture, the risk of a premature return increases. One's family situation and relationships are key reasons mentioned for refusing to accept an expatriate assignment in the first place.[22] Before a move as a family, it is important to be on the same page and discuss how the spouse will spend time, identify sources of social support, inquire into work and social activities for the spouse, and realistically examine the impact of the move for the whole family. If the expatriate is moving alone, then the risk is one of social isolation and loneliness.[23] Many companies have programs that facilitate spouses' adjustment. For example, some companies provide support to spouses in getting a job in the local market as part of their relocation packages. This policy is valuable due to the rise in the number of dual-career couples. When the

■ **FIGURE 15.1**   Factors Affecting Expatriate Adjustment

spouse is working in the same company, offering jobs for both may be another strategy in providing a type of support that will make a big difference in the adjustment of the expatriate.[24]

Language Ability

Not speaking the local language affects one's ability to adjust to the culture and social interactions. Language not only facilitates interpersonal communication but also affects power and status relationships. For example, research has shown that when multinational companies embrace a language as the official language of the company, those employees who speak that language fluently gain power and status over others who do not speak it well.[25]

 ## Manager's Toolbox
BEING EFFECTIVE IN GLOBAL TEAMS

In global organizations, there is often a need to work across borders. For example, a software development team may include employees from France, Russia, India, and the United States. Here are some tips on how to be more effective in these teams:[26]

1. **Do not confuse language fluency with job effectiveness.** It is likely that the team will include members with varying fluency in the language in which the team communicates. It is important for the team leader to understand that those who are the most articulate are not necessarily the best performers, and valuing their contributions more may affect team morale and sense of fairness.

2. **Be inclusive.** The team leader may create an inclusive climate by deliberately asking questions to the more silent members, giving members time to articulate their thoughts, and asking open-ended questions.

3. **Providing cultural training.** Providing training on how culture affects assumptions and attributions may facilitate more effective communication with those from different cultural backgrounds.

4. **Invest in relationship development.** When working with those from a different cultural upbringing, mistakes and misunderstandings are bound to happen. Forgiveness is easier to achieve if you have an existing relationship. Relating to your team members and bonding with them is not a waste of time: It is an investment that will pay off throughout the life of the project and beyond.

Further, host-country employees often try to make sense of expatriates' behavior, attempting to understand how well intentioned they are toward the local employees and how much respect they have toward their culture. One qualitative study in China found that when expatriates showed a willingness to learn the local language, local employees expressed more acceptance toward them. Such effort on the expatriates' part was interpreted as a sign of goodwill. Unfortunately, simple good intentions were not sufficient to build relationships over time. Trying but failing to speak the local language resulted in overreliance on a few people to interpret the work environment and difficulties getting work done and building relationships. Not showing any interest resulted in social isolation and being segregated from the host-country nationals.[27]

A survey of 13,000 people in 188 countries in 2017 ranked Bahrain as the best destination for expatriates. The country is known for being open and friendly to expatriates, and the expatriate population actually outnumbers the local population, creating a diverse and welcoming culture.[29]

Cultural Distance

The cultural distance between one's own country of origin and the destination has a negative effect on adjusting to a new culture.[28] At the same time, cultural similarity may be a double-edged sword. A U.S. expatriate moving to South Korea will certainly encounter unfamiliar situations. At the same time, some potential expatriates will opt out of this move due to expectations of such difficulties, which means that those interested in moving will be the ones who are motivated to invest time and effort in preparing for the move. In contrast, a U.S. expatriate moving to Australia may assume that given the similarity in language, the move will be free of cultural challenges. However, despite speaking the same language, there are clear and important cultural differences between the two countries, as well as different leadership styles and ways of doing business, which may lead to misunderstandings and frustrations.

Expatriate Personality

The expatriate's social and relational skills affect all three forms of adjustment. Expatriates need to be able to work with people who are different from themselves and influence them in ways that will facilitate their own adjustment, get accepted, and get things done. This is no small feat and requires exceptional relational skills. Further, the expat's self-confidence matters a great deal for successful adjustment.[30] Researchers also noted that learning-oriented expatriates who view their assignment as a challenge to master and expatriates who are sociable are more likely to seek support from locals, which should help them build a network of supportive relationships.[31]

Job Characteristics

Research shows that the two job-related factors that matter the most to expatriate adjustment are role clarity and role discretion. There needs to be crystal-clear communication between management and the expatriate with respect to expectations, and expatriates should be given autonomy to perform their jobs effectively.[32]

Support

For successful adjustment of expatriates to their work, two sources of organizational support seem critical: support from the host-country employees and support from the organization itself. Support of local coworkers matters a great deal. Local employees are in a position to interact with the expatriate every day, share information, and give tips about how to get things done, facilitating all three forms of adjustment. To prevent the new expatriate from being classified as an outsider, organizations sometimes resort to sending an expatriate with ties to the local context (such as sending an employee who identifies as ethnic Chinese to their operations in China). However, this practice is not always success-ful and actually may sometimes create hostility, envy, or resentment among local employ-ees.[33] Expatriates themselves also play a role in how much support they receive from local employees. Expatriates who are motivated to seek support from the "right" coworkers who are capable and motivated to help them are likely to establish support networks.[34]

Organizational support is also critical to expatriate adjustment. Expatriates who feel that the organization cares about them, values them, and is invested in them report higher levels of adjustment in their assignments.[35] Organizations can also support expatriates by providing logistical support. This involves taking care of mundane but important details of the move, such as identifying appropriate housing, finding schools for children moving with the expatriate, opening bank accounts, and other daily details that are bound to create stress for the expatriates.

Preparing Expatriates for Their Assignments

Organizations may do a great deal to facilitate expatriates' adjustment into their new locale in the predeparture stage. Preparation may facilitate quicker adjustment and prevent pre-mature departures. Organizations will need to ensure that they (a) select the right person, (b) prepare them for the role, and (c) provide ongoing support.

Selecting Expatriates

Historically, companies chose expatriates based on their specific job knowledge and skills. This approach was quickly revealed as misguided, as success in an expatriate assignment takes much more than being good at one's job. Just because someone is good at market-ing products in the United States is no guarantee that they will be equally good at doing so in Thailand. Experts recommend that the selection process also consider personality and social skills. Relational skills, or the ability to build effective relationships with key stakeholders, will be important. A **global mindset** is also important: Individuals who are open to learning about different cultures, have a sense of adventure, are comfort-able dealing with ambiguity, and have a nonjudgmental attitude toward those from other cultures are more likely to be successful. Assessing global mind-set skills as part of the selection process could be helpful.[36]

Identifying candidates who are excited about serving as expatriates also matters. When few candidates exist for an expatriate position, offering financial incentives may be an option, but companies often feel that pointing to developmental benefits of an expatriate assignment works better. For example, the Mexican multinational CEMEX faced resistance to expatriate assignments in the past, with headquarter employees not wanting to work outside of Mexico. Over time, by communicating the benefits of an expatriate assignment for employees' careers, the company was able to create a pool of interested candidates.[37]

Cultural Training

An important barrier to effectiveness in a new location is lack of understanding of cultural differences. Expatriates may be frustrated because their normal ways of behaving at work may no longer be appropriate. The feeling of disorientation individuals experience when they enter a new culture is called **culture shock**. For example, an expatriate who is used to relating to people and building quick relationships with others may realize that the idea of

Global mindset
Refers to being open to learning about different cultures, having a sense of adventure, being comfortable dealing with ambiguity, and having a nonjudgmental attitude toward those from other cultures

Culture shock The feeling of disorientation individuals experience when they enter a new culture

In 2017, 11% of *Fortune* 500 companies had foreign-born CEOs, including Sundar Pichai, CEO of Google, pictured here. Research shows that people with international experience are more effective and creative problem solvers and are promoted faster, pointing to the benefits of expatriate experience for companies and individuals.[38]

small talk is foreign in cultures such as Germany or Japan. In these cultures, relationships develop over a long period of time through mutually lived experiences and trust. Discussions of weather or traffic, or other lighthearted conversation that does not communicate anything real about the person, will not be useful in building relationships.[39] Understanding these and other cultural differences may facilitate the adjustment process by helping expatriates be attuned to instances when they need to vary either their own behavior or interpretations of others' actions.

Companies vary in the amount of cultural training they provide, and there are examples of companies that do a thorough job with expatriate training. For example, Nike assigns expatriates and their families a cultural trainer who will stay in touch with them throughout the assignment and help them adjust to and decode the new culture.[40]

Relocation Assistance

The amount of assistance and the form of assistance provided will vary by the level of resources the company can afford, the specific location one is moving into, and the organizational level of the expatriate. For example, moving to a big city in China such as Hong Kong, Shanghai, or Beijing will require different resources compared to moving from a large city to a less developed inland city in China such as Chengdu or Wuhan. Moving to a remote location may mean that the expatriate will need to deal with lack of adequate medical care, difficulty identifying international schools for kids, and lack of housing that matches what the expatriate is used to. The more declines expatriates are expected to experience in their quality of life relative to their home country, the more generous the expatriate relocation assistance and pay packages will need to be. Using the services of a global relocation services provider may make this process easier and more professional.

Organizations often cap the amount they pay as relocation assistance. For example, only 42% of companies participating in a survey reported that they pay the entire cost of relocation. Companies are more likely to pay a lump-sum amount when expatriates are low-level employees, as opposed to covering the costs on an ongoing basis.[41] Working with a relocation company may help expatriates avoid numerous hassles they would not even expect to encounter during their initial move.

Compensation

Staffing overseas positions with expatriates is expensive. When determining pay packages, it is important to ensure that the expatriate does not suffer a serious financial penalty as a result of accepting the assignment. Additionally, benefits such as travel insurance; home, auto, and property insurance; and health insurance must be provided. Expatriate compensation packages have become subject to increased scrutiny over the years, and many organizations have reduced the types of benefits and allowances they provide. For example, in the past, Ford used to allow expatriates to sell their homes to the company at an assessed value. Ford abandoned this policy following the 2008 recession. Although it still covers the full housing costs for expatriates, it does not provide support for the homes that are left behind.[42]

Companies make a choice regarding whether to make the home country or the host country pay the basis for expatriate pay. The approach chosen will depend on where the assignment is located. For example, assignments taking place in Hong Kong and Singapore are often on a "local-plus" package, given the high salaries, high quality of life, and high cost of living of these locations. The salary is localized, with a few expatriate benefits added to it such as housing and education allowances.[43]

When determining the pay and benefits packages, one size may not fit all, and it is important to consider the issues that are relevant for the expatriate and the family. For one family, educational opportunities for children may be the most important, whereas for another, finding employment for the spouse may be critical. Providing a compensation package that is consistent and fair while also considering the unique needs of each expatriate may increase the success of the assignment. For this purpose, one option is to use a **coreflex plan**, which provides some services (such as paying for movers and travel expenses) to all expatriates, with the remainder of benefits personalized to the unique situation of the expatriate (such as trips to look for a new house or assistance in identifying private schools). According to one estimate, 9% of companies currently have such plans in place, but these plans are expected to become more popular as companies become more cost conscious.[44]

Risk Management

Organizations need to ensure the safety and security of their employees when sending them overseas. The world is increasingly unpredictable, and political turmoil, health risks (remote location, unsanitary conditions), individual high crime rates (murder, theft, break-ins), organized crime (terrorism, gang activities, kidnappings), and natural risks (earthquakes, extreme weather) pose serious threats and uncertainty to companies operating in some regions. Certain areas may pose a threat to expatriates in particular, such as the increasing frequency of kidnappings of expatriates in oil-producing Nigeria.[45] In Latin America and Eastern Europe, someone who is dressed nicely may be subject to an "express kidnapping" in which they are forced to walk to an ATM and withdraw cash.[46] More familiar catastrophes also could occur while the employee is traveling: What happens if the expatriate has a heart attack on the plane?

Organizations are responsible for ensuring the safety of all employees, and securing the services of professional security consultants may be done in some locations. It may be impossible for a company doing overseas business to eliminate all risks, as many of these are inherent in doing business everywhere and are often unpredictable, but these risks must be managed. Companies should decide whether expatriates need to be sent to a particular location or whether employing local employees is possible. Regardless of whether expatriates or locals are employed, the company will need to take steps to keep employees safe. In some locations, this may involve having work performed in a barricaded compound or hiring bodyguards or providing bulletproof cars. A decision must be made regarding whether families are allowed to accompany the expatriate. Emergency evacuation procedures and protocols should be established. Finally, it is important to explain all the risks involved to prospective employees before they are sent, and proper training should be provided if they choose to accept the assignment.[47]

Coreflex plan
A plan that provides some services (such as paying for movers and travel expenses) to all expatriates, with the remainder of benefits personalized to the unique situation of the expatriate

Special Considerations Relating to Women and LGBTQ Employees as Expatriates

Women constitute 20% of the expatriate population. These numbers depend on location (higher in Asia, lower in Europe and Africa) and industry (higher in consumer goods, lower in energy), but women as a group experience particular challenges as expatriates.[48] Stereotypes about women's unwillingness to serve as expatriates and potential inability to operate in other cultures have been debunked. At the same time, organizational decision makers' worries about sending women as expatriates have been identified as a reason for the lower representation of women among expatriates.[49] Still, in cultures where sexism has been institutionalized, female expatriates report greater problems such as being excluded from social activities, being insulted, and experiencing physical violence.[50]

Research shows that organizational support and absence of family problems serve as buffers for female expatriates dealing with local employees' prejudices.[51] Despite challenges in some locations, organizations are advised against excluding female employees from expatriate opportunities. Instead, organizations may offer training to potential expatriates as well as work to introduce zero-tolerance policies in their subsidiaries regarding discrimination and harassment. By sending the signal that everyone is considered equally for expatriate positions and supported throughout the process, organizations benefit from the talent and skills of all their employees.

Similar concerns exist for lesbian, gay, bisexual, transgender, and queer/questioning (LGBTQ) employees. Research suggests that many LGBTQ employees are highly motivated to accept expatriate positions and have ways of facilitating their own adjustment such as via connections to the local LGBTQ community.[52] At the same time, serious concerns exist. More than 70 countries criminalize homosexuality, and 13 view it as punishable by death.[53] LGBTQ employees may also experience hurdles not experienced by other expatriates, such as difficulty obtaining visas for their spouses, lack of legal protection and presence of institutionalized harassment, and possibilities for social exclusion. Obtaining current information regarding the legal and social climate in the target location is important. The organization should educate prospective expatriates regarding what to expect, provide resources that are inclusive in language and content (such as spousal-support policies inclusive of same-sex couples and their children), and provide information and support throughout the assignment.[54]

Repatriation

In many cases, the conclusion of the expatriate assignment means repatriation, or relocating the expatriate to their country of origin. The repatriation process presents challenges. Expatriates are valuable to their companies given the investments the company made in their career development. However, many companies have difficulty retaining expatriates. According to one estimate, 38% of expatriates leave their company within 1 year of their return.[55]

Sometimes, repatriation is a challenge because expatriates may not be interested in going back. This may be due to financial reasons: An employee who is relocated from India to the United Kingdom will likely have had their salary adjusted to the higher-cost location, which means that they will experience a significant pay cut when they return to India. Further, expatriates may not have a desirable job waiting for them when they return home. In most cases, the company will have to find a new job for them, as their old job would have already been filled by someone else, and they may have outgrown their former job. Research has shown that perceptions of underemployment in the job they return to are a precursor to turnover intentions among expatriates.[56] Upon return, expatriates may also experience a reverse culture shock. These expatriates may find that they have changed during the assignment and that their home country and company have also changed during their absence, resulting in the feeling that their country of origin does not feel like home anymore.

Unfortunately, despite the cost of an expatriate assignment to a company, organizations do not always approach repatriation of expatriates in a systematic way and often do not know what to do with expatriates once they return. For example, a study by Ernst & Young suggested that 47% of responding companies reported doing little to help expatriates reintegrate into the company.[57] It is not surprising that when organizations are unable to absorb the additional experience and skills employees develop during an international assignment, the employees are likely to leave.

Alternatives to Long-Term Relocation Assignments

LO 15.5   Identify alternatives to long-term relocation assignments.

Organizations are increasingly designing short-term assignments to contain costs and reduce the disruptive effects of long-term stays on employees and their families. Instead of sending an employee as an expatriate for 3 years, the company may choose to send them for 3 months, extending the stay as needed or sending the employee multiple times. Extended business travel may be a useful way to meet short-term staffing needs. For example, tax season in Germany is in September, whereas it is in April in the United States, so KPMG brings in tax professionals from Germany to the United States to meet the high seasonal demand. eBay sends U.S.-based employees to Europe to cover for employees on maternity leave. Walmart has Action Learning Groups in which teams are sent to a region to solve specific business problems. It also has short-term internship programs of 12 weeks in different countries to ensure that best practices are shared.[58]

Short-term assignments usually do not have much of the organizational support involved for expatriates: Typically, there is no adjustment in pay or relocation allowances, and the company's investment may be limited to travel expenses for the expatriate to and from the location. Short-term assignments are also less burdensome for employees. In particular, employees with families may benefit from such assignments given the difficulty of moving an entire family overseas for several years. In short-term assignments, the employee's permanent job will usually not be given away, so repatriation will not be as challenging. The employee will typically retain their regular reporting relationships but most likely will also report to a local manager as well. As long as such arrangements meet business needs, there may be advantages for businesses (low cost) and employees (low risk while also carrying developmental benefits).[59]

Cross-border commuters represent another alternative to expatriate assignments. Employees may work in a different country during the week, returning home on weekends. These arrangements are popular in Europe. For example, it is not unusual for an employee to live in Italy and work in Switzerland. Such arrangements are often outside of formal mobility programs, but they still must be monitored. The company needs to comply with tax-withholding requirements in multiple countries, ensure that the employee has

Spotlight on Data and Analytics

TRACKING EXPATRIATES AROUND THE WORLD

A volcano is erupting in Bali. Do you know where your employees are? This question may not have an easy answer for global firms that operate in multiple countries and those that have expatriates, frequent business travelers, and "global nomads" who do not even have a permanent place of assignment.

In addition to knowing where everyone is physically, companies need to ensure that their expatriate experience is managed smoothly. This means making sure that every paycheck is correct, pre-assignment experiences and requirements are checked off, visas are valid, and medical benefits are up to date.

Each expatriate assignment generates valuable data that companies can use to continuously improve the experience and manage the repatriation process. Expatriate satisfaction surveys, turnover data, and performance data may be analyzed to gain clues as to which systematic problems exist in each country of operations.

Tracking such data may be handled via Excel or other in-house products. For companies that employ hundreds of expatriates, investing in tracking technology is another option. Regardless of the method used, integrating data generated from expatriates with the remainder of Human Resource Information Systems (HRIS) will provide benefits by making sense of how the company is managing the expatriate experience and what keeps expatriates committed to the company.[60]

the appropriate work permit, and fulfill data privacy and legal requirements.[61] Companies often find that these programs are expensive, given the need to pay for a hotel or a serviced apartment and to pay for travel during peak travel periods.[62]

In conclusion, increasing globalization of businesses introduces novel challenges for management of human resources. Managing a workforce that transcends local borders and managing employees who are mobile across borders are only two common challenges and ways in which HR can add value to businesses.

CHAPTER SUMMARY

HR faces many challenges when business goes global. One challenge is to determine the proper balance of global integration and local differentiation. There are advantages to standardizing HR practices, but local laws, differences in attitudes toward unions, national culture, and the reason the company chose to internationalize will influence how much standardization is appropriate. When operating in different countries, recruitment and selection, separations, compensation, and treatment of employees must consider local norms. An important HR challenge is to manage mobility of employees, either through short-term or longer-term expatriate assignments. There are both benefits and disadvantages to hiring expatriates. HR can add value by recognizing various kinds of adjustments expatriates and their families must make and by providing preparation and cultural training. Finally, organizations can be creative in devising alternatives to long-term relocation assignments.

KEY TERMS

international companies   356
multinational companies   357
transnational companies   357
offshoring   357
outsourcing   357
global integration   357

local differentiation   357
expatriate   363
organizationally assigned
    expatriate   363
self-initiated expatriate   363
cultural adjustment   364

work adjustment   364
interactional adjustment   364
global mindset   367
culture shock   367
coreflex plan   369

$SAGE edge™

Get the tools you need to sharpen your study skills. SAGE edge offers a robust online environment featuring an impressive array of free tools and resources.

Access practice quizzes, eFlashcards, video, and multimedia at **edge.sagepub.com/bauerbrief**

HR REASONING AND DECISION-MAKING EXERCISES

EXERCISE 15.1: DEVELOPING A GLOBAL MINDSET

Your company recently started marketing its products in different overseas markets, including China and France. Realizing that international expansion will drive the future of business, your CEO wants to make sure that managers over a certain organizational level all have "a global mindset." One idea the CEO has is to require all managers above a certain level to have at least 6 months of overseas experience to qualify for a promotion.

You are not really sure whether this is the right strategy. You worry that this will lead some high-potential individuals to quit or to feel resentment and a sense of unfairness. You agree that a global mindset is important to the future of business, but is requiring international experience for all managers the right way to go about ensuring it?

What would you advise your CEO that the company do? Develop a concrete proposal about how to develop a global mindset in the company and provide justification for your plan. Be sure to include a discussion of the resource requirements of your plan.

EXERCISE 15.2: ASSESSING THE EFFECTIVENESS OF EXPAT MANAGEMENT

You are the HR director of Moore Markets, a grocery retailer that is in the process of overseas expansion. The company is U.S. based and just opened up several stores and branch offices in Mexico, Canada, China, and Germany. You currently have more than 50 expatriates working in these countries. These employees have been deployed as needed, working on assignments that will last anywhere between 1 and 3 years. Anecdotally, you know that a few expatriates who repatriated from these assignments will quit within 6 months. You also know that several expatriates cut their assignments short and asked to return early. Expatriates also voiced concerns that local employees often compare their pay and benefits with what they perceive as generous expatriate packages, expressing resentment. You realize that you are not really tracking the return on investment of expatriates. You do not really know whether your company is doing a good job managing expatriates and whether the company is having systematic problems with them.

Questions

1. How would you go about measuring the effectiveness of your expatriate program? What type of information would you collect, and how? Develop a plan to collect the information you need.
2. Would you assess whether you are sending the right employees for these assignments? Describe what steps you would follow.
3. Effectiveness of expatriates relies on their ability to cooperate with local employees, and perceived unfairness and resentment on the part of locals could hamper expatriate effectiveness. What can you do to prevent such resentment?

ETHICAL MATTERS EXERCISE: MANAGING ETHICS GLOBALLY IN MULTINATIONALS

What do Rolls-Royce, Walmart, Royal Dutch Shell, and SAP have in common? These companies and others have faced investigations of corruption and bribing government officials to facilitate winning government contracts, getting permits, or obtaining licenses. A challenge all multinationals face is to uphold global ethical standards in diverse regions, including locations where anticorruption laws are loosely enforced or nonexistent and bribing government officials is considered a normal way of doing business. How can global businesses ensure that they uphold global principles of ethics in their operations around the world while conducting business effectively?

Global organizations will benefit from enforcing a culture of ethics and integrity throughout their operations. This seems like common sense, given that allowing bribery and corruption in some parts of their operations threatens the culture and reputation of the entire operation. It is also important to remember that even though local businesses may in fact be using bribes to speed the process of approvals or facilitate their operations, multinationals are often held to a different and higher standard in other countries, making their ethics violations all the more damaging. A few steps multinationals can take and HR can facilitate are as follows:

Commit to a culture of integrity. Multinationals should have top management who value and embrace ethics in global operations. This means a strong commitment for doing the right thing, dealing with unethical actions quickly, and holding people accountable.

Eliminate undue performance pressures. Often, unethical actions are a symptom of pressures for short-term results. When headquarters evaluate performance of subsidiaries using short-term results such as how quickly a store was opened, pressure increases on local employees to get things done at all costs. It also signals to third parties that the company is in a hurry, giving them leverage to pressure the company.

Provide training and policies. It is important to provide training not only about defining acceptable and unacceptable behaviors but also teaching employees what to do when confronted with questionable requests. Monitoring compliance via committees and audits can also help.

Eliminate a culture of silence. It is important to encourage people to speak up about questionable ethical behaviors. Giving employees anonymous ways of reporting unethical behaviors and ensuring that reports are followed by action will help create a culture of ethics.[63]

Questions

1. As an HR professional, suppose you are assigned to arrange for your company's international employees to receive ethics training to define acceptable and unacceptable behaviors and to know what to do when confronted with questionable requests. How would you develop a set of training objectives? Would you hire an outside training vendor, and if so, how would you select the vendor?

2. Find an example in the news or in the HR literature of a global company that was accused of corruption. How was the case resolved? What did the individuals involved do right, and what could they have done better?

Appendix A

Cases

CHAPTER 1
Human Resource Management

The Case of Chobani's Evolving HR Culture

Hamdi Ulukaya, founder and CEO of Chobani, LLC, left his family dairy business in Turkey to learn English in the United States. Soon after he arrived, he noticed that the strained yogurt popular in Greece and Turkey, known for its rich flavor and high levels of protein, was not widely available in U.S. grocery stores. In 2005, that realization and Ulukaya's dairy background led him to take the opportunity to purchase a 100-year-old dairy plant in central New York state. He started out small. As he recalls, "I hired five people from the 55 [applicants], and those five are still with me." It took 2 years of work to perfect the yogurt recipe; the company's first order didn't ship until 2007. However, Chobani caught on quickly, with annual sales of $1 billion in 2012. That same year, Chobani opened its second plant. In 2019, Chobani is the best-selling Greek yogurt in the United States, employs over 2,000 people, and boasts the world's largest yogurt plant at its state-of-the art, million-square-foot location in Twin Falls, Idaho.

However, the company has experienced its share of highs and lows. In 2013, Ulukaya was named the Ernst & Young World Entrepreneur of the Year, but Chobani was plagued with a recall of some of the yogurt produced in its new plant. Chobani recovered and in 2015 had sales of $1.6 billion. Again, in 2016, Chobani and its founder were

making headlines when Ulukaya surprised 2,000 full-time Chobani employees with shares worth 10% of the company, redeemable when Chobani is sold or goes public. Ulukaya tied the number of shares to the length of time an employee had been with Chobani so that the five original employees received the greatest number of shares. These shares come directly from Ulukaya, as he was the sole owner of the 100% independent company—a status that enabled him to create what he calls a "people-centered company." He said in a memo to employees that the shares were not just a gift. They were "a mutual promise to work together with a shared purpose and responsibility." In 2017, Chobani implemented a new paid parental leave policy offering 100% paid parental leave for 6 weeks for all full-time employees.

Along the way, Chobani's HRM system needed to evolve in response to the company's astronomical growth. How did Chobani's 30 full-time HR professionals help manage the 3,000 full- and part-time employees in Australia and the United States who make over 2.2 million cases of yogurt each week? Craig Gomez, Chobani's former chief people officer, describes how his experience in HR at PepsiCo, GE, and Cisco helped him strike a balance between where Chobani's HR had grown organically and where it needed to go. Gomez's strategy was to find solutions to existing organizational "pain points." He and his HR colleagues realized that they couldn't do everything all at once. "We have picked items that add tremendous value and do not unduly burden the client with administrative headaches," Gomez says. He further notes, "I think, with all due respect to all of my peers in HR, a lot of times HR comes at an organization with a set playbook and they just lead with a set list of things they think that every organization should have instead of really listening to the client and really matching up what they deliver with what the specific client's points of pain are."

When it comes to insights, Chobani's HR team has had a few. For example, they developed orientation programs that new employees can view on a laptop. They also realized that even though they couldn't hire every person who applied to work at Chobani, it is important to treat applicants with respect. Gomez explained, "We want to bring the same level of sensitivity to job applicants as we do

to consumers." As you will see in this textbook, these are HR insights that are backed up by research studies on the topics. As for Chobani, it is clear that HR is a partner in helping the business grow and generate solutions.

An important point in this case is the fact that organizations evolve. You will see examples throughout this book of small start-up companies, governmental agencies, and not-for-profit organizations as well as small, medium, and large organizations, including *Fortune* 500 companies. If you examine the histories of organizations, you can begin to see a pattern where today's large corporations often began as small start-ups employing just a handful of individuals. The HRM needs of start-up organizations certainly differ from those of large *Fortune* 500 companies, but the principles of HRM remain the same. Beginning with solid, tested HRM practices and ethical guidelines makes it much easier for organizations to stay effective as they grow.

Case Discussion Questions

1. Chobani has grown a great deal since its founding in 2005. How do you think growth has influenced its HR practices beyond what is mentioned in this case? Please share specific insights.

2. Craig Gomez, Chobani's former chief people officer, makes a strong case for HR being in the business of solving problems for the organization. Do you agree with this position? Why or why not?

3. Why do you think that Chobani's founder, Hamdi Ulukaya, gave away 10% of his

company to his current full-time employees? Do you think this is a wise idea or a foolish one? Why?

4. Do you consider Chobani's policy of offering 6 weeks of paid parental leave to all full-time employees a waste of money or a wise investment? Why? Be prepared to defend your response.

Click to learn more . . .

View Hamdi Ulukaya's story at https://youtu.be/578FODRPRa0

Sources: Case partially based on information in Eat This, Not That! (2018). 16 things you don't know about Chobani. https://www.eatthis.com/chobani/; Durisin, M. (2013). Chobani CEO: Our success has nothing to do with yogurt. *Business Insider.* http://www.businessinsider.com/the-success-story-of-chobani-yogurt-2013-5; Hager, H. (2012). HR shared services: It's not all Greek to Chobani. http://www.humanresourcesiq.com/hr-shared-services/articles/hr-shared-services-it-s-not-all-greek-to-chobani; *Industry News.* (2013). Chobani founder named world entrepreneur 2013. https://www.qsrmagazine.com/news/chobani-founder-named-world-entrepreneur-2013; McGregor, J. (2016). Chobani's CEO is giving up to 10 percent of his company to employees. *Washington Post.* https://www.washingtonpost.com/news/on-leadership/wp/2016/04/27/chobanis-ceo-is-giving-up-to-10-percent-of-his-company-to-employees/; Strom, S. (2016). At Chobani, now it's not just the yogurt that's rich. *New York Times.* http://www.nytimes.com/2016/04/27/business/a-windfall-for-chobani-employees-stakes-in-the-company.html?_r=0; Weisul, K. (2012). 6 hiring secrets from Chobani HR. *Inc.com.* http://www.inc.com/kimberly-weisul/hiring-secrets-chobani-hamdi-ulukaya-craig-gomez.html; Chobani. (2018). About Chobani. https://www.chobani.com/about

CHAPTER 2
Strategic HRM, Data-Driven Decision Making, and HR Analytics

The Case of Strategy and HR Analytics at Chevron

Chevron is a large energy company based in San Ramon, California. In 2014, the company launched a centralized human resource analytics team, which it refers to as a talent analytics team. *Human resource (HR) analytics* goes by different terms, such as people analytics, workforce analytics, human capital analytics, and talent analytics; it refers to the process of collecting, analyzing, and reporting people-related data for the purpose of improving decision making, achieving strategic objectives, and sustaining a competitive advantage.

From the beginning, Chevron's analytics team made it clear that its mission is to "support Chevron's business strategies with better, faster workforce decisions informed by data." To that end, R. J. Milnor, the former head of talent analytics for Chevron, stated that "[HR] analytics is really about informing and supporting business strategy, and we do that through people data." In other words, the analytics team at Chevron understands the important role that people data can play in strategy realization. After all, people are valuable resources for companies, and making data-driven and evidence-based decisions provides companies such as Chevron with an opportunity to attract, motivate, and retain talented people with the right knowledge, skills, and abilities.

Over time, Chevron's HR analytics team has moved from running simple descriptive analytics, which represent a snapshot of the past, to more advanced predictive and prescriptive analytics, which provide a glimpse into the future. As such, managing human resources at Chevron is now more forward thinking and proactive, which allows for more strategic thinking and informed action.

As an overarching strategic objective, Chevron's HR analytics team has been tasked with improving revenue per employee. The team also consults with other units and departments, including company leadership, when it comes to major decisions such as reorganization and restructuring. With respect to workforce planning, the team built models to forecast future talent demand and supply 10 years in the future. These models identified key drivers of talent demand and supply for different geographic locations and provided estimates of future attrition (e.g., turnover) with 85% accuracy. Knowing the key drivers—or predictors—of attrition is very important when it comes to making decisions about how to retain talented people who can help the organization achieve its strategic objectives.

In just a few short years, Chevron's HR analytics team has transformed the way the organization leverages data. By centralizing the HR analytics function, the team created an HR hub that collects data, performs data analytics, and reports findings to HR specialty areas spread across the company. Of note, centralizing the analytics function increased the productivity of analysts by approximately 30% and substantially reduced redundant HR reporting within at least one business unit.

Chevron also established a community of practice with hundreds of members, which include HR specialists, business partners, and analysts. The community of practice encourages members to discuss topics related to data analytics and data-driven decision making during virtual meetings. In doing so, HR and non-HR workers have an opportunity to learn from one another and to share different data-modeling approaches, techniques, and programs. Ultimately, this has led to an increase in the number of projects pursued by HR analysts and a decrease in the amount of time it takes to complete such projects.

The HR analytics team at Chevron has fundamentally changed the company's approach to human resource management. Merely introducing an HR analytics function, however, is by no means a panacea. In fact, failing to align HR analytics with

HR and business strategy can hinder the likelihood of success. As such, an organization will be best served by using HR analytics to inform and support strategy, as Chevron has done. In other words, HR analytics should be embedded into the fabric of the organization.

Case Discussion Questions

1. How has Chevron used HR analytics to inform and support organizational strategy?

2. Chevron's HR analytics team used statistical models to predict employee turnover with a high degree of accuracy. Based on your own knowledge and experiences, what are some key drivers (i.e., predictors) of employee turnover?

3. What are some different ways in which an organization might leverage HR analytics to attract, motivate, and retain talented people?

4. Chevron has established an HR-specific analytics team. From the perspective of organizational effectiveness, what are some potential advantages of having data analytics integrated directly into the HR function as opposed to a company-wide analytics team that supports HR and other functional areas?

Click to learn more . . .

To learn more about HR analytics at Chevron, check out the following video: https://youtu.be/LbxGL2TXza0

Sources: Collins, L., Fineman, D. R., & Tsuchida, A. (2017, February 28). People analytics: Recalculating the route. https://www2.deloitte.com/insights/us/en/focus/human-capital-trends/2017/people-analytics-in-hr.html#endnote-sup-16; Lewis, G. (2017, March 30). 3 ways data shapes the talent strategy at Tesla, Chevron, and LinkedIn. https://business.linkedin.com/talent-solutions/blog/talent-analytics/2017/3-ways-data-shapes-the-talent-strategy-at-tesla-chevron-and-linkedin; McKeon, A. (2017). How some companies reap rewards of people analytics tools. http://searchhrsoftware.techtarget.com/feature/How-some-companies-reap-rewards-of-people-analytics-tools; Thibodeau, P. (2018, February 14). HR is failing to use people analytics tools, new report says. http://searchhrsoftware.techtarget.com/news/252435104/HR-is-failing-to-use-people-analytics-tools-new-report-says

---

CHAPTER 3

Data Management and Human Resource Information Systems

Shifting to a Data-Driven Organization With HRIS: The Case of Nissan

In 1999, the Japanese carmaker Nissan was in trouble. The company had not been profitable for 8 years, its margins were low, and it was estimated that the car company gave away $1,000 for every car it sold in the United States. In addition, plant capacity was much larger than demand, leading to high overhead costs. In the hopes of turning things around, French carmaker Renault invested $5.4 billion in Nissan for an equity stake in the company. After their strategic alliance governed by cross-sharing agreements was struck, Renault-Nissan became the fourth-largest car company in the world. But the alliance made sense only if Nissan could turn things around. It was asked to do just that.

One of the major ways that Nissan set out to turn things around was to transform HR to a "shared services model." This entailed a multitier HR service delivery system in which employees first had access to technology that allowed them to answer their own questions and to make most of their HR-related decisions on their own. If employees still needed help, then their question could be escalated to the next level of service, which included sending a ticket to a shared service desk. Finally, if the HR concern was not resolved at that level, it was escalated to HR experts. This change was transformational in allowing HR staff to shift from spending much of their time on administrative and transactional activities to spending more time on activities associated with being a strategic business partner.

Today, Renault, Nissan, and Mitsubishi are all part of a unique strategic alliance partnership. However, in 2012, Nissan was running multiple non–cloud-based HR systems across its multiple regions without a way to link them. For example, Nissan ran SuccessFactors and Oracle's PeopleSoft in North America but SAP HR packages in Europe and outdated software in Japan. Through pressure from Nissan's board to streamline the HR systems, Alfonso Díez David, Alliance General Manager of Global Digital Human Resources at Renault-Nissan-Mitsubishi, was tasked with integrating and unifying all of Nissan's HR systems to achieve global consistency. The transition was not without its challenges, but after successfully piloting the Workday, Inc., platform in Hong Kong and South Africa, Nissan rolled it out to North America and Japan in 2016. By 2017, both the French carmaker Renault (with nearly 125,000 employees in 128 countries) and

Nissan (with nearly 140,000 employees in more than 160 countries) had a global cloud-based HR software system.

Díez David explains that the rationale behind the major investment in time and money to move to a single global HR system was to allow Nissan to compare "apples to apples" when it came to employees and HR. Another major driver was the desire to leverage HR analytics to manage their talent globally. The hope was to save time for HR staff by offloading common administrative HR tasks and allowing them time to focus on high-value data analytics to help Nissan become more efficient and profitable.

Díez David recommends several things when rolling out a major HRIS project such as this one, including

- being user centric,
- recruiting system champions to answer questions and help with trainings locally,
- focusing on data quality upfront to avoid problems later on, and
- investing in the management of data privacy concerns.

Of course, the changes made with Nissan's HR system and their global HRIS rollout are not the only factors influencing Nissan's successful turnaround. However, this case remains a valuable reminder of how important data management and HRIS are as a foundation to strong organizations.

Case Discussion Questions

1. Nissan underwent a great deal of change in a short period of time. How do you think the employees who were asked to make these changes reacted along the way?

2. Díez David shared four recommendations for those considering a major HRIS project. Can you think of other recommendations that might make sense to help the process go smoothly?

3. What role do you think HRIS played in Nissan's turnaround story?

4. Do you think there are any downsides to having a global HRIS in place? If so, what could be done to help mitigate those problems in the design and implementation phases?

Sources: Byrne, N. (2010). Nissan North American transforms HR services. https://www.hrexchangenetwork.com/hr-shared-services/articles/nissan-north-america-transforms-hr-services; Campbell, P. (2017). Renault-Nissan alliance becomes world's largest carmaker. *Financial Times.* https://www.ft.com/content/fe682336-7365-11e7-aca6-c6bd07df1a3c; Carey, S. (2017). Renault follows in Nissan's tracks with global Workday rollout for HR. ComputerWorldUK. https://www.computerworlduk.com/cloud-computing/what-expect-from-aws-reinvent-2016-3648942/; Ghosn, C. (2002). Saving the business without losing the company. *Harvard Business Review.* https://hbr.org/2002/01/saving-the-business-without-losing-the-company; Ghosn, C., & Ries, P. (2004). *Shift: Inside Nissan's historic revival.* Crown Business; McLain, S., & Stoll, J. (2017). Carlos Ghosn steps down as Nissan CEO. *Wall Street Journal.* https://www.wsj.com/articles/carlos-ghosn-resigns-as-nissan-ceo-1487807319; Statista. (2017). Number of Nissan employees from FY 2009 to FY 2016. https://www.statista.com/statistics/370511/number-of-nissan-employees/; Statista. (2017). Number of Renault Group employees between 2012 and 2016. https://www.statista.com/statistics/387166/number-of-renault-group-employees/

CHAPTER 4
Diversity, Inclusion, and Equal Employment Laws

Diversity Challenges in the Tech Industry: The Case of Pinterest

The San Francisco–based visual social media firm Pinterest is one of the first Silicon Valley companies that recognized the dismal state of diversity in the technology industry. In fact, a former Pinterest engineer, Tracy Chou, is credited with starting the movement toward more data-driven diversity management. The 2013 blog post Ms. Chou wrote, titled "Where Are the Numbers?" motivated tech giants such as Facebook and Google to reveal the number of women and minorities in their workforce, particularly in technology and leadership positions. Pinterest's own numbers were revealed in this management-authorized blog post, with the assumption that by releasing the figures and making a public commitment, its team of more than 700 employees would become more diverse.

Unfortunately, the results at the end of the first year of this experiment showed that it was business as usual. Similar to other companies, Pinterest was half White and 43% Asian. It had 42% women, but this was because of the inclusion of all business units in these calculations. Men dominated technology (79%), engineering (81%), and leadership positions (84%).

One year into its commitment, the numbers had barely moved, even though the company had instituted several initiatives: mentored female programming students; recruited at African American, Hispanic, and female engineering events; and invested in unconscious bias training. What had gone wrong? Even though recruiters brought in a more diverse pool of candidates, hiring managers continued to use the same selection criteria, including prioritizing hiring from a small set of Ivy League schools (that happen to have a less diverse body of graduates). In retrospect, even though top management wanted to diversify hiring, they had not made a business case to everyone in the company. Thinking in terms of diversity had not become a part of a widespread mentality; it had remained an HR initiative.

As part of an overhaul, the company entered 2016 with explicit goals: It announced that in 2016, 30% of its new engineers would be female, and 8% would be underrepresented minorities. It was careful to clarify that these were to be used as guidelines and not quotas. It also started a partnership with the consulting firm Paradigm. This firm uses HR analytics to examine how recruitment and selection techniques affect the diversity of hires and presents suggestions to remove barriers to diversity. For example, Paradigm recommended that Pinterest help employees better prepare for an interview at a Silicon Valley company. Companies in the tech industry are known for their unusual hiring techniques, ranging from casual dress codes for applicants to intense team interviews. By sharing information about what to expect as part of the hiring process, it was able to prepare applicants better, give them more clarity, and limit the influence of nonessential factors on interview performance. Asking employees to refer potential hires from underrepresented groups also worked, increasing the number of female and Hispanic applicants for engineering jobs. In the same time period, the company hired its first head of diversity. Pinterest instituted programs such as apprenticeship and summer internship programs to increase diversity. Broadening their university outreach partners was also helpful. To avoid potential bias, in meetings and interviews, they started introducing applicants with their academic major and not the name of the university. Finally, the company instituted the National Football League's so-called Rooney Rule, requiring that for each leadership position, at least one female and one underrepresented minority would be interviewed.

Early results are promising: In 2017, women constituted 29% of all technical roles, up from 21% in 2015, whereas underrepresented ethnicities rose from 3% to 9%. Pinterest remains committed to sharing what it learned and continuing its data-driven approach to understanding and promoting diversity. The technology industry's diversity problem has many sources, ranging from a "leaky pipeline" (which means that women and minorities leave the industry due to discrimination and other factors) to organizational cultures that do not internalize diversity as a competitive advantage. Efforts such as those at Pinterest are noteworthy for their transparency and for their willingness to be part of the solution.

Case Discussion Questions

1. What is the difference between diversity goals and diversity quotas? Why do you think Pinterest was careful to distinguish between the two?

2. What are some of the challenges to diversity management in the technology industry? List and discuss what prevents companies from attracting and retaining diverse talent.

3. Consider the initiatives with which Pinterest is experimenting. Which ones hold greater promise? What else would you suggest it do?

4. What are your thoughts about the central roles of sex and racial diversity in the technology industry's diversification efforts?

Click to learn more . . .

Read Tracy Chou's blog post at https://medium.com /@triketora/where-are-the-numbers-cb997a5725 2#.1305agqnk

Sources: Bellstrong, K. (2015, August 4). Why Pinterest's new diversity goals actually matter. Fortune.com. http://fortune .com/2015/08/03/pinterest-diversity-goals/; Cohen, D. (2017, December 20). Pinterest updated its progress on its 2017 diversity efforts. http://www.adweek.com/digital/pinterest-diversity-2017/; Guynn, J. (2015, July 31). Pinterest launches diversity project to see what sticks. *USA Today*; Kokalitcheva, K. (2016, January 21). Pinterest hires its first head of diversity. *Fortune.* https://www.forbes .com/sites/kathleenchaykowski/2016/01/06/pinterest-hires-its-first-head-of-diversity/#6dfe0a1a787f; Lorenzetti, L. (2015, August 4). What Pinterest is learning from Pittsburgh Steelers about diversity. *Fortune.* http://fortune.com/2015/07/30/pinterest-diversity-initiative; Rao, L. (2016, March 15). Tech's diversity fixer. *Fortune.* http://fortune.com/2016/03/15/tech-diversity-problem; Vara, V. (2015, November). Pinterest's great expectations. *Fast Company*, pp. 33–36.

CHAPTER 5
The Analysis and Design of Work

The Development of SHRM's Competency Model for HR Practice

HR systems are designed to give employers a competitive advantage by focusing on how to attract and hire the best talent, as well as how to develop, train, and retain employees. This includes aligning jobs with organizational goals and strategies.

So a key challenge for HR managers is to understand the tasks that need to be carried out by individual employees and how individual positions fit together to accomplish organizational goals. In addition, organizations must understand what knowledge, skills, abilities, and other characteristics (KSAOs) employees need to have to do their work most effectively. In short, a clear understanding of what employees do on their jobs and the skills employees need to do their jobs is the basis for building strong organizations.

This is true not only within organizations; it is true within specific professions as well. More and more, professions from health care to engineering are defining what skills and abilities are needed to carry out their work. This provides credibility for the profession as a whole, and it also helps define what is needed for licensure and certification of individuals to protect the public. For example, how would you feel if an unlicensed physician took care of you or a family member?

It is for these reasons that the HR profession, through the Society for Human Resource Management (SHRM; see Chapter 1), systematically developed a competency model that defines the competencies required for success in the HR profession. SHRM developed its competency model to guide HR practitioners in achieving their professional goals and thus is developmental in nature. The model includes nine key competencies, which are listed below.

- HR expertise (HR knowledge)
- Global and cultural effectiveness
- Relationship management
- Communication
- Consultation
- Critical evaluation
- Business acumen
- Ethical practice
- Leadership and navigation

Note that only one of the nine competencies is focused on technical knowledge of human resources. The other eight are less knowledge focused and reflect broader behaviors needed for success in organizations, including HR jobs. This is important since, according to the researchers who developed the SHRM competency model, successful HR practice entails more than just HR *knowledge;* it also requires the right *behaviors* for implementing this knowledge in an actual work organization.

A key aspect of SHRM's model is that it provides substantial detail in defining each competency, including the identification of subcompetencies. It also defines behaviors that reflect how each competency is manifested on the job. Finally, the model describes proficiency standards for each competency at four different career stages: early, mid, senior, and executive levels. As such, it serves as a helpful guide for HR professionals seeking to develop themselves to move on to the next stage of their careers. It is also helpful to organizational decision makers who want to know how best to develop and structure their HR functions.

To develop its HR competency model, SHRM used established best practices for analyzing jobs and building competency models. Moreover, as described in Chapter 1, SHRM used a multistage process involving tens of thousands of participants, which included the following steps:

- An initial sample of more than 1,000 HR professionals in more than 100 focus groups in 29 cities worldwide, together with a survey of 640 HR leaders, was used to generate model content.

- Once the model was developed, SHRM surveyed tens of thousands of HR experts to confirm the importance of each competency.

- SHRM then studied more than 800 HR professionals and their supervisors with the goal of assessing the degree to which the competencies—both technical and behavioral—predict the job performance of HR professionals. This last step in the analysis shows "where the rubber meets the road" by demonstrating the robustness of the model through empirical validation.

The development of the SHRM competency model was an impressive feat that resulted in an enduring instrument that provides substantial guidance for the development of HR professionals. Going forward, a key goal for the model is to gain HR professionals a place at the table among organizational decision makers.

Case Discussion Questions

1. Regardless of whether you plan to be an HR professional, how might you use this competency model for your professional development? Specifically, how would you go about gaining proficiency in each of these nine competencies? How might doing so help you succeed in your chosen occupation?

2. How might the robust empirical process used to develop the model be used to promote the model's credibility among business leaders? How would you argue in favor of the model to leaders in a government organization? In a multinational, private corporation?

3. What do you think about the relative value of each of the nine competencies at different career stages of HR practitioners? For example, how might an executive HR professional differ from an entry-level HR professional in their need for each of these competencies?

4. How do you think business schools and HR programs could use the model for curriculum development for both HR professionals and students in other fields of business administration?

5. How relevant do you think each of the nine competencies is for an employee's success in organizations, whether or not a person is associated with the HR function? Explain.

Click to learn more . . .
To learn more about the SHRM competency model development, click on this report:

https://www.shrm.org/learningandcareer/compe tency-model/pages/default.aspx

Sources: Campion, M. A., Fink, A. A., Ruggeberg, B. J., Carr, L., Phillips, G. M., & Odman, R. B. (2011). Doing competencies well: Best practices in competency modeling. *Personnel Psychology, 64,* 225–262; Shippmann, J. S., Ash, R. A., Battista, M., Carr, L., Eyde, L. D., Hesketh, B., . . . Sanchez, J. I. (2000). The practice of competency modeling. *Personnel Psychology, 53,* 703–740; Alonso, A., Kurtessis, J. N., Schmidt, A. A., Strobel, K., & Dickson, B. (2015). A competency-based approach to advancing HR. *People + Strategy, 28,* 38–44; Alonso, A. (2017, March 27). Certify this! The role of competency-based certification in HR. https://blog.shrm.org/blog/certify-this-the-role-of-competency-based-certification-in-hr; Society for Human Resource Management. (2012). SHRM Competency Model. https://www.shrm.org/LearningAndCareer/competency-model/Documents/ Full%20Competency%20Model%2011%202_10%201%202014.pdf; National Council of State Boards of Nursing, Inc. (NCSBN®). (2015). Report of findings from the 2014 Nurse Aide Job Analysis and Knowledge, Skill and Ability Study. https://www.ncsbn .org/15_2014NNAAP_Job_Analysis_vol65.pdf; American Association of Engineering Societies and U.S. Department of Labor. (2015). Engineering competency model. www.aaes.org/sites/default/files/Engineering%20Competency%20Model_Final_May2015.pdf

CHAPTER 6
Workforce Planning and Recruitment

Creating a College Recruitment Pipeline: The Case of PwC

PricewaterhouseCoopers (PwC) is one of the Big 4 accounting firms that, along with Deloitte, EY, and KPMG, handles 80% of auditing for all U.S. public companies. PwC provides tax, assurance, and advisory services to clients around the world and employs more than 250,000 people across 158 countries in 721 locations. The work can be demanding. To keep the new employee pipeline open, PwC focuses a great deal on its college relationships and recruiting from new college graduate programs. PwC has invested and continues to invest time, effort, and money toward these programs. Several of its recruitment activities are covered in this chapter. For example, as of 2016, PwC had hired more than 11,000 students per year via college campus recruiting programs and relationships and offers new college graduates $1,200 per year to help them pay off student debt. Legally, firms are prohibited from asking about employees' personal debt, but nationally, 71% of more than 44 million college graduates have student loan debt of $31,000 on average. Thus, this benefit has the potential to be highly attractive to college students weighing their options for employment after graduation.

PwC also offers CareerAdvisor, a website designed to help students assess their strengths and interests, maximize their resources to identify opportunities, prepare for the job search, and identify ways to present themselves to make the best impression. CareerAdvisor offers articles, videos, assessments, and tools to help students succeed in their new careers regardless of where they choose to go. It also introduced video interviewing to help busy students work around their schedules and classes. But PwC is also hoping that by offering innovative recruitment tools, its employment brand and reputation will be enhanced, which can help attract and hire the best candidates. Rod Adams, PwC's U.S. recruiting leader, noted that the use of video interviews helps to free up time during a site visit after an offer is made,

creating a more enjoyable experience. In his words, "It becomes a sell visit instead of an interview. The benefit is candidate experience because [candidates] come into the office, they're not nervous because they already have an offer, and they can really just absorb our environment and what we have to offer them versus worrying about their interview."

Finally, one major source of new employees is internships that turn into job offers. According to PwC, 90% of its interns receive full-time job offers (compared to the U.S. average of 72%). To help students prepare for internships, PwC offers information regarding what students can expect, including coaching and real-time development during internships. Its continued investment in its internship program has helped PwC earn the 12th spot on the 20 Most Prestigious Internships list for 2018, according to *Forbes*.

Following are some job search tips from Alexa Merschel, a PwC recruiter, who has hired more than 500 people after reviewing 8,000 résumés and interviewing thousands of applicants:

- Keep your résumé short and up-to-date.

- Include volunteer experience.

- Include the name of the company to which you are applying in your résumé's "objective."

- Make sure your phone's voicemail greeting sounds professional.

- Create a profile on LinkedIn and make sure it is complete.

- Network widely.

- If interviewed, come prepared with stories illustrating your initiative and leadership skills, and be ready to answer specific questions about your accomplishments and leadership skills.

PwC is also working toward other strategic recruiting goals such as gamified training solutions, which allow trainees to engage in work scenario role-playing online. Further, PwC maintains a robust alumni network, which lets it cultivate future employees and stay in touch with former employees as potential clients and returning employees.

Case Discussion Questions

1. Do you think PwC is offering the right mix of incentives to attract college graduates? Why or why not?

2. Are there other things PwC should consider doing to attract college students and graduates?

3. Do you think the tips shared by Alexa Merschel, a PwC recruiter, would be helpful at other firms or in other industries? Why or why not?

4. PwC offers 90% of its interns full-time employment. What do you see as the pros and cons of this approach?

Click to learn more . . .

Read more about PwC's college student programs for recruitment for college freshmen, sophomores, juniors, seniors, and fifth-year students at http://www.pwc.com/us/en/careers/campus/programs-events.html

Sources: Adams, S. (2014). Job search secrets from a campus recruiter. *Forbes*. http://www.forbes.com/sites/susanadams/2014/03/26/job-search-secrets-from-a-campus-recruiter/#eace97a236bf; PwC. (2017). Recruiting process. http://www.pwc.com/us/en/careers/campus/recruiting.html; PwC. (2017). Practice areas. http://www.pwc.com/us/en/careers/campus/why-pwc/what-we-do.html; NACE. (2016). Video interviewing helps PwC boost candidate experience. http://www.naceweb.org/s02102016/video-interviewing-helps-boost-candidate-experience.aspx; Malcolm, H. (2015). PwC to start giving employees $1,200 a year in student loan debt assistance. *USA Today*. http://www.usatoday.com/story/money/personalfinance/2015/09/22/pwc-offering-student-loan-assistance-to-employees/72565522/; Walker, J. (2010). PwC pays for priority: New recruiting tool for college students gives accounting firm top billing. *Wall Street Journal*. https://www.wsj.com/articles/SB10001424052748704029304575526641294699972; Statista. (2018). Number of PwC employees worldwide from 2013–2017, by region. https://www.statista.com/statistics/189763/number-of-employees-of-pwc-by-region-2010/

CHAPTER 7
Selection Processes and Procedures

Finding the Best Fit: The Case of Selection at Google

Acquiring the best talent provides organizations with an important competitive advantage, particularly when selection systems are aligned with strategic objectives. Chapter 6 pointed out one key aspect of hiring the best talent: the recruitment and selection funnel. As noted there, having more candidates to choose from in the funnel gives an organization the highest probability of hiring the best. In other words, all things being equal, it's better to choose from 10 qualified job candidates than from just two.

Now consider the size of the recruitment and selection funnel at Google, which is one of the most admired employers in the world and has been ranked at the top of *Fortune*'s list of "best companies to work for" for many years. By some estimates, Google receives as many as 2 million job applications each year but only hires about 5,000 of those applicants. So, the chances of an applicant landing a job at Google are about 1 in 400; it is not impossible to get a job there, but it is not going to be easy. One thing is certain: The recruitment and selection funnel works in Google's favor.

In addition to having more qualified applicants from which to choose, companies also need valid, job-related selection procedures to be able to choose among job candidates. As this chapter discusses, managers who simply choose candidates "from the gut" tend not to choose the people who are the best fit for the job. Rather, systematic and rigorous selection procedures, such as a structured interview process in which all candidates are asked the same job-related questions, lead to hiring the best talent. Google is a leader in this area, applying the top research practices to optimize its interview process. For example, Google found through its research that conducting four interviews is the best way to optimize selection decisions. This is likely because having more than one interviewer compensates for the biases of any single interviewer, and it also takes into account that a candidate may simply have had a "bad day" when they participated in an interview. Google

also found—again through robust analytics—that conducting many more interviews per candidate (e.g., 25) was not necessarily more effective and may in fact have made the selection process take too long. The point is that using research and analytics to understand the hiring process maximizes the chances of hiring success.

Other innovative approaches to recruitment and selection include Google's development of an international programming competition called Google Code Jam, which was established in 2003 to help the company identify top engineering talent. The competition culminates with the top 25 Code Jammers competing in the World Championship for $15,000 and bragging rights. Google sees this as a way to engage with the engineering community, celebrate those at the top of their game, and also consider top talent recruited in a unique way. Google seems to have leveraged the best of proven selection science as well as creative applicant cultivation to its advantage.

Case Discussion Questions

1. Although having more applicants to choose from is a good thing, can there be such a thing as too many applicants? For example, how might a company like Google process 2 million applicants per year, short of interviewing all candidates?

2. Although hiring "from the gut" is generally not the best approach to selection, do you think that this approach may have some advantages? If so, what are they? Do you think that this sort of approach enters into Google's hiring processes?

3. In addition to using interviews, how might Google select employees for certain jobs

such as programmers? How would you decide which types of assessment(s) are most important for hiring programmers that best fit the job?

4. Teamwork and being able to admit mistakes are also factors that seem to fit well with success at Google. How could these sorts of factors be assessed in the selection process?

Click to learn more . . .

Watch a video on getting a job at Google: https://www.youtube.com/watch?v=k-baHBzWe4k

Sources: https://code.google.com/codejam/; Fallows, J., & Coates, T. N. (2016, April 10). The science of smart hiring. *The Atlantic Monthly.* https://www.theatlantic.com/business/archive/2016/04/the-science-of-smart-hiring/477561/; Lamont, T. (2015, April 6). How to get a job at Google: Meet the man who hires and fires. *The Guardian.* https://www.theguardian.com/technology/2015/apr/04/how-to-get-job-at-google-meet-man-hires-fires; The 100 best companies to work for 2017. (2018). *Fortune.* http://beta.fortune.com/best-companies/

CHAPTER 8
Training, Development, and Careers

Using Training and Development to Drive Culture of Commitment: The Case of Igloo

Igloo, a Texas-based manufacturer of ice chests for more than 70 years, has undertaken a number of initiatives to train and develop its employees to promote its company culture of commitment. Igloo's operations in Texas employ 900 *associates*—the term Igloo uses for its employees. There are a number of key dimensions to Igloo's culture, such as trusting others, avoiding politics (decision making based on personal advantage), and promoting effective communication.

As keeper of the culture at Igloo, HR is central to promoting, supporting, and sustaining the culture. So, part of HR's job is to train associates on what Igloo's culture is, why it is important, and how to embrace it. This includes not only training on the culture for new hires during the onboarding process but also explaining the culture during annual goal-setting sessions, sales meetings, and strategic planning programs.

One key dimension of Igloo's culture of commitment is the "recipe for associate success." Training and development activities are a central part of this dimension, so Igloo has undertaken an ambitious training program for enhancing the skills of its associates. Part of the development of this training program included an assessment of training needs and tailoring the program to the needs of associates. The program's key features focus on training, but they also focus on the counseling and coaching of associates.

Further, Igloo developed a technical skills training program based on the latest neuroscience research on adult learning. This technical skills program includes these five steps:

- *Demonstration:* Knowledgeable associates show learners how to carry out the task at hand.

- *"By the numbers":* Highly technical work is broken down into established, standardized steps so that it is more easily taught and is taught in a consistent manner to different employees.

- *Role reversal:* Learners act as instructors themselves. That is, they "teach" the skill to instructors to demonstrate to instructors what they can actually do. The idea is that a person must be highly proficient before they can teach a skill to another person.

- *Practice with questions and answers:* Associates are given time to practice their new skills and ask questions about them so that they can build confidence.

- *Certification:* Final step in which Igloo determines whether associates are ready to go and "floor ready."

Igloo's culture of commitment demonstrates its emphasis on people—in short, safety and respect toward associates.

Case Discussion Questions

1. Igloo has developed its culture around associates who primarily work in manufacturing. How effective would this approach to implementing culture be in other industries, for example, commercial construction? A high-tech start-up?

2. What are some of the drawbacks to Igloo's approach to managing its culture? Where

might HR or top management face some challenges in the organization?

3. How would you decide what the appropriate culture is for an organization? How would you use the company's training and development function to help introduce and reinforce a new culture?

4. How might training be used to introduce a culture focused on respect for diversity? On employee safety?

5. What specific types of training content and exercises might you include if you were rolling out a training program for Igloo that was focused on its culture of commitment?

6. How would you assess the effectiveness of Igloo's efforts to introduce the culture of commitment? Consider (a) how you would know if the culture was actually adopted and (b) what metrics you might use to know whether the culture is actually supporting the success of the organization.

Click to learn more . . .

To learn more about how to transform culture like Igloo did, click on this article: https://www.corpmagazine.com/human-resources/cultural-commitment-creating-a-workplace-where-people-feel-valued/

Source: Winters, J. (2017, April). A principles-driven culture pushes Igloo to success. *TD: Training and Development,* pp. 36–40.

CHAPTER 9
Performance Management

Transforming Performance Management: The Case of Deloitte

Among companies that have made major changes in their approach to performance management, the multinational consulting firm Deloitte provides an interesting example. In 2013, Deloitte conducted an internal study that revealed it was spending around 2 million hours on performance management–related activities. Performance management consisted of annual evaluations in which managers and employees set goals at the beginning of the year and then rated progress made at the end of the year. Despite the time spent on them, the system did not provide adequate or timely feedback to employees, nor did it provide organizational decision makers with sufficiently accurate performance data to be used in important decisions such as incentive pay. The company decided to give the system a makeover but also to change the company's view of what performance management is and how to approach it.

This transformation effort began with identifying what Deloitte needed the system to be able to accomplish. Erica Bank, performance management leader at Deloitte, describes the objectives as threefold: fuel performance, see performance, and recognize performance. To fuel performance, a key tool in the revamped system is frequent meetings in which the employee and the manager have future-oriented conversations, called "check-ins" or "one-on-ones." Managers and employees are encouraged to briefly meet weekly or biweekly to discuss ongoing work and employee career development. To get the employees and managers started, HR gave them ideas of what to talk about and sent weekly e-mails asking whether they had met (i.e., rather than force compliance, they simply nudged). The frequency and regularity of these meetings would ensure that the feedback received would be timely.

To see performance, managers are now asked to rate each employee they work with at the end of each project using a simple, four-question survey:

- Given what I know of this person's performance, I would always want him/her on my team. (*Responses reported on a 5-point scale ranging from* strongly disagree *to* strongly agree.)

- This person is at risk for low performance (*yes/no*).

- Given what I know of this person's performance, and if it were my own money, I would award this person the highest possible compensation increase. (*Responses reported on a 5-point scale ranging from* strongly disagree *to* strongly agree.)

- This person is ready for promotion today (*yes/no*).

At a minimum, each employee is rated every quarter. Deloitte made the initial decision not to share each rating from individual managers with the employees, opting to share annual aggregated ratings with the rationale that this would allow managers to be more honest.

To recognize performance, Deloitte decided to use the performance ratings as a starting point. Chief Learning Officer Jeff Orlando notes that every "people decision" will be data informed but not data driven. HR and business leaders could use this information to decide whom to promote and whose performance needed intervention. The system is meant to help support (but not replace) decision makers in their efforts to recognize employee contributions.

Is the system working? Deloitte invested heavily in training managers on how the system would work and encouraged adoption by allowing them to opt in. Deloitte will, no doubt, continue to change and shape the system in keeping with evolving demands. The initial reactions of its own employees have been positive. In 2016, ALM Intelligence named Deloitte a global leader in performance management consulting, indicating that the company is a thought leader in this arena and shares its performance management experience with its clients as well.

Case Discussion Questions

1. Which aspects of Deloitte's new performance management system do you find most radical?

2. If you were a manager at Deloitte, how would you have reacted to such a system? Would your answer change if you were an employee?

3. What are your thoughts regarding measuring performance with four simple questions? Do you think these are the right questions? How would you know if a particular question is effective?

4. How would you motivate managers to conduct frequent check-in meetings with employees? How would you counter the argument that these meetings take a lot of time?

5. How transparent is this system? Do you think Deloitte's decision not to share individual ratings with employees is warranted?

Click to learn more . . .

Read the Deloitte University Press report titled "Performance Management Is Broken: Replace 'Rank and Yank' With Coaching and Development." https://dupress.deloitte.com/dup-us-en/focus/human-capital-trends/2014/hc-trends-2014-performance-management.html

Sources: Banks, E. (2016, January 13). Reinventing performance management at Deloitte. https://www.td.org/Publications/Blogs/Learning-Executive-Blog/2016/01/Reinventing-Performance-Management-at-Deloitte; Buckingham, M., & Goodall, A. (2015, April). Reinventing performance management. *Harvard Business Review,* pp. 40–50; Deloitte. (2016, August 1). Deloitte named a global leader in performance management consulting by ALM intelligence. https://www2.deloitte.com/global/en/pages/about-deloitte/articles/deloitte-performance-management-consulting-alm-intelligence.html; Lee, J. (2016). Traditional performance reviews get a makeover. *Benefits Canada, 40*(3), 42–43; Orlando, J. (2016, Summer). It all adds up to change at Deloitte. *People + Strategy*, p. 11; Orlando, J., & Bank, E. (2016, April). Case study: A new approach to performance management at Deloitte. *People + Strategy*, pp. 42–44.

CHAPTER 10
Managing Employee Separations and Retention

Analytics as a Retention Management Tool: The Case of the Trucking Industry

Long-haul trucking often conjures images of open roads and beautiful scenery. Drivers are admired for the freedom and independence that are often associated with this lifestyle. The reality, however, bears little resemblance to this picture. Today, professional truck drivers typically drive predetermined and optimized routes, with their stops, rests, and speed strictly regulated and watched. They are continuously monitored via video cameras and dashboard "black boxes" or electronic logging devices. They are solo workers, spending long hours in isolation, and with a median salary around $40,000 nationwide, it is not a scheme to get rich quickly. As a result, it is no surprise that there is a nationwide shortage of truck drivers, with estimates that by 2024, the size of the shortage will reach 175,000 drivers.

Freight companies and private companies that rely on truck drivers as a critical part of their logistics network find it extremely difficult to fill open positions. This is an industry in which there is great pressure to hire anyone who is qualified and interested. Once hired, the problem is to hold on to new hires, because the annual turnover rate has been 100% for several years in a row. These data do not only capture voluntary leavers; some drivers leave due to retirements, and others are dismissed for problematic behavior. Still, holding on to good drivers is likely to give employers a key advantage in this highly competitive field.

Many carriers now rely on external vendor-generated solutions or build their own algorithms to benefit from predictive analytics for driver retention. A major use of analytics occurs in the hiring process. If characteristics that predict which truckers will leave quickly can be identified, the company can be more selective in the hiring process or use targeted interventions to retain particular groups of applicants. For example, a Tacoma, Washington–based carrier, Interstate Distributor Co., found that the turnover rate was lower among drivers who were referred by other employees. Iowa-based Decker Truck Line, Inc. identified retention problems among drivers who were hired directly from driving school, which led Decker to require at least 1 year of experience.

In addition to selecting employees for retention, analytics can be used to identify areas of improvement on the job or during the hiring process. For example, an external vendor called Stay Metrics partnered with Professor Timothy Judge of Ohio State University to see which personal and job characteristics predicted turnover and to build a predictive model based on these factors. Their results showed that those who left within 90 days were more likely to be inexperienced, showed low satisfaction with their recruiter, were home less than they expected, and were dissatisfied with their dispatcher.

One of the improvements to the hiring process based on their findings is to have a consistent message during recruitment regarding how much time drivers may expect to spend at home. Using data routinely gathered during hiring and through employee attitude surveys and exit interviews, it is possible to identify factors contributing to driver turnover in the entire industry, as well as to turnover within the specific company. A Chicago-based vendor, Enlistics, has an app drivers may optionally log into via their Facebook account during hiring. If they choose to do this, information in their Facebook profiles becomes part of a model used to predict eventual turnover. For example, the company found in a different industry that applicants who use the expression "I am sick of . . ." in their social media profiles tend to have higher turnover rates.

Predictive analytics allow firms to make predictions about turnover risk of specific employees and intervene so that these high-risk employees are retained. For example, the trucking solutions vendor Omnitracs, LLC uses predictive analytics to assign drivers risk scores from 1 to 100 based on their likelihood to quit. Management periodically receives a list of high-risk employees. The next step is for a manager or HR representative to initiate a conversation with the driver to see what the problems might be. The system even sends prompts for a follow-up conversation with the driver. The users of these systems credit these solutions and the utilization of predictive analytics as a positive influence over their retention rates and an opportunity to make significant changes in their turnover rate.

Case Discussion Questions

1. What types of data, in addition to those mentioned in the case, do you think can be used to develop predictive models regarding turnover? If you were developing such a model, what information would you want to collect so that you could predict turnover? Would you advise a company to use all information available to it in these predictive models?

2. Do you think the determinants of why employees quit and why they are dismissed would be different? What factors would you expect to be more closely related to voluntary turnover? What factors are more likely to predict whether the employee is dismissed?

3. What are the pros and cons of using social media profiles to predict turnover? What do you think about the ethics of this practice?

4. What are your thoughts about identifying the specific employees with high risk for turnover and intervening directly with them? What advantages and risks do you see in this approach? Do you think this approach is better than checking in with all employees regularly?

Sources: U.S. Bureau of Labor Statistics. (2016). Heavy and tractor-trailer truck drivers. https://www.bls.gov/ooh/transportation-and-material-moving/heavy-and-tractor-trailer-truck-drivers.htm; Huff, A. (2015, November 24). Data analysis proves beneficial in driver recruiting, retention. http://www.ccjdigital.com/data-analysis-proves-beneficial-in-driver-recruiting-retention/; Huff, A. (2016, December 16). Stay metrics research shows root causes of early driver turnover. http://www.ccjdigital.com/stay-metrics-research-shows-the-root-causes-of-early-driver-turnover/; Huff, A. (2017, February 22). Predicting driver turnover: The model sends a message. http://www.ccjdigital.com/predicting-driver-turnover-the-model-sends-a-message/; Jaillet, J. (2017). Advanced tools help carriers keep, reward drivers before they quit. http://www.ccjdigital.com/tech-toolbox-retaining-drivers/; Kilcarr, S. (2014, September). New solutions being aimed at driver shortage. *Fleet Owner, 109*(9).

CHAPTER 11
Rewarding Employees

Equal Pay for the U.S. Women's National Soccer Team

Avoiding pay discrimination is an important consideration when designing and implementing a compensation system, and it is a focal point of several U.S. employment and labor laws. Perhaps most well known is the Equal Pay Act, signed into law by President John F. Kennedy in 1963. Since then, additional legislation like the Civil Rights Act of 1964 and the Lilly Ledbetter Fair Pay Act of 2009 have been introduced to ensure equal pay for equal work.

In recent years, pay disparities between men's and women's professional sports have received increased scrutiny. The U.S. women's soccer team has featured prominently on the international stage by winning major competitions, including Olympic gold medals in 1996, 2004, 2008, and 2012 and World Cup titles in 1991, 1999, 2015, and 2019. Some 30 million television viewers watched the U.S. women's team defeat Japan in the 2015 World Cup, and their 2019 defeat of the Netherlands smashed global ratings records. Yet despite all of their success, the U.S. women have not received equal pay from the U.S. Soccer Federation as compared to the pay the men have received.

On the surface, the pay received by top U.S. men's and women's soccer players appears somewhat comparable. For instance, the U.S. men's star goalkeeper, Tim Howard, was paid a salary of $398,495 during 2014, and the U.S. women's star goalkeeper, Hope Solo, was paid a salary of $366,000 in 2015. A closer look, however, reveals that Tim Howard played just 8 games, whereas Hope Solo played in 23 games. In other words, not only did Hope Solo make less overall, but Tim Howard's earnings came out to $49,812 per game, as compared to Hope Solo's earnings of $15,913 per game, which some have argued is compelling evidence of pay inequality. When looking farther down the list, even more striking pay differences appear. For example, the 50th-highest-paid U.S. men's player received $246,238 in cumulative pay between 2008 and 2016; in contrast, the 50th-highest-paid U.S. women's player received just $25,516 over that same period.

The differences in pay can be attributed to the pay structure and incentives: The U.S. Soccer Federation compensated men per game played, regardless of the outcome, whereas women were paid a base salary with relatively small financial incentives for winning games. Further, women received lower per diems to cover travel expenses and lower rates for sponsor appearances.

Some people contend that historically, women's soccer has generated less revenue than men's soccer and so argue that the ongoing pay discrepancy is justified. In contrast, those in favor of equal pay point to more recent data that show the U.S. women's team earned more revenue than the U.S. men's team in 2016. Some argue that the men and women do not perform equal work, pointing to the fact that, to qualify for the World Cup, the women's team must play 5 games over 2 weeks, whereas the men's team must play 16 games over a 2-year period. Because of this difference, some believe that the men's qualification schedule is more arduous than the women's, thereby warranting higher pay, but others argue that the women's schedule is more condensed and thus more intense.

The concern over equal pay came to a head in 2016 when five players from the U.S. women's team filed a formal complaint with the Equal Employment Opportunity Commission, a government body that investigates discrimination claims. In 2017, as part of a collective bargaining agreement, the U.S. women's team agreed to a new pay structure, which included a 30% increase in base pay as well as higher incentives for winning games. The new agreement did not yield pay equality between men and women, but it did take a large step toward closing the pay gap, moving the U.S. women's soccer team toward pay fairness.

Case Discussion Questions

1. Why do you think pay fairness is important for employee job performance and retention?

2. If you were a leader at the U.S. Soccer Federation, how would you have responded to the U.S. women's team assertion that pay inequality existed?

3. How do you define *equal work* when it comes to the men's and women's soccer players?

4. Given what is described in this case, why do you think these pay discrepancies exist? Do you think that they are fair or unfair? Why?

5. In your opinion, when it comes to equal pay, what is the next step for the U.S. women's soccer team?

Click to learn more . . .

Read a CBS News interview transcript with players from the U.S. women's national soccer team here: https://www.cbsnews.com/news/60-minutes -women-soccer-team-usa-gender-discrimination -equal-pay-2019-07-10/

Sources: Cauterucci, C. (2017, April 5). The U.S. women's soccer team finally has a better contract, but not equal pay. http:// www.slate.com/blogs/xx_factor/2017/04/05/the_u_s_women_s_soccer_team_finally_has_a_better_contract_but_not_ equal.html; Das, A. (2016, April 21). Pay disparity in U.S. soccer? It's complicated. *New York Times.* https://www.nytimes .com/2016/04/22/sports/soccer/usmnt-uswnt-soccer-equal-pay.html; Das, A. (2016, March 31). Top female players accuse U.S. soccer of wage discrimination. *New York Times.* https://www.nytimes.com/2016/04/01/sports/soccer/uswnt-us-women-carli-lloyd-alex-morgan-hope-solo-complain.html; Das, A. (2017, April 5). Long days, Google docs and anonymous surveys: How the U.S. soccer team forged a deal. https://www.nytimes.com/2017/04/05/sports/soccer/uswnt-us-soccer-labor-deal-contract.html; History: U.S. Soccer Team Honors. (n.d.). https://www.ussoccer.com/about/history/awards; O'Donnell, N. (2016, November 10). Team USA members on historic fight for equal pay in women's soccer. http://www.cbsnews.com/news/60-minutes-women-soccer-team-usa-gender-discrimination-equal-pay/

CHAPTER 12
Managing Benefits

Providing Benefits to Gig Workers at Care.com

A gig refers to a single project or task that an individual completes for pay, and individuals who complete gigs are often referred to as gig workers. Examples of gigs range from driving for Uber and Lyft to performing assignments for TaskRabbit and Postmates. Estimates suggest that more than 23 million Americans work in the gig economy, and a 2017 MetLife survey indicated that 51% of workers expressed interest in gig work instead of a full-time, salaried position at a single organization. Because many gig workers earn most of their income through part-time employment or independent contracts, they typically do not have access to the employer-sponsored benefits

that full-time employees have. As such, a common complaint among gig workers is the lack of certain voluntary benefits—something that an organization called Care.com has sought to change.

Founded in 2007, Care.com is the world's largest online marketplace aimed at connecting families with caregivers, babysitters, and nannies. The company's overarching objective is "to improve the lives of families and caregivers by helping them connect in a reliable and easy way." Care.com's online marketplace connects millions of families with gig workers who provide care services. Amid calls for added protections and benefits for gig workers, in 2016,

Care.com unveiled an initiative to contribute up to $500 per year to each care provider for health care, educational, and transportation expenses—a benefit that is relatively unheard of among gig workers.

Care.com funds this employee benefit with a portion of the transaction fee charged to families who use the company's services. In addition to having up to $500 to spend each year on qualified expenses, the benefit allows workers to roll unspent money forward to the following year. With health care costs increasing, $500 per year is likely not enough to pay for all health care, educational, and transportation expenses. However, the Patient Protection and Affordable Care Act provides workers who are not covered under employee health insurance with an opportunity to purchase relatively affordable health care policies. As such, when the $500-per-year sum is applied toward health care plan premiums, deductibles, and other expenses,

care providers at Care.com can significantly reduce their annual out-of-pocket expenditures.

Care.com's initiative was among the first of its kind and is at the forefront of a larger movement toward providing more benefits to gig workers. Some groups, such as the Independent Drivers' Guild in New York City, have advocated for legislation that would require a fee to be added to gig-economy transactions—similar to the one implemented by Care.com—to provide portable benefits that workers could use even after switching to new gigs. In Seattle, the city council voted unanimously to allow taxi and ride-sharing drivers for companies such as Lyft and Uber to unionize, which provides independent contractors and gig workers with greater influence when it comes to introducing and changing benefits. As more workers take on gigs, other companies and governments may initiate new benefits, policies, and practices out of consideration for gig workers.

Case Discussion Questions

1. What type of benefit did Care.com introduce for its gig workers? Why?

2. In addition to offsetting health care, educational, and transportation expenses, what other benefits could Care.com provide to its gig workers? What types of benefits would be most valuable to gig workers?

3. What effect might gig workers' ability to unionize have on their access to benefits?

4. In your opinion, in the future, will gig workers receive greater access to benefits, or will societal expectations of benefits

change such that gig workers no longer expect access to employer-sponsored benefits? Why?

Click to learn more . . .

To learn more about the challenges many gig workers face and how portable benefits might help, watch this video published by the *Wall Street Journal*:

https://www.wsj.com/video/series/financial-inclu sion-in-america/america-changing-workforce-ind ependent-and-gig-workers/A8D181BC-7494 -4D6D-BE8A-250EBDFD841F

Sources: Care.com introduces groundbreaking peer-to-peer benefits platform for caregivers. (2018). https://www.care.com/press-release-carecom-introduces-caregiver-benefits-platform-p1186-q81381650.html; Company overview. (2018). https://www.care.com/company-overview; Katz, L. F., & Krueger, A. B. (2016). The rise and nature of alternative work arrangements in the United States, 1995–2015. Working paper. https://benefittrends.metlife.com/us-perspectives/work-redefined-a-new-age-of-benefits/; Scheiber, N. (2016, September 14). Care.com creates a $500 limited for benefit gig-economy workers. *New York Times.* https://nyti .ms/2cM6luB; Semuels, A. (2017, November 6). Could a tax fix the gig economy? *The Atlantic.* https://www.theatlantic.com/business/archive/2017/11/gig-economy/544895/; Stonier, M. (2017, October 13). This state wants to offer universal benefits for gig workers. *Fortune.* http://fortune.com/2017/10/13/gig-economy-workers-benefits/; Torpey, E., & Hogan, A. (2016, May). Career outlook: Working in a gig economy. U.S. Bureau of Labor Statistics. https://www.bls.gov/careeroutlook/2016/article/what-is-the-gig-economy.htm

CHAPTER 13
Employee and Labor Relations

The First B Corp Certified U.S. Grocery Store: The Case of New Seasons Market

New Seasons Market is an Oregon-based grocery store chain founded in 2000 by three families who set the goal of "rethinking what a grocery store could be." The store is known for offering local and organic products. As of 2019, the company had 21 stores and more than 3,253 employees.

From the start, New Seasons Market was dedicated to both socially and environmentally responsible initiatives, including advocating for raising the minimum wage and the need for affordable housing. The stores divert more than 90% of all their waste from landfills via programs focused on composting, donations, and recycling. Fulfilling the company's mission statement "to be the ultimate neighborhood store," New Seasons Market offers events and classes, provides opportunities for its employees to do community volunteer work, and gives back 10% of after-tax profits to nonprofit organizations.

In 2013, New Seasons Market became the first grocery store in the United States to achieve B Corp certification. B Corps are for-profit companies that are certified by the nonprofit B Lab if they meet rigorous standards of social and environmental performance, accountability, and transparency and strive to use the power of markets to help solve social and environmental problems. B Corp certification is voluntary and can be changed at any time. B Lab is not a legal designation but it is seen by some as important. For example, Rose Marcario, CEO of Patagonia, argues, "The B Corp movement is one of the most important of our lifetime, built on the simple fact that business impacts and serves more than just stakeholders—it has an equal responsibility to the community and to the planet." While New Seasons Market is not a publicly traded company, one key aspect of B Corps in general is that they don't have to focus solely on maximizing shareholder value. More than 2,000 Certified B Corps exist in 50 countries across 130 industries. Many of these companies are small to medium sized, which is where much of the growth in this type of company has emerged. This certification is an independent, third-party certification that consists of an application of 170 questions covering such aspects of the business as energy efficiency and employee programs and practices. As a result of a company's answers to these questions, a total of 200 points is possible, but the certification does not expect that any company will ever be able to achieve a perfect score. In fact, a score of 80 points is enough to become certified. In its initial application, New Seasons Market earned 121 points, which is higher than the average of 97 points and higher than some companies known for their environmental and social responsibility missions, such as Patagonia. Other notable companies with B Corp certification include Ben & Jerry's (the first wholly owned subsidiary to get certified), Etsy, and Kickstarter. Natura, a Brazilian cosmetics company, became the first publicly traded Certified B Corp in 2014. Beyond those companies that formally apply for certification, more than 40,000 organizations use the free self-assessment tool available at www.bimpactassessment.net to help them benchmark and improve their social and environmental impact.

One major challenge for New Seasons Market is to manage relations with its workforce as the company continues to grow and expand into new parts of the country. Its expansion in 2016 to Mercer Island, Washington, was met with resistance by the United Food and Commercial Workers union's UFCW21 over the lack of a unionized workforce and concerns over the number of hours worked required for employees to receive benefits. Also, some workers in Portland, Oregon, began a union drive in 2017 as benefits were changing as part of the growth of the company.

Effectively managing employee relations will continue to be a major part of New Seasons Market's strategy for success.

Case Discussion Questions

1. If you were a manager at New Seasons Market, how would you have reacted to B Lab certification? Would your answer change if you were an employee?

2. What are your thoughts regarding the pros and cons of measuring social and environmental impact of organizations? How would you know if a particular question on the certification is effective?

3. Prior to reading this case, had you heard about B Corp certification? What new things did you learn about this concept from the case?

4. Do you agree or disagree with Patagonia CEO Rose Marcario that "the B Corp movement is one of the most important of our lifetime"? Please explain your answer.

5. Do you think that New Season Market's B Corp certification has positive or negative implications for employee relations? Please explain your answer.

Click to learn more . . .

To hear more about New Seasons Market becoming a B Corporation, view this YouTube video: https://youtu.be/Z9p88J9ZGeE

Sources: McIntosh, D. (2017). Union drive launches at New Seasons. nwLaborPress.org. https://nwlaborpress.org/2017/11/union-drive-launches-at-new-seasons/; Tu, J. I. (2016). Controversy, competition greet New Seasons Market as it opens on Mercer Island. *Seattle Times.* https://www.seattletimes.com/business/retail/controversy-competition-greet-new-season-market-as-it-opens-on-mercer-island/; Goodman, M. (2013). Make it good officially. *Entrepreneur.* http://www.bcorporation.net/sites/default/files/Entrepreneur_Mag_Feature.pdf; Freeland, C. (2013). Capitalism, but with a little heart. *New York Times.* http://www.nytimes.com/2013/07/19/us/19iht-letter19.html?_r=0; Why B Corps matter. http://www.bcorporation.net/what-are-b-corps/why-b-corps-matter; Taylor, N. (2017). New Seasons Market earns B Corp recertification. *Grocery Business.* http://www.winsightgrocerybusiness.com/new-seasons-market-earns-b-corp-recertification; New Seasons Market. Our story. https://www.newseasonsmarket.com/our-story/; B Corps. Our history. http://www.bcorporation.net/what-are-b-corps/the-non-profit-behind-b-corps/our-history; Honeyman, R. (2014). *The B Corp handbook: How to use business as a force for good.* Oakland, CA: Berrett-Koehler Publishers.

CHAPTER 14
Employee Safety, Well-Being, and Wellness

Putting the Brakes on Train Derailments: The Case of Public Railways

Supporting the safety of employees and customers is a stated goal for most organizations. Besides its importance for individual employees and for society more broadly, safety is linked to organizational success. For example, safety is directly linked to decreased liability, health, workers' compensation,

and medical costs. It is also associated with greater employee satisfaction and retention. And visible cases of lapses in safety can severely damage an organization's reputation.

The question, then, is why some organizations continue to struggle with supporting workplace safety despite the demonstrated value of doing so. Part of the problem is that employee and customer safety is the result of multiple, complicated factors, including organizational culture, climate, rules, and policies; leadership; employee training; and even employee health. It is also a function of the physical work environment and the safeguards that are put into place by the organization.

The passenger rail industry provides a vivid illustration of the multiple factors that can affect safety and the challenges organizations face in trying to improve safety. In recent years, there have been a number of high-profile cases of the failure of train safety systems, and some similar patterns emerge from these cases.

On September 29, 2016, a New Jersey Transit passenger train crashed in the Hoboken, New Jersey, station. Although it had been traveling at only 10 mph as it first entered the station, and even though the engineer had earlier sounded the horn to signal the train's approach, it suddenly accelerated to 21 mph within the station. The train was moving so quickly that it plowed through a train bumper and onto the platform, killing one person with falling debris and injuring 100 others. The engineer said he had no memory of the accident and woke up after the train had stopped. It was later found that he was severely overweight and was diagnosed with severe sleep apnea, a sleep disorder often associated with obesity and one that can cause people to fall asleep during the day. In addition, despite continued calls to include an automatic braking system, or to use a "positive train control" system, which notifies the engineer that the train is traveling too fast and can, if needed, even stop the train, the train did not have this type of technology. Note that this technology has been around for many years, and Congress has mandated that such systems be installed. However,

the deadline for the system's installation has been pushed back several times due to the high costs cited by the railroad industry.

Similarly, on January 4, 2017, a Long Island Railroad train crashed into the Brooklyn station, destroying a bumper, ramming into a room just beyond the end of the track, and injuring more than 100 people. Again, the engineer said he remembered approaching the station but had no memory of the crash. The National Transportation Safety Board found that he too was overweight and had sleep apnea. (After the crash, Long Island Railroad immediately started testing its engineers for sleep apnea; at one point, 8 of the 34 engineers that had been tested—nearly 25%— had sleep apnea.) Also, like the New Jersey Transit case, it had been recommended that positive train control be installed, but it was not in place on the Long Island line at the time of the crash.

On December 18, 2017, an Amtrak train traveling from Seattle, Washington, to Portland, Oregon, derailed just south of Seattle, killing four people and injuring dozens. At the time of the accident, the train was traveling into a curve at more than double the posted speed limit of 30 mph. Although at this writing the cause of the derailment is still under investigation, it appears that the engineers were not using their personal electronic devices; in other words, they were not distracted by them. A positive train control system had been installed on this line, but it was not yet in use. If it had been, it would have prevented the train from traveling too fast. The lack of a warning system has been cited as a factor that might have prevented the accident. Some analysts have also noted that although most railroads in the United States are behind in meeting their goals to install these types of automated safety systems due to costs, the railroads do continue to invest in other infrastructure such as new train stations.

Case Discussion Questions

1. Given the examples of these three organizations, why do you think that these types of accidents continue to occur? Consider multiple issues and stakeholders that might be affecting railroads' decisions about preventing accidents, including short-term versus long-term goals.

2. Based on these cases, do you think that these three organizations have a safety culture in which workers perceive that management views safety as a priority? Which factors in the cases make you say that? Could it be that the culture is positive in some ways but not in others? How might these cultures be improved?

3. Consider the multiple variables, including employee characteristics and behaviors, and factors in the physical environment that would help prevent transportation accidents such as these. Then develop a plan for a passenger railroad system that would help to prevent accidents.

4. What would be your argument to organizational leaders about the relative value of each of your suggestions? What data and metrics would you want to have available to you to make your arguments?

5. In two of the cases described here, the health of the engineers might have played a role in the accident. What is the employer's responsibility for monitoring and maintaining the health of their employees when it can have a direct impact on public safety?

Click to learn more . . .

Watch this video with the president of the National Safety Council on positive train control technology: https://youtu.be/PJqOfc93mtU

Sources: Associated Press. (2017). Video: Train crew not using electronic devices before crash. https://www.nytimes.com/aponline/2017/12/22/us/ap-us-train-derailment-washington-state.html; Barone, B. (2017). NJ: Engineers in LIRR and NJ Transit derailments had sleep apnea, NTSB says. *AM New York.* https://www.amny.com/transit/engineers-in-lirr-and-nj-transit-derailments-had-sleep-apnea-ntsb-1.14241007; Fitzsimmons, E. G. (2016). Train was traveling at twice the speed limit just before Hoboken crash. *New York Times.* https://www.nytimes.com/2016/10/07/nyregion/train-was-traveling-at-twice-the-speed-limit-just-before-hoboken-crash.html; McGeehan, P., Mazzei, P., & Johnson, K. (2017). Law requires life-saving braking device. Most trains don't have it. *New York Times.* https://www.nytimes.com/2017/12/20/us/amtrak-train-safety.html; Shepardson, D. (2017). U.S. Safety Board says train-crash engineers had undiagnosed sleep disorders. *Scientific American.* https://www.scientificamerican.com/article/u-s-safety-board-says-train-crash-engineers-had-undiagnosed-sleep-disorders/

CHAPTER 15
Opportunities and Challenges in International HRM

Talent Management in the Danger Zone: The Case of Mercy Corps

Consider the following job attributes: good pay and benefits and meaningful work where you are able to make a difference in people's lives, save them from danger, help them get jobs, and bring aid to places where it is needed most. You have opportunities to learn something new every day, and a lot of travel is involved. If this sounds like your dream job, note that the job is actually in a war or disaster zone with poor living conditions, scarce medical support, and physical danger. Many organizations encounter risks as they do business, but for an international nongovernmental organization (INGO) such as Mercy Corps, danger *is* the business.

Nongovernmental organizations (NGOs) are humanitarian nonprofit organizations that aim to effect change in environmental, social, human rights, or other issues, and as an INGO, Mercy Corps performs this mission on a global scale. Whether it is bringing relief to refugees in Syria, helping farmers in Ethiopia prepare for drought conditions, or providing educational and employment opportunities to marginalized populations in Nigeria, working in international tough spots is everyday work for Mercy Corps employees. The Portland, Oregon–based organization operates in 40 countries and employs around 4,000 employees, fewer than 200 of whom are based in the United States. The agency deploys talent to where it is needed, which may mean sending African employees to work in the Middle East or Indonesian employees to South Sudan.

To a degree, all companies struggle with hiring, onboarding, managing, and retaining talent. However, Mercy Corps' HR challenges put it in a category of its own. For example, even though there is a large pool of individuals who are interested in volunteering and making a difference through their work, Mercy Corps is often looking for a specific set of skills as well as experience living and working under dangerous and volatile conditions, leading the organization to compete with other NGOs for a very small pool of talent for hiring. In addition to skills, it seeks characteristics that will make someone resilient and adaptable: Sensitivity, flexibility, curiosity, and emotional stability under pressure are traits it looks for. CEO Neal Keny-Guyer views "cultural intelligence" as a critical competency in hiring.

In addition to finding the right talent, keeping them is another challenge. Once hired, onboarding matters a great deal to ensure that new hires can hit the ground running and be effective quickly. They need to ensure that employees can be transported to safety if problems arise, prevent burnout of employees through regular rest and recovery, and provide extensive training that will enable employees to function effectively in a given geography. For example, field workers are trained on topics such as curfews, travel restrictions, how to interact with locals, and communication procedures during emergencies (often by trainers with a military background). Finally, Mercy Corps cannot solely rely on its meaningful mission to attract and retain workers, given the intense competition for talent among INGOs seeking personnel with similar skill sets. Thus, developing an employer brand that supports and engages employees is among the responsibilities of its HR team.

Given how critical employees are to Mercy Corps' mission, it is no surprise that HR is a strategic partner within the company. To be effective, HR leaders of Mercy Corps need a deep understanding of the company's operations, which may explain the appointment of Nigel Pont, a former regional director for Middle Eastern Operations, to the role of chief people and strategy officer. Part of how Mercy Corps enables business success is to ensure that the local teams are supported by local HR teams and that local HR teams have a voice within the country-level operations.

A key initiative for Mercy Corps is to build in-house expertise in data analytics and ensure that data are harnessed to increase the efficiency of all of its operations. For example, data analytics can be used to forecast how many people will arrive at a specific aid distribution center, ensuring that sufficient staff and resources are available to meet the needs of new arrivals. With the help of a partnership with Cisco, the company aims to make faster, more accurate, and more effective decisions that will help it meet the humanitarian challenges it faces every day.

Case Discussion Questions

1. What do you think the unique and similar challenges are for NGOs versus for-profit companies in terms of HR and HR strategy?

2. What advantages do you think Mercy Corps has in recruiting, hiring, training, and managing employees relative to a domestic business? What are the challenges?

3. Cultural intelligence is the ability to work effectively across cultures. How do you think Mercy Corps can hire based on this skill? How can this skill be developed?

4. How do you think improved expertise in data analytics would affect the HR functions of Mercy Corps?

5. Organizations have a choice in centralizing or decentralizing their operations, including those of HR. To what degree do you think that centralized HR operations would be beneficial for Mercy Corps? Which operations would benefit from centralization? Which ones are better left to the discretion of local teams?

Click to learn more . . .

Watch the "culture and values" video of Mercy Corps: https://www.youtube.com/watch?v=qcBKc3WIMFs

---

Sources: Baker, L. (2016, March 28). A world on fire. *Oregon Business Magazine.* https://www.oregonbusiness.com/article/politics/item/16592-world-on-fire; Proulx, C. (2016, October 5). Five trends transforming the employee experience at INGOs. https://www.insidengo.org/blog/five-trends-transforming-employee-experience-ingos; Westcott, S. (2008, January 24). Recruiting in dangerous times. *Chronicle of Philanthropy.* https://www.philanthropy.com/article/Recruiting-in-Dangerous-Times/167475; Yoo, T., & Donald, A. (2017, September 7). Tech breakthroughs must reach the world's most vulnerable. https://medium.com/world-economic-forum/tech-breakthroughs-must-reach-the-worlds-most-vulnerable-61661c14f4cc; Yu, R. (2010, August 24). Fending off danger abroad. *USA Today,* Money, p. 1.

Appendix B

Data Analytics Exercises

These exercises provide additional learning opportunities to help you practice using data and analytics. The authors also created Excel extension exercises that accompany the data exercises so that you can apply what you learn using Excel. You can access the Excel extensions on the resource site at edge.sagepub.com/bauerbrief, where you will also find author tutorial PowerPoints that will walk you through how to complete each exercise.

CHAPTER 1

Data and Analytics Exercise: Correlation Does Not Equal Causation

Correlation is an important statistical tool, and it is used in different ways in the context of HRM. A correlation coefficient is a number that conveys two important pieces of information: sign and magnitude. The *sign* (positive or negative) refers to the direction of a relationship, and the size of that relationship is its *magnitude.*

A correlation coefficient can range from −1.00 to +1.00 (i.e., its greatest possible magnitude is 1.00, and its sign can be either positive or negative). A correlation coefficient of −1.00 indicates that two variables are "perfectly" correlated and share a negative (inverse) relationship such that as scores on one variable get larger, scores on the other variable get smaller. Conversely, a correlation of +1.00 indicates that two variables are perfectly correlated and share a positive relationship such that as scores on one variable get larger, scores on the other variable also get larger. Specifically, the absolute value of a correlation coefficient indicates how strong the relationship is, where an absolute value of 1.00 indicates a perfect relationship, and a value of 0.00 indicates

no relationship. In HRM, we often describe the size of a correlation using qualitative descriptors. For instance, we might describe a correlation coefficient of 0.10 as *small,* 0.30 as *medium,* and 0.50 as *large.* A correlation coefficient provides a very efficient description of how much two variables are related in terms of the sign and magnitude of their relationship.

With all that said, we must still remember that *correlation does not mean causation.* That is, two variables may covary with one another without being directly related. When a correlation is found between two variables that are not directly related, we refer to this as a *spurious correlation,* which may be the result of two variables that are not directly related but that share a common cause. For example, imagine that you find a large positive correlation (e.g., $r = .52$) between construction workers' self-reported annual consumption of ice cream and their level of self-reported job satisfaction. That is, as the amount of ice cream consumed by construction workers increases, their level of job satisfaction tends to increase as well. At first glance, we might look at this finding and conclude that ice cream consumption causes job satisfaction. Taking a closer look, we might think, "Well, this relationship doesn't make much sense given what we know about job satisfaction."

What, then, is a possible explanation for this potentially spurious correlation? The finding could be due to a third variable that causes both increases in ice cream consumption and increases in job satisfaction. Perhaps construction workers in this sample work in multiple locations around the United States. Accordingly, those who work in warmer climates consume more ice cream per year to cool off. In addition, those who work in warmer climates feel more satisfied with their job because they work outdoors in more pleasant temperatures. In this scenario, ice cream consumption does not cause job satisfaction, and job satisfaction does not cause ice cream consumption; rather, warmer climate is the common cause that leads to more ice cream consumption and higher job satisfaction, thereby resulting in the spurious correlation.

In sum, we should remain cautious when interpreting correlations and remind ourselves that *correlation does not equal causation*. To avoid making this mistake, we should evaluate each correlation coefficient through the lens of existing theory to make better decisions and draw more appropriate conclusions.

Excel Extension: Now You Try!

- On **edge.sagepub.com/bauerbrief,** you will find an Excel tutorial that shows how to compute a correlation coefficient, as well as a sample data set and questions to answer based on the data.

CHAPTER 2

Data and Analytics Exercise: Describing Your Data

Summarizing people data using descriptive analytics can provide valuable insights into the state of your company. Although there are a number of common HR metrics, such as turnover rate and yield ratio, often it is valuable to summarize basic demographic data, survey data, and performance data using descriptive statistics like frequency, percentage, mean, median, mode, and standard deviation. Part of the challenge is determining which descriptive statistic to use to describe a particular variable. Regarding quantitative variables, one can distinguish between categorical variables and continuous variables. Although variables can be described in even more specific terms, the categorical and continuous distinction is an important one.

A *categorical variable* consists of multiple levels, but these levels do not have a particular order or inherent numeric values. For example, race is typically operationalized as a categorical variable, where the levels of the race variable correspond to the different categories of race (e.g., Asian, Black, White), in no particular order. As another example, for reporting purposes to the Equal Employment Opportunity Commission, employee sex is often reported as a dichotomous categorical variable with the following levels: male and female. When we report categorical variables, we often use frequency or percentage to describe the data. For example, imagine that a company employs 230 female and 199 male employees. We could describe sex using two frequencies: frequency of females (230) and frequency of males (199). Alternatively, we could describe each level of the gender variable as a percentage. For example, 53.6% of employees identify as female (53.6% = 230/(230 + 199) × 100), and 46.4% identify as male (46.4% = 199/(230 + 199) × 100). Data visualizations like the bar charts shown in Figures 2.7 and 2.8 facilitate the communication of such descriptive analytics findings.

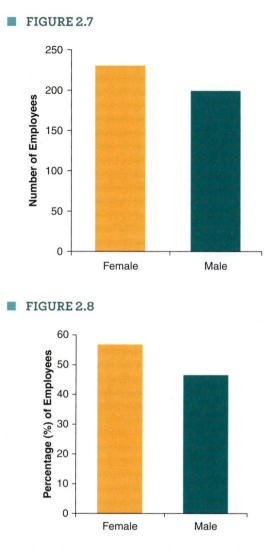

A *continuous variable* consists of a continuum of numerically ordered values. A classic example is employee age when measured in years. Years can be ordered such that we can say someone who is 39 years is older than someone who is 38 years, so one value is larger or higher than another value. Although many survey response scales technically represent what are referred to as ordinal variables, which are distinguishable from continuous variables, we often treat them like continuous variables for the purposes of data analysis. For instance, in an employee engagement survey, you might ask employees to respond to different survey items using a 5-point response scale ranging from *strongly disagree* (1) to *neither agree nor disagree* (3) to *strongly agree* (5).

To summarize employees' ages or their responses to the item "I am satisfied with my job," you could compute descriptive statistics of central tendency and/or dispersion. For example, you might find that the *mean* (average) employee age is 38.2 years with a *standard deviation* of 5.4 years. This means that the center of the distribution of employee ages is 38.2 years and that about two thirds of employees' ages fall within 5.4 years of 38.2 or, in other words, 32.8 to 43.6 years. Similarly, you might find that the mean response to the job satisfaction item is 3.0, which indicates that, on average, employees neither agree nor disagree with the statement "I am satisfied with my job." A standard deviation of 1.2 for responses on that item, however, indicates that approximately two thirds of employees' responses fall within 1.2 points above and below the mean or, in other words, 1.8 to 4.2. So, in that example, a large proportion of employees' responses varied anywhere from slightly dissatisfied to slightly satisfied with their job. When creating a data visualization for a mean, there are many options; Figures 2.9 and 2.10 provide examples.

■ FIGURE 2.9

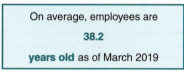

On average, employees are

38.2

years old as of March 2019

■ FIGURE 2.10

The average employee rating was **3.0** for the survey item *I am satisfied with my job*

In summary, descriptive analytics includes basic summary statistics and the data visualizations used to communicate those summary statistics. Identifying the difference between categorical and continuous variables is the first step toward picking the right statistic to summarize your data.

Excel Extension: Now You Try!

- On **edge.sagepub.com/bauerbrief,** you will find an Excel tutorial that shows how to compute descriptive analytics, as well as a sample data set and questions to answer based on the data.

CHAPTER 3
Data and Analytics Exercise: Data Cleaning

One of the overarching goals of any HRIS is to provide users with accurate data. Further, the integrity of the data directly influences the integrity of the insights gleaned from the data, or in other words: garbage in, garbage out. Unfortunately, the data that reside within an HRIS are not always what we would hope or expect for. There are a number of reasons for this, but one of the most common reasons is human error.

Imagine that your HRIS is built around a relational database consisting of a number of different tables. In one of the tables, you store basic employee information, such as employee ID, employee name, job level, location, and department.

Here is an excerpt of the table:

EMPLOYEE ID	EMPLOYEE NAME	JOB LEVEL	LOCATION	DEPARTMENT
EA44312	Kim, Yeongjin	1	beaverton	Customer Service
EB58521	Dowsett, Jane	3	Hillsboro	
EA64533	Henderson, Lynn	4	Hillsboro	
EA89575	Mitchell, Terrance	1	Hillsboro	Customer Service
ET58748	Smith, John	1	Beaverton	Customer Service
ET96461	Martinez, David	4	Beavertn	Marketing
EB11248	Liu, Patricia	11	Beaverton	Customer Service

First, take a close look at the Location field. Do you notice anything? Note how the Beaverton location is spelled with a capital "B" for three of the cases and how it is spelled without the "o" for one case. Most likely, this difference in spelling was the result of an error during data entry. Errors like this might not seem like such a big deal, but down the road, they can lead to issues when it comes to merging and analyzing the data. Namely, many software programs such as Microsoft Access Excel will treat the two different versions of the word *Beaverton* (i.e., Beaverton, Beavertn) location as two distinct categories. That is, instead of treating the Location field as a categorical variable with two levels (i.e., Beaverton, Hillsboro), the Location field will be treated as a categorical variable with the following three levels: Beaverton, Beavertn, and Hillsboro. If you were to create a PivotTable in Excel to determine the frequency (i.e., counts) of employees who work at each location, you would end up with the following frequency table:

Row Labels ▾	Count of Location
Beavertn	1
Beaverton	3
Hillsboro	3
Grand Total	**7**

Note how the frequency table correctly indicates that three employees work at the Hillsboro location but incorrectly indicates that three employees work at the Beaverton location and one employee works at the Beavertn location.

Second, take a close look at the rest of the table. Did you notice the missing data? Specifically, Jane Dowsett and Lynn Henderson are missing the names of the departments in which they work. More than likely, these two employees work in a department that has a name. As such, it is important that these missing data are found and the table is updated.

Third, in this organization, there are only seven job levels, where a 1 corresponds to entry-level jobs and a 7 corresponds to executive jobs. Now take a look at the Job Level field. Note how Patricia Liu has a job level of 11, which is clearly beyond the 1–7 range. This might mean that someone accidentally entered 1 twice by mistake, resulting in 11. Again, a simple Excel PivotTable can be used to create a frequency table that displays how many employees fall into each job level. The frequency table here shows in the left column that one of the job levels is 11, which is not correct.

Row Labels ▾	Count of Job Level
1	3
3	1
4	2
11	1
Grand Total	**7**

The best course of action is to prevent these errors in the first place. For instance, you can design tables with data validation rules that allow only predetermined values to be entered into cells (e.g., Beaverton, Hillsboro). Alternatively, in the context of a relational database, you can create a form that facilitates data entry by requiring data to be entered into certain fields and allowing only certain fields to be completed using drop-down menus with provided options.

If you still find yourself with "dirty" data, you will need to clean the data prior to analysis. Fortunately, Excel and other programs offer several tools that can facilitate the data-cleaning process, such as the PivotTable tool that was highlighted in the example.

Excel Extension: Now You Try!

- On **edge.sagepub.com/bauerbrief,** you will find an Excel tutorial that shows how to clean data, as well as a sample data set and tasks to follow using the data.

CHAPTER 4

Data and Analytics Exercise: Using the Chi-Square Test to Assess Disparate Impact

Given the downsides of the 4/5ths rule, including its high rate of false positives and its sensitivity to sampling errors, companies may rely on more sophisticated analyses. The 4/5ths rule is simply a "rule of thumb" adopted by the courts and is not based on a formal statistical test. An alternative method is the chi-square test.

Consider the following example. Assume that the use of a knowledge test resulted in the following distribution:

	PASS	FAIL	TOTAL
Men	70	90	160
Women	42	72	114
Total	112	162	274

These results indicate that if you disregard gender, 112 of 274 (40.9%) of all applicants passed the test, and 162 of 274 (59.1%) failed the test.

Now you need to calculate the distribution you would expect to see if gender plays no role. Without any systematic effects of gender, you would expect men and women to have the same pass and fail ratios. This is the *expected distribution*.

	PASS	FAIL	TOTAL
Men	65.4 (of 160 men, 40.9% should pass)	94.6 (of 160 men, 59.1% should fail)	160
Women	46.6 (of 114 women, 40.9% should pass)	67.4 (of 114 women, 59.1% should fail)	114
Total	112	162	274

Now you need to enter these data into Excel, as shown in the screenshot. Then insert the formula you see at the top into cell B12. This formula helps you perform a chi-square test. The result is the "*p*-value," which indicates whether the difference you observe

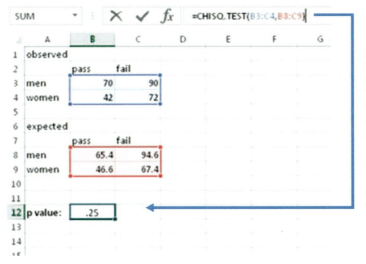

Use the formula listed at the top to calculate the p value for a chi-square difference test.

This test can easily be modified to have more than two groups (e.g., Whites, Hispanics, African Americans, and Asians).

between actual distribution and expected distribution is purely by chance, where a *p*-value lower than .05 is considered statistically significant. The result presented below has a *p*-value of .25, which is not statistically significant (which indicates that there is no evidence of a gender effect on selection).

Excel Extension: Now You Try!

- On **edge.sagepub.com/bauerbrief,** you will find an Excel tutorial that shows how to conduct a chi-square test, as well as a sample data set and questions to answer based on the data.

CHAPTER 5

Data and Analytics Exercise: Evaluating Task–KSAO Analysis Data

When conducting a task–KSAO analysis, a list of tasks and KSAOs is generated for a particular job. To determine which tasks and KSAOs to retain, as well as which KSAOs are most important for performing each task, different questionnaires are administered to subject matter experts (SMEs), who rate the criticality (importance) of the tasks and KSAOs.

Two simple descriptive analytics—the *mean* and the *standard deviation (SD)*—can be used to determine which tasks and KSAOs are most critical, as well as the level of agreement of SMEs' ratings. First, a mean (or average) is a measure of central tendency. Assuming that ratings fall in a normal bell-shaped distribution, the mean represents the most central—or average—rating. In the context of a task–KSAO analysis, the mean rating for a particular task or KSAO represents its level of criticality. So, if a task or KSAO has a higher mean than another task or KSAO, it signifies that it is more critical in the eyes of the SMEs. Second, a standard deviation (*SD*) is a measure of dispersion or variation. Assuming that ratings fall in a normal distribution, the *SD* represents how dispersed or spread out the ratings are around the mean. Thus, in the context of a task–KSAO analysis, a smaller *SD* indicates that there is more agreement in SME ratings for a particular task or KSAO. Further, assuming a normal distribution of SME ratings, 68% of scores will fall between 1 *SD* below and above the mean rating, and 95% of scores will fall within 2 *SD*s below and above the mean rating (as shown in the distribution below).

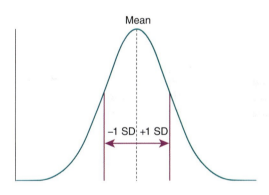

Excel software from Microsoft makes it easy to compute the mean and *SD* of a set of scores. To calculate the mean, use the =AVERAGE() function, and to calculate the *SD,* use the =STDEV.S() function. Within the parentheses of either function, simply enter the vector of scores for which you wish to calculate the mean or *SD*. For example, in the sample spreadsheet shown in the following Excel screenshot, to calculate the mean and *SD* of the first task criticality ratings (i.e., 4, 3, 4, 4, 5, 2, 4, 5), you would enter the following in cells J2 and K2, respectively: =AVERAGE(B2:I2) and =STDEV.S(B2:I2). The mean is 3.88, and the *SD* is .99.

Tasks	SME 1	SME 2	SME 3	SME 4	SME 5	SME 6	SME 7	SME 8	Mean	SD
1. Speaks with customers who are interested in new products.	4	3	4	4	5	2	4	5	3.88	.99
2. Works to solve customer complaints.	5	5	5	5	5	5	5	5		
3. Coordinates with supervisor to resolve customer problems.	4	4	5	4	4	4	5	4		
4. Stays abreast of current sales and specials provided by the company by checking company website.	2	1	3	4	2	2	5	1		
5. Uses telephone system to answer customer calls promptly.	3	3	4	3	4	3	4	4		
6. Uses computer to look up customer orders.	4	4	5	4	4	4	4	4		
7. Uses telephone system to notify customers about products received.	1	1	2	1	2	2	1	1		
8. Uses email system to notify customers about products received.	5	5	4	3	3	3	4	5		
9. Cleans office kitchen area when it is their turn to do so.	2	2	4	2	2	2	3	2		
10. Uses sit/stand desk correctly throughout the day to maintain own personal health.	4	3	4	4	4	5	3	4		
11. Provides customers with refunds, as appropriate, if there is any problem with the product.	1	1	1	1	1	1	1	1		

Excel Extension: Now You Try!

- On **edge.sagepub.com/bauerbrief,** you will find an Excel tutorial that shows how to calculate the means and *SD*s for the task criticality ratings, as well as a sample data set and questions to answer based on the data.

CHAPTER 6

Data and Analytics Exercise: The Transition Matrix and Evaluating Movement Into, Through, and Out of an Organization

Understanding how employees move into, through, and out of different jobs in an organization is important for planning and staffing purposes. So it would be helpful to have a statistic that can be used to analyze these employee transitions. The transition matrix—also known as a Markov matrix—is a useful tool for examining such patterns of movement. As shown in what follows, a transition matrix communicates the number of employees or the proportion of employees who began in one job in one time period and who ended up in other jobs in the

organization or even left the organization by another time period.

Transition Matrix With Raw Numbers

First, take a look at the transition matrix with raw numbers, wherein the numbers represent employees. If read from left to right across a given row, the sum of the row values represents total number of employees who had a particular job title in the earlier time period. For example, a total of 15 (14 + 1) employees held the Research Scientist job title in 2014. Further, each row indicates where employees ended up in

	2020			
	RESEARCH SCIENTIST	**RESEARCH ASSOCIATE**	**RESEARCH ASSISTANT**	**NOT IN ORGANIZATION**
2014 **RESEARCH SCIENTIST**	14			1
RESEARCH ASSOCIATE	4	26		4
RESEARCH ASSISTANT		11	43	2
NOT IN ORGANIZATION	1	2	12	

terms of their job titles at the later time period. For example, 14 of the 15 Research Scientists from 2014 were still Research Scientists at 2020, and 1 of 15 Research Scientists from 2014 exited the organization by 2020. Alternatively, if read from top to bottom by a given column, the sum of each overall column total represents how many employees held a given job title in 2020. For example, 20 (14 + 5 + 1) employees held the job title of a Research Scientist in 2020. Further,

14 of those 20 individuals were also Research Scientists in 2014, 5 were Research Associates in 2014 but are now Research Scientists, and 1 was not in the organization in 2014 but is now a Research Scientist. Accordingly, a transition matrix comprising raw numbers provides an indication of the number of employees who entered, moved within, and exited the organization, as well as which positions they held during their time in the organization.

	2020			
	RESEARCH SCIENTIST	**RESEARCH ASSOCIATE**	**RESEARCH ASSISTANT**	**NOT IN ORGANIZATION**
2014 **RESEARCH SCIENTIST**	.93			.07
RESEARCH ASSOCIATE	.14	.74		.10
RESEARCH ASSISTANT		.20	.77	.03
NOT IN ORGANIZATION	.06	.14	.80	

Transition Matrix With Proportions

Second, take a look at the transition matrix with proportions (bottom of p. A-35), wherein the values represent the proportion of employees from the earlier time period who hold various jobs at the later time period. The transition matrix with proportions is constructed to be read from left to right across a given row, as the sum of each row's proportions totals to 1.0. Further, each row indicates the proportion of employees from an earlier time period who ended up in the same or different jobs (or even out of the organization)

by a later time period. For example, .93 (or 93%) of individuals who held the job title of Research Scientist in 2014 continued to hold the title of Research Scientist in 2020, whereas .07 (7%) of individuals who held the job title of Research Scientist in 2014 left the organization by 2020.

The transition matrix can be a useful descriptive analytics tool, as it can be used to describe the way in which employees have moved into, through, and out of the organization in the past.

Excel Extension: Now You Try!

- On **edge.sagepub.com/bauerbrief,** you will find an Excel tutorial that shows how to create a transition matrix, as well as a sample data set and questions to answer based on the data.

CHAPTER 7

Data and Analytics Exercise: Weighting Predictors via Regression

One way to use analytics to show the validity of a selection procedure, or how well it predicts job performance, is though criterion-related validity. Criterion-related validity of selection procedures can be shown through a statistically significant correlation between a test and a job outcome like performance. Going one step further, regression can show a predicted score on the outcome based on a test.

For example, if you had a data set that allowed you to develop a regression equation (through a statistical program), you would get an equation in this form:

$$Y = bx + a$$

where Y is the predicted score on the outcome, X is the score a person obtained on the test, b is the weight of the test, and a is the constant or "y-intercept."

Let's say the specific equation you obtained from your data set was as follows:

$$Y = 3x + 1$$

In this case, if a person obtained a 5 on the test, their predicted score on outcome would be 16 ($3 \times 5 + 1 = 16$). Note that this is not the score that all people with a 5 would get but is rather a *predicted* score or their most likely score.

Now let's go through an example where you have given three tests to a group of employees (concurrent design). The tests are proactivity, emotional intelligence (EI), and situation judgment (SJT), all predicting customer service job performance. Imagine the resulting correlations between these four variables are as indicated in the table on the next page.

As indicated by the double asterisks (**) next to the correlation coefficients, all three tests have a significant correlation with customer service job performance. But the EI test and SJT are highly redundant, correlated .932. One of them should go.

Here is one way to settle this: You learn that the SJT costs $1 per person to administer, while the test of EI costs $10 per person. With

Correlations

		PROACTIVITY	EMOTIONAL INTELLIGENCE	SJT	CUSTOMER SERVICE
Proactivity	Pearson correlation	1	.318**	.237**	.391**
	Sig. (2-tailed)		.000	.000	.000
	N	300	300	300	300
Emotional intelligence	Pearson correlation	.318**	1	.932**	.426**
	Sig. (2-tailed)	.000		.000	.000
	N	300	300	300	300
SJT	Pearson correlation	.237**	.932**	1	.417**
	Sig. (2-tailed)	.000	.000		.000
	N	300	300	300	300
Customer service	Pearson correlation	.391**	.426**	.417**	1
	Sig. (2-tailed)	.000	.000	.000	
	N	300	300	300	300

**correlation is significant at the .01 level (2-tailed).

thousands of applicants, you are concerned about the relative utility of the EI, and so you decide to drop it.

Now you have to decide how to weight the two remaining tests: proactivity and SJT. To do so, you estimate a regression model with proactivity and SJT as the predictors and customer service as the outcome. In the following table, the regression weights (i.e., coefficients) are found in the column labeled "B Coefficients."

	B COEFFICIENTS	STANDARD ERROR	*t* STATISTIC	*p*-VALUE
Intercept	5.527	.539	10.249	.000
Proactivity	.385	.064	6.031	.000
SJT	.567	.085	6.714	.000

In this case, the weight of SJT is .567, and the weight of proactivity is .385. The constant is 5.527. So the equation then becomes:

Predicted customer service score = 5.527 + .567 (SJT score) + .385 (proactivity score)

So, if a person obtained a 10 on the SJT and a 10 on proactivity, their predicted customer service score would be:

$$Y = 5.527 + 5.670 + 3.850$$

$$Y = 15.047$$

Excel Extension: Now You Try!

- On **edge.sagepub.com/bauerbrief,** you will find an Excel tutorial that shows how to estimate a regression model.

CHAPTER 8

Data and Analytics Exercise: Evaluating a Training Program

Evaluation of training is important yet sometimes forgotten or ignored. But without thoughtful evaluation, a company might continue with a training program in which employees fail to demonstrate sufficient levels of proficiency on key training outcomes. If you recall, we can classify training outcomes using Kirkpatrick's four levels: (1) reactions, (2) learning, (3) behavior, and (4) results.

Different inferential statistical analyses, such as *t*-tests or analyses of variance (ANOVAs), can be used to evaluate training programs, and the most appropriate analysis will depend on the type of design used (e.g., posttest-only design with a control group). Before running inferential statistical analyses, however, it is useful to compute descriptive analytics (e.g., mean, standard deviation) and create charts to generate a basic understanding of how individuals performed on training outcomes.

On one hand, a *mean* is a measure of central tendency. It is the average score. In the training context, we often examine the mean of trained or untrained groups on some outcome measure. On the other hand, a *standard deviation (SD)* represents how dispersed or spread out the scores are around the mean. Thus, a larger *SD* indicates that there is more variation around the mean, whereas a smaller *SD* indicates that there is less variation.

In a normal distribution, 68% of scores fall between 1 *SD* below and above the mean, and 95% of scores fall within 2 *SDs* below and above the mean. If higher scores on a training outcome indicate better performance, organizations typically want to see a high mean coupled with a small *SD,* which would suggest that the average employee performed well and most employees performed at about the same level.

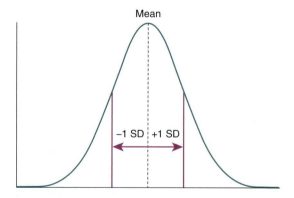

Fortunately, Excel makes it easy to compute the mean and *SD* of a set of scores. To calculate the mean, use the =AVERAGE() function, and to calculate the *SD,* use the =STDEV.S() function. Within the parentheses of either function, simply enter the vector of scores for which you wish to calculate the mean or *SD*. For example, to calculate the mean and SD for the set of training outcome scores (i.e., 7, 6, 4, 8, 6, 4) in the following Excel sheet, you would enter the

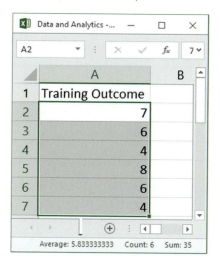

following in an empty cell: =AVERAGE(A2:A7) and =STDEV.S(A2:A7). Try this in Excel—you should get a mean of 5.83 and an *SD* of 1.60.

Now imagine that your company used a posttest-only with control group design to evaluate a safety training program. One group of trainees gets the new safety training program, and another group (control group) gets the old safety training program. The key training outcome is safety knowledge.

In this case, the big question is, *Did those in the new safety training program outperform those in the old safety training program?* Using an independent-samples *t*-test, we can assess whether two means are statistically different from one another. For example, if the *p*-value associated with the *t*-value we generate from the independent-samples *t*-test is less than the conventional cutoff of .05, then we can conclude that the difference in means between the trainees in the new and old safety programs is significant.

Excel Extension: Now You Try!

- On **edge.sagepub.com/bauerbrief,** you will find an Excel tutorial that shows how to conduct an independent-samples *t*-test, as well as a sample data set and questions to answer based on the data.

CHAPTER 9
Data and Analytics Exercise: Using Data Analytics to Understand Performance

It helps to understand what factors contribute to improving performance. Organizations may use predictive analytics to find the answers to this question. For example, let's assume that managers just measured employees' of performance using the company's performance appraisal form. Assume that you have information on four criteria that could affect performance:

- Product knowledge (results of a test the employees took part in)
- Personality (a measure of employee extraversion)

- Time management skills (evaluated by each associate's manager)
- Cooperativeness (evaluated by team members)

Which of these metrics are in fact good predictors of performance ratings? This is important information for the organization. For example, if we find that product knowledge is an important predictor, we can increase investment in training on product knowledge. If extraversion is an important predictor, then we could select employees based on extraversion.

EMPLOYEE	PRODUCT KNOWLEDGE	EXTRAVERSION	TIME MANAGEMENT	COOPERATIVENESS	PERFORMANCE RATING
1	3.75	2.33	2.67	4.67	4
2	3.4	3.8	4.4	2.5	2.5
3	3	2.33	4	4	4.33
4	4	4.67	4.33	4	4
5	4.8	3.75	3.33	3.4	3
6	3.5	2.67	4	4	4
7	4	2.6	3.5	4	4.6
8	5	5	5	2.67	2
9	4	4.6	5	2	2
10	3.4	2	2.3	4.3	4
11	4.5	2.5	4.4	3	4.5
12	3.5	2.3	4.5	3.6	4.3
13	3.8	2.1	2.8	5	5
14	3.7	5	3.2	3.5	4.3
15	3.4	4.5	4.3	5	3.4
16	4.3	4.8	3.75	3.33	3.4
17	4.8	3.5	3.67	4	4
18	3.5	3.67	4	4	4
19	3.5	5	4.4	4	3.4
20	5	2.3	4.5	4.3	5

The table shown above includes the data set we will analyze. To understand which of the four potential predictors are related to performance ratings, you could use simple bivariate correlations. However, you have four predictors and one outcome. If you use correlations, you will look at each relationship in isolation. In reality, our four predictors may be correlated with each other. This means that you may find that each of the four is correlated with performance ratings, but we would not know which ones are the best predictors once the others are accounted for.

For this reason, we will perform a regression analysis on these data. Note that this is actually a very small sample size to perform this analysis, but let's do it for illustration purposes.

We will use the "Data Analysis" function of Excel. (You can perform these analyses very easily in the statistics software SPSS or using a regression calculator that may be found online as well.) Once you click on Data Analysis, you will be able to perform a regression analysis, as shown on the next page (A).

Now we will indicate the range of input. We marked the location of performance ratings under the Y range and the location of the other four variables under the X range. We included variable labels in the selection and then checked the "Labels" box to indicate that the selection includes variable names at the top (next page, B).

(A)

| From HTML | From Text | New Database Query | | Refresh All | | Edit Links | | Sort | Filter | Advanced | Text to Columns |

A24

Data Analysis

Analysis Tools

Moving Average
Random Number Generation
Rank and Percentile
Regression
Sampling
t-Test: Paired Two Sample for Means
t-Test: Two-Sample Assuming Equal Variances
t-Test: Two-Sample Assuming Unequal Variances

OK

Cancel

					G
13	3.8	2.1	2.8	5	5
14	3.7	5	3.2	3.5	4.3
15	3.4	4.5	4.3	5	3.4
16	4.3	4.8	3.75	3.33	3.4
17	4.8	3.5	3.67	4	4
18	3.5	3.67	4	4	4
19	3.5	5	4.4	4	3.4
20	5	2.3	4.5	4.3	5

(B)

Regression

Input

Input Y Range: $F$1:$F$21

Input X Range: $B$1:$E$21

☑ Labels   ☐ Constant is Zero

☐ Confidence Level: 95 %

OK

Cancel

Output options

○ Output Range:
● New Worksheet Ply:
○ New Workbook

Residuals

☐ Residuals   ☐ Residual Plots
☐ Standardized Residuals   ☐ Line Fit Plots

Normal Probability

☐ Normal Probability Plots

Once you hit OK, you will see a new sheet with the output (next page, C).

Now let's take a look at the sections we marked in (C). *R*-square tells us the percentage variance in performance ratings that is being explained by the four variables in our model. An *R*-square of 64% means that the four variables explain 64% of the differences in performance ratings.

(C)

	A	B	C	D	E	F	G	H	I	J
SUMMARY OUTPUT										
Regression Statistics										
Multiple R	0.79765741									
R Square	0.63625735									
Adjusted R S	0.53925931									
Standard Err	0.58922527									
Observations	20									
ANOVA										
	df	*SS*	*MS*	*F*	*Significance F*					
Regression	4	9.1094587	2.27736467	6.55948661	0.00293277					
Residual	15	5.2077963	0.34718642							
Total	19	14.317255								
	Coefficients	*Standard Error*	*t Stat*	*P-value*	*Lower 95%*	*Upper 95%*	*Lower 95.0%*	*Upper 95.0%*		
Intercept	2.23158768	1.81013451	1.23282975	0.23661228	-1.6266227	6.08979805	-1.6266227	6.08979805		
Product Knov	0.12193257	0.23449962	0.51996917	0.61067371	-0.3778915	0.62175669	-0.3778915	0.62175669		
Extraversion	-0.3491473	0.13565507	-2.5737874	0.02117445	-0.6382893	-0.0600054	-0.6382893	-0.0600054		
Time manag	0.02621841	0.22534763	0.11634651	0.90892133	-0.4540987	0.50653552	-0.4540987	0.50653552		
Cooperativen	0.58024875	0.21603593	2.68589001	0.01693088	0.11977906	1.04071844	0.11977906	1.04071844		

The *p*-values tell us about the statistical significance of each predictor. This is an indicator of the probability that the relationship you observe between each predictor and the outcome is actually not different from zero. High *p*-values mean that there is a very good chance that any relation you observe is really due to chance. Small *p*-values indicate that the chance of the observed relationship being zero is really small. In this output, the *p*-values are smaller than .05 for extraversion and cooperativeness. In other words, these are the predictors to pay attention to.

Finally, take a look at the "coefficients" column for extraversion and cooperativeness. Do you see anything interesting here? The sign of the extraversion coefficient is negative. This means that extraversion is actually *negatively* related to performance ratings. Using these data, you would conclude that in this company, introverted employees are actually higher performers. In contrast, there seems to be a positive relationship between cooperativeness and performance ratings. These results would help you make decisions such as where to invest your selection and training budget and where not to.

Excel Extension: Now You Try!

- On **edge.sagepub.com/bauerbrief,** you will find an Excel tutorial that shows how to estimate a regression model, as well as a sample data set and questions to answer based on the data.

CHAPTER 10

Data and Analytics Exercise: How High Is Your Turnover?

Shaffer Technologies is an educational software firm in the San Francisco area. This firm had the following number of departures and number of employees during the past calendar year:

MONTH	NUMBER OF DEPARTURES	NUMBER OF EMPLOYEES
January	24	1,070
February	88	1,347
March	67	1,213
April	29	1,200
May	45	1,422
June	77	1,277
July	74	1,286
August	18	1,109
September	34	1,272
October	14	1,000
November	63	1,263
December	72	1,435

1. Using the formula presented in Chapter 10, calculate the annual overall turnover rate for this firm.

2. How would you decide whether this turnover rate is excessive for this firm? Explain the steps you would follow to make this decision.

3. Let's focus only on January. Assume that out of the 24 employees who are shown as departures, 2 left voluntarily, 9 of them are on FMLA leave, 5 of them were temporary agency workers who were let go, 2 retired, 4 were terminated for cause, and 2 were put on unpaid leave. What is the monthly turnover rate for January?

Excel Extension: Now You Try!

- On **edge.sagepub.com/bauerbrief,** you will find an Excel tutorial that shows how to calculate turnover rates, as well as a sample data set and questions to answer based on the data.

CHAPTER 11
Data and Analytics Exercise: Evaluating Pay Compression

The compa-ratio can be a useful metric when investigating whether pay compression might be an issue for those employees who work the same job and thus belong to the same pay grade. For this exercise, you will calculate compa-ratios for individual employees using the following formula:

$$\text{Compa-ratio for one employee} = \frac{\text{Actual pay of employee}}{\text{Midpoint of pay grade}}$$

For example, if an employee earns $42,000/year and the midpoint of the employee's pay grade is $40,000, then the compa-ratio will be equal to 1.05 ($42,000/$40,000 = 1.05). Because this compa-ratio value is greater than 1.00, it indicates that the employee is paid more than the midpoint of the pay grade. If the compa-ratio had been less than 1.00, then it would have indicated that the employee was paid less than the midpoint of the pay grade. Now let's imagine that there are 100 total employees who work the same job, and we compute compa-ratios for each of them. In addition to each employee's compa-ratio, we also know the length of time (in years) that the employee has worked in that position (i.e., tenure). Using the compa-ratio and tenure variables, we can construct a scatterplot to understand how these employees are compensated relative to their length of tenure.

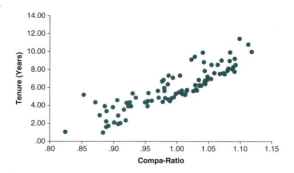

The scatterplot indicates that employees with higher compa-ratios tend to have worked in the job more years. In other words, there does not appear to be evidence of pay compression, as individuals who have worked fewer years in the job tend to earn less pay relative to the midpoint than those who have worked more years.

Excel Extension: Now You Try!

- On **edge.sagepub.com/bauerbrief,** you will find an Excel tutorial that shows how to compute compa-ratios, as well as a sample data set and questions to answer based on the data.

CHAPTER 12

Data and Analytics Exercise: Evaluating Employees' Satisfaction With Benefits

Offering the right mix of benefits can be quite challenging. Employers want to manage costs while also providing benefits that attract, motivate, and retain potential and current employees, and employees want benefits that meet their needs. Even the best assortment of benefits offerings can face problems if program details are not properly communicated and explained to employees. Employee surveys can be a powerful data collection tool when used to understand employees' attitudes toward benefits and how to improve benefits offerings.

Imagine an employee survey with items (e.g., questions) pertaining to the following attitudinal and behavioral concepts: overall benefits satisfaction, turnover intentions, and attendance at a benefits information session. Overall benefits satisfaction and turnover intentions are assessed with five-item measures, where employees rated each item using a 1 = *strongly disagree* and 5 = *strongly agree* response scale. An example item for overall benefits satisfaction is: "I am satisfied with the company's current medical plan offerings." A sample item for turnover intentions is: "I am considering leaving the organization in the next 6 months." A single item is used to assess attendance at a benefits information session, such that employees respond either "yes, I attended" or "no, I did not attend."

In what follows, we include a sample of employee response data for illustration purposes, where each row contains a unique employee's data and each column contains employees' scores on each of the three attitudinal and behavioral concepts. To simplify things, the averages of employees' responses (i.e., scores) on the five-item measures for overall benefits satisfaction and turnover intentions have already been computed.

OVERALL BENEFITS SATISFACTION	TURNOVER INTENTIONS	ATTENDED A BENEFITS INFORMATION SESSION
3.78	2.87	Yes
4.60	1.91	Yes
3.19	2.14	Yes
4.12	1.90	Yes
3.88	2.90	Yes
3.84	1.64	Yes
4.68	1.63	Yes
3.46	3.29	Yes
3.26	2.45	Yes
4.52	2.07	Yes
2.06	2.98	No
2.84	2.97	No
3.63	3.01	No
3.36	3.17	No
3.64	3.45	No
2.84	4.09	No
2.71	3.40	No
2.84	3.14	No
2.86	2.83	No
2.93	2.66	No

Given these data, we will attempt to answer the following questions:

- Is there a negative correlation between overall benefits satisfaction and turn-over intentions, such that employees with higher overall satisfaction with benefits offerings have fewer intentions to leave the company?

- Do employees who attended a benefits information session have higher overall satisfaction with their benefits than employees who did not?

To answer the first question, we can use simple linear regression, where overall benefits satisfaction is specified as the predictor variable and turnover intentions is specified as the outcome variable. Using Excel, we find the following:

	COEFFICIENTS	STANDARD ERROR	t STATISTIC	p-VALUE	LOWER 95%	UPPER 95%
Intercept	4.81	.61	7.89	.00	3.53	6.09
Overall benefits satisfaction	-.60	.17	-3.49	.00	-.97	-.24

The results indicate that the regression coefficient for overall benefits satisfaction in relation to turnover intentions is –.60, which means that the association between the two variables is negative. Such an association means that for every 1-point increase in overall benefits satisfaction, we tend to see turnover intentions drop by .60 points. The corresponding p-value is less than the conventional two-tailed cutoff (alpha) value of .05, which means we can treat the regression coefficient of –.60 as being statistically significant. Together, these two pieces of information provide evidence that, indeed, employees with higher overall satisfaction with benefits offerings have fewer intentions to leave the company.

Regarding the second question, we can run an independent-samples t-test using Excel to determine whether the average overall benefits satisfaction score for those who attend a benefits information session is significantly higher than the average overall benefits satisfaction score for those who did not attend a session.

	YES	NO
Mean	3.93	2.97
Variance	.29	.22
Observations	10	10
Pooled variance	.26	
Hypothesized mean difference	0	
df	18	
t Statistic	4.22	
P(T ≤ t) one-tail	.00	
t Critical one-tail	1.73	
P(T ≤ t) two-tail	.00	
t Critical two-tail	2.10	

The results indicate that the t statistic that corresponds to the difference between the two means (averages) is 4.22, and the associated two-tailed p-value is less than the conventional cutoff of .05. Based on this information, we have evidence that in fact there is a statistically significant difference between the average overall benefits satisfaction score for those who attended a benefits information session and the average overall benefits satisfaction score for those who did not attend a session. To determine whether those who attended the information session had a higher average, we can look at the mean scores. The mean for the group of employees who indicated "yes, I attended" was 3.93, whereas the mean for those who indicated "no, I did not attend" was 2.97. Thus, we found support that indeed those who attended an information session tended to have higher satisfaction with the company's current benefits offerings.

Excel Extension: Now You Try!

- On **edge.sagepub.com/bauerbrief,** you will find an Excel tutorial that shows how to estimate a regression model and conduct an independent-samples *t*-test, as well as a sample data set and questions to answer based on the data.

CHAPTER 13

Data and Analytics Exercise: Using Opinion Survey Data to Gauge Employee Satisfaction

Gathering and analyzing opinion survey data from existing employees is a common practice for medium and large businesses. However, small businesses can also benefit from this activity. It doesn't have to be a long, time-intensive survey to help small businesses track how satisfied their employees are over time. Such data can also be helpful in understanding reactions to organizational changes because you have the data both before and after.

1. Imagine that all of your employees have been filling out an anonymous survey every year

they have been with your small but growing organization. In 2010, there were eight employees. Since 2010, you've been averaging hiring around three new employees each year but sometimes only one in a given year.

2. You want to analyze the data to see what trends are occurring in terms of their overall job satisfaction scores for each year, which range from 1 (*completely dissatisfied*) to 7 (*completely satisfied*). The data from those annual surveys appear in the following table.

	2010	2011	2012	2013	2014	2015	2016	2017	2018
1									5.1
2							6.2	5.9	5.0
3				4.5					
4	7.0	6.8	5.1	2.0					
5	5.9	5.8	5.8	5.6	5.7	5.9	5.6	5.8	5.9

(Continued)

(Continued)

6	6.3	6.2	6.5	5.9	6.1	6.6	6.3	6.3	5.8
7	6.4	6.6	6.7	4.1	5.1	5.5	6.2	5.8	5.1
8	4.0	4.0	4.0	4.0	4.0	4.0	4.0	4.0	4.0
9						6.2	5.9	5.0	5.0
10					5.0	5.0	5.0	5.0	5.0
11				7.0	6.8	6.6	6.0	5.3	5.0
12				5.0	5.0	5.0	5.0	5.0	5.0
13		6.0	6.0	3.8	5.0	5.2	5.1	5.6	5.4
14									7.0
15									6.8
16								7.0	7.0
17				4.0	5.2	5.2	5.4	5.5	5.5
18						4.0	3.8	3.6	3.0
19			7.0	6.2	6.8	6.0	6.1	6.4	6.0
20						6.6	6.0	5.3	5.0
21		6.0	6.0	5.0	6.0	6.0	6.0	6.0	6.0
22								6.3	6.4
23						5.4	5.3	5.5	5.7
24						5.4	5.3	5.5	5.7
25					1.0	1.0	1.0	1.0	1.0
26	7.0	7.0	7.0	7.0	7.0	7.0	7.0	7.0	7.0
27				5.5	4.9	5.1	5.4	5.5	5.5
28				4.0	5.2	5.1	5.5		
29			2.0	2.0	2.0	2.0	2.0	2.0	2.0
30							5.0	5.0	5.0
31				5.9	5.4	5.2	5.5	5.5	6.1
32				5.4	5.9	5.1	5.5	5.6	5.7
33			5.1	5.4	5.9	5.1	5.5	5.6	5.7

34				6.4	6.1	5.3	5.1	4.8	4.2
35	7.0	7.0	7.0	7.0	7.0	7.0	7.0	7.0	7.0
36									
37	5.3	5.6	5.3	5.4	5.9	5.1	5.5	5.6	5.7
38								5.3	5.7

Questions to Address

1. Do you have any concerns about these data? Why or why not?

2. Are the survey data truly anonymous? Explain your rationale.

3. What questions would you ask about these data?

4. What action would you take based on these data?

Excel Extension: Now You Try!

- On **edge.sagepub.com/bauerbrief,** you will find an Excel tutorial that shows how to compute means and standard deviations and how to create a heat map table, as well as a sample data set and questions to answer based on the data.

CHAPTER 14
Data and Analytics Exercise: Investigating Employee Stress

Recall that employee stress can lead to workplace accidents, as well as to lower productivity and higher turnover. Stress can be conceptualized as a process involving stressors and strain, where stressors are demands in the environment to which a person must respond and strain refers to a person's reaction to stressors. Employees' perceptions of stressors and strain can be measured using surveys, and the data from such surveys can be used to understand which organizational units perceive the highest levels of stressors and strain and whether stressors and strain are associated with important outcomes, such as employee attitudes (e.g., job satisfaction, turnover intentions) and performance.

Regression analysis can be used to understand whether the relationship between a stressor or strain variable and an outcome variable is statistically significant and, if so, the direction of the association (positive vs. negative). For example, consider the following data set. It contains employees' perceptions of a common workplace stressor called interpersonal conflict and their turnover intentions. Each row represents a unique employee's set of responses to the different survey questions, and the numeric scores associated with each variable represent the employee's average response to items/questions associated with that particular variable.

SURVEY NUMBER	INTERPERSONAL CONFLICT	TURNOVER INTENTIONS
1	4.6	4.1
2	4.7	3.4
3	3.7	4.0
4	3.9	3.1
5	3.6	3.7
6	2.0	3.9
7	3.3	2.9
8	2.9	3.4
9	3.2	3.7
10	2.9	4.0
11	2.9	3.4
12	3.1	3.4
13	3.3	3.8
14	2.0	2.9
15	2.5	3.4
16	2.3	2.5
17	2.5	2.7
18	3.5	2.3
19	2.6	2.1
20	1.4	1.5

If you were to plug these variables into a simple linear regression analysis, wherein interpersonal conflict is entered as a predictor variable and turnover intentions is entered as an outcome variable, you would find that the association between the two variables is statistically significant because the p-value equals .03, which is less than the conventional cutoff of .05. Further, the unstandardized regression coefficient for interpersonal conflict is .58, which means that the association is positive and that for every 1.0-point increase in interpersonal conflict scores, turnover intentions scores tend to increase by .58 points. An excerpt from the regression analysis output is provided.

	COEFFICIENTS	STANDARD ERROR	t STATISTIC	p-VALUE	LOWER 95%	UPPER 95%
Intercept	1.20	.80	1.50	.15	–.48	2.88
Interpersonal conflict	.58	.24	2.37	.03	.06	1.09

If the regression coefficient for interpersonal conflict had been nonsignificant (i.e., the p-value were equal to or greater than .05), then we would conclude that there is no association between the two variables.

Excel Extension: Now You Try!

- On **edge.sagepub.com/bauerbrief,** you will find an Excel tutorial that shows how to estimate a regression model, as well as a sample data set and questions to answer based on the data.

CHAPTER 15

Data and Analytics Exercise: Managing Expatriates Using Data

Ettinger Manufacturing currently has 30 expatriates working in three countries. They perform similar jobs, and they started their expatriate assignments at about the same time. A sample of the data collected from them is shown here. What would you do with such data to understand how best to manage expatriates at Ettinger Manufacturing? For example, consider conducting a one-way ANOVA to see if there are differences based on location, or an independent-samples t-test to see if predeparture training makes a difference.

EXPATRIATE ID	ASSIGNMENT SATISFACTION	FAMILY SATISFACTION	PAY SATISFACTION	COWORKER SATISFACTION	RECEIVED PREDEPARTURE TRAINING (1 = YES)	LOCATION
1	4.57	3.55	2.70	2.85	1	Turkey
2	5.00	3.00	3.30	2.55	1	Turkey
3	4.14	3.19	3.00	3.19	1	Turkey

(Continued)

(Continued)

4	4.71	3.56	3.38	2.88	1	Turkey
5	4.57	4.13	3.13	3.25	1	Turkey
6	4.57	4.31	3.06	1.81	1	Turkey
7	4.14	3.00	2.58	1.50	0	Turkey
8	3.00	2.69	3.38	1.63	1	Turkey
9	1.57	1.38	1.50	1.13	0	Turkey
10	2.71	3.42	3.08	1.08	0	Turkey
11	3.14	2.50	3.31	1.31	1	Canada
12	3.86	2.88	3.00	1.88	1	Canada
13	3.86	2.83	2.67	1.17	0	Canada
14	2.71	1.95	2.05	1.40	0	Canada
15	3.86	3.25	2.25	1.80	1	Canada
16	3.57	2.82	2.57	1.57	1	Canada
17	4.71	4.00	2.42	1.17	0	Canada
18	4.86	3.50	1.69	1.13	0	Canada
19	4.00	3.15	2.05	1.55	1	Canada
20	2.71	2.63	2.13	1.63	0	Canada
21	4.00	2.78	2.84	1.84	0	Spain
22	3.00	1.38	2.13	1.50	0	Spain
23	3.50	1.90	2.70	1.20	1	Spain
24	3.57	2.50	1.38	1.00	1	Spain
25	3.29	2.75	2.63	2.38	1	Spain
26	3.00	2.75	2.63	1.63	1	Spain
27	4.86	4.06	2.75	2.19	1	Spain
28	4.43	3.19	3.00	1.94	1	Spain
29	4.57	3.69	3.44	2.38	0	Spain
30	4.00	3.50	2.94	2.44	0	Spain

Excel Extension: Now You Try!

- On **edge.sagepub.com/bauerbrief,** you will find an Excel tutorial that shows how to estimate a regression model, an independent-samples *t*-test, and a one-way analysis of variance, as well as a sample data set and questions to answer based on the data.

Glossary

360-degree feedback Multiple-rater systems, which present employees with feedback from different stakeholders and have the potential to provide rich information

4/5ths (or 80%) rule According to this rule, one group's selection ratio may not be less than 80% of the majority group's ratio

Absenteeism Unscheduled absences from work

Adhocracy culture Organizations with adhocracy cultures are creation focused and emphasize entrepreneurship, flexibility, risk taking, and creativity

Alternative dispute resolution Methods of resolving disputes that do not involve litigation

Anchoring bias The tendency when making a judgment to rely on the first piece of information that one receives

Anonymous data Pieces of information that cannot be linked to any information that might identify an individual, thereby disclosing the individual's identity

Applicant reactions A job applicant's perspective regarding the selection procedures they encounter and the employer that uses them

Applicant tracking system (ATS) An internal system that offers a centralized way to house employee data and to enable electronic business processes related to recruitment

A-S-A framework The process of attraction, selection, and attrition that defines an organization's culture

Assessment center A specific type of work sample, often used for manager selection

Availability bias The tendency to rely more on information that is readily available than alternative information

Behavior/behavior criteria Actual behavior on the job that is an outcome of training

Behavioral interview A type of structured selection interview that uses questions about how applicants handled a work-related situation in the past

Benchmark job A key job that is common across different organizations in terms of its job description

Benchmarking The measurement of the quality of an organization's practices in comparison with those of a peer organization

Benefits Employee rewards that are sometimes referred to as indirect pay and include health, life, and disability insurance; retirement programs; and work–life balance programs

Biases A tendency, feeling, or opinion, especially one that is preconceived, unreasoned, and unsupported by evidence

Big data Large amounts of unstructured, messy, and sometimes quickly streaming data, which can be described in terms of volume, variety, velocity, and veracity

Biographical data (biodata) Information about a job applicant based on their personal history that can be used to make selection decisions

Blockchain A distributed incorruptible digital technology infrastructure that maintains a fully encoded database that serves as a ledger where all transactions are recorded and stored

Bona fide occupational qualification (BFOQ) A particular instance where a normally legally protected characteristic (such as age or gender) is an essential necessity of a job

Boomerang employees Former employees who rejoin an organization

Bridge employment Reducing one's hours or reducing job demands within the same or a different organization in preparation for full retirement

Business ethics A system of principles that govern how business operate, how decisions are made, and how people are treated

Calibration meeting A meeting in which groups of managers come together and discuss the ratings they will give their employees before ratings are finalized

Candidate experience A term for applicant reactions often used by employers

Career management The continual process of setting career-related goals and planning a route to achieve those goals

Case studies A managerial training method wherein participants analyze and discuss a difficult business case

Central tendency error The tendency to rate most employees in the middle category

Clan culture Organizations with clan cultures are collaboration and people oriented and value cohesion, employee empowerment, and team players

Cognitive ability test A measure of the ability to perceive, process, evaluate, compare, create, understand, manipulate, or generally think about information and ideas

Collective bargaining The process of negotiating in good faith toward agreed terms on wages, hours, and working conditions

Compa-ratio A ratio that reflects how much employees are actually paid for a given job or pay grade as compared to the espoused pay structure and policies, and it can be used to assess whether systematic compression or inversion is occurring

Compensable factors The common dimensions by which jobs vary in terms of worth to the organization

Compensation Employee reward that includes base pay and variable pay and is sometimes referred to as direct pay

Competency A cluster of knowledge, skills, abilities, and other characteristics (KSAOs) necessary to be effective at one's job

Competency modeling A type of job analysis with the goal of understanding what types of attributes and behaviors are required for a group of jobs, perhaps over an entire organization

Confidential data Information for which individuals' identities are known by the researchers due to the linking of a name or code but are not generally disclosed or reported

Consolidated Omnibus Budget Reconciliation Act (COBRA) Introduced in 1985 to protect employees' and their beneficiaries' health care coverage for a designated amount of time in the event of job loss, work-hour reductions, or another major occurrence

Contingent employees Employees who are hired for a limited, fixed term such as a short-term contract or a project consulting contract

Coreflex plan A plan that provides some services (such as paying for movers and travel expenses) to all expatriates, with the remainder of benefits personalized to the unique situation of the expatriate

Critical incident method A method through which managers identify examples of exceptionally high and low incidents of performance and document them in narrative form

Critical incidents technique A technique that involves asking SMEs to describe critical job situations that they frequently encounter on the job

Cultural adjustment Adjusting to the new culture one is now living in, including factors such as transportation, entertainment, health system, education, and general living conditions

Culture shock The feeling of disorientation individuals experience when they enter a new culture

Cybersecurity Data security applied to information accessible through the Internet

Data flow diagrams Depict the logical design of how data move from one entity to the next and how data are processed within an information system

Data lake Stores a vast amount of raw data in its native (and often unstructured) format

Data privacy Individual's control over the collection, storage, access, and reporting of their personal data

Data security Protective measures taken to prevent unauthorized access to employee data and to preserve the confidentiality and integrity of the data

Data-driven decisions Decisions that are made based on the analysis and interpretation of relevant, accurate, and timely data

Defined-benefit plan Also known as a traditional pension plan, a type of retirement plan in which the employer provides plan participants with a preestablished benefit to be paid out over a fixed time period

Defined-contribution plan A type of retirement plan in which the employee and/or employer contributes to an investment fund

Descriptive analytics Focuses on understanding what has already happened, which implies a focus on the past

Dismissal Employment termination because the worker fails to meet organizational expectations

Disparate (or adverse) impact When employers use seemingly neutral criteria that have a discriminatory effect on a protected group

Disparate treatment Treating different groups of applicants or employees differently because of their race, color, religion, sex, or national origin

Diversity Real or perceived differences among people with respect to sex, race, ethnicity, age, physical and mental ability, sexual orientation, religion, and attributes that may affect their interactions with others

Educational-assistance program A program whereby the employer provides financial assistance for employee educational expenses

e-HRM Internet-based information systems and technology that span across organizational levels

eLearning Training that is delivered through an online platform via computers or mobile devices

Emotional intelligence (EI) One's ability to recognize and appraise emotions in oneself and others and behave accordingly

Employee relations The collective relationships between different employees as well as between employees and management in an organization

Employee Retirement Income Security Act (ERISA) Introduced in 1974 to establish minimum standards for many private employers' health care plans to protect employees

Employee wellness programs Organizational initiatives that promote the health, fitness, and well-being of workers

Employment at will When organizations have the right to terminate the employment of anyone at any time, and employees have the right to quit at any time

Enterprise resource planning (ERP) Integrated business management software intended to coordinate and integrate processes and data across different functional areas of a company

Equal Employment Opportunity Commission (EEOC) An independent federal agency that ensures compliance with the law and provides outreach activities designed to prevent discrimination

Ergonomic design Fitting the physical aspects of the job to the human body

Executive coaching Individual advice and counseling to managers regarding their work and careers

Executive orders Presidential orders that carry the force of law

Expatriate A person who is living and working in a different country than their country of origin

Expectancy theory A theory that suggests that if a person sees that their efforts will lead to greater performance, and if they believe that performance will lead to an outcome that they value, they will be more motivated

External equity The extent to which the pay for a particular job is competitive and fair relative to the pay of the same or similar jobs at other organizations

External recruitment An employer's actions that are intended to bring a job opening to the attention of potential job candidates outside of the organization and, in turn, influence their intention to pursue the opportunity

Fair Labor Standards Act (FLSA) Enacted in 1938, this act introduced major provisions aimed at regulating overtime pay, minimum wage, hours worked, and recordkeeping

Family and Medical Leave Act (FMLA) Introduced in 1993 to protect employees' job security when they need to take unpaid leave due to family or medical issues

Family-to-work conflict When nonwork responsibilities interfere with work responsibilities

Federal Insurance Contributions Act (FICA) A federal payroll tax paid by both employees and employers that funds current Social Security beneficiaries

Feedback culture A culture in which employees and managers feel comfortable giving and receiving feedback

Five-factor model (FFM) A model of normal adult personality that includes the dimensions of Openness to Experience, Conscientiousness, Extraversion, Agreeableness, and Neuroticism

Flexible benefit plans Offer employees some degree of choice for the employer-sponsored voluntary benefits they select and the benefits they are able to receive on a pretax basis

Flextime A work arrangement in which workers can choose from a number of work schedules

Forced distribution Also known as stack rankings; involves the rater placing a specific percentage of employees into categories such as exceptional, adequate, and poor performer categories

Forecasting The act of determining estimates during workforce planning regarding what specific positions need to be filled and how to fill them

Frame of reference (FOR) training Training that involves raters observing specific instances of performance through videotapes or vignettes and then telling them the "true score" and why raters should rate in a particular way

Games and simulations A type of managerial training in which teams challenge each other as if they were businesses in competition

Gamification Training that is made into a game or competition among employees in terms of scores on their training performance

Gig economy The prevalence of temporary employment positions, where individuals are employed as independent workers instead of actual employees of an organization

Global integration When a company standardizes its HR practices around the world

Global mindset Refers to being open to learning about different cultures, having a sense of adventure, being comfortable dealing with ambiguity, and having a nonjudgmental attitude toward those from other cultures

Halo error Basing performance ratings on one or two performance dimensions, with one prominent dimension positively affecting how the employee is perceived on other dimensions

Harassment Unwelcome behaviors based on sex, race, religion, national origin, and other protected characteristics

Health Insurance Portability and Accountability Act (HIPAA) Introduced in 1996 to add protections to the portability of employees' health care coverage and ensure the privacy and security of employees' health care data

Hierarchy culture Organizations with hierarchy cultures focus on control and value being efficient, timely, and consistent

High-performance work practices Bundles of HR universal best HR practices, such as promoting within the organization and offering training

Hiring manager The person who asked for the role to be filled and/or to whom the new hire will be reporting as their manager

Hostile work environment Behavior that contributes to an environment that a reasonable person would find offensive

HR business partner Someone who serves as a consultant to management on HR-related issues

HR generalist A person who fulfills an HR generalist function attends to multiple HR functions

HR specialist A person who fulfills an HR specialist function attends to all aspects of one specific HRM function

Human capital The knowledge, skills, and abilities that people embody across an organization

Human resource (HR) analytics The process of collecting, analyzing, interpreting, and reporting people-related data for the purpose of improving decision making, achieving strategic objectives, and sustaining a competitive advantage

Human resource information systems (HRIS) Systems used to collect, store, manage, analyze, retrieve, and report HR data and allow for the automation of some HR management functions

Human resource management (HRM) The decisions and actions associated with managing individuals throughout the employee life cycle to maximize employee and organization effectiveness

Inclusive environments Organizations or groups in which individuals, regardless of their background, are treated with dignity and respect, included in decision making, and valued for who they are and what they bring to the group or organization

Individual equity The fairness of how pay is administered and distributed to individual employees working similar jobs within the same organization

Informational interview The exchange of information between an individual and an organizational representative

with the goal of learning more about the organization and its industry

Integrity test A test specifically developed to assess applicants' tendency toward counterproductive and antisocial behavior

Interactional adjustment The comfort felt with interacting with local individuals inside or outside work

Internal equity The fairness of pay rates across jobs within an organization

International companies Companies that export or import, but their investments are within one home country

Involuntary turnover An employee terminated by the organization against their own wishes

Job (job classification) A group of related duties within an organization

Job analysis The analysis of work and the employee characteristics needed to perform the work successfully

Job Characteristics Model (JCM) The first complete model of job design, explaining which job characteristics are the most important to increasing worker motivation and productivity

Job crafting Redesigning one's own job to fit one's needs (e.g., abilities, interests, personality)

Job Demands-Resources Model (JDR) This model emphasizes that job demands, such as workload and time pressure, can be counteracted by characteristics such as job control, participation, and supervisor support

Job descriptions Job descriptions provide the title and purpose of the job, as well as a general overview of the essential tasks, duties, and responsibilities (i.e., observable actions) associated with the job

Job design The process of identifying how a job's characteristics are experienced from the employee's perspective to enhance well-being and performance

Job embeddedness model A model that explains that employees stay because of their links to others and fit

with the context at work and in their communities, and how much they would have to sacrifice by leaving their work and communities

Job enlargement The addition of more responsibilities to a job so that it is less boring and more motivating for workers

Job enrichment Allowing workers to have greater decision-making power

Job rotation Rotating employees from one job to another, allowing them to learn new skills

Job specifications Job specifications focus on the characteristics of an employee who does the job

KSAOs Knowledge, skills, abilities, and other characteristics employees need to have to do their work most effectively

Labor Management Relations Act (1947) Also known as the Taft-Hartley Act; amended the National Labor Relations Act and restricts the activities and power of labor unions

Labor market conditions The number of jobs available compared to the number of individuals available with the required KSAOs to do those jobs

Labor relations Managing in response to labor laws relating to unions and collective bargaining

Labor–Management Reporting and Disclosure Act (LMRDA) (1959) Requires labor organizations to report financial transactions and administrative practices of unions, employers, and labor consultants

Layoffs Organizationally initiated termination of employment due to economic or strategic reasons

Leadership development The formal and informal opportunities for employees to expand their KSAOs

Learning criteria Measures of whether the trainee actually gained some sort of knowledge or skill while in training

Leniency error The tendency of a rater to rate most employees highly

Life insurance program Provides financial compensation for designated beneficiaries when the insured individual dies

Little data Structured data that are gathered in small volumes, usually for a previously planned purpose

Local differentiation When organizations vary their HR practices in consideration of the local environment

Long-term disability insurance A form of income protection for employees that is similar to short-term disability insurance, except it offers longer-term benefits activated once short-term disability insurance benefits expire

Management by objectives (MBOs) A management strategy where organizational goals are translated into department- and individual-level goals

Market culture Organizations with market cultures are characterized by competition and are characterized as aggressive, competitive, and customer oriented

Market review The process of collecting pay data for benchmark jobs from other organizations

Metacognitive skills A person's ability to step back and assess their own skill, performance, or learning

Mindfulness training Teaches a person to be present in the moment and to notice things around them in a nonjudgmental way

Mission A core need that an organization strives to fulfill and represents the organization's overarching purpose

Multifactor authentication An extra layer of security that requires an additional piece of information that only the user would know

Multinational companies Companies operating in multiple countries but with clearly designated headquarters in their home country

Multiple-hurdle approach When a series of selection procedures are administered sequentially and applicants must pass each hurdle to move to the next one

National Labor Relations Act Stipulates that employees protected under the act have a right to discuss pay as part of activities related to collective bargaining and protection, thereby providing an avenue through which employees may uncover pay discrimination

National Labor Relations Board (NLRB) An independent U.S. governmental agency, the NLRB is tasked with supervising union elections and is empowered to investigate suspected unfair labor practices

Near misses Situations in which an accident could have occurred but did not

Needs assessment A systematic evaluation of the organization, the jobs, and the employees to determine where training is most needed and what type of training is needed

Occupational Safety and Health Administration (OSHA) Under the U.S. Department of Labor, OSHA's purpose is to ensure safe and healthy working conditions for employees by setting and enforcing safety and health standards

Office of Federal Contract Compliance Programs (OFCCP) A division of the Department of Labor, monitors EEO compliance of federal contractors

Offshoring When companies produce physical goods or perform some of their operations overseas

Onboarding (organizational socialization) The process of helping new employees adjust to their new organizations by imparting to them the knowledge, skills, behaviors, culture, and attitudes required to successfully function within the organization

Open offices An office arrangement in which employees work in open spaces

Organizational culture Assumptions shared by organization members, which affect their actions, thoughts, and perceptions

Organizationally assigned expatriate When an expat is sent by the organization for a predetermined time to work in an overseas operation

Orientation program A specific type of training designed to help welcome, inform, and guide new employees

Outsourcing Moving some operations of the organization to a different organization

Overconfidence bias The tendency for an individual to be more confident in their own beliefs than reality would suggest

Paid time off (PTO) A program that provides employees with compensation when they take time away from work, subject to employer approval

Patient Protection and Affordable Care Act (PPACA) Introduced in 2010 to provide rights and protections associated with access to health care coverage

Pay compression Occurs when more recently hired employees with less experience earn nearly as much or the same as more experienced, longer-tenured employees in the same job or when employees in a lower-level job earn nearly as much or the same as employees in a higher-level job

Pay-for-performance programs Compensation programs that reward employees based on the behaviors they actually exhibit at work and for the results or goals they actually achieve

Pay structure The way in which an organization applies pay rates and financial rewards to different jobs, skills, or competencies

Performance appraisal A measurement of employee performance

Performance improvement plan (PIP) Plan aimed at helping poor performers be accountable to meeting performance standards

Performance management The process of measuring, communicating, and managing employee performance

Perquisites (perks) Nonmonetary services or benefits provided by an employer

Personally identifiable data Data readily linked to specific individuals

Point-factor method A job evaluation approach in which a team of subject matter experts systematically identifies compensable factors and develops and applies scales and weights for compensable factors, ultimately resulting in points being assigned to different jobs to describe their relative worth

Position Duties that can be carried out by one person

Prescriptive analytics Focuses on what actions should be taken based on what is likely to happen in the future

Predictive analytics Focuses on what is likely to happen in the future based on available data

Progressive discipline The process of using increasingly severe steps to correct a performance problem

Pulse surveys Short, frequent surveys

Qualitative data Nonnumeric information that includes text or narrative data, such as interview transcripts

Quantitative data Numeric data that can be counted or measured in some way

Quid pro quo harassment Involves making employment decisions contingent on sexual favors

Reactions criteria The assessment of how trainees react to training such as whether they thought it was valuable

Realistic job preview (RJP) Offers potential applicants a realistic view of

the actual job, including both positive and negative information

Reasonable accommodation An accommodation provided to employees to help them perform their jobs that is reasonable given a firm's resources

Recency error When a rater focuses on the most recent employee behaviors they have observed rather than focusing on the entire rating period

Recruitment The process of identifying a group of individuals (employees or potential applicants) who possess the KSAOs to fill a particular role

Relational returns Nonmonetary incentives and rewards, such as new learning and developmental opportunities, enriched and challenging work, job security, and recognition

Reliability The consistency of measurement

Results criteria Whether the training actually translates into improved organizational outcomes

Reward system The policies, procedures, and practices used by an organization to determine the amount and types of returns individuals, teams, and the organization receive in exchange for their membership and contributions

Right-to-work state laws Vary from state to state but generally prohibit requiring employees to join a union or pay regular or fair-share union dues to obtain or keep a job

Role-plays When trainees act in managerial situations such as counseling a difficult subordinate

Safety climate The shared understanding that workers have about the importance of safety

Safety committee Provides employees with a voice and an opportunity to participate in safety-related decisions in the organization

Safety compliance behavior The extent to which workers follow the safety rules and regulations

Safety knowledge Workers' understanding of how to protect themselves and others on the job

Safety motivation Workers' perceived value for safety and desire to perform safely on the job

Safety officer An individual who is assigned to support safety and health issues in the workplace such as the promotion of safe practices and compliance with safety policies and rules

Safety participation behavior Employees' willingness to support safety among their coworkers

Scientific process A method used for systematic and rigorous problem solving that is predicated on the assumption that knowledge requires evidence

Selection interview A traditional job interview

Self-efficacy A person's belief that they can accomplish a task

Self-initiated expatriate A skilled professional who moves to a different country for a specific period of time with the intention of gaining overseas work experience

Severance pay Payments made to departing employees during organizationally initiated turnover

Severity error The tendency to rate almost all ratees low

Sexual harassment Unwanted advances and other harassment that are sexual in nature

Short-term disability insurance A form of income protection for employees who temporarily become unable to work as a result of an illness or injury

Similarity-attraction hypothesis The theory that individuals prefer others who are similar to them

Site visit When a job applicant agrees to physically go to the organization's location to meet with and to be interviewed by its representatives

Situational interview A type of structured interview in which job applicants are asked what they would do in a hypothetical work-related situation

Situational judgment tests (SJTs) A test that captures some of the realism of work sample tests but in a format (e.g., multiple-choice) that can be used more easily with large numbers of applicants

SMART goals Goals that are specific, measurable, aggressive, realistic and time bound

Social Security Act Passed by Congress in 1935 as part of the New Deal to help the United States recover from the Great Depression by providing economic security for old-age individuals and, later, additional programs for mothers and children in need, individuals with disabilities, the unemployed, and those whose family members have died

Stakeholders A number of different groups that an organization must appeal to, including customers and investors

Stereotypes Overly simplified and generalized assumptions about a particular group that may not reflect reality

Strain A person's reaction to stressors, such as heart disease, burnout, or depression, or behavioral outcomes such as low performance and turnover

Strategic human resource management The process of aligning HR policies and practices with the objectives of the organization, including employee, operational, stakeholder, and financial outcomes

Strategy A well-devised and thoughtful plan for achieving an objective

Strategy implementation The enactment of a strategic plan

Stressors Demands in the environment to which a person must respond

Structured interview An interview in which all job applicants are asked the same, job-related questions

Subject matter experts (SMEs) People (e.g., employees, supervisors) who provide information about the job

Succession management The process of identifying and developing successors at all levels of the organization

Succession planning Taking stock of which employees are qualified to fill positions that are likely to be vacated soon

Systems perspective The view of how all pieces of a system and its subsystems fit together

Talent analysis The process of gathering data to determine potential talent gaps, or the difference between an organization's talent demand and the available talent supply

Talent pool A group of individuals (employees or potential applicants) who possess the KSAOs to fill a particular role

Tardiness Being late to work without giving advance notice

Tasks The elements of a job analysis that are typically used to describe the job itself

Team appraisals A team evaluation in which goals and performance are evaluated at the team level

Telecommuting A work arrangement in which an employee is not physically at an office or other location but instead works a substantial amount of time away from the office

Total compensation Package of compensation and benefits that employees receive

Total Worker Health™ (TWH™) An integrated approach to safety, well-being, and wellness

Traditional-pay programs A payment program that is based on the content of employees' job descriptions, job titles, and/or organizational levels

Trainee motivation The sustained motivation of employees during the training process, which is a predictor of training success

Training transfer Whether the training results in changes in job performance

Transnational companies Companies that have operations in multiple countries and do not view themselves as belonging to any one country

Two-step authentication An extra layer of security that requires an additional piece of information that only the user would know

Unconscious bias Stereotypes individuals hold that reside beyond their conscious awareness

Unemployment insurance Payment made to unemployed individuals

Unfair labor practices Defined in the United States as actions taken by either unions or employers that violate the National Labor Relations Act or other legislation. Such acts are investigated by the National Labor Relations Board

Unfolding model of turnover A model that recognizes that employees often leave without lining up a new job and that turnover is often a result of "shocks" to the system

Uniform Guidelines on Employee Selection Procedures Guidelines adopted by the EEOC, the Department of Labor, and the Department of Justice, which outline how selection systems can be designed to comply with EEO laws

Unstructured interview When the interviewer has a conversation with a job applicant with no fixed set of questions for each applicant

Utility The monetary value of an HR function (e.g., a selection procedure)

Validity The accuracy of a measure, or the degree to which an assessment measures what it is supposed to measure

Values Parameters and guidelines for decision making that help an organization realize its vision

Vision An extension of an organization's mission that describes what the organization will look like or be at some point in the future

Voluntary turnover A departure initiated by an employee

Well-being A worker's well-being is composed of their safety, health, satisfaction, and engagement

Work adjustment Feeling comfortable at work and with one's new tasks

Work sample A sample or example of the work produced by an applicant

Workers' compensation Program funded entirely by the employer in the form of payroll taxes that provides medical coverage and income replacement for an individual who is injured or becomes ill on the job due to an accident or hazard at work

Workflow analysis A broad, organization-level focus on work within the organization and within organizational units and the input needed

Workforce labor shortages Labor market conditions where there are more jobs available than workers to fill them

Workforce labor surplus (or slack) Labor market conditions where there is more available labor than organizations need

Workforce planning The process of determining what work needs to be done in both the short and long term and coming up with a strategy regarding how positions will be filled

Workplace bullying Consistent mistreatment by others in the workplace

Work-to-family conflict When work interferes with nonwork responsibilities

Wrongful dismissal A dismissal that violates the law

Notes

CHAPTER 1

1. Employee relations best practices: Costco's approach to HR. http://i-sight.com/resources/employee-relations-best-practices-costco/; Chu, J., & Rockwood, K. (2008). CEO interview: Costco's Jim Sinegal. https://www.fastcompany.com/1042487/ceo-interview-costcos-jim-sinegal; La Monica, P. R. (2015). The best CEOs of the year are.... *CNN Money.* http://money.cnn.com/gallery/investing/2015/12/23/best-ceos-2015/; 11 reasons to love Costco that have nothing to do with shopping. *Huffington Post.* http://www.huffingtonpost.com/2013/11/19/reasons-love-costco_n_4275774.html; https://www.marketwatch.com/investing/stock/cost

2. Nutt, P. C. (2002). *Why decisions fail.* Oakland, CA: Berrett-Koehler.

3. Coff, R. W. (2002). Human capital, shared expertise, and the likelihood of impasse on corporate acquisitions. *Journal of Management, 28*, 107–128.

4. Virgin Air website. (2015, January 26). Why is looking after your employees so important? https://www.virgin.com/entrepreneur/why-is-looking-after-your-employees-so-important

5. Schein, E. (1996). Culture: The missing concept in organization studies. *Administrative Science Quarterly, 41*, 229–240; Cameron, K. S., & Quinn, R. E. (1999). *Diagnosing and changing organizational culture: Based on the competing values framework.* Reading, MA: Addison-Wesley; Huselid, M. A. (1995). The impact of human resource management practices on turnover, productivity, and corporate financial performance. *Academy of Management Journal, 38*, 635–672; Pfeffer, J. (1998). *The human equation: Building profits by putting people first.* Boston, MA: Harvard Business School Press; Pfeffer, J., & Veiga, J. F. (1999). Putting people first for organizational success. *Academy of Management Executive, 13*, 37–48; Welbourne, T., & Andrews, A. (1996). Predicting performance of Initial Public Offering firms: Should HRM be in the equation? *Academy of Management Journal, 39*, 910–911.

6. Cameron, K. S., & Quinn, R. E. (1999). *Diagnosing and changing organizational culture: Based on the competing values framework.* Reading, MA: Addison-Wesley.

7. Schein, E. (1996). Culture: The missing concept in organization studies. *Administrative Science Quarterly, 41*, 229–240.

8. Zielinski, D. (2015, November). The gamification of recruitment. *HR Magazine*, 59–60.

9. U.S. Department of Commerce, U.S. Census Bureau. (2014). The baby boom cohort in the United States: 2012-2060. https://www.census.gov/prod/2014pubs/p25-1141.pdf

10. U.S. Bureau of Labor Statistics. http://www.bls.gov/opub/reports/womens-earnings/archive/highlights-of-womens-earnings-in-2014.pdf

11. Pew Research Center. (2015). Projected U.S. population by race and Hispanic origin, 2015–2065, with and without immigrants entering 2015–2065. http://www.pewhispanic.org/2015/09/28/modern-immigration-wave-brings-59-million-to-u-s-driving-population-growth-and-change-through-2065/ph_2015-09-28_immigration-through-2065-a2-06/

12. Dougherty, C. (2008, August 14). Whites to lose majority status in US by 2042. *Wall Street Journal*, p. A3.

13. U.S. Bureau of Labor Statistics. (2016). Employment situation summary Table A. Household data, seasonally adjusted. http://www.bls.gov/news.release/empsit.a.htm

14. Edelman, D. J. (2015). Freelancing in America: 2015. http://www.slideshare.net/upwork/2015-us-freelancer-survey-53166722/1

15. Torpey, E., & Hogan, A. (2016). Working in a gig economy. U.S. Department of Labor, Bureau of Labor Statistics. http://www.bls.gov/careeroutlook/2016/article/what-is-the-gig-economy.htm

16. Krantz, M. (2015, July 15). 10 U.S. companies take the most foreign money. *USA Today.* http://americasmarkets.usatoday.com/2015/07/15/10-u-s-companies-take-the-most-foreign-money/

17. Intel. (2015). Celebrating 50 years of Moore's Law. http://download.intel.com/newsroom/kits/ml50/pdfs/moores-law-50-years-infographic-entire.pdf

18. Liberatore, S. (2016). What happens in an Internet second. *Daily Mail.* http://www.dailymail.co.uk/sciencetech/article-3662925/What-happens-Internet-second-54-907-Google-searches-7-252-tweets-125-406-YouTube-video-views-2-501-018-emails-sent.html; Pappas, S. (2016). How big is the Internet, really? LiveScience. http://www.livescience.com/54094-how-big-is-the-Internet.html; http://www.Internetlivestats.com/one-second/

19. Wetherill, D. (2016). Broken links: Why analytics investments have yet to pay off. *The Economist.* http://www.zsassociates.com/-/media/files/publications/public/broken-links-why-analytics-investments-have-yet-to-pay-off.pdf?la=en

20. Deloitte University Press. (2015). Global human capital trends 2015: Leading in the new world of work. http://www2.deloitte.com/content/dam/Deloitte/at/Documents/human-capital/hc-trends-2015.pdf

21. SHRM Foundation. (2015). What's next? Use of workforce analytics for competitive advantage. https://www.shrm.org/about/foundation/ShapingtheFuture/Documents/EIU%20Theme%203%20Analytics%20Report-FINAL.pdf

22. Business ethics and compliance timeline. (2018). https://www.ethics.org/eci/research/free-toolkit/ethics-timeline

23. Ethical education in business schools. (2004). http://www.aacsb.edu/~/media/AACSB/Publications/research-reports/ethics-education.ashx

24. Hunter, S. T., Bedell, K. E., & Mumford, M. D. (2007). Climate for creativity: A quantitative review. *Creativity Research Journal, 19*, 69–90; Zohar, D., & Luria, G. (2005). A multilevel model of safety climate: Cross-level relationships between organization and group-level climates. *Journal of Applied Psychology, 90*, 616–628; Mayer, D. M., Kuenzi, M., & Greenbaum, R. L. (2010). Examining the link between ethical leadership and employee misconduct: The mediating role of ethical climate. *Journal of Business Ethics, 95*, 7–16.

25. Society for Human Resource Management (2019). https://www.shrm.org

26. Bureau of Labor Statistics, *U.S. Department of Labor, Occupational Outlook Handbook,* 2016–17 Edition, Human Resources Managers. (2018). http://www.bls.gov/ooh/management/human-resources-managers.htm

27. Glassdoor.com. (2018). 25 best jobs in America. https://www.glassdoor.com/List/Best-Jobs-in-America-LST_KQ0,20.htm

28. Westfall, B. (2019). Study: What employers are looking for in HR positions. http://new-talent-times.softwareadvice.com/what-employers-look-for-hr-jobs-0514/

29. Lengnick-Hall, M. L., & Aguinis, H. (2012). What is the value of human resource certification? A multi-level framework for research. *Human Resource Management Review, 22*, 246–257.

30. Campion, M. A., Fink, A. A., Ruggeberg, B. J., Carr, L., Phillips, G. M., & Odman, R. B. (2011). Doing competencies well: Best practices in competency modeling. *Personnel Psychology, 64*, 225–262; Shippman, J. S., Ash, R. A., Battista, M., Carr, L., Eyde, L. D., Hesketh, B., . . . Sanchez, J. I. (2000). The practice of competency modeling. *Personnel Psychology, 53*, 703–740; SHRM. (2016). The SHRM Competency Model. https://www.shrm.org/LearningAndCareer/competency-model/PublishingImages/pages/default/SHRM%20Competency%20Model_Detailed%20Report_Final_SECURED.pdf

31. U.S. Bureau of Labor Statistics. (2017). Industrial-organizational psychologists. https://www.bls.gov/oes/current/oes193032.htm

32. Academy of Management. (2018). https://aom.org/; Society for Industrial-Organizational Psychology. (2018). What is I-O? www.siop.org

33. EEOC. (2018). Charge statistics FY 1997 through FY 2017. https://www.eeoc.gov/eeoc/statistics/enforcement/charges.cfm

CHAPTER 2

1. Abelson, J. (2005, July 13). Gillette and P&G shareholders approve takeover. *New York Times.* http://www.nytimes.com/2005/07/13/business/worldbusiness/gillette-and-pg-shareholders-approve-takeover.html?_r=0; Kanter, R. M. (2009, October). Mergers that stick. https://hbr.org/2009/10/mergers-that-stick; Sierra-Cedar 2016–2017 HR Systems Survey White Paper, 19th Annual Edition. (n.d.). http://www.sierra-cedar.com/white-papers/; Sorkin, A. R., & Lohr, S. (2005, January 28). Procter said to reach a deal to buy Gillette in $55 billion accord. *New York Times.* http://www.nytimes.com/2005/01/28/business/procter-said-to-reach-a-deal-to-buy-gillette-in-55-billion-accord.html

2. SAS Institute, Inc. (n.d.). Jim Goodnight, co-founder & CEO. http://www.sas.com/en_us/company-information/leadership/jim-goodnight.html

3. Strategy. In *Merriam-Webster's online dictionary.* http://

www.merriam-webster.com/dictionary/strategy

4. Hambrick, D. C., & Fredrickson, J. W. (2001). Are you sure you have a strategy? *Academy of Management Executive, 15,* 48–59.

5. U.S. Securities and Exchange Commission. (2018, September 29). Elon Musk settles SEC fraud charges; Tesla charged with and resolves securities law charge. https://www.sec.gov/news/press-release/2018-226

6. Hamilton, A. (2008, October 29). Best inventions of 2008: Invention of the year. http://content.time.com/time/specials/packages/article/0,28804,1852747_1854195,00.html

7. Boudette, N. E. (2017, July 3). Tesla's first mass-market car, the Model 3, hits production this week. https://www.nytimes.com/2017/07/03/business/tesla-model-3-elon-musk.html; Boudreau, J. (2012, June 22). Tesla Motors begins delivering Model S electric cars in Silicon Valley milestone. http://www.mercurynews.com/2012/06/22/tesla-motors-begins-delivering-model-s-electric-cars-in-a-silicon-valley-milestone-2/

8. Hull, D. (2016, November 1). Tesla sees SolarCity boost in 3 years as Musk hits critics. http://www.bloomberg.com/news/articles/2016-11-01/tesla-motors-says-solarcity-will-add-to-tesla-s-balance-sheet

9. Gans, J. (2016, July 25). Why Elon Musk's new strategy makes sense. *Harvard Business Review.* https://hbr.org/2016/07/why-elon-musks-new-strategy-makes-sense

10. Learned, E. P., Christensen, C. R., Andrews, K. R., & Guth, W. D. (1969). *Business policy: Text and cases.* Homewood, IL: R. D. Irwin.

11. Porter, M. E. (1980). *Competitive strategy: Techniques for analyzing industries and competitors.* New York, NY: Free Press.

12. Guth, W. D., & MacMillan, I. C. (1986). Strategy implementation versus middle management self-interest. *Strategic Management Journal, 7,* 313–327; When CEOs talk strategy, is anyone listening? (2013, June). https://hbr.org/2013/06/when-ceos-talk-strategy-is-anyone-listening; Eisenhardt, K. M. (1989). Agency theory: An assessment and review. *Academy of Management Review, 14,* 57–74; Wright, P. M., Smart, D. L., & McMahan, G. C. (1995). Matches between human resources and strategy among NCAA basketball teams. *Academy of Management Journal, 38,* 1052–1074.

13. Schuler, R. S., & Jackson, S. E. (1987). Linking competitive strategies with human resource management practices. *The Academy of Management Executive, 1,* 207–219.

14. Ferris, G. R., Barnum, D. T., Rosen, S. D., Holleran, L. P., & Dulebohn, J. H. (1995). Toward business–university partnerships in human resource management: Integration of science and practices. In G. R. Ferris, S. D. Rosen, & D. T. Barnum (Eds.), *Handbook of human resource management* (pp. 1–16). Cambridge, MA: Blackwell.

15. Huselid, M. A., Becker, B. E., & Beatty, R. W. (2005). *The workforce scorecard: Managing human capital to execute strategy.* Cambridge, MA: Harvard Business Review Press; Kaplan, R. S., & Norton, D. P. (1996, July/August). Using the balanced scorecard as a strategic management system. *Harvard Business Review,* pp. 75–85.

16. Huselid, M. A. (1995). The impact of human resource management practices on turnover, productivity, and corporate financial performance. *Academy of Management Journal, 38,* 635–672; Pfeffer, J. (1998). Seven practices of successful organizations. *California Management Review, 40,* 96–124.

17. Huselid, M. A. (1995). The impact of human resource management practices on turnover, productivity, and corporate financial performance. *Academy of Management Journal, 38,* 635–672.

18. Tzabbar, D., Tzafrir, S., & Baruch, Y. (2016). A bridge over troubled water: Replication, integration and extension of the relationship between HRM practices and organizational performance using moderating meta-analysis. *Human Resource Management Review, 27,* 134–148.

19. Boxall, P., & Macky, K. (2009). Research and theory on high-performance work systems: Progressing the high-involvement stream. *Human Resource Management Journal, 19,* 3–23.

20. Huselid, M. A. (1995). The impact of human resource management practices on turnover, productivity, and corporate financial performance. *Academy of Management Journal, 38,* 635–672.

21. Rasmussen, T., & Ulrich, D. (2015). Learning from practice: How HR analytics avoids being a management fad. *Organizational Dynamics, 44,* 236–242.

22. Dineva, B. (2015, May 11). Data: Referrals strongly impact retention and depend on employee performance. https://business.linkedin.com/talent-solutions/blog/2015/05/data-referrals-strongly-impact-retention-and-depend-on-employee-performance; Lewis, G. (2017, March 30). 3 ways data shapes the talent strategy at Tesla, Chevron, and LinkedIn. https://business.linkedin.com/talent-solutions/blog/talent-analytics/2017/3-ways-data-shapes-the-talent-strategy-at-tesla-chevron-and-linkedin;

Kazmierczak, K. (2015, March 9). Tesla Motors—growing rapidly and strategically. http://www.hci.org/blog/tesla-motors-growing-rapidly-and-strategically

23. Lepak, D. P., Liao, H., Chung, Y., & Harden, E. E. (2006). A conceptual review of human resource management systems in strategic human resource management research. *Research in Personnel and Human Resources Management, 25*, 217–271.

24. Angrave, D., Charlwood, A., Kirkpatrick, I., Lawrence, M., & Stuart, M. (2016). HR and analytics: Why HR is set to fail the big data challenge. *Human Resource Management Journal, 26*, 1–11; Lohr, S. (2013, April 20). Big data, trying to build better workers. *New York Times.* http://www.nytimes.com/2013/04/21/technology/big-data-trying-to-build-better-workers.html; Ransbotham, S., Kiron, D., & Prentice, P. K. (2016, March 8). Hard work behind analytics success: Why competitive advantage from analytics is declining and what to do about it. *MIT Sloan Management Review;* Silverman, R. E., & Waller, N. (2015, March 13). The algorithm that tells the boss who might quit. *Wall Street Journal.* http://www.wsj.com/articles/the-algorithm-that-tells-the-boss-who-might-quit-1426287935; Streitfield, D. (2015, August 17). Data-crunching is coming to help your boss manage your time. *New York Times.* http://www.nytimes.com/2015/08/18/technology/data-crunching-is-coming-to-help-your-boss-manage-your-time.html

25. Lewis, G. (2017, March 30). 3 ways data shapes the talent strategy at Tesla, Chevron, and LinkedIn. https://business.linkedin.com/talent-solutions/blog/talent-analytics/2017/3-ways-data-shapes-the-talent-strategy-at-tesla-chevron-and-linkedin

26. SHRM Foundation. (2016, May). *Use of workforce analytics for competitive advantage.* https://www.shrm.org/about/foundation/shapingthefuture/documents/eiu%20theme%203%20analytics%20report-final.pdf

27. *Global human capital trends 2015.* (2015). Westlake, TX: Deloitte University Press.

28. Davenport, T. (n.d.). In praise of "light quants" and "analytical translators." https://www2.deloitte.com/us/en/pages/deloitte-analytics/articles/in-praise-of-light-quants-and-analytical-translators.html

29. SHRM Foundation. (2016, May). Use of workforce analytics for competitive advantage. https://www.shrm.org/about/foundation/shapingthefuture/documents/eiu%20theme%203%20analytics%20report-final.pdf

30. Cascio, W. (1991). *Costing human resources: The financial impact of behavior in organizations* (3rd ed.). Boston, MA: PWS-Kent; Mobley, W. H. (1982). *Employee turnover: Causes, consequences, and control.* Menlo Park, CA: Addison-Wesley.

31. Fitz-Enz, J. (1997). It's costly to lose good employees. *Workforce, 76*(8), 50–52; Hale, J. (1998). Strategic rewards: Keeping your best talent from walking out the door. *Compensation and Benefits Management, 14*, 39–50.

32. EEOC convenes meeting to discuss "Big Data" analytics. (2016, October 14). *The National Law Review.* http://www.natlawreview.com/article/eeoc-convenes-meeting-to-discuss-big-data-analytics

33. The White House. (2016, May 4). Big risks, big opportunities: The intersection of big data and civil rights. https://obamawhitehouse.archives.gov/blog/2016/05/04/big-risks-big-opportunities-intersection-big-data-and-civil-rights

34. Knaflic, C. N. (2015). *Storytelling with data: A data visualization guide for business professionals.* Hoboken, NJ: John Wiley.

35. Potts, R., & LaMarsh, J. (2004). *Managing change for success: Effecting change for optimum growth and maximum efficiency.* London, UK: Duncan Baird.

36. Agencies. (2006, March 17). L'Oréal buys Body Shop for £652m. https://www.theguardian.com/business/2006/mar/17/retail.money; http://www.thebodyshop-usa.com/about-us/aboutus_anita-roddick.aspx; Build for the future: Our values performance 2014/2015 & our new commitment. (2016). https://www.thebodyshop.com/medias/Values-Report-2015-6.pdf?context=pdf/ha8/h40/9089793032222.pdf/

CHAPTER 3

1. Rooney, B. (2010, February 5). Buffett's Berkshire loses top S&P credit rating. *CNN Money.* http://money.cnn.com/2010/02/05/news/companies/Berkshire_Hathaway_credit_rating/index.htm, https://www.adp.com/solutions/large-business/services/benefits-administration/analytics-and-decision-support.aspx; Nash, K. S. (2016, May 31). ADP's CIO says algorithms measure employee flight risk. *Wall Street Journal.* http://blogs.wsj.com/cio/2016/05/31/adp-algorithms-tackle-employee-flight-risk/; U.S. Bureau of Labor Statistics, Labor Force Statistics from the Current Population Survey. http://data.bls.gov/timeseries/LNS14000000; Carsten, J. M., & Spector, P. E. (1987). Unemployment, job satisfaction, and employee turnover: A meta-analytic test of

the Muchinsky model. *Journal of Applied Psychology, 72,* 374–381; U.S. Bureau of Labor Statistics, Job Openings and Labor Turnover Survey. http://data.bls.gov/timeseries/JTS00000000TSR

2. Tannenbaum, S. I. (1990). Human resource information systems: User group implications. *Journal of Systems Management, 41,* 27–32.

3. Ruël, H., Bondarouk, T., & Looise, J. K. (2004, February). E-HRM: Innovation or irritation. An explorative empirical study in five large companies on web-based HRM. *Management Review,* pp. 364–380.

4. Miracle, K. (2004). Case study: The City of Virginia Beach's innovative tool for workforce planning. *Public Personnel Management, 33,* 449–458.

5. Beulen, E. (2008). *The contribution of a global service provider's human resources information system (HRIS) to staff retention in emerging markets—comparing issues and implications in six developing countries.* Paper presented at the Information Systems Workshop on Global Sourcing: Services, Knowledge, and Innovation.

6. Kavanaugh, M. J., Thite, M., & Johnson, R. D. (2015). *Human resource information systems: Basics, applications, and future directions.* Thousand Oaks, CA: Sage, p. 6.

7. Carlson, K. D., & Kavanaugh, M. J. (2015). HRIS in action from HR metrics and workforce analytics chapter. Reprinted with permission from Kavanaugh, M. J., Thite, M., & Johnson, R. D. (2015). *Human resource information systems: Basics, applications, and future directions.* Thousand Oaks, CA: Sage.

8. Maier, C., Laumer, S., Eckhardt, A., & Weitzel, T. (2013). Analyzing the impact of HRIS implementations on HR personnel's job satisfaction and turnover intention. *Journal of Strategic Information Systems, 22,* 193–207.

9. Maier, C., Laumer, S., Eckhardt, A., & Weitzel, T. (2012). Analyzing the impact of HRIS implementation on HR personnel's job satisfaction and turnover intention. *Journal of Strategic Information Systems, 22,* 193–207.

10. Marler, J. H., & Floyd, B. D. (2015). Database concepts and applications in HRIS. In M. J. Kavanagh, M. Thite, & R. D. Johnson (Eds.), *Human resource information systems: Basics, applications, and future directions* (3rd ed.). Thousand Oaks, CA: Sage.

11. SHRM. (2015). Designing and managing a human resource information system. https://www.shrm.org/resourcesandtools/tools-and-samples/toolkits/pages/managingahumanresourceinformationsystem.aspx

12. Cleveland, W. S., Diaconis, P., & McGill, R. (1982). Variables on scatterplots look more highly correlated when the scales are increased. *Science, 216,* 1138–1141.

13. Knaflic, C. N. (2015). *Storytelling with data: A data visualization guide for business professionals.* Hoboken, NJ: John Wiley.

14. Knaflic, C. N. (2015). *Storytelling with data: A data visualization guide for business professionals.* Hoboken, NJ: John Wiley.

15. Hussain, Z., Wallace, J., & Cornelius, N. E. (2007). The use and impact of human resource information systems on human resource management professionals. *Information & Management, 44,* 74–89; Lawler, E. E., Levenson, A., & Boudreau, J. W. (2004). HR metrics and analytics: Use and impact. *Human Resource Planning, 26,* 15–29; Ngai, E. W. T., & Wat, F.

K. T. (2006). Human resource information systems: A review and empirical analysis. *Personnel Review, 35,* 297–314.

16. Beadles, N., Lowery, C., & Johns, K. (2005). The impact of human resource information systems: An exploratory study in the public sector. *Communications of the IIMA, 5,* 39–46; Bussler, L., & Davis, E. (2002). Information systems: The quiet revolution in human resource management. *Journal of Computer Information Systems, 42,* 17–20; Hussain, Z., Wallace, J., & Cornelius, N. E. (2007). The use and impact of human resource information systems on human resource management professionals. *Information & Management, 44,* 74–89.

17. Stone, E. F., & Stone, D. L. (1990). Privacy in organizations: Theoretical issues, research findings, and protection mechanisms. *Research in Personnel and Human Resources Management, 8,* 349–411.

18. Lukaszewski, K. M., Stone, D. L., & Stone-Romero, E. F. (2008). The effects of the ability to choose the type of human resources system on perceptions of invasion of privacy and system satisfaction. *Journal of Business & Psychology, 23,* 73–86.

19. Eddy, E. R., Stone, D. L., & Stone-Romero, E. E. (1999). The effects of information management policies on reactions to human resource information systems: An integration of privacy and procedural justice perspectives. *Personnel Psychology, 52,* 335–358.

20. SHRM. (2016). *SHRM survey findings: Using social media for talent acquisition: Recruitment and screening.* Alexandria, VA: Society for Human Resource Management. https://www.shrm.org/hr-today/trends-and-forecasting/research-and-surveys/Documents/

SHRM-Social-Media-Recruiting-Screening-2015.pdf

21. Rao, P. S., Frenkel, S., & Schreuer, M. (2018). Mark Zuckerberg to meet European Parliament members over Facebook's data use. *New York Times.* https://www.nytimes.com/2018/05/16/technology/zuckerberg-europe-data-cambridge-analytica.html; Snell, J., & Care, D. (2013). Use of online data in the Big Data Era: Legal issues raised by the use of web crawling and scraping tools for analytics purposes. *Bloomberg Law.* https://www.bna.com/legal-issues-raised-by-the-use-of-web-crawling-and-scraping-tools-for-analytics-purposes/

22. SHRM. (2014). Record-keeping policy: Safeguarding Social Security numbers. https://www.shrm.org/ResourcesAndTools/tools-and-samples/policies/Pages/cms_015266.aspx

23. Stallings, W., & Brown, L. (2015). *Computer security: Principles and practice* (3rd ed.). Boston, MA: Pearson.

24. Naylor, B. (2016). One year after OPM data breach, what has the government learned? *NPR.* http://www.npr.org/sections/alltechconsidered/2016/06/06/480968999/one-year-after-opm-data-breach-what-has-the-government-learned; Sanders, S. (2015). Massive data breach puts 4 million federal employees' records at risk. *NPR.* http://www.npr.org/sections/thetwo-way/2015/06/04/412086068/massive-data-breach-puts-4-million-federal-employees-records-at-risk

25. Lomas, N. (2016). Zuckerberg's Twitter, Pinterest, LinkedIn accounts hacked. *Tech Crunch.* https://techcrunch.com/2016/06/06/zuckerbergs-twitter-pinterest-linkedin-accounts-hacked/

26. Anthes, M. (2018). Three ways blockchain will disrupt traditional business and impact marketing in 2018. *Forbes.* https://www.forbes.com/sites/forbesagencycouncil/2018/01/29/three-ways-blockchain-will-disrupt-traditional-business-and-impact-marketing-in-2018/#4b2d39915e26

27. Anthes, M. (2018). Three ways blockchain will disrupt traditional business and impact marketing in 2018. *Forbes.* https://www.forbes.com/sites/forbesagencycouncil/2018/01/29/three-ways-blockchain-will-disrupt-traditional-business-and-impact-marketing-in-2018/#4b2d39915e26

28. Brown, G., & Smit, N. (2017). Will blockchain disrupt the HR technology landscape? *Deloitte.* https://www2.deloitte.com/nl/nl/pages/human-capital/articles/will-blockchain-disrupt-the-hr-technology-landscape.html

29. EMI Blogger. (2017). Data breach stats show almost 1.4B records were compromised in 2016. https://cybersec.buzz/data-breach-stats-show-almost-1-4b-data-records-compromised-2016/; Leech, M. (2017). Data breach statistics 2017: First half results are in. https://blog.gemalto.com/security/2017/09/21/new-breach-level-index-findings-for-first-half-of-2017/

30. Rayome, A. D. (2017). Negligent employees are no. 1 cause of cybersecurity breaches at SMBs. *TechRepublic.* https://www.techrepublic.com/article/report-negligent-employees-are-no-1-cause-of-cybersecurity-breaches-at-smbs/;2017 state of cybersecurity in small & medium sized businesses. https://keepersecurity.com/2017-State-Cybersecurity-Small-Medium-Businesses-SMB.html

31. SHRM. (2015). How to select an HRIS. https://www.shrm.org/resourcesandtools/tools-and-samples/how-to-guides/pages/howtoselectanhrissystem.aspx

32. Wilson-Evered, E., & Hartel, C. E. J. (2009). Measuring attitudes to HRIS implementation: A field study to inform implementation methodology. *Asia Pacific Journal of Human Resources, 47,* 374–384.

33. Kavanaugh, M. J., & Johnson, R. D. (2018). *Human resource information systems* (4th ed.). Thousand Oaks, CA: Sage.

34. SHRM. (2015). Designing and managing a human resource information system. https://www.shrm.org/resourcesandtools/tools-and-samples/toolkits/pages/managingahumanresourceinformationsystem.aspx

35. Dery, K., Hall, R., Wailes, N., & Wiblen, S. (2013). Lost in translation? An actor-network approach to HRIS implementation. *Journal of Strategic Information Systems, 22,* 225–237.

36. Virgin Pulse. (n.d.). Personalized wellbeing. https://www.virginpulse.com/our-products/; EEOC Enforcement Guidance on the Americans with Disabilities Act and Psychiatric Disabilities. (1997). https://www.eeoc.gov/policy/docs/psych.html

CHAPTER 4

1. Ruiz, R. (February 3, 2019). Raising the next STEM generation. https://mashable.com/feature/san-francisco-schools-stem-diversity/#NKx44GUg_Zqi; Ward, M. (November 20, 2017). Salesforce CEO Marc Benioff: There's no finish line when it comes to equality. https://www.cnbc.com/2017/11/20/marc-benioff-theres-no-finish-line-when-it-comes-to-equality.html

2. Bell, M. P. (2012). *Diversity in organizations.* Mason, OH: Cengage.

3. U.S. Bureau of Labor Statistics. (2016). Labor force statistics from the current population survey. https://www.bls.gov/cps/cpsaat11.htm

4. Bell, S. T., Villado, A. J., Lukasik, M. A., Belau, L., & Briggs, A. L. (2010). Getting specific about demographic diversity variable and team performance relationship: A meta-analysis. *Journal of Management, 37,* 709–743; Roberge, M. E., & van Dick, R. (2010). Recognizing the benefits of diversity: When and how does diversity increase group performance? *Human Resource Management Review, 20,* 295–308.

5. Boehm, S. A., Kunze, F., & Bruch, H. (2014). Spotlight on age-diversity climate: The impact of age-inclusive HR practices on firm-level outcomes. *Personnel Psychology, 67,* 667–704; Chrobot-Mason, D., & Aramovich, N. P. (2013). The psychological benefits of creating an affirming climate for workplace diversity. *Group & Organization Management, 38,* 659–689; Nishii, L. H. (2013). The benefits of climate for inclusion for gender-diverse groups. *Academy of Management Journal, 56,* 1754–1774.

6. van Dijk, H., van Engen, M. L., & van Knippenberg, D. (2012). Defying conventional wisdom: A meta-analytical examination of the differences between demographic and job-related diversity relationships with performance. *Organizational Behavior and Human Decision Processes, 119,* 38–53.

7. Diel, S. (2010, November 4). TIAA-CREF chief Roger W. Ferguson Jr. tells Birmingham audience that diverse companies outperform others. *The Birmingham News;* Reuters (2008, April 4). Chief is selected at TIAA-CREF. *New York Times;*

Carter, D. A., Simkins, B. J., & Simpson, W. G. (2003, February 4). Corporate governance, board diversity, and firm value. *The Financial Review.*

8. Miller, T., & Triana, M. D. C. (2009). Demographic diversity in the boardroom: Mediators of the board diversity-firm performance relationship. *Journal of Management Studies, 46,* 755–786.

9. Anonymous. (2017, June 7). These are the women CEOs leading *Fortune* 500 companies. *Fortune.* http://fortune.com/2017/06/07/fortune-500-women-ceos/; Mariño, K. J. (2016). Top 10 Latino CEOs at *Fortune* 500 companies you should know about. *Latin Post.* http://www.latinpost.com/articles/107285/20160108/top-10-latino-ceos-at-fortune-500-companies-you-should-know-about.htm

10. Sacco, J. M., & Schmitt, N. (2005). A dynamic multilevel model of demographic diversity and misfit effects. *Journal of Applied Psychology, 90,* 203–231.

11. Shaver, K. (2015, March 25). Female dummy makes her mark on male-dominated crash tests. *Washington Post.*

12. U.S. Department of Labor. (2016). Equal employment opportunity. https://www.dol.gov/general/topic/discrimination

13. EEOC. (2018). Filing a lawsuit. https://www.eeoc.gov/employees/lawsuit.cfm

14. EEOC. (2016). Employees and job applicants. https://www.eeoc.gov/employees/index.cfm

15. U.S. Bureau of Labor Statistics. (2016, January 15). Women's earnings 83 percent of men's, but vary by occupation. http://www.bls.gov/opub/ted/2016/womens-earnings-83-percent-of-mens-but-vary-by-occupation.htm

16. EEOC. (2010). Walmart to pay more than $11.7 million to settle

EEOC sex discrimination suit. https://www.eeoc.gov/eeoc/newsroom/release/3-1-10.cfm

17. Fitzke, S., Gorajski, S., & Parker, B. (2015, March). Weigh EEOC guidance when considering criminal histories. *HR Specialist: Minnesota Law, 8*(3), 6; National origin discrimination: What managers need to know. (2015, May). *HR Specialist: Minnesota Employment Law, 4;* Zachary, M. K. (2015). Labor law for supervisors: Language requirements and the law. *Supervision, 76*(5), 19–23.

18. EEOC. (2002). Title VII: BFOQ. https://www.eeoc.gov/eeoc/foia/letters/2002/titlevii_bfoq.html; Shorter, T. N., McLaughlin, C. L., & O'Day, T. (2007). Can we use gender in our hiring decisions? The discrimination Bona Fide Occupational Qualification (BFOQ) applied to health care. http://www.gklaw.com/news.cfm?action=pub_detail&publication_id=544

19. Progress Illinois. (2016, September 20). Appeals court sides with Chicago female paramedics in sex discrimination suit. http://progressillinois.com/news/content/2016/09/20/appeals-court-sides-chicago-female-paramedics-sex-discrimination-suit

20. FindLaw. (2019). Equal pay and discrimination against women. http://employment.findlaw.com/employment-discrimination/equal-pay-and-discrimination-against-women.html

21. Gurrieri, V. (2016). Sheet metal union to pony up $1.6m in EEOC race bias case. www.law360.com/articles/784572

22. Wickham, A. (2016). Accenture reaches $500k settlement in bias class action. http://www.law360.com/articles/851153/accenture-reaches-500k-settlement-in-bias-class-action

23. EEOC. (2016). Pregnancy discrimination. https://www

.eeoc.gov/eeoc/publications/fs-preg.cfm

24. Rhodan, M. (2015, March 26). Supreme Court rules in favor of protecting pregnant women in the workplace. *Time;* Supreme Court creates new pregnancy discrimination framework. (2015, May). *HR Specialist: California Employment Law, 9*(5), 7.

25. EEOC. (2016). Age discrimination. https://www.eeoc.gov/laws/types/age.cfm

26. *Gross v. FBL Financial Services.* http://caselaw.findlaw.com/us-supreme-court/557/167.html

27. Anonymous. (2016, July 7). EEOC issues new guidance on leave and the ADA. *Payroll Manager's Letter,* pp. 6–7.

28. Mook, J. R. (2010, September 9). Five steps to protect your company from claims under new ADA. http://www.hrhero.com/hl/articles/2010/09/09/five-steps-to-protect-your-company-from-claims-under-new-ada/

29. EEOC proposed rule clarifies wellness rules under GINA. (2016, January). *HR Specialist: California Employment Law, 10*(1), 7; GINA Genetic Information Nondiscrimination Act. http://ginahelp.org/#

30. Miller, S. (2015). United States District Court for the Northern District of Georgia finds employer liable for violation of Genetic Information Nondisclosure Act (GINA) in the case of the "devious defecator." *American Journal of Law & Medicine, 41,* 684–687.

31. EEOC. (2016). Equal Pay Act of 1963 and Lilly Ledbetter Fair Pay Act of 2009. https://www.eeoc.gov/eeoc/publications/brochure-equal_pay_and_ledbetter_act.cfm

32. Human Rights Campaign. (2016). http://www.hrc.org/state_maps; Sangha, K. K. (2015). LGBT protection in the workplace: A survey of state and local laws.

33. Frankel, A. (2017, September 11). How Trump DOJ's about-face on LGBT workplace bias could backfire at Scotus. https://www.reuters.com/article/us-otc-lgbt/how-trump-dojs-about-face-on-lgbt-workplace-bias-could-backfire-at-scotus-idUSKCN1BM2DD

34. EEOC. (2016). What you should know about EEOC and the enforcement protections for LGBT workers. https://www.eeoc.gov/eeoc/newsroom/wysk/enforcement_protections_lgbt_workers.cfm

35. Munoz, S. T., & Kalteux, D. M. (2016, March). LGBT, the EEOC, and the meaning of "sex." *The Florida Bar Journal,* pp. 43–48.

36. Joiner, E., & Lyons, A. (2016, Summer). Creating an inclusive workplace for LGBT employees. *Corporate Counsel Litigation, 30,* 3.

37. Cheri Gay, V. (2015). 50 years later . . . still interpreting the meaning of "because of sex" within Title VII and whether it prohibits sexual orientation discrimination. *The Air Force Law Review, 73,* 61–109; More reason for sexual orientation policy: EEOC files first Title VII gay-bias suit. (2016, April). *The HR Specialist, 14*(4), 3; Munoz, S. T., & Kalteux, D. M. (2016, March). LGBT, the EEOC, and the meaning of "sex." *The Florida Bar Journal,* pp. 43–48.

38. Maechtlen, L. (2016, August 19). EEOC loses landmark transgender discrimination case. http://www.workplaceclassaction.com/2016/08/eeoc-loses-landmark-transgender-discrimination-case/

39. King, E. B., & Cortina, J. M. (2010). The social and economic imperative of lesbian, gay, bisexual, and transgendered supportive organizational policies. *Industrial and Employment Relations Today, 42,* 57–68.

40. Joiner, E., & Lyons, A. (2016, Summer). Creating an inclusive workplace for LGBT employees. *Corporate Counsel Litigation, 30,* 3.

41. Grant, A. (2017, October 26). World's 100 most successful LGBT executives and business leaders, 2017. http://ceoworld.biz/2017/10/26/worlds-100-most-successful-lgbt-executives-and-business-leaders-2017/; Hewett, J. (March 4, 2016). Alan Joyce says management diversity was key to getting Quantas through turbulent times. https://www.theaustralian.com.au/business/in-depth/perpetual/alan-joyce-says-management-diversity-was-key-to-getting-qantas-through-turbulent-times/news-story/5afe123042f7d2e20b8d3a5f001477b8

42. SHRM. (2015). Affirmative action: General: When would my company need to have an affirmative action program? https://www.shrm.org/resourcesandtools/tools-and-samples/hr-qa/pages/whenisanaapneeded.aspx

43. Benn, K. (2016, April 21). Uber settles two class actions with drivers for up to $100M. https://www.law360.com/articles/787770/uber-settles-2-class-actions-with-drivers-for-up-to-100m; Wood, R. (2015, June 16). W. FedEx settles independent contractor mislabeling case for $228 million. *Forbes.* http://www.forbes.com/sites/robertwood/2015/06/16/fedex-settles-driver-mislabeling-case-for-228-million/#199f59165f5a

44. Leslie, L. M., Mayer, D. M., & Kravitz, D. A. (2014). The stigma of affirmative action: A stereotyping-based theory and meta-analytic test of the consequences for performance. *Academy of Management Journal, 57,* 964–989.

45. SHRM. (2015, November 9). Affirmative action: General: When would my company need to have an affirmative action program? https://www.shrm.org/resourcesandtools/tools-and-samples/hr-qa/pages/whenisanaapneeded.aspx

46. EEOC. (2018). Enforcement guidance on vicarious employer liability for unlawful harassment by supervisors. https://www.eeoc.gov/policy/docs/harassment.html

47. Phillis, M. (2016, June). You have a chief diversity officer, but is your workplace inclusive? *Workforce,* pp. 20–21.

48. Huet, E. (2015, July 17). Women who code: We have to start making commitments on diversity. *Forbes;* Goodman, N. (2016, September/October). Diversity is reality; inclusion is a choice. *Training,* pp. 56–57.

49. Dobbin, F., & Kalev, A. (2016, July/August). Why diversity programs fail. *Harvard Business Review.* https://hbr.org/2016/07/why-diversity-programs-fail

50. Cox, J., & Musaddique, S. (2018, February 12). Lloyds banking group sets ethnic diversity target. http://www.independent.co.uk/news/business/news/lloyds-bank-ethnic-diversity-target-bame-increase-numbers-ftse-100-a8207046.html

51. Zakrzewski, C. (2015, August 5). Corporate news: Intel seeks to boost diversity in hiring. *Wall Street Journal,* p. B9.

52. Morgan, W. B., Dunleavy, E., & DeVries, P. D. (2016). Using big data to create diversity and inclusion in organizations. In S. Tonidandel, E. King, & J. Cortina (Eds.), *Big data at work: The data science revolution and organizational psychology* (pp. 310–335). New York, NY: Routledge.

53. Morse, G. (2016, July/August). Designing a bias-free organization. *Harvard Business Review, 94*(7/8).

54. Waxer, C. (2015, April). Combating the diversity dearth with analytics. *Computerworld,* pp. 11–18.

55. Smith, A. (2016, July/August). Analyzing pay. *HR Magazine,* pp. 69–72.

56. Murray, S. (2014, April 1). How one company put women in charge. http://blogs.wsj.com/atwork/2014/04/01/how-one-company-put-women-in-charge/; Petrilla, M. (2014, December 11). How analytics helped Kimberly-Clark solve its diversity problem. *Fortune.* http://fortune.com/2014/12/10/kimberly-clark-dodsworth-diversity/

57. Bridgeford, L. C. (2015, September). Experts discuss big data's effect on hiring, bias claims. *HR Focus,* pp. 4–6; Macheel, T. (2016, September 8). Women in banking: Is big data a weapon of mass discrimination? *American Banker.* https://www.americanbanker.com/opinion/women-in-banking-is-big-data-a-weapon-of-mass-discrimination

58. McGowan, K. (2016, July 29). When is big data bad data? When it causes bias. http://www.bna.com/big-data-bad-n73014445584

59. Jensen, C. (2016, October 5). Entrepreneurship puts returning citizens back in the game. http://streetsense.org/article/entrepreneurship-returning-citizens-jobs-reentry/#.WBE3YuErL-Y; National Employment Law Project. (2016, December 1). Ban the box: US cities, counties, and states adopt fair hiring policies. http://www.nelp.org/publication/ban-the-box-fair-chance-hiring-state-and-local-guide/; Second chance employment. (n.d.). http://www.daveskillerbread.com/media/second-chance-employment/; Schmitt, J., & Warner, K. (2010, November). Ex-offenders and the labor market. http://cepr.net/documents/publications/ex-offenders-2010-11.pdf; Smialek, J. (2014, February 7). Putting released prisoners back to work. *Bloomberg;* Vega, T. (2015, October 30). Out of prison and out of work: Jobs out of reach for former inmates. http://money.cnn.com/2015/10/30/news/economy/former-inmates-unemployed/

CHAPTER 5

1. U.S. Office of Personnel Management. (2007). Delegated examining operations handbook: A guide for federal agency examining offices. https://www.opm.gov/policy-data-oversight/hiring-information/competitive-hiring/deo_handbook.pdf

2. U.S. Office of Personnel Management. (2007). Delegated examining operations handbook: A guide for federal agency examining offices. https://www.opm.gov/policy-data-oversight/hiring-information/competitive-hiring/deo_handbook.pdf; PDRI. (2014). Validating the global competency model. https://www.pdri.com/images/uploads/PDRI_EP_CM_IBM_FW.pdf

3. Alonso, A. (2017, March 27). Certify this! The role of competency-based certification in HR. https://blog.shrm.org/blog/certify-this-the-role-of-competency-based-certification-in-hr; Society for Human Resource Management. (2012). SHRM Competency Model. https://www.shrm.org/LearningAnd Career/competency-model/Documents/Full%20Competency%20Model%2011%202_10%201%20 2014.pdf; National Council for Therapeutic Recreation Certification. (2015). 2014 CTRS job analysis report. http://nctrc.org/wp-content/uploads/2015/02/RP1-MM6-nctrc-job-analysis-report.pdf; National Council of State Boards

of Nursing, Inc. (NCSBN®) (2015). Report of findings from the 2014 Nurse Aide Job Analysis and Knowledge, Skill and Ability Study. https://www.ncsbn.org/15_2014NNAAP_Job_Analysis_vol65.pdf

4. Morgeson, F. P., & Dierdorff, E. C. (2011). Work analysis: From technique to theory. In S. Zedeck (Ed.), *APA handbook of industrial and organizational psychology* (Vol. 2, pp. 3–41). Washington, DC: APA.

5. U.S. Office of Personnel Management. (2007). Delegated examining operations handbook: A guide for federal agency examining offices. https://www.opm.gov/policy-data-oversight/hiring-information/competitive-hiring/deo_handbook.pdf

6. PDRI. (2014). Validating the global competency model. https://www.pdri.com/images/uploads/PDRI_EP_CM_IBM_FW.pdf

7. Brannick, M. T., Levine, E. L., & Morgeson, F. P. (2007). *Job and work analysis: Methods, research, and applications for human resource management.* Thousand Oaks, CA: Sage; Cascio, W. F., & Aguinis, H. (2011). *Applied psychology in human resource management* (7th ed.). Upper Saddle River, NJ: Prentice Hall; Morgeson, F. P., & Dierdorff, E. C. (2011). Work analysis: From technique to theory. In S. Zedeck (Ed.), *APA handbook of industrial and organizational psychology* (Vol. 2, pp. 3–41). Washington, DC: APA.

8. Brannick, M. T., Levine, E. L., & Morgeson, F. P. (2007). *Job and work analysis: Methods, research, and applications for human resource management.* Thousand Oaks, CA: Sage; Cascio, W. F., & Aguinis, H. (2011). *Applied psychology in human resource management* (7th ed.). Upper Saddle River, NJ: Prentice Hall.

9. Uniform Guidelines on Employee Selection Procedures.

(1978). *Federal Register, 43,* 38290–38315.

10. Mook, J. R. (2010, September 9). Five steps to protect your company from claims under new ADA. http://www.hrhero.com/hl/articles/2010/09/09/five-steps-to-protect-your-company-from-claims-under-new-ada/

11. Morgeson, F. P., & Dierdorff, E. C. (2011). Work analysis: From technique to theory. In S. Zedeck (Ed.), *APA handbook of industrial and organizational psychology* (Vol. 2, pp. 3–41). Washington, DC: APA.

12. Burroughs, A. (2017, January 3). The digitalization of retail means broad continuous change. *Smart Business.* http://www.sbnonline.com/article/digital-transformation-retail-broad-continuous-change/

13. The EDISON project. (n.d.). http://edison-project.eu/; The EDISON data science framework (EDSF). (n.d.). http://edison-project.eu/sites/edison-project.eu/files/attached_files/node-488/edison-general-introduction-edsf.pdf

14. Brannick, M. T., Levine, E. L., & Morgeson, F. P. (2007). *Job and work analysis: Methods, research, and applications for human resource management.* Thousand Oaks, CA: Sage; Gatewood, R., Feild, H., & Barrick, M. (2011). *Human resource selection.* Mason, OH: Cengage Learning.

15. Brannick, M. T., Levine, E. L., & Morgeson, F. P. (2007). *Job and work analysis: Methods, research, and applications for human resource management.* Thousand Oaks, CA: Sage.

16. Brannick, M. T., Levine, E. L., & Morgeson, F. P. (2007). *Job and work analysis: Methods, research, and applications for human resource management.* Thousand Oaks, CA: Sage; Gatewood, R., Feild, H., & Barrick, M. (2011). *Human resource selection.* Mason, OH: Cengage Learning.

17. Flanagan, J. C. (1954). The critical incident technique. *Psychological Bulletin, 51,* 327–358.

18. McCormick, E. J., Jeanneret, P. R., & Mecham, R. C. (1972). A study of job characteristics and job dimensions as based on the position analysis questionnaire (PAQ). *Journal of Applied Psychology, 56,* 347–368.

19. Brannick, M. T., Levine, E. L., & Morgeson, F. P. (2007). *Job and work analysis: Methods, research, and applications for human resource management.* Thousand Oaks, CA: Sage; Gatewood, R., Feild, H., & Barrick, M. (2011). *Human resource selection.* Mason, OH: Cengage Learning.

20. Peterson, N. G., Mumford, M. D., Borman, W. C., Jeanneret, P. R., Fleishman, E. A., Levin, K. Y., . . . Dye, D. M. (2001). Understanding work using the Occupational Information Network (O*NET): Implications for practice and research. *Personnel Psychology, 54,* 451–492.

21. Alonso, A. (2017, March 27). Certify this! The role of competency-based certification in HR. https://blog.shrm.org/blog/certify-this-the-role-of-competency-based-certification-in-hr; Campion, M. A., Fink, A. A., Ruggeberg, B. J., Carr, L., Phillips, G. M., & Odman, R. B. (2011). Doing competencies well: Best practices in competency modeling. *Personnel Psychology, 64,* 225–262; Shippmann, J. S., Ash, R. A., Battista, M., Carr, L., Eyde, L. D., Hesketh, B., . . . Sanchez, J. I. (2000). The practice of competency modeling. *Personnel Psychology, 53,* 703–740.

22. Campion, M. A., Fink, A. A., Ruggeberg, B. J., Carr, L., Phillips, G. M., & Odman, R. B. (2011). Doing competencies well: Best practices in competency modeling. *Personnel Psychology, 64,* 225–262; PDRI. (2014). Validating the global competency model. https://www.pdri.com/

images/uploads/PDRI_EP_CM_IBM_FW.pdf; Sanchez, J. I., & Levine, E. L. (2009). What is (or should be) the difference between competency modeling and traditional job analysis? *Human Resource Management Review, 19,* 53–63; Shippmann, J. S., Ash, R. A., Battista, M., Carr, L., Eyde, L. D., Hesketh, B., . . . Sanchez, J. I. (2000). The practice of competency modeling. *Personnel Psychology, 53,* 703–740.

23. Parker, S. K. (2014). Beyond motivation: Job and work design for development, health, ambidexterity, and more. *Annual Review of Psychology, 65,* 661–691; Parker, S. K., Morgeson, F. P., & Johns, G. (2017). One hundred years of work design research: Looking back and looking forward. *Journal of Applied Psychology, 102,* 403–420.

24. Parker, S. K., Morgeson, F. P., & Johns, G. (2017). One hundred years of work design research: Looking back and looking forward. *Journal of Applied Psychology, 102,* 403–420.

25. Hackman, J. R., & Oldham, G. R. (1976). Motivation through the design of work: Test of a theory. *Organizational Behavior and Human Performance, 16,* 250–279.

26. Demerouti, E., Bakker, A. B., Nachreiner, F., & Schaufeli, W. B. (2001). The job demands–resources model of burnout. *Journal of Applied Psychology, 86,* 499–512; Hackman, J. R., & Oldham, G. R. (1975). Development of the job diagnostic survey. *Journal of Applied Psychology, 60,* 159–180; Karasek, R. A. (1979). Job demands, job decision latitude, and mental strain: Implications for job redesign. *Administrative Science Quarterly, 24,* 285–308.

27. Morgeson, F. P., & Humphrey, S. E. (2006). The Work Design Questionnaire (WDQ): Developing and validating a comprehensive measure for assessing job design and the nature of work. *Journal of Applied Psychology, 91,* 1321–1399.

28. Humphrey, S. E., Nahrgang, J. D., & Morgeson, F. P. (2007). Integrating motivational, social, and contextual work design features: A meta-analytic summary and theoretical extension of the work design literature. *Journal of Applied Psychology, 92,* 1332–1356.

29. Truxillo, D. M., Cadiz, D. A., Rineer, J. R., Zaniboni, S., & Fraccaroli, F. (2012). A lifespan perspective on job design: Fitting the job and the worker to promote job satisfaction, engagement, and performance. *Organizational Psychology Review, 2,* 340–360.

30. Zaniboni, S., Truxillo, D. M., & Fraccaroli, F. (2013). Differential effects of task variety and skill variety on burnout and turnover intentions for older and younger workers. *European Journal of Work and Organizational Psychology, 22,* 306–317; Zaniboni, S., Truxillo, D. M., Fraccaroli, F., McCune, E. A., & Bertolino, M. (2014). Who benefits from more tasks? Older versus younger workers. *Journal of Managerial Psychology, 29,* 508–523.

31. Zaniboni, S., Truxillo, D. M., Rineer, J. R., Bodner, T. E., Hammer, L. B., & Krainer, M. (2016). Relating age, decision authority, job satisfaction, and mental health: A study of construction workers. *Work, Aging and Retirement, 2,* 428–435.

32. Bouville, G., Dello Russo, S., & Truxillo, D. (2018). The moderating role of age in the job characteristics–absenteeism relationship: A matter of occupational context? *Journal of Occupational and Organizational Psychology, 91,* 57–83.

33. Parker, S. K. (2014). Beyond motivation: Job and work design for development, health, ambidexterity, and more. *Annual Review of Psychology, 65,* 661–691; Tims, M., Bakker, A. B., & Derks, D. (2012). Development and validation of the job crafting scale. *Journal of Vocational Behavior, 80,* 173–186.

34. Lebowitz, S. (2015). A Yale professor explains how to turn a boring job into a meaningful career. *Business Insider.* http://www.businessinsider.com/turn-a-boring-job-into-a-meaningful-career-job-crafting-2015-12; Wrzesniewski, A., & Dutton, J. E. (2001). Crafting a job: Revisioning employees as active crafters of their work. *Academy of Management Review, 26,* 179–201.

35. Parker, S. K. (2014). Beyond motivation: Job and work design for development, health, ambidexterity, and more. *Annual Review of Psychology, 65,* 661–691.

36. Rudolph, C. W., Katz, I. M., Lavigne, K. N., & Zacher, H. (2017). Job crafting: A meta-analysis of relationships with individual differences, job characteristics, and work outcomes. *Journal of Vocational Behavior, 102,* 112–138.

37. Heuvel, M., Demerouti, E., & Peeters, M. C. (2015). The job crafting intervention: Effects on job resources, self-efficacy, and affective well-being. *Journal of Occupational and Organizational Psychology, 88,* 511–532; Kooij, D. T., van Woerkom, M., Wilkenloh, J., Dorenbosch, L., & Denissen, J. J. (2017). Job crafting towards strengths and interests: The effects of a job crafting intervention on person–job fit and the role of age. *Journal of Applied Psychology, 102,* 971–981.

38. Fell, S. S. (2015). How telecommuting reduced carbon footprints at Dell, Aetna and Xerox. *Entrepreneur.* https://

www.entrepreneur.com/article/245296

39. Gajendran, R. S., & Harrison, D. A. (2007). The good, the bad, and the unknown about telecommuting: Meta-analysis of psychological mediators and individual consequences. *Journal of Applied Psychology, 92,* 1524–1541; Tobak, S. (2017). IBM signals end of telecommuting craze. *Entrepreneur.* https://www.entrepreneur.com/article/294656

40. Pofeldt, E. (2015). Shocker: 40% of workers now have "contingent" jobs, says U.S. government. *Forbes.* https://www.forbes.com/sites/elainepofeldt/2015/05/25/shocker-40-of-workers-now-have-contingent-jobs-says-u-s-government/#4ad6ceec14be

41. Fisher, S. L., & Connelly, C. E. (2017). Lower cost or just lower value? Modeling the organizational costs and benefits of contingent work. *Academy of Management Discoveries, 3,* 165–186; Pofeldt, E. (2015, May 25). Shocker: 40% of workers now have "contingent" jobs, says U.S. government. *Forbes;* Tran, M., & Sokas, R. K. (2017). The gig economy and contingent work: An occupational health assessment. *Journal of Occupational and Environmental Medicine, 59,* e63–e66.

42. Society for Human Resource Management. (2012). SHRM competency model. https://www.shrm.org/LearningAndCareer/competency-model/Documents/Full%20Competency%20Model%2011%202_10%201%202014.pdf; Department of Labor. (n.d.). O*NET Database. https://www.onetcenter.org/dictionary/21.3/excel/work_styles.html

CHAPTER 6

1. U.S. Bureau of Labor Statistics. (2017). Occupational outlook handbook: Water and wastewater treatment plant and system operators. https://www.bls.gov/ooh/production/water-and-wastewater-treatment-plant-and-system-operators.htm; The Conference Board. (2014). International comparisons of annual labor force statistics. https://www.conference-board.org/ilcprogram/index.cfm?id=25444; Top 10 reasons to get a career in the water treatment industry (2018). http://watergrades.com/1960/top-10-reasons-to-get-a-career-in-the-water-treatment-industry/; Roberts, B. (2010). Can they keep our lights on? SHRM. https://blog.shrm.org/workforce/can-they-keep-our-lights-on; Nursing shortage. (2018). http://www.nursingworld.org/nursingshortage

2. Sullivan, J. (2002). Why you need workforce planning. *Workforce.* http://www.workforce.com/2002/10/24/why-you-need-workforce-planning/

3. Boston, W. (2016). BMW loses core development team of its i3 and i8 electric vehicle line. *Wall Street Journal.* https://www.wsj.com/articles/bmw-loses-core-development-team-of-its-i3-and-i8-electric-vehicle-line-1461086049

4. Day, D. (2007). Developing leadership talent. SHRM Foundation. https://www.shrm.org/foundation/ourwork/initiatives/resources-from-past-initiatives/Documents/Developing%20Leadership%20Talent.pdf

5. U.S. Bureau of Labor Statistics. (2017). About BLS. https://www.bls.gov/bls/infohome.htm

6. NACE. (2016). Trends: Fewer women in computer sciences. http://www.naceweb.org/talent-acquisition/trends-and-predictions/trends-fewer-women-in-computer-sciences/; Sherman, E. (2015, March 26). Report: Disturbing drop in women in computing field. *Fortune.* http://fortune.com/2015/03/26/report-the-number-of-women-entering-computing-took-a-nosedive/

7. The Conference Board. (2014). International comparisons of annual labor force statistics. https://www.conference-board.org/ilcprogram/index.cfm?id=25444

8. Jobvite. (2016). Jobvite recruiter national report: The annual social recruiting survey. http://web.jobvite.com/Q316_Website_2016RecruiterNation_LP.html

9. Schwartz, N. D., & Wingfield, N. (2017). Amazon to add 100,000 jobs as bricks-and- mortar retail crumbles. *New York Times.* https://www.nytimes.com/2017/01/12/business/economy/amazon-jobs-retail.html?_r=0; Swartz, J. (2017). Amazon is creating 100,000 U.S. jobs, but at what cost? *USA Today.* https://www.usatoday.com/story/tech/columnist/2017/01/13/amazons-jobs-creation-plan-comes-amid-labor-pains/96488166/

10. Berman-Gorvine, M. (2013). Boeing soars over potential talent gaps with its workforce planning strategies. *Bloomberg.* https://www.bna.com/boeing-soars-potential-n17179872416/

11. U.S. Bureau of Labor Statistics. (2016). Foreign-born workers: Labor force statistics. https://www.bls.gov/news.release/pdf/forbrn.pdf

12. Barber, A. E. (1998). *Recruiting employees: Individual and organizational perspectives.* Thousand Oaks, CA: Sage; Kim, Y., & Ployhart, R. E. (2014). The effects of staffing and training on firm productivity and profit growth before, during, and after the great recession. *Journal of Applied Psychology, 99,* 361–389.

13. Sullivan, J. (2012). Recruiting has the highest business impact of any HR function. www.ere.net; Boston Consulting Group.

(2018). http://www.bcg.com/ expertise/capabilities/people-organization/human-resources .aspx

14. Bauer, T. N., & Green, S. G. (1994). Effect of newcomer involvement in work-related activities: A longitudinal study of socialization. *Journal of Applied Psychology, 79,* 211–223; Major, D. A., Kozlowski, S. W., Chao, G. T., & Gardner, P. D. (1995). A longitudinal investigation of newcomer expectations, early socialization outcomes, and the moderating effects of role development factors. *Journal of Applied Psychology, 80,* 418–431; Saks, A. M. (1994). A psychological process investigation for the effects of recruitment source and organization information on job survival. *Journal of Organizational Behavior, 15,* 225–244; Wanous, J. P., Poland, T. D., Premack, S. L., & Davis, K. S. (1992). The effects of met expectations on newcomer attitudes and behaviors: A review and meta-analysis. *Journal of Applied Psychology, 77,* 288–297.

15. Truxillo, D. M., Cadiz, D. M., & Rineer, J. R. (2014). *The aging workforce: Implications for human resource management research and practice* (S. Jackson, Ed.). Oxford, UK: Oxford Handbooks Online: Business & Management. https:// www.researchgate.net/ publication/282348874_The_ Aging_Workforce_Implications_ for_Human_Resource_ Management_Research_and_ Practice

16. Truxillo, D. M., & Bauer, T. N. (2015). *Maximizing candidate and recruiter experiences and organizational outcomes.* Findly White Paper. Available upon request from the first author.

17. Glassdoor.com. (2017). 50 best jobs in America. https://www .glassdoor.com/List/Best-Jobs-in-America-LST_KQ0,20.htm

18. Jobvite. (2016). Jobvite recruiter national report: The annual social recruiting survey. http://web.jobvite.com/Q316_ Website_2016RecruiterNation_ LP.html

19. Baert, S. (2017). Facebook profile picture appearance affects recruiters' first hiring decisions. *New Media & Society, 20,* 1220–1239.

20. Jobvite. (2016). Jobvite recruiter national report: The annual social recruiting survey. http://web.jobvite.com/Q316_ Website_2016RecruiterNation_ LP.html

21. Jobvite. (2016). Jobvite recruiter national report: The annual social recruiting survey. http://web.jobvite.com/Q316_ Website_2016RecruiterNation_ LP.html

22. Carlson, K. D., Connerley, M. L., & Mecham, R. L. (2002). Recruitment evaluation: The case for assessing the quality of applicants attracted. *Personnel Psychology, 55,* 461–490; Collins, C. J., & Han, J. (2004). Exploring applicant pool quantity and quality: The effects of early recruitment practice strategies, corporate advertising, and firm reputation. *Personnel Psychology, 57,* 685–717.

23. Huselid, M. A. (1995). The impact of human resource management practices on turnover, productivity, and corporate financial performance. *Academy of Management Journal, 38,* 635–872.

24. Indiana Department of Child Services. (2011). Family case manager. http://www.in.gov/ dcs/3209.htm

25. Jones, B. I. People management lessons from Disney. https:// cdns3.trainingindustry .com/media/3532077/ disneypeoplemanagement lessons.pdf

26. Breaugh, J. A., Macan, T. H., & Grambow, D. M. (2008). Employee recruitment: Current knowledge and directions for future research. In G. P. Hodgkinson & J. K. Ford (Eds.), *International review of industrial and organizational psychology* (Vol. 23, pp. 45–82). New York, NY: John Wiley; Breaugh, J. A. (2008). Employee recruitment: Current knowledge and important areas for future research. *Human Resource Management Review, 18,* 103–118; Earnest, D. R., Allen, D. G., & Landis, R. S. (2011). Mechanisms linking realistic job previews with turnover: A meta-analytic path analysis. *Personnel Psychology, 64,* 865–897.

27. Burkus, D. (2016). Why Amazon bought into Zappos' "pay to quit" policy. *Inc.* http://www.inc.com/ david-burkus/why-amazon-bought-into-zappos-pay-to-quit-policy.html; Snyder, B. (2015). 14% of Zappos' staff left after being offered exit pay. *Fortune.* http://fortune.com/2015/05/08/ zappos-quit-employees/

28. SHRM. (2016). Talent acquisition: Selection. *HRToday.* https://www.shrm.org/hr-today/ trends-and-forecasting/research-and-surveys/Documents/Talent-Acquisition-Selection.pdf

29. Day, D. (2007). Developing leadership talent. SHRM Foundation. https://www .shrm.org/foundation/ourwork/ initiatives/resources-from-past-initiatives/Documents/ Developing%20Leadership%20 Talent.pdf

30. Garland, P. (2016, September). Why people quit their jobs. *Harvard Business Review.* https:// hbr.org/2016/09/why-people-quit-their-jobs

31. Weber, L., & Kwoh, L. (2013). Beware the phantom job listing. *Wall Street Journal.* https://www .wsj.com/articles/SB100014241 27887323707064578229661268 628432

32. CareerXroads. (2015). Source of hire report. http://www .slideshare.net/gerrycrispin/

2015-careerxroads-source-of-hire-report-56847680

33. Zimmerman, E. (2006). The boom in boomerangs. Workforce Management Online. http://www.workforce.com/section/06/feature/24/25/79/%20index.html

34. Rediff. (2014, July 15). Hiring former employees is beneficial. http://www.rediff.com/money/report/hiring-former-employees-is-beneficial/20140715.htm

35. Shipp, A. J., Furst-Holloway, S., Harris, T. B., & Rosen, B. (2014). Gone today but here tomorrow: Extending the unfolding model of turnover to consider boomerang employees. *Personnel Psychology, 67,* 421–462; Tugend, A. (2014). Employees who leave increasingly return to the fold. *New York Times.* https://www.nytimes.com/2014/07/26/your-money/employees-who-leave-are-increasingly-returning-to-the-fold.html; Zottoli, M. A., & Wanous, J. P. (2000). Recruitment source research: Current status and future directions. *Human Resource Management Review, 10,* 353–383.

36. Zimmerman, E. (2006). The boom in boomerangs. Workforce Management Online. http://www.workforce.com/section/06/feature/24/25/79/%20index.html

37. Nitsch v. DreamWorks Animation SKG Inc., 14-cv-04062, U.S. District Court, Northern District of California (San Jose) (2016); Rosenblatt, J. (2017). Disney agrees to pay $100 million to end no-poaching lawsuit. *Bloomberg.* https://www.bloomberg.com/news/articles/2017-02-01/disney-agrees-to-pay-100-million-to-end-no-poaching-lawsuit

38. Zimmerman, E. (2006). The boom in boomerangs. *Workforce.* http://www.workforce.com/2006/01/25/the-boom-in-boomerangs/

39. WorldatWork. (2014, June). Bonus programs and practices. https://www.worldatwork.org/adimLink?id=75444

40. Bock, L. (2015). *Work rules! Insights from inside Google that will transform how you live and lead.* New York, NY: Twelve.

41. Jobvite. (2015). The Jobvite recruiter nation survey. https://www.jobvite.com/wp-content/uploads/2015/09/jobvite_recruiter_nation_2015.pdf

42. SHRM. (2016). Designing and managing successful employee referral programs. https://www.shrm.org/resourcesandtools/tools-and-samples/toolkits/pages/tk-designingandmanagingsuccessfulemployeereferralprograms.aspx

43. Lublin, J. S. (2012). More executive recruiting shifts in-house. *Wall Street Journal.* https://www.wsj.com/articles/SB10000872396390443294904578046421729938416

44. Bersin, J. (2013). Corporate recruiting explodes: A new breed of service providers. *Forbes.* https://www.forbes.com/sites/joshbersin/2013/05/23/corporate-recruitment-transformed-new-breed-of-service-providers/#3648c3c840a9

45. Agnvall, E. (2007). Job fairs go virtual. *HR Magazine.* https://www.shrm.org/hr-today/news/hr-magazine/Pages/0707agenda_empstaff.aspx

46. Roheling, M. V., & Cavanaugh, M. A. (2000). Student expectations of employers at job fairs. *Journal of Career Planning & Employment, 60,* 48–53.

47. Spors, K. K. (2007, June 4). For company in remote location, ex-residents offer promising pool. *Wall Street Journal.* https://www.wsj.com/articles/SB118081823563622771

48. NACE. (2016). Campus ambassadors help Rosetta extend its reach. http://www.naceweb.org/talent-acquisition/branding-and-marketing/campus-ambassadors-help-rosetta-extend-its-reach/

49. NACE. (2012). The skills and qualities employers want in their class of 2013 recruits. http://www.naceweb.org/s10242012/skills-abilities-qualities-new-hires/; Stone, C., van Horn, C., & Zukin, C. (2012, May). *Chasing the American dream: Recent college graduates and the Great Recession.* Report from the John J. Heldrich Center for Workforce Development at Rutgers University; Taylor, M. S. (1988). Effects of college internships on individual participants. *Journal of Applied Psychology, 73,* 393–401.

50. Zhao, H., & Liden, R. C. (2011). Internship: A recruitment and selection perspective. *Journal of Applied Psychology, 96,* 221–229.

51. Jobvite. (2015). 2015 Recruiter nation survey. http://web.jobvite.com/Q315_Website_2015RecruiterNation_LP.html

52. Jobvite. (2016). Jobvite recruiter national report: The annual social recruiting survey. http://web.jobvite.com/Q316_Website_2016RecruiterNation_LP.html

53. Jobboard Finder. (2018). https://www.jobboardfinder.net/jobboard-51job-china

54. Statista. (2018). Number of LinkedIn members from 1st quarter 2009 to 3rd quarter 2016 (in millions). https://www.statista.com/statistics/274050/quarterly-numbers-of-linkedin-members/

55. Budzienski, J. (2015). 3 ways to be constantly recruiting star talent through social media. *Entrepreneur.* https://www.entrepreneur.com/article/245295

56. Sharma, P. (2016). How Disney and 5 other top employers use Twitter to recruit. http://

theundercoverrecruiter.com/how-disney-and-5-other-top-employers-use-twitter-to-recruit/

57. Arnold, J. T. (2009). Twittering and Facebooking while they work. *HR Magazine, 54,* 12, 53–55.

58. Osawa, J., & Mozur, P. (2012). In China, recruiting gets social. *Wall Street Journal.* https://www.wsj.com/articles/SB10000872396390444226904577561643928840040

59. Crispin, G., & Hoyt, C. (2015). Source of hire 2015. *CareerXroads.* http://www.slideshare.net/gerrycrispin/2015-careerxroads-source-of-hire-report-56847680

60. Bonet, R., Cappelli, P., & Hamori M. (2013). Labor market intermediaries and the new paradigm for human resources. *The Academy of Management Annals, 7,* 341–392.

61. Donham, C. (2013). Five things to know about working with staffing firms. *Workforce Magazine.* http://www.workforce.com/2013/10/16/five-things-to-know-about-working-with-staffing-firms/

62. Zappe, J. (2005, June). Temp-to-hire is becoming a full-time practice at firms. *Workforce Magazine,* pp. 82–85.

63. Collamer, N. (2014). 10 great sites to find gigs and part-time work. *Forbes.* https://www.forbes.com/sites/nextavenue/2014/04/04/10-great-sites-to-find-gigs-and-part-time-work/#50b0009f5502; Flandez, R. (2008). Help wanted—and found. *Wall Street Journal.* https://www.wsj.com/articles/SB122347721312915407

64. Jobvite. (2016). Jobvite recruiter national report: The annual social recruiting survey. http://web.jobvite.com/Q316_Website_2016RecruiterNation_LP.html

65. NACE. (2017). Benchmarks: Diversity recruiting efforts, target groups. http://www.naceweb.org/talent-acquisition/trends-and-predictions/benchmarks-diversity-recruiting-efforts-target-groups/

66. Kelleher, K. (2017). Uber is facing a leadership crisis that could cause lasting damage. *Time.* http://time.com/4687491/uber-travis-kalanick-crisis-pr-brand-ipo-image-sexism-privacy/

67. Bock, L. (2015). *Work rules! Insights from inside Google that will transform how you live and lead.* New York, NY: Twelve; Lang, J., & Zapf, D. (2015). Quotas for women can improve recruitment procedures: Gender as a predictor of the frequency of use of passive job search behavior and the mediating roles of management aspirations, proactivity, and career level. *Journal of Personnel Psychology, 14,* 131–141.

68. ERE. (2017). 5 keys to recruiting women for your workforce. www.eremedia.com

69. Gaucher, D., Friesen, J., & Kay, A. C. (2011). Evidence that gendered wording in job advertisements exists and sustains gender inequality. *Journal of Personality and Social Psychology, 101,* 109–128; Wild, J. (2017, March 7). Wanted—a way with words in recruitment ads. *Financial Times.* https://www.ft.com/content/9974b0ce-e7bb-11e6-967b-c88452263daf

70. fastaff. (2016). Male nursing statistics. http://www.fastaff.com/blog/male-nursing-statistics

71. Avery, D. R., & McKay, P. F. (2006). Target practice: An organizational impression management approach to attracting minority and female job applicants. *Personnel Psychology, 59,* 157–187.

72. Highhouse, S., Stierwalt, S. L., Bachiochi, P., Elder, A. E., & Slaughter, J. E. (1999). Effects of advertised human resource management practices on attraction of African American applicants. *Personnel Psychology, 52,* 425–442; Slaughter, J. E., Sinar, E., & Bachiochi, P. D. (2002). Black applicants' reactions to affirmative action plans: Effects of plan content and previous experience with discrimination. *Journal of Applied Psychology, 87,* 333–344.

73. Avery, D. R., Hernandez, M., & Hebl, M. (2004). Who's watching the race? Racial salience in recruitment advertising. *Journal of Applied Social Psychology, 34,* 146–161; Walker, H. J., Feild, H. S., Bernerth, J. B., & Becton, J. B. (2012). Diversity cues on recruitment websites: Investigating the effects on job seekers' information processing. *Journal of Applied Psychology, 97,* 214–224.

74. Avery, D. R. (2003). Reactions to diversity in recruitment advertising—are differences black and white? *Journal of Applied Psychology, 88,* 672–679.

75. Truxillo, D. M., Cadiz, D. M., & Hammer, L. B. (2015). Supporting the aging workforce: A review and recommendations for workplace intervention research. *Annual Review of Organizational Psychology and Organizational Behavior, 2,* 351–381.

76. Ng, T. W. H., & Feldman, D. C. (2008). The relationship of age to tend dimensions of job performance. *Journal of Applied Psychology, 93,* 392–423.

77. Ng, T. W. H., & Feldman, D. C. (2012). Examining six common stereotypes about older workers with meta-analytical data. *Personnel Psychology, 65,* 821–858.

78. Truxillo, D. M., Cadiz, D. M., & Rineer, J. R. (2014). *The aging workforce: Implications for human resource management*

research and practice (S. Jackson, Ed.). Oxford, UK: Oxford Handbooks Online: Business & Management. https://www.researchgate.net/publication/282348874_The_Aging_Workforce_Implications_for_Human_Resource_Management_Research_and_Practice

79. Freudenheim, M. (2005, March 23). More help wanted: Older workers please apply. *New York Times*, p. A1.

80. Evans, M. (2017, February 24). The stubborn problem of ageism in hiring. https://www.citylab.com/work/2017/02/ageism-in-hiring-is-rife-and-not-easy-to-fix/517323/; McGuireWoods. (2017, March 6). Are college recruiting programs age discrimination? http://www.lexology.com/library/detail.aspx?g=c08e77fc-9c83-4630-9344-b4d9e80136d4

81. SHRM. (2016). Employing military personnel and recruiting veterans: What HR can do. https://www.shrm.org/ResourcesAndTools/hr-topics/benefits/Documents/10-0531%20Military%20Program%20Report_FNL.pdf

82. Meinert, D. (2016). Why hiring veterans makes good business sense. *HR Magazine*. https://www.shrm.org/hr-today/news/hr-magazine/1116/pages/why-hiring-veterans-makes-good-business-sense.aspx

83. Stone, C., & Stone, D. L. (2015). Factors affecting hiring decisions about veterans. *Human Resource Management Review, 25*, 68–79.

84. EEOC Compliance Manual. (2006). https://www.eeoc.gov/policy/docs/race-color.html; EEOC Prohibited Employment Policies/Practices. https://www.eeoc.gov/laws/practices/; Harris, M. M. (2006). EEOC is watching you: Recruitment discrimination comes to the forefront. https://www.eremedia.com/ere/eeoc-is-watching-you-recruitment-discrimination-comes-to-the-forefront/

85. NACE. (2015). Measuring your organization's quality of hire. http://www.naceweb.org/s10212015/measuring-quality-of-hire.aspx

86. SHRM. (2016). Talent acquisition: Selection. *HR Today*. https://www.shrm.org/hr-today/trends-and-forecasting/research-and-surveys/Documents/Talent-Acquisition-Selection.pdf

87. Hausknecht, J. P. (2010). Candidate persistence and personality test practice effects: Implications for staffing system management. *Personnel Psychology, 63*, 299–324; Walker, H. J., Helmuth, C., Feild, H. S., & Bauer, T. N. (2015). Watch what you say: Job applicants' justice perceptions from initial organizational correspondence. *Human Resource Management, 54*, 999–1011; Walker, J., Bauer, T. N., Cole, M. S., Bernerth, J. B., Feild, H. S., & Short, J. C. (2013). Is this how I will be treated? Reducing uncertainty through recruitment interactions. *Academy of Management Journal, 56*, 1325–1347.

88. Harris, M. M., & Fink, L. S. (1987). A field study of applicant reactions to employment opportunities: Does the recruiter make a difference? *Personnel Psychology, 40*, 765–784.

89. Boswell et al. (2003). Individual job-choice decisions and the impact of job attributes and recruitment practices: A longitudinal field study. *Human Resource Management, 42*, 23–37; Chapman, D. S., Uggerslev, K. L., Carroll, S. A., Piasentin, K. A., & Jones, D. A. (2005). Applicant attraction to organizations and job choice: A meta-analytic review of the correlates of recruiting outcomes. *Journal of Applied Psychology, 90*, 928–944; Rynes, S. L., Bretz,

R. D., Jr., & Gerhart, B. (1991). The importance of recruitment in job choice: A different way of looking. *Personnel Psychology, 50*, 309–339.

90. Disney. (n.d.). https://www.youtube.com/watch?v=Lv7o-Q4IbjY

91. Boswell, W. R., Roehling, M. V., LePine, M. A., & Moynihan, L. M. (2003). Individual job-choice decisions and the impact of job attributes and recruitment practices: A longitudinal field study. *Human Resource Management, 42*, 23–37; Rynes, S. L., Bretz, R. D., & Gerhart, B. (1991). The importance of recruitment in job choice: A different way of looking. *Personnel Psychology, 50*, 309–339; Turban, D. B., Campion, J. E., & Eyring, A. R. (1995). Factors related to job acceptance decisions of college recruiters. *Journal of Vocational Behavior, 47*, 193–213.

92. Boswell, W. R., Roehling, M. V., LePine, M. A., & Moynihan, L. M. (2003). Individual job-choice decisions and the impact of job attributes and recruitment practices: A longitudinal field study. *Human Resource Management, 42*, 23–37; Lievens, F., & Highhouse, S. (2003). The relation of instrumental and symbolic attributes to a company's attractiveness as an employer. *Personnel Psychology, 56*, 75–102; Uggerslev, K. L., Fassina, N. E., & Kraichy, D. (2012). Recruiting through the stages: A meta-analytic test of predictors of applicant attraction at different stages of the recruiting process. *Personnel Psychology, 65*, 597–660.

93. Cable, D. M., & Yu, K. Y. T. (2006). Managing job seekers' organizational image beliefs: The role of media richness and media credibility. *Journal of Applied Psychology, 91*, 828–840.

94. Dishman, L. (2015). A former Google recruiter reveals the biggest résumé mistakes. Fast Company. https://www.fastcompany.com/3052371/hit-the-ground-running/a-former-google-recruiter-reveals-the-biggest-resume-mistakes

95. Google. (2017). How we review applications (and what happens next). https://careers.google.com/how-we-hire/apply/

96. The Conference Board. (2017). CEO challenge 2017: Meeting the customer relationships/corporate brand and reputation challenge. https://www.conference-board.org/publications/publicationdetail.cfm?publicationid=7400& centerId=9

97. Murphy, B. (2018). Wendy's can't stop trolling McDonald's on Twitter. Inc. https://www.inc.com/bill-murphy-jr/wendys-cant-stop-trolling-mcdonalds-on-twitter-heres-latest-burn.html; Whitten, S. (2017). A Wendy's tweet just went viral for all the wrong reasons. CNBC. http://www.cnbc.com/2017/01/04/wendys-saucy-tweets-are-hit-and-miss-on-social-media.html

98. van Hoye, G., & Lievens, F. (2009). Tapping the grapevine: A closer look at word-of-mouth as a recruitment source. Journal of Applied Psychology, 94, 341–352.

99. Griepentrog, B. K., Harold, R. M., Holtz, B. C., Klimoski, R. J., & Marsh, S. M. (2012). Integrating social identity and the theory of planned behavior: Predicting withdrawal from an organizational recruitment process. Personnel Psychology, 65, 723–753.

100. Bauer, T. N., & Aiman-Smith, L. (1996). Green career choices: The influence of ecological stance on recruiting. Journal of Business and Psychology, 10, 445–458; Gully, S. M., Phillips, J. M., Castellano, W. G., Han, K., & Kim, A. (2013). A mediated moderation model of recruiting socially and environmentally responsible job applicants. Personnel Psychology, 66, 935–973.

101. Dineen, B. R., Ash, S. R., & Noe, R. A. (2002). A web of applicant attraction: Person–organization fit in the context of web-based recruitment. Journal of Applied Psychology, 87, 723–734; Swider, B. W., Zimmerman, R. D., & Barrick, M. R. (2015). Searching for the right fit: Development of applicant person–organization fit during the recruitment process. Journal of Applied Psychology, 100, 880–893.

102. Doyle, A. (2016, July 5). How to avoid identity theft when you are job searching. https://www.thebalance.com/how-to-avoid-identity-theft-when-you-are-job-searching-2062151; Feldman, D. C., & Klaas, B. S. (2002). Internet job hunting: A field study of applicant experiences with on-line recruiting. Human Resource Management, 41, 175–192; Gohring, N. (2009, January 23). Monster.com reports theft of user data. PCWorld. http://www.pcworld.com/article/158270/monster_reports_theft.html; Gueutal, H., & Stone, D. L. (2005). The brave new world of eHR: Human resources in the digital age. New York, NY: John Wiley.

CHAPTER 7

1. Friedman, T. L. (2014). How to get a job at Google. New York Times. https://www.nytimes.com/2014/02/23/opinion/sunday/friedman-how-to-get-a-job-at-google.html?_r=0; United States Office of Personnel Management. (2008). Structured interviews: A practical guide. https://www.opm.gov/policy-data-oversight/assessment-and-selection/structured-interviews/guide.pdf

2. Deutschman, A. (2004). Inside the mind of Jeff Bezos. Fast Company. https://www.fastcompany.com/50541/inside-mind-jeff-bezos

3. Nisen, M. (2013). It takes Mayo Clinic 3 whole years to decide if a doctor's good enough for them. Business Insider. http://www.businessinsider.com/mayo-clinics-hiring-process-is-incredibly-rigorous-2013-2

4. Chamorro-Premuzic, T. (2015). 3 emerging alternatives to traditional hiring methods. Harvard Business Review. https://hbr.org/2015/06/3-emerging-alternatives-to-traditional-hiring-methods

5. Society for Industrial and Organizational Psychology (SIOP). (2003). Principles for the validation and use of personnel selection procedures (4th ed.). Bowling Green, OH: Author; Uniform Guidelines on Employee Selection Procedures. (1978). Federal Register, 43, 38290–38315.

6. Gatewood, R., Feild, H., & Barrick, M. (2011). Human resource selection. Mason, OH: Cengage Learning.

7. Society for Industrial and Organizational Psychology (SIOP). (2003). Principles for the validation and use of personnel selection procedures (4th ed.). Bowling Green, OH: Author; Uniform Guidelines on Employee Selection Procedures. (1978). Federal Register, 43, 38290–38315.

8. Kuncel, N. R., Klieger, D. M., Connelly, B. S., & Ones, D. S. (2013). Mechanical versus clinical data combination in selection and admissions decisions: A meta-analysis. Journal of Applied Psychology, 98, 1060–1072.

9. Gatewood, R., Feild, H., & Barrick, M. (2011). Human resource selection. Mason, OH: Cengage Learning.

10. Society for Industrial and Organizational Psychology (SIOP). (2018). *Principles for the validation and use of personnel selection procedures* (5th ed.). Cambridge, MA: Cambridge University Press; *Uniform Guidelines on Employee Selection Procedures*. (1978). *Federal Register, 43,* 38290–38315.

11. Biddle Consulting Group. (2013). *Content-related and criterion-related validation study of CritiCall.* http://ww1.prweb .com/prfiles/2013/09/19/ 11143327/Florida%20 Highway%20Patrol%20 CritiCall%20Content%20and%20 Criterion%20Validation%20 Report%209-3-13.pdf

12. Wilhelmy, A., Kleinmann, M., König, C., Melchers, K., & Truxillo, D. M. (2016). How and why do interviewers try to make impressions on applicants? A qualitative study. *Journal of Applied Psychology, 101,* 313–332.

13. Blackman, M. C. (2002). Personality judgment and the utility of the unstructured employment interview. *Basic and Applied Social Psychology, 24,* 241–250; Dipboye, R. L., Macan, T., & Shahani-Denning, C. (2012). The selection interview from the interviewer and applicant perspectives: Can't have one without the other. In N. Schmitt (Ed.), *The Oxford handbook of personnel assessment and selection* (pp. 323–352). New York, NY: Oxford University Press; Wilhelmy, A., Kleinmann, M., König, C., Melchers, K., & Truxillo, D. M. (2016). How and why do interviewers try to make impressions on applicants? A qualitative study. *Journal of Applied Psychology, 101,* 313–332.

14. Arvey, R. D., & Campion, J. E. (1982). The employment interview: A summary and review of recent research. *Personnel Psychology, 35,* 281–322; Janz, T. (1982). Initial comparisons of patterned behavior description interviews versus unstructured interviews. *Journal of Applied Psychology, 67,* 577–580; Latham, G. P., Saari, L. M., Pursell, E. D., & Campion, M. A. (1980). The situational interview. *Journal of Applied Psychology, 65,* 422–427; Levashina, J., Hartwell, C. J., Morgeson, F. P., & Campion, M. A. (2014). The structured employment interview: Narrative and quantitative review of the research literature. *Personnel Psychology, 67,* 241–293.

15. Friedman, T. L. (2014). How to get a job at Google. *New York Times.* https://www.nytimes .com/2014/02/23/opinion/ sunday/friedman-how-to-get-a-job-at-google.html?_r=0

16. Campion, M. A., Palmer, D. K., & Campion, J. E. (1997). A review of structure in the selection interview. *Personnel Psychology, 50,* 655–702; Chapman, D. S., & Zweig, D. I. (2005). Developing a nomological network for interview structure: Antecedents and consequences of the structured selection interview. *Personnel Psychology, 58,* 673–702; Hartwell, C. J., & Campion, M. A. (2016). Getting on the same page: The effect of normative feedback interventions on structured interview ratings. *Journal of Applied Psychology, 101,* 757–778.

17. Blacksmith, N., Willford, J. C., & Behrend, T. S. (2016). Technology in the employment interview: A meta-analysis and future research agenda. *Personnel Assessment and Decisions, 2,* 12–20.

18. Bye, H. H., & Sandal, G. M. (2016). Applicant personality and procedural justice perceptions of group selection interviews. *Journal of Business and Psychology, 31,* 569–582.

19. Kantrowitz, T. M. *Global assessment trends 2014.* CEB-SHL Talent Management. https:// www.cebglobal.com/content/ dam/cebglobal/us/EN/regions/ uk/tm/pdfs/Report/gatr-2014 .pdf

20. Barrick, M. R., & Mount, M. K. (1991). The Big Five personality dimensions and job performance: A meta-analysis. *Personnel Psychology, 44,* 1–26.

21. International Personality Item Pool: a scientific collaboratory for the development of advanced measures of personality traits and other individual differences. http://ipip.ori.org/

22. Goldberg, L. R. (1999). A broad-bandwidth, public domain, personality inventory measuring the lower-level facets of several five-factor models. *Personality Psychology in Europe, 7,* 7–28; International Personality Item Pool: A scientific collaboratory for the development of advanced measures of personality traits and other individual differences. http://ipip.ori.org/

23. Morgeson, F. P., Campion, M. A., Dipboye, R. L., Hollenbeck, J. R., Murphy, K., & Schmitt, N. (2007). Reconsidering the use of personality tests in personnel selection contexts. *Personnel Psychology, 60,* 683–729.

24. Crant, J. M. (1995). The Proactive Personality Scale and objective job performance among real estate agents. *Journal of Applied Psychology, 80,* 532–537; Spitzmuller, M., Sin, H. P., Howe, M., & Fatimah, S. (2015). Investigating the uniqueness and usefulness of proactive personality in organizational research: A meta-analytic review. *Human Performance, 28,* 351–379.

25. Cullen, K. L., Edwards, B. D., Casper, W. C., & Gue, K. R. (2014). Employees' adaptability and perceptions of change-related uncertainty: Implications for perceived organizational support, job satisfaction, and

performance. *Journal of Business and Psychology, 29,* 269–280.

26. U.S. Department of Labor. (2009). Other workplace standards: Lie detector tests. https://www.dol.gov/compliance/guide/eppa.htm

27. Marcus, B., Lee, K., & Ashton, M. C. (2007). Personality dimensions explaining relationships between integrity tests and counterproductive behavior: Big Five, or one in addition? *Personnel Psychology, 60,* 1–34; Sackett, P. R., & Wanek, J. E. (1996). New developments in the use of measures of honesty, integrity, conscientiousness, dependability, trustworthiness, and reliability for personnel selection. *Personnel Psychology, 49,* 787–829.

28. Ones, D. S., Viswesvaran, C., & Schmidt, F. L. (1993). Comprehensive meta-analysis of integrity test validities: Findings and implications for personnel selection and theories of job performance. *Journal of Applied Psychology, 78,* 679–703.

29. Ones, D. S., Viswesvaran, C., & Schmidt, F. L. (2012). Integrity tests predict counterproductive work behaviors and job performance well: Comment on Van Iddekinge, Roth, Raymark, and Odle-Dusseau. *Journal of Applied Psychology, 97,* 537–542; Sackett, P. R., & Schmitt, N. (2012). On reconciling conflicting meta-analytic findings regarding integrity test validity. *Journal of Applied Psychology, 97,* 550–556; Van Iddekinge, C. H., Roth, P. L., Raymark, P. H., & Odle-Dusseau, H. N. (2012). The criterion-related validity of integrity tests: An updated meta-analysis. *Journal of Applied Psychology, 97,* 499–530.

30. Berry, C. M., Sackett, P. R., & Wiemann, S. (2007). A review of recent developments in integrity test research. *Personnel Psychology, 60,* 271–301; Marcus, B., Lee, K., & Ashton, M. C. (2007). Personality dimensions explaining relationships between integrity tests and counterproductive behavior: Big Five, or one in addition? *Personnel Psychology, 60,* 1–34.

31. Guion, R. M. (1998). *Assessment, measurement, and prediction for personnel decisions.* Mahwah, NJ: Lawrence Erlbaum.

32. Schmidt, F. L., & Hunter, J. E. (1998). The validity and utility of selection methods in personnel psychology: Practical and theoretical implications of 85 years of research findings. *Psychological Bulletin, 124,* 262–274.

33. Ones, D. S., Dilchert, S., & Viswesvaran, C. (2012). Cognitive abilities. In N. Schmitt (Ed.), *The Oxford handbook of personnel assessment and selection* (pp. 179–224). New York, NY: Oxford University Press; Roth, P. L., Bevier, C. A., Bobko, P., Switzer, F. S., & Tyler, P. (2001). Ethnic group differences in cognitive ability in employment and educational settings: A meta-analysis. *Personnel Psychology, 54,* 297–330; Ryan, A. M., & Powers, C. (2012). Workplace diversity. In N. Schmitt (Ed.), *The Oxford handbook of personnel assessment and selection* (pp. 814–831). New York, NY: Oxford University Press.

34. Ones, D. S., Dilchert, S., & Viswesvaran, C. (2012). Cognitive abilities. In N. Schmitt (Ed.), *The Oxford handbook of personnel assessment and selection* (pp. 179–224). New York, NY: Oxford University Press; Schmidt, F. L., & Hunter, J. (2004). General mental ability in the world of work: occupational attainment and job performance. *Journal of Personality and Social Psychology, 86,* 162–173.

35. Guion, R. M. (1965). *Personnel testing.* New York, NY: McGraw-Hill.

36. Wonderlic. (2012). Client stories: Subway restaurants. https://www.wonderlic.com/wp-content/uploads/2017/04/subwayRestaurants_cs.pdf

37. Gatewood, R., Feild, H., & Barrick, M. (2011). *Human resource selection.* Mason, OH: Cengage Learning.

38. Salovey, P., & Mayer, J. D. (1990). Emotional intelligence. *Imagination, Cognition and Personality, 9,* 185–211.

39. Joseph, D. L., Jin, J., Newman, D. A., & O'Boyle, E. H. (2015). Why does self-reported emotional intelligence predict job performance? A meta-analytic investigation of mixed EI. *Journal of Applied Psychology, 100,* 298–342; Joseph, D. L., & Newman, D. A. (2010). Emotional intelligence: An integrative meta-analysis and cascading model. *Journal of Applied Psychology, 95,* 54–78.

40. A video game that slays hiring bias and airdrops you into the right job. (2016, October 12). *Fast Company.* https://www.fastcompany.com/3063881/a-video-game-that-slays-hiring-bias-and-airdrops-you-into-the-right-job; Gamification in recruitment: Psychometric selection for diverse talent. (2016, August 1). *Personnel Today.* http://www.personneltoday.com/hr/gamification-recruitment-psychometric-selection-diverse-talent/; Riley, P. (2015). Should we play? Gamification in assessment and selection. *Assessment and Development Matters, 7,* 13–16. http://ptc.bps.org.uk/sites/ptc.bps.org.uk/files/Documents/Assessment%20%26%20Development%20Matters/Should%20we%20Play%20-%20Philippa%20Riley.pdf

41. Block, K. (2016). I hire engineers at Google. Here's what I look for (and why). *Fast Company.* https://www.fastcompany.com/3062713/i-hire-engineers-at-google-heres-what-i-look-for-and-why

42. JetBlue: hiring crewmembers with the skills to thrive. (2019). https://rework.withgoogle.com/case-studies/JetBlue-hiring-crewmembers-with-skills-to-thrive

43. Hausknecht, J. P., Day, D. V., & Thomas, S. C. (2004). Applicant reactions to selection procedures: An updated model and meta-analysis. *Personnel Psychology, 57,* 639–683; Schmidt, F. L., & Hunter, J. E. (1998). The validity and utility of selection methods in personnel psychology: Practical and theoretical implications of 85 years of research findings. *Psychological Bulletin, 124,* 262–274.

44. Bauer, T. N., Truxillo, D. M., Mack, K., & Costa, A. B. (2011). Applicant reactions to technology-based selection: What we know so far. In N. T. Tippins & S. Adler (Eds.), *Technology-enhanced assessment* (pp. 190–223). San Francisco, CA: Jossey-Bass.

45. Christian, M. S., Edwards, B. D., & Bradley, J. C. (2010). Situational judgment tests: Constructs assessed and a meta-analysis of their criterion-related validities. *Personnel Psychology, 63,* 83–117; Lievens, F., & Sackett, P. R. (2012). The validity of interpersonal skills assessment via situational judgment tests for predicting academic success and job performance. *Journal of Applied Psychology, 97,* 460–468.

46. Arthur, W., Day, E. A., McNelly, T. L., & Edens, P. S. (2003). A meta-analysis of the criterion-related validity of assessment center dimensions. *Personnel Psychology, 56,* 125–153; Schmidt, F. L., & Hunter, J. E. (1998). The validity and utility of selection methods in personnel psychology: Practical and theoretical implications of 85 years of research findings. *Psychological Bulletin, 124,* 262–274.

47. Lievens, F., & De Soete, B. (2012). Simulations. In N. Schmitt (Ed.), *The Oxford handbook of personnel assessment and selection* (pp. 383–410). New York, NY: Oxford University Press.

48. http://www.siop.org/lec/2009/reynolds_bio.aspx; http://www.ddiworld.com/company/our-management-team/douglas-reynolds

49. Schmidt, F. L., & Hunter, J. E. (1998). The validity and utility of selection methods in personnel psychology: Practical and theoretical implications of 85 years of research findings. *Psychological Bulletin, 124,* 262–274.

50. Cucina, J. M., Caputo, P. M., Thibodeaux, H. F., & Maclane, C. N. (2012). Unlocking the key to biodata scoring: A comparison of empirical, rational, and hybrid approaches at different sample sizes. *Personnel Psychology, 65,* 385–428; Gatewood, R., Feild, H., & Barrick, M. (2011). *Human resource selection.* Mason, OH: Cengage Learning.

51. Schmidt, F. L., & Hunter, J. E. (1998). The validity and utility of selection methods in personnel psychology: Practical and theoretical implications of 85 years of research findings. *Psychological Bulletin, 124,* 262–274.

52. Schmidt, F. L., & Hunter, J. E. (1998). The validity and utility of selection methods in personnel psychology: Practical and theoretical implications of 85 years of research findings. *Psychological Bulletin, 124,* 262–274.

53. Hausknecht, J. P, Day, D. V., & Thomas, S. C. (2004). Applicant reactions to selection procedures: An updated model and meta-analysis. *Personnel Psychology, 57,* 639–683.

54. Gatewood, R., Feild, H., & Barrick, M. (2011). *Human resource selection.* Mason, OH: Cengage Learning.

55. Gatewood, R., Feild, H., & Barrick, M. (2011). *Human resource selection.* Mason, OH: Cengage Learning; Society for Human Resource Management. (2010, January 22). Background checking: Conducting reference background checks: SHRM poll. *Survey Findings.* http://www.shrm.org/Research/SurveyFindings/Articles/Pages/ConductingReferenceBackgroundChecks.aspx

56. The White House. (2016). White House launches the fair chance business pledge. https://obamawhitehouse.archives.gov/the-press-office/2016/04/11/fact-sheet-white-house-launches-fair-chance-business-pledge; https://www.laboremploymentlawblog.com/2017/07/articles/background-investigations/criminal-background-checks/; https://www.shrm.org/resourcesandtools/legal-and-compliance/state-and-local-updates/xperthr/pages/ban-the-box-laws-by-state-and-municipality-.aspx

57. Chicago to pay $3.8 million as part of Fire Department gender bias case. (2016, December 9). *Chicago Tribune.* http://www.chicagotribune.com/news/local/politics/ct-chicago-fire-department-lawsuit-gender-bias-met-20161209-story.html

58. Baker, T. A., & Gebhardt, D. L. (2012). The assessment of physical capabilities in the workplace. In N. Schmitt (Ed.), *The Oxford handbook of personnel assessment and selection* (pp. 274–296). New York, NY: Oxford University Press; Courtright, S. H., McCormick, B. W., Postlethwaite, B. E., Reeves, C. J., & Mount, M. K. (2013). A meta-analysis of sex differences in physical ability: Revised estimates and strategies for reducing differences in selection

contexts. *Journal of Applied Psychology, 98,* 623–641.

59. Van Iddekinge, C. H., Lanivich, S. E., Roth, P. L., & Junco, E. (2016). Social media for selection? Validity and adverse impact potential of a Facebook-based assessment. *Journal of Management, 42,* 1811–1835.

60. Bernerth, J. B., Taylor, S. G., Walker, H. J., & Whitman, D. S. (2012). An empirical investigation of dispositional antecedents and performance-related outcomes of credit scores. *Journal of Applied Psychology, 97,* 469–478.

61. Harold, C. M., Holtz, B. C., Griepentrog, B. K., Brewer, L. M., & Marsh, S. M. (2016). Investigating the effects of applicant justice perceptions on job offer acceptance. *Personnel Psychology, 69,* 199–22; McCarthy, J. M., Bauer, T. N., Truxillo, D. M., Anderson, N. R., Costa, A. C., & Ahmed, S. M. (2017). Applicant perspectives during selection: A review addressing "so what?," "what's new?," and "where to next?" *Journal of Management, 43,* 1693–1725.

62. Steiner, K. (2017). Bad candidate experience cost Virgin Media $5M annually—and how they turned it around. https://business.linkedin.com/talent-solutions/blog/candidate-experience/2017/bad-candidate-experience-cost-virgin-media-5m-annually-and-how-they-turned-that-around

63. Bauer, T. N., Truxillo, D. M., Sanchez, R. J., Craig, J., Ferrara, P., & Campion, M. A. (2001). Applicant reactions to selection: Development of the Selection Procedural Justice Scale (SPJS). *Personnel Psychology, 54,* 387–419; Gilliland, S. W. (1993). The perceived fairness of selection systems: An organizational justice perspective. *Academy of Management Review, 18,*

694–734; Hausknecht, J. P., Day, D. V., & Thomas, S. C. (2004). Applicant reactions to selection procedures: An updated model and meta-analysis. *Personnel Psychology, 57,* 639–683; McCarthy, J. M., Bauer, T. N., Truxillo, D. M., Anderson, N. R., Costa, A. C., & Ahmed, S. M. (2017). Applicant perspectives during selection: A review addressing "so what?," "what's new?," and "where to next?" *Journal of Management, 43,* 1693–1725.

64. Anderson, N., Salgado, J. F., & Hülsheger, U. R. (2010). Applicant reactions in selection: Comprehensive meta-analysis into reaction generalization versus situational specificity. *International Journal of Selection and Assessment, 18,* 291–304; Hoang, T. G., Truxillo, D. M., Erdogan, B., & Bauer, T. N. (2012). Cross-cultural examination of applicant reactions to selection methods: United States and Vietnam. *International Journal of Selection and Assessment, 20,* 209–219; Steiner, D. D., & Gilliland, S. W. (1996). Fairness reactions to personnel selection techniques in France and the United States. *Journal of Applied Psychology, 81,* 134–141.

65. Gilliland, S. W. (1993). The perceived fairness of selection systems: An organizational justice perspective. *Academy of Management Review, 18,* 694–734; Hausknecht, J. P., Day, D. V., & Thomas, S. C. (2004). Applicant reactions to selection procedures: An updated model and meta-analysis. *Personnel Psychology, 57,* 639–683.

66. Truxillo, D. M., Bauer, T. N., Campion, M. A., & Paronto, M. E. (2002). Selection fairness information and applicant reactions: A longitudinal field study. *Journal of Applied Psychology, 87,* 1020–1031;

Truxillo, D. M., Bodner, T. E., Bertolino, M., Bauer, T. N., & Yonce, C. A. (2009). Effects of explanations on applicant reactions: A meta-analytic review. *International Journal of Selection and Assessment, 17,* 346–361.

67. CandE Awards. (2018). CandE winners. https://www.thetalentboard.org/cande-awards/cande-winners/#2018ranking

68. Guion, R. M. (2011). *Assessment, measurement, and prediction for personnel decisions.* New York, NY: Routledge.

69. Based on information contained in 74,000 data records breached on stolen Coca-Cola laptops. (2014, January 27). *Infosecurity Magazine.* http://www.infosecurity-magazine.com/view/36627/74000-data-records-breached-on-stolen-cocacola-laptops-/; Are you doing enough to protect your sensitive HR data? (2016, October 19). *People HR.* https://www.peoplehr.com/blog/index.php/2016/10/19/are-you-doing-enough-to-protect-your-sensitive-hr-data/

CHAPTER 8

1. Kirkpatrick, D. L., & Kirkpatrick, J. D. (2006). *Evaluating training programs: The four levels.* San Francisco, CA: Berrett-Kohler; Russell, G. (2017, March). Program measurements get streamlined. *TD: Training and Development,* pp. 24–27.

2. Size of training industry. (2017). https://www.trainingindustry.com/wiki/entries/size-of-training-industry.aspx

3. Goldstein, I. L., & Ford, J. K. (2002). *Training in organizations: Needs assessment, development, and evaluation* (4th ed.). Belmont, CA: Wadsworth Cengage Learning.

4. Rients, S. (2017, February 1). Compliance training doesn't have to be boring. Association for Talent Development. https://www.td.org/Publications/Magazines/TD/TD-Archive/2017/02/Compliance-Training-Doesnt-Have-to-Be-Boring; *Uniform Guidelines on Employee Selection Procedures*. (1978). *Federal Register, 43,* 38290–38315.

5. Goldstein, I. L., & Ford, J. K. (2002). *Training in organizations: Needs assessment, development, and evaluation* (4th ed.). Belmont, CA: Wadsworth Cengage Learning.

6. Kraiger, K., Ford, J. K., & Salas, E. (1993). Application of cognitive, skill-based, and affective theories of learning outcomes to new methods of training evaluation. *Journal of Applied Psychology, 78,* 311–328; Salas, E., Tannenbaum, S. I., Kraiger, K., & Smith-Jentsch, K. A. (2012). The science of training and development in organizations: What matters in practice. *Psychological Science in the Public Interest, 13,* 74–101.

7. Colquitt, J. A., LePine, J. A., & Noe, R. A. (2000). Toward an integrative theory of training motivation: A meta-analytic path analysis of 20 years of research. *Journal of Applied Psychology, 85,* 678–707; Goldstein, I. L., & Ford, J. K. (2002). *Training in organizations: Needs assessment, development, and evaluation* (4th ed.). Belmont, CA: Wadsworth Cengage Learning.

8. Kruger, J., & Dunning, D. (1999). Unskilled and unaware of it: How difficulties in recognizing one's own incompetence lead to inflated self-assessments. *Journal of Personality and Social Psychology, 77,* 1121–1132.

9. Goldstein, I. L., & Ford, J. K. (2002). *Training in organizations: Needs assessment, development, and evaluation* (4th ed.). Belmont, CA: Wadsworth Cengage Learning.

10. Goldstein, I. L., & Ford, J. K. (2002). *Training in organizations: Needs assessment, development, and evaluation* (4th ed.). Belmont, CA: Wadsworth Cengage Learning.

11. Arthur, W., Jr., Bennett, W., Jr., Edens, P. S., & Bell, S. T. (2003). Effectiveness of training in organizations: A meta-analysis of design and evaluation features. *Journal of Applied Psychology, 88,* 234–245; Goldstein, I. L., & Ford, J. K. (2002). *Training in organizations: Needs assessment, development, and evaluation* (4th ed.). Belmont, CA: Wadsworth Cengage Learning.

12. Wilks, K. (2015). Learning to fly from the ground up. https://news.delta.com/learning-fly-ground

13. Goldstein, I. L., & Ford, J. K. (2002). *Training in organizations: Needs assessment, development, and evaluation* (4th ed.). Belmont, CA: Wadsworth Cengage Learning; Villado, A. J., & Arthur W., Jr. (2013). The comparative effect of subjective and objective after-action reviews on team performance on a complex task. *Journal of Applied Psychology, 98,* 514–528.

14. Goldstein, I. L., & Ford, J. K. (2002). *Training in organizations: Needs assessment, development, and evaluation* (4th ed.). Belmont, CA: Wadsworth Cengage Learning.

15. Global investment in learning technology firms surpasses previous year's record. (2017, April). *TD: Talent Development,* p. 19; Adkins, S. S. (2017, January). The 2016 global learning technology investment patterns. http://www.metaari.com/assets/Metaari_s-Analysis-of-the-2016-Global-Learning-Technology-Investment-Pat25875.pdf

16. Slade, T. (2017, March). Five lessons for new eLearning designers. *TD: Training and Development,* pp. 60–64.

17. Bell, B. S., & Kozlowski, S. W. (2002). Adaptive guidance: Enhancing self-regulation, knowledge, and performance in technology-based training. *Personnel Psychology, 55,* 267–306; Bell, B. S., & Kozlowski, S. W. (2008). Active learning: Effects of core training design elements on self-regulatory processes, learning, and adaptability. *Journal of Applied Psychology, 93,* 296–316; Sitzmann, T., Kraiger, K., Stewart, D., & Wisher, R. (2006). The comparative effectiveness of web-based and classroom instruction: A meta-analysis. *Personnel Psychology, 59,* 623–664.

18. SAP Learning Hub. https://training.sap.com/shop/learninghub

19. https://training.sap.com/shop/learninghub

20. Baldwin, T. T. (1992). Effects of alternative modeling strategies on outcomes of interpersonal-skills training. *Journal of Applied Psychology, 77,* 147–154; Bandura, A. (1977). *Social learning theory.* Englewood Cliffs, NJ: Prentice Hall; Taylor, P. J., Russ-Eft, D. F., & Chan, D. W. (2005). A meta-analytic review of behavior modeling training. *Journal of Applied Psychology, 90,* 692–709.

21. Alhejji, H., Garavan, T., Carbery, R., O'Brien, F., & McGuire, D. (2016). Diversity training programme outcomes: A systematic review. *Human Resource Development Quarterly, 27,* 95–149; Dobbin, F., & Kalev, A. (2016, July–August). Why diversity programs fail and what works better. *Harvard Business Review,* pp. 52–60; Kalinoski, Z. T., Steele-Johnson, D., Peyton, E. J., Leas, K. A., Steinke, J., & Bowling, N. A. (2013). A meta-analytic evaluation of diversity training outcomes. *Journal of Organizational Behavior, 34,* 1076–1104; Lindsey, A., King,

E., Hebl, M., & Levine, N. (2015). The impact of method, motivation, and empathy on diversity training effectiveness. *Journal of Business and Psychology, 30,* 605–617; Manjoo, F. (2014). Exposing hidden bias at Google. *New York Times.* http://www.nytimes.com/2014/09/25/technology/exposing-hidden-biases-at-google-to-improve-diversity.html

22. Salas, E., DiazGranados, D., Klein, C., Burke, C. S., Stagl, K. C., Goodwin, G. F., & Halpin, S. M. (2008). Does team training improve team performance? A meta-analysis. *Human Factors, 50,* 903–933.

23. Center for Creative Leadership. (n.d.). https://www.ccl.org/people/cindy-mccauley-2/; The long view: Cindy McCauley. (2017, February). *TD: Training and Development,* pp. 62–63.

24. Bono, J. E., Purvanova, R. K., Towler, A. J., & Peterson, D. B. (2009). A survey of executive coaching practices. *Personnel Psychology, 62,* 361–404; Goldstein, I. L., & Ford, J. K. (2002). *Training in organizations: Needs assessment, development, and evaluation* (4th ed.). Belmont, CA: Wadsworth Cengage Learning.

25. Hülsheger, U. R., Feinholdt, A., & Nübold, A. (2015). A low-dose mindfulness intervention and recovery from work: Effects on psychological detachment, sleep quality, and sleep duration. *Journal of Occupational and Organizational Psychology, 88,* 464–489; Roeser, R. W., Schonert-Reichl, K. A., Jha, A., Cullen, M., Wallace, L., Wilensky, R., . . . Harrison, J. (2013). Mindfulness training and reductions in teacher stress and burnout: Results from two randomized, waitlist-control field trials. *Journal of Educational Psychology, 105,* 787–804.

26. Schaufenbruel, K. (2015, December 29). Why Google, Target, and General Mills are investing in mindfulness. *Harvard Business Review.* https://hbr.org/2015/12/why-google-target-and-general-mills-are-investing-in-mindfulness; Wieczner, J. (2016, March 12). Meditation has become a billion dollar business. *Fortune.* http://fortune.com/2016/03/12/meditation-mindfulness-apps/

27. Landers, R. N., & Armstrong, M. B. (2017). Enhancing instructional outcomes with gamification: An empirical test of the technology-enhanced training effectiveness model. *Computers in Human Behavior, 71,* 499–507; Santhanam, R., Liu, D., & Shen, W. C. M. (2016). Research Note—Gamification of technology-mediated training: Not all competitions are the same. *Information Systems Research, 27,* 453–465.

28. Bauer, T. N., Bodner, T., Erdogan, B., Truxillo, D. M., & Tucker, J. S. (2007). Newcomer adjustment during organizational socialization: A meta-analytic review of antecedents, outcomes, and methods. *Journal of Applied Psychology, 92,* 707–721; Saks, A. M., Uggerslev, K. L., & Fassina, N. E. (2007). Socialization tactics and newcomer adjustment: A meta-analytic review and test of a model. *Journal of Vocational Behavior, 70,* 413–446.

29. Klein, H. J., & Polin, B. (2012). Are organizations on board with best practices onboarding? In C. Wanberg (Ed.), *The Oxford handbook of organizational socialization* (pp. 267–287). New York, NY: Oxford University Press.

30. Bauer, T. N., & Erdogan, B. (2016). *Organizational behavior.* Boston, MA: Flat World Knowledge; Durett, J. (2006, March 1). Technology opens the door to success at Ritz-Carlton. http://www.managesmarter.com/msg/search/article_display.jsp?vnu_content_id=1002157749; Elswick, J. (2000, February). Puttin' on the Ritz: Hotel chain touts training to benefit its recruiting and retention. *Employee Benefit News, 14,* 9; The Ritz-Carlton Company: How it became a "legend" in service. (2001, January–February). *Corporate University Review, 9,* 16.

31. Personal communication with Talya N. Bauer.

32. Bauer, T. N. (2015). Onboarding: The critical role of hiring managers. *SuccessFactors.* https://www.researchgate.net/publication/286447336_The_critical_role_of_the_hiring_manager_in_new_employee_onboarding

33. Ashford, S. J., & Black, J. S. (1996). Proactivity during organizational entry: The role of desire for control. *Journal of Applied Psychology, 81,* 199–214.

34. Ellis, A. M., Nifadkar, S. S., Bauer, T. N., & Erdogan, B. (2017). Your new hires won't succeed unless you onboard them properly. *Harvard Business Review.* https://hbr.org/2017/06/your-new-hires-wont-succeed-unless-you-onboard-them-properly

35. Alliger, G. M., Tannenbaum, S. I., Bennett, W., Jr., Traver, H., & Shotland, A. (1997). A meta-analysis of the relations among training criteria. *Personnel Psychology, 50,* 341–358.

36. Bushée, D. (2017, March). Analyze this. *TD: Training and Development,* pp. 28–29; Ketter, P. (2017, April). Artificial intelligence creeps into talent development. *TD: Talent Development,* pp. 22–25.

37. McIntosh, C. (2017, June). Swapping training delivery for knowledge building. *TD: Talent Development,* pp. 60–61.

38. Association Adviser. (2015). Professional development vs.

career management. http://www
.associationadviser.com/index
.php/professional-development-
career-management/

39. Are you ready to take on a
brand new challenge? (2019).
https://jobs.raytheon.com/
college-jobs

40. Allen, T. D., Eby, L. T., Poteet, M.
L., Lentz, E., & Lima, L. (2004).
Career benefits associated with
mentoring for protégés: A meta-
analysis. *Journal of Applied
Psychology, 89,* 127–136.

41. *Fortune.* (2017). 100 Best
companies to work for,
Genentech. http://fortune
.com/best-companies/2015/
genentech-9/; Training. (2015).
2015 best practice and outstanding
training initiative award winners.
https://trainingmag.com/trgmag-
article/2015-best-practice-and-
outstanding-training-initiative-
award-winners

42. National Institutes of Health.
(2018). NIH Ethics Program.
https://ethics.od.nih.gov/
training.htm; Raicu, I. (2017, May
26). Rethinking ethics training
in Silicon Valley. *The Atlantic.*
https://www.theatlantic.com/
technology/archive/2017/05/
rethinking-ethics-training-in-
silicon-valley/525456/

CHAPTER 9

1. Cunningham, L. (2015, July
21). In big move, Accenture will
get rid of annual performance
reviews and rankings.
Washington Post. https://www
.washingtonpost.com/news/
on-leadership/wp/2015/07/21/in-
big-move-accenture-will-get-rid-
of-annual-performance-reviews-
and-rankings/; Rafter, M. V.
(2017, January/February). Upon
further review. http://www
.workforce.com/2017/01/10/
upon-further-review/

2. SHRM. (2014, October 20).
HR professionals' perceptions

about performance management
effectiveness. https://www
.shrm.org/hr-today/trends-
and-forecasting/research-
and-surveys/Pages/2014-
performance-management.aspx#
sthash.DoYdBNJT.dpuf

3. Mohan, P. (2017). Ready to
scrap your annual performance
reviews? Try these alternatives.
Fast Company. https://www
.fastcompany.com/40405106/
ready-to-scrap-your-annual-
performance-reviews-try-these-
alternatives

4. Fleck, C. (2016, June). An
algorithm for success. *HR
Magazine,* pp. 130–135; Roberts,
G. (July, 2016). Predictive
analytics is essential to your
candidate pre-screening
process—Here's why! *Workforce
Solutions Review,* pp. 36–37.

5. Bretz, R. D., Milkovich, G. T.,
& Read, W. (1992). The current
state of performance appraisal
research and practice: Concerns,
directions, and implications.
Journal of Management, 18, 321–
352; DeNisi, A. S., & Murphy, K.
R. (2017). Performance appraisal
and performance management:
100 years of progress? *Journal
of Applied Psychology, 102,*
421–433; Landy, F. J., & Farr, J.
L. (1980). Performance rating.
Psychological Bulletin, 87, 72–107.

6. Pyrillis, R. (2011, May 5). Is
your performance review
underperforming? http://www
.workforce.com/2011/05/05/
is-your-performance-review-
underperforming/

7. Taylor, M. S., Tracy, K. B.,
Renard, M. K., Harrison, J. K.,
& Carroll, S. J. (1995). Due
process in performance
appraisal: A quasi-experiment
in procedural justice.
*Administrative Science Quarterly,
40,* 495–523.

8. DeNisi, A., & Smith, C. E.
(2014). Performance appraisal,
performance management, and
firm-level performance: A review,

a proposed model, and new
directions for future research.
*Academy of Management Annals,
8,* 127–179.

9. Behson, S. (2016, April 6). Work–
life balance is easier when your
manager knows how to assess
performance. *Harvard Business
Review,* pp. 2–4.

10. Heidemeier, H., & Moser, K.
(2009). Self-other agreement in
job performance ratings: A meta-
analytic test of a process model.
Journal of Applied Psychology, 94,
353–370.

11. Locke, E., & Latham, G. P. (1990).
*A theory of goal setting & task
performance.* Englewood Cliffs,
NJ: Prentice Hall.

12. Ordóñez, L. D., Schweitzer, M.
E., Galinsky, A. D., & Bazerman,
M. H. (2009, February). Goals
gone wild: The systematic side
effects of overprescribing goal
setting. *Academy of Management
Perspectives,* pp. 6–14.

13. Griswold, A. (2017, February 27).
Uber is designed so that for one
employee to get ahead, another
must fail. https://qz.com/918582/
uber-is-designed-so-that-for-
one-employee-to-succeed-
another-must-fail/

14. O'Boyle, E., & Aguinis, H.
(2012). The best and the rest:
Revisiting the norm of normality
of individual performance.
Personnel Psychology, 65, 79–119.

15. Cappelli, P., & Tavis, A. (2016,
October). The performance
management revolution:
The focus is shifting from
accountability to learning.
Harvard Business Review,
pp. 58–61.

16. Mohan, P. (2017). Ready to
scrap your annual performance
reviews? Try these alternatives.
Fast Company. https://www
.fastcompany.com/40405106/
ready-to-scrap-your-annual-
performance-reviews-try-these-
alternatives

17. Levy, P. E., & Williams, J. R.
(2004). The social context of

performance appraisal: A review and framework for the future. *Journal of Management, 30,* 881–905.

18. Mohan, P. (2017). Ready to scrap your annual performance reviews? Try these alternatives. *Fast Company.* https://www.fastcompany.com/40405106/ready-to-scrap-your-annual-performance-reviews-try-these-alternatives

19. Antonioni, D. (1994). The effects of feedback accountability on upward appraisal ratings. *Personnel Psychology, 47,* 349–356.

20. Hekman, D. R., Aquino, K., Owens, B. P., Mitchell, T. R., Schilpzand, P., & Leavitt, K. (2010). An examination of whether and how racial and gender biases influence customer satisfaction. *Academy of Management Journal, 53,* 238–264.

21. Farh, J. L., & Werbel, J. D. (1986). Effects of purpose of the appraisal and expectation of validation on self-appraisal leniency. *Journal of Applied Psychology, 71,* 527–529; Heidemeier, H., & Moser, K. (2009). Self–other agreement in job performance ratings: A meta-analytic test of a process model. *Journal of Applied Psychology, 94,* 353–370.

22. Seifert, C. F., Yukl, G., & McDonald, R. A. (2003). Effects of multisource feedback and a feedback facilitator on the influence behavior of managers toward subordinates. *Journal of Applied Psychology, 88,* 561–569.

23. Nyberg, A. J., Pieper, J. R., & Trevor, C. O. (2016). Pay-for-performance's effect on future employee performance: Integrating psychological and economic principles toward a contingency perspective. *Journal of Management, 42,* 1753–1783.

24. Cohen-Charash, Y., & Spector, P. E. (2001). The role of justice in organizations: A meta-analysis. *Organizational Behavior and Human Decision Processes, 86,* 278–321.

25. Goler, L., Gale, J., & Grant, A. (2016, November). Let's not kill performance evaluations yet. *Harvard Business Review,* pp. 91–94.

26. Caprino, K. (2016, December 13). Separating performance management from compensation: New trend for thriving organizations. *Forbes.* https://www.forbes.com/sites/kathycaprino/2016/12/13/separating-performance-management-from-compensation-new-trend-for-thriving-organizations/; Papp, F. (2017, March 14). Avaloq: Employees evaluate team performance. http://www.finews.com/news/english-news/26590-avaloq-where-employees-get-to-decide-about-bonuses

27. Wayne, S. J., & Liden, R. C. (1995). Effects of impression management on performance ratings: A longitudinal study. *Academy of Management Journal, 38,* 232–260.

28. Bretz, R. D., Milkovich, G. T., & Read, W. (1992). The current state of performance appraisal research and practice: Concerns, directions, and implications. *Journal of Management, 18,* 321–352.

29. Freeman, M. (2016, July 26). Qualcomm enters $19.5 million gender bias settlement. *San Diego Union Tribune.* http://www.sandiegouniontribune.com/business/technology/sdut-qualcomm-lawsuit-gender-bias-women-stem-2016jul26-story.html; Freeman, M. (2016, July 27). Qualcomm settles gender-discrimination lawsuit. *Los Angeles Times.* http://www.latimes.com/business/la-fi-qualcomm-women-20160727-snap-story.html; Sanford Heisler Sharp LLP. (2016). Qualcomm gender discrimination class action–$19.5 million settlement. https://sanfordheisler.com/case/qualcomm-gender-discrimination-class-action/

30. Harari, M. B., Rudolph, C. W., & Laginess, A. J. (2015). Does rater personality matter? A meta-analysis of rater Big Five–performance rating relationships. *Journal of Occupational and Organizational Psychology, 88,* 387–414.

31. Robbins, R. L., & DeNisi, A. S. (1994). A closer look at interpersonal affect as a distinct influence on cognitive processing in performance appraisal. *Journal of Applied Psychology, 79,* 341–353.

32. Levy, P. E., & Williams, J. R. (2004). The social context of performance appraisal: A review and framework for the future. *Journal of Management, 30,* 881–905.

33. Villanova, P., Bernardin, H. J., Dahmus, S. A., & Sims, R. L. (1993). Rater leniency and performance appraisal discomfort. *Educational & Psychological Measurement, 53,* 789–799.

34. Fludd, V. (2016, March). Performance management for managers. *TD,* p. 12.

35. Arvey, R. D., & Murphy, K. R. (1998). Performance evaluation in work settings. *Annual Review of Psychology, 49,* 141–168; Athey, T. R., & McIntyre, R. M. (1987). Effects of rater training on rater accuracy: Levels-of-processing theory and social facilitation theory perspectives. *Journal of Applied Psychology, 72,* 567–572.

36. Lebowitz, S. (2015, June 15). Here's how performance reviews work at Google. *Business Insider.* http://www.businessinsider.com/how-google-performance-reviews-work-2015-6

37. Sitrin, C. (2017, June 13). Here's what Eric Holder's law firm thinks Uber should do to fix its

toxic culture. Retrieved June 20, 2017, from https://www.vox.com/technology/2017/6/13/15793712/uber-holder-report-sexual-harassment-travis-kalanick

38. DeNisi, A. S., & Peters, L. H. (1996). Organization of information in memory and the performance appraisal process: Evidence from the field. *Journal of Applied Psychology, 81,* 717–737.

39. Goler, L., Gale, J., & Grant, A. (2016, November). Let's not kill performance evaluations yet. *Harvard Business Review,* pp. 91–94.

40. Pulakos, E. D., Hanson, R. M., Arad, S., & Moye, N. (2015). Performance management can be fixed: An on-the-job experiential learning approach for complex behavior change. *Industrial and Organizational Psychology, 8,* 51–76.

41. Meinecke, A. L., Klonek, F. E., & Kauffeld, S. (2017). Appraisal participation and perceived voice in annual appraisal interviews: Uncovering contextual factors. *Journal of Leadership & Organizational Studies, 24,* 230–245.

42. Porath, C. (2016). Give your team more effective positive feedback. *Harvard Business Review.* https://hbr.org/2016/10/give-your-team-more-effective-positive-feedback

43. Hoffman, L. (2017, April 21). Goldman goes beyond annual review with real-timeemployee feedback; changesare part of bigger shift in the way companies track andgrade workers' performance. *Wall Street Journal.* https://www.wsj.com/articles/goldman-goes-beyond-annual-review-with-real-time-employee-ratings-1492786653

44. SHRM. (2017, March 6). How to establish a performance improvement plan. https://www.shrm.org/resourcesandtools/tools-and-samples/how-to-guides/pages/performanceimprovementplan.aspx

45. Egan, M. (2016, September 9). Workers tell Wells Fargo horror stories. http://money.cnn.com/2016/09/09/investing/wells-fargo-phony-accounts-culture/index.html?iid=EL; Egan, M. (2017, January 6). Wells Fargo's notorious sales goals to get a makeover. http://money.cnn.com/2017/01/06/investing/wells-fargo-replace-sales-goals-fake-accounts/index.html

CHAPTER 10

1. Kaplan, D. A. (2013, January 17). Mars incorporated: A pretty sweet place to work. *Fortune.* http://fortune.com/2013/01/17/mars-incorporated-a-pretty-sweet-place-to-work/; Moss, D. (2016, September 20). Profiles in HR: Tracey Wood, Mars Chocolate North America. https://www.shrm.org/hr-today/news/hr-magazine/1016/pages/profiles-in-hr-tracey-wood-mars-chocolate-north-america.aspx; Zimmerman, K. (2016, August 8). Are rotational programs the key to retaining millennial employees? *Forbes.* https://www.forbes.com/sites/kaytiezimmerman/2016/08/08/can-a-millennial-quarter-life-crisis-be-cured-by-their-employer/

2. Glebbeek, A. C., & Bax, E. H. (2004). Is high employee turnover really harmful? An empirical test using company records. *Academy of Management Journal, 47,* 277–286.

3. Maurer, R. (2017, March 21). Data will show you why your employees leave or stay. https://www.shrm.org/resourcesandtools/hr-topics/talent-acquisition/pages/data-retention-turnover-hr.aspx

4. Allen, D. G., Bryant, P. C., & Vardaman, J. M. (2010). Retaining talent: Replacing misconceptions with evidence-based strategies. *Academy of Management Perspectives, 24,* 48–64.

5. Based on Glebbeek, A. C., & Bax, E. H. (2004). Is high employee turnover really harmful? An empirical test using company records. *Academy of Management Journal, 47,* 277–286.

6. Griffeth, R. W., Hom, P. W., & Gaertner, S. (2000). A meta-analysis of antecedents and correlates of employee turnover: Update, moderator tests, and research implications for the next millennium. *Journal of Management, 26,* 463–488.

7. Harter, J. K., Schmidt, F. L., & Hayes, T. L. (2002). Business-unit-level relationship between employee satisfaction, employee engagement, and business outcomes: A meta-analysis. *Journal of Applied Psychology, 87,* 268–279.

8. Mitchell, T. R., & Lee, T. W. (2001). The unfolding model of voluntary turnover and job embeddedness: Foundations for a comprehensive theory of attachment. *Research in Organizational Behavior, 23,* 189–246.

9. Anonymous. (2015, October). Talent quitting time. *Harvard Business Review,* p. 34; Anonymous. (2016, September). Talent: Why people quit their jobs. *Harvard Business Review,* pp. 20–21.

10. Hom, P. W., Lee, T. W., Shaw, J. D., & Hausknecht, J. P. (2017). One hundred years of employee turnover theory and research. *Journal of Applied Psychology, 102,* 530–545.

11. Krell, E. (2012, April). 5 ways to manage high turnover. *HR Magazine,* pp. 63–64.

12. Staley, O. (2017, February 14). Employers are creepily analyzing

your emails and Slack chats to see if you're happy. https://qz.com/910394/employers-are-using-sentiment-analysis-and-analyzing-your-emails-and-slack-chats-to-see-if-youre-happy-at-work; Waddell, K. (2017, September 29). The algorithms that tell bosses how employees are feeling. https://www.theatlantic.com/technology/archive/2016/09/the-algorithms-that-tell-bosses-how-employees-feel/502064/; Zielinski, D. (2017, May 15). Artificial intelligence and employee feedback. https://www.shrm.org/resourcesandtools/hr-topics/technology/pages/-artificial-intelligence-and-employee-feedback.aspx

13. Anonymous. (2014, November). One engagement question a week helps company maintain culture, manage turnover. *HR Focus, 91*(11), pp. 1–2; Fox, A. (2012, July). Drive turnover down. *HR Magazine,* pp. 23–27.

14. Anonymous. (2008, July). How to learn more from exit interviews. *HR Focus,* pp. 3–6; Spain, E., & Groysberg, B. (2016, April). Making exit interviews count. *Harvard Business Review,* pp. 88–95.

15. Heavey, A. L., Holwerda, J. A., & Hausknecht, J. P. (2013). Causes and consequences of collective turnover: A meta-analytic review. *Journal of Applied Psychology, 98,* 412–453.

16. Burry, M. (2017, April 23). Top 15 companies that offer tuition reimbursement programs. https://www.thebalance.com/companies-offer-tuition-reimbursement-4126637

17. Benson, G. S., Finegold, D., & Mohrman, S. A. (2004). You paid for the skills, now keep them: Tuition reimbursement and voluntary turnover. *Academy of Management Journal, 47,* 315–331.

18. Goler, L. (2015, December 16). What Facebook knows about engaging millennial employees. *Harvard Business Review.* https://hbr.org/2015/12/what-facebook-knows-about-engaging-millennial-employees

19. Hoffman, R. (2014, September 1). Four reasons to invest in a corporate alumni network. https://business.linkedin.com/talent-solutions/blog/2014/09/four-reasons-to-invest-in-a-corporate-alumni-network

20. Apy, F. A., & Ryckman, J. (2014). Boomerang hiring: Would you rehire a past employee? *Employment Relations Today,* pp. 13–19.

21. Shipp, A., Furst-Holloway, S., Harris, T. B., & Rosen, B. (2014). Gone today but here tomorrow: Extending the unfolding model of turnover to consider boomerang employees. *Personnel Psychology, 67,* 421–462.

22. Swider, B. W., Liu, J. T., Harris, T. B., & Gardner, R. G. (2017). Employees on the rebound: Extending the careers literature to include boomerang employees. *Journal of Applied Psychology, 102,* 890–909.

23. Fox, A. (2014, April). Keep your top talent: The return of retention. *HR Magazine,* pp. 31–40; Hamori, M., Koyuncu, B., Cao, J., & Graf, T. (2015, Fall). What high-potential young managers want? *MIT Sloan Management Review,* pp. 61–68; Knight, R. (2015, September 29). When the competition is trying to poach your top employee. *Harvard Business Review.* https://hbr.org/2015/09/when-the-competition-is-trying-to-poach-your-top-employee

24. Leonard, D., Swap, W., & Barton, G. (2014, December 2). What's lost when experts retire. *Harvard Business Review,* pp. 2–4.

25. Wang, M., & Shultz, K. S. (2010). Employee retirement: A review and recommendations for future investigation. *Journal of Management, 36,* 172–206.

26. Ostrower, J. (2017, July 31). The U.S. will face a staggering shortage of pilots. Retrieved August 16, 2017, from http://money.cnn.com/2017/07/27/news/companies/pilot-shortage-figures/index.html

27. Fisher, G. G., Chaffee, D. S., & Sonnega, A. (2016). Retirement timing: A review and recommendations for future research. *Work, Aging and Retirement, 2,* 230–261.

28. EEOC. (2000). EEOC compliance manual. https://www.eeoc.gov/policy/docs/benefits.html#VI.%20Early%20Retirement%20Incentives

29. Skarlicki, D. P., & Folger, R. (1997). Retaliation in the workplace: The roles of distributive, procedural, and interactional justice. *Journal of Applied Psychology, 82,* 434–443.

30. Berman-Gorvine, M. (2016, February). Having a toxic worker costs employers minimum of $12,500. *HR Focus, 2,* 10.

31. Doyle, A. (2016, October 17). Exceptions to employment at will. https://www.thebalance.com/exceptions-to-employment-at-will-2060484; Holzschu, M. (2017). Just cause vs. employment-at-will. https://www.businessknowhow.com/manage/justcausevsfreewill.htm; National Conference of State Legislatures. (2017). The at-will presumption and exceptions to the rule. http://www.ncsl.org/research/labor-and-employment/at-will-employment-overview.aspx

32. Wood, M. S., & Karau, S. J. (2009). Preserving employee dignity during the termination interview: An empirical examination. *Journal of Business Ethics, 86,* 519–534.

33. DePree, C., & Jude, R. K. (2007, August). Ten practical suggestions for terminating an employee. *The CPA Journal, 77*(8), 62–63.

34. Knight, R. (2016, February 5). The right way to fire someone. *Harvard Business Review.* https://hbr.org/2016/02/the-right-way-to-fire-someone

35. Matousek, M. (2018, March 21). 2 veteran United flight attendants won $800,000 in a lawsuit after a supervisor made an absurd claim about iPads. *Business Insider.* http://www.businessinsider.com/united-flight-attendants-lawsuit-against-airline-2018-3; Nicholson, K. (2018, March 7). Two former United airlines employees awarded $800,000 in age discrimination lawsuit. https://www.denverpost.com/2018/03/06/united-airlines-age-discrimination-lawsuit/

36. Wadors, P. (2015, October 2). Letting good people go when it's time. *Harvard Business Review.* https://hbr.org/2015/10/letting-good-people-go-when-its-time

37. Zillman, C. (2015, September 20). The 10 biggest corporate layoffs of the past two decades. *Fortune.* http://fortune.com/2015/09/20/biggest-corporate-layoffs/

38. Datta, D. K., Guthrie, J. P., Basuil, D., & Pandey, A. (2010). Causes and effects of employee downsizing: A review and synthesis. *Journal of Management, 36,* 281–348.

39. Pugh, S. D., Skarlicki, D. P., & Passell, B. S. (2003). After the fall: Layoff victims' trust and cynicism in re-employment. *Journal of Occupational and Organizational Psychology, 76,* 201–212.

40. Davis, P. R., Trevor, C. O., & Feng, J. (2015). Creating a more quit-friendly national workforce? Individual layoff history and voluntary turnover. *Journal of Applied Psychology, 100,* 1434–1455.

41. Datta, D. K., Guthrie, J. P., Basuil, D., & Pandey, A. (2010). Causes and effects of employee downsizing: A review and synthesis. *Journal of Management, 36,* 281–348.

42. Keim, A. C., Landis, R. S., Pierce, C. A., & Earnest, D. R. (2014). Why do employees worry about their jobs? A meta-analytic review of predictors of job insecurity. *Journal of Occupational Health Psychology, 19,* 269–290; Sverke, M., & Hellgren, J. (2002). The nature of job insecurity: Understanding employment uncertainty on the brink of a new millennium. *Applied Psychology: An International Review, 51,* 23–42.

43. Koller, F. (2010). *Spark: How old-fashioned values drive a twenty-first century corporation.* New York, NY: PublicAffairs.

44. Becker, S. (2017, January 8). Job search? These 5 companies have policies that prevent layoffs. https://www.cheatsheet.com/money-career/job-search-these-companies-have-policies-that-prevent-layoffs.html/?a=viewall; Van Gorder, C. (2015, January 26). A no-layoffs policy can work, even in an unpredictable economy. *Harvard Business Review.* https://hbr.org/2015/01/a-no-layoffs-policy-can-work-even-in-an-unpredictable-economy

45. Maingault, A. (2009, July). Layoff criteria, severance pay, student interns. *HR Magazine,* p. 16.

46. Kalev, A. (2016, July 26). How "neutral" layoffs disproportionately affect women and minorities. *Harvard Business Review.* https://hbr.org/2016/07/how-neutral-layoffs-disproportionately-affect-women-and-minorities

47. Anonymous. (2009, February). Know your layoff rules and procedures. *HR Focus.* U.S. Department of Labor. WARN advisor. https://webapps.dol.gov/elaws/eta/warn/faqs.asp

48. Anonymous. (2009, February). Know your layoff rules and procedures. *HR Focus, 86,* 2; SHRM (2012, December 27). What is the California WARN act and how does it differ from federal WARN? https://www.shrm.org/resourcesandtools/tools-and-samples/hr-qa/pages/californiawarnact.aspx

49. Anonymous. (2009, February). Know your layoff rules and procedures. *HR Focus, 86,* 2.

50. Blau, G., Petrucci, T., & McClendon, J. (2012). Effects of layoff victims' justice reactions and emotional responses on attitudes toward their previous employer. *Career Development International, 17,* 500–517.

51. Richter, M., König, C. J., Koppermann, C., & Schilling, M. (2016). Displaying fairness while delivering bad news: Testing the effectiveness of organizational bad news training in the layoff context. *Journal of Applied Psychology, 101,* 779–792.

52. Anonymous. (2009, November). Exclusive survey results: How employers are handling severance. *HR Focus, 86,* 7–13.

53. EEOC. (2009). Understanding waivers of discrimination claims in employee severance agreements. https://www.eeoc.gov/policy/docs/qanda_severance-agreements.html#II

54. Anonymous. (2014, February). Cutting staff? Offering outplacement services benefits everyone, survey finds. *HR Focus,* p. 16.

55. Martin, H. J., & Lekan, D. F. (2007). Reforming executive outplacement. *Organizational Dynamics, 37,* 35–46.

56. Maertz, C. P., Wiley, J. W., LeRouge, C., & Campion, M. A. (2010). Downsizing effects on survivors: Layoffs, offshoring, and outsourcing. *Industrial Relations, 49,* 275–285.

57. Wadors, P. (2015, October 2). Letting good people go when it's time. *Harvard Business Review.* https://hbr.org/2015/10/letting-good-people-go-when-its-time

58. Vickers, M. H., & Parris, M. A. (2009). Layoffs: Australian executives speak of being

disposed of. *Organizational Dynamics, 39,* 57–63.

59. Vickers, M. H., & Parris, M. A. (2009). Layoffs: Australian executives speak of being disposed of. *Organizational Dynamics, 39,* 57–63.

60. Pete, J. S. (2014, November 3). Robocall to 100 Ford workers: "You are fired." http://www.nwitimes.com/business/local/robocall-to-ford-workers-you-re-fired/article_3b821381-0a50-5631-847d-6647a51f8d6c.html

61. Nobel, C. (2015, January 7). The quest for better layoffs. http://hbswk.hbs.edu/item/the-quest-for-better-layoffs

CHAPTER 11

1. Cohen, P. (2015, July 31). A company copes with backlash against the raise that roared. *New York Times.* https://www.nytimes.com/2015/08/02/business/a-company-copes-with-backlash-against-the-raise-that-roared.html?smid=fb-nytimes&smtyp=cur&_r=1; Cohen, P. (2015, April 13). One company's new minimum wage: $70,000 a year. *New York Times.* https://www.nytimes.com/2015/04/14/business/owner-of-gravity-payments-a-credit-card-processor-is-setting-a-new-minimum-wage-70000-a-year.html; Drew, K. (2017, June 21). Seattle company paying $70K salaries to employees expands, workers see housing boom. http://komonews.com/news/local/seattle-company-with-70k-salaries-for-employees-doubles-office-space; Kahneman, D., & Deaton, A. (2010). High income improves evaluation of life but not emotional well-being. *Proceedings of the National Academy of Sciences, 107,* 16489–16493; Keegen, P. (n.d.).

Here's what really happened at that company that set a $70,000 minimum wage. https://www.inc.com/magazine/201511/paul-keegan/does-more-pay-mean-more-growth.html

2. U.S. Bureau of Labor Statistics. (2018). Employer costs for employee compensation—March 2018 (USDL-18-0944). https://www.bls.gov/news.release/pdf/ecec.pdf

3. Quest for kudos: Korn Ferry survey finds highly skilled professionals are motivated more by recognition and meaningful work than by pay. (2017, July 27). https://www.kornferry.com/press/quest-for-kudos-korn-ferry-survey-finds-highly-skilled-professionals-are-motivated-more-by-recognition-and-meaningful-work-than-by-pay/

4. Judge, T. A., Piccolo, R. F., Podsakoff, N. P., Shaw, J. C., & Rich, B. L. (2010). The relationship between pay and job satisfaction: A meta-analysis of the literature. *Journal of Vocational Behavior, 77,* 157–167.

5. Humphrey, S. E., Nahrgang, J. D., & Morgeson, F. P. (2007). Integrating motivational, social, and contextual work design features: A meta-analytic summary and theoretical extension of the work design literature. *Journal of Applied Psychology, 92,* 1332–1356; Judge, T. A., Heller, D., & Mount, M. K. (2002). Five-factor model of personality and job satisfaction: A meta-analysis. *Journal of Applied Psychology, 87,* 530–541; Kaplan, S., Bradley, J. C., Luchman, J. N., & Haynes, D. (2009). On the role of positive and negative affectivity in job performance: A meta-analytic investigation. *Journal of Applied Psychology, 94,* 162; Kinicki, A. J., McKee-Ryan, F. M., Schriesheim, C. A., & Carson, K. P. (2002). Assessing the construct validity

of the job descriptive index: A review and meta-analysis. *Journal of Applied Psychology, 87,* 14–32; Kooij, D. T., Jansen, P. G., Dikkers, J. S., & De Lange, A. H. (2010). The influence of age on the associations between HR practices and both affective commitment and job satisfaction: A meta-analysis. *Journal of Organizational Behavior, 31,* 1111–1136.

6. Newman, J. M., Gerhart, B., & Milkovich, G. T. (2017). *Compensation* (12th ed.). Boston, MA: McGraw-Hill.

7. D'Onfro, J. (2015, April 17). The truth about Google's famous "20% time" policy. *Business Insider.* http://www.businessinsider.com/google-20-percent-time-policy-2015-4

8. Newman, J. M., Gerhart, B., & Milkovich, G. T. (2017). *Compensation* (12th ed.). Boston, MA: McGraw-Hill.

9. Kilgour, J. G. (2008). Job evaluation revisited: The point factor method: The point factor method of job evaluation consists of a large number of discretionary decisions that result in something that appears to be entirely objective and, even, scientific. *Compensation & Benefits Review, 40,* 37–46; SHRM. (2016, October 27). Performing job evaluations. https://www.shrm.org/resourcesandtools/tools-and-samples/toolkits/pages/performingjobevaluations.aspx

10. ADP. (n.d.). https://www.adp.com; Benchmark. (n.d.). http://www.payscale.com/hr/product-benchmark; Smith, A. (2016, July 1). HR's role in pay analyses. https://www.shrm.org/hr-today/news/hr-magazine/0716/pages/hrs-role-in-pay-analyses.aspx

11. Weber, C. L., & Rynes, S. L. (1991). Effects of compensation strategy on job pay decisions.

Academy of Management Journal, 34, 86–109.

12. Barcellos, D. (2005). The reality and promise of market-based pay. *Employment Relations Today, 32*, 1–10.

13. U.S. Department of Labor. (n.d.). Wage and hour division: Compliance assistance–wages and the Fair Labor Standards Act (FLSA). https://www.dol.gov/whd/flsa/

14. U.S. Department of Labor. (2018). Wage and hour division: Fact Sheet #17A: Exemption for executive, administrative, professional, computer & outside sales employees under the Fair Labor Standards Act (FLSA). https://www.dol.gov/whd/overtime/fs17a_overview.pdf

15. U.S. Department of Labor. (n.d.). Wage and hour division: Overtime pay. https://www.dol.gov/whd/overtime_pay.htm

16. U.S. Department of Labor. (n.d.). Wage and hour division: Minimum wage. https://www.dol.gov/whd/minimumwage.htm

17. U.S. Department of Labor. (2008). Wage and hour division: Fact Sheet #22: Hours worked under the Fair Labor Standards Act (FLSA). https://www.dol.gov/whd/regs/compliance/whdfs22.pdf

18. U.S. Department of Labor. (2008). Wage and hour division: Fact Sheet #21: Recordkeeping requirements under the Fair Labor Standards Act (FLSA). https://www.dol.gov/whd/regs/compliance/whdfs21.pdf

19. U.S. Government Publishing Office. (1954, August 16). Title 26–Internal Revenue Code. https://www.gpo.gov/fdsys/pkg/USCODE-2011-title26/pdf/USCODE-2011-title26.pdf

20. Domonoske, C. (2017). Secret Service, agents settle over racial discrimination allegations. *NPR*. https://www.npr.org/sections/thetwo-way/2017/01/18/510396659/secret-service-agents-settle-over-racial-discrimination-allegations; Hassan, A. (2017). A Secret Service agent's path from recruitment to bias lawsuit. *New York Times*. https://www.nytimes.com/2017/02/25/us/secret-service-bias-lawsuit-ray-moore.html?_r=0; Secret Service penalized in discrimination case. (2008). *NBC News*. http://www.nbcnews.com/id/28303789/ns/us_news-crime_and_courts/t/secret-service-penalized-discrimination-case/#.WgspAFtSzIV; U.S. Department of Homeland Security. (2017, January 17). Statement by Secretary of Homeland Security Jeh C. Johnson on U.S. Secret Service resolution. https://www.dhs.gov/news/2017/01/17/statement-secretary-homeland-security-jeh-c-johnson-us-secret-service-resolution; U.S. Secret Service inspector destroyed documents. (2008, February 21). https://www.rcfp.org/browse-media-law-resources/news/us-secret-service-inspector-destroyed-documents

21. March, J. G., & Simon, H. A. (1958). *Organizations*. Oxford, UK: Wiley.

22. Carrell, M. R., & Dittrich, J. E. (1976). Employee perceptions of fair treatment. *Personnel Journal, 55*, 523–524.

23. Amabile, T. M. (1993). Motivational synergy: Toward new conceptualizations of intrinsic and extrinsic motivation in the workplace. *Human Resource Management Review, 3*, 185–201; Herzberg, F. (1966). *Work and the nature of man*. Cleveland, OH: World.

24. Amabile, T. M. (1993). Motivational synergy: Toward new conceptualizations of intrinsic and extrinsic motivation in the workplace. *Human Resource Management Review, 3*, 185–201; Deci, E. L., & Ryan, R. M. (2000). The "what" and "why" of goal pursuits: Human needs and the self-determination behavior. *Psychological Inquiry, 11*, 227–268.

25. Cerasoli, C. P., Nicklin, J. M., & Ford, M. T. (2014). Intrinsic motivation and extrinsic incentives jointly predict performance: A 40-year meta-analysis. *Psychological Bulletin, 140*, 980–1008.

26. Porter, L. W., & Lawler, E. E. (1968). *Managerial attitudes and performance*. Homewood, IL: Irwin; Vroom, V. H. (1964). *Work and motivation*. New York, NY: John Wiley.

27. Cable, D. M., & Judge, T. A. (1994). Pay preferences and job search decisions: A person–organization fit perspective. *Personnel Psychology, 47*, 317–348; Le Blanc, P. V., & Mulvey, P. W. (1998). Research study: How American workers see the rewards of work. *Compensation & Benefits Review, 30*, 24–28.

28. WorldatWork. (2016). Compensation programs and practices survey. https://www.worldatwork.org/adimLink?id=80656

29. Newman, J. M., Gerhart, B., & Milkovich, G. T. (2017). *Compensation* (12th ed.). New York, NY: McGraw-Hill.

30. Saunders, N. (2016). Motivate and retain top talent with spot awards. https://blogs.sap.com/2016/05/23/motivate-and-retain-top-talent-with-spot-awards/

31. Rynes, S. L., Gerhart, B., & Parks, L. (2005). Personnel psychology: Performance evaluation and pay for performance. *Annual Review of Psychology, 56*, 571–600.

32. Deming, W. E. (1986). *Out of the crisis*. Cambridge, MA: MIT Center for Advanced Engineering Study; Pfeffer J. (1998). *The human equation*. Boston, MA: Harvard Business School Press.

33. Rynes, S. L., Gerhart, B., & Parks, L. (2005). Personnel psychology: Performance evaluation and pay for performance. *Annual Review of Psychology, 56,* 571–600.

34. Kaufman, R. T. (1992). The effects of Improshare on productivity. *Industrial Labor Relations Review, 45,* 311–322.

35. Hafner, K. (2005, February 1). New incentives for Google employees: Awards worth millions. *New York Times.* http://www.nytimes.com/2005/02/01/technology/new-incentive-for-google-employees-awards-worth-millions.html

36. Leitman, I. M., Levin, R., Lipp, M. J., Sivaprasad, L., Karalakulasingam, C. J., Bernard, D. S.,... & Shulkin, D. J. (2010). Quality and financial outcomes from gainsharing for inpatient admissions: A three-year experience. *Journal of Hospital Medicine, 5,* 501–507.

37. Designing and managing incentive compensation programs. (2018, January 12). https://www.shrm.org/resourcesandtools/tools-and-samples/toolkits/pages/designingincentivecompensation.aspx

38. French, J. L. (1987). Employee perspectives on stock ownership: Financial investment or mechanism of control. *Academy of Management Review, 12,* 427–435.

39. Bob's Red Mill. (n.d.). Proudly employee-owned. https://www.bobsredmill.com/bobs-way-meet#ESOP

40. Newman, J. M., Gerhart, B., & Milkovich, G. T. (2017). *Compensation* (12th ed.). Boston, MA: McGraw-Hill.

41. Newman, J. M., Gerhart, B., & Milkovich, G. T. (2017). *Compensation* (12th ed.). Boston, MA: McGraw-Hill.

42. Blinder, A. (1990). *Paying for productivity.* Washington, DC: Brookings Institution.

43. Hegarty, W. H., & Sims, H. P. (1978). Some determinants of unethical decision behavior: An experiment. *Journal of Applied Psychology, 63,* 451.

44. Barro, J. (2016). Wells Fargo's scandal is a cautionary tale about incentive pay. *Business Insider.* http://www.businessinsider.com/wells-fargos-scandal-is-a-cautionary-tale-about-incentive-pay-2016-9

45. Bomey, N., & McCoy, K. (2017). Wells Fargo clawing back $75.3 million more from former execs in fake accounts scandal. *USA Today.* https://www.usatoday.com/story/money/2017/04/10/wells-fargo-compensation-clawback/100276472/

46. Carey, K. (2017). The little-known statistician who taught us to measure teachers. *New York Times.* https://www.nytimes.com/2017/05/19/upshot/the-little-known-statistician-who-transformed-education.html?_r=0; Chetty, R., Friedman, J. N., & Rockoff, J. E. (2014). Measuring the impacts of teachers II: Teacher value-added and student outcomes in adulthood. *The American Economic Review, 104,* 2633–2679; Dee, T. S., & Keys, B. J. (2004). Does merit pay reward good teachers? Evidence from a randomized experiment. *Journal of Policy Analysis and Management, 23,* 471–488; Hanushek, E. A. (2011). The economic value of higher teacher quality. *Economics of Education Review, 30,* 466–479; Johnson, S. M. (2012). Having it both ways: Building the capacity of individual teachers and their schools. *Harvard Educational Review, 82,* 107–122; Murnane, R., & Cohen, D. (1986). Merit pay and the evaluation problem: Why most merit pay plans fail and a few survive. *Harvard Educational Review, 56,* 1–18; Woessmann, L. (2011). Cross-country evidence on teacher performance pay. *Economics of Education Review, 30,* 404–418; Yuan, K., Le, V. N., McCaffrey, D. F., Marsh, J. A., Hamilton, L. S., Stecher, B. M., & Springer, M. G. (2013). Incentive pay programs do not affect teacher motivation or reported practices: Results from three randomized studies. *Educational Evaluation and Policy Analysis, 35,* 3–22.

CHAPTER 12

1. Care.com introduces groundbreaking peer-to-peer benefits platform for caregivers. (2018). https://www.care.com/press-release-carecom-introduces-caregiver-benefits-platform-p1186-q81381650.html; Company overview. (2018). https://www.care.com/company-overview; Katz, L. F., & Krueger, A. B. (2016). The rise and nature of alternative work arrangements in the United States, 1995–2015. Working paper. https://benefittrends.metlife.com/us-perspectives/work-redefined-a-new-age-of-benefits/; Scheiber, N. (2016, September 14). Care.com creates a $500 limited for benefit gig-economy workers. *New York Times.* https://nyti.ms/2cM6luB; Semuels, A. (2017, November 6). Could a tax fix the gig economy? *The Atlantic.* https://www.theatlantic.com/business/archive/2017/11/gig-economy/544895/; Stonier, M. (2017, October 13). This state wants to offer universal benefits for gig workers. *Fortune.* http://fortune.com/2017/10/13/gig-economy-workers-benefits/; Torpey, E., & Hogan, A. (2016, May). Career outlook: Working in a gig economy. U.S. Bureau of Labor Statistics. https://www.bls.gov/careeroutlook/2016/article/what-is-the-gig-economy.htm

2. U.S. Bureau of Labor Statistics. (2018, June 8). News release: Employer costs for employee compensation—March 2018. USDL-18-0944. https://www.bls.gov/news.release/pdf/ecec.pdf

3. Society for Human Resource Management. (2017). 2017 strategic benefits survey: Strategize with benefits. SHRM. https://www.shrm.org/hr-today/trends-and-forecasting/research-and-surveys/pages/strategize-with-benefits.aspx; Society for Human Resource Management. (2018). 2018 employee benefits: The evolution of benefits. SHRM. https://www.shrm.org/hr-today/trends-and-forecasting/research-and-surveys/Documents/2018%20Employee%20Benefits%20Report.pdf

4. U.S. Bureau of Labor Statistics. (2018, June 8). News release: Employer costs for employee compensation—March 2018. USDL-18-0944. https://www.bls.gov/news.release/pdf/ecec.pdf; Beam, B. T., & McFadden, J. J. (2007). *Employee benefits* (8th ed.). Chicago, IL: Dearborn Financial Publishing.

5. U.S. Social Security Administration. (2018). https://www.ssa.gov/

6. U.S. Social Security Administration. Updated 2018. (2018). https://www.ssa.gov/pubs/EN-05-10003.pdf

7. U.S. Social Security Administration. (2018). Retirement benefits. https://www.ssa.gov/benefits/retirement/

8. U.S. Social Security Administration. (2018). Survivors benefits. https://www.ssa.gov/benefits/survivors/

9. U.S. Social Security Administration. (2018). Disability benefits. https://www.ssa.gov/benefits/disability/; U.S. Social Security Administration.

(2018). Types of beneficiaries. https://www.ssa.gov/oact/ProgData/types.html

10. U.S. Social Security Administration. (2018). Medicare benefits. https://www.ssa.gov/benefits/medicare/

11. Posthuma, R. A. (2009). Workers' compensation. SHRM. https://www.shrm.org/academicinitiatives/universities/teachingresources/Documents/Workers%27%20Comp%20IM%20Final.pdf

12. U.S. Department of Labor. (2018). Unemployment insurance. https://www.dol.gov/general/topic/unemployment-insurance

13. U.S. Department of Labor. (2018). Wage and Hour Division (WHD): Family and Medical Leave Act. https://www.dol.gov/whd/fmla/

14. U.S. Department of Labor. (2018). Health plans & benefits: ERISA. https://www.dol.gov/general/topic/health-plans/erisa

15. U.S. Department of Labor. (2018). Health plans & benefits: Continuation of health coverage—COBRA. https://www.dol.gov/general/topic/health-plans/cobra; U.S. Department of Labor. (2018). History of EBSA and ERISA. https://www.dol.gov/agencies/ebsa/about-ebsa/about-us/history-of-ebsa-and-erisa

16. U.S. Department of Labor. (2018). Health plans & benefits: Portability of health coverage. https://www.dol.gov/general/topic/health-plans/portability; U.S. Department of Labor. (2018). History of EBSA and ERISA. https://www.dol.gov/agencies/ebsa/about-ebsa/about-us/history-of-ebsa-and-erisa

17. HealthCare.gov. (2018). Health coverage rights and protections. https://www.healthcare.gov/health-care-law-protections/; U.S. Internal Revenue Service. (2018). Employer shared responsibility

provisions. https://www.irs.gov/affordable-care-act/employers/employer-shared-responsibility-provisions; U.S. Government Publishing Office. (2010, March 23). Public Law 111-148—Mar. 23, 2010. https://www.gpo.gov/fdsys/pkg/PLAW-111publ148/pdf/PLAW-111publ148.pdf

18. U.S. Internal Revenue Service. (2017). Publication 969 (2017), health savings accounts and other tax-favored health plans. https://www.irs.gov/publications/p969

19. Society for Human Resource Management. (2014, December 11). Disability benefits: What are short-term disability and long-term disability? https://www.shrm.org/resourcesandtools/tools-and-samples/hr-qa/pages/stdandltd.aspx

20. Society for Human Resource Management. (2014, December 11). Disability benefits: What are short-term disability and long-term disability? https://www.shrm.org/resourcesandtools/tools-and-samples/hr-qa/pages/stdandltd.aspx

21. Society for Human Resource Management. (2018). 2018 employee benefits: The evolution of benefits. SHRM. https://www.shrm.org/hr-today/trends-and-forecasting/research-and-surveys/Documents/2018%20Employee%20Benefits%20Report.pdf

22. Beam, B. T., & McFadden, J. J. (2007). *Employee benefits* (8th ed.). Chicago, IL: Dearborn Financial Publishing; Society for Human Resource Management. (2015, April 24). Pension plan: Defined benefit: General: What is a defined benefit plan? https://www.shrm.org/resourcesandtools/tools-and-samples/hr-qa/pages/whataredefinedbenefitplans.aspx

23. Beam, B. T., & McFadden, J. J. (2007). *Employee benefits* (8th ed.). Chicago, IL: Dearborn Financial Publishing; U.S. Department of Labor. (2018). Types of retirement plans. https://www.dol.gov/general/topic/retirement/typesofplans

24. U.S. Internal Revenue Service. (2018). Definitions. https://www.irs.gov/retirement-plans/plan-participant-employee/definitions

25. U.S. Internal Revenue Service. (2018). 401(k) plan overview. https://www.irs.gov/retirement-plans/plan-sponsor/401k-plan-overview

26. U.S. Internal Revenue Service. (2018). 401(k) plans. https://www.irs.gov/retirement-plans/401k-plans

27. U.S. Internal Revenue Service. (2018). Tax-sheltered annuity plans. https://www.irs.gov/retirement-plans/irc-403b-tax-sheltered-annuity-plans

28. U.S. Internal Revenue Service. (2018). Choosing a retirement plan: 403(b) tax-sheltered annuity plan. https://www.irs.gov/retirement-plans/choosing-a-retirement-plan-403b-tax-sheltered-annuity-plan

29. U.S. Internal Revenue Service. (2018). Definitions. https://www.irs.gov/retirement-plans/plan-participant-employee/definitions

30. U.S. Internal Revenue Service. (2018). Employee stock ownership plans (ESOPs). https://www.irs.gov/retirement-plans/employee-stock-ownership-plans-esops; U.S. Internal Revenue Service. (2018). Definitions. https://www.irs.gov/retirement-plans/plan-participant-employee/definitions

31. Sammer, J. (2016, February 4). ESOPs turn workers into owners. https://www.shrm.org/resourcesandtools/hr-topics/benefits/pages/esops-workers-owners.aspx

32. Beam, B. T., & McFadden, J. J. (2007). *Employee benefits* (8th ed.). Chicago, IL: Dearborn Financial Publishing; U.S. Department of Labor. (2018). Types of retirement plans. https://www.dol.gov/general/topic/retirement/typesofplans; U.S. Internal Revenue Service. (2018). Choosing a retirement plan: Money-purchase plan. https://www.irs.gov/retirement-plans/choosing-a-retirement-plan-money-purchase-plan

33. Beam, B. T., & McFadden, J. J. (2007). *Employee benefits* (8th ed.). Chicago, IL: Dearborn Financial Publishing.

34. Foster, A. C. (1997). Employee benefits: Life insurance. U.S. Bureau of Labor Statistics. https://www.bls.gov/opub/mlr/cwc/life-insurance.pdf

35. Blanco, R. M. (2012). Life insurance benefits: Variations based on workers' earnings and work schedules. U.S. Bureau of Labor Statistics. https://www.bls.gov/opub/mlr/cwc/life-insurance-benefits-variations-based-on-workers-earnings-and-work-schedules.pdf

36. The Kaiser Family Foundation and Health Research & Educational Trust. (2017). *Employer health benefits*. Menlo Park, CA: Henry J. Kaiser Family Foundation.

37. Goetzel, R. Z., Henke, R. M., Tabrizi, M., Pelletier, K. R., Loeppke, R., Ballard, D. W., . . . Serxner, S. (2014). Do workplace health promotion (wellness) programs work? *Journal of Occupational and Environmental Medicine, 56,* 927–934; Mattke, S., Liu, H., Caloyeras, J., Huang, C. Y., Van Busum, K. R., Khodyakov, D., & Shier, V. (2013). Workplace wellness programs study. *Rand Health Quarterly, 3*(2), 7; Gebhardt, D. L., & Crump, C. E. (1990). Employee fitness and wellness programs in the workplace. *American Psychologist, 45,* 262–272; Parks, K. M., & Steelman, L. A. (2008). Organizational wellness programs: A meta-analysis. *Journal of Occupational Health Psychology, 13,* 58–68.

38. Society for Human Resource Management. (2017). *2017 Employee benefits: Remaining competitive in a challenging talent marketplace.* Alexandria, VA: Author.

39. U.S. Department of Labor. (2018). Holiday pay. https://www.dol.gov/general/topic/wages/holiday

40. Sammer, J. (2017, January 9). Employers are banking on paid time off. https://www.shrm.org/resourcesandtools/hr-topics/benefits/pages/banking-on-paid-time-off.aspx

41. Smith, A. (2017, April 6). SHRM to Congress: Make comp time available to businesses. https://www.shrm.org/resourcesandtools/legal-and-compliance/employment-law/pages/shrm-congress-comp-time-businesses.aspx; Society for Human Resource Management. (2016, August 31). Legal & regulatory: Compensatory time: Is compensatory time allowed in the private sector? https://www.shrm.org/resourcesandtools/tools-and-samples/hr-qa/pages/iscompensatorytimeallowedintheprivatesector.aspx

42. U.S. Bureau of Labor Statistics. (2016). Employment characteristics of families (USDL-16-0795). https://www.bls.gov/news.release/famee.nr0.htm; U.S. Bureau of Labor Statistics. (2013). Women in the labor force: A databook. http://stats.bls.gov/cps/wlf-databook-2012.pdf; U.S. Bureau of Labor Statistics. (2015a). Employment characteristics of families (USDL-15-0689). https://www.bls.gov/news.release/archives/famee_04232015.pdf;

U.S. Bureau of Labor Statistics. (2015b). Unpaid eldercare in the United States: Data from the American Time Use Survey (USDL-15-1851). https://www.bls.gov/news.release/pdf/elcare.pdf

43. The state of child care in the U.S. (2018). https://www.care.com/care-index

44. Dalton, M. (2017, December 21). Companies realize benefits of pitching in for child care. https://www.wabe.org/companies-realize-benefits-pitching-child-care/

45. Hopkins, J. (2016, September 15). Understanding the tax benefits of 529 plans. *Forbes.* https://www.forbes.com/sites/jamiehopkins/2016/09/15/understanding-the-tax-benefits-of-529-plans/#3a7cf53a19aa

46. Kenney, J., & Mason, L. (2012, February 17). Strengthen employee loyalty with corporate 529 plans. SHRM. https://www.shrm.org/resourcesandtools/hr-topics/benefits/pages/529plans.aspx; LearnVest. (2017, April 1). College savings plans: The next big employee benefit? *Forbes.* https://www.forbes.com/sites/learnvest/2017/04/01/college-savings-plans-the-next-big-employee-benefit/#46fcae6272ce; Ward, L. (2016, March 27). The latest corporate benefit: The 529 plan. *Wall Street Journal.* https://www.wsj.com/articles/the-latest-corporate-benefit-the-529-plan-1459130786

47. Society for Human Resource Management. (2015, November 14). Designing and managing educational assistance programs. https://www.shrm.org/resourcesandtools/tools-and-samples/toolkits/pages/educationalassistanceprograms.aspx; U.S. Congress. (2013, January 2). H.R.8—American Taxpayer Relief Act of 2012. https://www.congress.gov/bill/112th-congress/house-bill/8/text?overview=closed

48. Sammer, J. (2014, July 10). The case for legal services and ID theft benefits. SHRM. https://www.shrm.org/resourcesandtools/hr-topics/benefits/pages/legal-services.aspx

49. Federal Trade Commission. (2014, February). Consumer Sentinel Network: Data book. SHRM. https://www.shrm.org/ResourcesAndTools/hr-topics/benefits/Documents/sentinel-cy2013.pdf

50. Stewart, J. B. (2013, March 15). Looking for a lesson in Google's perks. *New York Times.* http://www.nytimes.com/2013/03/16/business/at-google-a-place-to-work-and-play.html

51. D'Onfro, J. (2015, April 7). Here are all of Google's employees, and how much they cost the company. *BusinessInsider.* http://www.businessinsider.com/cost-benefit-of-google-perks-2015-4

52. U.S. Internal Revenue Service. (2018). Section 125: Cafeteria plans: Modification of application of rule prohibiting deferred compensation under a cafeteria plan. https://www.irs.gov/pub/irs-drop/n-05-42.pdf; U.S. Internal Revenue Service. (2017). Employer's tax guide to fringe benefits (Publication 15-B). https://www.irs.gov/publications/p15b#en_US_2017_publink1000193624

53. Liptak, A. (2015, June 26). Supreme Court ruling makes same-sex marriage a right nationwide. *New York Times.* https://www.nytimes.com/2015/06/27/us/supreme-court-same-sex-marriage.html; *United States v. Windsor.* (2013). https://www.law.cornell.edu/supremecourt/text/12-307; Bernard, T. S. (2015, August 20). Gay couple are eligible for Social Security benefits, U.S. decides.

New York Times. https://www.nytimes.com/2015/08/21/business/gay-couples-are-eligible-for-benefits-us-decides.html; Scheiber, N. (2016, December 2). Walmart settles discrimination suit over benefits for same-sex spouses. *New York Times.* https://www.nytimes.com/2016/12/02/business/walmart-same-sex-discrimination-lawsuit.html?_r=0; U.S. Equal Employment Opportunity Commission. (2019). What you should know about EEOC and the enforcement protections for LGBT workers. https://www.eeoc.gov/eeoc/newsroom/wysk/enforcement_protections_lgbt_workers.cfm; Freur, A. (2017, July 27). Justice Department says rights law doesn't protect gays. *New York Times.* https://www.nytimes.com/2017/07/27/nyregion/justice-department-gays-workplace.html

54. Kass, E. M. (2017, July 19). Moving the meter on benefits utilization. https://www.benefitnews.com/news/moving-the-meter-on-benefits-utilization; Work redefined: A new age of benefits. (2017). https://benefittrends.metlife.com/us-perspectives/work-redefined-a-new-age-of-benefits/

55. Hennessey, H. W., Perrewe, P. L., & Hochwarter, W. A. (1992). Impact of benefit awareness on employee and organizational outcomes: A longitudinal field examination. *Benefits Quarterly, 8,* 90–96.

56. Society for Human Resource Management. (2017). 2017 strategic benefits survey: Strategize with benefits. SHRM. https://www.shrm.org/hr-today/trends-and-forecasting/research-and-surveys/pages/strategize-with-benefits.aspx

57. Wilson, M., Northcraft, G. B., & Neale, M. A. (1985). The

perceived value of fringe benefits. *Personnel Psychology, 38*(2), 309–320.

58. Richardson, C. M. (1998). Ethics and employee benefits. *Benefits Quarterly, 14,* 9–16.

CHAPTER 13

1. History of the coalition of Kaiser Permanente unions. (n.d.). https://www.union coalition.org/who-we-are/

2. Lazes, P. M., Figueroa, M., & Katz, L. (2012). How labor–management partnerships improve patient care, cost control, and labor relations. http://digitalcommons .ilr.cornell.edu/reports/59/

3. Agrawal, N. (2017). Kaiser nurses reach tentative labor agreement with Los Angeles Medical Center. *Los Angeles Times.* http://www.latimes.com/business/la-fi-kaiser-nurses-agreement-20170217-story.html

4. Meinert, D. (2014). Be fair, be consistent, avoid lawsuits. *HR Magazine.* https://www.shrm .org/hr-today/news/hr-news/pages/be-fair-be-consistent-avoid-lawsuits.aspx

5. Buttigieg, D. M., Deery, S. J., & Iverson, R. D. (2007). An event history analysis of union joining and leaving. *Journal of Applied Psychology, 92,* 829–839; Cohen-Charash, Y., & Spector, P. E. (2001). The role of justice in organizations: A meta-analysis. *Organizational Behavior≈and Human Decision Processes, 86,* 278–321; Colquitt, J. A., Scott, B. A., Rodell, J. B., Long, D. M., Zapata, C. P., Conlon, D. E., & Wesson, M. J. (2013). Justice at the millennium, a decade later: A meta-analytic test of social exchange and affect-based perspectives. *Journal of Applied Psychology, 98,* 199–236.

6. Doucouliagos, C. (1995). Worker participation and productivity in labor-managed and participatory capitalist firms: A meta-analysis. *Industrial and Labor Relations Review, 49,* 58–77.

7. Matsakis, L. (2018). Why Amazon really raised its minimum wage to $15. *Wired.* https://www.wired.com/story/why-amazon-really-raised-minimum-wage/

8. Gabler, N. (2016). The magic in the warehouse. *Fortune.* http://fortune.com/costco-wholesale-shopping/; Taube, A. (2014). Why Costco pays its retail employees $20 an hour. *Business Insider.* http://www.businessinsider.com/costco-pays-retail-employees-20-an-hour-2014-10

9. Robinson, J. (2015). 6 inspiring employee handbook examples. *Nasdaq.* http://www .nasdaq.com/article/6-inspiring-employee-handbook-examples-cm459464

10. Strauss, K. (2017). 10 companies that offer unlimited vacation time. *Forbes.* https://www.forbes.com/sites/karstenstrauss/2017/07/19/10-companies-offering-unlimited-vacation-time/#6fa1a10c2082

11. SHRM. (2011). Dress & appearance: Body odor, what should HR do when an employee's body odor is affecting the workplace? https://www .shrm.org/resourcesandtools/tools-and-samples/hr-qa/pages/bodyodoraffectingworkplace .aspx

12. Pew Research. (2010). Millennials: Confident. Connected. Open to change. http://www.pewsocialtrends .org/2010/02/24/millennials-confident-connected-open-to-change/

13. Oliver, C. (2015). Tattoos in the workplace: Laws for covering art. *NBC News.* http://www.nbc-2 .com/story/28241652/tattoos-in-the-workplace-laws-of-covering-art

14. Lucas, S. (20114). Nordstrom's awesome employee handbook is a myth. *CBS News MoneyWatch.* https://www.cbsnews.com/news/nordstroms-awesome-employee-handbook-is-a-myth/; Lutz, A. (2014). Nordstrom's employee handbook has only one rule. *Business Insider.* http://www .businessinsider.com/nordstroms-employee-handbook-2014-10

15. Greenhouse, S. (2010). Company accused of firing over Facebook post. *New York Times.* http://www.nytimes.com/2010/11/09/business/09facebook.html

16. Types of Unions: Industrial and Craft Unions. Unions vary depending on the type of work their members do. The two types of unions are industrial unions and craft unions. Industrial unions cover all workers who are employed within a given industry. For example, the National Education Association represents teachers from a variety of fields and types of educational institutions, and the Order of Railway Conductors of America represents railroad workers. Conversely, craft unions represent individuals with a specific trade across different employers and locations. Examples include unions of plumbers, electricians, and ironworkers. Craft unions emerged from the guild system of the Middle Ages, with the first craft union within the United States being shoemakers in Philadelphia during colonial times. United States History. (2017). Craft unions. http://www.u-s-history.com/pages/h1746.html.

17. National and International Unions. Internationally, the largest union is the All-China Federation of Trade Unions,

a state-controlled union comprising more than 280 million members. In 2006, Walmart had unionized employees working in its Chinese stores represented by this union. In the United States, the largest unions are much smaller, with the National Education Association having more than 2 million members and Service Employees International Union having close to 2 million members. Within the United States, many national unions are affiliated with the American Federation of Labor and Congress of Industrial Organizations (AFL-CIO). It is not a union but rather an association designed to help advocate for union worker rights nationally. UNITE HERE was established in 2004 via mergers with other unions and represents workers in industries such as airports, food service, hotels, textiles, transportation, and gaming. It is the fastest-growing union in the private sector within the United States with more than 270,000 members. It is affiliated with the AFL-CIO along with 55 other unions representing 12.5 million working people. Groll, E. (2013). The world's most powerful labor unions. *Foreign Policy.* http:// foreignpolicy.com/2013/09/02/ the-worlds-most-powerful-labor-unions/; China's growing labour movement offers hope for workers globally. (2015). *The Conversation.* http:// theconversation.com/chinas-growing-labour-movement-offers-hope-for-workers-globally-39921; Mernit, J. L. (2017). How millennials are trying to revive the labor movement. *Fast Company.* https://www.fastcompany .com/40497318/how-millennials-are-trying-to-revive-the-labor-movement; UNITEHERE. http://

unitehere.org/who-we-are/; AFL-CIO. (2017). Our affiliated unions. https://aflcio.org/about/ our-unions-and-allies.

Local Unions. Although national and international unions have a great deal of collective power due to their size and many local unions belong to national unions, for most union members, their local union has a greater impact on their day-to-day working lives. For example, union members elect local union officials such as the president, vice president, and secretary of the union. These individuals often form the team that negotiates with the organization during collective bargaining. It is possible for a bargaining team to be appointed to engage in bargaining on behalf of the local union members.

Youngblood, S. A., DeNisi, A. S., Molleston, J. L., & Mobley, W. H. (1984). The impact of work environment, instrumentality beliefs, perceived union image, and subjective norms on union voting intentions. *Academy of Management Journal, 27,* 576–590.

18. Baker, D. (2015). Labor unions: The folks who gave you the weekend. *Huffington Post.* https:// www.huffingtonpost .com/dean-baker/labor-unions-the-folks-wh_b_8101242.html

19. Baugher, J. E., & Roberts, J. T. (2004). Workplace hazards, unions, and coping styles. *Labor Studies Journal, 29,* 1–24.

20. Western, B., & Rosenfeld, J. (2011). Unions, norms, and the rise in U.S. wage inequality. *American Sociological Review, 76,* 513–537.

21. Long, G. I. (2013). Differences between union and nonunion compensation, 2001–2011. *Monthly Labor Review.* https:// www.bls.gov/opub/mlr/2013/04/ art2full.pdf; Luhby, T. (2015). Want a raise? Join a union. *CNN Money.* http://money.cnn

.com/2015/02/24/news/economy/ union-wages/index.html

22. U.S. Bureau of Labor Statistics. (2016). Union members—2016. https://www.bls.gov/news .release/pdf/union2.pdf

23. Wallace, G. (2015). Facebook's bus drivers set for raises after union vote. *CNN Money.* http://money.cnn.com/ 2015/02/22/technology/ facebook-bus-drivers-union/ index.html?iid=EL; Wong, Q. (2015). Facebook approves union contract for shuttle bus drivers. http://www.siliconbeat. com/2015/03/12/facebook-approves-union-contract-for-shuttle-drivers/

24. Modern Survey. (2015). Employee engagement and unions. http:// www.modernsurvey.com/ resources/whitepapers; Tyler, J. (2009). Employee engagement and labor relations. *Gallup News Business Journal.* http://news.gallup.com/ businessjournal/122849/ employee-engagement-labor-relations.aspx

25. Laroche, P. (2016). A meta-analysis of the union–job satisfaction relationship. *British Journal of Industrial Relations, 54,* 709–741.

26. Becker, B. E., & Olson, C. A. (1992). Unions and firm profits. *Industrial Relations, 31,* 395–415.

27. Doucouliagos, C., & Laroche, P. (2003). What do unions do to productivity? A meta-analysis. *Industrial Relations, 42,* 650–691.

28. Cooke, W. N., & Meyer, D. G. (1990). Structural and market predictors of corporate labor relations strategies. *Industrial and Labor Relations Review, 43,* 280–293.

29. Martin, C. J. (2016). Business and labor don't have to be enemies. *Washington Post.* https://www .washingtonpost.com/news/ in-theory/wp/2016/08/04/ business-and-labor-dont-have-to-be-enemies/?tid=a_

inl&utm_term=.51822ef21a8a;
The World Bank. (2017). Ease of
Doing Business Index. https://
data.worldbank.org/indicator/
IC.BUS.EASE.XQ?year_high_
desc=false

30. Durham, C. (2017). Court
upholds T-Mobile's positive
workplace environment rules.
SHRM. https://www.shrm.org/
resourcesandtools/legal-and-
compliance/employment-law/
pages/court-report-positive-
workplace-rules.aspx

31. U.S. Department of Labor.
(2018). https://www.dol.gov/
general/aboutdol/majorlaws;
https://www.dol.gov/olms/regs/
compliance/LMRDAQandA
.htm#quest1

32. SHRM. (2016). https://www
.shrm.org/resourcesandtools/
legal-and-compliance/
employment-law/pages/norris-
laguardia-act.aspx

33. Dunn, M., & Walker, J. (2016).
Union membership in the United
States. https://www.bls
.gov/spotlight/2016/union-
membership-in-the-united-
states/pdf/union-membership-
in-the-united-states.pdf

34. Marsh, J. M., Bloom, H. M.,
& Rosen, P. B. (2017). Unions
winning more elections, but
organizing fewer new workers.
https://www.laborandcollective
bargaining.com/2017/03/articles/
collective-bargaining/unions-
winning-elections-organizing-
fewer-new-workers/#page=1;
Swift, A. (2017). Labor union
approval best since 2003, at 61%.
Gallup News. http://news.gallup
.com/poll/217331/labor-union-
approval-best-2003.aspx

35. Employee involvement—
European Works Councils. (n.d.).
http://ec.europa.eu/social/main
.jsp?catId=707&langId=en&
intPageId=211

36. NHO. (2013). Basic labour law.
https://www.nho.no/en/Business-
in-Norway/Basic-Labour-Law/

37. Wingfield, N., & Eddy, M. (2013).
In Germany, union culture
clashes with Amazon's labor
practices. *New York Times.* http://
www.nytimes.com/2013/08/05/
business/workers-of-amazon-
divergent.html

38. Calderone, M. (2017). The
Huffington Post ratifies union
contract. *Huffington Post.* https://
www.huffingtonpost.com/entry/
huffington-post-union-contract_
us_588f7523e4b0c90efefed41a

39. https://unionbase.org/;
Wartzman, R. (2017). Meet
the millennial who's trying to
save the labor movement with
a Facebook for unions. https://
www.fastcompany.com/
40461691/meet-the-millennial-
whos-trying-to-save-the-labor-
movement-with-a-facebook-for-
unions

40. National Labor Relations
Board. (2002). Your government
conducts an election, For you—
on the job. Information for voters
in NLRB elections. https://www
.nlrb.gov/sites/default/files/
attachments/basic-page/node-
3024/election.pdf

41. National Labor Relations Board.
(2000). https://www.nlrb.gov/
rights-we-protect/whats-law/
employees/i-am-represented-
union/decertification-election

42. Marsh, J. M., Bloom, H. M.,
& Rosen, P. B. (2017). Unions
winning more elections, but
organizing fewer new workers.
https://www.laborandcollective
bargaining.com/2017/03/articles/
collective-bargaining/unions-
winning-elections-organizing-
fewer-new-workers/#page=1

43. Tinsley, C. H. (2001). How
negotiators get to yes: Predicting
the constellation of strategies
used across cultures to negotiate
conflict. *Journal of Applied
Psychology, 86,* 583–593.

44. Cutcher-Gershenfeld,
J. (1991). The impact on
economic performance of a
transformation in workplace

relations. *Industrial Labor
Relations Review, 44,* 241–260.

45. Deery, S. J., & Iverson, R. D.
(2005). Labor–management
cooperation: Antecedents
and impact on organizational
performance. *Industrial and
Labor Relations Review, 58,*
588–609.

46. O'Connor, K. M., & Arnold, J.
A. (2001). Distributive spirals:
Negotiation impasses and
the moderating role of self-
efficacy. *Organizational Behavior
and Human Decision Processes,
84,* 148–176.

47. Griffiths, J. (2016). China on
strike. *CNN.* http://www.cnn
.com/2016/03/28/asia/china-
strike-worker-protest-trade-
union/index.html

48. U.S. Bureau of Labor Statistics.
(2017). Major work stoppages.
https://www.bls.gov/news
.release/wkstp.htm

49. U.S. Bureau of Labor Statistics.
(n.d.). Frequently asked questions
(FAQs). Work stoppages. https://
www.bls.gov/wsp/wspfaq.htm

50. SHRM. (2012). Grievance
procedures: What are the steps
typically found in a grievance
procedure? https://www.shrm
.org/resourcesandtools/tools-
and-samples/hr-qa/pages/
aresolutionformanagementand
employees.aspx

51. Hastings, R. R. (2012). Measure
grievances to minimize costs.
SHRM. https://www.shrm.org/
resourcesandtools/hr-topics/
employee-relations/pages/
measuregrievancestominimize
costs.aspx

52. History.com. (2008). Writers'
strike ends after 100 days.
http://www.history.com/
this-day-in-history/writers-
strike-ends-after-100-days;
Klowden, K., Chatterjee,
A., & DeVol, R. (2008). The
writers' strike of 2007–2008:
The economic impact of
digital distribution. *Milken
Institute Review.* http://

www.milkeninstitute.org/ publications/view/347; Macaray, D. (2013). The 2007–2008 writers strike. *Huffington Post.* https://www.huffingtonpost .com/david-macaray/ the-200708-writers- strike_b_3840681.html; Ng, D., James, M., & Faughnder, R. (2017). They avoided a strike, but negotiations between writers and studios were a true Hollywood thriller. *Los Angeles Times.* http://www.latimes .com/business/hollywood/ la-fi-ct-writers-guild-no-strike- 20170501-story.html

CHAPTER 14

1. Milligan, S. (2017, September). Employee wellness blows up. *HR Magazine,* pp. 60–67; Johnson & Johnson. (2017). Health and wellness at work. https://www. jnj.com/caring/patient-stories/ health-and-wellness-at-work; Johnson & Johnson. (2016). The healthiest workforce. https://www.jnj.com/about-jnj/ company-statements/healthiest- workforce; Johnson & Johnson. (2018). Our approach to health and wellness. https://www .jnj.com/jjhws; Moran, G. (2017). This is the future of corporate wellness programs. *Fast Company.* https://www .fastcompany.com/40418593/ this-is-the-future-of-corporate- wellness-programs; Quinton, S. (2013). The Johnson & Johnson workout program: Improving productivity with diet and exercise. *The Atlantic.* https:// www.theatlantic.com/business/ archive/2013/06/the-johnson- amp-johnson-workout-program- improving-productivity-with- diet-and-exercise/425994/; Thompson, M. (2017). How to launch a corporate wellness program that works. *Forbes.*

https://www.forbes.com/sites/ melissathompson/2017/03/03/ how-to-launch-a-corporate- wellness-program-that- works/#51d4f8e51a56

2. McGeehan, P., Mazzei, P., & Johnson, K. (2017). Law requires life-saving braking device. Most trains don't have it. *New York Times.* https://www.nytimes. com/2017/12/20/us/amtrak- train-safety.html; Shepardson, D. (2017). U.S. Safety Board says train-crash engineers had undiagnosed sleep disorders. *Scientific American.* https://www .scientificamerican.com/article/ u-s-safety-board-says-train- crash-engineers-had- undiagnosed-sleep-disorders/

3. Workplace well-being. (2018). International Labor Organization. http://www.ilo .org/safework/areasofwork/ workplace-health-promotion- and-well-being/WCMS_118396/ lang—en/index.htm

4. About OSHA. (n.d.) https://www .osha.gov/about.html; State Plans. https://www.osha.gov/dcsp/osp/ index.html

5. About NIOSH. (2018). http:// www.cdc.gov/niosh/about/ default.html

6. Leigh, J. P. (2011). Economic burden of occupational injury and illness in the United States. *Milbank Quarterly, 89,* 728–772.

7. America's safest companies awards: 2017 America's Safest Companies. (2017). EHS Today. http://www.ehstoday.com/ americas-safest-companies- awards/2017-america-s-safest- companies

8. Musik, T. (2017, August 27). Preventing serious injuries and fatalities. *Safety + Health Magazine.* http://www .safetyandhealthmagazine .com/articles/16087-preventing- serious-injuries-and-fatalities

9. Musik, T. (2017). Preventing serious injuries and fatalities.

Safety + Health Magazine. http:// www.safetyand healthmagazine.com/ articles/16087-preventing- serious-injuries-and-fatalities

10. Neal, A., & Griffin, M. A. (2006). A study of the lagged relationships among safety climate, safety motivation, safety behavior, and accidents at the individual and group levels. *Journal of Applied Psychology, 91,* 946–953.

11. Triangle Shirtwaist Factory Fire. (2009). http://www.history.com/ topics/triangle-shirtwaist-fire

12. IEEE. (2014). *Workplace safety monitoring using RFIT sensors.* https://ieeexplore.ieee.org/ document/7034494/; National Institute for Occupational Safety and Health. (2018). *Direct reading and sensor technology.* https:// www.cdc.gov/niosh/topics/drst/ default.html

13. Edelson, J. (2017, December 13). Hotels add panic buttons to protect housekeepers from guests. *Bloomberg.* https:// www.bloomberg.com/news/ articles/2017-12-13/hotels- add-panic-buttons-to-protect- housekeepers-from-guests

14. Clarke, S. (2006). The relationship between safety climate and safety performance: A meta-analytic review. *Journal of Occupational Health Psychology, 11,* 315–327; Zohar, D., & Luria, G. (2005). A multilevel model of safety climate: Cross-level relationships between organization and group- level climates. *Journal of Applied Psychology, 90,* 616–628.

15. Zohar, D., & Polachek, T. (2014). Discourse-based intervention for modifying supervisory communication as leverage for safety climate and performance improvement: A randomized field study. *Journal of Applied Psychology, 99,* 113–124.

16. Occupational Safety and Health Administration. (n.d.). Workplace violence.

https://www.osha.gov/SLTC/workplaceviolence/

17. Hershcovis, M. S. (2011). "Incivility, social undermining, bullying . . . oh my!": A call to reconcile constructs within workplace aggression research. *Journal of Organizational Behavior, 32,* 499–519.

18. Campbell, A. F. (2016). Why violence against nurses has spiked in the last decade. *The Atlantic.* https://www.theatlantic.com/business/archive/2016/12/violence-against-nurses/509309/; OSHA. (2016). Guidelines for preventing workplace violence for healthcare and social service workers. https://www.osha.gov/Publications/osha3148.pdf

19. McGeehan, P., Mazzei, P., & Johnson, K. (2017). Law requires life-saving braking device. Most trains don't have it. *New York Times.* https://www.nytimes.com/2017/12/20/us/amtrak-train-safety.html

20. Shepardson, D. (2017). U.S. Safety Board says train-crash engineers had undiagnosed sleep disorders. *Scientific American.* https://www.scientificamerican.com/article/u-s-safety-board-says-train-crash-engineers-had-undiagnosed-sleep-disorders/

21. Federal Motor Carrier Safety Administration. (2018). Driving when you have sleep apnea. https://www.fmcsa.dot.gov/driver-safety/sleep-apnea/driving-when-you-have-sleep-apnea

22. Wallace, J. C., & Chen, G. (2005). Development and validation of a work-specific measure of cognitive failure: Implications for occupational safety. *Journal of Occupational and Organizational Psychology, 78,* 615–632.

23. Society for Human Resource Management. (2016). Developing effective safety management programs. https://www.shrm.org/resourcesandtools/tools-and-samples/toolkits/pages/developingsafetymanagementprograms.aspx

24. OSHA. (2018). Emergency preparedness and response. https://www.osha.gov/SLTC/emergencypreparedness/index.html; OSHA. (2018). Evacuation and shelter in place. https://www.osha.gov/SLTC/emergencypreparedness/gettingstarted_evacuation.html

25. OSHA. (2018). Frequently asked questions. https://www.osha.gov/OSHA_FAQs.html#!employerassist; OSHA. (2016). Inspections. https://www.osha.gov/OshDoc/data_General_Facts/factsheet-inspections.pdf

26. U.S. Department of Labor. (2013). Fact sheet: Your rights as a whistleblower. https://www.osha.gov/OshDoc/data_General_Facts/whistleblower_rights.pdf

27. Druley, K. (2017). OSHA's top-10 most cited violations for fiscal year 2017. *Safety + Health Magazine.* http://www.safetyandhealthmagazine.com/articles/16362-oshas-top-10-most-cited-violations-for-2017; OSHA. (2015). Job safety and health: It's the law. https://www.osha.gov/Publications/poster.html; OSHA fines employer $105,000 for retaliating against employee who complained about mold exposure. (2016). *National Law Review.* https://www.natlawreview.com/article/osha-fines-employer-105000-retaliating-against-employee-who-complained-about-mold; https://www.osha.gov/OshDoc/data_General_Facts/whistleblower_rights.pdf

28. OSHA. (2018). Ergonomics. https://www.osha.gov/SLTC/ergonomics

29. Total Worker Health in Action! (2016). https://www.cdc.gov/niosh/twh/newsletter/twhnewsv5n3.html

30. Stromberg, J. (2014). Five health benefits of standing desks. *Smithsonian.* https://www.smithsonianmag.com/science-nature/five-health-benefits-standing-desks-180950259/

31. Boubekri, M., Cheung, I. N., Reid, K. J., Wang, C. H., & Zee, P. C. (2014). Impact of windows and daylight exposure on overall health and sleep quality of office workers: A case-control pilot study. *Journal of Clinical Sleep Medicine, 10,* 603–611.

32. Evans, G. W., & Johnson, D. (2000). Stress and open-office noise. *Journal of Applied Psychology, 85,* 779–783; Konnikova, M. (2014, January 7). The open-office trap. *The New Yorker.* http://www.newyorker.com/business/currency/the-open-office-trap

33. Whitaker, P. (2017, December 12). UK high court: Employers may be vicariously liable for employee data breaches. *The National Law Review.* https://www.natlawreview.com/article/uk-high-court-employers-may-be-vicariously-liable-employee-data-breaches

34. Marvin, R. (2017). The best employee monitoring software of 2018. *PC Magazine.* https://www.pcmag.com/roundup/357211/the-best-employee-monitoring-software; Shartonn, B. R., & Neuman, K. L. (2017). The legal risks of monitoring employees online. *Harvard Business Review.* https://hbr.org/2017/12/the-legal-risks-of-monitoring-employees-online

35. American Psychological Association. (2017). 2017 work and well-being survey. http://www.apaexcellence.org/assets/general/2017-work-and-well-being-survey-results.pdf; Careercast. (2017). 2017 stressful jobs reader survey. http://www.careercast.com/career-news/2017-stressful-jobs-reader-survey

36. Newport, F., & Harter, J. (2016). U.S. workers' satisfaction with

job dimensions increases. http://news.gallup.com/poll/195143/workers-satisfied-job-dimensions.aspx

37. Wallace, J. C., & Chen, G. (2005). Development and validation of a work-specific measure of cognitive failure: Implications for occupational safety. *Journal of Occupational and Organizational Psychology, 78*, 615–632.

38. Gonzalez-Mulé, E., & Cockburn, B. (2017). Worked to death: The relationships of job demands and job control with mortality. *Personnel Psychology, 70*, 73–112; Workers in stressful, low-control jobs have higher risk of early death: Study. (2016). *Safety + Health Magazine.* http://www.safetyandhealthmagazine.com/articles/14913-workers-in-stressful-low-control-jobs-have-higher-risk-of-early-death-study

39. Dill, K. (2014). Survey: 42% of employees have changed jobs due to stress. *Forbes.* https://www.forbes.com/sites/kathryndill/2014/04/18/survey-42-of-employees-have-changed-jobs-due-to-stress/#607fbecc3380

40. Liu, S., Wang, M., Zhan, Y., & Shi, J. (2009). Daily work stress and alcohol use: Testing the cross-level moderation effects of neuroticism and job involvement. *Personnel Psychology, 62*, 575–597.

41. Demerouti, E., Bakker, A. B., Nachreiner, F., & Schaufeli, W. B. (2001). The job demands-resources model of burnout. *Journal of Applied Psychology, 86*, 499–512; Schaufeli, W. B., & Taris, T. W. (2014). A critical review of the Job Demands-Resources Model: Implications for improving work and health. In G. F. Bauer & O. Hämmig (Eds.), *Bridging occupational, organizational and public health* (pp. 43–68). Dordrecht, The Netherlands: Springer.

42. Klass, P. (2017). Taking care of the physician. *New York Times.* https://www.nytimes.com/2017/11/13/well/family/taking-care-of-the-physician.html

43. Saad, L. (2014). The "40-hour" work week is actually longer—by seven hours. http://news.gallup.com/poll/175286/hour-workweek-actually-longer-seven-hours.aspx

44. Morris, D. Z. (2017). New French law bars work emails after hours. *Fortune.* http://fortune.com/2017/01/01/french-right-to-disconnect-law/

45. Allen, T. D., Johnson, R. C., Saboe, K. N., Cho, E., Dumani, S., & Evans, S. (2012). Dispositional variables and work–family conflict: A meta-analysis. *Journal of Vocational Behavior, 80*, 17–26.

46. Kossek, E. E., Hammer, L. B., Thompson, R. J., & Buxbaum, L. B. (2014). *Leveraging workplace flexibility for engagement and productivity.* Alexandria, VA: SHRM.

47. Brenoff, A. (2013). 8 reasons why employees never want to leave this amazing company. https://www.huffingtonpost.com/2013/11/18/best-places-to-work_n_4240370.html; Meaningful work, life balance makes SAS one of the world's best workplaces. (n.d.). https://www.sas.com/en_us/news/press-releases/2017/october/gptw-multinational.html

48. Masterson, L. (2017). Nurses are burnt out. Here's how hospitals can help. https://www.healthcaredive.com/news/nurses-are-burnt-out-heres-how-hospitals-can-help/442640/

49. Wellness Council of America (WELCOA). (2018). The benefits of stress management for employees. https://www.welcoa.org/blog/benefits-stress-management-employees/

50. Tepper, B. J., Simon, L., & Park, H. M. (2017). Abusive supervision. *Annual Review of Organizational Psychology and Organizational Behavior, 4*, 123–152; Yang, L. Q., Caughlin, D. E., Gazica, M. W., Truxillo, D. M., & Spector, P. E. (2014). Workplace mistreatment climate and potential employee and organizational outcomes: A meta-analytic review from the target's perspective. *Journal of Occupational Health Psychology, 19*, 315–335.

51. Kantor, J. (2014, August 13). Working anything but 9 to 5. *New York Times.* http://www.nytimes.com/interactive/2014/08/13/us/starbucks-workers-scheduling-hours.html

52. Mäkikangas, A., Kinnunen, S., Rantanen, J., Mauno, S., Tolvanen, A., & Bakker, A. B. (2014). Association between vigor and exhaustion during the workweek: A person-centered approach to daily assessments. *Anxiety, Stress, & Coping, 27*, 555–575; Sonnentag, S., & Fritz, C. (2007). The Recovery Experience Questionnaire: Development and validation of a measure for assessing recuperation and unwinding from work. *Journal of Occupational Health Psychology, 12*, 204–221.

53. Shen, L. (2016). These 19 great employers offer paid sabbaticals. *Forbes.* http://fortune.com/2016/03/07/best-companies-to-work-for-sabbaticals/

54. Herrera, T. (2017). Take naps at work. Apologize to no one. *New York Times.* https://www.nytimes.com/2017/06/23/smarter-living/take-naps-at-work-apologize-to-no-one.html; Six companies (including Uber) where it's OK to nap. (2015). *Inc.* https://www.inc.com/zoe-henry/google-uber-and-other-companies-where-you-can-nap-at-the-office.html

55. Druley, K. (2016). Keeping aging workers safe. *Safety + Health Magazine.* http://www.safetyandhealthmagazine.com/articles/15023-aging-workers; Loch, C. H., Sting, F. J., Bauer, N., & Mauermann, H. (2010). How BMW is defusing

the demographic time bomb. *Harvard Business Review, 88,* 99–102.

56. Loehr, J., & Schwartz, T. (2001). The making of a corporate athlete. *Harvard Business Review.* https://hbr.org/2001/01/the-making-of-a-corporate-athlete

57. SHRM. (2015). What is a wellness program? https://www.shrm.org/resourcesandtools/tools-and-samples/hr-qa/pages/whatarewellnessbenefits.aspx

58. Rand Corporation. (2014). Do wellness programs save employers money? (2014). https://www.rand.org/content/dam/rand/pubs/research_briefs/RB9700/RB9744/RAND_RB9744.pdf

59. Mattke, S., Liu, H., Caloyeras, J. P., Huang, C. Y., Van Busum, K. R., Khodyakov, D., & Shier, V. (2013). *Workplace wellness programs study.* https://www.rand.org/pubs/research_reports/RR254.html

60. Milligan, S. (2017). Employers take wellness to a higher level. *HR Magazine.* https://www.shrm.org/hr-today/news/hr-magazine/0917/pages/employers-take-wellness-to-a-higher-level.aspx

61. SHRM. (2014). Measuring wellness: From data to insights. The Economist Intelligence Unit. https://www.shrm.org/ResourcesAndTools/hr-topics/benefits/Documents/EIU_HUMANA_WEB_FINAL_0.pdf

62. Bertolini, M. T. (n.d.). Forget ROI: Aetna's CEO's perspective on wellness & functionality. http://www.corporatewellnessmagazine.com/cwminterviews/aetna-ceo-perspective-on-wellness-functionality

63. Rand Corporation. (2014). Do wellness programs save employers money? (2014). https://www.rand.org/content/dam/rand/pubs/research_briefs/RB9700/RB9744/RAND_RB9744.pdf

64. Rand Corporation. (2014). Do wellness programs save employers money? (2014). https://www.rand.org/content/dam/rand/pubs/research_briefs/RB9700/RB9744/RAND_RB9744.pdf; Harris, M. M. (2016). The business case for employee health and wellness programs. Society for Industrial and Organizational Psychology. http://www.siop.org/WhitePapers/casehealth.pdf

65. Purcell, J. (2016). Meet the wellness programs that save companies money. *Harvard Business Review.* https://hbr.org/2016/04/meet-the-wellness-programs-that-save-companies-money

66. SHRM. (2016). Designing and managing wellness programs. https://www.shrm.org/resourcesandtools/tools-and-samples/toolkits/pages/designingandmanaging wellness programs.aspx; Martis, L. (2018). 7 companies with epic wellness programs. https://www.monster.com/career-advice/article/companies-good-wellness- programs; Milligan, S. (2017). Employers take wellness to a higher level. *HR Magazine.* https://www.shrm.org/hr-today/news/hr-magazine/0917/pages/employers-take-wellness-to-a-higher-level.aspx; Mattke, S., Liu, H., Caloyeras, J. P., Huang, C. Y., Van Busum, K. R., Khodyakov, D., & Shier, V. (2013). *Workplace wellness programs study.* https://www.rand.org/pubs/research_reports/RR254.html; 10 great examples of workplace wellness programs. (2018). https://risepeople.com/blog/workplace-wellness-programs/ Milligan, S. (2017). Employers take wellness to a higher level. *HR Magazine.* https://www.shrm.org/hr-today/news/hr-magazine/0917/pages/employers-take-wellness-to-a-higher-level.aspx

67. Milligan, S. (2017). Employers take wellness to a higher level. *HR Magazine.* https://www.shrm.org/hr-today/news/hr-magazine/0917/pages/employers-take-wellness-to-a-higher-level.aspx

68. SHRM. (2014, August 12). Employee assistance program (EAP): General. What is an employee assistance program? https://www.shrm.org/resourcesandtools/tools-and-samples/hr-qa/pages/whatisaneap.aspx

69. 10 great examples of workplace wellness programs. (2017). https://risepeople.com/blog/workplace-wellness-programs/

70. International Employee Assistance Association. (2011, October). Definitions of an employee assistance program (EAP) and EAP core technology. http://www.eapassn.org/about/about-employee-assistance/eap-definitions-and-core-technology; SHRM. (2015). Managing employee assistance programs. https://www.shrm.org/resourcesandtools/tools-and-samples/toolkits/pages/managingemployeeassistance programs.aspx

71. SHRM. (2015). Managing employee assistance programs. https://www.shrm.org/resourcesandtools/tools-and-samples/toolkits/pages/managingemployeeassistance programs.aspx

72. American Psychiatric Association. (2016). Employee assistance programs: an often overlooked resource. https://www.psychiatry.org/news-room/apa-blogs/apa-blog/2016/07/employee-assistance-programs-an-often-overlooked-resource; Dunning, M. (2014). Employee assistance programs underutilized by employees. http://www.businessinsurance.com/article/20140105/NEWS03/301059979

73. SHRM. (2016). Designing and managing wellness programs. https://www.shrm.org/resourcesandtools/tools-and-samples/toolkits/pages/designingandmanaging wellness programs.aspx; Harris, M. M. (2016). The

business case for employee health and wellness programs. Society for Industrial and Organizational Psychology. http://www.siop .org/WhitePapers/casehealth.pdf; Mattke, S., Liu, H., Caloyeras, J. P., Huang, C. Y., Van Busum, K. R., Khodyakov, D., & Shier, V. (2013). *Workplace wellness programs study*. https://www .rand.org/pubs/research_reports/ RR254.html; Milligan, S. (2017, August 21). Employers take wellness to a higher level. *HR Magazine*. https://www .shrm.org/hr-today/news/hr-magazine/0917/pages/ employers-take-wellness-to-a-higher-level.aspx

74. Beckman, K. (2017, June 28). Wearables technology gains traction in workplace safety. http://www.businessinsurance .com/article/00010101/ NEWS08/912314133/Wearables-technology-gains-traction-in-workplace-safety; Harvard Business School Cold Call Podcast. (2018, January 4). How to monetize happiness. https:// hbswk.hbs.edu/item/how-to-monetize-happiness?cid=wk-rs; Kahn, J. (2017). Fitness tracking startups are sweating due to EU privacy regulators. *Bloomberg*. https://www.bloomberg.com/ news/articles/2017-09-11/ fitness-tracking-startups-are-sweating-due-to-eu-privacy-regulators; Moran, G. (2017). This is the future of corporate wellness programs. *Fast Company*. https:// www.fastcompany .com/40418593/this-is-the-future-of- corporate-wellness-programs; Sly, L. (2018). US soldiers are revealing sensitive and dangerous information by jogging. *Washington Post*. https:// www.washingtonpost .com/world/a-map-showing-the-users-of-fitness-devices-lets-the-world-see-where-us-soldiers-are-and-what-they-are-doing/2018/01/28/86915662-

0441-11e8-aa61-f3391373867e_story. html?utm_term=.11e2967e71a4; Vanderkam, L. (2015). The darkside of corporate wellness programs. *Fast Company*. https:// www.fastcompany.com/3047115/ the-dark-side-of-corporate-wellness-programs

75. Hammer, L. B., Johnson, R. C., Crain, T. L., Bodner, T., Kossek, E. E., Davis, K. D., . . . Berkman, L. (2016). (2016). Intervention effects on the safety compliance and citizenship behaviors: Evidence from the work, family, and health study. *Journal of Applied Psychology, 101*, 190–208; Hurtado, D. A., Okechukwu, C. A., Buxton, O. M., Hammer, L., Hanson, G. C., Moen, P., . . . Berkman, L. F. (2016). *Journal of Epidemiology and Community Health, 70*, 1155–1161; Olson, R., Crain, T. L., Bodner, T. E., King, R., Hammer, L. B., Klein, L. C., . . . Buxton, O. M. (2015). A workplace intervention improves sleep: Results from the randomized controlled Work, Family, and Health study. *Sleep Health, 1*, 55–65; Zohar, D., & Luria, G. (2005). A multilevel model of safety climate: Cross-level relationships between organization and group-level climates. *Journal of Applied Psychology, 90*, 616–628; Zohar, D., & Polachek, T. (2014). Discourse-based intervention for modifying supervisory communication as leverage for safety climate and performance improvement: A randomized field study. *Journal of Applied Psychology, 99*, 113–124; Olson, R., Wipfli, B., Thompson, S. V., Elliot, D. L., Anger, W. K., Bodner, T., . . . Perrin, N. (2016). Weight control intervention for truck drivers: The SHIFT randomized controlled trial, United States. *American Journal of Public Health, 106*, 1698–1706.

76. Total worker health. (2015). https://www.cdc.gov/niosh/twh/ totalhealth.html

77. Total worker health in action! (2017, December). https://www .cdc.gov/niosh/twh/newsletter/ twhnewsv6n4.html#Promising

78. Anger, W. K., Elliot, D. L., Bodner, T., Olson, R., Rohlman, D. S., Truxillo, D. M., . . . Montgomery, D. (2015). Effectiveness of total worker health interventions. *Journal of Occupational Health Psychology, 20*, 226–247.

79. Milligan, S. (2017, August 21). Employers take wellness to a higher level. *HR Magazine*. https://www.shrm.org/hr-today/ news/hr-magazine/0917/pages/ employers-take-wellness-to-a-higher-level.aspx

80. Isaac, M., Benner, K., & Frenkel, S. (2017). Uber hid 2016 breach, paying hackers to delete stolen data. *New York Times*. https:// www.nytimes.com/2017/11/21/ technology/uber-hack.html; Email top attack vector in healthcare cyberattacks. (2017, December 12). *HIPAA Journal*. https://www.hipaajournal .com/email-top-attack-vector-healthcare-cyberattacks/; Smith, A. (2016, January 8). Employee training to reduce cybersecurity breaches underused. https://www .shrm.org/resourcesandtools/ legal-and-compliance/state-and-local-updates/pages/training-reduces-cybersecurity-breaches .aspx

CHAPTER 15

1. Churchard, C. (2013, August 23). Totally worth it. *People Management*, pp. 36–38; Hong, H. J., & Doz, Y. (2013, June). L'Oréal masters multiculturalism. *Harvard Business Review*. https://hbr .org/2013/06/loreal-masters-multiculturalism; L'Oréal.

(2016). Key figures. http://www.loreal.com/group/our-activities/key-figures; Meyer, E. (2015, October). When culture doesn't translate. *Harvard Business Review*. https://hbr.org/2015/10/when-culture-doesnt-translate

2. Petroff, A., & Cornevin, O. (2017, January 2). France gives workers "right to disconnect" from office email. http://money.cnn.com/2017/01/02/technology/france-office-email-workers-law/index.html

3. McCarthy, N. (2017, June 20). Which countries have the highest level of union membership? *Forbes*. https://www.forbes.com/sites/niallmccarthy/2017/06/20/which-countries-have-the-highest-levels-of-labor-union-membership-infographic/#262682c233c0

4. Farndale, E., & Paauwe, J. (2007). Uncovering competitive and institutional drivers of HRM practices in multinational corporations. *Human Resource Management Journal, 17,* 355–375.

5. Vaiman, V., & Brewster, C. (2015). How far do cultural differences explain the differences between nations? Implications for HRM. *International Journal of Human Resource Management, 26,* 151–164.

6. Brewster, C., Sparrow, P., & Harris, H. (2005). Towards a new model of globalizing HR. *International Journal of Human Resource Management, 16,* 949–970.

7. Morris, S. S., Wright, P. M., Trevor, J., Stiles, P., Stahl, G., et al. (2009). Global challenges to replicating HR: The role of people, processes, and systems. *Human Resource Management, 48,* 973–995.

8. Thite, M., Wilkinson, A., & Shah, D. (2012). Internationalization and HRM strategies across subsidiaries in multinational corporations from emerging economies: A conceptual framework. *Journal of World Business, 47,* 251–258.

9. Budhwar, P. S., Varma, A., & Patel, C. (2016). Convergence-divergence of HRM in the Asia-Pacific: Context-specific analysis and future research agenda. *Human Resource Management Review, 26,* 311–326.

10. Overman, S. (2016, February). Tapping talent around the globe. *HR Magazine,* pp. 47–51.

11. WillisTowersWatson. (2017, September 18). A global approach to company car benefits policy. https://www.willistowerswatson.com/en-LB/insights/2017/09/A-global-approach-to-company-car-benefits-policy

12. Aon. (2017, September). Revisiting 13th and 14th month bonus rules in Latin America, Europe, Africa and Asia. https://radford.aon.com/insights/articles/2017/13th-and-14th-Month-Bonus-Rules-in-Latin-America-Europe-Africa-and-Asia

13. Central Intelligence Agency. (2017). *The world factbook*. https://www.cia.gov/library/publications/the-world-factbook/fields/2177.html

14. Claus, L. (2010, February). International assignees at risk. *HR Magazine,* pp. 73–75; EEOC. (2003). Employee rights when working for multinational employers. https://www.eeoc.gov/facts/multi-employees.html; Maurer, R. (2014, November). The rise of the accidental expat. *HR Magazine,* p. 12; Simms, J. (2017, February 21). The tricky logistics of global mobility—and HR's crucial role in getting it right. *People Management,* pp. 46–48.

15. Onley, D. S. (2014, January). Terminating overseas employees. *HR Magazine,* pp. 33–36.

16. Burgess, M. (2018, January 2). What is GDPR? WIRED explains what you need to know. http://www.wired.co.uk/article/what-is-gdpr-uk-eu-legislation-compliance-summary-fines-2018; Wright, A. D. (2017, July 31). HR urged to prepare for new data protection law in Europe. https://www.shrm.org/resourcesandtools/hr-topics/global-hr/pages/hr-urged-to-prepare-for-new-data-protection-law-in-europe.aspx

17. Doke, D. D. (January 4, 2016). Adidas: Where talent rules. http://www.recruiter.co.uk/news/2015/12/adidas-where-talent-rules

18. Harzing, A. W., Pudelko, M., & Reiche, S. (2016). The bridging role of expatriates and inpatriates in knowledge transfer in multinational corporations. *Human Resource Management, 55,* 679–695.

19. Harzing, A. W. (1995). The persistent myth of high expatriate failure rates. *International Journal of Human Resource Management, 6,* 457–475; Naumann, E. (1993). Organizational predictors of expatriate job satisfaction. *Journal of International Business Studies, 24,* 61–79.

20. Anonymous. (2009). Best expatriate assignments require much thought, even more planning. *HR Magazine, 2009 HR Trendbook,* 74–75.

21. Bhaskar-Shrinivas, P., Harrison, D. A., Shaffer, M. A., & Luk, D. M. (2005). Input-based and time-based models of international adjustment: Meta-analytic evidence and theoretical extensions. *Academy of Management Journal, 48,* 257–281.

22. Everson, K. (2014, July). Relocation sector keeps moving right along. *Workforce,* p. 93.

23. Clouse, M. A., & Watkins, M. D. (2009, October). Three keys to

getting an overseas assignment right. *Harvard Business Review,* pp. 115–119.

24. Clemetson, L. (2010, December 15). The globe-trotters. *Workforce Management, 89.* http://www.workforce.com/2010/12/15/special-report-on-globalization-the-globe-trotters/

25. Marschan-Piekkari, R., Welch, D., & Welch, L. (1999). In the shadow: The impact of language on structure: Power and communication in the multinational. *International Business Review, 8,* 421–440.

26. Molinsky, A. L. (2012, January/February). Code switching between cultures. *Harvard Business Review,* pp. 140–141; Molinsky, A. (2014, January 30). Encourage foreign-born employees to participate more in meetings. *Harvard Business Review.* https://hbr.org/2014/01/encourage-foreign-born-employees-to-participate-more-in-meetings; Molinsky, A. L. (2014, July 15). Adapt to a new culture—but don't go too far. *Harvard Business Review.* https://hbr.org/2014/07/adapt-to-a-new-culture-but-dont-go-too-far; Neeley, T., & Kaplan, R. S. (2014, September). What's your language strategy? *Harvard Business Review,* pp. 70–76.

27. Zhang, L. E., & Harzing, A. W. (2016). From dilemmatic struggle to legitimized indifference: Expatriates' host country language learning and its impact on the expatriate–HCE relationship. *Journal of World Business, 51,* 774–786.

28. Peltokorpi, V. (2008). Cross-cultural adjustment of expatriates in Japan. *International Journal of Human Resource Management, 19,* 1588–1606.

29. Anonymous. (2017, May 8). What is it like to live and work in Bahrain? https://www.expatfocus.com/c/aid=4190/articles/bahrain/what-is-it-like-to-live-and-work-in-bahrain/;

Steverman, B. (2017, September 6). The best and worst countries to live and work in, according to expats. https://www.bloomberg.com/news/articles/2017-09-06/the-u-s-and-u-k-are-getting-worse-and-worse-expats-say

30. Bhaskar-Shrinivas, P., Harrison, D. A., Shaffer, M. A., & Luk, D. M. (2005). Input-based and time-based models of international adjustment: Meta-analytic evidence and theoretical extensions. *Academy of Management Journal, 48,* 257–281.

31. Farh, C. I. C., Bartol, K. M., Shapiro, D. L., & Shin, J. (2010). Networking abroad: A process model of how expatriates form support ties to facilitate adjustment. *Academy of Management Review, 35,* 434–454.

32. Bhaskar-Shrinivas, P., Harrison, D. A., Shaffer, M. A., & Luk, D. M. (2005). Input-based and time-based models of international adjustment: Meta-analytic evidence and theoretical extensions. *Academy of Management Journal, 48,* 257–281.

33. Fan, S. X., Cregan, C., Harzing, A. W., & Köhler, T. (2018). The benefits of being understood: The role of ethnic identity confirmation in knowledge acquisition by expatriates. *Human Resource Management, 57,* 327–339.

34. Farh, C. I. C., Bartol, K. M., Shapiro, D. L., & Shin, J. (2010). Networking abroad: A process model of how expatriates form support ties to facilitate adjustment. *Academy of Management Review, 35,* 434–454.

35. Kraimer, M. L., Wayne, S. J., & Jaworski, R. A. (2001). Sources of support and expatriate performance: The mediating role of expatriate adjustment. *Personnel Psychology, 54,* 71–99.

36. Anonymous. (2009). Best expatriate assignments require much thought, even more

planning. *HR Magazine, 2009 HR Trendbook,* 74–75.

37. Anonymous. (2011, March). Developing your global know-how. *Harvard Business Review,* pp. 71–75.

38. Gillenwater, S. (2017, June 16). Today's immigrant CEOs: Bringing a global sensibility to American business. https://www.salesforce.com/blog/2017/06/immigrant-ceos-global-sensibility-business.html; Maddux, W. W., Galinsky, A. D., & Tadmor, C. T. (2010, September). Be a better manager: Live abroad. *Harvard Business Review,* p. 24.

39. Molinsky, A., & Hahn, M. (2015, April 8). Building relationships in cultures that don't do small talk. *Harvard Business Review.* https://hbr.org/2015/04/building-relationships-in-cultures-that-dont-do-small-talk

40. Frase, M. (2007, February). The road to (inland) China. *HR Magazine,* pp. 71–78.

41. Everson, K. (2014, July). Relocation sector keeps moving right along. *Workforce, 93.*

42. Clemetson, L. (2010, December 15). The globe-trotters. *Workforce Management, 89.* http://www.workforce.com/2010/12/15/special-report-on-globalization-the-globe-trotters

43. Anonymous. (2010). Pay variations in Asia. *HR Magazine, 2010 Trendbook,* p. 6.

44. Gale, S. F. (2017, November/December). Finding agility in employee mobility. *Workforce,* pp. 58–59.

45. Refworld. (2014, July 31). Nigeria: Kidnapping for ransom, including frequency, profile of victims and kidnappers; response by authorities (2013–2014). http://www.refworld.org/docid/546dc1724.html

46. Bureau of National Affairs. (2011, January). Kidnappings remain a concern for firms doing business abroad. *HR Focus,* pp. 6–8.

47. Wright, A. D. (2011, December). Open for business? *HR Magazine,* pp. 105–107.

48. Bruning, N. S., & Cadigan, F. (2014). Diversity and global talent management: Are there cracks in the glass ceiling and glass border? *People & Strategy, 37*(3), 18–21.

49. Varma, A., & Russell, L. (2016). Women and expatriate assignments: Exploring the role of perceived organizational support. *Employee Relations, 38,* 200–223.

50. Bader, B. (2018, February 6). Do female expats experience a greater level of discrimination? *People Management.* https://www.peoplemanagement.co.uk/voices/comment/female-expats-greater-discrimination

51. Shen, J., & Jiang, F. (2015). Factors influencing Chinese female expatriates' performance in international assignments. *International Journal of Human Resource Management, 26,* 299–315.

52. McPhail, R., McNulty, Y., & Hutchings, K. (2016). Lesbian and gay expatriation: Opportunities, barriers, and challenges for global mobility. *International Journal of Human Resource Management, 27,* 382–406.

53. Fenton, S. (2016, May 17). LGBT relationships are illegal in 74 countries, research finds. https://www.independent.co.uk/news/world/gay-lesbian-bisexual-relationships-illegal-in-74-countries-a7033666.html

54. Florian, J. (2018, April 2). Sending LGBTQ employees abroad poses challenges, requires planning. https://www.bna.com/sending-lgbtq-employees-b57982090600/

55. Bolino, M. C., Klotz, A. C., & Turnley, W. H. (2017, April 18). Will refusing an international assignment derail your career? *Harvard Business Review.* https://hbr.org/2017/04/will-refusing-an-international-assignment-derail-your-career

56. Kraimer, M. L., Shaffer, M. A., & Bolino, M. C. (2009). The influence of expatriate and repatriate experiences on career advancement and repatriate intentions. *Human Resource Management, 48,* 27–47.

57. Clemetson, L. (2010, December 15). The globe-trotters. *Workforce Management, 89.* http://www.workforce.com/2010/12/15/special-report-on-globalization-the-globe-trotters

58. Anonymous. (2011, March). Developing your global know-how. *Harvard Business Review,* pp. 71–75.

59. Krell, E. (2011, December). Taking care of business abroad. *HR Magazine,* pp. 44–48.

60. Hannibal, E., Traber, Y., & Jelinek, P. (2015, April). Tracking your expatriate software. *HR Magazine,* pp. 63–65.

61. Maurer, R. (2014, November). The rise of the accidental expat. *HR Magazine,* p. 12.

62. Simms, J. (2017, February 21). The tricky logistics of global mobility—and HR's crucial role in getting it right. *People Management,* pp. 46–48.

63. Albanese, C., DiPasquale, S., & Gilblom, K. (2017, December 20). Eni, Shell to face trial in Italy in $1 billion bribery case. *Bloomberg.* https://www.bloomberg.com/news/articles/2017-12-20/eni-shell-to-face-trial-in-italy-over-1-billion-bribery-case; Anonymous. (2017, January 18). Rolls-Royce apologises after £671m bribery settlement. *BBC.* http://www.bbc.com/news/business-38644114; Auchard, E., & Brock, J. (2017, October 26). SAP faces U.S. probe into South Africa kickback allegations. https://www.reuters.com/article/us-sap-se-corruption-safrica/sap-faces-u-s-probe-into-south-africa-kickback-allegations-idUSKBN1CV0ZW; Currell, D., & Davis Bradley, T. (2012, September). Greased palms, giant headaches. *Harvard Business Review.* https://hbr.org/2012/09/greased-palms-giant-headaches; Heineman, B. W. (2014, May 15). Who's responsible for the Walmart Mexico scandal? *Harvard Business Review.* https://hbr.org/2014/05/whos-responsible-for-the-walmart-mexico-scandal; Paine, L. S. (2010, June). The China rules. *Harvard Business Review,* pp. 103–108.

Index